Thinking Like a Planet

Thinking Like a Planet
The Land Ethic and the Earth Ethic

J. Baird Callicott

OXFORD
UNIVERSITY PRESS

OXFORD
UNIVERSITY PRESS

Oxford University Press is a department of the University of Oxford.
It furthers the University's objective of excellence in research, scholarship,
and education by publishing worldwide.

Oxford   New York
Auckland   Cape Town   Dar es Salaam   Hong Kong   Karachi
Kuala Lumpur   Madrid   Melbourne   Mexico City   Nairobi
New Delhi   Shanghai   Taipei   Toronto

With offices in
Argentina   Austria   Brazil   Chile   Czech Republic   France   Greece
Guatemala   Hungary   Italy   Japan   Poland   Portugal   Singapore
South Korea   Switzerland   Thailand   Turkey   Ukraine   Vietnam

Oxford is a registered trademark of Oxford University Press
in the UK and certain other countries.

Published in the United States of America by
Oxford University Press
198 Madison Avenue, New York, NY 10016

© Oxford University Press 2013

Library of Congress Cataloging-in-Publication Data
Callicott, J. Baird.
Thinking like a planet : the land ethic and the earth ethic / J. Baird Callicott.
pages cm
ISBN 978-0-19-932489-7 (pbk. : alk. paper) — ISBN 978-0-19-932488-0 (hardcover : alk. paper)
1. Environmental ethics.   2. Climatic changes—Moral and ethical aspects.   I. Title.
GE42.C353 2013
179'.1—dc23
2013016146

For Theo Callicott, my grandson

Contents

Acknowledgments

The only people to read and comment on the whole of this work in manuscript form are the two scholars chosen to review it by Oxford University Press: David Schmidtz, who identified himself from the outset, and David Henderson. Both offered valuable criticisms and suggestions for improving various chapters and the book as a whole, which is indeed better for their advice. Canadian philosopher Antoine Dussault read and commented on Part One; and from him I learned much and incorporated much of what I learned. Curt Meine, among other accomplishments, Aldo Leopold's biographer, and Buddy Huffaker, president and executive director of the Aldo Leopold Foundation, offered valuable advice for improving Chapter 1. I am grateful to Oxford University Press acquisitions editors Hallie Stebbens, who enthusiastically endorsed this project, and to Lucy Randall, who expertly and efficiently advised and guided me through the contract and submissions processes. I thank Balamurugan Rajendran of Newgen Knowledge Works Pvt. Ltd., the project manager, who, with great courtesy and care oversaw the turning of my manuscript into a book. I thank Matt Story for creating the index. Patterson Lamb and I were the copy editors. We are responsible for the surviving errors in the minutia of punctuation and style.

An explicit tenet of my philosophy is that thoughts are publicly ambient, not privately cogitated things. Thus I regard myself not as an individually creative thinker, but as a memeticist sequencing one segment of the evolving human memome. This book could, therefore, only exist because the field of environmental philosophy emerged in the 1970s and has flourished ever since. I am indebted to the whole community of environmental philosophers, living and dead, in whose universe of discourse this book takes its place. I thank the provosts (past and present, since my arrival in 1995) of the University of North Texas and the deans (past and present, also since then) of the UNT College of Arts and Sciences for subsidizing my research and providing me with the space (literal as well as figurative) to interact with my colleagues across the campus, with my fellow denizens of the Environmental Education, Science, and Technology building, and with fellow members of and students (graduate and undergraduate) in the UNT Department of Philosophy and Religion Studies. They too have provided a thinking community from which this book has emerged.

I am most grateful to have been the son of my late father, Burton Callicott, who made the painting titled "New Moon 2," a photograph of which graces the cover of this book; and I thank my sister, Alice Callicott, for blessing my use of the image. Last, I thank Priscilla Solis Ybarra, with whom I have engaged in an ongoing critical conversation for upwards of fifteen years. More than anyone else, she has expanded the horizons of my vision and opened up new doors of perception—as well as keeping me abreast, to the limits of my fading capacities, with new technologies.

Introduction

The idea for this book began to occur to me in Cambridge, Massachusetts, as I was participating in a small conference titled "Buddhist Ecology and Environmental Studies" at the Harvard Center for the Study of World Religions in December of 2005. There a delegation of Buddhist scholars, from Dongguk University in Seoul, South Korea, met with a group of American scholars, mostly from the Greater Boston area, to explore the conference theme. I had devoted a chapter and a half to Buddhism in my 1994 book, *Earth's Insights: A Multicultural Survey of Ecological Ethics from the Mediterranean Basin to the Australian Outback*.[1] And I suppose it was for that reason that I was invited to participate. But I am by no means an expert on Buddhism. For *Earth's Insights* I learned only enough about it to suggest—at a level of detail appropriate to a global survey of world religions and select indigenous traditions—how ecologically consonant environmental ethics have been and might be developed within several prominent strains of Buddhism. My secondhand account focused on Thervada, Hua-Yen, Tendai, Shingon, and Zen Buddhism. For me to address the Dongguk and local specialists in attendance about the potential for ecological ethics in Korean Buddhism would have been presumptuous, to say nothing of embarrassing. However, just as there are many kinds of Buddhism, so also are there many kinds of ecology. Therefore, to engage the conference theme—Buddhist Ecology and Environmental Studies—not only must one first ask, "What Buddhism?" one must also ask "What Ecology?" I left the first question for the other participants to answer and dwelled instead on the second in my conference paper.[2]

Many of us in environmental philosophy and ethics have an impression of ecology derived from the paradigm prevailing in the early 1970s, when our philosophical subdiscipline first emerged. That paradigm was set out with force and authority by Eugene P. Odum in the then-leading textbook, *Fundamentals of Ecology*.[3] According to Odum, ecosystems were the central objects of ecological study; and, undisturbed by human activities, "mature" ecosystems were believed to be in a highly organized state of self-regulating dynamic equilibrium.[4] Odum had given a sophisticated and detailed formulation to a tradition of thought in ecology going back to its beginnings as a science.[5] In Odum's masterly hands the ecosystem concept was successor to Frederic Clements's claim that, just as single-celled organisms eventually evolved to form multi-celled organisms, so multi-celled organisms eventually evolved to form super-organisms.[6] There is some historical irony in this line of conceptual development, because Arthur Tansley had first delineated the ecosystem concept in 1935 as an alternative to the super-organism idea, of which he was sharply critical.[7] However that may be, for Clements, ecology was the physiology of homeostatic super-organisms, while for Odum ecology studied the functional units of homeostatic ecosystems and their harmonious integration—which is to say pretty much the same thing in different words.

1

Clements's paradigm was opposed by his contemporary, Henry Gleason, who publicly doubted the existence of super-organisms.[8] Gleason pointed out that such putative entities were difficult to bound spatially with any precision—one species of super-organism, say, an oak-hickory hardwood forest, often blended into another, say, a long-grass prairie. Equally difficult to bound in time were the successional stages in the putative development (ontogeny) of a super-organism from herbaceous weeds through shrubs and brush to the supposedly self-sustaining and self-reproducing climax type. Moreover, close, quantitative comparison of several alleged instances of the same species of super-organism indicated that no two were as similar in composition and structure as are individuals of the same species of multi-celled organisms.

Nevertheless, so suggestive and enthralling was the Clementsian super-organism paradigm that Gleason was virtually ignored in his own era, the first quarter of the twentieth century.[9] Back then, ecology was a brand new science and Clements's paradigm allowed ecological studies to be conceived as analogs of familiar biological studies. Ecology could have its own form of taxonomy (types of forests, grasslands, deserts), anatomy (physical structure—canopy, understory, root system), physiology (producers, consumers, decomposers), and ontogeny (succession). Quantitative study of vegetation, however, by John Curtis, Robert Whittaker, and their students in the 1950s, began to confirm Gleason's rival "individualistic" paradigm: that each plant species is "a law unto itself"; that species which are often found together are simply adapted to similar "gradients" of temperature, moisture, soil pH, and the like; and that associations of similarly adapted species, far from being super-organisms, are better thought of as mere coincidences.[10] The emergence of paleoecology—the study of past plant associations by examining their constituents' pollens preserved in peats—further confirmed the Gleasonian paradigm. In the course of the flow and ebb of ice over the continents during the Pleistocene, plants had formed associations different from those found presently and, during the Holocene, had come together from different directions at different rates of speed.[11] Thus, the idea that a contemporary forest is a functionally integrated unit was hard to credit in the light of these two lines of evidence to the contrary.

From the point of view of the classic and now superseded Clements-Odum paradigm, the delicate functional equilibria of ecosystems were upset mainly by external disturbances of sufficient magnitude, visited on them by human activities: timber harvesting; strip mining; plowing; urban, suburban, and exurban development.[12] In the 1980s, ecologists began to study the ecological role of "natural" disturbances—by fire, flood, drought, frost, ice, wind, pestilence, disease, volcanic eruption—and found them to be more common and frequent than had been supposed.[13] Indeed, so common and frequent are natural disturbances that they, rather than long-enduring homeostatic states, are the norm rather than the exception for most landscapes. Ecologists soon began to identify and measure various "disturbance regimes"—the periodic recurrences of fire, flood, drought, and other disturbances, and their ecologic effects.[14] Simultaneously, demographers began to recalculate the size of the Pre-Columbian human population in the Western hemisphere, taking into account the devastating impact of Old World diseases on New World peoples, and revised their estimates upward by a factor of ten.[15] In short, landscapes the world over have been subject to both natural and anthropogenic disturbance for thousands of years.

The implicit stochasticity at the heart of the Gleasonian idea—that groups of plants are coincidental assemblages—and the ubiquity of disturbance in nature undermined the Clementsian dogma that succession proceeds through determinate steps to a climax condition (Odum's mature ecosystem). These climax associations or mature ecosystems were supposed to be self-maintaining and -reproducing until reset by some exogenous, most probably anthropogenic, disturbance—only to go through the same successional series to the same endpoint. But, as it turns out, there are no end states, *teloi*, toward which nature aims. Rather, what there is is endless, direction-less change.[16]

[margin note: Teleological Man vs. Directionless Nature]

Indeed, that ecosystems exist as independent biophysical objects is dubious. Ecologists from Clements to Odum believed that super-organisms/ecosystems had evolved through natural selection. Those kinds that were most stable (persistent, resistant, and resilient) and self-regulating out-competed those that were less so.[17] That idea was debunked by evolutionary biologist G. C. Williams, who sharply and persuasively criticized the concept of group selection in the 1960s.[18] How could ecosystems evolve by natural selection if they were so ephemeral, on the evolutionary temporal scale, and lacked a genome of their own? Further, the isolation of an ecosystem as an object of study is partially artificial.[19] If, for example, an aquatic community ecologist is studying predator-prey relationships among fishes in a lake, the shoreline of the lake bounds the ecosystem spatially and a period of time measured in years bounds it temporally; if another ecologist is studying the process of eutrophication in the same lake, the watershed surrounding the lake bounds the ecosystem spatially and a period of time measured in decades bounds it temporally. The object of study is in effect defined, both spatially and temporally, by the ecological question posed. How can ecosystems be real, independent biological objects—comparable in that regard to organisms—if they morph from one size and shape to another and from one life span to another, depending on how ecologists interrogate them?[20]

[margin note: Challenge: ecosystems as independent biological organisms]

In my Buddhist-ecology conference paper I pointed out that this ground-sea paradigm shift in ecology had serious implications for environmental ethics, and most especially for the holistic Leopold land ethic—which I had long championed—because the land ethic is based squarely on evolutionary biology and ecology.[21] The evolutionary foundations of the Leopold land ethic involve the unorthodox concept of group selection (which, however, may now be returning to some modicum of respectability). That's trouble enough, but the ecological foundations of the Leopold land ethic appear to be hopelessly obsolete. The summary moral maxim, or "golden rule," of the land ethic is "A thing is right when it tends to preserve the integrity, stability, and beauty of the biotic community. It is wrong when it tends otherwise."[22] Have coincidences any integrity to preserve? Have periodically disturbed, ever-changing landscapes any stability to preserve? That leaves only the beauty of the biotic community as an environmental-ethical norm, but isn't beauty, notoriously, in the eye of the beholder? More basic still, are biotic communities actual biological entities or are they, as Gleason suspected, figments of the overwrought ecological imagination?

As bearer of these sad tidings regarding *fin de millennium* ecology, I felt like the pro-verbial skunk at the Buddhist-ecology garden party. After I had presented a PowerPoint summary of my paper, Michael McElroy, a distinguished Earth-systems scientist, pre-sented one of his.[23] The contrast was stark. He began with a biography of planet Earth from its condensation in a spinning mass of gas and dust some 4.6 billion years ago through the gravitational and thermal sorting of materials into a core, inner and outer mantle, crust, hydrosphere, and atmosphere. He went on to describe such geological processes as mantle convection and plate tectonics, the uplifting of mountains, and their eventual mechanical and chemical weathering. He speculated on the origin of life on Earth some 3.5 billion years ago and the evolution of eukaryotic unicellular organ-isms 1.5 billion years ago from prokaryotic bacteria and blue-green algae. He described the first known global crisis for life on Earth, about two billion years ago, when oxygen, a waste product of photosynthesis, began to accumulate in the atmosphere and hydro-sphere, mortally threatening most of Earth's organisms that had evolved in an anaero-bic environment and relegating the survivors to anoxic microenvironments or *refugia* in, among other places, deep sediments and the guts of animals. That crisis, however, afforded the opportunity for oxygen-tolerant and oxygen-demanding respiratory organisms to evolve and to colonize dry land—because enough ozone (O_3) formed in the stratosphere to shield the naked surface of the Earth from excessive ultraviolet radiation from the Sun, which would otherwise have been lethal for living things.

McElroy carried his story through the great Late Permian mass extinction event about 250 million years ago and that at the end of the Cretaceous period some sixty-five million years ago. He went on to characterize the current state of the planet and the changes of geologic proportions—especially altering the chemistry of the atmosphere—that we *Homo sapiens* are now imposing on it.

Three things struck me about McElroy's conference presentation. The first was the spatial and temporal scales on which it focused: spatially the scale was planetary (if not solar-systemic); temporally the scale was geological. The second was its ontological focus: the Earth, an entity the actual existence of which is subject only to what might be called metaphysical doubt—the sort of doubt that Descartes is famous for—not to scientific doubt. The actual existence of super-strings in quantum physics and of super-organisms (or ecosystems) in ecology is subject to scientific doubt, but not the actual existence of planet Earth. Third, while at geological scales of time, the chemistry of the Earth's atmosphere and hydrosphere and its climate have fluctuated radically, at organismic and ecological temporal scales, they have fluctuated within narrow bounds. In short, at the planetary spatial scale and at humanly meaningful and practical tem-poral scales, the Earth's climate has remained relatively stable and its biogeochemistry has remained relatively homeostatic.

The disparity between my presentation and McElroy's troubled me and I contin-ued to think about it after the conference was over. It soon dawned on me that what was needed was an Earth ethic to complement the land ethic. I had already argued, in several papers published over the previous decade, that, appropriately revised, the land ethic could be accommodated to the currently prevailing neo-Gleasonian paradigm in ecology.[24] But the land ethic is nevertheless limited in application. It is, after all, the *land* ethic. Leopold himself seems to have thought little about the oceans, and so the question has been raised: Is it possible to extend the foundations of the land ethic to the sea or do we need to develop a completely independent sea ethic? (At different times and in different venues I have given mutually contradictory answers to that question.)[25] But even if the land ethic could be stretched (paradoxically, given its name) to embrace the sea, it would not constitute a genuine Earth ethic.

Why? Because the land ethic is spatially and temporally scaled to the size and dynamics of biotic communities and ecosystems—however imprecise and variable their spatial and temporal boundaries, and whether they are terrestrial or marine. But our most pressing environmental concerns have become global in spatial scale and proportionately protracted in temporal scale—global climate change, the threat of mass species extinction, and the erosion of the stratospheric ozone to the point of a "hole" appearing in it during the austral summer over the South Pole. These concerns came to public attention in the 1980s and together represent a *second wave of the environmental crisis*, the first wave of which crested in the 1960s. The first wave of the environmental crisis was all about pollution and resource depletion, which are spatially circumscribed—pollution, for example, coming from tailpipes, tankers, smokestacks, sewer outfalls, and spray nozzles. And, by implementing various conservation measures and switching to alternative technologies and resources, we can at least envision their remedies occurring over the span of a human lifetime. While global climate change is, of course, not unrelated to both local sources of pollution and the depletion of specific resources, the problem and its solution are orders of magnitude greater in both spatial and temporal scale.[26] The climate change that we are most concerned about is planetary in spatial scale. Further, it may not fully kick in for several decades into the future, when many of us—me included—will be dead and gone. But only by decisively and collectively acting now, can we delay its onset and diminish its magnitude, although we can no longer hope to prevent its occurrence.[27] And if we act now, we can hope to reverse global climate change, although the global climate may not return to Holocene norms for centuries or millennia to come. I do not mean to imply that micro-, local-, and regional-climate changes (associated with, say, deforestation) are not pressing concerns; I only mean to suggest that they are less fearsome and, if they can be disentangled from global climate change, they can be reversed in decades (by, say, afforestation).

Finally, I remembered that we have the germ of a true Earth ethic already to hand. And it was sketched by none other than Aldo Leopold himself in a manuscript, which had lain unpublished for more than half a century, innocuously titled "Some Fundamentals of Conservation in the Southwest" and dated 1923. Eugene C. Hargrove found it among Leopold's papers in the archives of the University of Wisconsin and secured permission from the Leopold family to publish it in the first volume of *Environmental Ethics* (the journal) in 1979.[28] In the last of its three sections, titled "Conservation as a Moral Issue," Leopold conceived of an ethic concerned not for biotic communities and ecosystems, but for the whole Earth and for the whole extent of its biography. At thirty-six years of age, this was Leopold's first sortie into environmental ethics and he sketched a sweeping moral vision in a prose poem that was as remarkable for its compelling literary beauty as for its expansive scope and scientific and philosophical sophistication.

As to scientific sophistication, in "Some Fundamentals" Leopold anticipates the outlines of biogeochemistry—then, of course unbeknownst to him, gestating in the mind of Vladimir Vernadsky in Russia. *Biosfera*, Vernadsky's field-defining work, was published in Russian in 1926 (and, translated into French, *La Biosphère* was published in 1929).[29] Vernadsky's son, George, was a member of the Yale University faculty in Russian history and, by that stroke of luck, the great Yale ecologist G. E. Hutchinson became acquainted with Vladimir Vernadsky's work and facilitated the publication of a summary of his science of biogeochemistry in English in the mid-1940s.[30] Building, to some extent, on Hutchinson's Vernadsky-inspired work, James Lovelock and Lynn Margulis developed a globally scaled systems science in the 1970s and 1980s under the rubric of the Gaia hypothesis.[31] Thus Leopold seems to have entertained essentially Gaian speculations at about the same time as Vernadsky, perhaps even earlier, although unlike Vernadsky, Leopold never developed them at greater length.

As to philosophical sophistication, Leopold hints, in "Some Fundamentals," at basing an Earth ethic on personal, professional, and social self-respect—which would make it a form of multi-level virtue ethics—as well as basing such an ethic on concern for future human generations. More fully, however, he explores grounding an Earth ethic on an essentially Kantian concept of respect—for living, not necessarily rational, beings—and in doing so he anticipates the approach to environmental ethics more fully developed by Albert Schweitzer, at about the same time, and, more rigorously as well as more fully, by "biocentric" environmental philosophers in the 1980s and '90s, such as Paul W. Taylor, James P. Sterba, and Gary Varner.[32] Schweitzer and the latter-day biocentrists limited their ethic of respect for life to individual living beings—that is, to organisms in the conventional sense of the term. In sharp contrast, Leopold suggested, in accordance with his Gaian speculations, that the Earth itself is a living being—which, per se, should command our respect. In a foundational paper in environmental ethics, Kenneth E. Goodpaster briefly ruminated on the possibility of extending a biocentric ethic to the "biosystem" (or biosphere, we must suppose he meant), per se—Gaia by another name.[33] Respect for ordinary (multi-celled) living organisms—for which Schweitzer, Taylor, Sterba, and Varner exclusively pled—Leopold may have assumed, but did not specifically mention in "Some Fundamentals."

The spatio-temporal scale of the Leopold Earth ethic is its principal asset. Its *spatial* scale is commensurate with the scale of our most pressing contemporary environmental concerns—once more: anthropogenic global climate change, mass extinction, and damage to the ozone membrane of the upper atmosphere. But just as the land ethic is rendered problematic by the contemporary neo-Gleasonian paradigm in ecology, so the Earth ethic may be rendered problematic by its very scalar proportions, especially the proportions of its *temporal* scale. Are there spatio-temporal scalar limits to ethics, to moral concern? For example, can we—or should we—be ethically concerned about life on an Earth-like planet in another solar system? Can we—or should we—be ethically concerned about events that occurred or will occur on Earth in the distant past or in the distant future? In other words, how wide and long can our moral sensibilities range? If they are limited in spatio-temporal scope, does the Leopold Earth ethic exceed those limits? If a non-anthropocentric Earth ethic as sketched by Leopold is literally far-fetched, what about the cogency of an anthropocentric Earth ethic, at which he also hints—one rooted in virtuous self-respect and in responsibility to future generations, to both "immediate posterity" and the "Unknown Future"? And if we do have responsibility to distant future generations, as well as to those to whom we can relate in some personal way, are those responsibilities to the *individual members* of those distant future generations or to those generations collectively? Can intergenerational ethics, in other words, be individualistic or must they be holistic? If necessarily holistic, then to what human "thing," what entity, do we of the present have duties and obligations?

This book is divided into two parts—Part One: The Land Ethic, and Part Two, the Earth Ethic. I begin Part One with a chapter devoted to the philosophical burden of *A Sand County Almanac and Sketches Here and There*, Leopold's masterpiece and the literary context of "The Land Ethic," its capstone essay. In Chapter 1, I argue that *Sand County* has a single overarching and unifying theme—the exposition and promulgation of an evolutionary-ecological worldview and its axiological (ethical and aesthetical) and normative (practical moral) implications. In Chapter 2, I provide a detailed account of the Leopold land ethic and its Humean philosophical and Darwinian evolutionary foundations. In Chapter 3, I provide an account of its ecological scientific foundations and indicate how the land ethic can be updated to meet the challenge posed by the changes here just indicated in its scientific foundations. Because the land ethic is informed by evolutionary biology and ecology, in Chapter 3, I also address the prohibition of deriving value from fact and *oughts* from *ises*—sometimes carelessly called "the Naturalistic Fallacy"—that cloistered twentieth-century moral philosophy and prohibited it from having any legitimate intercourse with science. In Chapter 4, I demonstrate that this sequestration of ethics from science is historically anomalous and indeed a historical aberration and pathology. And in Chapter 5, I indicate how the science of ethics is now flourishing in the twenty-first century and is, furthermore, vindicating a Humean and Darwinian approach to ethics.

For those readers who are well acquainted with my earlier work, the account, justification, revision, and defense of the land ethic in Part One will be generally familiar and new only to the extent of including new details, increased historical depth, and new developments in the exciting contemporary science of ethics. Here I reprise my account, justification, and defense of the land ethic and my suggested revision of it—in light of developments in evolutionary biology and ecology that took place after Leopold sketched it—for three reasons. First, precisely because the land ethic is familiar and my treatment of it, though far less so, is also familiar, a well-established model of what an environmental ethic is and what its foundations are can here serve as a kind of benchmark or template for a similar account of the Leopold Earth ethic—for which no account, justification, or defense has so far appeared by me or anyone else. Second, an account of the land ethic can serve as a kind of foil for an account of the Earth ethic, revealing not only the necessary formal elements of any environmental ethic, but also bringing into sharp contrast differences in the philosophical and scientific substance that gives content to the formal structure that any well-formed

Earth ethic complements land ethic

environmental ethic should have. Third, I do not suggest that the Earth ethic should replace or supersede the land ethic, but that the Earth ethic should complement the land ethic. Appropriately updated and revised, the land ethic still serves, better than any other, to address our still very real and very grave environmental concerns at ecological spatial and temporal scales.

In Chapter 6, the first chapter of Part Two, I provide a detailed account of the Leopold Earth ethic and the several philosophical foundations for it that Leopold suggests in "Conservation as a Moral Issue," the third section of "Some Fundamentals of Conservation in the Southwest." In Chapter 6, as I also do in Chapter 1, I indulge myself in a polemical digression. Bryan G. Norton has long challenged my interpretation of Aldo Leopold's philosophy and offered up his own interpretation of it, placing Leopold in the tradition of American Pragmatism; making of him a lifelong disciple of Arthur Twining Hadley; and also making of him, as is Norton himself, an unregenerate anthropocentrist. Norton's interpretation of Leopold's philosophy has mostly centered on "Thinking Like a Mountain" in *A Sand County Almanac*, and on "Conservation as a Moral Issue." In Chapter 1, I dispute Norton's interpretation of "Thinking Like a Mountain" and, in Chapter 6, I dispute his interpretation of "Conservation as a Moral Issue."

In Chapter 7, I explore the scientific and metaphysical foundations of a non-anthropocentric Earth ethic such as Leopold broaches in "Some Fundamentals of Conservation in the Southwest." In the third section, "Conservation as a Moral Issue," of that essay Leopold several times refers to and quotes "the Russian philosopher [P. D.] Ouspensky" from his book *Tertium Organum*, published in English in 1920.[34] We can overlook the fact that Ouspensky hardly qualifies as a philosopher and also what Leopold's enthusiasm for Ouspensky says about Leopold's critical faculties in 1923, let alone his intellectual tastes. Of far greater worth is exploring the thought of another Russian philosopher, and also a contemporary of Leopold, Vladimir Vernadsky. Ouspensky does not seem to have been influenced by Vernadsky; nor could Leopold have been, except were he accustomed to reading French, but, in some inexplicable and uncanny way, Leopold's speculations about a living Earth have a remarkable similarity to those of Vernadsky. Further, how do Leopold's Gaian speculations compare with other expressions of planetary holism and panpsychism that were roughly contemporary with his own and Vernadsky's or developed a little later, such as those of Teilhard de Chardin?[35]

In Chapter 8 of Part Two, I explore the support that might be found in contemporary environmental ethics—Kantian biocentrism—for the kind of non-anthropocentric Earth ethic to which Leopold gives the most concentrated attention in "Conservation as Moral Issue." In Chapter 9, I explore the possibility that "natural-contract" ethics (developed by Michel Serres and recently hinted at by James Lovelock) and virtue ethics (suggested by Leopold himself in "Conservation as a Moral Issue" and recently endorsed most notably by Dale Jamieson and Ron Sandler) might provide support for an Earth ethic, such as Leopold envisioned in 1923. Natural-contract ethics and virtue ethics are both essentially anthropocentric. In Chapter 10, I review and critique the prevailing ethical über-paradigm in mainstream moral philosophy, Rational

Individualism—which, as Jamieson demonstrates, "collapses" in the face of the spatial and especially the temporal scales of global climate change. This discussion too is a bit polemical as I have long championed a communitarian and holistic approach to ethics rooted in the moral sentiments—in human (and Humean) emotions—in contrast with the prevailing individualistic approach rooted in rationality. In Chapter 11, I argue that my long-championed communitarian and holistic ethical paradigm is mandated by the spatial and temporal scales of global climate change and vindicated by the contemporary science of ethics. That is, I demonstrate that the Humean-Darwinian foundations of the land ethic—now so well validated by the contemporary science of ethics—can also coherently undergird responsibility to future human generations and therefore can also serve as the foundations for an international and intergenerational anthropocentric Earth ethic. Thus can the land ethic and the Earth ethic, in its anthropocentric form, be reconciled and unified in theory as well as be complementary in practice.

The word *anthropocentric* appears to be deceptively straightforward, simply meaning human-centered. Correlatively, *non-anthropocentric* means not human-centered. That *anthropocentrism* and *non-anthropocentrism*—the philosophical expressions of anthropocentric and non-anthropocentric doctrines—are more complicated concepts than the use of just these two words (and their syntactical variants) would imply will become evident as the analysis of the land ethic and the Earth ethic unfolds in the chapters that follow this introduction. So here at the outset, let me distinguish three primary senses in which *anthropocentrism* and *non-anthropocentrism* are used, each indicated by a distinct adjective.

Aristotle called the study of being qua being "first philosophy" because it is prior, not necessarily in the temporal order in which a philosopher takes it up, but prior in the very architecture of philosophical thought. The study of such foundational concepts is called *metaphysics*. Accordingly, we might denominate as *metaphysical anthropocentrism* the doctrine that human beings occupy a privileged place in the order of being. Aristotle himself was a metaphysical anthropocentrist because he thought that human beings, albeit animals, were uniquely rational animals and thus occupied a higher and more privileged place in the order of being than do all other animals. The biblical worldview is also metaphysically anthropocentric because Genesis declares that human beings were uniquely created in the image of God and thus assigned an exalted and privileged place in the hierarchy of creation. To think that human beings do not occupy a vaunted and privileged place in the order of being is to espouse *metaphysical non-anthropocentrism*. One reason that the theory of evolution is, by some, reviled and rejected is because it is metaphysically non-anthropocentric.

Limiting membership to all and only human beings in what Richard Routley calls the "base class" of an ethic—the set of entities to which ethical regard is appropriately directed—may be called *moral anthropocentrism*.[36] *Moral non-anthropocentrism* enlarges the base class of an ethic to include some non-human beings. Animal liberation and animal rights, for example, are morally non-anthropocentric, as, apparently, is the land ethic. The base class of the land ethic is, however, far wider than those of animal liberation and animal rights, because it includes plants as well as animals and also soils and waters; the land ethic's base class even includes the biotic community per se or "as such." Moral anthropocentrism is often justified by appeal to metaphysical anthropocentrism. Kant, for example, justified limiting ethical regard to all and only rational beings (the class of which, as far as he knew, is coextensive with the class of human beings) by appeal to the metaphysical claim that only rational (human) beings were ends in themselves and autonomous. But moral anthropocentrism need not be justified by appeal to metaphysical anthropocentrism. The anthropocentric utilitarianism, for example, prevailing in neoclassical economic theory is not justified by appeal to metaphysical anthropocentrism; rather, its anthropocentrism seems to be unapologetically arbitrary. Various approaches to an anthropocentric Earth ethic reviewed and developed in Chapters 9 and 10 are not justified by appeal to metaphysical anthropocentrism, but neither is their moral anthropocentrism arbitrary. Indeed quite the opposite; they are, rather, unequivocally based on metaphysical non-anthropocentrism and quite consistently and unparadoxically so.

A third species of anthropocentrism—that might be called *tautological anthropocentrism*—is occasionally invoked. All human experience, including all the ways that human beings experience value, is human experience and therefore tautologically anthropocentric. Tautological anthropocentrism is humanly inescapable. Indeed, the term *tautological non-anthropocentrism* is oxymoronic and names nothing real or possible. One may value intrinsically various non-human beings and, for that reason, regard them ethically—and if so, one would be a moral non-anthropocentrist. Nevertheless, for a human being to value non-human beings intrinsically is a human act of valuing; and all human valuing is human valuing—and thus tautologically anthropocentric. Militant moral anthropocentrists sometimes cryptically conflate tautological anthropocentrism with moral anthropocentrism in order to dismiss moral non-anthropocentrism as incoherent or self-contradictory. As noted, tautological non-anthropocentrism is indeed incoherent and self-contradictory, but moral non-anthropocentrism is entirely coherent and self-consistent. The claim that all human beings are tautologically anthropocentric is trivially true or analytically true and is, therefore, a hollow claim not worth making—except for purposes of sophistical argumentation.

Further complicating matters is the concept designated by the term *anthropomorphic*, meaning having a human form. The ancient Greek gods and goddesses were *physically anthropomorphic*, portrayed in the bodily form of human beings and thus the Olympian religion of the ancient Greeks involved anthropomorphism. The animal characters in *The Wind and the Willows* by Kenneth Grahame are not physically anthropomorphic; rather they are psychologically *anthropomorphic*— they experience the world like human beings do. They are also *culturally anthropomorphic*—they wear clothes, live in houses, row boats, drive automobiles, and speak English. As detailed and documented in Chapter 1, in *A Sand County Almanac* Aldo Leopold's characterization of animals is often anthropomorphic—psychologically anthropomorphic, but neither physically nor culturally anthropomorphic. Making matters more complicated still, in "Some Fundamentals of Conservation in the

Southwest," Leopold uses the word *anthropomorphic*, when he evidently means *anthropocentric*.

Finally, moral anthropocentrism and moral non-anthropocentrism may be either individualistic or holistic or both at once. *Individualistic moral anthropocentrism* admits into the base class of ethics only individual human beings and excludes human collectives such as families, societies, nation-states, global civilization, and *Homo sapiens* (the species). *Holistic moral anthropocentrism* admits both individual human beings and human collectives into the base class of ethics. Fascism is a form of holistic moral anthropocentrism that admits human collectives, especially the nation-state, into the base class of ethics, but effectively excludes individual human beings. The Earth ethic that I commend in Chapter 11 as theoretically the most plausible and pragmatically the most serviceable of conceivable alternatives is an instance of holistic moral anthropocentrism. *Individualistic moral non-anthropocentrism* admits only individual human and non-human beings into the ethical base class and excludes non-human collectives such as non-human species, biotic communities, ecosystems, and the biosphere. Animal liberation, animal rights, and most expressions of biocentrism are instances of individualistic moral non-anthropocentrism. *Holistic moral non-anthropocentrism* admits non-human collectives into the ethical base class. The land ethic is apparently an instance of holistic moral non-anthropocentrism. Environmental fascism would be a form of holistic moral non-anthropocentrism that excludes individual human and non-human beings from the base class of ethics. The land ethic has been accused of being an instance of environmental fascism, but, in Chapter 2, I indicate otherwise: the land ethic is an addendum to all our familiar human-oriented ethics, not a substitute for them. Among my principal philosophical tasks in this study is to unify, theoretically, our familiar human-oriented ethics, the land ethic, and also the Earth ethic—to articulate a theory of ethics, in other words, that will embrace them all.

The term *anthropogenic* figures prominently in the previous discussion and occasionally in the chapters that follow and is conceptually unproblematic. It simply means human-caused or human-generated.

I bring this introduction to a close by posing and trying persuasively to answer two related questions one of which is essentially existential, the other essentially strategic: (1) Why the Leopold *Earth* ethic and (2) Why the *Leopold* Earth ethic?

The first question might be rephrased as follows: Isn't the land ethic up to the job of meeting the challenges of the second wave of the environmental crisis? If the answer to that question is Yes, then isn't a new Earth ethic otiose? In "The Land Ethic," Leopold seems expressly to address one salient challenge of the second wave of the environmental crisis—species extinction. He states, for example, that "wildflowers and songbirds…are entitled to continuance" and "should continue as a matter of biotic right."[37] Leopold did not, however, comprehend the full scale of species extinction that snapped into clear focus only in the last quarter of the twentieth century with the recognition that the planet is on the precipice of only the sixth mass extinction event in the entire biography of the Earth.[38] The extinctions that the land ethic specifically addresses are local and regional; the sixth mass extinction is not only of planetary spatial scale, its temporal scale is multi-millennial—only after several million years following a mass extinction event does Earth's biodiversity recover.[39] Latterly, we are morally concerned not only about species extinction but also about biodiversity loss. And the very concept of *biodiversity* is more than the sum of its parts, the several species that compose it. As the bumper sticker reminds us, "extinction is forever"—true enough for individual species extinctions; but, as the fossil record demonstrates, biodiversity loss is not forever; biodiversity comes back.[40] The erosion of Earth's protective ozone membrane and global climate change exacerbate biodiversity loss as photo-sensitive species are pushed over the brink of extinction by the former phenomenon and, by the latter, those that cannot move uphill or farther north fast enough. Stratospheric ozone thinning, global climate change, and biodiversity loss are more a matter of Earth ethics than land ethics given the spatial and temporal scales of these unwelcome phenomena.

Once more, however, let me emphasize—and at the risk of being repetitive I shall reiterate it in subsequent chapters of this book because it is so very important: *the Earth ethic complements and supplements the land ethic; it does not succeed or replace it.* No, not any more than that the land ethic succeeds or replaces our venerable human ethics, as I explain in Chapter 2. To say that because the land ethic addresses, by implication, the challenges of the second wave of the environmental crisis, we don't need a new-fangled Earth ethic is like saying we don't need a non-anthropocentric land ethic because our venerable anthropocentric ethics address the challenges of the first wave of the environmental crisis. Bryan Norton, for one, has long argued just that— we don't need a non-anthropocentric land ethic—because it is hard to think of any environmental damage that does not adversely affect human beings, if not always in material ways then in psycho-spiritual ways.[41] Perhaps. But don't we need as many moral reasons as philosophers can muster up to meet the challenges of both waves of the environmental crisis? Just as the non-anthropocentric land ethic complements and supplements anthropocentric utilitarian and deontological environmental ethics, so the Earth ethic in both its non-anthropocentric and anthropocentric formulations complements and supplements the land ethic.

In a single system of moral philosophy, which I attempt to achieve in this book, ontological pluralism and deontological pluralism must be tempered by theoretical monism. That is, the many disparate objects of moral concern and the many disparate duties and obligations generated by one's relationships with those many and diverse objects of moral concern must be theoretically unified if one's moral philosophy is to be coherent and self-consistent. In the concluding chapter, Chapter 11, I indicate how the land ethic and the Earth ethic can be embraced by a single ethical theory, by a single overarching moral philosophy.

I turn now to the second question, Why the *Leopold* Earth ethic? Leopold wrote a single section of a single paper in 1923 on the possibility of a biosphere-scaled environmental ethic that he himself never saw fit to publish. Nor did he ever subsequently develop his faint sketch of an Earth ethic anywhere else. Why not the *Vernadsky* Earth ethic or the *Lovelock* Earth ethic or just the plain, no-brand-name Earth ethic? Why drag Leopold's name into it—or anyone else's other than my own for that matter? My answer is fourfold: the first personal, the second and third historical, and the fourth philosophical.

First, the personal answer: my work has long been associated with the Leopold legacy. While I suppose that I could develop a biosphere-scaled environmental ethic with only passing reference to Leopold, I want to establish continuity between such an ethic and my older exposition of the biotic-community-scaled land ethic in numerous essays, many collected in *In Defense of the Land Ethic* and *Beyond the Land Ethic*. Otherwise it might seem as if I just saw Al Gore's infomercial, *An Inconvenient Truth*, and jumped on the latest bandwagon to pass my way.

Second, Leopold has street cred in the environmental-movement 'hood like nobody else, not Thoreau, not Muir, not Pinchot. When Leopold talks, people listen. That's the second answer.

Third, Leopold deserves credit for first speculating about an Earth ethic however fleetingly. He is often called a prophet and in most cases for good reason.[42] He noticed the environmental crisis a decade and a half before most anyone else did. His "The Land Ethic" in *A Sand County Almanac* was published two and a half decades before anyone else thought that working out environmental ethics was a worthwhile thing to do. And he was a few years ahead of Vernadsky and half a century ahead of Lovelock in thinking ethically—if they ever really did—on a biospherical scale. Leopold deserves credit for conceiving the Earth ethic.

Fourth, the philosophical and the most important answer: the most compelling Earth ethic is built upon the same essentially Humean theoretical foundations that ground the land ethic. The Earth ethic that I ultimately commend in this book is, in the last analysis, a companion and complement to the land ethic and together they are components of a new comprehensive environmental philosophy for the twenty-first century.

Because it is the textual basis for the Leopold Earth ethic and because it is less well known and accessible than *Sand County*'s "The Land Ethic," "Some Fundamentals of Conservation in the Southwest" is published in its entirety as an appendix in this book.

Part One
The Land Ethic

1

A Sand County Almanac

"The Land Ethic" is the capstone essay of Aldo Leopold's enduring masterpiece, *A Sand County Almanac*. That essay has been scrutinized and analyzed by environmental philosophers—including by this environmental philosopher—for nearly half a century. Relatively little philosophical attention has been paid to other essays in the book, with the exception of "Thinking Like a Mountain," on which much philosophical attention has been lavished in the voluminous writings of Bryan G. Norton. But practically no philosophical attention has been paid to the book as a whole. As Ashley Pryor laments, "As a brief survey of environmental-ethics textbooks will confirm, the majority of academic philosophers who engage with Leopold read 'The Land Ethic' in isolation from the rest of Leopold's extensive body of written work."[1] Because "The Land Ethic" is the climax, the culmination, the denouement of *A Sand County Almanac*, a thorough treatment of "The Land Ethic" (and of the land ethic)—which is what I provide in the first half of this book—would be incomplete without a thorough understanding of the literary context in which it is situated. Thus the first chapter of this book on the conceptual foundations of the Leopold land ethic and the little known and so-far unanalyzed Leopold Earth ethic begins with a brief introduction to the author and an analysis of his revered classic. In the second half of this book, I engage with a bit of the rest of Leopold's extensive body of work, especially with "Some Fundamentals of Conservation in the Southwest."

1.1 THE AUTHOR

Aldo Leopold was born on January 11, 1887, into a prosperous, public-spirited commercial family of German descent—a family keenly interested in the natural sciences and the fine and liberal arts. He was born in Burlington, Iowa, a Mississippi River town. As a boy, Leopold showed an avid interest in natural history, especially bird watching, and an enthusiasm for hunting. His father, Carl, an impassioned hunter himself, imparted to his sons both extraordinary venatic skills and ethical restraints in the pursuit of game. The teenaged Leopold was sent to the elite Lawrenceville School in New Jersey, which prepared him for matriculation into Yale University, where, after five years, he was graduated from the Yale Forest School, with a master's degree, in 1909. That year he joined the US Department of Agriculture Forest Service and was posted to the Southwest Territories—then they had not yet become states—of Arizona and New Mexico.[2]

Leopold steadily rose in the ranks of the Service, but he was less interested in its principal remit, timber production, than with the "thifty" condition of the forest itself.[3] As he would later characterize it, he was interested in the "beauty" of the national forest lands as well as their "utility."[4] Leopold was, accordingly, alarmed at soil erosion, caused by livestock grazing and fire suppression; and he was interested in the animals inhabiting the national forests—only in part because he was an ardent hunter.[5] In his wide-ranging Forest Service fieldwork, Leopold also developed a love for roadless travel by horse, pack train, and canoe. Consistent with all these concerns and interests, he was among the first civil servants to propose a system of wilderness reserves in the US National Forests.[6]

In 1924, Leopold was posted to the USDA Forest Products Laboratory in Madison, Wisconsin. He was not happy in that post and resigned from the Service in 1928 to become a consultant to the Sporting Arms and Ammunition Manufacturers' Institute, conducting game surveys and overseeing wildlife research in the midwestern states. Leopold was barely able to support a wife and five children during the ensuing Great Depression but used the involuntary leisure it afforded him to write a field-defining text, *Game Management*, published in 1933. That book led to an appointment at the University of Wisconsin as professor of game management in the Department of Agricultural Economics. Leopold remained a college professor for the rest of his life, eventually heading his own Department of Wildlife Management (later to become the Department of Wildlife Ecology). From that position he assumed a leadership role in the American conservation movement. Leopold was among the founders of the Wilderness Society (1935) and the Wildlife Society (1936) and he served the Ecological Society of America as president (1947), among other similar organizational offices and services.[7]

In 1935, Leopold bought eighty acres (~40 hectares) of exhausted farmland on the Wisconsin River, some fifty miles (~80 kilometers) north of Madison, which he planned to use for waterfowl hunting. The farmhouse had burned down and the only standing building was a chicken coop or cow shed full of manure. Leopold and his family converted that building into a camp cabin—adding a bunkroom and a fireplace and chimney. They dubbed it "the shack." The Leopolds soon turned to the task of planting pine trees and prairie vegetation. Although the concept had not been fully articulated by then, theirs was among the first projects of ecological restoration.

1.2 THE PROVENANCE OF THE BOOK

In the early 1940s, at the behest of the New York publisher Alfred A. Knopf, Leopold began work, in a desultory way, on a book of nature essays. The publisher asked him to write "'a personal book recounting adventures in the field…warmly, evocatively, and vividly written…a book for the layman…[with] room for the author's opinions on ecology and conservation…worked into a framework of actual field experience.'"[8] Leopold's plan was to revise and include some very argumentative pieces that he had already written and published in various venues during the 1930s, along with some more descriptive, less judgmental pieces that he was writing for *The Wisconsin Agriculturist and Farmer*. Despite the initial provision of "room for the author's opinions on ecology and conservation," the editors at Knopf found that kind of essay to be repetitive and tedious. They decided that what they really wanted was "a book purely of nature observations."[9] Further, they found Leopold's essays to be not only scattered in subject matter, but also in place (from the Southwest to the Midwest, from Canada to Mexico), and time (from Leopold's boyhood to his early days in the forest service to his latter days as a college professor). His essays, therefore, lacked the classic Aristotelian unities of time and place, which characterized nature-writing genre exemplars, such as *The Natural History of Selborne* by Gilbert White; *Walden; or Life in the Woods*, by Henry David Thoreau; and *The Outermost House: A Year on the Great Beach of Cape Cod* by Henry Beston. Leopold's essays also varied radically in length—"Draba," for example, filling only half a page, "Good Oak," twelve pages.

In response to these criticisms, Leopold struggled throughout the decade to produce a book that had all the qualities that Knopf first suggested: a book that was personal, addressed to a broad lay audience, and opinionated—all worked into a framework of actual field experience. He declined to write a book of "mere natural history" (as he styled it), a book "purely of nature observations" (as they did).[10] And so Knopf declined to publish the manuscript as submitted in 1947. It was also rejected by Macmillan and the University of Minnesota Press. Bitterly disappointed, Leopold discarded the more conventional Foreword he had written by way of an introduction in July 1947 and replaced it with a new, pithier Foreword written in March 1948.[11] He then relinquished the task of finding a publisher to his son, Luna, who sent it to William Sloan Associates and to Oxford University Press. Oxford immediately accepted it for publication without critical comment or demand for extensive revision. Difficulty finding a publisher for the book on which he had worked so hard was not the only trouble plaguing Leopold's life at that time. He was suffering from "tic douloureux" (trigeminal neuralgia), an excruciatingly painful irritation of a facial nerve and from vehement political opposition to his management plan for reducing the size of the deer herd in northern Wisconsin. Just a week after receiving the good news from Oxford, Leopold died—pleased at least by this long-awaited happy outcome—at age sixty-one, on April 21, 1948.[12]

Because Luna Leopold had already taken on a substantial role in getting his father's manuscript accepted for publication, he guided it through the production process. He proceeded on the principle that the eventual book should be as faithful as possible to the volume that his father had crafted. Leopold's own title, *Great Possessions*, was, however, wisely discarded. He had titled the first and longest of the three parts of his book, "A Sauk County Almanac," because "the shack" and its environs, the setting of Part I, were located in Sauk County, Wisconsin (named for the American Indian tribe that had once lived there). No one now knows who suggested that "Sauk County" be changed to "Sand County"—but whoever deserves the credit, it was stroke of genius. There is no Sand County, Wisconsin, but the shack and its environs are located in the sandy outwash plain of the glacier that covered half the state, bisecting it from the northwest to the southeast, as recently as twelve thousand years ago. The region was (and is) known in Wisconsin as "the sand counties" or "the central sands." And so the book was published in 1949 as *A Sand County Almanac and Sketches Here and There*.[13]

1.3 THE UNITY OF *A SAND COUNTY ALMANAC*–AN EVOLUTIONARY-ECOLOGICAL WORLDVIEW

For Knopf and the other publishers who had rejected Leopold's manuscript, the main issue could be boiled down to one thing, "unity." And upon first encounter, the book does appear to be a hodgepodge of variegated materials.

Part I shifts from casually following a skunk track in the first essay; to making firewood from a lightning-killed oak, in the second (all the while providing an environmental history of the ground in which the good oak was rooted); to migrating geese in the third; then on to loving descriptions of various humble plants (such as draba) and animals (such as woodcock); to episodes of fishing and hunting; to activities of ecological restoration, such as tree planting and culling. To mute the jarring effect of their disparate subject matter, Leopold obligingly supplied the essays of Part I, but only of Part I, with the Aristotelian unities of time and place. They are organized by the months of the calendar year; and the place in which they are set is the shack landscape—Leopold's Waldenesque "week-end refuge from too much modernity." (In the "Foreword," Leopold informally refers to Part I as the "shack sketches.")[14]

Part II, "Sketches Here and There," gently transitions from the well-circumscribed shack environs to Wisconsin at large. Then the setting of the essays shifts a little farther away to the neighboring states of Illinois and Iowa, then it jumps to the more distant American Southwest (Arizona and New Mexico), then turns sharply south to Chihuahua and Sonora in Mexico; then moves back north to Oregon and Utah and finally to Manitoba in Canada. Sketches here and there indeed!—all loosely organized by state or province and scattered across the whole North American continent. And again, the subject matter ranges just as widely in Part II as in Part I: from threatened cranes to the extinct passenger pigeon to canoing on a river in "Wisconsin"; from a bus journey through corn fields to a brutal youthful hunting vignette in "Illinois and Iowa"; from climbing mountains to exterminating bears and wolves in "Arizona and New Mexico"; from parrots in the Sierra Madre mountains to the delta of the Colorado River and to a mountain stream in "Chihuahua and Sonora"; from an invasive species of grass in "Oregon and Utah" to a lonely, wild marsh in "Manitoba."

In Part III, "The Upshot," Leopold totally abandons any attempt to supply a transparent (and artificial) literary device of unification. It consists of four longer "philosophical" essays, the first two of which are strident rebukes of unethical hunting practices, while the third is a poignant appeal for wilderness preservation. The fourth is "The Land Ethic," which Leopold himself had placed first in the final section, but was moved (again wisely) to the climactic conclusion of Part III and of the book as a whole.

Were the editors at Knopf right to complain that the manuscript Leopold submitted lacked unity? Leopold thought not. He had taken their criticisms to heart and worked to overcome their concerns and replied of his submitted essays: "I still think that they have a unity as they are."[15] The book has become a classic of conservation philosophy, the bible of the contemporary environmental movement. Translated into a dozen languages, it has universal appeal. Evidently in *A Sand County Almanac* as in the United

States of America, *e pluribus unum*, from many one. But what is its principle of unity, what makes of that variegated many a unified whole?

There is one underlying, persistent thematic thread that Leopold weaves through the fabric of his masterpiece from the first pages to the last: the exposition and promulgation of an evolutionary-ecological worldview and its axiological (ethical and aesthetical) and normative (practical moral) implications. Leopold's bold project in *A Sand County Almanac* is nothing short of worldview remediation. And, whether consciously or not, I think that his prospective publishers sensed that and reacted negatively—not to the book's lack of unity, but to its very radical and revolutionary unifying theme. They were afraid that the book-buying public would be offended: "What we like best is the nature observations, and the more objective narratives and essays. We like less the subjective parts—that is, the philosophical reflections which are less fresh and which one reader finds sometimes 'fatuous.' The ecological argument almost everyone finds unconvincing."[16] Leopold's was an unsettling book, an affront to postwar blue-skies optimism and American self-satisfaction.

Luna Leopold edited a second book by his father titled *Round River: From the Journals of Aldo Leopold*, published by Oxford in 1953. The raw and often graphic journals, most of them narratives of Leopold's hunting adventures, were never written for publication and proved to be an embarrassment, threatening to tarnish Leopold's reputation among the more tender-hearted constituents of the conservation community. Rachel Carson, in particular, found them to be unworthy of the author of *A Sand County Almanac* (to put her point circumspectly). The essays on conservation in *Round River* were quietly culled away from the journal material and interpolated into *A Sand County Almanac* and published by Oxford in 1966 as *A Sand County Almanac with Other Essays on Conservation from Round River*. There they constitute a new Part III, and Part III of the original was reorganized to become Part IV of the expanded edition. *A Sand County Almanac* needed the essays from *Round River* about like I need another hole in the head. Don't get me wrong. They are all great essays, comparable in quality to those of the *Almanac*. But the carefully crafted unity that Leopold imparted to his masterpiece was destroyed by that ill-advised and thoughtless outrage. Ballantine Books began publishing the mutilated text in 1970 in the form of a cheap paperback—which has now, unfortunately, become the most commonplace edition. Needless to say, my analysis here is of the book that Leopold himself assembled.

1.4 THE ARGUMENT OF THE FOREWORD— TOWARD WORLDVIEW REMEDIATION

Leopold plainly and guilelessly announces the nature of his project in the "Foreword," but with such charm and indirection that the enormous scope and scale of it might easily be missed: "Conservation is getting nowhere," he writes, "because it is incompatible with our Abrahamic *concept* of land."[17] One of Leopold's favorite rhetorical devices is synecdoche, letting the part stand for the whole.[18] Our Abrahamic concept of land is, more forthrightly put, our inherited biblical worldview. In accordance with that worldview, Leopold claims, "We abuse land because we regard it as a commodity belonging to us."[19] Toward the end of the book, in "The Land Ethic," Leopold evokes the same synecdoche for the biblical worldview once more: "Abraham knew what the land was for: it was to drip milk and honey into Abraham's mouth. At the present moment, the assurance with which we regard this assumption is inverse to our education."[20]

Leopold here anticipates the (in)famous environmental critique of the biblical worldview by historian Lynn White Jr. at the zenith of public awareness of and concern about an "environmental crisis." White laid ultimate blame for what he called "the ecologic crisis" on the biblical ideas that "man" is created in the "image of God," given "dominion" over the rest of creation, and charged to "subdue" it.[21] Whether Leopold and White correctly understand the particulars of the biblical worldview or how it has shaped Christendom's cultural attitudes toward the natural world is another question, which has been much debated. My present point is that Leopold *thought* that the biblical worldview is incompatible with conservation. Grafted on to the biblical foundations of the twentieth-century Western worldview was the emergence—following World War II—of mass consumerism: "our bigger and better society is now like a hypochondriac, so obsessed with its own economic health as to have lost the capacity to remain healthy. The whole world is so greedy for more bathtubs [another synecdoche] that it has lost the stability necessary to build them or even to turn off the tap."[22]

Rather than accommodate conservation to that toxic mix of biblical dominionism and mass consumerism, Leopold instead proposed to replace it with a more coherent and comprehensive alternative: "I suppose it may be said that these essays tell the company how it may get back in step."[23] Thoreau, as everyone knows, claimed to step to the beat of a "different drummer" and was proud to be out of step with the company—nineteenth-century American cultural attitudes and values.[24] Leopold boldly insists that the company—twentieth-century Western civilization—get in step with the better beat of the drummer to which he had learned to march.

"When we see land as a community to which we belong," Leopold continues, "we may begin to use it with love and respect.... That land is a community is the basic concept of ecology, but that land is to be loved and respected is an extension of ethics. That land yields a cultural harvest is a fact long known but latterly often forgotten."[25] To repeat, my central claim is this: *A Sand County Almanac*, at first blush a mere hodgepodge of charming but disparate vignettes, has a single overarching and unifying theme and purpose—the exposition and promulgation of an evolutionary-ecological worldview and its axiological and normative implications. "These essays," Leopold goes on, "attempt to weld these three concepts"—the community-concept of ecology, ethics, and aesthetics (the cultural harvest yielded by land).[26]

On February 11, 1948, Roberts Mann, the superintendent of conservation for the Forest Preserve District of Cook County (Chicago) Illinois and a friend of Leopold, wrote to share his chagrin and amusement over some "kick-back" he received for a piece he had published in his organization's *Nature Bulletin*. Mann's article was titled "Lincoln and Darwin"—who were both born on February 12, 1809. The kick-back from some readers was motivated by religious antagonism to Darwin's theory of evolution apparently worked to a fever pitch by Mann's association of Illinois's most distinguished native son with Darwin-the-devil-incarnate, in the minds of the back-kickers. Several days later, Leopold replied to Mann. "I liked your page on Darwin and Lincoln," he wrote, "and was also surprised about the protest. Of course neither of us really ought to be surprised because if one carries the ecological idea far enough, one ultimately gets over into philosophy."[27] Leopold's own exploration of an evolutionary-ecological philosophy was fully expounded in his manuscript. And, perhaps inspired by this exchange with Mann, he wrote a new Foreword for it sometime during the weeks following. The 1948 Foreword contrasted the evolutionary-ecological philosophy with the philosophy of those who were threatened by it, but, apparently unlike Mann, Leopold introduced and explored the new philosophy in a disarming style.

1.5 THE ARGUMENT OF PART I– THE INTERSUBJECTIVE BIOTIC COMMUNITY–INTRODUCED

"Nothing could be more salutary," Leopold concludes the Foreword, "than a little healthy contempt for a plethora of material blessings. Perhaps such a *shift of values* can be achieved by reappraising things unnatural, tame, and confined in terms of things natural, wild, and free."[28] Turn the page, and Leopold's effort to induce a culture-wide "shift of values"—a wholesale paradigm shift—begins right on the downbeat. The first (and only) essay in "January," the first section of Part I, "the shack sketches" is "January Thaw." The author is awakened by dripping water and goes outside to see what's up. He follows a skunk track "curious *to deduce* his *state of mind* and *appetite*, and destination if any."[29] The ecologist, like a natural-history version of Sherlock Holmes, deduces hidden facts from readily perceptible clues. To be an ecologist is a mind-challenging, adventurous occupation. (And we readers secretly want to be Dr. Watsons to his Holmes—sharing in the fun of discovery, by following the lead of the masterly sleuth.) Leopold first comes upon "[a] meadow mouse, startled by my approach, [who] darts damply across the skunk track." The eco-detective's mind starts to work: "Why is he abroad in daylight? Probably because he *feels grieved* about the thaw."[30] Leopold goes on gently to satirize the prevailing metaphysical and moral anthropocentrism of the Abrahamic worldview by comparing it with the microtocentrism of a mouse's worldview: "The mouse is a sober citizen who *knows* that grass grows in order that mice may store it as underground haystacks, and that snow falls in order that mice may build subways from stack to stack: supply, demand, and transport all neatly organized"—but "the thawing sun has mocked the basic premises of the microtine economic system."[31] Just what is being mocked here and by whom?

Putting all such things in pluralistic post-modern perspective, Leopold follows by treating his reader to a buteocentric worldview: The author sees "A rough-legged hawk…sailing over the meadow. Now he stops, hovers like a kingfisher, and then drops like a feathered bomb into the marsh. He does not rise again, so I am sure he has caught and is now eating some worried mouse-engineer.…The rough-legged has no *opinion* why grass grows, but he is *well aware* that snow melts in order that hawks may again catch mice."[32]

For most of Leopold's contemporaries, one unwelcome implication of the theory of evolution, of which ecology is but an extension, is that "man" is an animal no more exalted or privileged in the larger scheme of things than any other animal. We humans know by the most incontrovertible evidence—introspection—that we have states of mind and appetites, feelings and passions. To impute states of mind and appetites, feelings and passions to the other animals is therefore perfectly consistent with the evolutionary-ecological worldview. Leopold thus freely indulges in the anthropomorphic personification of other animals as central to his project of worldview remediation. The community concept—"the basic concept of ecology"—has an interior, a subjective, as well as an exterior, objective aspect. The shack sketches are full of "scientific natural history," as the British ecologist and Leopold's friend, Charles Elton, defined *ecology*—all sorts of interesting and engaging ecological observations.[33] But Leopold also subtly works at portraying the intersubjectivity, the interiority of the biotic community.

1.6 THE ARGUMENT OF PART I– THE INTERSUBJECTIVE BIOTIC COMMUNITY–DRIVEN HOME

Leopold first blithely disregards the nearly universal skepticism about animal minds, not only evinced by those under the sway of the biblical worldview, which posits a metaphysical divide between humans and animals, but also evinced by his fellow scientists under the sway of Logical Positivism. He eventually confronts it, however, in "The Geese Return" in the "March" section of Part I. To do so, he begins by reinforcing his conflation of the human and animal worlds with a comparison that decidedly favors the animal:

A March morning is only as drab as he who walks in it without a glance skyward, ear cocked for geese. I once knew a lady, *banded* by Phi Beta Kappa, who told me that she had never heard or seen the geese that twice a year proclaim the revolving seasons to her well-insulated roof. Is education possibly trading awareness for things of lesser worth? The goose who trades his is soon a pile of feathers.[34]

Leopold then goes on to pique skepticism about animal minds to the point of outrage: "The geese that proclaim the seasons to our farm are aware of many things, including the Wisconsin statutes."[35] That, of course, is, on the face of it, ridiculous. Geese may be "aware of many things"—or they may not be—but they are not aware of the laws of the state of Wisconsin. Certainly not. But they *are* aware of the effect on human behavior of those Wisconsin statutes governing waterfowl hunting: "The southbound November flocks pass over us high and haughty, with scarcely a honk of recognition for their favorite sandbars and sloughs....November geese are aware that every marsh and pond bristles from dawn till dark with hopeful guns."[36] And we can believe that they are indeed. However, "March geese are a different story."

That point scored, Leopold steps up his anthropomorphic personification of geese. The gabbling geese "*debate* the merits of the day's dinner."[37] Their gathering is a "spring goose *convention*" whereat "one notices the prevalence of singles—lone geese that do much flying about and much *talking*."[38] Thus, "One is apt to impute a disconsolate tone to their honkings and to jump to the conclusion that they are broken-hearted *widowers*, or *mothers* hunting lost *children*."[39] However, "[t]he seasoned ornithologist knows that such subjective interpretation of bird behavior is…"[40] Leopold does not say "unscientific" or "unverifiable," but simply "risky." He then tells a tale of data-gathering by his graduate students counting "for half a dozen years the number of geese comprising a flock," followed by "mathematical analysis," all indicating that "lone geese in spring are probably just what our fond imaginings had first suggested. They are bereaved survivors of the winter's shooting, searching in vain for their kin. Now I am free to grieve with and for the lone honkers."[41]

Unstated but scarcely unnoticeable in this vignette is the background evolutionary assumption that if we are entitled confidently to impute states of mind to our fellow humans—on the basis of what we know of our own states of mind, their behavior, and our knowledge of human social structures—we are no less entitled confidently to impute states of mind to our fellow voyagers in the odyssey of evolution on the basis of what we know of our own states of mind, their behavior, and our knowledge of their social structures. To the Positivist complaint that we can never directly observe the state of mind of another animal and verify our hypotheses concerning their thoughts and feelings, Leopold need only reply that we can never directly observe the states of mind of another human being. The only consciousness that one can directly observe is one's own—a somewhat unsettling realization, enticing a few idiosyncratic skeptics to espouse solipsism.[42] But how can one seriously doubt that the state of mind of a person whose face reddens, fists clench, and neck veins swell, upon suffering an insult added to an injury, would be exactly one's own if one were standing in the other's shoes. Of course, we can never be as confident that we know other animal minds as well as we think we know other human minds, but that they have minds and that they share with us a full suite of basic animal appetites, passions, and feelings—hunger, thirst, sexual craving, fear, and rage—is beyond doubt, from an evolutionary-ecological point of view.

Having not only blithely insisted upon the existence of non-human animal subjectivity but defended the scientific legitimacy of anthropomorphically personifying animals, Leopold is free to indulge in sympathetically imagining animal consciousness throughout the remainder of Part I. The instances are too numerous to document and dissect here. But they contribute immeasurably to the charm of the shack sketches and much endear their author to his readers. As a college professor who has taught logic to dull pupils, I will share my favorite instance and leave it at that. Recounting a partridge hunt in "Red Lanterns," Leopold notes that

My dog, by the way, thinks that I have much to learn about partridges, and, being a professional naturalist, I agree. He persists in tutoring me, with the calm patience of a professor of logic, in the art of drawing deductions from an educated nose. I delight in seeing him deduce a conclusion, in the form of a point, from data that are obvious to him, but speculative to my unaided eye. Perhaps he hopes his dull pupil will one day learn to smell.[43]

In Part I, Leopold's project of worldview remediation is approached relentlessly, but also indirectly and subliminally. Jumping right up on a soapbox and preaching a new gospel is hardly ever effective. In Part I, he never refers to evolution or ecology by name. Leopold is keenly aware that his readers' wariness must be overcome by charm and humor and that his message must be conveyed obliquely. The voice is first-person singular—"I." The tense is present. The author's persona is warm, amiable, intelligent, literate, witty, wry, ironic, entertaining, and self-confident. He seems only to observe and describe, to share his experience and knowledge. Yes, he gently criticizes and sometimes ridicules human foibles and follies, but never stridently or bitterly—rather, always tastefully, understatedly, and with a touch of ironic humor.

1.7 THE ARGUMENT OF PART II–THE EVOLUTIONARY ASPECT: TIME AND TELOS

In Part II, "Sketches Here and There," the voice shifts from the first-person singular to the first-person plural—to "we"—and the tense shifts from present to past. It's not about what I (the author) see and do, think and feel, but about what *we*, collectively, as a culture, believe. And it's about how *our* prevailing attitudes and values have led *us* astray in our relationship with things natural, wild, and free. It's also about how those attitudes and values must change if they are to accord with what evolutionary biology and ecology—now by name—have revealed to *us*, not only about nature but about ourselves and our place in nature.

James Brown, "the Godfather of Soul," introduced many innovations to American music. Arguably his greatest was a heavy emphasis on "The One," the first beat of every four-beat measure (as opposed to the emphasis on the second and fourth in traditional blues and jazz).[44] Leopold was ahead of his time in this particular as in so many others. Just as the one, "January Thaw," of Part I, gets right on the evolutionary-ecological groove, "Marshland Elegy," the first essay in Part II, "Sketches Here and There," also hits that theme hard right from the downbeat.

In my opinion, "Marshland Elegy" is the most beautiful piece in the book, from a purely literary point of view. It begins with a visual metaphor: a bank of fog covering a crane marsh as the "white ghost of a glacier" that covered the place thousands of years ago—thus immediately evoking deep time.[45] Several paragraphs further, the metaphorically evoked temporal scale of evolution becomes explicit: "A sense of time lies thick and heavy on such a place. Yearly since the ice age it has awakened each spring to the clangor of cranes.... An endless caravan of generations has built of its own bones this bridge into the future, this habitat where the oncoming host again may live and breed and die."[46]

For many of Leopold's contemporaries, as for many of our own, another unwelcome implication of the theory of evolution is its purposelessness. In Aristotelian terms, there is no "final cause" in evolutionary processes, no *telos*, no goal. Evolution proceeds by what the Greeks called chance, necessity, and fortune—chance genetic mutation, natural selection, and a little good or bad luck is what drives evolutionary development. Skunks, mice, hawks, geese, cranes, and humans have all just been spit out by the blind forces of nature, from an evolutionary point of view, happy (or unhappy, as the case may be) accidents. For Woody Allen this cosmic purposelessness leads to a profound (and comic) existential funk.[47] If the filmmaker is at all representative, people seem to want to feel that they have an important place in the grand scheme of things, that their lives have meaning, that we are here for a reason. The Abrahamic (biblical) worldview provides us with an exalted place in the cosmos, tells us the reason we exist, and gives a meaning from on high to our lives; the Darwinian (evolutionary-ecological) worldview does not.

Leopold squarely confronts that obstacle to the popular embrace of the evolutionary-ecological worldview by asking "To what end?" (this age-old annual cycle of living, breeding, and dying). And answers, cryptically, "Out on the bog a crane, gulping some luckless frog, springs his ungainly hulk into the air and flails the morning sun with mighty wings. The tamaracks re-echo his bugled certitude. He seems to know."[48]

So deep runs the desire for a transcendent cosmic purpose to give meaning to life that Peter Fritzell, one of the (otherwise probative) contributors to *Companion to A Sand County Almanac: Interpretive and Critical Essays*, insisted that Leopold meant that there *is* a final cause, an end, a *telos*—*we* just do not know what it is. But cranes do. Fritzell writes, "humans do not know, perhaps cannot know, 'to what end,' however much they may wish to. The crane, on the other hand,…'seems to know'—not only where he came from but also where he and his marshes are going—a quality of knowledge man can perceive perhaps, but which he cannot capture in language."[49] I think that Fritzell badly misses Leopold's point. There is no ultimate end. Leopold's point is that the question—To what end?—does not occur to the crane nor is he troubled by the fact that there is none. Every day, I read some lines by Matthew Arnold that are literally inscribed on stone in my study: "Is it so small a thing/To have enjoyed the sun,/To have lived light in the spring,/To have loved, to have thought, to have done?"[50] Why must we have a preordained *telos* to give meaning to our existence and a raison d'etre? Isn't it enough that we exist at all? Shouldn't we simply accept the mystery of our existence and pay it the homage that it deserves by giving it a meaning of our own making?

Wait a while. Perhaps there is an end: an end of another kind than that desired by those who *do* ask the question and *are* troubled by the absence of a satisfactory scientific answer. Aristotle draws a distinction that is often forgotten in contemporary teleology/ateleology debates, the distinction between "extrinsic" or "transcendent" and "intrinsic" or "immanent" ends. Some activities are their own ends (such as gazing at the moon, playing tennis, or making love); other activities we do for some end other than themselves (such as doing onerous, mind-numbing labor for the sake of earning a wage or traveling a long time in a cramped airplane seat to reach a distant destination). For Aristotle, intrinsic or immanent ends are superior to extrinsic or transcendent ends. Life might be understood to be an intrinsic or immanent end; we might live it for its own sake. The crane lives his to its fullest and with robustness of spirit. That's what the crane knows, if he knows anything—not where he came from and where he and his marshes are going. And that's what he has to teach Woody Allen, Peter Fritzell, and any of Leopold's readers who may be alienated by the *extrinsic, transcendent* purpose-lessness—the holy *sunyata*, the emptiness—at the core of the evolutionary-ecological worldview.

1.8 THE ARGUMENT OF PART II–THE EVOLUTIONARY ASPECT: BEAUTY, KINSHIP, AND SPIRITUALITY

"Marshland Elegy" has a personal significance for me. Not only did it awaken in me the profound potential in the evolutionary-ecological worldview for a naturalistic aesthetic and spirituality; it awakened in me a lifelong romance with cranes. "[O]ur appreciation of the crane grows," Leopold writes,

> with the slow unraveling of earthly history. His tribe, we now know, stems out of the remote Eocene. When we hear his call we hear no mere bird. We hear the trumpet in the orchestra of evolution. He is the symbol of our untamable past, of that incredible sweep of millennia that underlies and conditions the daily affairs of birds and men. And so they live and have their being—these cranes—not in the constricted present, but in the wider reaches of evolutionary time.[51]

After reading this passage for the first time, my very perceptual experience of cranes changed. No longer were they just large birds differing from herons in flying with neck outstretched rather than crooked into an S shape. They were flying fossils, only an evolutionary step or two removed from the pterosaurs from which they evolved. They were to me indeed "wildness incarnate," a living bridge across the Quaternary and Neogene periods into the Paleocene. Incidentally, the sentence—"We hear the trumpet in the orchestra of evolution"—was deleted from the four-part expanded (and apparently bowdlerized!) version of the book published by Oxford as *A Sand County Almanac with Other Essays on Conservation from Round River* in 1966 and by Ballantine in 1970. Were the Oxford and Ballantine editors of the popular paperback as leery of Leopold's forthright evolutionary proselytizing in 1966 as were the editors of Knopf in 1948? As noted in 1.3, sticking the essays on conservation from *Round River* into *Sand County* destroyed the beautiful unity of the book as Leopold had left it. And by deleting a key sentence of the original, the cutting edge of Leopold's overall argument was dulled.

In Part II's "On a Monument to the Pigeon," Leopold meditates at the gravesite of the extinct passenger pigeon in Wyalusing State Park at the confluence of the Wisconsin and Mississippi rivers. In that essay, he further develops the profound potential in the evolutionary-ecological worldview for a naturalistic spirituality and environmental ethic:

> It is a century now since Darwin gave us the first glimpse of the origin of species. We know now what was unknown to all the preceding caravan of generations: that men are only fellow-voyagers with other creatures in the odyssey of evolution. This new knowledge should have given us, by this time, *a sense of kinship* with fellow creatures; a wish to live and let live; *a sense of wonder* over the magnitude and duration of the biotic enterprise.[52]

Leopold follows with a pot shot at the smug metaphysical anthropocentrism of the worldview he essays to remediate: "Above all we should, in the century since Darwin, have come to know that man, while now captain of the adventuring ship, is hardly the sole object of its quest, and that his prior assumptions to this effect arose from the simple necessity of whistling in the dark."[53]

1.9 THE ARGUMENT OF PART II—THE ECOLOGICAL ASPECT

The ecological aspect of the evolutionary-ecological worldview is developed in Part II's "Odyssey," the essay following, at one remove, the evolution-themed "Marshland Elegy." Prior to European settlement, X, an atom of unspecified species (probably calcium), is dislodged from the limestone (calcium carbonate) substrate of the western Wisconsin prairie by a bur-oak root. He begins to cycle through the biota—first into one of the bur oak's acorns, which is eaten by a deer, which is eaten by an Indian. After the death and decay of the Indian, it is taken up by bluestem (a prairie grass) and then goes back into the soil. "Next he entered a tuft of side-oats gramma [another prairie grass], a buffalo, a buffalo chip, and again the soil. Next a spiderwort [a prairie flower], a rabbit, and an owl." And so the story goes, cycle after cycle, each one as detailed as the one before. (As an environmental-education exercise, I once observed children set to the task of drawing and painting X's odyssey. They were kept quiet and busy for a whole day.) After European settlement, "Y began a succession of dizzying annual trips through a new grass called wheat…his trip from rock to river completed in one short century"; and then, in a flash, from river to "his ancient prison, the sea."[54]

At the Yale School of Forestry and Environmental Studies, during the centennial celebration of Leopold's graduation in 2009, the distinguished ecologist Gene Likens, a founder of the famous Hubbard Brook Research Foundation, said that he had spent his whole career just putting numbers on X and Y. And indeed, when it was first published in 1942, Leopold was expressing, in a scientifically informed literary genre, state-of-the-art ecosystem ecology. In 1935, Arthur Tansley coined the term "ecosystem."[55] Tansley expanded the purview of ecology from the biota (relationships among plants and animals) to the "inorganic 'factors'"—for "there is constant interchange of the most various kinds within each [eco]system, not only between the organisms but between the organic and the inorganic."[56] Building on Tansley's work, in 1942, Raymond Lindeman incorporated the concept of energy flow into the nascent ecosystem paradigm in ecology.[57] Less than a decade after the introduction of the ecosystem idea, Leopold was conceptually, albeit not quantitatively, articulating both its main research components—materials cycling, in "Odyssey" (first published in 1941) and energy flows in "A Biotic View of Land" (first published in 1939).[58] He cut, edited, and pasted extensive passages from the latter into "The Land Ethic." Leopold actually anticipated Lindeman's focus on energy by several years, but thought that energy, like materials, cycled. However, unlike materials, such as the atoms of "Odyssey," energy makes a one-way trip through the biota, from solar source to entropic sink as Lindeman clearly understood. (See 3.8, 3.9, and 3.12 for a more detailed discussion of Leopold's place in the history of ecosystem ecology.)

In the "Chihuahua and Sonora" section of Part II, Leopold elaborates the "harmony-of-nature" ecological trope as a two-tiered metaphor. A fast-running mountain stream in northern Mexico, the Gavilan, produces an array of sounds, for which there are few adequate words in English. Even Leopold, among the great masters of the language, comes up only with "the tinkle of waters."[59] Gently moving waters also gurgle; and rapids roar. Be all that as it may, to characterize the panoply of sounds made by a mountain stream as a "song" is the first tier of the metaphor. "This song of the waters is audible to every ear, but there is other music in these hills, by no means audible to all."[60] That other "music" is the second tier of the metaphor.

> To hear even a few notes of it…you must know the speech of hills and rivers. Then on a still night, when the campfire is low and the Pleiades have climbed over rimrocks, sit quietly and listen for a wolf to howl, and *think hard* of everything you have seen and tried to understand. Then you may hear it—a vast pulsing harmony—its score inscribed on a thousand hills, its notes the lives and deaths of plants and animals, its rhythms spanning the seconds and the centuries.[61]

This "music" is as cerebral and metaphysical as the Pythagorean harmony of the spheres.

1.10 THE ARGUMENT OF PART II–THE PIVOTAL TROPE: "THINKING LIKE A MOUNTAIN"

"Thinking Like a Mountain," is all about predator-prey population dynamics and the relationship of those dynamics to vegetation cover and soil stability. In his early Forest-Service days, Leopold was a zealous advocate of predator extermination because, as he simply and candidly explains, he "thought that because fewer wolves meant more deer, . . . no wolves would mean hunter's paradise."[62] And so, when given "a chance to kill a wolf," he and his crew "were pumping lead into the pack" that had appeared unexpectedly below the escarpment where they were distractedly eating lunch.[63] They succeeded in mortally wounding the alpha female. In perhaps the most oft-quoted lines in Part II, Leopold sounds her death knell: "We reached the old wolf in time to watch a fierce green fire dying in her eyes. I realized then, and have known ever since, that there was something new to me in those eyes—something known only to her and to the mountain."[64] Subsequent experience revealed just what the wolf and the mountain know:

> Since then I have lived to see state after state extirpate its wolves. I have watched the face of many a newly wolfless mountain, and seen the south-facing slopes wrinkle with a maze of new deer trails. I have seen every edible bush and seedling browsed, first to anaemic desuetude, and then to death. I have seen every edible tree defoliated to the height of a saddlehorn....In the end the starved bones of the hoped-for deer herd, dead of its own too much, bleach with the bones of the dead sage, or molder under the high-lined junipers.[65]

Bryan G. Norton foregrounds another important ecological insight embedded in "Thinking Like a Mountain": "For Leopold, learning to think like a mountain was to recognize the importance of multiple temporal scales and the associated hidden dynamics that drive them."[66] Norton provides no textual support for this statement and his extensive elaboration of it in his book *Sustainability*, but it is supported by this passage in the essay:

> I now suspect that just as a deer herd lives in mortal fear of its wolves, so does a mountain live in mortal fear of its deer. And perhaps with better cause, for while a buck pulled down by wolves can be replaced in two or three years, a range pulled down by too many deer may fail of replacement in as many decades.[67]

The temporal scale of wolf-deer predator-prey population dynamics is measured in years; that of vegetational succession is measured in decades. Further, as Norton goes on to note, "These normally slow-scaled ecological dynamics [vegetative succession, in this case] if accelerated by violent and pervasive changes [to the faster-scaled dynamics of the ecological processes embedded in them, wolf-deer predator-prey population dynamics, in this case] can create havoc with established evolutionary opportunities and constraints."[68]

In addition to these ecological insights, "Thinking Like a Mountain" is also, much more importantly, about a moment of epiphany in the course of Leopold's own process of worldview remediation. Though set in the Southwest and describing an event that took place in 1909, it was written much later, in 1944, in response to criticism by one of Leopold's former students, Albert Hochbaum, who was reading Leopold's manuscript as it was taking shape.[69] In a letter to Leopold, Hochbaum wrote, "You have sometimes followed trails like anyone else that lead up wrong alleys....Your lesson is much stronger, then, if you try to show how your own attitude towards your environment has changed....That's why I suggested the wolf business. I hope that you will have at least one piece on wolves alone."[70] After reading Leopold's draft of "Thinking Like a Mountain," Hochbaum replied that it "fills the bill perfectly."[71]

In the tale Leopold tells, the dying eyes of the old she-wolf mutely ask her slayer, just as the voice of Jesus asked Saul of Tarsus on the road to Damascus, "Why persecutest thou me?" (Acts 22:7). We too can live and learn, just as did Leopold himself. We too can change our worldview, just as he himself did. Saul of Tarsus rejected his pagan worldview and adopted the Christian worldview and, to mark the transition his name changed from Saul to Paul and he became Paul "the Apostle." Leo (as he was called by his forest-service compatriots), the zealous predator exterminator—yes, in his Southwest days he was a very zealous advocate of predator extermination—became one of the twentieth century's most eloquent advocates and ardent protectors of predators. Leo's transformations, no less than Saul's, involved a profound paradigm shift, a worldview change. Maybe, Leopold hoped, he was but a harbinger of the worldview transformation that society as a whole was poised to undergo.

Gavin Van Horn points to another element in the essay that supports this epiphanic interpretation. "Perhaps the only time Leopold directly quoted Thoreau in his published writing," Van Horn notes, "was in the final paragraph of 'Thinking Like a Mountain,'..."—the famous line from Thoreau's essay, "Walking": "in wildness is the preservation of the world."[72] But Leopold either misquoted or deliberately changed one word: "In wildness," Leopold writes, "is the *salvation* of the world."[73] Van Horn points out that

> Though only a single word, the alteration is significant....It could be that Leopold, working from memory, inadvertently slipped at this point in the essay. More likely, however, is that the word substitution was neither a slip of the mind or the pen. Leopold's meticulous character and his penchant for continually re-drafting and editing his essays...suggest that [he] was carefully choosing his words while quoting from such a revered source. Whether to jolt the reader with a "mistaken" word, because of the suggestive redemptive connotations, or both, by using "salvation" rather than "preservation," Leopold underscored his own conversion experience in the essay and implied that the "hidden" knowledge of what has "long [been] known among mountains"...requires a similar *cultural conversion.*[74]

A Sand County Almanac is crafted to nudge that process of "cultural conversion" along. The confessional "Thinking Like a Mountain" demonstrates that worldview remediation is possible. It also demonstrates how a worldview remediator like Leopold can draw on the imagery and power of the very same traditional worldview that he is hoping to replace with the scientific worldview that he is striving to explicate and promulgate. The epiphany and conversion of Saul of Tarsus to Paul the Apostle was immediate, the epiphany and conversion of Leo-the-predator-exterminator to Aldo-the-predator-protector was gradual and protracted—a signal difference. But the impact that the essay makes on the reader is, as in the biblical paradigm that Leopold is mirroring, immediate and palpable. Thus the retold experience effects an immediate epiphany and conversion in the reader, even though it took the author thirty years to fully appreciate the significance of his youthful experience.

1.11 NORTON'S NARROW INTERPRETATION OF LEOPOLD'S WORLDVIEW-REMEDIATION PROJECT

Norton agrees that in "Thinking Like a Mountain," Leopold was out to change his readers' worldview. But that worldview change, Norton wishes us to believe, was far more modest than a wholesale shift from the prevailing militantly anthropocentric biblical dominionism leavened with consumerism to a non-anthropocentric evolutionary-ecological worldview. "Leopold's most important discovery," Norton asserts, is "the recognition that we act, learn, and evaluate within a multiscalar world. Leopold's greatest contribution is not in musings about extending moral considerability"—not, in other words, in bequeathing the land ethic to us—"but in reconstituting the perceptual field of *environmental managers*. He transformed that world into *the world of the adaptive manager*, measuring, testing, and evaluating within a complex dynamic system."[75] Fortunately, Leopold's own conception of the world of the adaptive manager is set out in an address to fellow wildlife managers in 1940. In that address Leopold clearly states that a seismic shift in values across Western culture is the worldview change that he has in his managerial sights:

> Our profession began with the job of producing something to shoot. However important that may seem to us, it is not very important to the emancipated moderns who no longer feel soil between their toes.
>
> We find that we cannot produce much to shoot until the landowner changes his ways of using his land, and he cannot change his ways until his teachers, bankers, customers, editors, governors, trespassers *change their ideas* about what land is for. To *change ideas* about what land is for is to *change ideas* about what anything is for.
>
> Thus we started to move a straw, and end up with the job of moving a mountain.[76]

Norton seems keen to counter the overwhelming impact that "Thinking Like a Mountain"—centrally located in and functioning as the pivotal essay of *A Sand County Almanac*—has actually had on its readers' sensibility and worldview. Leopold's arresting image—"a fierce green fire"—has become an iconic symbol for the contemporary environmental movement.[77] That the tempo of the dynamics of the world we live in is multiscalar is certainly an important element of the evolutionary-ecological worldview. But this is what readers remember most vividly about "Thinking Like a Mountain": that fierce green fire dying in the eyes of the old mother wolf; the remorse that the more mature Leopold evinces for his murderous and thoughtless act committed thirty-five years before, as finally he publicly confesses it; and his subsequent conversion to a whole 'nother way of thinking that was indeed decidedly non-anthropocentric—both metaphysically and morally non-anthropocentric (as distinguished in the Introduction). The most recent piece of evidence for my claim about what is truly memorable about "Thinking Like a Mountain" is the recent film (2011) documenting Leopold's life and thought, which is not titled "The World of the Adaptive Manager, Aldo Leopold" or "A Multiscalar World: Aldo Leopold the Anthropocentrist"; it is titled "Green Fire: Aldo Leopold and a Land Ethic for Our Time."

Just as Norton is keen narrowly to circumscribe the scope of the worldview remediation that Leopold was attempting to effect—limiting it to the outlook of "environmental managers," not to that of the public at large, and the shift of outlook among environmental managers to "the world of an *adaptive* manager"—Norton is also keen to narrow the range of Leopold's value pluralism to include only anthropocentric values:

> By reconstituting our perception of natural systems as multiscalar, Leopold encouraged a pluralistic approach to evaluation, an approach according to which humans may, and eventually must, evaluate changes that emerge on multiple scales, including the scale of individual economic activity and community-wide, multigenerational scales. By placing all of these evaluations within a reconfigured perceptual field, however, Leopold also eliminated appeal to values that transcend human experience. He was in this sense unquestionably an anthropocentrist.[78]

 Indeed in one sense—a trivial sense—Leopold was unquestionably an anthropocentrist. He was, as are we all, *tautologically* anthropocentric (as distinguished in the Introduction from *metaphysical* and *moral* anthropocentrism). All human values are…well, human values. If we value other-than-human beings intrinsically, such valuing remains human valuing. If we imagine the subjectivity of another kind of animal, such imagining is a human experience. By definition, then, we cannot transcend human experience, but there is no substance and no bite to such a truism. Leopold was demonstrably neither a metaphysical nor a moral anthropocentrist—he was not someone, that is, who values only human beings and/or the human species intrinsically and on that basis limits moral regard to human beings or to human communities or to the human species. Certainly Leopold was a value pluralist. He contrasted "value in the philosophical sense"—intrinsic value by another name (as explained in 1.13) with "mere economic value" and attributed the former to land. But he also acknowledged the importance of human-centered values at the scale of individual economic activity. Indeed, toward the end of "The Land Ethic," Leopold notes that "It of course goes without saying that economic feasibility limits the tether of what can or cannot be done *for* land. It always has and always will."[79]

Norton simply cannot be right to insist that Leopold intended to *eliminate* appeal to values that transcend human experience in any but a trivially true sense. If so, why would Leopold bother, in Part I of the *Almanac*, to invite his readers to try to transcend human experience by asking them to imagine experiencing the world as a horny skunk, just woken from hibernation; a worried meadow mouse, feeling grieved about a January thaw; an opinionated rough-legged hawk, enjoying a meadow-mouse lunch; talkative, broken-hearted geese, searching in vain for their kin; and a professorial pointer disappointed in his dull pupil? Norton insinuates that Leopold was an unregenerate metaphysical and moral anthropocentrist because, like everyone else, he is necessarily tautologically anthropocentric. But if so, *Sand County*'s Part I and Part II would be working at cross purposes; and "The Land Ethic" of Part III would be little more than a postscript consisting of idle "musings about extending moral considerability" to "soils, waters, plants, and animals, or collectively: the land."[80] If Norton is to be believed, Leopold was only doodling when there he wrote, "a land ethic changes the role of *Homo sapiens* from conqueror of the land community to plain member and citizen of it. It implies respect for his fellow-members and also for the community as such."[81] In 2.17, I provide a full and nuanced discussion of the anthropocentrism/non-anthropocentrism question concerning the land ethic. My decades-long debate with Norton about whether Leopold was an anthropocentrist or a non-anthropocentrist surfaces again in connection with the Earth ethic in 6.10 and again in 9.2.

1.12 THE ARGUMENT OF PART III–TO "SEE" WITH THE ECOLOGIST'S "MENTAL EYE"

The *penultimate goal* of Leopold's central task of worldview remediation is to cultivate in his readers his own settled *perception* of the world organized by way of the conceptual framework of the seasoned naturalist and professional ecologist that he had become—organized by way of the evolutionary-ecological worldview. In "Song of the Gavilan" the mode of perception is aural and the goal is to "hear" the harmony of nature—less with the bodily ear than with the Pythagorean ear of the ecologist's mind. In "Conservation Esthetic" in *Sand County*'s Part III, "The Upshot," Leopold articulates a visual metaphor complementing the aural metaphor of "Song of the Gavilan." The goal is for the reader to come to "see" the world, if not with the Buddha eye of the classical Japanese Zen master, Dogen, then with the ecological eye of Aldo Leopold—to see with the eye of the ecologist's mind.

As Leopold notes in "Conservation Esthetic," there was no greater American woodsman than Daniel Boone, but

> Boone's reaction depended not only on the quality of what he saw, but on the quality of the *mental eye* with which he saw it. Ecological science has wrought a change in the mental eye. It has disclosed origins and functions for what to Boone were only facts. It has disclosed mechanisms for what to Boone were only attributes.... [C]ompared with the competent ecologist of the present day, Boone saw only the surface of things. The incredible intricacies of the plant and animal community—*the intrinsic beauty* of the organism called America, then in the full bloom of her maidenhood—were as invisible and incomprehensible to Daniel Boone as they are today to Babbitt.[82]

Babbitt is the title character—a militantly ignorant real estate salesman, booster, and social climber—of a novel by Sinclair Lewis, satirizing the prevailing middle-class American beliefs, attitudes, and values of the 1920s. Leopold's *ultimate goal* is to draw out the axiological and normative implications of the evolutionary-ecological world-view—to bring to light its values and derive from it an environmental ethic. That is the principal burden of Part III of *A Sand County Almanac*, "The Upshot."

1.13 THE ARGUMENT OF PART III–AXIOLOGICAL IMPLICATIONS OF THE EVOLUTIONARY-ECOLOGICAL WORLDVIEW

Here we encounter one of the most disastrous shibboleths of twentieth-century philosophy, the so-called naturalistic fallacy: the dogma that science and ethics belong to separate universes of discourse, nor ever the twain should have permissible intercourse and legitimate issue. Facts and values, ethics and science, *ises* and *oughts* were relegated by twentieth-century philosophers to hermetically sealed compartments of thought and speech.[83] Thus, the very idea that the evolutionary-ecological worldview has ethical and aesthetic implications became a philosophical anathema. The derivation of *oughts* from *ises*, values from facts, ethics from science is alleged to be a fallacy of formal logic. With the improbable assistance of Immanuel Kant, in 3.1–3.5, I provide a full exposition of the naturalistic fallacy—actually David Hume's Is/Ought Dichotomy—and indicate how Hume himself explains the way in which facts inform values and ought-statements can be legitimately derived from is-statements.[84] Suffice it to say here that the sciences and the facts they disclose do inform our values and transform our ethics—and well they should. The scientific fact that *Homo sapiens* is a single species, originating in Africa and, from there, spreading all across the planet, makes belief in the superiority of any single human "race" untenable. Indeed racism is based on the false belief that race is a biological taxon analogous to species, but we know now—thanks to the human genome project, thanks to science—that it is not. We properly correct false values—racism, misogyny, homophobia, xenophobia—by appeal to the facts disclosed by science all the time. And there is nothing in the least fallacious about that.

The axiological implications of the evolutionary-ecological worldview that Leopold derives in "The Land Ethic" are straightforward and direct.

As indicated in the Introduction, moral anthropocentrism is the doctrine that the "base class" of an ethic—the set of entities meriting ethical regard—is constituted exclusively by human beings. Moral anthropocentrism is conventionally justified by appeal to metaphysical anthropocentrism. In the Abrahamic worldview moral anthropocentrism is justified by appeal to the metaphysical doctrine that humans are uniquely created in the image of God; in the modern philosophical tradition, best articulated by Immanuel Kant, moral anthropocentrism is justified by appeal to the metaphysical doctrine that humans are rational and autonomous—and while there may be other rational and autonomous beings in the universe, human beings are the only ones so far encountered. From the perspective of moral anthropocentrism, all that is non-human has but instrumental value to intrinsically valuable humans. But the theory of evolution undercuts all the traditional markers of human exceptionalism, as Darwin persuasively demonstrates in *The Descent of Man*—a point effectively made by both Peter Singer and James Rachels (as detailed and documented in 5.1 and 5.2) in service of animal-welfare ethics.

In accordance with both the metaphysical and moral non-anthropocentrism of the evolutionary-ecological worldview that Leopold is propounding and promulgating in *A Sand County Almanac* (pace Norton to the contrary), he effectively attributes intrinsic value to "land." Anything that has mere instrumental value can, as Kant first noted, be assigned a price, by means of which its relative instrumental value can be expressed:

> Whatever has reference to general human inclinations and needs [human desires or preferences] has a market price; whatever, without supposing any need, accords with a certain taste [objects of aesthetic delight, such as environmental "amenities"]…has an affective price [a shadow price]; but that which constitutes the condition under which alone something can be an end in itself has not merely a relative worth, i.e., a price, but has an intrinsic worth, i.e., a dignity.[85]

While Leopold does not specifically say that land has "intrinsic value," he uses words that clearly indicate that that is what he has in mind. Moreover, like Kant, he contrasts things that have intrinsic value with those that have merely instrumental value by associating the latter with economic valuation. Here is what Leopold does say about the value of land: "It is inconceivable to me that an ethical relation to land can exist without love, respect, and a high regard for its value. By value, I of course mean something far broader than mere economic value: I mean value in the philosophical sense."[86] In contrasting the kind of value he has in mind with "mere economic value"—price, to which everything of instrumental value is subject—Leopold could only mean by "value in the philosophical sense" what we environmental philosophers call "intrinsic value."[87]

1.14 THE ARGUMENT OF PART III–THE NORMATIVE IMPLICATIONS OF THE EVOLUTIONARY-ECOLOGICAL WORLDVIEW

The normative implications of the evolutionary-ecological worldview that Leopold derives in "The Land Ethic" are also straightforward and direct, but a little more complex.

From Darwin himself in *The Descent of Man*, Leopold took the idea that human ethics evolved by natural selection as a means to social integration. As Plato long ago observed, injustice (and immorality more generally) breeds enmity, hatred, and ultimately faction; it divides rather than unites.[88] If, due to internal faction and conflict, a society disintegrates, then, as solitaries, its erstwhile members could hardly survive and reproduce. Their lying, larcenous, murderous genes would be winnowed from the gene pool, while those of the compassionate, sympathetic, and sociable members of well-integrated cooperative communities would be conserved. Darwin also imagined how societies might have expanded over time and, correlative to that expansion, how human ethics expanded to become both more complex and more inclusive. Darwin even envisioned the expansion of ethics to eventually become inclusive of all humanity, indeed inclusive of all sentient beings. (See 2.5 and 2.6 for a full discussion and documentation.)

Leopold's vision went further still. To the evolutionary foundations provided by Darwin, Leopold added those of ecology. Ecology, especially as articulated by Charles Elton, represents plants and animals in terms of a social analogy—as members of biotic communities.[89] From an evolutionary point of view, human beings are also members of biotic communities. Therefore, if ethics evolved by natural selection as a means to social integration and if humans are members of biotic as well as human societies or communities, then a land ethic follows logically (Table 1.1). To avoid the disintegration of the biotic communities of which we humans are members and on which we humans depend for our very survival, we must expand the scope of our ethics to include our fellow members and those communities per se—not only the fellow members of our human communities and those communities per se, but the fellow members of our biotic communities and those communities per se. (See 2.7 for a full discussion and documentation.)

Table 1.1 Structure of Leopold's Project of Worldview Remediation—The Exposition and Promulgation of an Alternative Evolutionary-Ecological Worldview in *A Sand County Almanac and Sketches Here and There* and Its Axiological and Normative Implications

	Foreword	Part I	Part II	Part III
Voice	Condensed, pointed, but circumspect	First-person singular, descriptive, experiential	First-person plural expository, didactic	Impersonal, axiological, normative
Theme	Worldview remediation	Objective and intersubjective biotic-community membership	Evolutionary-ecological worldview exposed	Aesthetic and ethical implications promulgated

1.15 THE PERSUASIVE POWER OF LEOPOLD'S STYLE OF WRITING

Leopold's project in *A Sand County Almanac*—the exposition and promulgation of an evolutionary-ecological worldview and its axiological and normative implications—is a grand one, to be sure. He is trying to effect a sea change in popular consciousness. The actual evolutionary and ecological concepts that he propounds and promulgates are, however, pretty basic. Necessarily so, given the lay audience that he is addressing and its limited capacity for either profundity or subtlety. Indeed, Leopold produced exactly the book that Knopf first said they wanted him to write: "a personal book recounting adventures in the field... warmly, evocatively, and vividly written....a book for the layman... [with] room for the author's opinions on ecology and conservation... worked into a framework of actual field experience." That sort of book does not lend itself to a sustained, well-developed discussion of evolutionary biology and ecology, let alone value theory and moral philosophy. Why then has it become a great book? It is, by no means, unique, the only book of its kind from its era. There is, for example, *A Naturalist on Rona: Essays of a Biologist in Isolation* by Frank Frasier Darling, published by Oxford's Clarendon Press in 1939; *Road to Survival* by William Vogt, produced in 1948 by the same publisher, William Sloan, that was favorably considering Leopold's manuscript but that did not do so as quickly as Oxford.[90] Even more similar to *A Sand County Almanac* is *Adventures with a Texas Naturalist* by Roy Bedichek, published in 1947, two years *before* Leopold's book appeared—so there can be no suspicion that Bedicheck was imitating or echoing Leopold. In his introduction to a recent new edition, contemporary nature writer Rick Bass comments, perceptively, that Bedichek's *Adventures with a Texas Naturalist* "has much the same strength and message as Leopold's *A Sand County Almanac*."[91] If so, why have few outside a small circle of Texan environmentalists and historians ever heard of Roy Bedichek or his book? And the flip side of that question: why the virtual apotheosis of Leopold and the canonization of *Sand County*?

The simple and shallow answer is that Leopold had the good sense to write a slender volume of short essays—the longest of which, "The Land Ethic" is just twenty-five pages—in all, just 226 pages, typeset in a large font-size and illustrated by some thirty drawings (by Charles W. Schwartz), about half of which occupy a full page. Bedichek's book is half again as many pages long with half again as many words to a page and with half as many illustrations (by Ward Lockwood). Leopold knew how to give his message impact. His prose is condensed, heavy with import. It makes its mark in the mind and leaves a lasting impression. His book has risen above others like it from the same era mainly because of the way in which it is written.

John Tallmadge's "Anatomy of a Classic" in *Companion to* A Sand County Almanac, provides an analysis of Leopold's style. Central to it are Leopold's use of "techniques of compression."[92] One such technique is "concentration." While recording many natural facts, only those that "serve the theme and thrust of the essay" are included—"eliminating whatever does not advance the plot."[93] As a result, "Each word drops into place with that sense of inevitability that Dylan Thomas said he found in all good poetry... as if chosen with the utmost care."[94] Another technique is "engagement"—inviting "the reader to contribute [what] the text does not provide, thereby reducing the amount of explanation while increasing the density of implication."[95] Leopold's devices of engagement are "synecdoche, allusion, irony, understatement, and rhetorical questions."[96] I have already noted and commented on Leopold's use of synecdoche. In addition to "Abraham" as a surrogate for the Bible, Leopold frequently makes "Babbitt" a surrogate for the typical mindless American cipher. In other passages already quoted we find examples of all these devices. As Tallmadge notes, "Because the narrator does not browbeat us with verbiage, we feel respected, as if he valued our time, and so we are more inclined to listen. Here we feel is a writer who has taken pains to find exactly the right words to express the distilled wisdom of his life."[97]

One important aspect of Leopold's style, noted by Tallmadge, is its biblical resonance, especially resonance with the parables of Jesus in the New Testament: "A parable conveys novel ideas by means of familiar facts and situations, as in the well-known parables of Jesus....Eventually we realize that Leopold's 'sketches' are really parables and that this parabolic style accounts more than anything else for the book's perennial freshness."[98] As noted in 1.10, in addition to parables, "Thinking Like a Mountain" almost transparently mirrors the dramatic story of Paul's conversion on the road to Damascus.

In the 1920s, Leopold gave close study to the Bible—not, I think, for devotional as much as for rhetorical inspiration.[99] During this period he wrote a playful, irreverent piece titled "The Forestry of the Prophets," based on "a purely amateur study of the Books of the Prophets of the Old Testament" from which he gleaned and commented on the occasional bits of forest lore and fable that they contain.[100] In other essays from the same period, one finds Leopold making obvious attempts to mimic biblical diction and phrasing. For example, in "Some Fundamentals of Conservation in the Southwest"—the 1923 source for the Earth ethic developed in Part Two of this book—Leopold writes, "Erosion eats into our hills like a contagion, and floods bring down the loosened soil upon our valleys like a scourge."[101] By the time he assembled his masterpiece, he had perfected his rhetorical skills; but as Tallmadge notes, "Like hand-rubbed wood, its surface conceals its craft."[102] So, for example, in a passage already quoted from "Marshland Elegy" Leopold employs a biblical phrase, but redacts it just enough that its effect on the reader is more subliminal than conscious: "And so they live and have their being—these cranes." Had he written, as he may have at first been tempted to write, "And so they live, *and move*, and have their being—these cranes," the full phrase would be immediately recognizable as biblical (Acts 17:28). And thus its subliminal effect and power would have been canceled.

The ultimate use of irony, then, in *A Sand County Almanac*, is Leopold's deployment of the rhetorical power of biblical phrasing (e.g., "live and have their being"), biblical narratives (e.g., Paul on the Road to Damascus), and biblical literary forms (e.g., parables) to undercut the Bible-sourced aspect of the worldview that he sought to replace with the evolutionary-ecological worldview. To undercut its other aspects—consumerism and the associated commodification of nature and the reduction of its value to dollars and cents and the reduction of its wholeness to an aggregate of parts—Leopold deploys all these Bible-derived rhetorical devices, the frequent use of the "Babbitt" synecdoche, and the many more darts and arrows in his rhetorical quiver that Tallmadge identifies, irony principal among them. We have been conditioned to hear the words of the Bible as revealed truth. Thanks to Leopold's well-concealed craft, we receive the words of *A Sand County Almanac* as similarly revealed truth. It is no wonder, nor is it any accident, that Leopold is called a prophet and his wonderful book is called a bible.[103]

1.16 THE NEW SHIFTING PARADIGM IN ECOLOGY AND THE EVOLUTIONARY-ECOLOGICAL WORLDVIEW

A Sand County Almanac was published more than half a century ago and between then and now (as noted in the Introduction) both evolutionary biology and certainly ecology have undergone a series of profound changes. Is the evolutionary-ecological worldview that *Sand County* so persuasively exposes and promulgates still tenable? Does the Leopold land ethic, grounded in that worldview, remain relevant to our present environmental concerns?

The land ethic obviously seems to assume as definitive the biotic-community paradigm most clearly and elegantly expressed by the aforementioned Charles Elton in *Animal Ecology*, which represents plants and animals as occupying "niches," playing "roles," and pursuing "professions" in the "economy of nature."[104] After the deconstruction of the "community unit" theory by the likes of R. H. Whittaker, John T. Curtis, and Robert P. McIntosh (described and documented in the Introduction) do ecologists still believe that biotic communities exist as robust entities?[105] And if they do, do biotic communities have any integrity and stability to be preserved?

Philosophers call questions about the existence of this or that *ontological* questions. Does God exist? Do Platonic forms exist? Do ghosts exist? Do electrons exist? Do quarks exist? Do biotic communities exist?—a question more fully addressed in 3.14. Existence may come in degrees. As the aforementioned Tansley noted in the paper in which he coined the word *ecosystem*, "the systems we isolate mentally are not only included as parts of larger ones, but they also overlap, interlock, and interact with one another. The *isolation is partly artificial*, but it is the only possible way in which we can proceed."[106] Do ecosystems exist?—say the Greater Yellowstone Ecosystem or a prairie soil ecosystem—a question more fully addressed in 3.15. Yes, but when we come to isolate them, to bound them, for purposes of ecological study, we partly create them. Perhaps we might best say that ecosystems exist potentially, like electrons, and their existence is fully actualized when ecologists isolate them for purposes of study, just as electrons emerge fully into existence when quantum physicists measure them.

Leopold's project of worldview remediation in *A Sand County Almanac* is far more artful and beguiling than it had been a decade earlier. In a piece titled "The Arboretum and the University," published in 1934, Leopold more harshly perp-walked the prevailing cultural "world view" (his term) and boldly looked to ecology for a replacement:

> For twenty centuries or longer, all civilized *thought* has rested on one basic premise: that it is the destiny of man to exploit and enslave the earth. The biblical injunction to "go forth and multiply" is merely one of many dogmas which imply this attitude of *philosophical* imperialism. During the past few decades, however, a new science called ecology has been unobtrusively spreading a film of doubt over this heretofore unchallenged "world view." Ecology tells us that no animal—not even man—can be regarded as independent of his environment.

Plants, animals, men, and soil are a community of interdependent parts, *an organism*. No organism can survive the decadence of a member. Mr. Babbitt is no more a separate entity than is his left arm or a single cell of his biceps....It may flatter our ego to be called the sons of man, but it would be nearer the truth to call ourselves the brothers of our fields and forests.[107]

The (evolutionary-)ecological worldview that Leopold here alludes to is the super-organism paradigm championed by F. E. Clements, the dean of American ecology during its first quarter-century of existence as a distinct scientific discipline.[108] The next year (1935), Tansley introduced a new paradigm in ecology—the ecosystem paradigm—which is often characterized as a radical departure from Clementsian organicism.[109] As detailed in 3.12, while denying that "mature, well-integrated plant communities" were well-enough integrated to qualify as organisms, Tansley repeatedly declares that they are "quasi-organisms," existing in a state of "dynamic equilibrium," evolved to persist in that happy state by "natural selection."[110] As also detailed in 3.12, by mid-century, E. P. Odum had virtually returned the dominant ecosystem paradigm in ecology to its Clementsian roots, characterizing ecosystems in organismic terms.[111] *A Sand County Almanac* reflects the state of ambiguity in ecology about the (evolutionary-)ecological worldview at mid-century. The dominant image of land that Leopold promulgates there is, of course, the Eltonian "biotic community," but, with his "fountain-of-energy" trope, first published a decade before he edited and pasted it into "The Land Ethic," Leopold also anticipated the way that Raymond Lindeman would integrate Tansley's ecosystem concept with Elton's pyramid of numbers and render Elton's qualitative idea of food chains quantitatively as conduits of measurable energy.[112] Leopold also invoked the idea of "land health."[113] But health is a state of an organism; and indeed, in the same passage, Leopold used the phrase "land the collective *organism*."[114] On the other hand, he expressed reservations about the "balance-of-nature" idea and invoked "the mental image of land as a biotic *mechanism*."[115] So, is land an organism, a biotic community, an energy-metabolizing and nutrient-cycling ecosystem, or is it a mechanism?

As detailed in 3.13, late-twentieth-century hierarchy theory actually provides a theoretical integration of these once-disparate paradigms in ecology.[116] Community ecology focuses on interactive *components*, the specific plants and animals that perform various jobs in the economy of nature. Ecosystem ecology focuses on the *processes* that those components carry out, irrespective of the specific identity of the components; and it focuses on fluxes of energy and materials through the system. In hierarchy theory, three hierarchical levels must be isolated: the mid-level may be regarded as the "organic" object of inquiry; the level beneath it consists of various "mechanisms" and the level above it is the "context" or "environment" on which it draws for materials and energy.[117] Consider oneself as an organic object of study. One's various organs—the heart pumping blood, the lungs oxygenating the blood, the kidneys cleansing the blood—are the mechanisms that, when appropriately integrated and coordinated, perform organic functions. And one's environment is the context in which one exists and the source of one's energy and materials in the form of food (other organisms), air, and water. Analogously, consider Lindeman's Cedar Bog Lake as the organic object of his ecological study. The photosynthesis of the algae and other aquatic plants and the dynamics of the food web and its predator-prey interactions are the mechanisms, and the surrounding watershed is the context or environment. Arguably, in mixing his ecological metaphors in the way that he does in *Sand County*, Leopold vaguely anticipates the development of hierarchy theory in ecology.

In the decades following the publication of *Sand County*, the truly radical contemporary critique of Clementsian organicism by H. A. Gleason (see 3.13 for the historical details)—which made Tansley's seem tame by comparison—was revived as the "individualistic paradigm" in ecology, according to which each species is "law unto itself" and biotic communities are coincidental aggregates of species adapted to similar environmental gradients.[118] The ecological impact of natural disturbance was acknowledged and emphasized and "disturbance regimes" were identified.[119] Anthropogenic disturbance, moreover, was recognized to be long-standing and ubiquitous, requiring humans to be factored in to ecological studies on a par with other ecologically significant agents.[120] Urban ecology thus emerged as no less worthy or oxymoronic a field of study in ecology than tropical ecology or grassland ecology.[121]

So, from our vantage point in the second decade of the twenty-first century, we might well ask, Is there anything that can be characterized as an evolutionary-*ecological* worldview? And, if so, in what does an evolutionary-*ecological* worldview consist? Does ecology, that is, no less than the theory of evolution, provide us with a network of concepts, a cognitive framework, that functions as a lens through which our sensory experience is classified and organized to form a coherent whole, an evolutionary cum ecological worldview? I believe that it does, but it poses as formidable an expository challenge to contemporary philosophers as it did to Leopold. His challenge was that of a trailblazer into terra incognita; Leopold pioneered the philosophy of ecology. Our challenge is to follow him, but we must do so into a denser and more tangled thicket of scientific ideas than those that he encountered. For all the competing metaphors that ecology had spawned by the mid-twentieth century—super-organism, biotic community/economy of nature, ecosystem, mechanism—few doubted that biotic communities were ontologically robust and had integrities and were stable. Now ecologists present us with a view of a world that is dynamic at every scale, with no stable equilibrium in sight, a world constantly undergoing disturbance, dissolution, and reorganization. A land ethic without reference to integrity and stability is possible, as I argue in 3.16 and 3.17.[122] It is just not as easy as it was a half-century or so ago to articulate a coherent evolutionary-*ecological* worldview and work through its axiological and normative implications.

And what about an *evolutionary*-ecological worldview? The most fundamental pillars of an evolutionary (ecological) worldview remain unchanged. Life on Earth has existed for some 3.5 billion years. However it first emerged, complex life forms including the complex form named *Homo sapiens*, evolved from simpler ones—"descent with modification." Ontological questions haunt the evolutionary aspect of the evolutionary-ecological worldview no less than the ecological aspect. What is the ontological status of genes? They cannot be material entities, as organisms inherit the *same genes* from their parents, but not the same atoms and molecules composing their parents' DNA. As argued in 4.13 the ontology of a gene is more like that of Platonic form than that of Democritean atom. What is the ontology of the relationship between genotypes and phenotypes? Are groups of social organisms ontologically robust enough to be subject to natural selection? Evolutionary *theory* has also radically changed—and more recently than ecological theory—in recognizing the role of serial endosymbiosis, Lamarckian inheritance, and multi-level selection alongside competition, Darwinian inheritance, and individual selection.[123] To accommodate these new theoretical developments in evolutionary biology, the venerable two-kingdom Linnaean taxonomy was revised to become first a five-kingdom (monera, protista, fungi, plantae, animalia) and later a three-domain (bacteria, archaea, eukaryota) taxonomy.[124] These radical changes in evolutionary biology are, however, less problematic, from the point of view of the land ethic, than the radical changes in ecology. Indeed, especially in the case of multi-level selection, they directly corroborate the evolutionary foundations of the land ethic (as detailed and documented in 5.8). And in turning on its head the Clementsian characterization of ecosystems as super-organisms—organisms are now being characterized as super-ecosystems—contemporary evolutionary biology supplies both the land ethic and the Earth ethic with a thoroughly holistic moral ontology (as detailed and documented in 11.2).

1.17 THE CHALLENGE BEFORE US

However formidable the task before us, humanists of the third millennium must rise to the challenge. That challenge is even more formidable now that we confront a threat that Leopold himself never anticipated—global climate change. In addition to articulating a coherent evolutionary-ecological worldview and an associated land ethic, we environmental philosophers are challenged to add another story to the conceptual edifice of environmental ethics: a biospheric or Gaian worldview and an associated Earth ethic. The future of global civilization is at grave risk of collapse if the prevailing collective delusion—the old "Abrahamic concept of land" married to cornucopian consumerism and rugged individualism—is allowed to stand unopposed and unreplaced. Like Leopold, we have to call it out by name and not shrink from enumerating its many absurdities and megalomaniacal conceits. But that is only half the task. Like Leopold, we also have viscerally to appreciate and effectively to communicate the very real aesthetic and spiritual potentiality of the evolutionary-ecological worldview that we have to offer as an alternative—thanks in large part to him. And we have to range in thought further than Leopold himself ventured in *A Sand County Almanac* and viscerally experience and effectively communicate a planetary Gaian consciousness, wedding the insights of geophysics and biogeochemistry to those of ecology and evolutionary biology. In this dimension of our challenge, Leopold cannot lead the way forward, but he did point out the way in his 1923 essay, "Some Fundamentals of Conservation in the Southwest." We would do well to consult his signage with the greatest of care and receptivity.

The Abrahamic worldview has a legion of critics—from the Lynn Whites and Ian McHargs of the 1960s to the Richard Dawkinses and Daniel Dennetts of the present.[125] Leopold may not be alone in appreciating the positive aesthetic and spiritual potentiality in the scientific worldview—Thomas Berry also comes to mind—but he is one of the few who did.[126] So let us pick up the standard from the prematurely fallen Leopold and press forward with the creative and affirmative as well as the critical vocation to which he was called. In the chapters that follow, I provide a detailed critical examination of the conceptual foundations of the familiar Leopold land ethic and, using what can be learned from doing so, turn to the detailed development of the conceptual foundations of a heretofore barely sketched Leopold Earth ethic.

2

The Land Ethic: A Critical Account
of Its Philosophical and Evolutionary
Foundations

In Chapter 1, I provide an analysis of the larger whole, *A Sand County Almanac and Sketches Here and There*, of which "The Land Ethic" is the crowning part—the capstone essay, the climax, the denouement. The land ethic represents the axiological (ethical and aesthetical) and normative (practical moral) implications of an evolutionary-ecological worldview, which is gradually exposed and promulgated in the preceding parts of the book. In *Sand County*'s Part I, readers are introduced to an evolutionary-ecological worldview—circumspectly and indirectly through narrative description, vicarious sensory experience, and imaginative engagement. In *Sand County*'s Part II, readers are introduced to an evolutionary-ecological worldview also by means of narrative accounts of the author's experience on his own journey of discovery and conversion, but more directly, more urgently, and certainly more confrontationally than in Part I. In Chapter 1, I also portrayed the land ethic of *Sand County*'s Part III with a broad brush, indicating its principal conceptual features. In this chapter I begin to paint a picture of it in much more detail.

2.1 THE ODYSSEUS VIGNETTE

Aldo Leopold begins "The Land Ethic" with a vignette about Odysseus's homecoming to Ithaca, an island off the western coast of the Greek mainland after being gone for twenty years.

> When god-like Odysseus returned from the wars in Troy, he hanged all on one rope a dozen slave-girls of his household whom he suspected of misbehavior during his absence.
>
> This hanging involved no question of propriety. The girls were property. The disposal of property was then, as now, a matter of expediency, not of right and wrong.
>
> Concepts of right and wrong were not lacking from Odysseus's Greece: witness the fidelity of his wife through the long years before his black-prowed galleys clove the wine-dark seas for home.[1]

After so long a time, Odysseus was believed by many to be dead. A central theme of the *Odyssey* is the ravages upon his estate wreaked by more than a hundred boorish suitors for his wife Penelope's hand in marriage and, by that token, possession of his kingdom.[2] Disguised as a beggar, and with the help of his son Telemachus, his faithful servants, and the goddess Athena, Odysseus kills them all—thus avenging their insults, plunder, and, most serious, their plot to assassinate Telemachus. Having himself observed the maidservants sneaking out to have sex with some of the suitors, and confirming his suspicions by the testimony of Telemachus, he orders their death by sword, but Telemachus prefers to visit a more ignominious death on them by hanging.

Several aspects of Leopold's allusion to these events in the later books of the *Odyssey* are problematic.[3] First, Leopold remembers that Odysseus did the hanging, but it was actually done by Telemachus. Second, Leopold suggests that the execution of the slave girls was based on suspicion alone, while in fact Odysseus had solid evidence of their disloyal "misbehavior." Third, Leopold characterizes their execution as an act of "expediency" not "propriety"; but it was not utterly unjustified, however harsh. Fourth, it is unfortunate that Leopold chose to make his point—which I will get to shortly—by a story about slave *girls*, raising the whole question of patriarchy and gender-related oppression. Though gender-related oppression is not unimportant or irrelevant to environmental ethics, as ecofeminists have amply demonstrated, the gender of the slaves is beside the point that Leopold wants to make.[4] The gender issue that he inadvertently raises is further compounded by the evidence Leopold offers to show that the Greeks were not totally bereft of ethics: Odysseus's wife's sexual fidelity. That, to be sure, was a virtue practiced by Penelope. But it was not a virtue practiced by Odysseus, of whom it was neither expected nor demanded. And that invites the reflective reader to wonder about another important, but ancillary issue: double standards in Greek sexual ethics.

In any case, the point Leopold wants to make is twofold. The main point is that although the ancient Greeks certainly had ethics, to own human property and dispose of it as they would was outside the scope of their ethics. The corollary point of this vignette is initially implicit, but is stated explicitly a few paragraphs further on in the next section of the essay: "There is as yet no ethic dealing with man's relation to land and to the animals and plants which grow upon it. Land, like Odysseus's slave-girls, is still property. The land-relation is still strictly economic, entailing privileges but not obligations."[5] Like Odysseus, we too have our ethics, but to own "real" property as we call it—land—and dispose of it as we will is currently well outside the scope of those ethics. By our current ethical standards, Odysseus (and Telemachus) behaved badly—first by enslaving human beings and second by executing some of them summarily. Leopold implicitly suggests that as ethics further evolve to embrace "the land," future generations will judge us badly for enslaving and abusing it.

2.2 EXPANSION OF THE SCOPE OF ETHICS OVER TIME (?)

Why does Leopold invoke the *Odyssey* at the beginning of "The Land Ethic"? Perhaps because Homer's epics are the first recorded "literature" (they were originally preserved in the living memories of rhapsodes and recited orally) in Western civilization—to the origins of which Leopold directs his reader's attention. Over the course of Western civilization, of which Homer's epics are foundational texts, Leopold thinks that ethics have expanded in scope: "During the three thousand years which have since elapsed"—since Odysseus caused his slave girls to be executed—"ethical criteria have been extended to many fields of conduct, with corresponding shrinkages in those judged by expediency only."[6] Let me represent Leopold's claim about the expansion of the scope of ethics diagrammatically (Figure 2.1). The large black circles represent the universe of human actions—all that it is possible for humans to do. The small white circles represent the portion of that universe covered by ethics. Over three thousand years, the ethics-covered portion increased, Leopold claims.

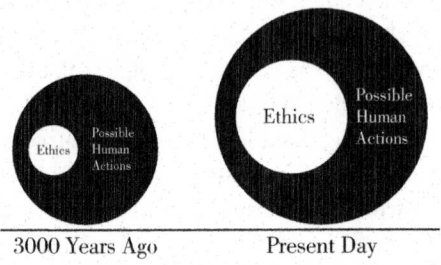

3000 Years Ago   Present Day

Figure 2.1 The circles represent the universe of possible human actions. The ovals within the circles represent the portion of that universe covered by ethics. Over 3000 years, both the universe of possible human actions and relative portion of them covered by ethics has increased.

The diagram also indicates that the universe of possible human actions has expanded by several orders of magnitude: Odysseus could not travel from Troy to Ithaca by air, for example, or communicate with Telemachus by email. Leopold appears to be well aware of the correlative expansion in the universe of possible human actions: "The complexity of cooperative mechanisms has increased with population density, and with the efficiency of tools. It was simpler, for example, to define the anti-social uses of sticks and stones in the days of the mastodons than of bullets and billboards in the age of motors."[7]

Leopold's claim about the expansion of the ethics-covered portion of possible human actions and the corresponding shrinkage in the portion remaining to expediency is debatable. Slavery existed legally in the United States, a country founded on Enlightenment ideals of human dignity and equality, less than a century before Leopold wrote. On the other hand, a mere seven or eight centuries after the Trojan war, which took Odysseus away from home, and a mere two or three centuries after the *Odyssey* was written down, Democritus, Protagoras, Socrates, Plato, and Aristotle were systematically articulating ethical ideals and their philosophical foundations; nor is it at all clear that modern ethical ideals and their philosophical foundations—articulated by Hobbes, Locke, Hume, Kant, and Bentham—are more advanced. The course of ethical expansion in the West, if any, appears not to have been steady but to have been characterized by progress followed by regress. Even though Aristotle was his tutor, Alexander the Great slaughtered his way from the Nile to the Indus and back. After the ethical advances of Jesus and the advent of Christianity, bloody gladiator shows continued to be staged in Rome and other venues in the Mediterranean basin; and later, in the very name of Christianity, brutal Crusades were launched and Inquisitions conducted.[8] Arguably, the nadir of the history of Western morality came in the twentieth century with Hitler's Germany—only a few years before Leopold wrote "The Land Ethic." But in the same year, 1948, that Leopold put the finishing touches on his essay, the United Nations adopted the Universal Declaration of Human Rights—doubtless in part as a repudiation of the Nazi holocaust. That certainly expanded the scope of ethics. Following Leopold's death came the civil rights movement, women's liberation, stronger rights for children, and robust animal-welfare ethics and correlative regulations for the use of domestic animals in scientific research and agriculture.

2.3 ETHICAL CRITERIA/NORMS/IDEALS VERSUS (UN)ETHICAL BEHAVIOR/PRACTICE

Here a distinction might be drawn to make better sense of and tentatively to affirm Leopold's claim about moral progress. Surely Leopold is right that, over three thousand years, ethical "*criteria*," moral *norms* or *ideals*, were expanded, even though actual *behavior* often violated those criteria—that is, failed to measure up to those norms or ideals. The expansion may not have been steady, but Leopold doesn't claim that it was. Thus, for example, while the Declaration of Independence upholds the ideals of human dignity and equality, the US Constitution and US law and practice, during the slavery era—and then after emancipation, during the Jim Crow era—flouted those ideals. Indeed, one of the strongest motives leading to the abolition of slavery in the United States—and the eventual award of equal civil rights to all Americans—was the discrepancy between professed American ideals and actual American practices. Similarly, the Crusades and the Inquisition were betrayals of Christian ethics, not appropriate expressions of Christianity.

One important function of ethics is to govern human behavior. And, as Plato noted in the *Republic* and elsewhere, morality is a form of *self*-governance. When it fails in that function, it can have another: to provide oneself and others norms in reference to which one can criticize one's own behavior and that of others. The state of ethical development—of criteria, ideals, to say nothing of behavior—in Odysseus's Greece provided him no norms in reference to which he or others might have censured his behavior toward his wayward maidservants. Similarly, the state of ethical development—of criteria, of ideals—in Leopold's Western civilization provided no norms by reference to which one might criticize behavior affecting land, still then unquestionably a servant and slave. As Leopold comments, "The farmer who clears the woods off a 75 per cent slope, turns his cows into the clearing, and dumps its rainfall, rocks, and soil into the community creek is still (if otherwise decent) a respected member of society."[9] As ethical progress continues, and ethical criteria are extended to environmental fields of conduct, as surely they shall be, Leopold implicitly suggests that future generations will look back on our treatment of land with the same condescending disapprobation that we, at Leopold's behest, look back on Odysseus's treatment of his slave girls.

2.4 ETHICS ECOLOGICALLY (BIOLOGICALLY) SPEAKING

Leopold goes on to assert that a biological approach to understanding this "extension of ethics" to more and more "fields of conduct" can be illuminating: "This extension of ethics," he writes, has "so far [been] studied only by philosophers"—the implication being that it has not been adequately or at least not scientifically studied. But it "is actually a process in ecological evolution."[10] Leopold goes on to develop this point:

> Its sequences may be described in ecological [biological] as well as in philosophical terms. An ethic, ecologically [biologically] is a limitation on freedom of action in the struggle for existence. An ethic, philosophically, is a differentiation of social from anti-social conduct. These are two definitions of one thing. The thing has its origins in the tendency of interdependent individuals or groups to evolve modes of co-operation.[11]

Up to this point, the words that appear in "The Land Ethic" were borrowed directly from "The Conservation Ethic," published in 1933.[12] The only revision that Leopold made from the earlier text was to change "biological" and "biologically" to "ecological" and "ecologically." That redaction, in my opinion, sacrifices precision of expression for cachet, but it is perfectly understandable in light of the singular theme of the whole book—cultivating an evolutionary-*ecological* worldview. "The Land Ethic" is a part— the axiological-and-normative-implications part—of that worldview (as detailed in 1.13 and 1.14). Irrespective of whether a more illuminating study of ethics than that provided by philosophers is broadly biological or more narrowly ecological, Leopold suggests that the best system of ideas for understanding ethics is generally evolutionary. Leopold invokes "evolution" by name and alludes, more particularly, to Darwin's original account of evolution with the phrase "struggle for existence."

In the hagiography, Leopold is represented as broadly educated and, throughout his life, as reading widely—and doubtless that's all true.[13] But Leopold does not here exhibit a familiarity with the way ethics is actually portrayed in the Western philosophical canon. In fact, the "definitions" of this "thing" called ethics, as Leopold presents them here—"a limitation on freedom of action in the struggle for existence" and "a differentiation of social from anti-social conduct"—are not, respectively, ecological (or biological) versus philosophical ways of defining ethics. They are, rather, two central moments of a single account of ethics "exclusively from the side of natural history" developed by Darwin himself in *The Descent of Man*.[14]

How could *any* limitation on freedom of action have evolved *and* grown in scope, given the relentless and universal struggle for existence? The very idea of ethics presents

Darwin with an evolutionary paradox—a paradox that continued to engage the ingenuity of evolutionary biologists and psychologists in the second half of the twentieth century and is still engaging their ingenuity in the first decades of the twenty-first century (as detailed and documented in 4.9–4.17 and 5.8–5.16).

2.5 DARWIN'S ACCOUNT OF THE ORIGIN OF ETHICS BY NATURAL SELECTION

Darwin's own resolution of that paradox is simple, straightforward, and elegant—as all good scientific explanations should be. Ethical conduct is conducive to social integration while unethical or "anti-social conduct" leads to social disintegration. As Darwin vividly notes, "No tribe could hold together if murder, robbery, treachery, etc. were common."[15] For some species, and most especially for *Homo sapiens*, the struggle for existence is more efficiently prosecuted collectively in socially integrated, cooperative groups. Thus natural selection favored *individuals* who would limit their freedom of action in the struggle for existence and only thus could they "evolve modes of co-operation." Those who would not limit their freedom of action in the struggle for existence and instead indulged in "anti-social conduct" either destroyed the social groups to which they belonged or they were expelled from those social groups. In either case, those who thus found themselves prosecuting the struggle for existence as solitaries were less successful in that enterprise than those who were members of socially integrated groups and who prosecuted the struggle for existence collectively, in cooperation with their fellow members. Thus those who engaged in "social…conduct" as opposed to "anti-social conduct" (the differentiation between which Leopold regards as the philosophical definition of ethics) passed on the capacity for and tendency to a "limitation on their freedom action in the struggle for existence" (the ecological or biological definition of ethics, according to Leopold) to their offspring, whether as a genetic or as a cultural legacy or as a bit of both.

Darwin suggests that human ethics eventually evolved from the platform of the "parental and filial affections" common to all mammals and perhaps to some other vertebrates.[16] Such affections bond parent(s) and offspring, at least until the latter are able to fend for themselves. If these affections chance to linger and become more widely diffused—to siblings, aunts, uncles, cousins—a small group will be similarly bonded, thus forming a rudimentary society. As these "social instincts and sympathies" are strengthened, through natural selection, together with adaptive social behaviors, individual members will mutually benefit from cooperative defense, both against natural enemies and other groups of the same species; cooperative exploitation of resources; and cooperative offspring rearing.

While the members of many other species also live in affectionally bonded social groups, only *Homo sapiens* evolved ethics proper. Darwin appears to think of ethics proper as *codes* of conduct—and language is required for codifying socially appropriate (and inappropriate) types of behavior. Setting aside the possibility that cetaceans may have evolved something functionally equivalent to human language, *Homo sapiens* appears to be the only species with languages capable of codifying socially appropriate (and inappropriate) types of behavior. In addition to language, Darwin thinks that both intelligence and imagination are necessary for codes of conduct to be formulated. Intelligence is necessary to discern the socially conducive and socially destructive effects of various behaviors and inductively to generalize those observations into types or kinds of behavior—such as charity (of whatever kind) or murder (by whatever means). Imagination is necessary to bring the socially destructive effects of various behaviors graphically to mind so as to register on the naturally selected moral sentiments and "moral sense"—the title of Darwin's chapter on ethics in *The Descent of Man.*

2.6 DARWIN'S ACCOUNT OF THE EXTENSION OF ETHICS

Darwin is careful to make the boundaries of ethics coextensive with the perceived boundaries of the correlative cooperative societies that constituted the social environment in which socially conducive forms of behavior and the feelings that motivate them were selected. "The virtues which must be practised, at least generally," he writes, "by rude men so that they may associate together in a body are those which are still recognized as the most important. But they are practised almost exclusively in relation to the men of the same tribe."[17] Not only have ethics been "extended" to more and more "fields of conduct," they have been extended to more and more persons. Nor is this in the least problematic. The 1948 United Nations Declaration of Universal Human Rights, as the name suggests, extended ethics to every human being. To be sure, there remain those who do not recognize ethics to be so universally extended; indeed some recognize them to apply no more widely than do the "rude men" Darwin had in mind. However, again we may deploy the distinction between ideals or norms and their behavioral implementation: ethics have evolved to the extent that those who do not recognize their universal human application are subject to moral censure for not doing so.

Up to this point, Darwin's account of the origin of ethics by natural selection seems consistent with the basic principles of *Darwinian* evolution, according to which natural selection ranges over traits manifested by individual specimens. Parental and filial affections, social instincts and sympathies, socially conducive forms of behavior are all individually variable psychological or behavioral traits. However, the next step in Darwin's account involves the controversial concept of group selection. Once ethics evolved, what is the evolutionary mechanism by which they were "extended" to more and more "fields of conduct" and to more and more persons (maidservants, for example), the phenomenon to which Leopold calls attention at the beginning of "The Land Ethic"? The success of the collective, cooperative prosecution of the struggle for existence by *Homo sapiens* resulted, we may suppose, in population growth; and, we may also suppose that internally ethical human groups found themselves in competition with other internally ethical human groups for the limited means of survival. If competing groups merged to form larger groups they would be able to out-compete their smaller, and thus weaker, rivals. And so when larger groups coalesced, with correspondingly more widely extended ethics, they even more efficiently and successfully survived and flourished—forcing their competitors also to unite or to be exterminated. This process of merger and ethical extension was repeated throughout human history: clans or gens, the ur-societies of *Homo sapiens*, merged to form tribes; tribes merged to form "nations," or what today are called "ethnic groups"; ethnic groups merged to form nation-states or countries (Figure 2.2).

Clan ⇒ Tribe ⇒ Nation ⇒ Nation-State ⇒ (Global Village)

Figure 2.2 Social-ethical evolution in *The Descent of Man*; parentheses indicate that the global-village stage had not emerged when *The Descent of Man* was in preparation by Darwin.

By Darwin's time, the nation-state stage marked the limits this process of social merger had reached. Darwin's England was a nation-state; so were Spain and France; and, with the annexation of Venice in 1866 and Rome in 1870, Italy had become a nation-state the year before the first edition of *The Descent of Man* was published; and in that year, 1871, Germany was unified as a nation-state.[18] Darwin looked forward to the continuation of this merger process to its next stage—which was formally declared in 1948, but which is still very much a work in progress—the global village (as it is sometimes called) and its correlative ethic of universal human rights:

> As man advances in civilization, and small tribes are united into larger communities, the simplest reason would tell each individual that he ought to extend his social instincts and sympathies to all the members of the same nation, though personally unknown to him. This point being once reached, there is only an artificial barrier to prevent his sympathies extending to the men of all nations and races.[19]

While Darwin's foreseeing the emergence of a universal human community is remarkable, more remarkably still, he anticipates something approaching an environmental ethic. He goes on immediately to write that

> Sympathy beyond the confines of man, that is, humanity to the lower animals, seems to be one of the latest moral acquisitions....This virtue, one of the noblest with which man is endowed, seems to arise incidentally from our sympathies becoming more tender and more widely diffused, until they are extended to all sentient beings.[20]

I say "something approaching an environmental ethic" because what Darwin here clearly anticipates is the development of animal liberation (about which more in 5.2 and 5.3). For some non-anthropocentric ethicists, animal liberation has been a theoretical terminus.[21] But for others it is a theoretical basis for further extending ethics to the whole of the organic environment—to all animals, not just sentient ones, and to plants as well as animals—and to the organic environment as a whole.[22] Furthermore, note that, for Darwin, an extension of ethics to sentient beings arises "incidentally," not as a matter of the same "reason" that should move individuals to extend their ethics to "all the members of the same nation." Presumably, with the emergence of an international human community—a global village—reason would also move individuals to widen the scope of their ethics to encompass "the men of all nations and races." For the reasoning involved in all such extensions is that the boundaries of the moral community are coextensive with the boundaries of the perceived social community. And sentient beings, so far as Darwin knew, did not form a community with man.[23] To suggest that not only sentient animals, but that also plants and even soils and waters form a community with man was the value Leopold added to Darwin's account of the origin and development of ethics.

2.7 THE COMMUNITY CONCEPT IN ECOLOGY

While the opinion of historians of ecology is not unanimous, most agree that a necessary and sufficient condition for the emergence of ecology as a "self-conscious science" in the last decade of the nineteenth century was the prior emergence of the theory of evolution in the mid-nineteenth century.[24] The ideas of natural selection and adaptation direct attention to the environmental context of species and their relationships with other species and with such physical and chemical aspects of the environment as temperature, moisture, salinity, acidity, and the like. Indeed, the ecological concept of niches—to which species are adapted and into which they fit—seems virtually entailed by the evolutionary concepts of natural selection and adaptation. The ecologist who first most fully developed the niche notion was Charles Elton—who is notable among those who credit Darwin with stimulating the development of ecology. Leopold became acquainted with Elton in 1931 at a conference in Canada on population cycles in sub-arctic mammals, and they remained friends until Leopold's death.[25] Elton provided an alternative to Clements's super-organism paradigm in ecology. Rather than thinking of the functional relationship of proximate species on the landscape as like the functional relationship of organs in an organism, Elton suggested that ecological relationships be conceived as analogous to functional roles in a human society or community. Each plant and animal had a "profession" in the "economy of nature." As Elton, a gifted writer, vividly expressed this then-new community paradigm in ecology, "When an ecologist says, 'there goes a badger' he should include in his thoughts some definite idea of the animal's place in the community to which it belongs, just as if he had said, 'there goes the vicar.'"[26]

If Darwin did not think of animals and plants as forming a community with human beings—because ecology had not yet emerged as a distinct science and the community paradigm in ecology had not yet been conceived—Leopold certainly did. To reach a land ethic, he seems to have taken the outlines of Darwin's account of the evolution and development of human ethics and added to its basic conceptual architecture the

Eltonian community concept in ecology. Leopold writes, "All ethics so far evolved rest upon a single premise: that the individual is a member of a community of interdependent parts."[27] That distills Darwin's account down to its essence. Then Leopold adds the Eltonian element: ecology "simply enlarges the boundaries of the community to include soils, waters, plants, and animals, or collectively: the land."[28] From that follows "a land ethic" which "changes the role of *Homo sapiens* from conqueror of the land community to plain member and citizen of it" and "implies respect for his fellow-members and also respect for the community as such."[29] To paraphrase Darwin, once we realize—thanks to ecology—that we belong to a biotic community, the simplest reason should tell us that we ought to extend ethical regard to all the members of that community, however greatly they differ from us in form, and to the community as such.

2.8 THE HUMEAN FOUNDATIONS OF DARWIN'S EVOLUTIONARY ACCOUNT OF THE MORAL SENSE

As Leopold's land ethic appears to rest squarely on conceptual foundations supplied by Darwin in *The Descent of Man*, Darwin's account of the origin, evolution, and development of ethics appears to rest squarely on even more fundamental conceptual foundations supplied by David Hume in *An Enquiry Concerning the Principles of Morals*.[30] In his chapter on "The Moral Sense," Darwin eclectically cites and sometimes quotes a number of notable moral philosophers, including Hume, but also including Adam Smith, Immanuel Kant, John Stuart Mill, and Henry Sidgwick.[31] The centrality in his account of what Darwin calls the "all important emotion of sympathy" and the peculiar kind of pleasure animals derive from fulfilling their social instincts suggests that Darwin conceives ethics to be rooted in sentiments, feelings, and emotions—as did Hume (and as did Adam Smith, for that matter)—and not, as Kant believed, in reason alone.[32] Nor, despite quoting Mill and Sidgwick, has Darwin much to say about utility or happiness and so he seems to be no more inclined to the utilitarian conception of ethics than to the Kantian (or deontological) conception of them.[33]

Hume himself devotes much discussion to utility, but does so to explain why human beings experience a peculiar kind of pleasure in beneficent acts, both their own and those of others. The reason we regard such acts as morally good, Hume claims, is because of the particular pleasure they afford us, and the reason that nature has made us to experience such a pleasure when contemplating them is because of their utility. The utilitarians cut out the affective middle man, so to speak, and made a calculation of utility the direct measure of an action's moral value. And they defined utility in terms of happiness and made happiness to consist of pleasure and the absence of pain. While for Hume *a special kind of pleasure* was a *marker* of utility, for the utilitarians pleasure in all its forms was the *currency* of utility and the quantity (and for Mill quality) of pleasure was the *measure* of utility. Thus, in emphasizing the moral sense and sentiments and relating them to the integrity and stability of society or community, while hardly mentioning happiness and pleasure and pain, Darwin's understanding of the conceptual foundations of ethics is clearly Humean, and while Hume himself extensively discusses utility, he was not a precursor of utilitarianism as it eventually took shape in the works of Bentham and Mill.

Indeed, Darwin's evolutionary account of ethics completes Hume's moral science (detailed and documented in 4.3 and 5.11–5.16). Hume regards himself as recording the "facts" of moral psychology by "following the experimental method," which he takes to consist of empirical observation and induction.[34] We are ethical beings, Hume concludes, because we have "some internal sense or feeling which nature has made universal in the whole species."[35] But both why and how nature has made such a sense or feeling universal in the whole species, Hume is at an utter loss to explain—except by appeal to the will of a Supreme Being (about whose existence we know Hume to be skeptical).[36] Darwin explains why, naturalistically: because *Homo sapiens* is an intensely social species and ethical approbation and disapprobation are the way human beings differentiate socially conducive from socially destructive conduct, to employ Leopold's turn of phrase. And Darwin explains how: the evolutionary mechanism of natural selection. To be sure, the forms of human societies and their associated cultures differ greatly. And thus the ways various human groups spell out the differentiation between socially conducive and socially destructive conduct also differ greatly in their particulars. Nevertheless, as under-determined capacities, the moral sense and sentiments are universal, as are a few core precepts—a condemnation of murder, robbery, treachery, etc., to employ Darwin's turn of phrase.

2.9 UNIVERSALISM AND RELATIVISM: HUME AND DARWIN

Hume's empirical moral science—fact gathering through observation and inductive generalization—is biased by a limited sample set. Hume's observations were limited to his own eighteenth-century British society and to classical Western literature and history. Darwin, on the other hand, was made vividly aware of the immense differences in moral sensibilities and precepts among human beings by his exposure to a variety of non-Western societies and cultures during his *Beagle* voyage. His evolutionary account of ethics serves to explain the differences as well as the commonalities. All *Homo sapiens* are social and thus all have some ethics; and in all ethics there are core precepts endorsed by all, even by "rude men so that they may associate together in a body" and these are "still recognized as the most important." In *The Descent of Man*, Darwin regales his readers with a wide variety of anecdotal evidence of strongly held moral convictions among members of non-Western societies that run counter to his own and presumably to those of his Western (and Westernized) readers.

We should hardly be surprised that because societies differ from one another, the kinds of conduct conducive to the sustenance of one society might differ, sometimes radically, from the kinds of conduct conducive to the sustenance of a very different society. For example, among peoples practicing a highly mobile, foraging way of life, respect for private property is a less highly esteemed virtue than gift giving.[37] Possessions are few and simple to begin with, as they must be portable; and resources are subject both to fortune and to cycles of abundance and scarcity.[38] So gifts to others, when one's own fortunes are good and plenty abounds, is not very costly; and the goodwill such gifts generate may be a saving grace when one's own fortunes are bad and the necessities of life are elusive or out of season.[39] On the other hand, among peoples practicing a sedentary, agrarian way of life, food is produced by foresight and labor and stored for off-season consumption; and implements, furniture, and the like can be accumulated.[40] Failure to respect private property can rend such a society asunder and prodigal generosity could encourage laziness and imprudence. Thus the respect for private property is a more highly esteemed virtue than gift giving among peoples practicing a sedentary, agrarian way of life.

Darwin also observes that cultural moral codes can assume a life of their own and develop according to an obscure internal dialectic—sometimes to the point that they themselves can become dysfunctional, that is, destructive to the society that they originally evolved to sustain. He recounts an anecdote from West Australia about a man who felt obliged to murder a woman from a distant tribe because his own wife had died from disease. The white farmer, for whom the man worked, vigorously discouraged the practice of this tradition. But, feeling increasingly morose by the weight of his unfulfilled "moral" obligation (as he believed it to be), the man committed the "crime" (in the estimation of his employer) anyway—despite his employer's threat to punish him with imprisonment for life. Darwin then comments, "The breach of a rule held sacred by the tribe, will thus, as it seems, give rise to the deepest feelings,—and this quite apart from the social instincts, excepting in so far as the rule is grounded on the judgment of the community."[41] In other words, there is nothing in such a rule of causally unrelated compensatory murder that sustains the society for which it is a rule, except for the very general meta-principle that adhering to socially sanctioned rules is conducive to maintaining social organization. And such a rule could be counterproductive if it were to set in motion—as very likely it would—a spiral of revenge murders between the two affected tribes. Finally, Darwin remarks, "How so many strange superstitions have arisen throughout the world, we know not."[42] Neither did Darwin know anything of genes nor certainly anything of memes. But just as there is genetic drift as well as genetic adaptation, so apparently can there be memetic drift as well as memetic adaptation. (See 5.10 for further discussion of topics closely related to the topic of this section.)

2.10 HOW HUME ANTICIPATES DARWIN'S ACCOUNT OF THE ORIGIN AND EXPANSION OF ETHICS

The very title of the chapter "The Moral Sense," in which Darwin accounts for the origin, evolution, and development of ethics in the *Descent of Man*, alludes to Hume. And the core of Darwin's discussion there can be understood to be an elaboration of the following paragraph from Hume's *An Enquiry Concerning the Principles of Morals*:

> But suppose the conjunction of the sexes to be established in nature, a family immediately arises, and particular rules being requisite for its subsistence, these are immediately embraced, though without comprehending the rest of mankind within their prescriptions. Suppose that several families unite together into one society which is totally disjoined from all others, the rules which preserve the peace and order enlarge themselves to the utmost of that society, but…lose their force when carried one step farther. But again suppose that several distinct societies maintain a kind of intercourse for mutual convenience and advantage, the boundaries of justice grow still larger, in proportion to the largeness of men's views and the force of their mutual connections. History, experience, reason sufficiently instruct us in this natural progress of human sentiments.[43]

2.11 SHADES OF THE SOCIAL-CONTRACT THEORY OF ETHICS IN "THE LAND ETHIC"

There is ample reason to suppose that Leopold was familiar with "The Moral Sense" in *The Descent of Man*. His rhetoric seems to allude to Darwinian evolution in his discussion of the origin and development of ethics and, more generally, Leopold's formal schooling centered on the biological sciences and his lifelong professional activities as forester, game manager, and wildlife ecologist were informed by the biological sciences. On the other hand, there is no reason to suppose that Leopold was familiar with Hume's *Enquiry*. The way Leopold himself construes what he calls "The Ethical Sequence" suggests, however, that his reading of Darwin was not fresh and that he was not at all well versed in the several distinct and mutually inconsistent theories of ethics in the Western philosophical canon. He seems to think that before we evolved ethics there was an "original free-for-all competition" among human beings.[44] This phrase evokes the so-called state of nature foundational to the social-contract theory of the origin of ethics, classically articulated by many of the philosophers (derided as "sophists" by Plato) contemporary with Socrates, and, among early modern philosophers, by Thomas Hobbes in the seventeenth century and by Jean-Jacques Rousseau a century later (detailed and documented in 9.4).

The social contract theory assumes that all "men" are egoistic—that is, motivated only by self-interest—and that ethics is essentially a matter of *enlightened* self-interest. In the state of nature, human life—in Hobbes's famous characterization—is "*solitary, poor, nasty, brutish, and short.*"[45] Finding such a situation intolerable, human beings called a meeting, hammered out some rules to live by, and designated a sovereign power to enforce them. That's how both society and the ethics that make it possible originated in social-contract theory. Such a scenario is preposterous from an evolutionary point of view, because human beings could not have become human in anything other than in an intensely social—and thus already rudimentarily ethical—context. Even without the benefit of a well-formed theory of human evolution, Hume points out the implausibility of the state of nature posited in the social-contract theory of the origin of ethics: "Whether such a condition of human nature could ever exist…may justly be doubted. Men are necessarily born in a family society at least and are trained up by their parents to some rule of conduct and behavior."[46] Moreover, the social-contract theorists do not recognize the existence of the social instincts and sympathies, a point that Hume emphatically rejects: "We must renounce the theory which accounts for every moral sentiment by the principle of self-love. We must adopt a more *public affection* and allow that the *interests of society* are not, *even on their own account*, entirely indifferent to us."[47]

And this is not the only anomaly in Leopold's discussion of "The Ethical Sequence." Probably because he confuses the atomized "state of nature" in the social-contract theory of the origin of ethics with Darwin's very different natural-history theory of the origin of ethics (in which the evolutionary ancestors of moral "man" were already one among many socially incorporated species of animals), Leopold claims that "The first ethics dealt with the relation between individuals; the Mosaic Decalogue is an example."[48] Unless God is to be counted among "individuals," this cannot be true—because several of the Ten Commandments concern duties to God. Moreover, Old Testament ethics in general seem less concerned with relations among individuals than with those of the whole community—the nation of Israel, a stiff-necked people—with their jealous and wrathful God and with other neighboring nations. "Later accretions," Leopold goes on to declare, "dealt with the relation between the individual and society. The Golden Rule tries to integrate the individual to society; democracy to integrate social organization to the individual."[49] It seems that with its emphasis on "others" severally that the Christian Golden Rule comes closer to dealing with relations between individuals than does the Mosaic Decalogue. With its emphasis on individual liberty, however, Leopold seems to be correct that democracy aims to accommodate social organization to the inalienable rights of individuals. In any case, Darwin's account of the ethical sequence in regard to the relations between the individual and society is the inverse of Leopold's:

> We have now seen that actions are regarded by savages, and were probably so regarded by primeval man, as good or bad, solely as they obviously affect the welfare of the tribe,—not that of the species, nor that of an individual member of the tribe. This conclusion agrees well with the belief that the so-called [by Hume] moral sense is aboriginally derived from the social instincts, for both relate at first exclusively to the community.[50]

Whatever their historical order, Leopold suggests that in addition to both individuals and society, "a third element" needs to be added to the scope of ethics: land, the biotic community—both fellow-members (individuals) and the biotic community (or society) as such.[51] My point here is that Leopold assumes that, as we presently find it, ethics has a holistic as well as individualistic dimension. Clearly, Darwin concurs; and indeed Darwin—I think correctly—makes the holistic dimension of ethics more primitive and primary than the individualistic dimension. Does Hume also consider ethics to have a holistic as well as an individualistic dimension? Some scholars think not.

2.12 INDIVIDUALISM IN (BENTHAMIC) UTILITARIANISM AND (KANTIAN) DEONTOLOGY

In general, modern ethical theory has assumed an ontology of social atomism, the view that a society or community is reducible to an aggregate of individuals (see 10.4 and 11.1 for a full *critical* discussion).[52] Jeremy Bentham, the founder of the utilitarian school, provides the clearest possible declaration of the atomic view of society:

> The interest of the community is one of the most general expressions that can occur in the phraseology of morals....When it has a meaning, it is this. The community is a fictitious *body*, composed of the individual persons who are considered as constituting as it were its *members*. The interest of the community then is what?—the sum of the interests of the several members who compose it. It is vain to talk of the interest of the community, without understanding what is the interest of the individual.[53]

The two main streams of modern ethical theory, moreover, are tailored to an atomic or individualistic moral ontology (as detailed and documented in 10.5–10.6 and 11.1).

Immediately following this reductive comment about the interest of the community, Bentham goes on to declare that "A thing is said to promote the interest of the individual, when it adds to the sum total of his pleasures: or, what comes to the same thing, to diminish the sum total of his pains."[54] Because the community as such can experience neither pleasure nor pain, from a utilitarian point of view, the idea that a community or a society per se can be benefited or harmed is nonsensical—as all benefit and harm is a matter of pleasure and pain, respectively.

Kant is the fountainhead of the other great tradition of modern ethical theory, deontology. For Kant, the only beings worthy of ethical regard are rational beings, and communities as such are no more rational than they are sentient. Thus also, from a Kantian or deontological point of view, the idea that communities per se are proper objects of ethical concern is nonsensical. Unlike Bentham and Kant, Hume does not specify a psychological capacity—such as sentience or rationality—that a being must have in order to be a fitting object of moral regard. Michael Slote calls Hume's an "agent-based"—as opposed to the currently prevailing "patient-based"—theory of ethics.[55] For Hume, that is, moral regard is based not on the capacities of its objects, but on the intentional capacities of moral subjects—on ethical feelings or moral sentiments, such as sympathy, beneficence, and patriotism. And just as our moral sentiments are many, so are their proper objects. Other sentient beings may be fitting objects of sympathy; God may be a fitting object of awe and reverence; other rational beings may be fitting objects of respect; societies may be fitting objects of allegiance; and nations may be fitting objects of patriotism.

2.13 HOLISM IN HUME'S MORAL PHILOSOPHY

I contend that Hume's ethical theory has a holistic dimension—because he regards society or community per se as a proper object of at least some of the moral sentiments, such as loyalty, allegiance, and patriotism. Flowing perhaps from the ingrained biases against ethical holism characteristic of philosophers steeped in mainstream modern ethical theory, three scholars have challenged my contention. Gary Varner states flatly that "sympathetic concern for communities as such has no historical antecedent in David Hume."[56] With Varner I agree: *sympathetic* concern for communities has no historical antecedent in David Hume's moral philosophy, but sympathy is not the only moral sentiment to play a role in Hume's moral philosophy. Similarly, Alan Carter argues that Hume cannot have thought that societies or communities per se were proper objects of the moral sentiments because, in *A Treatise of Human Nature*, all the moral sentiments are reducible to sympathy and we can only sympathize with sentient beings.[57] That may be so, but the *Treatise* was not the only exposition of Hume's moral philosophy, nor is it Hume's final statement of his moral philosophy. Y. S. Lo also incorrectly privileges the *Treatise*, claiming that "[T]extual evidence from David Hume's *A Treatise of Human Nature* does not support [a] holistic environmental ethic....Based on Hume's reductionist account of the mind...a Humean account of the community should be similarly reductionist....[H]olism is at least foreign to, and at worst incompatible with, Hume's philosophy."[58]

Books I and II of Hume's *Treatise* were published in 1739 and Book III in 1740, when he was in his late twenties. The *Treatise* was not as widely read and discussed as Hume had hoped that it would be. He extensively reworked the third book of the *Treatise*, focusing on ethics, and that revised discussion of ethics was published as *An Enquiry Concerning the Principles of Morals* in 1752, when Hume was in his early forties. In his 1776 autobiography, *My Own Life*, he stated that "my *Inquiry Concerning Human Morals*...is of all my writings, historical, philosophical, or literary, incomparably the best."[59] Whose thinking does not mature and change between their twenties and forties? Both Lo and Carter want to make Hume's thinking in the *Enquiry Concerning the Principles of Morals* subordinate to, and force it to be consistent with, what they believe to be his thinking in *A Treatise of Human Nature*. But Hume himself regarded the *Enquiry* to better represent his thinking than anything else he ever wrote, presumably including the *Treatise*. And in the *Enquiry*, again and again, Hume indicates that society per se is a proper object of ethical (if not sympathetic) concern. In addition to the foregoing, here are a few more of many examples.

> We may observe that in displaying the praises of any humane, beneficent man there is one circumstance which never fails to be amply insisted upon—namely

the happiness and satisfaction derived to society from his intercourse and good offices.[60]

The happiness of mankind, *the order of society, the harmony of families,* the mutual support of friends are always considered as the result of the gentle dominion over the breasts of men.[61]

And if the principles of humanity are capable, in many instances, of influencing our actions, they must, at all times, have some authority over our sentiments and give us a general approbation of what is *useful to society,* and blame of what is dangerous or pernicious.[62]

It appears that a tendency to *public good* and to the promoting of peace, harmony, and *order in society* does always, by affecting the benevolent principles of our frame, engage us on the side of the social virtues... [so] that everything which promotes the *interests of society* must communicate pleasure, and what is pernicious give uneasiness.[63]

Are not justice, fidelity, honor, veracity, allegiance, chastity esteemed solely on account of their tendency to promote *the good of society?*[64]

That should suffice. And let me expressly note that Hume is perfectly capable of referring to "others" severally and reductively when that is in fact his meaning. It is perhaps possible to insist, despite his own choice of words, that when Hume refers, as just illustrated, to the "happiness" and "satisfaction" of society, happiness and satisfaction being states of consciousness, that he could only mean the happiness and satisfaction of the members of society individually and aggregatively. But by a similarly strict analysis of language, when Hume refers, as just illustrated, to the "order" of society and the "harmony" of families, order and harmony being states of wholes, not their constituent parts, he cannot be intelligibly supposed to mean the order and harmony of the members of society individually. Of course, conceptually disentangling moral concern for individuals severally from moral concern for society per se is not easy, because the two are so intimately connected. Murder, robbery, treachery, etc. are perpetrated on individuals, but, as Darwin notes, if they were common, no tribe could hold together; and, according to Darwin, *for that reason* they "are branded with everlasting infamy."

However hard it may be to disentangle individualistic and holistic concern, Hume does not quail. He explicitly draws a distinction between harm to individuals and harm to society as a whole in "Appendix III—Some Further Considerations with Regard to Justice" of the *Enquiry.* There he writes, "For if it be allowed (what is, indeed, evident) that the particular consequences of a particular act of justice may be hurtful to the public as well as to individuals; it follows that every man, in embracing that virtue, must have an eye to the whole plan and system, and must expect the concurrence of his fellows in the same conduct and behavior."[65] The kind of justice that Hume discusses exclusively in the *Enquiry* is distributive justice and the closely associated concept of private property. Hume here envisions a circumstance in which upholding property rights (say, the right of a landowner obstinately to refuse to sell to a developer) might harm both individuals severally and the public collectively (say, individuals in need of housing or convenient shopping, and a municipality in need of an expanded tax base). His point is that even when a particular act of justice, such as the one here illustrated, harms both individuals and the public, we still generally concur that it is right because property rights are foundational to society as we know it. But if that weren't clear enough, Hume concludes Appendix III by considering acts of injustice and indisputably distinguishing between the harm such acts inflict on individuals and the harm they inflict on the community as a whole:

> We may just observe, before we conclude this subject, that, after the laws of justice are fixed by views of general utility, the injury, the hardship, the harm, which result to any individual from a violation of them, enter very much into consideration, and are a great source of that universal blame, which attends every wrong or iniquity.... *What injures the community, without hurting any individual,* is often more lightly thought of. But where the greatest public wrong is also conjoined with a considerable private one, no wonder the highest disapprobation attends so iniquitous a behavior.[66]

2.14 HOLISM IN "THE LAND ETHIC"

To be sure, our moral outrage at acts of injustice is amplified if these acts injure individuals as well as threaten the good order of society, but my point simply is that Hume takes it for granted that injury to the community is not a shorthand way of referring to the aggregate injuries of its several members. Therefore, evidently and incontestably, there is a holistic aspect to Hume's moral philosophy. I dwell on the holistic aspect of Hume's moral philosophy only because it has been vigorously contested. Suffice it to say, in concluding this digression, that Leopold identifies two historical foci of ethical relationships: (a) between individuals severally and (b) between individuals and the societies per se that they compose. He thinks that the historical order in which these aspects of ethics developed was first (a) between individuals severally and later (b) between individuals and the societies per se that they compose, while Darwin—more truly, in my opinion—regards the historical order of their development inversely: first b then a. Darwin's account of the origin and evolution of ethics completes Hume's even more fundamental moral philosophy; and in that philosophy we find provision for both the individualistic and holistic aspects of ethics that Leopold identifies. Leopold then goes on to assert the "evolutionary possibility and ecological necessity" of an "extension of ethics" to a "third element in human environment"—the biotic community.[67] His proposed "land ethic" would also have an individualistic and holistic aspect: "respect for... fellow-members" and also "respect for the community as such." Note, in light of Varner's misdirected criticism, Leopold does not say "sympathetic concern" for the community as such, but *respect* for the community as such. Surely the notion that we can have respect for non-individuals is entirely familiar and uncontroversial: respect for the law; respect for the office of president of the United States, even when the officeholder proves to be unworthy of respect; respect for the sovereignty of a nation state; and so on; and so on; and so on.

As "The Land Ethic" proceeds from start to finish, the individualistic aspect recedes from view and by the end of the essay it is altogether eclipsed by the holistic aspect. In a middle section titled "Substitutes for a Land Ethic," Leopold declares that "Wildflowers and songbirds…are members of the biotic community and…are entitled to continuance" despite their lack of "economic use."[68] But the context suggests that what entities Leopold thinks are entitled to continuance are species populations of wildflowers and songbirds—not individual wildflowers and songbirds, whose lives are naturally ephemeral in any case. He also seems to have species, not specimens, in mind when he writes, in the same section, that "birds should continue as a matter of biotic right" and that "no special interest has a right to exterminate them for the sake of a benefit, real or fancied, to itself."[69] An individual bird may be killed, but it would be odd to say that it was "exterminated"; rather species populations are the sorts of things that are exterminated. He goes on to lament "the impending erasure of *the* timber wolf."[70] And then he makes it very clear that, under the regime of a land ethic, "biotic" rights pertain to fellow-members of the biotic community only as species not as specimens: "Some *species* have been 'read out of the party' by economic-minded foresters because they grow too slowly, or have too low a sale value to pay as timber crops."[71] In the final section—"The Outlook"—of the essay, fellow-members are altogether left out of the famous summary moral maxim or golden rule of the land ethic and only the community (as such) is mentioned: "A thing is right when it tends to preserve the integrity, stability, and beauty of the biotic community. It is wrong when it tends otherwise."[72]

Why do fellow-members diminish in importance as "The Land Ethic" progresses toward its climax? Note that in the "ethical sequence" to which Leopold calls attention, the Darwinian progression is just the opposite. According to Darwin, once more, "actions are regarded by savages, and were probably so regarded by primeval man, as good or bad, solely as they obviously affect the welfare of the tribe,—not that of the species, nor that of an individual member of the tribe." But as ethics evolved or developed, moral regard for individuals grew to the point that, in democratic societies, inalienable rights to life, liberty, and the pursuit of happiness are asserted on behalf of individuals, sometimes against the interests of society as a whole. The reason that the tendency in the recent development of ethics away from a holistic and toward an individualistic emphasis is reversed in the land ethic may be because the basic structure of biotic communities is very different from that of human communities. Indeed, biotic communities are only communities by analogy. Thus one should expect that the precepts of a correlative land ethic will be very different indeed from those of the various human ethics that are correlative to various actual human communities.

2.15 THE LAND ETHIC AND THE PROBLEM OF ECOFASCISM RESOLVED

Already noted (2.9) are differences in the ethical precepts of foraging societies and agrarian societies, which are derived from their differing structures and the general fact that ethical behaviors and the feelings that motivate them were naturally selected because they help hold societies together, help to preserve their integrity and stability. As to biotic communities, according to Charles Elton, "the ground plan of every...community is much the same" and "food is the burning question in animal society" and "food is the factor which...forms the connecting link between members of the community."[73] Food is the currency of the economy of nature and it passes not from hand to hand as does money or bartered goods or gifts in human economies, but from stomach to stomach. While individual fellow members of biotic communities deserve respect, they have no right to life as links in food chains. Leopold has been excoriated as something of a hypocrite for at once advocating a land ethic and continuing to hunt "game" avidly.[74] But hunting, killing, and eating our fellow-members of the biotic community is perfectly consistent with his land ethic, because food is the factor that forms the connecting link between members of the community. The integrity and stability of the biotic community depend on the maintenance of species populations, the specimens of which eat and are eaten in turn. (In 3.8, I indicate how Leopold anticipated Raymond Lindeman in realizing that the burning question in biotic communities is not really food but energy released by metabolizing food.)

Animal-welfare ethics have been either irrelevant to conservation and environmental concerns or an impediment to them—as when animal-welfare advocates, informed by animal-welfare ethics, oppose the preservation of plant species by means of killing the feral animals that threaten them. Conservationists, qua conservationists, are simply not concerned about the welfare of individual organisms; rather they are concerned, among other things, about the "continuance" of species. The Leopold land ethic has become popular among contemporary conservationists and environmentalists largely because of its holistic cast.[75] To many philosophers, however, steeped in the individualistic bias of both mainstreams of modern moral philosophy—utilitarianism and deontology—holism in ethics is anathema. The Leopold land ethic has, accordingly, been decried as "environmental fascism"—because the interests of individual members of biotic communities are subordinated to the good order of their respective wholes.[76] And it would seem to follow inexorably that because *Homo sapiens* is, according to Leopold, also but a "plain member and citizen" of the biotic community, the land ethic would subordinate individual *human* interests, as well as the interests of specimens of other species, to the integrity, stability, and beauty of the biotic community. If that were so, any but the most extreme misanthropist would recoil in horror from the land ethic. Nor should any philosopher be satisfied with an ad hoc remedy—just arbitrarily excepting *Homo sapiens* from the logic of the land ethic.

But in fact the communitarian conceptual architecture foundational to the land ethic does not entail the subordination of individual human interests to the integrity, stability, and beauty of the biotic community. To be sure, individual *Homo sapiens* are

s and citizens of the biotic community, indeed, *plain* members and citizens,
so nor any less so than individual specimens of other species. But, just as
lividual *Homo sapiens* also remain members and sometimes citizens of other
ies—clans (extended families), tribes, nations (ethnic groups), nation-states
....tries), the global village (the international community)—each with its own associated ethic. The land ethic is one of several ethical "accretions," according to Leopold,
the envisioned next "step in a sequence."[77] An accretion is an "external addition."[78] The
land ethic thus does not replace all the previous steps in the ethical sequence; it is
 an addendum to them. The land ethic may well require the subordination of some
individual human interests to the integrity, stability, and beauty of the biotic com-
munity—those that are weak or trivial—but the ethic of democratic nation-states and
that of the global village uphold the rights of individual human beings to life, liberty,
property, and the pursuit of happiness (Figure 2.3).

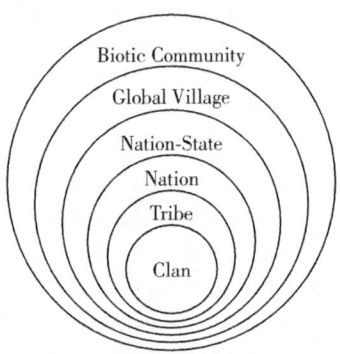

Figure 2.3 Hierarchical structure of community memberships.

As among all the previous steps in the sequence, the additional duties and obligations of the land ethic must be reconciled with the duties and obligations of the
foregoing accretions. Thus we search for ways that we can respect human rights and
individual civil and economic liberties while preserving other species and maintaining biological integrity and ecosystem health. When that is not possible—just as it is
sometimes not possible to reconcile tribal mores, such as "female circumcision," with
universal human rights—then we must prioritize the conflicting duties and obligations generated by our membership in the biotic community with those generated by
our memberships in other communities. I suggest the following two "second-order
principles" for prioritizing among conflicting first-order principles, the duties and
obligations generated by different community memberships.[79]

2.16 PRIORITIZING CROSS-COMMUNITY DUTIES AND OBLIGATIONS

The first second-order principle (SOP1) is that the duties and obligations generated
by memberships in our more intimate and venerable communities take precedence

over those generated by memberships in the larger, more impersonal, and more recently evolved (or more recently recognized) communities. The "family society," as Hume calls it, is the most intimate and venerable of all communities and so, in general, extended-family duties and obligations would eclipse those generated by all other community memberships, in accordance with SOP1.

The second second-order principle (SOP2) is that stronger duties and obligations take precedence over weaker ones. Members of family societies have an obligation to, say, observe the birthdays of fellow members, but that is a relatively weak obligation in comparison with the obligation to, say, care for infant and aged fellow members. No less than within communities, the relative strength of duties and obligations can be compared between communities. Thus the basic human right of a young woman to autonomy over her own body and to sexual fulfillment is stronger than her duty to honor the ethnic tradition of female circumcision, although the ethnic community is more intimate and venerable than is the global village to which the ethic of universal human rights is correlative.

Finally, I suggest applying a third-order principle (TOP) specifying the sequence in which the two second-order principles are consulted and which to honor if they give counterindications: first apply SOP1 to any given conflict among duties and obligations generated by multiple community memberships, then apply SOP2. If SOP2 countermands SOP1, the TOP requires that SOP2 trump the ruling of SOP1.[80]

While the apparent formalism of this approach to resolving conflicts between duties and obligations generated by multiple community memberships may smack of algorithmic certainty, I would most emphatically protest that there is nothing certain about it. Moral decision making is not an exact science—pace Bentham's hedonic calculus and its many successors in the utilitarian tradition—nor will everyone applying these second- and third-order principles come to the same decisions. Imagine a case of conflict between the duties and obligations generated by membership in a biotic community and membership in a nation-state. The economic activity (say, logging) of some of my fellow Americans threatens to exterminate a species (say, the northern spotted owl or the red-cockaded woodpecker). I agree with Aldo Leopold that bird species should have a biotic right to continuance and with Holmes Rolston that speciescide is "super-killing" requiring "super justification" and thus that we have a very strong land-ethical duty to preserve species.[81] Thus I would decide that saving an endangered species should take priority over the economic liberty of my fellow citizens of our democratic nation-state when their exercise of that liberty threatens such a species. Others of goodwill—even those who recognize the existence of biotic communities and acknowledge the correlative land-ethical duties and obligations it generates—might well come to a different decision.

2.17 IS THE LAND ETHIC ANTHROPOCENTRIC OR NON-ANTHROPOCENTRIC?

To conclude this chapter and anticipate the next, I pose the question: Is the land ethic anthropocentric or non-anthropocentric? Please recall the distinction between metaphysical and moral anthropocentrism (drawn in the Introduction). Moral anthropocentrism is the view that humans alone are the proper beneficiaries of ethics. Moral anthropocentrism is conventionally justified by appeal to metaphysical anthropocentrism. There is no question that the land ethic is non-anthropocentric, metaphysically speaking. From the point of view of evolutionary-ecological metaphysics, humans are fellow-voyagers with other creatures in the odyssey of evolution, plain members and citizens of the biotic community. Rather, the question posed here is whether the land ethic might be anthropocentric or non-anthropocentric, morally speaking, despite lacking support for moral anthropocentrism derived from metaphysical anthropocentrism. Is it genuinely about benefiting fellow-members of the biotic community and the biotic community as such or is it really about only benefiting humans and various human communities? The answer is that the land ethic is both anthropocentric and non-anthropocentric depending on whether we engage it phenomenologically or scientifically.

As Leopold makes clear, he believes that the phenomenology of ethics—the way we experience ethics—involves the other-oriented moral sentiments. As he says, "We can be ethical only in relation to something we can see, feel, understand, love, or otherwise have faith in." And he says that "It is inconceivable to me that an ethical relation to land can exist without love, respect, and admiration for land, and a high regard for its value." Lest one suppose that by "value," Leopold might mean that land has only instrumental value to human beings, Leopold goes to insist that "By value, of course I mean something far broader than mere economic value; I mean value in the philosophical sense"—that is, intrinsic value (as noted in 1.13). As the land ethic is lived—as it is experienced viscerally—the land ethic is genuinely and sincerely non-anthropocentric.

But we may step back from ethical experience and examine ethical phenomena from what phenomenologists call the perspective of naturalism—that is, a more disinterested scientific perspective.[82] From that perspective, the land ethic may appear to be anthropocentric, or perhaps better sociocentric. According to Leopold,

> An ethic may be regarded as a mode of guidance for meeting ecological situations so new or intricate, or involving such deferred reactions, that *the path of social expediency* is not discernible to the average individual. Animal instincts [including, presumably, the "social instincts" to which Darwin so frequently refers] are modes of guidance for the individual in meeting such situations. Ethics are possibly a kind of *community instinct* in-the-making.[83]

Scott Lehmann nicely expresses the dual anthropocentric/non-anthropocentric aspects of the land ethic:

> Leopold argues that we shall be most successful in promoting human welfare if we look to the welfare of the land....The more direct approach of simply assessing actions in terms of their consequences for human welfare is not a feasible alternative to the land ethic, in Leopold's view. First, the complexity of the biosphere and our ignorance of its relations of interdependence make such

assessment impossible. Second, the assessors are apt to have a narrow vis[on]
of human welfare: they may discount the future,…or place their own inter[est]
above those of others. Only a love for the land, Leopold thinks, can meet [those]
needs.[84]

From an evolutionary point of view, what *all* ethics are ultimately about is sur-vival and reproductive success for both individuals and communities. But the path to this end of inclusive fitness is difficult to discern. Nature has taken reproduction out of the hands of our calculative intelligence and placed it instead in the hands of our sexual instincts and impulses. So also has nature in effect taken what Lehman calls "human welfare"—collectively understood, broadly conceived, and over the long term—out of the hands of our calculative intelligence (long before we evolved calcu-lative intelligence) and placed it instead in the more reliable but cruder hands of our social instincts and sympathies. From a lived, phenomenological, experiential perspec-tive, sexual activity is an end in itself, motivated by desire and rewarded with a pecu-liar, intense physically local pleasure, followed by a more diffusely pleasant afterglow. Reproduction is at best an afterthought to sexual gratification—indeed, more often, no thought at all. From a lived, phenomenological, experiential perspective, ethics are an expression of other-oriented intentional feelings, our moral sentiments. We are motivated by love, respect, sympathy, beneficence, magnanimity, loyalty, allegiance, patriotism, reverence…and we are rewarded by a peculiar warm, low-intensity psy-chological pleasure when we act on these motivations. Thus, because the land ethic specifically focuses our other-oriented intentional sentiments on the biotic commu-nity and its fellow members (lest we as well as Leopold forget them), it is morally non-anthropocentric. But from a disinterested, analytic, scientific perspective, ethics are subtly and indirectly self-serving: they enable individuals and communities to sur-vive, flourish, and reproduce themselves. Thus the land ethic is, from this point of view, morally anthropocentric.

In the next several chapters, I more closely examine the relationship of science and ethics—first, the way science informs the land ethic, then how ethics has itself been assimilated to science, and finally how the land ethic fares from the point of view of the scientific accounts of ethics that have come along after Darwin's, on which Leopold relied.

3

The Land Ethic (an Ought): A Critical Account of Its Ecological Foundations (an Is)

In Chapter 2, I argue that Charles Darwin's account of the origin and evolution of ethics in the *Descent of Man* is central to the philosophical foundations of the Leopold land ethic. There, I also argue that the community paradigm in ecology, as articulated by Charles Elton in *Animal Ecology*, is a signal element in Leopold's move from Darwin's general account of ethics to a land ethic. In this chapter, I review other ways that the theory of evolution informs the *worldview* in which the land ethic is embedded. I then move on to the central topic of this chapter: the very complex way in which various paradigms in ecology, not just the "community concept," inform the land ethic. This cozy relationship between the biological sciences and the land ethic, however, flies in the face of a specter that mercilessly haunted twentieth-century moral philosophy and threatens to spook the moral philosophy of the twenty-first—unless it is exorcised once and for all. Ironically, it is the shade of David Hume—ironic because Hume's general moral philosophy was incorporated into Darwin's account of the origins and evolution of ethics and is, therefore, the intellectual substratum on which the conceptual foundations of the land ethic rest. More ironic still, because Hume's general moral philosophy is the root from which contemporary evolutionary moral psychology now flowers forth (detailed and documented in 5.9). So I begin this chapter with a discussion of the Humean Is/Ought Dichotomy that benights and confounds moral philosophy to this day. This phantasm goes by several names. In addition to the Is/Ought Dichotomy, it is also called the Fact/Value Dichotomy and the Naturalistic Fallacy.

3.1 MOORE'S NATURALISTIC FALLACY

The Naturalistic Fallacy is, however, a misnomer—a legacy not of Hume, but of G. E. Moore.[1] What Moore meant by the Naturalistic Fallacy is not entirely clear to me, nor does it seem to be entirely clear to Moore himself.[2] This much *is* clear, however: Moore thought that good was a "non-natural" property possessed by good things. Some things are intrinsically good; others are instrumentally good, because they are productive of intrinsically good things.

A natural or empirical property is a property apprehensible by our senses—either unaided or augmented by instruments, such as microscopes and spectrometers—or otherwise capable of being directly experienced. Being spherical is a natural property; so is being jealous—a state of consciousness that is directly experienced. Having a nucleus is a natural property of eukaryotic cells apprehensible by our senses, but only with the aid of microscopes. Putatively non-natural moral and aesthetic properties are not empirical. They are not supposed to be apprehended by our senses, aided or unaided, nor are they otherwise supposed to be directly experienced. Rather, they are supposed to be apprehended by a special intuitive faculty, according to Moore. To commit the Naturalistic Fallacy is to claim that exhibiting some natural property is what makes something good. Moore was out to discredit the traditional utilitarians, who, as noted in 2.8, believed that the only intrinsically good thing was pleasure. But because pleasure is experienced sensuously or at least empirically, pleasure is a natural property. And thus to claim that the property of being pleasurable or being pleasure-producing is what makes good things good (intrinsically or instrumentally, respectively) is to commit the Naturalistic Fallacy.

Moore claimed to prove his point with the Open Question. The question, Are all bachelors unmarried men? is closed because no man who is a bachelor can by that very token be married. One can, however, ask, Is pleasure really good? and the question is open because one might intelligibly—and possibly truthfully—answer No. In the *Gorgias*, for example, Plato's answer to that question is a resounding No. Bentham, of course, would not agree with Plato—and why not, because the question is indeed open. The good and the pleasant cannot therefore be the same thing, Moore argued, and the same Open-Question argument would apply to any other naturalistic candidate for the nature of the good.

In environmental ethics, a case might be made that both neo-utilitarians, such as Peter Singer, and deontologists such as Tom Regan and Paul Taylor, commit the Naturalistic Fallacy in declaring that the goodness (intrinsic value or inherent worth) of an entity turns on its being sentient, a subject of a life, or being a teleological center of a life, respectively. To make intrinsic value a supervenient property—that is, a property that piggybacks on another objective property—might be a way for Singer, Regan, and Taylor to circumvent the accusation that they commit the Naturalistic Fallacy.

3.2 HUME'S IS/OUGHT DICHOTOMY AND THE LAND ETHIC

In any case, the Naturalistic Fallacy is not a formal fallacy of logic. The Is/Ought Dichotomy, however, is supposed to be a formal fallacy of logic—which may explain why it has been confused with Moore's Naturalistic Fallacy. In the case of the Is/Ought Dichotomy, the putative formal fallacy is illegitimately to derive an ought-statement, a prescription, an imperative, from an is-statement, a description, a declarative. Here is the passage in Hume's *A Treatise of Human Nature* that has, in the minds of many twentieth-century ethicists, made science irrelevant to ethics and ethics independent of science:

> In every system of morality, which I have hitherto met with, I have always remark'd that the author proceeds for some time in the ordinary way of

reasoning, and establishes the being of a God, or makes observations concerning human affairs; when of a sudden I am surpriz'd to find, that instead of the usual copulations of propositions, *is*, and *is not*, I meet with no proposition that is not connected with an *ought* or an *ought not*. This change is imperceptible; but is, however, of the last consequence. For as this *ought* or *ought not*, expresses some new relation or affirmation, 'tis necessary that it should be observ'd and explain'd; and at the same time that a reason should be given, for what seems altogether inconceivable, how this new relation can be a deduction from others, which are entirely different from it.[3]

Darwin seems untroubled by the logical relationship between declarative statements and imperative statements. For example, as highlighted in 2.6, he writes, "As man advances in civilization, and small tribes *are* united into larger communities, the simplest reason would tell each individual that he *ought* to extend his social instincts and sympathies to all the members of the same nation, though personally unknown to him."[4] Indeed, I am aware of no nineteenth-century moral philosophers who were vexed by the logical relationship between is-statements and ought-statements. But— perhaps because twentieth-century philosophy became obsessed with the analysis of language and with the relationship between statements, propositions, and the entities to which they refer—this passing comment of Hume's in the *Treatise* was received like a divine revelation by the rank-and-file moral philosophers of that century. A physical theory that violated the second law of thermodynamics would be rejected as untenable. Similarly, many philosophers regard an ethical theory to be equally untenable that violates the prohibition of deriving prescriptions from descriptions. Indeed, twentieth-century British moral philosopher R. M. Hare called the Is/Ought Dichotomy "Hume's Law."[5]

Max Black, a more circumspect contemporary of Hare, notes "the remarkable influence this passage has exerted," and in consequence he "propose[s] to assign to the principle that only factual statements can follow from exclusively factual statements the title 'Hume's Guillotine.'"[6] Apropos the fact that most executioners deploying Hume's Guillotine otherwise pay no attention whatever to Hume's moral philosophy, I should observe the anachronism: the *Treatise* was published in 1739 and Hume died in 1776, while the guillotine was invented by Joseph-Ignace Guillotine in the 1790s and became emblematic of the Reign of Terror following the French Revolution.[7] Nonetheless, Black's epithet is perfectly fitting; "Madame Gillotine," as the device was known in the dark days of the Terror, took the lives of thousands of victims in the last decade of the eighteenth century.[8] Likewise, Hume's Guillotine has been invoked thousands of times by twentieth-century ethicists as a means of summarily decapitating an opponent's argument and striking terror into the heart of any other philosophers who might dare to derive *ought*s from *is*es.

Leopold, in "The Land Ethic," appears to follow the pattern of argument noticed and censured by Hume. Instead of establishing the being of a God, he establishes the being of a biotic community; and "makes observations concerning human affairs" in regard to land. Then he goes on to conclude, among other things, that because "these creatures *are* members of the biotic community,…birds *should* [another word for *ought*] continue as a matter of biotic right."[9] So great a shibboleth had become the Is/Ought Dichotomy—"Hume's Law"—in twentieth-century moral philosophy that Leopold felt a need at least to acknowledge, in "The Conservation Ethic," that for some of his readers no connection between science and ethics was legitimate. He wisely rejects such an unbridgeable lacuna as a dogmatic philosophical presumption unworthy of the open-mindedness typical of science: "Some scientists will dismiss this matter forthwith on the ground that ecology has no relation to right and wrong. To such I reply that science, *if not philosophy*, should by now have made us cautious about dismissals."[10] This remark was deleted when Leopold worked parts of "The Conservation Ethic" into "The Land Ethic."

3.3 HOW HUME BRIDGES THE LACUNA BETWEEN IS-STATEMENTS AND OUGHT-STATEMENTS

Alasdair MacIntyre argues that by "deduction" Hume does not mean formal logico-mathematical entailment but, in line with "ordinary eighteenth-century use," he meant "'inference' and 'infer' [rather] than 'entailment' and 'entail.'"[11] Further, MacIntyre notes, when he meant logico-mathematical entailment, Hume "always uses the term 'demonstrative arguments.'"[12] On this point, MacIntyre concludes that "Hume, then, in the celebrated passage, does not mention entailment. What he does is ask how and if moral rules may be inferred from factual statements, and in the rest of Book III of the *Treatise* he provides an answer to his own question."[13]

Indeed, Hume's observation about inferring imperative from declarative statements comes at the conclusion of an argument central to his moral philosophy: that right and wrong, good and evil, virtuousness and viciousness are not properties—either natural or non-natural—of objects or actions. According to Hume, one function of the faculty of reason is to discern all *objective* matters of fact, among them the properties of objects or actions. If good and evil, right and wrong, virtuousness and viciousness are not objective matters of fact discernible by reason, then by what means do they so palpably manifest themselves to us? Hume's example of a vicious action is "willful murder."

> Examine it in all lights, and see if you can find that matter of fact, or real existence, which you call vice....The vice entirely escapes you, as long as you consider the object. You never can find it, till you turn your reflection into your own breast, and find a sentiment of disapprobation, which arises in you, toward this action. Here is a matter of fact; but 'tis the object of feeling, not of reason. It lies in yourself, not in the object. So that when you pronounce any action or character to be vicious, you mean nothing, but that from the constitution of your nature you have a feeling or sentiment of blame from the contemplation of it.[14]

Note that Hume here commits Moore's Naturalistic Fallacy because he equates vice—evil, the contrary of good—with a natural property: "a feeling or sentiment of blame." But so what? That is of no consequence for the matter at hand; and Moore's ethical theory is hardly now anything more than a historical curiosity. Immediately after declaring the Is/Ought Dichotomy, Hume goes on to the conclusion that he draws from his observation regarding every system of morality that he has hitherto met with:

> But as authors do not commonly use this precaution, I shall presume to recommend it to readers; and am persuaded, that this small attention would subvert all the vulgar systems of morality, and let us see, that the distinction of vice and virtue is not founded merely on the relations of objects, nor is perceived by reason."[15]

Thus, when Hume's Is/Ought Dichotomy is located in the context of the argument of the *Treatise* in which it is found, we discover that there *is* a logical link between is-statements and ought-statements—between declaratives and imperatives, descriptions and prescriptions. The usually missing link is a statement referring to subjective sentiments or feelings. Willful murder combines malice with violence. So much reason can disclose. In addition, it arouses feelings of fear and loathing in those who witness or contemplate it. Because of these sentiments, we pronounce it vicious; and then declare that one ought not to commit willful murder.

The "vulgar systems of morality," in short, turn on an enthymeme, an argument with an unstated premise. Consider, in light of the larger context of Hume's argument in the *Treatise*, that typical vulgar system founded on the being of a God, who demands that His name not be taken in vain.

(P) God exists and is sorely offended when His name is taken in vain.
(C) Therefore, you ought not to take God's name in vain.

The unstated premise is one referring to the subjective emotional state of those persuaded by the moralist's establishment of the being of a God: they *fear* their God's wrath or *desire* to please their God in hope of a reward. The fully stated argument then would run something like this.

(P1) God exists and is sorely offended when His name is taken in vain.
(P2) You fear God and/or desire to please God
(C)   Therefore, you ought not to take the name of God in vain.

MacIntyre's "interpretation of the 'is' and 'ought' passage...can now be stated compendiously" and he states my interpretation, as well, both succinctly and authoritatively:

> Hume is not in this passage asserting the autonomy of morals—for he did not believe in it; and he is not making a point about entailment—for he does not mention it. He is asserting that the question of how the factual basis of morality is related to morality is a crucial logical issue, reflection on which will enable one to realise how there are ways in which this transition can be made and ways in which it cannot. One has to go beyond the passage to see what these are; but if one does so it is plain that we can connect the facts of the situation

with what we ought to do only by means of one of those concepts which Hume treats under the heading of the passions.... Hume is not as [A. N.] Prior seems to indicate, trying to say that morality lacks a basis; he is trying to point out the nature of that basis.[16]

3.4 HOW KANT INFERS OUGHT-STATEMENTS FROM IS-STATEMENTS IN HYPOTHETICAL IMPERATIVES

Grant, for the sake of argument, that by *deduction* Hume meant "entailment" as those twentieth-century philosophers, such as Prior and Hare, assume in self-assured ignorance of both general eighteenth-century usage and Hume's own consistent use of the phrase "demonstrative argument" when he means formal validity or entailment. Can the affective link between is-statements and ought-statements be a matter of *formal logic* and not merely a psychological link? Kant—who credited reading Hume for waking him from his dogmatic slumber—thought that is-statements can sometimes *entail* ought-statements.[17] According to Kant, "All imperatives are expressed by an 'ought'"; and "[a]ll imperatives command either hypothetically or categorically. The former present the practical necessity of a possible action as a means to achieving something else which one desires."[18] Hypothetical imperatives are expressed in an *if…then…*form. The phrase following the *if* is the hypothetical element; that following the *then* is the imperative element.

Suppose, accordingly, that I am a student's faculty advisor and I say to that student, "You ought to take biology." And the student asks, "Why?" And I reply, "You just said that you want to go on to medical school and become a physician; you cannot get into medical school if you haven't taken biology. Therefore, IF you *desire* to get into medical school and become a physician, THEN you *ought* to take biology." Kant calls this kind of hypothetical imperative a "problematical" imperative of "skill." It is problematical because the subjective desire or "inclination" may or may not be present. Suppose further that my advisee replies, "No, you misheard me; I said that I want to get an MBA from business school and become an investment banker, not an MD from medical school and become a physician." To which I would reply, "Oh, then you *ought not* to take biology; instead you *ought* to take economics."

Kant also identifies another kind of hypothetical imperative, the "assertorical" imperatives of "prudence." Not everyone wants to be a physician and not everyone wants to be an investment banker. But everyone does want to be happy. To this universally desired end there is a set of means, which, given the end, ought to be undertaken. IF you *desire* to be happy, THEN you *ought* (a) to refrain altogether from tobacco; (b) to drink alcohol only moderately; (c) not to engage in risky sexual behavior; (d) to avoid eating a steady diet of junk food; (e) to conserve your financial resources;…and so on and so forth—the usual litany of imperatives we hear from our mothers and others concerned with our well-being. Now according to Kant, the logical link between the is-statement, *X is what I desire*, and the imperative, *I ought to do Y* as the means to achieve X, is the strongest of all possible logical links: analyticity. According to Kant, the ought-statement is indeed *entailed* by the is-statement:

> How an imperative of skill is possible requires no particular discussion. Whoever wills the end...wills also the indispensable means to it that lie in his power. This proposition, in what concerns the will, is analytical; for in willing an object as my effect, my causality as an acting cause, i. e., the use of means, is already thought, and the imperative derives the concept of necessary actions to this end from the concept of willing this end.[19]

Kant goes on to say that the logical link between assertorical imperatives of prudence and their hypotheses would also be analytical, if only we had as clear and self-consistent an idea of happiness and what means are necessary to achieving that end, as we have of being a physician or an investment banker and what means are necessary for achieving those ends. The categorical imperative has, by definition, no antecedent hypothesis, and thus its logical necessity is more difficult to comprehend. Kant eventually locates the logical necessity of the categorical imperative in pure reason—and its most fundamental logical law of non-contradiction—free of all empirical content, independent of all human "inclination"; that is, free of all human desires, passions, sentiments, and feelings. Kant dismisses Hume's ethical theory as "practical anthropology," grounded in human nature, while he believed that his own ethical theory transcends the specific features of human nature and thus obligates all rational beings anywhere in the universe, whatever their specific physical or psychological peculiarities might be. According to MacIntyre, to think that Hume prohibits the derivation of ought-statements from is-statements is to assimilate Hume's ethics to Kant's: "Hume becomes in this light an exponent of the autonomy of morality and in this at least is akin to Kant....Here it is outside my scope to argue against Kant; all I want to do is to prevent Hume from being classified with him on this issue."[20] Kant himself, it is worth noting, also draws a sharp contrast between his own ethics and that of Hume's.

The fact that Kant believes that ought-statements may be validly derived from is-statements does not make it so. Were I to claim that it is so because Kant said that it was so would be for me to commit the informal logical fallacy of Appeal to Authority and put me in the company of those who seem so ready to appeal to the authority of Hume with unreflective and unscholarly prattle about "Hume's Law." But the fact that Kant believes that ought-statements may be validly derived from is-statements should give us pause and make us, as Leopold warned, "cautious about dismissals." It should make us receptive to carefully revisiting the Is/Ought Dichotomy with a newly reopened mind—a mind, on this particular, wakened from its dogmatic slumber.

3.5 THE SPECTER OF HUME'S IS/OUGHT DICHOTOMY FINALLY EXORCISED

In Hume's utterly human moral philosophy all imperatives are, as it were, hypothetical. Ought-statements are logically inferred from *objective* is-statements (statements referring to "relations of objects…perceived by reason") AND to is-statements referring to *subjective* passions, desires, sentiments, and feelings. So to take Hume's own example, a "vulgar" moral philosopher may make a series of is-statements consisting of "observations concerning human affairs" say, that willful murder is (a) physically possible, (b) often tempting to commit, and (c) sometimes actually committed. He or she may then go on to say that one ought not to commit willful murder. The logical link between the series of objective is-statements and the ought-statement is an unstated subjective premise referring to the sentiment of disapprobation regarding willful murder very commonly found in the human breast, if not universally found there. To make this Humean deduction of an ought-statement from an is-statement entirely clear, let me express it premise by premise and do so by analogy with an instance of Kant's problematical hypothetical imperative of skill:

(1) It *is* the case that to enroll in medical school one must have taken biology in college. (I'm just assuming that this premise is true for the sake of argument.)
(2) It *is* the case that you, an undergraduate, desire to enroll in medical school, after you are graduated from college, and eventually become a physician.
(3) Therefore, you *ought* to take biology.

(1) Willful murder *is* physically possible, often tempting to commit, and sometimes committed.
(2) We human beings, presumably you among us, *are* so constituted as to feel a strong disapprobation regarding willful murder.
(3) Therefore, you *ought* not to commit, aid, or abet willful murder and you *ought* morally to censure those who do.

Y. S. Lo claims that analogies like this with Kantian hypothetical imperatives do not help illuminate how Hume's Is/Ought Dichotomy can be bridged. She invokes the murders in Shakespeare's *Hamlet* as counter-examples. If such an is-to-ought transition as in this example of willful murder drawn from Hume and analyzed by parity of reasoning with a Kantian hypothetical imperative "seems legitimate to you," writes Lo, "but the is-to-ought transitions of the same form in the cases of *Hamlet*…do not, that is because you do not think that Hamelt ought to be poisoned."[21] To consider but the first case of willful murder in that doleful tragedy, the logical necessity of Claudius committing willful murder might indeed be expressed as a hypothetical imperative of skill—and a problematical one to be sure. Claudius wants to be King of Denmark. The only means available to achieve his end is to murder the incumbent king, Claudius's brother and Hamlet's father, and marry Gertrude, Queen of Denmark and Hamlet's mother. Therefore, Claudius ought to murder his brother, the king. As Lo points out, this hardly amounts to a valid moral argument. But no one, least of all Kant, thinks that it is a valid *moral* argument. It is, however, according to Kant, a valid problematical-hypothetical-imperative-of-skill argument. For as Kant expressly points out,

Whether the end is…good is not in question at all, for the question is only of what must be done in order to attain it. The precepts to be followed by a physician in order to cure his patient and by a poisoner to bring about certain death are of equal value in so far as each does that which will perfectly accomplish his purpose.[22]

Like Lo, perhaps Kant has *Hamlet* in mind, because the method Claudius chooses for murdering the incumbent king is poisoning. (Not only does he poison his brother, but he used poison to attempt to murder Hamlet, an attempt that goes awry and Claudius winds up killing Gertrude instead.) For Kant, incidentally, no argument whatsoever involving a hypothetical imperative is a valid *moral* argument. Only the categorical imperative is a moral imperative. And it is supreme; it trumps all hypothetical imperatives—certainly all problematical imperatives of skill, and, indeed, all assertorical imperatives of prudence. Nor would Lo's counter-example of murder in *Hamlet* be a true counter-example for it would not be a valid *moral* argument in Hume's system either. While for Hume all imperatives are, as it were, hypothetical, conditioned by subjective desires, passions, emotions, feelings, and sentiments, only prescriptive arguments conditioned by such *moral* sentiments as sympathy, beneficence, loyalty, and the like are valid *moral* arguments. As Hume puts this point with characteristic force,

Avarice, ambition, vanity, and all passions…comprised under the denomination of *self-love* are here excluded from our theory concerning the origin of morals, not because they are too weak, but because they have not a proper direction for that purpose.…

When a man denominates another his *enemy*, his *rival*, his *antagonist*, his *adversary* [as Claudius denominates Hamlet when Claudius realizes that Hamlet contemplates avenging his father's murder] he is understood to speak the language of self-love and to express sentiments peculiar to himself and arising from his particular circumstances and situation. But when he bestows on any man the epithets of *vicious*, or *odious*, or *depraved* [Hamlet denominates Claudius a "villain"], he then speaks another language and expresses sentiments in which he expects all his audience to concur with him. He must here depart from his private and peculiar situation and must choose a point of view common to him with others: he must move some universal principle of the human frame and touch a string to which all mankind have an accord and symphony.[23]

3.6 THE ROLES OF REASON AND FEELING IN HUME'S ETHICAL THEORY GENERALLY AND LEOPOLD'S LAND ETHIC PARTICULARLY

From a Humean point of view, in all circumstances of choice, like that faced by Claudius, between a moral and an immoral (or amoral) action, a person is moved to act on one or the other of two kinds of feelings: the selfish passions, such as avarice, ambition, and vanity, on the one hand; or the sociable moral sentiments, such sympathy, beneficence, and loyalty, on the other. Moral choice is not a matter of acting on reason rather than "inclination" (passion, desire, emotion, or sentiment) as Kant subsequently insisted. On the contrary, for Hume, reason by itself can never move us to act at all; and a passion can only be opposed by another passion. In the *Treatise*, however, Hume does provide an important supporting role for reason in choosing a course of action:

> [R]eason, in a strict and philosophic sense, can have an influence on our conduct only after two ways: Either when it excites a passion by informing us of the existence of something which is a proper object of it; or when it discovers the connection of causes and effects, so as to afford us the means of exerting any passion.[24]

In "The Land Ethic" Leopold uses reason (in the form of ecology) to influence our conduct in both ways. He reveals a proper object of our community-oriented passions—the biotic community—toward which, on the basis of such sentiments, we might conduct ourselves more respectfully. And he discovers for us the connection of causes and effects, affording us the means of exerting our passions. For example, the American Southwest, "when grazed by livestock, reverted through a series of worthless grasses, shrubs, and weeds to a condition of unstable equilibrium."[25] Leopold redirects or transfers our righteous indignation regarding the loss of natural beauty—for the conversion of a healthy and productive country into a "wrecked landscape"—toward its cause: livestock grazing. That feeling of indignation might motivate us to demand that our political representatives regulate or altogether prohibit livestock grazing in the region or reform grazing practices so that they imitate the patterns of grazing by native wild species, such as bison. In the *Enquiry*, Hume is less laconic in describing the differing roles of feeling and reason in ethics:

> The final sentence...which pronounces characters and actions amiable or odious, praiseworthy or blamable; that which stamps on them the mark of honor or infamy, approbation or censure; that which renders morality an active principle and constitutes virtue our happiness and vice our misery...I say that this final sentence depends on some internal sense or feeling which nature has made universal in the whole species. But in order to pave the way for such a sentiment and give a proper discernment of its object, it is often necessary, we find, that much reasoning should precede, that nice distinctions be made, just conclusions drawn, distant comparisons formed, complicated relations examined, and general facts fixed and ascertained.[26]

More reliably than any other method of reasoning, science ascertains and fixes general facts; examines complicated relations; forms distant comparisons; draws justified conclusions; and makes nice distinctions. The role of science in ethical deliberation is to bring facts, relations, analogies, conclusions, and distinctions before the jury of our moral sentiments for judgment or action. Further, because the moral sentiments are universal psychological traits of the human species—no less so than such physical traits as opposable thumbs and a bipedal gait—our moral differences of opinion turn not on differences of feeling but on the reasoning preceding the final sentence of feeling. As MacIntyre notes, Hume thought that "if all factual disagreements were resolved, no moral disagreements would remain" and his opinion on this head is a further reason that our "interpretation of the 'is' and 'ought' passage [should be] accepted; but on the standard interpretation it remains an odd and inexplicable belief of Hume's."[27] Thus the Humean theoretical foundations of the Leopold land ethic provide for a wholly rational and cognitive resolution for all ethical disputes—or at least all those within the same moral culture, mindful of the way our universally human ethical sensibilities are differently molded in different cultural contexts, as noticed in 2.8 and 2.9 and detailed in 5.9 and 5.10.

Here we find a supreme irony: Hume's moral philosophy, grounded in humanly universal moral sentiments, makes the resolution of all differences in moral judgment turn on reason—ascertaining and nailing down general *facts*, examining complicated *causal relations, comparing* novel situations to more familiar ones, *drawing conclusions* from such analogies, and *making fine distinctions*. Take Leopold's land-ethical analysis of the environmental deterioration of the Southwest as an illustration. As a matter of *fact*, the vegetation of the area used to be dominated by grass; but by the time Leopold arrived, it was dominated by brush.[28] The *causes* of this transformation of the region to a new, unstable, and undesirable domain of ecological attraction are, he discovered, livestock grazing and fire suppression.[29] Leopold compared this region to "India," which was also "devoid of any sod-forming grass," but was "settled, apparently without wrecking the land, by the simple expedient of carrying the grass to the cow, rather than vice versa."[30] He also compared this region to the "Mississippi valley" that "when subjected to the particular mixture of cow, plow, fire, and axe of the pioneer, became bluegrass" and "Western Europe," which is also the locus of a biotic community that is "tough, elastic, resistant to strain."[31] Leopold thus concluded that the conventional pastoral methods that Americans inherited from their European ancestors were disastrous when practiced in the Southwest. He drew the fine distinction that what is land-ethically permissible in one place—livestock grazing in Western Europe and in Eastern North America—is land-ethically impermissible in another place, the American Southwest.

3.7 HOW THE GENERAL THEORY OF EVOLUTION INFORMS THE LAND ETHIC

In 2.5 and 2.6, I indicate how Darwin's account of the origin and evolution of ethics was the foundation on which Leopold built the land ethic. And, as I also indicate in 2.7, ecology informs the land ethic. It establishes the existence of biotic communities, while the overall argument of *The Descent of Man* also establishes the general evolutionary fact that *Homo sapiens* are plain members and citizens of biotic communities. In an elegy for an extinct species, "On a Monument to the Pigeon" (documented in 1.8), Leopold provides the most succinct summary of the relevant justified conclusions of evolutionary biology.

Many of the complicated relations in evolutionary theory have changed "since Darwin gave us the first glimpse of the origin of species," and some remain matters of dispute among contemporary evolutionary biologists.[32] Darwin, for example, knew nothing of genes, nor, therefore, could the neo-Darwinian concept of genetic mutation be an element of his own theory of evolution. And some evolutionary biologists dispute the fundamental Darwinian orthodoxy that the principal force driving evolutionary change is natural selection.[33] The luckiest, not necessarily the fittest, may have survived; and as much change may be attributable to random genetic drift as to determinant selection.[34] More radically still, some evolutionary biologists think that both Darwin himself and the neo-Darwinians have myopically stressed competition as a driver of evolutionary change to the neglect of symbiosis—and their point of view is now becoming mainstream.[35]

But the justified conclusions of evolutionary biology that Leopold evokes throughout *Sand County* and pointedly in "On a Monument to the Pigeon," are beyond scientific dispute. *Homo sapiens* is an evolved species. We are literally kin to all other species and share common ancestors with them—with some, more recent common ancestors than with others—traceable on the tree of life. The "duration of the biotic enterprise"—going back some three and a half billion years—is truly immense; indeed, it is mind-boggling.[36] And "the magnitude…of the biotic enterprise"—the sheer exuberance of the biota, the literally uncountable diversity of life, both extant and extinct—is equally immense and mind-boggling.[37] Further, to describe evolution as an "odyssey" is to suggest that it is a wandering journey without a destination, a process without a goal or purpose. That evolution is an ateleological process is also beyond scientific dispute; and certainly the idea that "man" is the end of the process of evolution—"the sole object of its quest"—is, as Leopold suggests, but a childish notion born of both ignorance and arrogance.[38]

Note how Leopold, very much in the manner abstractly set forth by Hume, submits these justified conclusions of evolutionary biology to the final sentence—the judgment—of his reader's moral sense and expects them to touch a string to which all mankind have an accord and symphony. Learning of our "kinship with fellow creatures" in the "odyssey of evolution" should excite our universal human feelings of fellowship; and those feelings of fellowship, Leopold supposes, would be attended by a "wish"—a moral desire—"to live and let live."[39] Contemplating the immensity of "the magnitude and duration of the biotic enterprise" should, Leopold also supposes, play upon our universal human "sense of wonder"—our universal human capacity for awe when contemplating the sublime.[40]

3.8 HOW ECOSYSTEM ECOLOGY INFORMS
THE LAND ETHIC–BEYOND THE BIOTA

The land ethic is more sensitive to the changes in ecology that have occurred during the nearly century and a quarter since Leopold articulated it than to those in evolutionary biology. Community ecology—especially as it is developed by Charles Elton in his 1927 book, *Animal Ecology*—was the principal body of general facts, complicated relations, and justified conclusions that Leopold submits to the final sentence of those of his readers' moral sentiments that are excited by the prospect of community and community membership.[41] I sketch the Eltonian community paradigm in ecology in 2.7.

One finds, however, aspects of the more recent ecosystem paradigm also strongly represented in "The Land Ethic." One of the ecological concepts that Elton developed was the pyramid of numbers. Leopold made this concept and associated image the central trope for the longest section, "The Land Pyramid," of "The Land Ethic." As noted in 1.9, this section was adapted for "The Land Ethic" from "A Biotic View of Land," a plenary address to a joint meeting of the Society of American Foresters and the Ecological Society of America in the summer of 1939 and published later that year in the *Journal of Forestry*.[42] That article is remarkable because it partially anticipates the integration of Elton's pyramid-of-numbers concept with Arthur Tansley's ecosystem concept—which integration Raymond Lindeman fully effected in "The Trophic-Dynamic Aspect of Ecology," published in *Ecology* in 1942.[43] Once again Leopold proves to be a prophet—this time of the eventual shape of the ecosystem paradigm in ecology. However, as shortly to be shown, and as is often the case with prophets, he gets it almost—but not quite—right.

Tansley coined the term "ecosystem" in a 1935 article in *Ecology*, "The Use and Abuse of Vegetational Concepts and Terms."[44] To the biota (plants + animals), Tansley adds the abiotic elements of soil, water, and air as proper objects of ecological study and suggests that all together they (the biota + their abiotic environments) form "systems in the sense of the physicist."[45] Tansley expresses displeasure with the biotic-community concept and insists that

> The more fundamental conception is, as it seems to me, the whole system (in the sense of physics), including not only the organism complex, but the whole complex of physical factors forming what we call the environment of the biome—the habitat factors in the widest sense. Though the organisms may claim our primary interest, when we are trying to think fundamentally we cannot separate them from their environment, with which they form one physical system....These *ecosystems*, as we may call them, are of the most various kinds and sizes.[46]

In his popular and influential history of ecology, *Nature's Economy*, Donald Worster claims that "For the time, all that Tansley's new approach to ecology seemed to indicate was a shift toward an emphasis on energy flow."[47] Nowhere, however, in "Use and Abuse" does Tansley evoke the way energy flows through ecosystems and how consideration of energy flows can explain the structure of food chains and the pyramid of numbers. Indeed, the word "energy" appears but once in that article in the unrelated phrase "intellectual energy" (that is, effort).[48] The idea that energy flows through ecosystems and that such energy-flows explain the structure of food chains and the pyramid of numbers was crystallized by Lindeman, but it seems to have been first perceived—albeit through a glass darkly—by Leopold. For Elton, as noted in 2.15, "food is the burning question in animal society."[49] His pyramid of numbers is based on the obvious fact that prey species must be more numerous than their predators. And he traces the way herbivores are eaten by omnivores that are, in turn, eaten by carnivores, forming "food chains." When the organisms that eat and decompose plant and animal detritus—dead leaves, wood, skin, hair, bones, and such—are taken into account, it appeared to Elton that food chains are linked at either end to form a "food cycle."

However, while food may well be the burning question in *animal societies*, it could hardly be the burning question in *biotic communities*, nor certainly in *ecosystems*, for plants do not feed, except in a metaphorical sense. It was Lindeman who first *clearly* realized that the burning question—a metaphor more apt than perhaps Elton realized—in whole ecosystems was not food but energy. Plants use radiant solar energy to decouple the carbon atom from the oxygen atoms in atmospheric carbon dioxide (CO_2) and to combine the hydrogen in water (H_2O) with the reduced carbon to form carbohydrates (such as $C_6H_{12}O_6$, glucose), expelling the excess oxygen atoms (O_2) to the atmosphere as waste. Animals then eat plants and "burn" their carbohydrates, that is, recombine the carbon and hydrogen atoms with oxygen to reconstitute carbon dioxide and water, and, more to the present point, use the energy released in the process of oxidation to circulate fluids, carry on other physiological processes, and move around. What cycles is not food, per se, but matter—in addition to carbon, hydrogen, and oxygen, "nutrients," such as nitrogen, phosphorous, potassium, calcium, and iron. Energy, on the other hand, does not cycle; but, consistent with the laws of thermodynamics, it flows through ecosystems from radiant solar source to the thermal sink of outer space.

3.9 HOW ECOSYSTEM ECOLOGY INFORMS THE LAND ETHIC–A FOUNTAIN OF ENERGY

By 1939, Leopold had made the conceptual leap from food to energy, thus anticipating Lindeman, but, curiously, he remained as confused as Elton about the difference between nutrient *cycles* and energy *flows*. In "The Land Pyramid" section of "The Land Ethic," Leopold, with his signature poetic flourish, provides a quasi-ecosystemic "mental image of land":

> Plants absorb energy from the sun. This energy flows through a circuit called the biota, which may be represented by a pyramid consisting of layers. The

bottom layer is the soil. A plant layer rests on the soil, an insect layer on the plants, a bird and rodent layer on the insects, and so on up through various animal groups to the apex layer, which consists of the larger carnivores.[50]

So far so good, energy flows upward through food chains from plants, at the bottom of the trophic pyramid, through the large carnivores at the top. Leopold then goes on to emphasize the numbers aspect of the pyramid—"for every carnivore there are hundreds of his prey, thousands of their prey, millions of insects, uncountable plants"— and that the "pyramid is a tangle of chains" forming "a highly organized structure."[51] But then Leopold falls into Elton's error of conflating energy flows and material cycles:

> Land, then, is not merely soil; it is a fountain of energy flowing through a circuit of soils, plants, and animals. Food chains are the living channels which conduct energy upward; death and decay return it to the soil. The circuit is not closed; some energy is dissipated in decay, some is added by absorption from the air, some is stored in soils, peats, and long-lived forests; but it is a sustained circuit, like a slowly augmenting revolving fund of life.[52]

In "A Biotic View of Land," Leopold even provided a diagram of the pyramid of numbers and its associated energy *cycle*. (Leopold's diagram was purely conceptual and did not aim to express actual numbers or relative proportions [Figure 3.1]. Lindeman included a similar diagram in his landmark paper that did represent actual numbers and relative proportions, included here for comparison's sake [Figure 3.2].)

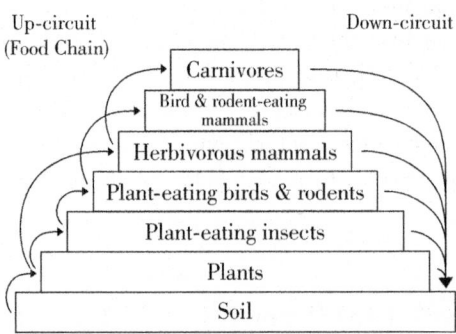

Figure 3.1 *A rendering of Leopold's "fountain of energy" as he represented it in "A Biotic View of Land," published in the* Journal of Forestry *in 1939.*

Up until this point, "The Land Pyramid" subsection of "The Land Ethic" was adapted from "A Biotic View of Land" with only cosmetic redaction. Compounding his Eltonian error, Leopold then added the following two sentences to the paragraph just quoted: "There is always a net loss [of energy] by downhill wash, but this is normally small and offset by the decay of rocks. It [energy] is deposited in the ocean and, in the course of geologic time, raised to form new lands and new pyramids."[53] One can only

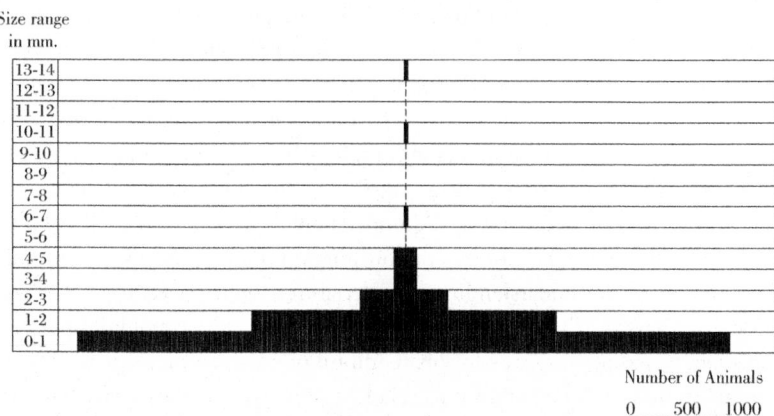

Size range
in mm.

Number of Animals

0   500   1000

Figure 3.2 *A rendering of the pyramid of numbers reproduced in Raymond Lindeman, "The Trophic-Dynamic Aspect of Ecology," published in* Ecology *in 1942 with the caption "Fig. 2. Eltonian pyramid of numbers, for floor-fauna invertebrates of the Panama rain forest (from Williams '41)." Lindeman cites E. C. Williams, "An Ecological Study of the Floor Fauna of the Panama Rain Forest,"* Bulletin of the Chicago Academy of Sciences 6 *(1941): 63–124.*

suppose that if Lindeman, then a graduate student at the University of Minnesota, was not in Leopold's audience when he read his plenary address to the ecologists assembled at the joint meeting of the Society of American Foresters (SAF) and the Ecological Society of America (ESA), G. E. Hutchinson would have been. And Lindeman came under Hutchinson's influence, which he generously acknowledged publicly, when he was a post-doctoral fellow at Yale, during the time he was developing his landmark paper. One can, therefore, only speculate that Leopold's (1939) insight, however con-fused—that energy, not food, was the currency of the economy of nature—was an actual moment in the development of ecosystem ecology. Lindeman does not cite Leopold's "A Biotic View of Land" in "The Trophic-Dynamic Aspect of Ecology," while he does cite Elton's *Animal Ecology* and, indeed, titles a section of his article "The Eltonian Pyramid."[54] The energy-flow perspective, central to ecosystem ecology, had its origins in Elton's (1927) concept of food chains and the pyramid of numbers and in Tansley's (1935) addition of abiotic to biotic elements, all integrated into systems. It culminates in Lindeman's (1942) sharp distinction between cycling materials and through-flowing energy. Did Leopold's 1939 plenary address at the joint SAF-ESA meeting directly influ-ence Lindeman, or indirectly influence him through Hutchinson? We are left to wonder.

And we might also wonder—while we are at it—why Leopold did not correct his misconception of energy as "a slowly augmenting *revolving* fund of life" when he was transforming large parts of "A Biotic View of Land" into "The Land Pyramid" in 1947, five years after Lindeman's field-defining article. Already, Leopold had himself vividly portrayed *materials* cycling. Beloved by readers of *Sand County*, "Odyssey" depicts the journeys through the "biota" of two "atoms"—"X" and "Y" of unspecified species— mined from a "limestone ledge" by "a bur-oak root" (documented and detailed in 1.9). The journey of X through the unbroken prairie and its diverse biota is long, compared with that of Y through the simplified biota after the prairie was converted to wheat, corn, and alfalfa monocultures. "Odyssey" was first published in 1942 and was thus written, one must suppose, before Leopold could have read and digested Lindeman's work.[55] Therefore it appears that Leopold had anticipated both the pillars of ecosystem ecology—energy transfers and materials cycling—before Lindeman integrated them in "The Trophic-Dynamic Aspect of Ecology." To be sure, Leopold failed to understand that energy flows, not cycles, but he did understand that energy is more fundamental than food—that energy, not food is the burning question in the biotic community. On the other hand, his understanding of materials retention, cycles, and leakage in the biota was flawless, as "Odyssey" proves. It is regrettable that Leopold did not correct his misunderstanding of energy for his rendition of ecosystem ecology in "The Land Pyramid" section of "The Land Ethic." Had he done so, it would have been state of the art.

3.10 HOW ORGANISMIC ECOLOGY INFORMS THE LAND ETHIC

Even more venerable than the biotic-community paradigm in ecology is the super-organism paradigm, vigorously espoused and championed by ecology's first dean, Frederic Clements (discussed more fully in the Introduction).[56] One finds vestiges of it too in "The Land Ethic." For example, in "Land Health and the A-B Cleavage" section of "The Land Ethic," Leopold writes, "A land ethic, then, reflects the existence of an ecological conscience, and this in turn reflects a conviction of individual responsibility for the health of the land. Health is the capacity of the land for self-renewal. Conservation is our effort to understand and preserve this capacity."[57] Health and its conceptual contrariety, disease, are states of organisms. To speak (metaphorically?) of "land health" is to assimilate land to an organism. Concluding the section, Leopold abandons circumlocution and directly assimilates land to an organism: "In all these cleavages, we see repeated the same basic paradoxes: man the conqueror *versus* man the biotic citizen; science the sharpener of his sword *versus* science the searchlight on his universe; land the slave and servant *versus* land the *collective organism*."[58]

Leopold's simplistic and reductive "factors" approach to game management, expounded in his 1933 textbook, *Game Management*, was not working as well in practice as he had anticipated in theory.[59] Perhaps for this reason, he became convinced that the workings of land were too complex to be easily manipulated to achieve predictable results.[60] The factors were food, water, minerals (primarily salt), cover, and agents of mortality (principal among them, predators). Provide game species with the first four and limit the fifth and managers could grow "wild crops" with the same alacrity and the same degree of success that farmers grow domestic crops.[61] By the early 1940s, Leopold seems to have become almost as unequivocal as Clements in his treatment of the ecological level of biological organization as itself being literally organismic. For example, in "Wilderness as a Land Laboratory," he writes, "There are two organisms in which the unconscious automatic processes of self-renewal have been supplemented by conscious interference and control. One of these is man himself (medicine and public health). The other is land (agriculture and conservation)."[62] (This paragraph found its way into *Sand County*'s Upshot essay "Wilderness.")[63] By the end of that decade (and of his own life), Leopold's reversion to ecological organicism had become thorough-going, as documented in the posthumous collection of his essays *For the Health of the Land*, especially two therein: "Biotic Land-Use" and "The Land-Health Concept and Conservation."[64]

3.11 HOW MECHANISTIC ECOLOGY INFORMS THE LAND ETHIC

The difficulty of sorting out and making sense of this eclectic mixture of ecological paradigms—the Eltonian community paradigm, the Tansleyan-Lindemanic ecosystem paradigm, and the Clementsian organismic paradigm—in "The Land Ethic" is compounded by Leopold's occasional description of land in mechanistic terms. Early on in the essay, in reference to the origin and evolution of ethics, he writes, "The complexity of cooperative *mechanisms* has increased with population density and the efficiency of tools."[65] Leopold implicitly evokes a mechanical model of human society when, in the "The Community Concept" section, he remarks, "In human history, we have learned (I hope) that the conqueror role is eventually self-defeating. Why? Because it is implicit in such a role that the conqueror knows, *ex cathedra*, just what makes the *community clock* tick."[66] Seamlessly transitioning from the human to the biotic community and perhaps alluding to his own frustrations with game management, he goes on to comment that "The ordinary citizen today assumes that science knows what makes the *community clock* tick; the scientist is equally sure that he does not."[67] Then, in the next sentence, he switches from the synecdocheal "clock" to that which it paradigmatically represents: "He [the scientist] knows that the *biotic mechanism* is so complex that its workings may never be fully understood."[68] Further, in the "Ecological Conscience" section Leopold refers to the Wisconsin Soil Conservation District Law as "a beautiful piece of *social machinery*."[69] And at the end of the "Substitutes for a Land Ethic" section he returns to the clock synecdoche, now (jarringly?) juxtaposed with the organismic adjective "healthy" and the biotic-community concept:

> To sum up: A system of conservation based solely on economic self-interest is hopelessly lopsided. It tends to ignore, and thus eventually to eliminate, many elements of the *land community* that lack commercial value, but that are (as far as we know) essential to its *healthy* functioning. It assumes, falsely, I think, that the economic parts of the *biotic clock* will function without the uneconomic parts.[70]

Then, Leopold sustains the mechanistic metaphor as he opens the next section, "The Land Pyramid": "An ethic to supplement and guide the economic relation to land presupposes the existence of some mental image of land as a *biotic mechanism*. We can be ethical only in relation to something we can see, feel, understand, love, or otherwise have faith in."[71] Is it humanly (Humeanly) possible to have an ethical relationship with a mechanism? We can see, feel, and perhaps understand a mechanism, but can we love it and have faith in it? In any case, however, Leopold, as noted, goes on to sketch a quasi-ecosystemic picture of land as a "fountain of energy." Is Leopold haphazardly mixing his ecological metaphors and ecological paradigms: community, ecosystem, organism, mechanism? Or does he present a more integrated and coherent mental image of land than meets the eye? Donald Worster, for one, expresses his frustration at Leopold's apparent lack of a coherent ecological worldview:

> [W]hile he came to view the land as a "single organism," he persisted in describing it as "an ecological mechanism," in which man functions as one important cog....This vacillation between root metaphors might be construed as casual or superficial, but such a defense ignores the fact that "organism" and "mechanism" had been around for at least three centuries, and during that time had been consistently identified with fundamentally antithetical world views.[72]

As evident from both "Some Fundamentals of Conservation in the Southwest" and "The Conservation Ethic," Leopold was aware of that. The antithesis between the mechanistic and organismic worldviews is a central theme of the former; and in the latter, Leopold laments the dominance of "mechanical ingenuity" over the wisdom of "applied biology" in the present "machine age." It is also a central organizing antithesis in Worster's *Nature's Economy*, wherein the pre-history and history of ecology are sorted dichotomously into "imperial" (reductive, mechanistic, quantitative, predictive, and managerial) and "arcadian" (holistic, organismic, qualitative, descriptive, emergent, and adaptive) traditions. Worster seems annoyed that Leopold cannot be neatly shoehorned into one or the other of these categories.

3.12 HOW THE ECOSYSTEM PARADIGM RETURNS ECOLOGY TO ITS ORGANISMIC ROOTS

While Worster may be right that the organismic and mechanistic worldviews are both centuries old and, for most of that time, antithetical, he is wrong to cast ecosystem ecology into the mechanistic bin. Because of Tansley's evocation of physicists and physics, when he introduced the ecosystem concept, and because of the post–World War II collaboration between ecosystem ecologists (Eugene P. Odum among them) and the US Atomic Energy Commission, Worster consigns ecosystem ecology to the "imperial" tradition, not the "arcadian." Whatever its associations—conceptual and institutional—ecosystem ecology turned out to be, if not arcadian, then certainly organismic. Indeed, in the hands of Eugene P. Odum, the dean of mid-twentieth-century ecology, fully fledged ecosystem ecology was the Clementsian super-organism paradigm in ecology redux. Two other notable historians of ecology agree with my assessment. Directly contradicting Worster, Robert P. McIntosh claims that "The holistic tradition in natural history and early ecology of the unity of nature, the chain of being, or the balance of nature [Worster's arcadian tradition] is seen as antecedent to the ecosystem concept."[73] Indeed, he goes on, "Several ecosystem ecologists suggested this residue of Clementsian ecology as essentially the Clementsian approach cast in the context of the ecosystem by E. P. Odum."[74] Joel B. Hagen affirms McIntosh's assessment:

> Eugene Odum, trained within a basically Clementsian tradition, has always stressed the organismal attributes of ecosystems: development, metabolism, and homeostasis....Arthur Tansley first presented the ecosystem concept within the context of a critique of holism....Ironically, as it evolved, the eco-system context became closely identified with the very philosophy Tansley so adamantly opposed. This change came about primarily through the writings of Eugene Odum and Howard Odum, strong defenders of holism.[75]

However, even Tansley's opposition to organicism and holism can be exaggerated (as noted in 1.16). While Tansley did indeed adamantly insist, contrary to Clements, that ecosystems were not literally organisms, he repeatedly characterizes them as "quasi-organisms," stresses their dynamic equilibria, and suggests that they evolved by natural selection, just as organisms proper do. In "Use and Abuse," Tansley reaffirms the conclusion he drew in an earlier paper:

> Briefly my conclusion was that mature well-integrated plant communities (which I identified with plant associations) had enough of the characters of organisms to be considered *quasi-organisms*, in the same way that human soci-eties are habitually so considered. Though plant communities are not and can-not be so highly integrated as human societies and still less than certain animal communities such as those of termites, ants, and social bees, the comparison with an organism is not merely loose analogy but is firmly based, at least in the case of the more complex and highly integrated communities, on the close inter-relations of the parts of their structure, of their behavior as wholes, and on a whole series of other characters which Clements...was the first to point out.... There is in fact a kind of natural selection of incipient systems, and those which can attain the most stable equilibria survive the longest.[76]

In the late 1930s and throughout the 1940s, Leopold was (a) asserting a Clementsian organicism and (b) thinking at the cutting edge of ecosystem ecology, anticipating, however imperfectly, Lindeman's field-defining discussion and mensuration of energy flowing through ecosystems. Because Clements's super-organism concept was ecol-ogy's inaugural paradigm, later supplanted first by the community concept and then the ecosystem concept, Leopold's blunt declaration in *Sand County*'s "Wilderness" that land is an organism and his use of the land-health metaphor in "The Land Ethic" seems retrogressive in relation to the dialectical history of ideas in ecology. On the contrary, as Leopold appears intuitively to realize, the development of ecosystem ecology—to which, whether acknowledged or not, Leopold contributed in both "A Biotic View of

Land" and "Odyssey"—would represent a return, in a much more sophisticated form, to Clementsian organicism.

Further, as the remark by Tansley indicates, in the first half of the twentieth century, social-insect communities and human societies were "habitually" characterized by organic metaphors. Most notably, William Morton Wheeler, an American social entomologist, championed the conception of termitaria, ant hills, and bee hives as holistic organisms; and Émile Durkheim, a French sociologist, characterized modern industrial societies, in which divisions of labor were well articulated, in functional organismic terms.[77] Therefore, we can conclude that three of the paradigms in ecology—biotic community, super-organism, and ecosystem—that Leopold rhetorically mixes together, seemingly so haphazardly, were in fact historically well integrated by the time Leopold was composing *A Sand County Almanac*.

3.13 HOW LEOPOLD ANTICIPATES HIERARCHY THEORY IN "THE LAND ETHIC"

But what about the mechanical paradigm? In respect to integrating the organic and mechanistic ways of thinking in ecology, Leopold may have been further ahead of his time—more prophetic, in a word—than in integrating environmental concern and ethics. Hierarchy theory in ecology calls attention to the way biological organization is hierarchically ordered and resolves the age-old (Worster got that right!) tension between organicism and mechanism. As to hierarchical organization, cells compose multi-celled organisms, and multi-celled organisms (along with extant single-celled organisms) compose biotic communities/Clementsian super-organisms/ecosystems. As noted in 1.16, to resolve the tension between organicism and mechanism, hierarchy theory offers a perspectival approach.[78] Reductive mechanical explanations of higher-level emergent phenomena are cast in terms of entities and processes occurring at lower levels of organization. The higher level of organization is the "organism," the lower level is the "mechanism," and the whole is greater than the sum of the parts.[79] Thus, pace Worster, Leopold does not confuse his readers and contradict himself when he characterizes "land" in both mechanistic and organismic terms. Rather, in the manner of the contemporary hierarchy theorists, by a "biotic mechanism" he may be understood to refer to, say, predator-prey interactions—interactions among the organisms (themselves not machines) composing it—as the explanation for, say, the amplitude and frequency of the demographic periodicities, an emergent property, in the land organism. (To my question, Why do we call the science of sub-atomic phenomena "quantum mechanics" when those phenomena are anything but mechanical in kind?, a physicist told me that the nomenclature was essentially hierarchical—the sub-atomic phenomena are down-scale to phenomena at the scale of atoms and explain, among other things, the various properties of various atoms.)

Invocation of hierarchy theory in ecology here brings to the fore the doubts about the robust ontology of land organisms. These doubts come in several forms. As noted in 1.16, Henry A. Gleason was the first ecologist to doubt the existence of Clementsian super-organisms or, by their other name, of organismic communities.[80] He argued that they were better conceived to be coincidences. No one would suppose that organisms proper are randomly assembled entities, but the paradigmatic human communities, in respect to which biotic communities are metaphoric analogs, are also subject to all the ontological suspicions raised by Gleason. Consider contemporary American municipalities, paradigm cases of proper human communities. They rarely have sharp spatial boundaries separating them from neighboring communities, as most have sprawled beyond their posted city limits, and many often gradually merge into one another. The temporal boundaries between their successional seres are no more clearly demarcated than those of biotic communities, as they go from, say, agrarian villages to manufacturing towns to bedroom suburbs. They are demographically dynamic as some people move in and others move away. And the people who find themselves together in a municipal human community are there because they are adapted to similar socioeconomic gradients, nor is everyone strongly connected to everyone else. If there is, for example, a university in a municipality, one will find a lot of college professors and students and few of them if there isn't; if there are also factories in the same municipality one will also find wage laborers and salaried managers. While professors and their students in municipal communities are as closely coupled as predators and their prey in biotic communities (perhaps not a good analogy), the citizens in the industrial sector of the municipal economy might have little interaction with those in the academic sector—as is the case in, say, New Haven, Connecticut.

Both paradigmatic human communities and their biotic analogs are presently understood to be self-organizing systems.[81] The old holism-versus-reductionism dichotomy—or holological-versus-mereological, as G. E. Hutchinson characterized it—is as obsolete as the organicism-versus-mechanism dichotomy in contemporary ecology.[82] Individual human beings and individual plants and animals act and interact in various ways—each, as it were, according to its own lights or, as Gleason put it, each "is a law unto itself."[83] In the seemingly random and, technically speaking, chaotic process, patterns begin to emerge when we shift focus—scale up—from the individual agents to the dynamic systems that take form. The enormous computational power of contemporary computers and new techniques of computer modeling, such as cellular automata and multi-agent-based models, enable ecologists, with the help of mathematicians, to simulate and analyze such self-organizing, complex systems and their emergent properties.[84]

3.14 ECOLOGICAL ONTOLOGY AND THE COMMUNITY PARADIGM IN ECOLOGY

But are such systems real entities? Perhaps one way of providing a definitive answer would be to say that if systems exhibit properties that cannot be intelligibly attributed to their components, then they are real. A property cannot exist unless the entity that it is the property of exists. Municipalities have transportation and communications networks. Their citizens, individually, do not. Thus municipalities, by this criterion, are real entities. Similarly, biotic communities have food chains and niches. The plants and animals composing them do not. Thus biotic communities, by this criterion, are real entities.

But do biotic communities really have niches? Due to the influence of Charles Elton's *Animal Ecology*, the French word "niche" became a standard term in community ecology. Its first lexical definition is a "recess in a wall especially for a statue" and so the term has a spatial air about it, even when adapted for its special, more abstract use in community ecology.[85] Indeed, "niche" suggests a space occupied by an object. Accordingly, niche theory was developed in a quasi-geometrical form by G. E. Hutchinson, who expressed the ecological parameters of a niche in terms of an "n-dimensional hypervolume."[86] Hutchinson expressed each of the "ecological factors"—biotic and abiotic—that a species requires to survive and successfully reproduce as a "dimension." When all such dimensions are specified, its niche can be abstractly characterized as its hypervolume. The species is analogous to a statue, its niche is analogous to a nook in a wall, and the wall is analogous to a biotic community.

When Hutchinson conceptualized niche theory in community ecology in terms of n-dimensional hypervolumes, he considered species as given entities and was concerned to organize all the ecological factors they required to survive and reproduce into a quasi-geometrical whole, their unique niches. But we can reverse figure and ground, and consider the niche as a given n-dimensional hypervolume to which species are adapted. Consider the following analogy. We might begin with a statue of a given height, width, and depth and ask what are the dimensions of a nook in a wall which we must find in order to accommodate it. Basically, that's the way Hutchinson was thinking. Or we might begin with the dimensions of various nooks already existing in a wall and ask how corresponding statues might be carved to fit into them. This is the way an evolutionary ecologist might think. According to this way of thinking, communities do indeed have niches, just as walls do indeed have nooks and crannies. And if walls are real, then, by analogy, so are communities. (A dogmatic reductionist might question the existence of walls and insist that they are but an aggregation of stones.)

Another ontological criterion—another reality check, as it were—for biotic communities is "downward causation." If a biotic community is, as a whole, a causal agent, it must be an entity. Species are adapted to ecological niches. Niches set the stage of the ecological theater on which the evolutionary play unfolds, to adapt another one of Hutchinson's metaphors.[87] Thus biotic communities exert downward causation on their components because they provide the niches to which those components are adapted. One might say somewhat metaphorically that biotic communities sculpt their component species. Of course, among the dimensions of one component's niche will be other components (what species the species of interest eats and what species eat it, for example); and so not only are species sculpted by their niches, their niches too are partly shaped by them—sort of like a cavity-nesting bird that may modify a nook it happens to find, better to accommodate its own dimensions. Thus we might think of the causal relationship between a biotic community and its component species as reciprocal rather than exclusively downward. But the ontological status of communities would remain unchanged. In order for a community to be both agent and patient in a reciprocal causal relationship, it must be an actual entity of some sort.

3.15 ECOLOGICAL ONTOLOGY AND THE ECOSYSTEM PARADIGM IN ECOLOGY

If Gleason and his successors cast doubts on the ontological status of biotic communities, Tansley himself casts doubts on the ontology of ecosystems. According to Tansley, "from the point of view of the ecologist," ecosystems "are the basic units of nature on the face of the earth."[88] But as noted in the Introduction, ecosystem ontology is driven by ecological epistemology. That is, the boundaries of an ecosystem are determined by the scientific questions ecologists pose. The Greater Yellowstone Ecosystem will, for example, be bounded one way by an ecologist studying the keystone-species function of reintroduced wolves and in another way by an ecologist studying the impact of the introduced lake trout on the native cutthroat trout. Having just characterized them as "basic units of nature," Tansley acknowledges that it is difficult "to isolate [eco] systems mentally for the purposes of study" and that "[t]he isolation is partly artificial, but is the only possible way in which we can proceed."[89] Paradigmatic entities, however, do not seem difficult to isolate, nor does their isolation seem at all artificial. An astronomer studying the conversion of hydrogen to helium in the sun and another studying the phenomenon of sun spots would have little reason to disagree about the circumscription of the object—the sun—that they are both studying. And it seems quite ridiculous, even impious, to say that the existence of the sun, as a unit of nature, is partly artificial.

Nevertheless, Tansley claims that what one might call *the isolation problem* is by no means unique to ecosystems and puts the following things in the same ontological boat with them: "a solar system, a planet, a climatic region, a plant or animal community, an individual organism, an organic molecule or an atom."[90] On reflection, Tansley may be wiser here than conventional wisdom. No entity exists in isolation from others that affect it to one degree or another. The sun is affected by the other stars in the galaxy and by the black hole at the galaxy's center; and the planets are affected by the sun, the other planets, and their respective moons. Individual organisms, from an ecosystemic perspective, appear to be dissipative structures through which energy and materials pass, no more substantial as entities than vortices and standing waves in flowing water.[91] Further, with the advent of the National Institutes of Health human biome project, purportedly "individual" organisms are themselves being reconceived as super-ecosystems (as detailed and documented in 11.2). Tansley reminds us that our perceptions of nature are biased by "[o]ur natural human prejudices."[92] Thus, we readily identify individual organisms as robust entities because we conceive of ourselves as individual organisms (although among evolutionary biologists, at least, that self-image is beginning to change) and we would like to think that we ourselves are robust entities. And Tansley reminds us also that ontology is not binary—real or unreal—but that there is an ontological gradient, along which entities may be arrayed: "Some of the systems are more isolated in nature, more autonomous, than others."[93] Both the sun and the Earth may lie toward the robust end of the ontological spectrum, while ecosystems may lie toward the opposite end. But ecosystems are not—like God, ghosts, and gremlins—off the ontological gradient altogether.

Thus land communities/ecosystems/super-organisms are real, existing entities. They may exist less robustly than stars, planets, and *perhaps* individual organisms, but they are by no means chimera of the perfervid imaginations of ecologists, as Gleason insinuated when he claimed that they "represent merely abstract extrapolations of the ecologist's mind."[94]

3.16 THE "FLUX OF NATURE" PARADIGM SHIFT IN CONTEMPORARY ECOLOGY AND "THE LAND ETHIC"

Leopold was also aware that what he called "land" was ever changing. However, he seems not to have fully appreciated the multiple scales at which land undergoes natural change—in the "The Land Ethic," at any rate (see my summary of Bryan G. Norton's analysis of "Thinking Like a Mountain" in 1.10 and 1.11)—nor to have anticipated the idea of disturbance regimes. He writes: "When a change occurs in one part of the circuit, many other parts must adjust themselves to it. Change does not necessarily obstruct or divert the flow of energy; evolution is a long series of self-induced changes, the net result of which has been to elaborate the flow mechanism and to lengthen the circuit."[95] (Here, incidentally, Leopold uses the term "mechanism" perfectly in accord with its current usage in hierarchy theory. Ecosystems are the objects of interest here and more especially the way energy flows through them. Food chains and their components interlaced into food webs constitute the down-level mechanism for the up-level energy-flow phenomenon in ecosystems.) The only directionless natural change that Leopold recognizes in "The Land Ethic" seems to be *evolutionary* change. He was certainly aware of successional change, but it was only after Leopold's time that ecologists realized that such change was directionless and did not terminate in a relatively static climax condition. And, as noted in the Introduction and in 1.16, ecologists have more recently identified a plethora of natural disturbances that also drive ceaseless, directionless changes in the land. Consistent with the then-current Clementsian thinking in ecosystem ecology, Leopold seems to regard significant change visited on ecosystems as largely anthropogenic.

The anthropogenic changes that Leopold laments are as follows. (1) "[C]hange in the composition of floras and faunas"—(a) "larger predators are lopped off the apex of the pyramid" and (b) "[d]omesticated species from other lands are substituted for wild ones, and wild ones are moved to new habitats," (c) constituting a "world-wide pooling of faunas and floras."[96] (2) "Agriculture" makes "overdrafts on the soil" leading to "erosion."[97] (3) "Industry" engages in (a) "polluting waters" and (b) "obstructing them with dams."[98] (4) "Transportation brings about another basic change: the plants and animals grown in one region are now consumed and returned to the soil in another."[99]

Ecologists are now keenly aware that natural change in the composition of floras and faunas also occurs by natural processes other than evolution. Indeed, somewhat ironically, given the influence on Leopold of his 1927 book, *Animal Ecology*, Charles Elton's 1958 book, *The Ecology of Invasions by Animals and Plants*, demonstrated that the floral and faunal components of ecosystems are constantly changing—both with and without human assistance.[100] And local extinction of larger predators also happens naturally.

Even though Leopold expressly recognizes only evolutionary change as natural, in "The Land Ethic," he nevertheless provides the key to evaluating anthropogenic change, not in reference to stable equilibria but in reference to the spatial and temporal scales of natural change: "Evolutionary changes, however, are usually slow and local. Man's invention of tools has enabled him to make changes of unprecedented violence, rapidity, and scope."[101] To evolutionary change, we may add directionless successional change, natural invasions and extirpations of floras and faunas, and the whole suite of changes driven by natural disturbances—by volcanic rains of ash and flows of lava, lightning strikes, wildfires, high winds, floodwaters, frosts, ice-heaves, pests, diseases, and so on and so forth. Some of these changes are violent, and some occur on temporal scales that are very rapid, relative to evolutionary changes, and on spatial scales that are relatively wide. Nevertheless, the temporal and spatial scales of ceaseless and direction-less successional change and that of disturbance-driven natural change provide norms in reference to which we can evaluate anthropogenic change (and non-change).

Hurricanes, for example, strike the Atlantic and Gulf coasts of North America nearly every year, blowing down trees and eroding the barrier islands in their paths.[102] Anthropogenic coastal development has similar effects. Depending on its intensity and path, a hurricane's swath of destruction might extend, with diminishing degrees of devastation, over a fifty-mile stretch of coast.[103] While some five hurricanes, on average, make landfall every three years on the eastern and southern coasts of North America, the frequency with which the same stretch of coast sustains a "direct hit" varies by location. That frequency runs from a high of one direct hit every nine and eleven years for the Miami and Cape Hatteras regions, respectively, to one direct hit every thirty-three and thirty-four years for the Apalachicola, Florida, and Savannah, Georgia, regions, respectively, with an average frequency of about twenty-one years.[104] Depending on the frequency of the hurricane disturbance regime, there is time—more or less, depending on location and luck, because the hurricane disturbance regime is quite stochastic—for the dunes to be rebuilt by the prevailing winds and currents and the vegetation to be reestablished successionally.[105] Shoreline development, how-ever, might extend very nearly continuously for three or four hundred miles along the coasts and, unlike a hurricane, beach development doesn't hit and then go quickly away. So, what is land-ethically wrong with beach development? Not that it disturbs the barrier islands and coastal forests, for they are disturbed naturally by hurricanes and other forces of nature. It's that beach-development disturbance occurs at spatial and temporal scales that greatly exceed those of such natural disturbances as hurri-canes. Similarly, we might land-ethically evaluate the clearcutting of inland forests by reference to the temporal and spatial scales of similar natural disturbances by wind, wildfire, or insect infestation.

By the same token, we might land-ethically evaluate the anthropogenic suppression of natural disturbance regimes, such as those by fire and flood. A century or more of fire suppression in the United States has resulted in a buildup of fuel and the correlative risk of catastrophic forest fires.[106] The historic fire regime is a good norm for prescribed low-intensity understory burns as a tool of forest management.[107] A quarter century of flood control in the Colorado River has threatened some of its native species of fish—particularly those that depend on the floodwaters to deposit gravel and sand shoals in the riverbed on which they spawn.[108] The historic spring flood regime in the Colorado River is the proper norm for release of a pulse of water from the Glen Canyon dam as a tool of fish management in the river.

3.17 A REVISED SUMMARY MORAL MAXIM FOR THE LAND ETHIC

Every great and enduring ethic has a summary moral maxim. That of the Christian ethic is "Do unto others as you would have them do unto you"—the Golden Rule. The summary moral maxim of the Aristotelian virtue ethic is the Golden Mean: always choose the mean between the extremes of excess (too much) and defect (too little). That of Kantian deontology is the categorical imperative: "Act only according to that maxim by which you can at the same time will that it should become a universal law." The summary moral maxim of utilitarianism is the greatest happiness principle: "Act so as to achieve the greatest happiness of the greatest number [of people]." That of Gifford Pinchot's Resource Conservation Ethic echoes utilitarianism's greatest happiness principle: "The greatest good of the greatest number in the long run." The summary moral maxim of the Aldo Leopold land ethic is, of course, "A thing is right when it tends to preserve the integrity, stability, and beauty of the biotic community. It is wrong when it tends otherwise."[109]

Developments in ecology after the publication of *Sand County* in 1949 have undermined the cogency of the land ethic's summary moral maxim. Are biotic communities ontologically robust enough and well enough integrated to have an integrity that can be preserved? That's doubtful, given the frequent and stochastic ingress and egress of their component species. Given their constant, directionless successional change and the ubiquity of the natural disturbances visited on them, certainly biotic communities have little stability to be preserved. Which leaves only their beauty to be preserved. Conventionally, beauty is regarded not as an actual property of an object, but as an aesthetic response in subjects to objects—it's "in the eye of the beholder." But if beauty is merely in the eye of the beholder, we hardly have a steadfast norm for assessing things land-ethically right and things land-ethically wrong.

There is good evidence, however, that by "beauty," in reference to land, Leopold means pretty much what he means by "land health." And by "land health" Leopold means self-sustaining and self-renewing normal ecosystemic functioning. Leopold's equation of "beauty" and "land health" and his association of them with normal ecosystemic functioning is most clearly evinced in "Land Pathology," written in 1935 and finally published in 1991, and in a section titled "Esthetics" in a 1946 paper of his, "The Land Health Concept and Conservation," that remained unpublished until 1999.[110] However, if beauty is, more objectively, another name for ecosystem health, ecosystems can remain healthy—that is, can function normally—while undergoing a wide variety of anthropogenic changes. Leopold was convinced that land health depended on biotic integrity; that is, that an ecosystem's normal functioning depended on the full complement of native species belonging to its associated biotic community. But beginning with Lindeman's 1942 paper, ecosystem ecologists regard an ecosystem's biota as mere moments in the complementary processes of materials cycling and energy flow. The specific identity of the organisms carrying out those processes is of functional consequence only when some species perform various ecosystem functions in ways that are appreciably different from the way others belonging to the same guild perform them. Hence, ecosystems may remain healthy—beautiful—when economically more valuable species are substituted for economically less valuable ones, provided the former adequately carry out the same ecosystem functions as the latter. Certainly a gardened world consisting of a congeries of beautiful/healthy/normally functioning ecosystems would be far better than our current "world of wounds," but would such a norm be strict enough for assessing things land-ethically right and things land-ethically wrong? I doubt that Leopold would think so. Therefore, even reinterpreted ecologically, the beauty of the biotic community alone is an inadequate norm for a land ethic.

In sum, the summary moral maxim of the land ethic must be thoroughly reformulated in light of developments in ecology since the mid-twentieth century. Leopold certainly thought of natural *processes* as taking place on multiple temporal scales, as Bryan G. Norton points out in his interpretation of "Thinking Like a Mountain" (documented and detailed in 1.10 and 1.11). Leopold also acknowledged the existence of natural *change*, including changes in ecosystem processes, but he seems to have thought of *natural* change primarily on a very slow evolutionary temporal scale. But even so, he thereby incorporates the concept of inherent environmental change and the crucial norm of scale into the land ethic. In light of more recent developments in ecology, we can add norms of scale to the land ethic for both climatic and ecological dynamics—such as directionless succession and natural disturbance—for purposes of land-ethically evaluating anthropogenic changes in nature. One hesitates to edit Leopold's elegant prose, but as a stab at formulating a dynamized summary moral maxim for the land ethic, I will hazard the following: *A thing is right when it tends to preserve the beauty of the biotic community and to disturb it only at normal spatial and temporal scales. It is wrong when it tends otherwise.*

4

The Land Ethic and the Science of Ethics: From the Seventeenth through the Twentieth Centuries

As Chapters 2 and 3 amply indicate, the Leopold land ethic evinces a complicated relationship to science, not surprisingly as Leopold himself was more scientist than philosopher. (1) Toward the beginning of "The Land Ethic," Leopold insinuates that an ecological (or, more basically, a biological) understanding of the "thing" (called ethics) may be more illuminating than a philosophical understanding of it. (2) Leopold builds the land ethic on the biological (or more specifically, evolutionary) account of ethics that Darwin provides in *The Descent of Man*. (3) Darwin in turn, builds on Hume's moral philosophy, and Hume himself claimed to be providing an empirically inductive, descriptive science of ethics. (4) The land ethic is informed (a) by a more general evolutionary worldview in which *Homo sapiens* is considered to be an evolved species that is phylogenetically kin to all other species, kin to some more closely than to others; and (b) by various paradigms in ecology, but especially by the Eltonian biotic-community paradigm. The previous chapter begins (3.1–3.5) by dispelling one impediment to a cozy relationship between science and ethics—the notorious Is/Ought Dichotomy, sometimes invoked by a misnomer, the Naturalistic Fallacy. I begin this chapter by tracing the surprisingly long history of the science of ethics. This phrase, "science of ethics," is ambiguous. In some contexts it may be understood to mean that ethics is or could itself become a science in the same sense that physics is a science. In other contexts it may be understood to mean a scientific study of the phenomenon of ethics in the same sense that sociology or psychology study other human behavioral phe-nomena, such as sport or sex. For the time being, I leave the phrase "science of ethics" deliberately ambiguous. This chapter concludes with a discussion of the implications for the land ethic of one especially dramatic moment in the long history of the science of ethics, the emergence of sociobiology in the last quarter of the twentieth century.

4.1 HOBBES'S SCIENCE OF ETHICS

Darwin may have been the first to provide an account of ethics "exclusively from the side of natural history," but he was by no means the first to envision a science of ethics. As just now noted (and also in passing in 2.8), Hume considers himself to be doing a kind of moral science in *An Enquiry Concerning the Principles of Morals*, but neither was *he* the first to envision a science of ethics. That distinction belongs to Thomas Hobbes, as far as I can determine. Hobbes was a contemporary of René Descartes, who dreamed of a wonderful new physical science, expressed most fully in *Principia Philosophiae*, published in 1644. Hobbes's objections to Descartes's *Meditationes de Prima Philosophia*, first published in 1641, were conveyed to the author via a mutual acquaintance, Marin Mersenne. Descartes published Hobbes's objections, together with those of others, and his replies in an addendum to the second edition of the *Meditationes* in 1642.[1] Hobbes corresponded with Descartes directly in 1644. His *Leviathan* was published in 1651. Isaac Newton brought Descartes's dream into a waking reality with his *Philosophiae Naturalis Principia Mathematica*, published in 1687.[2] In the *Leviathan*, Hobbes actually anticipates two of Newton's three laws of motion.[3] Hobbes seems to have reasoned somewhat as follows: the speculative natural philosophy of the ancients was transformed—by Copernicus, Kepler, Gassendi, Galileo, and Descartes—into a promising new science of nature. In addition to natural philosophy, we inherited from the ancients an equally speculative tradition of moral philosophy. Surely, then, the speculative moral philosophy of the ancients can also be transformed into a science of ethics.

While some of the cognitive substance of Newton's *Principia* can be found in Hobbes's *Leviathan*—reductionism, mechanism, materialism, a privileging of locomotion—Newton's scientific method (about which more in 4.3) cannot. Hobbes was especially contemptuous of the methods of the Scholastic philosophers, who built elaborate metaphysical systems on the authority of two source texts—the Bible and the corpus of Aristotle—that had been reconciled and synthesized by Thomas Aquinas in the thirteenth century. Just as "analytic philosophy" still dominates the philosophy departments of the most prestigious universities in the United States, Britain, and Australia as the twenty-first century unfolds, so Thomism and, *eo ipso*, Aristotelianism still dominated the centers of academic power and prestige in Europe as the seventeenth century unfolded. Thus Hobbes takes every opportunity to disparage the "Schoolmen" and "Scholastics," and their secular authority, Aristotle. Nonetheless, the paradigm of science that Hobbes hopes to emulate in the *Leviathan* is hardly less ancient than Aristotelian logic: plane geometry as systematized by Euclid, who was born two years before Aristotle died, and who lived and worked in Alexandria under the reign of the first Ptolemy, a general in the army of Alexander, and later regent of the new capital of Egypt founded in the name of his late, great king.[4]

Accordingly, Hobbes reduces his subject, human nature, to its simplest elements; sets out definitions; formulates axioms; and reasons deductively to (in his estimation) irrefutable conclusions, which he brazenly denominates "Laws of Nature"—some nineteen of them.[5] The human nature that Hobbes so treats of is psychological—of sense, of imagination, of speech, of reason, and so on—but the manner of treatment is mechanical. Sensation occurs when an external object either directly, as in the cases of touch and taste, or indirectly, as in the cases of sound and sight, causes a motion in the organs of sense, thence communicated to the brain by the nerves, which he conceives as taut strings or wires. Hobbes even explains the apparent location of such sensations as color on the objects themselves—in contrast to odors, which are sensed as located in our own noses—as owing to a counter-motion in the brain, which propels such sensations back toward the objects that produced them.[6] Imagination is but a kind of residual motion of sense; and thought is but a residual motion of imagination.[7] All allegedly abstract ideas for which there is no original in the domain of sense—Hobbes's pet peeve in this regard is the Schoolmen's concept of transubstatiation—are but (literal) nonsense and the words signifying them are but empty and meaningless sounds.[8] In addition to the "vital motions"—of the heart, lungs, and digestive organs—there are "voluntary motions" driven by bivalent "endeavor" (*conatus* in Hobbes's own Latin translation of the *Leviathan*, published 1668, discussed in 8.7), experienced as two primitive emotions, desire and aversion.[9] Desire moves us toward its objects; aversion moves us away from its objects. All the more subtle emotions are variations of these two. Love, for example, is desire of objects present, while hope is desire of objects absent plus the belief that they are obtainable.[10]

The relationship between Hobbes's moral science and the emerging early modern natural science appears to be analogical. Each human individual is an endeavoring or conative social atom propelled on its inertial course by desire and aversion. Hobbes's (in)famous "state of nature" in which there is a "war...of every man against every man" is analogous to physical atoms colliding in free space.[11] The most basic desire of all is for self-preservation. And the only condition conducive to self-preservation is peace. Thus, to put an end to the war of each against all is in the vital interest of everyone. That is, in other words, to leave the state of nature and enter into a peace-securing social contract is the only way people can survive and flourish, which we all desire above all else.[12] From these premises, Hobbes deduces, as theorems, his moral "laws of nature." While Descartes himself rejected atomism—vigorously championed by another of Descartes' correspondents, Pierre Gassendi—more deeply Hobbes seems to have shared Descartes's conviction that all physical phenomena could be exhaustively described by geometry. As humans are but physical beings—according to Hobbes, if not according to Descartes—our various motions, both vital and voluntary, can be exhaustively described by geometry, and ethics can be rendered scientific by the application to it of the demonstrative method of geometry.

4.2 LOCKE'S SCIENCE OF ETHICS

An Essay Concerning Human Understanding is a treatise on epistemology, not ethics, but there John Locke characterizes himself as an "underlaborer" to Newton.[13] Locke, nonetheless, expressly declines to "meddle" as Hobbes had done, "with the physical consideration of the mind;...or by what motions our spirits or alterations of our bodies we come to have any sensation by our organs, or any ideas of our understandings."[14] He characterizes his "method" in the *Essay* as "historical," not scientific.[15] However, in Book IV, Chapter III of the *Essay*, titled "The Extent of Human Knowledge," Locke avers in passing, apparently under the influence of Hobbes, that in principle we "might place morality amongst the sciences capable of demonstration: wherein I doubt not but from self-evident propositions, by necessary consequences as incontestable as those in mathematics, the measures of right and wrong might be made out to anyone that will apply himself with the same indifference and attention to the one as to the other of these sciences."[16]

Locke goes on to give two reasons why no moral science actually exists. First, moral ideas cannot be represented symbolically or diagrammatically as can circles, triangles, and other mathematical ideas, but instead rely entirely on words—which, except for the few onomatopoeia, are not copies or images of the ideas they stand for. Second, moral ideas, Locke thinks, are more complex than mathematical ideas. Still, Locke holds out hope that these difficulties might be overcome by analyzing complex ethical ideas into their simplest parts and providing those with sound and steady definitions. However, a third, essentially political obstacle lies in the way of such a Euclidean ethics. Because partiality in the domain of ethics (lack of "indifference") is greater than in mathematics, religious and political propagandists "cram their tenets down men's throats…and will not let truth have fair play in the world, or men the liberty to search after it."[17] Some things, it seems, never change.

Even though Locke begins the *Essay* with a paean to Newton, he is more skeptical about the possibility of natural science—not to be confused with mathematical science—than he is about that of a moral science. For concerning bodies, our knowledge can "never penetrate to the internal fabric and real essences" of them.[18] Whereas "morality is the proper science and business of mankind in general (who are both concerned and fitted to search out their *summum bonum*)."[19] That's because if we can know the internal fabric and essences of anything, it is of ourselves by introspection and of our societies and polities, because we make or create them. God alone knows the internal fabric and real essences of bodies, for the same reason: as their Maker, He created them. As the *Essay* resolutely confines itself to epistemology, Locke does not attempt actually to work out a demonstrative science of ethics in any detail, as Hobbes had done. Instead, he gives a substantive example or two of the kinds of propositions that it would contain: "[w]here there is no property there is no injustice"; and "[n]o government allows absolute liberty"; and he leaves it at that.[20]

4.3 HUME'S SCIENCE OF ETHICS

The foregoing are two canonical seventeenth-century conceptions of a science of ethics modeled on geometry. In the eighteenth century, David Hume, as noted in 2.8 and at the beginning of this chapter, also envisioned a science of ethics and set out his "experimental method" in the first section of *An Enquiry Concerning the Principles of Morals*.[21] This way of characterizing his method may occasion confusion in the minds of Hume's present readers, for many of whom the experimental method is so called because it turns on an *experimentum crucis*.[22] When phenomena predicted by a theory or hypothesis are found by experiment, the theory or hypothesis is confirmed; when not, it is falsified.[23] A famous example of the former is the experiment conducted in 1919 by Arthur Eddington proving that starlight is bent as it passes through the gravitational field of the sun, confirming Einstein's General Theory of Relativity.[24] A famous example of the latter is the interferometer experiment conducted in 1887 by Albert

Michelson and Edward Morley to measure the speed of the Earth relative to the luminiferous ether, which was supposed to be at rest and spread evenly through space.[25] It was not realized at the time, but the negative results of that and subsequent versions of the experiment falsified the hypothesis that an ether existed that is the substance of light waves, as air is the substance of sound waves.[26]

The potential for misunderstanding Hume's self-styled experimental method—not to be confused with that idealized in twentieth-century philosophy of science—is compounded because Hume goes on immediately to explain that he will be "deducing general maxims."[27] For, in the experimental method as we now understand it (thanks to such twentieth-century philosophers of science as Karl Popper), the predicted phenomena must be rigorously *deduced* from the theory or hypothesis in question in order to set up an *experimentum crucis*.[28] At the dawn of the Scientific Revolution, Newton used the phrase *experimentum crucis* (traceable to Francis Bacon) in his famous 1671 letter in *Philosophical Transactions* on light and color. Thanks to Alasdair MacIntyre (detailed and documented in 3.3), we know that by "deducing," Hume did not mean what that word currently means in logic, philosophy of science, and science itself. Indeed, Hume's actual method—although he too pretends to offer up an *experimentum crucis*—is better characterized, in contemporary terminology, as "empirical" not "experimental," and "inductive" not "deductive."[29] He will begin, that is, by "collecting and arranging the estimable and blamable qualities of men."[30] In common among such qualities, by a process of induction, he will "find those universal principles from which all censure or approbation is ultimately derived."[31]

Hume goes on immediately to contrast his essentially empirical and inductive approach to a science of ethics with the reductive and deductive (that is, "demonstrative") approach envisioned by Hobbes and Locke—and actually attempted by the former:

> The other scientific method, where a general abstract principle is first established, and is afterwards branched out into a variety of inferences and conclusions, may be more perfect in itself, but suits less the imperfections of human nature and is a common source of illusion and mistake, in this as well as in other subjects. Men are now cured of their passion for hypotheses and systems in natural philosophy, and will harken to no arguments but those which are derived from experience. It is full time they should attempt a like reformation in all moral disquisitions and reject every system of ethics, however subtle or ingenious, which is not founded on fact and observation.[32]

Like Locke, Hume invokes Newton by name and Newton's "chief rule of philosophizing," which is, according to Hume, "where any principle has been found to have great force and energy in one instance, to ascribe it a like energy in all similar instances."[33] In the third book of his *Principia*, Newton does indeed specify four "rules of reasoning in philosophy," the third of which he characterizes as the "foundation of all philosophy."[34] I can discern no clear correlation between Newton's own formulation of this rule—"The qualities of bodies, which admit neither intension nor remission of degrees, and which are found to belong to all bodies within the reach of our experiments, are to be esteemed the universal qualities of all bodies whatsoever"—and Hume's redaction of it. Not to digress too far into this matter, but Newton's elaboration of his third rule of reasoning in philosophy appears to endorse what logicians call the "fallacy of division"—inferring the properties of parts from the properties of the whole of which they are parts. Newton provides the following illustration of the application of this rule: "we therefore justly infer the hardness of the undivided particles not only of the bodies we feel but all others" from "the hardness of the whole."[35] This is how Newton justifies his tenet that the atoms or corpuscles ("the undivided particles"), which are not "within the reach of our experiments" (that is, experience), but which he imagines to compose all the objects that we sense, are themselves also hard. But so far has contemporary science departed from such an inference that atoms are represented to be composed of entities—ultimately either quarks or superstrings—whose properties not only lie beyond all our capacities of sensation, even augmented by the most powerful microscopes, but lie indeed beyond all our capacities of imagination.[36] Certainly, no quantum physicist supposes that the ultimate constituents of macroscopic material objects are hard because macroscopic material objects are hard![37]

However confused Hume may have been about Newton's chief rule of philosophizing, not to mention however fallacious Newton's foundation-of-all-philosophy rule may have been, Hume's characterization of the "experimental method" in science and the way he favorably contrasts it with that based on "hypotheses" is true to Newton's use of both the former phrase and the latter term. Newton's fourth rule of philosophical reasoning in his 1687 *Principia* is this: "In experimental philosophy we are to look upon propositions collected by general induction from phænomena as accurately or very nearly true, notwithstanding any contrary hypotheses that may be imagined, till such time as other phænomena occur, by which they may either be made more accurate, or liable to exceptions. This rule we must follow, that the argument of induction may not be evaded by hypotheses."[38]

The demonstrative science of ethics envisioned by Hobbes and Locke and the inductive science of ethics envisioned by Hume differ not only in method but also in effect. That of Hobbes and Locke would be prescriptive or normative; that of Hume would be descriptive and explanatory. Hobbes deduces "laws of nature" and Locke considers how "from self-evident propositions, by necessary consequences as incontestable as those in mathematics the measures [norms] of right and wrong might be made out." Hume, on the other hand, provides what Kant later calls a "practical anthropology"— a description of human morality as he finds it and a theory of why human morality is as it is.[39] Indeed, Hume provides a propaedeutic to Darwin's nineteenth-century natural history of ethics (detailed in 2.8–2.10). Hume is clearly aware of the distinction between a prescriptive or normative and descriptive and explanatory science of ethics. He begins "Part II" (the final part) of the "Conclusion" of the *Enquiry* with the following words: "Having *explained* the moral approbation attending merit or virtue, there remains nothing but briefly to consider men's *obligation* to it."[40] All that Hume manages to do, however, is to note that while virtue has been misrepresented "by many divines and some philosophers" in terms of "austerities and rigors, suffering, and self-denial," properly portrayed it is attractive in its own right and serves to make the virtuous individual happy, as well as benefiting and delighting those around him or her. In 5.13, I return to the problem of how the descriptive-explanatory science-of-ethics tradition, ancestral to the Leopold land ethic, can have normative or prescriptive bite.

4.4 KANT'S SCIENCE OF ETHICS

Normative force, in any case, is surely a hallmark of a third science-of-ethics tradition begun in the eighteenth century, the Kantian tradition. While Hobbes had characterized the moral theorems he deduces as "Laws of Nature," Kant envisions a science parallel to physics and its laws of nature in which one finds "laws of freedom." Kant's science-of-ethics project is confidently begun with the very first words of the *Foundations of the Metaphysics of Morals*: "Ancient Greek Philosophy was divided into three *sciences*: physics, ethics, and logic. This division conforms perfectly to the nature of the subject."[41] Logic, according to Kant,

> is occupied with the form of understanding and reason itself and with the universal rules of thinking.... Material philosophy, however, which has to do with definite objects and the laws to which they are subject is itself divided into two parts. This is because these laws are either laws of nature or laws of freedom. The *science* of the former is called physics and that of the latter ethics.[42]

Between logic and physics lies a "metaphysics of nature" and between logic and ethics lies a "metaphysics of morals."[43] The metaphysical domain in either case is concerned in part with the fitting of the purely formal laws of logic to its respective objects: natural phenomena, on the one hand, and the will, on the other. Kant is a thoroughgoing dualist, in the manner of Descartes. A human being consists of two natures: a physical body together with its "inclinations"—passions, desires, hopes, fears—and a rational essence, that is both originative of and subject to the laws of freedom. While the laws of Newtonian physics may be several and less than seamlessly unified—the three laws of motion and the law of gravity, for example—there is ultimately but one Kantian law of freedom, the categorical imperative, albeit expressed in three intertwined formulations. And the categorical imperative is an application to the will of the most fundamental law of logic, the law of non-contradiction.

For an action to be ethical, the maxim on which it is based must be capable of universalization. Simply understood, a maxim is a statement of what one is contemplating doing. Kant's favorite example is making a false promise, making a promise that one intends not to keep. Is it ethical to do that? To answer that question, we ask another: what would happen if one's maxim—"make a false promise"—were to become, Kant first says, "a universal law," then, as it were, "a universal law of nature"— a law, that is, as unexceptionable and as inviolable as, say, the law of gravity?[44] Thus universalized, the maxim would become self-contradictory. Were the maxim "make a false promise" to become a universal law, no one would believe anyone's promises, and promise making would cease be a form of communication. Self-contradiction become action is self-cancellation. In our actual, not our idealized moral lives, we are caught in what Kant calls a "contradiction of the will."[45] We will that the opposite, "keep thy promises," of our own maxim, "make false promises," be a universal law binding on everyone (else); and then we will that we alone be excused from abiding by it in deference to our own inclinations.

The reasons that Kant thinks of the science of ethics as discovering the laws of *freedom* are two. First, as rational moral agents, we are "autonomous," self-regulating. The moral law flows from our own rational essence and thus it is self-generated and self-imposed. A clear example of what Kant calls a "heteronomous"—or other-regulated—ethic would be biblical morality in which God generates moral laws or commandments, imposes them on us, and terribly sanctions disobedience and generously rewards obedience. Second, as physical beings we would seem, like all physical phenomena in the then prevailing Newtonian-Laplacean worldview, to be causally determined. Freedom in such a worldview is an illusion born of ignorance. Our minds are not large enough to comprehend the full suite of causes determining our behavior, and thus we suppose ourselves to be free. But we are more than physical beings, in Kant's estimation; we are also rational beings and when we choose to act on the dictates of reason, we interdict the chain of physical causes that determine the behavior of non-rational beings, such as machines and animals. Thus, in so far forth, we are genuinely, not just seemingly, free—hence, the "laws of freedom."

4.5 THE UTILITARIAN SCIENCE OF ETHICS

The other great school of ethics dating to the late eighteenth century is, of course, utilitarianism. Nor should we now be surprised that its founder, Jeremy Bentham, also sought to establish a "moral science."[46] And, with a little help from Adam Smith, he was ultimately successful in doing so, although the science that emerged, economics, is not usually thought of as moral—but the antithesis of morality, nor, universally, as scientific, for that matter. According to Bentham,

> By the principle of utility is meant that principle which approves or disapproves of every action whatsoever, according to the tendency which it appears to have to augment or diminish the happiness of the party whose interest is in question: …I say of every action whatsoever: and therefore not only of every action of a private individual, but of every measure of government.[47]

In classical utilitarianism, *happiness* is defined in terms of pleasure and pain; the more of the former and the less of the latter that one experiences the happier one is. Further, according to Bentham, the happiness of a society is constituted by the sum of the happiness of the individuals who compose it (documented in 2.12). He developed a "hedonic calculus"—as it came to be called—to quantify pleasures and pains for purposes of comparison and rational choice. Bentham (followed by John

Stuart Mill in this particular) seems to have conceived the utilitarian moral science more in accord with the deductive-prescriptive method of Hobbes and Locke than the inductive-descriptive method of Hume. Both Bentham and Mill consider the principle of utility to be beyond proof—because it is self-evident and axiomatic—that from which proof begins, not that in which it ends.[48] However, unlike Hobbes, who was perfectly content to suppose his Laws of Nature to be universally applicable to everyone, Bentham allows each person to be the arbiter of his or her own happiness. "Pushpin," a simple-minded eighteenth-century game, Bentham said notoriously, "is as good as poetry."[49] For happiness, modern economics substitutes the concept of welfare and defines *welfare*, not in terms of pleasure and pain, but in terms of *preference satisfaction*.[50] Like Bentham, modern economics regards each person as the best judge of their own welfare and treats the welfare of the community as additive rather than emergent—and terms it "aggregate utility."[51] And in place of Bentham's primitive hedonic calculus, modern economics has developed benefit-cost analysis to determine the aggregate utility, expressed in a monetary metric, of various laws and policies of government, corporate decisions, and private choices.[52]

4.6 HOW LOGICAL POSITIVISM CLEAVED APART SCIENCE AND ETHICS

There is no reason here to rehearse Darwin's nineteenth-century evolutionary natural history of ethics, which is fully summarized in 2.5 and 2.6. Nor is there a reason to cast about for more examples in the Western-philosophy canon of attempts to formulate a science of ethics. The immediate reasons for here sampling the history of ideas about a science of ethics in the modern Western canon of philosophy up to and through Darwin are two sides of one coin: on the one side, to indicate that the pursuit of a legitimate science of ethics—even, indeed, a normative science of ethics—has a very long and respectable philosophical pedigree; and, on the other, to indicate how anomalous is the wedge driven between science and ethics in mainstream twentieth-century philosophy. One might well wonder what happened? The short answer is this: Logical Positivism and, more generally, analytic philosophy happened.

Logical Positivism and analytic philosophy were a dialectical response to metaphysics gone mad in the nineteenth century. Kant's self-styled "Copernican revolution" in the eighteenth century limited all knowledge to phenomena as filtered through the subjective "forms of intuition" (space and time) and "categories of the understanding" (among them, cause and effect).[53] Kant allowed that "noumenal" things-in-themselves—both objects and subjects—actually existed but were beyond our ken. G. E. Schultze pointed out that since cause and effect were among the subjective categories of the understanding, cause and effect could obtain only among phenomena, not between noumenal things-in-themselves and the phenomena we actually experience and conceptually organize.[54] Hence things-in-themselves could not be the external causes of phenomena and thus had no metaphysical role to play. Following Schultze, J. G. Fichte steered German philosophy toward a fully fledged idealism in which all existence was limited to subjective phenomena; all existence was purely mental; only minds and their ideas exist.[55] This trend culminated in the early nineteenth-century Absolute Idealism of G. W. F. Hegel and F. W. J. von Schelling, in which any distinction between object and subject was erased.[56] German Absolute Idealism crossed the North Sea and took hold of British philosophy during the late nineteenth century, in the work, most notably, of T. H. Green, F. H. Bradley, and Bernard Bosanquet.[57] Disgusted by what appeared to them to be undisciplined metaphysical claptrap, early twentieth-century philosophers, both German and British—F. L. G. Frege and Ludwig Wittgenstein (a German-speaking Viennese of Jewish ancestry), among the former, and G. E. Moore and Bertrand Russell, among the latter—were determined to silence all such metaphysical discourse by policing language.

At the core of Logical Positivism is the claim that only two kinds of statements are meaningful: (1) those of logic and mathematics that are analytic, the truth or falsity of which can be determined by an analysis of the meaning of the words or signs composing them; and (2) those of science that are empirical, the truth or falsity of which can be determined by reference to observable facts.[58] This constraint on meaningful discourse certainly undermined metaphysical prattle about the Absolute, but it also undermined ethics, especially anything like a normative science of ethics. In his (in)famous "A Lecture on Ethics," Wittgenstein writes,

> And now I must say that if I were to contemplate what Ethics really would have to be if there were such a science, this result seems to me quite obvious...that nothing we could ever think or say should be the thing....[I]f a man could write a book on Ethics which really was a book on Ethics, this book would, with an explosion, destroy all the other books in the world. Our words used as we use them in science, are vessels capable only of containing and conveying meaning and sense, *natural* meaning and sense....I see now that these nonsensical expressions were not nonsensical because I had not yet found the correct expressions, but that their nonsensicality was their very essence. For all I wanted to do with them was *to go beyond* the world and that is to say beyond significant language....Ethics so far as it springs from the desire to say something about the ultimate meaning of life, the absolute good, the absolute valuable, can be no science. What it says does not add to our knowledge in any sense.[59]

So, from the point of view of Logical Positivism, our moral declamations are full of sound and fury, signifying nothing. As literally nonsense, they are like inarticulate vocalizations. To contemplate rape and say "rape is absolutely wrong" is similar to watching the performance of a lousy entertainer and hissing to express displeasure. Similarly to contemplate charity and say "charity is intrinsically good" is similar to watching the performance of a wonderful entertainer and clapping to express enjoyment. "Good" and "evil" have as much or as little sense as "boo!" and "hooray!" So far from being a prescriptive or normative science, even a potentially prescriptive or normative science, ethical discourse is on a par with the vocalizations of a chimpanzee—from the point of view of Logical Positivism, which, either overtly or covertly, dominated Anglo-American analytic philosophy for much of the twentieth century.

4.7 AYER'S MIGRATION OF A SCIENCE OF ETHICS FROM PHILOSOPHY TO THE SOCIAL SCIENCES

In the sixth chapter of his enormously influential *Language, Truth, and Logic*, A. J. Ayer provided a clearer and more systematic discussion of ethics from a logical-positivist point of view than one finds in Wittgenstein's colorful, but only suggestive remarks on ethics. First, Ayer distinguished between normative/prescriptive ethics and descriptive ethics. The former would include "propositions" such as those presented in 4.6: "rape is absolutely wrong" and "charity is intrinsically good."[60] These are mere "emotive ejaculations."[61] Like some other utterances that are neither true nor false—such as shouting "Hey, don't!" or "Come on!"—they function to influence the behavior of others: to discourage sexual assault and encourage generosity, in the case of these examples. A descriptive ethics would "describe the phenomena of moral experience, and their causes."[62] Neither of these kinds of ethics, however, belong to the then newly constricted province of philosophy, according to Ayer. Normative ethics is a part of everyone's life, including the lives of philosophers—not, however, in their professional capacity, but in their capacity as moral (or immoral) persons, choosing courses of action and judging the actions of others, according to the dictates of their idiosyncratic emotions. Descriptive ethics belongs to the sciences of psychology and sociology, not to philosophy. Philosophy does, however, properly engage in what eventually came to be called "metaethics": "A strictly philosophical treatise on ethics," according Ayer, "should therefore make no pronouncements. But it should, by giving an analysis of ethical terms, show what is the category to which all such pronouncements belong."[63] And that category is, once more, "emotive ejaculations."

The historical review here has revealed three conceptions of a science of ethics: (1) a deductive (or demonstrative) normative (or prescriptive) science of ethics, envisioned by Hobbes, Locke, and Bentham; (2) a transcendental a priori normative science of ethics, envisioned by Kant; and (3) an empirical and inductive descriptive science of ethics, envisioned by Hume. Ayer argued that the first was a chimera and that the third was a perfectly possible science, but one that belonged to the domain of psychology and sociology, not philosophy. As to the *science* of ethics envisioned by Kant, Ayer does not discuss it in *Language, Truth, and Logic*, but doubtless had he done so, he would have dismissed it as hopelessly metaphysical. His few comments on Kant appear to ignore a distinction basic to Kant's ethics—that between autonomy and heteronomy. In Ayer's view, "one of the chief causes of moral behavior is fear, both conscious and unconscious of a god's displeasure, and fear of the enmity of society. And this, indeed, is the reason why moral precepts present themselves to some people [presumably to Kant] as 'categorical' commands."[64] Finally, Ayer summarily dismisses Kant's theory of ethics because Kant "fail[s] to recognize that ethical concepts are pseudo-concepts and consequently indefinable."[65] Here, in any case, are his concluding remarks on the possibility of a science of ethics:

> The...task of describing the different feelings that the different ethical terms are used to express, and the different reactions that they customarily provoke is a task for the psychologist. There cannot be any such thing as ethical science, if by ethical science one means the elaboration of a "true" system of morals. For we have seen that, as ethical judgments are mere expressions of feeling, there can be no way of determining the validity of any ethical system, and indeed no sense in asking whether any such system is true. All that one may legitimately inquire in this connection is, what are the moral habits of a given person or group of people, and what causes them to have precisely those habits and feelings? And this inquiry falls wholly within the scope of the existing social sciences.[66]

Thus, due to the considerable influence of Logical Positivism, generally, and A. J. Ayer, more particularly, the pursuit of a *science* of ethics was largely abandoned by twentieth-century philosophers and was instead taken up by psychologists and sociologists—as if responding to Ayer's assignment of the task. As such a science was now none of their lofty business, twentieth-century analytic philosophers, with few exceptions, ignored it as beneath their contempt. On the other hand, as I note and critically review in 5.1 and 5.2, normative ethics continued to be pursued by twentieth-century moral philosophers—largely dropping all pretense to make a science of such. And this, as I show in 5.11 and 5.12, not in defiance of Logical Positivism's dictates, but altogether under the aegis of its severe constraints on meaningful discourse.

4.8 KOHLBERG'S SOCIAL SCIENCE OF ETHICS

Initially, the treatment of ethics in the "existing social sciences" was pursued independently of the biological treatment Darwin had given it in *The Descent of Man*. The best-known and most influential social science of ethics was offered up by Lawrence Kohlberg in the field of developmental psychology.[67] Kohlberg adapted the general pattern of *cognitive* development hypothesized by Jean Piaget, with whom he studied, to *moral* development. Piaget had a background in natural history, having taken a youthful interest in birds and mollusks, and he employed evolutionary concepts in his approach to developmental psychology, but his constructivist theory of cognitive development owed more to Kant's epistemology than to Darwin's evolutionary biology.[68] Following Kant, Piaget regarded knowledge as less impressed on the mind's *tabula rasa* from external stimuli, as in the empirical tradition of Hobbes and Locke, than as generated by the mind's own organizing structures. These, however, underwent several age-related stages of development, beginning with sensory-motor organization, as infants grasp and manipulate objects, culminating in the mature adult capacity for abstract thought.[69] Similarly, Kohlbergian age-related stages of moral development begin with uncomprehending responses to reward and punishment and end with an essentially Kantian conception of morality in terms of autonomous universal and self-consistent principles.[70] Indeed, Kohlberg appears in part to have arranged the historical smorgasbord of canonical Western theories of ethics into a developmental sequence—for one finds, along the way, vestiges of social-contract theory and ultilitarianism.

The developmental psychology of Piaget and Kohlberg conforms to the hypothetico-deductive-experimental standards of scientific method set out by Logical Positivism. Hypotheses about cognitive and moral development from infancy to maturity are generated on the basis of observation and induction; from them various predictions are rigorously deduced; experiments are designed to test the predictions; and, as the experiments validate the predictions, the hypotheses are confirmed. A well-verified scientific description of cognitive and moral development is thus generated.

That the paradigmatic social science of ethics was a species of *developmental* psychology is, perhaps, not accidental—because an implicit normative dimension comes with the concept of development. Never to achieve the ability to think abstractly or to act guided by universal principles of justice is to be incomplete, to be at an arrested stage of cognitive or moral development.[71] This may not be the kind of normativity envisioned by Hobbes and Locke (demonstrative proof) or rejected by Wittgenstein and Ayer (objective moral truth), but it is psychologically normative, albeit subtly and cryptically so. Thus, Kohlberg's treatment politicized moral science, as it suggested that the moral sentiments and socially embedded forms of ethical sensibility more frequently evinced by girls and women than by boys and men were immature. As Aristotle alleged that women, lacking a penis, were physically incomplete men, so Kohlberg seemed—surely without intending it—to be alleging that women were morally incomplete men.

4.9 GILLIGAN'S SOCIAL SCIENCE OF ETHICS

Carol Gilligan, a younger colleague of Kohlberg at Harvard, along with other female developmental psychologists, provided a feminist countertheory of moral development that did not privilege male ethical sensibilities.[72] Gilligan's developmental moral science was revolutionary—not, however, so much from a scientific point of view as from an ethical and even metaphysical point of view (pace the Logical Positivists). Kohlberg's stress on justice harks back to the oldest concept in Western moral discourse. In Hesiod's *Theogony*, Zeus introduces Justice into the violent and disorderly world of the Titans and punishes acts of injustice among mortals.[73] The kind of justice that Zeus brings to the cosmos is essentially distributive justice—the fair division of scarce resources. (He divides the cosmos among himself and his two brothers, Poseidon and Hades, by lot: the bright sky falling to himself, the foaming sea to Poseidon, and dank Tartarus to the unfortunate Hades, the earth remaining a commons.) The just distribution of political power, not resources, is a central topic of discussion in Plato's *Republic*. As thought about distributive justice evolved—in, for example, John Rawls's *Justice as Fairness*—closely allied with the concept of justice is the concept of impartiality.[74] A just person is not biased or prejudiced and does not play favorites. Justice is blind. Gilligan introduced a brand new moral concept into ethics: care. Over three thousand years, the concept of justice has been nicely parsed into its various subtypes: distributive, retributive, representative, and so on. The various forms of care—such as that given by doctors and nurses to patients, by parents to children, by adult children to their aged parents, by lovers to one another—have yet to be so clearly distinguished. But care is both necessarily and legitimately partial and particular, not impartial and universal.[75]

Further, as Rawls's famous "original position" behind a "veil of ignorance" imaginatively demonstrates, the classic moral subject is also universalized—a "rational" egoistic individual stripped of any particularity, knowing not its eventual race, gender, relatives, friends, sexual orientation, intellectual capacities or bents, tastes, preferences, and even its notion of the good. The individuality of these individuals in the original position is strictly monadic; they differ in number only, like so many distinct but otherwise identical hydrogen atoms. This universalistic conception of individuality is, according to Gilligan, male-biased, because women individuate and identify themselves in terms of their relationships. Metaphysically speaking, the individuality of a typically female moral subject is constituted by internal relationships; male moral subjects are individuated essentially—exclusively by their innate rationality, and their relationships are altogether of the external kind.[76] Thus Gilligan revolutionizes the metaphysics of morals by positing an alternative ontology of ethical subjects. Ethical subjects are conceived, in Gilligan's ethics of care, as the nexuses of webs of social relationships, not as social atoms (more fully elaborated in 11.1–11.2)—which had been either explicitly or implicitly assumed to be the nature of ethical subjects in Western moral philosophy at least since Hobbes.

4.10 GROUP SELECTION IN DARWIN'S SCIENCE OF ETHICS

While social scientists, more especially developmental psychologists, were busy working at a science of ethics, evolutionary biologists were doing so as well. Through the first third of the twentieth century there was no compelling reason for evolutionary biologists to do more than embellish and refine Darwin's account of the origin and evolution of ethics in *The Descent of Man*. As noted in 2.6, however, Darwin's evolutionary account of ethics casually employed the concept of group selection, as well as individual selection, and that concept would eventually come under fierce attack and rejection.

For many species, according to Darwin, and especially for *Homo sapiens*, being a member of a cooperative group enhances individual survival and reproductive success. And for *Homo sapiens* if not for other species, internal cooperation—indeed the very existence of a stable human group—depends on ethics ("No tribe could hold together..."). A tendency on the part of individuals toward unethical behavior ("murder, robbery, treachery &c.") would result in either banishment of the offending individuals or the disintegration of the cooperative group. Banishment or disintegration would require individuals to pursue the struggle for existence and reproductive success as solitaries. But survival and reproductive success for a solitary human being is next to impossible. Hence, cooperative group members and, *eo ipso*, tolerably ethical individuals would survive and successfully reproduce in greater numbers than unethical and unstintingly competitive individuals. Thus, an individual disposition toward ethical behavior is favored by natural selection as a condition for being a group member.

Note that Darwin's evolutionary just-so story in *The Descent of Man* explains the *origin* of ethics without appeal to group selection, but the increasing complexity and reach of ethics—what Leopold called the "extension" of ethics—does involve appeal to group selection in his account. It does because *groups* of *Homo sapiens*, which were both internally more cooperative and larger, out-competed rival groups that were less so. Thus, by group selection: from clans or gens there evolved tribes; from tribes, nations; from nations, countries or nation-states; and from nation-states the global village—each with its peculiar and supportive ethical precepts.

Darwin was aware of this shift from individual to group selection in his account as he moved from the evolutionary origin of ethics to its extension in step with the evolution of human societies:

> It must not be forgotten that although a high standard of morality gives but a slight or no advantage to each individual man and his children over other men of the same tribe, yet that an increase in the number of well-endowed men and an advancement in the standard of morality will certainly give an immense advantage to one tribe over another. A tribe including many members who, from possessing in a high degree the spirit of patriotism, fidelity, obedience, courage, and sympathy, were always ready to aid one another, and to sacrifice themselves for the common good, would be victorious over most other tribes; *and this would be natural selection.* At all times throughout the world tribes have supplanted other tribes; and as morality is one important element in their success, the standard of morality and the number of well-endowed men will thus everywhere tend to rise and increase.[77]

4.11 GROUP SELECTION IN WYNNE-EDWARDS'S EVOLUTIONARY BIOLOGY

British evolutionary biologist V. C. Wynne-Edwards provided a more focused and sustained brief for group selection, nor did he confine his discussion to human groups.[78] He expressly noted, "It is part of our Darwinian heritage to accept the view that natural selection operates at two levels, discriminating on the one hand in favor of individuals that are better adapted and consequently leave more surviving progeny than their fellows; and on the other hand between one species and another where their interests overlap and conflict, and where one proves more efficient in making a living than the other."[79] Selection between species was explored by Georgy Gause and denominated "competitive exclusion" by Garret Harden.[80] Wynne-Edwards offered an extended case for a level of selection between these two widely recognized levels, selection operating on competing animal populations or societies of the same species.

Among other social phenomena, Wynne-Edwards argued that members of many animal societies limited their individual reproductive potential, so that the group of which they were members would not exceed the carrying capacity of its environment or range. Like Darwin's account of the origin and extension of ethics in *The Descent of Man*, Wynne-Edwards combined notions of both individual and group selection. Those groups that grew beyond the carrying capacities of their environments would suffer a catastrophic population crash and most of their reproductively exuberant members and their offspring would die. On the other hand, those groups that did not grow beyond the carrying capacities of their environments would not suffer a population crash and their reproductively restrained members would survive to reproduce, albeit moderately. Hence, demographically steady-state groups would competitively replace demographically oscillating groups. Therefore, because natural selection favors demographically steady-state groups, natural selection also favors the reproductively self-restrained individuals composing such groups. Wynne-Edwards summarized his general argument for group selection in the following words—concluding, tellingly, with an explicit reference to morality:

> Survival is the supreme prize in evolution; and there is consequently great scope for selection between allied races or species. Some prove to be better adapted socially and individually than others, and tend to outlive them, and sooner or later to spread and multiply by colonizing the ground vacated by less successful neighboring communities.
>
> Evolution at this level can be ascribed, therefore, to what is here termed group-selection—still an intraspecific process, and, for everything concerning population dynamics, much more important than selection at the individual level. The latter is concerned with the physiology and attainments of the individual as such, the former with the viability of and survival of the stock or race as a whole. Where the two conflict, as they do when the short-term advantage of the individual undermines the future safety of the race, group-selection is bound to win, because the race will suffer and decline, and be supplanted by another in which antisocial advancement of the individual is more rigidly inhibited. In our own lives, of course, we recognize the conflict as a moral issue, and the counterpart of this must exist in all social animals.[81]

In the early twentieth century, there was even rampant speculation about the existence of group minds, especially in association with animal societies, such as those of termites and ants, which were so well integrated that they had many characteristics of a single, spatially disjoint organism.[82] A vertebrate example of a phenomenon that seemed inexplicable by any other hypothesis than a conscious and volitional mind at work at the social level of biological organization was the apparently orchestrated pattern of movement of a flock of small birds, flying close together, wheeling and turning in unison.[83] Wynne-Edwards was an accomplished ornithologist and field biologist and sometimes his sober accounts of the dynamics of group behavior may have suggested to some more mystically inclined readers the work of a group mind.

4.12 WILLIAMS'S ATTACK ON GROUP SELECTION

In any case, during the 1930s, the so-called modern synthesis integrated Gregor Mendel's genetics with Charles Darwin's theory of evolution by descent with modification and natural selection.[84] After the Modern Synthesis, the hypothesis of heritable self-restraint for the good of the group would have to be consistent with a genetics-fortified theory of evolution. And one major problem with group selection is that groups do not themselves have heritable genes that natural selection can favor or disfavor. The same might be said about selection at the level of species or the principle of competitive exclusion, to which Wynne-Edwards assimilated group selection by analogy—the competitive exclusion of one group or community by another is analogous to the competitive exclusion of one species by another. But a species may be regarded as a gene *pool* with a common genome and so competitive exclusion might rather be more analogous to competition between genetically endowed individuals. Indeed the competitive exclusion of one species by another might be reducible to the replacement, one by one, of the individuals of species A by those of species B.

George C. Williams, in the name of neo-Darwinian orthodoxy, launched a crusade against the need for group selection to explain any significant biological phenomenon, including phenomena of population dynamics, social phenomena, and ecological phenomena. Williams first drew a sharp distinction between the concepts of an adaptive function and an incidental effect. Earthworms, for example, condition soil but that is not the adaptive ecological function of their alimentary canals; it is a fortuitous incidental effect of the true adaptive function of their digestive tracts, which is to metabolize organic detritus. Then he invoked the principle of parsimony—that is, he whetted Occam's razor: "the principle of parsimony demands that we recognize adaptation at the level necessitated by the facts and no higher."[85] With these principles of argument in place, he proceeded systematically to review all the phenomena of population dynamics, social phenomena, and ecological phenomena explained by Wynne-Edwards and others by appeal to group selection and offered a counterexplanation appealing only to natural selection of favorable genetic alleles among competing individual organisms. To Wynne-Edward's central argument, Williams replies,

> Frequent contact with competitors would often be a reliable sign that to reproduce at all would require great effort and hazard to the somatic investment, and that any resulting offspring would be exposed to shortages and perhaps

accidental death from the competitive interactions of the adults. It may be adaptive to act on the assumption that reproduction is not worth the effort in crowded situations. The expected reaction would be to postpone reproduction and search for a less crowded area. There is no reason to suppose, as Wynne-Edwards and others have done, that such restraints on reproduction are designed to prevent the population from overtaxing its resources. They are adequately explained as adaptations whereby an individual can adjust to the probable outcome of trying to reproduce.[86]

As we see, from this brief extract, Williams's orthodox explanations of the various phenomena that Wynne-Edwards and others explained by appeal to group selection are inherently no more compelling or plausible. The manifest argument in their favor is simply that they are more parsimonious. There may be other, more insidious reasons why Williams was considered for most of the rest of the twentieth century to have decisively refuted group selection. I suggest the following. While Wynne-Edwards writes in a graceful and humane style reminiscent of Darwin's, Williams evinces an irascibility and zealousness born of an evolutionary fundamentalist crushing a threatening heresy. Williams appeared to be the champion of hard science, reductionism, positivism, and ruthless competition among individuals while Wynne-Edwards appeared to be the champion of speculative theory, superfluity, metaphysics, and even mysticism. Frans de Waal has a similar assessment: After Williams, the neo-Darwinian

idiom is almost derisive in its characterization of animals. Given the image of biologists as nature buffs, it may be shocking for outsiders to learn that the current scientific literature routinely depicts animals as "suckers," "grudgers," and "cheaters" who act "spitefully," "greedily," and "murderously."…If animals do show tolerance or altruism, these terms are often placed in quotation marks lest their author be judged hopelessly romantic or naïve.[87]

4.13 HUXLEY'S AND WILLIAMS'S ANTI-NATURAL (AND ANTI-LOGICAL) VIEW OF ETHICS

But what about the origin and nature of human ethics, over the long course of the reign of King Williams in evolutionary biology? Williams himself, ironically, appears to believe that ethics is anti-natural. In this opinion he expressly follows T. H. Huxley, who was Darwin's ally and an ardent defender of the latter's account of the origin of species by descent with modification and natural selection, but who regarded ethics as essentially opposed to natural selection. Huxley's account of ethics is hardly coherent, as he himself seems to realize. He styles natural selection "the cosmic process" and, here in agreement with Darwin, states that "man, physical, intellectual, and moral, is…purely a product of the cosmic process."[88] But in practically the same breath he opposes human ethics to the cosmic process and brazenly declares that "if the conclusion that the two are antagonistic is logically absurd, I am sorry for logic."[89] While it is difficult to make good sense of Huxley and Williams, both appear to think that human ethics is artificial, a product of human intelligence, which has somehow managed to transcend human nature. Their philosophical antecedent is clearly Hobbes rather than Hume (Huxley, revealingly, opposes "the state of nature" to the "state of art"). Williams's view of nature is even darker than that of Hobbes and Huxley. While Huxley had presumed to judge nature by the standards of human ethics and "condemned" it for its "indifference," Williams accuses nature of "gross immorality."[90] Williams summarizes his take as follows: "Huxley viewed the cosmic process as an enemy that must be combated. I take a similar, but more extreme position, based both on the more extreme contemporary view of natural selection [mainly owing to Williams himself] "as a process for maximizing selfishness, and the longer list of vices now assignable to the enemy."[91]

A science of ethics cannot rest on a position that is "logically absurd." Both Wynne-Edwards and Williams consider the most elementary form of Darwinian natural selection to operate on individual organisms—their difference of opinion lying in the difference between their respective answers to the question, Does it operate on higher levels of organization, such as populations, and societies as well? The modern synthesis, however, is even more reductive. The gene is the entity on which natural selection operates, as Richard Dawkins clearly and persuasively argues.[92] However reductive—it may be worth noting—the ontology of the modern synthesis paradoxically involves an abandonment of materialism. Individual flesh-and-blood organisms are composed of complex carbon-based molecules. When organisms die, the molecules composing them decay—that is, they are resolved into their elemental constituents. Before they die, the genes of some organisms are bequeathed to progeny—the *same* genes, say, the genes for blue eyes and blonde hair, but *not* the same molecules composed of the same atoms. Genes, thus, are not themselves complex carbon-based molecules; they are not strands of deoxyribonucleic acid. They are, rather, the replicable sequence of the adenine, guanine, thymine, and cytosine bases that compose strands of DNA. To make an analogy, the A, C, G, T nucleotide bases are like letters that combine to spell words. The *same* word may be written many times in many places in many materials, in books, say, or on blackboards with ink or with chalk. In short, a gene is no more material a thing than is a word. It is rather more of a Platonic form than a physical object uniquely located in space and time.

4.14 SOCIOBIOLOGY: WILSON'S NEO-DARWINIAN ACCOUNT OF THE ORIGIN OF ETHICS

In any case, how could ethics be accounted for—logically—in the ultra-reductive neo-Darwinian (and in a sense neo-Platonic) climate of evolutionary opinion in the last quarter of the twentieth century? In the mid-1970s, Edward O. Wilson elaborated a "new synthesis"—no less ambitious and momentous than the Modern Synthesis on which it was built—sociobiology. If the modern synthesis absorbed Mendelian genetics into Darwinian evolutionary theory, Wilson's self-styled new synthesis even more ambitiously aims to absorb the social sciences into the biological sciences. Wilson had a good start as a social entomologist; his task would be to extend a gene-based account of the particulars of haplodiploidal insect societies to diploidal vertebrate, mammalian, and finally human societies.[93] And the first chapter of *Sociobiology: The New Synthesis* was titled "The Morality of the Gene."

As Darwin himself observed, ethics is a phenomenon unique to *Homo sapiens*—if, for no other reason, because ethics is codified in *codes* of conduct and codification is a linguistic form of expression. In other words, no robust language, no ethics proper. But as Hume observed, human ethical behavior is motivated by other-regarding sentiments, such as sympathy and benevolence; and it is selfless, not selfish. Thus, to locate ethics in the wider spectrum of animal behavior, "altruism"—biologically defined as self-sacrificing behavior performed for the benefit of other phenotypes—was chosen to serve as a surrogate for ethics among other animals. According to Wilson, "the central theoretical problem of sociobiology [is] how can altruism, which by definition reduces personal fitness, possibly evolve by natural selection?"[94] And, also according to Wilson, "the answer is kinship":

> If the genes causing the altruism are shared by two organisms because of common descent, and if the altruistic act by one organism increases the joint contribution of these genes to the next generation, the propensity to altruism will spread through the gene pool. This occurs even though the altruist makes less of a contribution to the gene pool as the price of its altruistic act.[95]

This idea was not original with Wilson. The term "kin selection" was coined by John Maynard Smith in 1964 as a neo-Darwinian alternative to group selection; and the concept it labels was fully explored by W. D. Hamilton in the same year.[96] It may go back to J. B. S. Haldane—if a famous, but possibly apocryphal, anecdote is true. As I remember hearing it told, Haldane was asked by someone in a bar if he would risk his own life to save his brother's. Pausing to jot down some figures on a paper napkin he replied, "No, but I would to save *two* brothers, one brother and one sister, two sisters, four nephews and/or nieces, eight first cousins," and so on—these numbers corresponding to the fraction of genes he shared with these relatives: .5 with a sibling; .25 with a nephew or niece, and so on.

In addition to kin selection, neo-Darwinians recognize reciprocal altruism to be consistent with the assumption that the great prize in evolution is not personal survival, as Wynne-Edwards declares, but inclusive fitness—maximizing the representation of one's own genes in future generations.[97] The concept of reciprocal altruism is summed up in the popular adage, "I'll scratch your back, if you scratch mine." To account for altruism in its myriad biological manifestations, Wilson resorted primarily to kin selection rather than reciprocal altruism. Following Robert Trivers, he regarded the latter as useful, for the purpose of serving the presumed evolutionary *summum bonun* of inclusive fitness, only in "an advanced, personalized society, where individuals are identified and the record of their acts is weighed by others."[98] (In addition to human societies, Wilson would include those of wild dogs, wolves, monkeys, and apes as "advanced and personalized.") That's mainly because cheaters could exploit altruists and eventually drive the latter to extinction. However, as Robert Axelrod and W. D. Hamilton later showed with simple "games," like Prisoner's Dilemma, given the right quantitative assignment of rewards and penalties for altruism and cheating, populations of impersonal automata will stabilize at a certain percentage of cooperators and defectors, oscillating periodically around a point of equilibrium.[99]

4.15 THE FALLACIES OF DIVISION AND COMPOSITION IN THE SOCIOBIOLOGICAL SCIENCE OF ETHICS

As a science of ethics, sociobiology is beclouded by a penumbra of conceptual confusions. The most fundamental and vitiating of these is the frequent tendency of neo-Darwinists to commit the logical fallacies of division and composition. In 4.3, Newton was caught committing the former—attributing to its parts properties of a whole. The fallacy of composition is the complement of the fallacy of division—attributing to a whole the properties of its parts. Our genes are said to be "selfish." That's the fallacy of division. Oft-times we human beings, and indeed oft-times our fellow mammals, behave selfishly, but it makes as little sense to say that genes are selfish as to say that genes are smug or arrogant or manifest any other psychologically motivated behavior of complex organisms.[100] The expression "selfish gene" is literally nonsensical; indeed it is as nonsensical as the expression "lavender electron." Writes Wilson,

> Natural selection is the process whereby certain genes gain representation in the following generations *superior to* [more neutrally described: "*in greater numbers than*"] that of other genes located at the same chromosome positions. When new sex cells are manufactured in each generation, the *winning* [more neutrally described in the passive voice: "*the selected*"—whether randomly, by the way, or environmentally] genes are pulled apart and reassembled to manufacture new organisms that, on average, contain a higher proportion of the same genes.[101]

Genes do not in fact *compete* with one another and *win* or *lose*. These are but metaphorical ways of describing an essentially passive stochastic-statistical process. But grant that genes are "selfish." Wilson goes on to state that "the individual organism is only their vehicle, part of an elaborate device to preserve and spread them with the least possible biochemical perturbation."[102] One device of selfish genes is to "manufacture" altruistic organisms, which is precisely what the concept of kin selection was conceived to explain. The fallacy of composition is to conclude that because our genes are selfish then *we* are necessarily selfish and that the manifestly altruistic behavior of psychologically motivated complex organisms is somehow illusory. But in fact sociobiology affirms and explains not only altruistic *behavior*, but also the genuinely and sometimes ardently felt *feelings* motivating it. An uncle risking his own life by dashing in front of a speeding automobile to gather up and carry away his nephew in order save the toddler from being run over and killed is not consciously performing a Haldanean calculation before acting. (If he were, he would only so act for the sake of four nephews.) Rather, his behavior is "shaped by the emotional control centers in the hypothalamus and limbic system of the brain... [which] flood our consciousness with all the emotions—hate, love, guilt, fear, and others—that are consulted" not only "by ethical philosophers who wish to intuit the standards of good and evil" but by ordinary people who want to do what is good and noble, and occasionally what is heroic.[103]

In explaining the peculiarities of sexual behavior evolutionary biologists and sociobiologists often attribute to non-human animals sophisticated calculations and "strategies" employed by females to get genetically superior males to fertilize their eggs and by males to impregnate as many females as they possibly can. Williams sets out the conceptual foundations of the sociobiological battle of the sexes:

> A female may need to mate with a male to produce offspring, but a single mating may be enough to fertilize all the eggs she has or all she can produce in a breeding season. Mating once with the best male available can be a better strategy than mating once with the best and once with the second best....For the male, reproductive success may be largely a matter of how many females he can inseminate. He can be expected to make use of every opportunity to fertilize eggs and to seek out or try to produce such opportunities.[104]

Animals are not consciously trying "to produce offspring." Females are not devising "strategies" to maximize the fitness of their progeny. Males are not looking for an "opportunity to fertilize eggs"; they are not even looking for opportunities to "inseminate" females. Not only non-human animals—such as birds, whose sexual behavior is frequently discussed by Williams and Wilson—even human animals are rarely engaged in such reproductive calculations and strategies. I doubt that Haldane, to elaborate on the legendary story of his barroom synopsis of kin selection, would be thinking about fertilizing eggs and producing offspring had the person testing his heroism been an attractive graduate student he was trying to seduce. Judging from our own human experience, powerful impulses, far removed from cool reproductive calculations and deliberate genetic strategies, motivate sexual behavior. Among humans, and doubtless among some other animals, cool calculations and deliberate strategies are indeed often employed in sexual contexts, but (please forgive the vulgarism) in order to get laid or (more respectably) to win love, not to maximize the representation of the schemers' genes in future generations. Were it otherwise, how utterly contradictory and inexplicable would be the precautions (by means of condoms, birth control pills, vasectomies) often taken by the most ardent human pursuers of casual sex to avoid fertilizing eggs and producing offspring.

My point here is much the same as that concerning "selfish" genes and genuinely altruistic organisms. Genes that orchestrate conscious, quasi-conscious, or purely instinctive sexual behaviors, such as male aggression and promiscuity and female selectivity and cuckoldry, that, on average, result in fertilizing eggs and producing many and fit offspring are fixed in populations of sexually dimorphous animals by natural selection. Such genes themselves have no motives, conscious or unconscious; and to imply otherwise is to commit the fallacy of division. Nor are the motives of the genes—if genes had motives, which they certainly do not—the motives of the vehicular organisms whose behavior they orchestrate; and to imply otherwise is to commit the fallacy of composition. Regarding "gene-centric sociobiologists," de Waal puts my point this way: "Underlying their position is a monumental confusion between process and outcome....Human and other animals have been endowed with a capacity for genuine love, sympathy, and care—a fact that can and will one day be fully reconciled with the idea that genetic self-promotion drives the evolutionary process."[105]

4.16 SOCIOBIOLOGY AND BIOLOGICAL DETERMINISM

The habitual commission of the fallacies of division and composition in the sociobiological literature has led to another family of conceptual confusions beclouding sociobiology that might be generally characterized as alleged "biological determinism." And that is what led, primarily, to sociobiology's infamy and eventually made of it virtually an intellectual pariah. Sociobiology alienated many social scientists, who, understandably, resented the claim that their several disciplines should be eventually absorbed into biology.[106] About this, Wilson is blunt: "If we consider man in the free spirit of natural history...the humanities and social sciences shrink to specialized branches of biology."[107] *Shrink*! It also attracted the hostility of feminists and other representatives of social reform movements, because it seemed that sociobiology essentialized certain patterns of behavior and social relationship that reformists hoped to change—such as male dominance over females, male promiscuity and polygyny, tribalism and xenophobia, to mention but a few.[108] If such patterns of behavior and social relationship were genetically fixed or biologically determined they would be recalcitrant to change by means of habituation, training, and education. Moreover, if they were "natural," then they would not only be difficult to alter but also difficult to criticize; that is, they would be quasi-normative (a point to be explored more fully in 5.13). To put it in a nutshell, sociobiology renewed the contentious nature-nurture controversy, apparently weighing in heavily on the nature side of the debate. Setting aside the resentment of being shrunk, social scientists and social reformers were, for different reasons, partisans of nurture. Thus did sociobiology attract much enmity.

4.17 THE EVOLUTIONARY FOUNDATIONS OF THE LAND ETHIC IN LIGHT OF THE MODERN AND THE NEW SYNTHESES IN EVOLUTIONARY BIOLOGY

How do the evolutionary foundations of the land ethic stand up to the challenges of the Modern Synthesis and the New Synthesis (albeit that the latter synthesis merits capitalization remains questionable) in evolutionary biology? They are partly reinforced and partly undermined.

On the one hand—to the extent that group selection remains an anathema in the natural history of ethics (an important contingency)—they are undermined, because what Leopold calls the "ethical sequence," which he seems to have garnered from Darwin's natural history of ethics in *The Descent of Man,* appears to involve the concept of group selection. On the other hand, as argued here, sociobiology—despite widespread misunderstanding, especially among sociobiologists themselves—plausibly accounts for genuine altruism and, more generally, all the other other-regarding feelings that motivate ethical behavior. Sociobiology, therefore, is solidly in the Humean-Darwinian tradition of ethical theory, locating the ultimate source of ethics in other-regarding feelings, not in reason alone. However, the cornerstone of the sociobiological account of the origin of altruistic (other-regarding) feelings—the concept of kin selection—would appear to limit the extent of ethics to kin. But as also strenuously argued here, evolved emotions and the inclusive fitness that they enhance are not one and the same thing. Lust is naturally selected as a means to propagate genes, but lust is not experienced as a desire to propagate genes or to reproduce or to get eggs fertilized. Similarly, such other-regarding feelings as sympathy and beneficence may have evolved by natural selection to enhance inclusive fitness, but actually feeling sympathy and benevolence are not in any way connected to a desire to increase the probability that the genes of the one feeling those feelings, shared with the objects of those feelings, will be transmitted in greater numbers to future generations. Thus once the moral sentiments evolved by kin selection in small, genetically related primal human societies they might be showered upon unrelated members of the larger societies that later eventuated. The desires, passions, sentiments and other behavior motivators "devised" by our genes achieve the "goals" of their "designers" indirectly; they are crude, blunt instruments easily deflected from the *teloi* they evolved to serve.

Wilson provides an analogous example of the way feelings that were naturally selected for one purpose were directed beyond their evolved targets in changed social circumstances. Brother-sister sexual aversion evolved because of "inbreeding pathology"—the instance of stillbirths, mental retardation, various physical deformities and morbidities—caused by the expression of recessive genes shared by siblings at homozygous sites on the human genome. Matings of siblings would thus produce less fit offspring, on average, than matings of individuals who are less closely related. Thus ur-human brothers and sisters who chanced to experience mutual sexual aversion would enjoy a marked increase in inclusive fitness in comparison with those who experienced mutual sexual attraction, and so mutual sexual aversion between brothers and sisters became a naturally selected heritable trait—later much reinforced culturally, one might add, by taboos or expressly codified prohibitions. Wilson reports that unrelated children reared in a family-like Israeli-kibbutz setting also apparently experienced mutual sexual aversion: "Among 2,769 marriages recorded, none was between members of the same kibbutz peer group who had been together since birth."[109] Thus feelings of mutual sexual aversion, naturally selected by the incidence of inbreeding pathology in the absence of such feelings, are directed beyond their evolved targets in changed social circumstances.

Therefore, expansion of ethics to unrelated members of larger and larger societies is not inconsistent with the sociobiological hypothesis that ethics evolved by means of kin selection. Finally, if ethics are biologically determined, how can changes in the content of ethics, as well as their scope, be consistent with a sociobiological science of ethics? How the genetically endowed moral sentiments are to be codified and manifested is, in Wilson's words, "genetically underprescribed."[110] In short, ethics are not wholly determined by biology; indeed, they are not in fact biologically *determined* at all; rather, ethics are biologically *under*determined. How the genetically endowed moral sentiments are to be codified and manifested is prescribed—determined—by culture.

Here another analogy is useful. To speak a language is a naturally selected universally heritable trait in *Homo sapiens*.[111] But the huge variety of mutually unintelligible languages and the many mutually unintelligible dialects within some of them indicates that human language, though certainly genetically based, is genetically underprescribed or underdetermined. Indeed, language is doubly underdetermined. What language one first learns to speak is determined by the culture one is born into. And having learned to speak a language, what is appropriate to say to whom is also partially prescribed by cultural conventions. We human beings are genetically endowed with moral sentiments; they are part of our biology. Toward whom they are to be directed, how, and under what circumstances, however, is a matter not of biology but of culture. Aldo Leopold hoped to recast his culture and ours so that the moral sentiments would be directed toward "plants, animals, soils, and waters: or collectively the land." That aspiration is in no way thwarted by sociobiology.

Still, the Leopold land ethic might be undermined, as noted at the beginning of this chapter, by its dependence, via Darwin, on group selection. In the next chapter, I consider the science of ethics after the rise and fall of sociobiology and how the land ethic fares in the light of those developments—which include, surprisingly, a rehabilitation of the concept of group selection. Before that, however, I review the impact of Darwin, such as it has been, and of sociobiology and its successors, such as it has been, on late twentieth and early twenty-first-century mainstream moral philosophy.

5

The Land Ethic and the Science of Ethics: In the Light of Evolutionary Moral Psychology

Between 1936, when *Language, Truth, and Logic* was published, and 1975, when *Sociobiology: The New Synthesis* was published, I am aware of only one notable philosopher—Anthony Flew—to give any serious attention to evolution and ethics.[1] He was concerned, however, not with Darwin's account of the origin and evolution of ethics in *The Descent of Man* and the way it was revised after the Modern Synthesis, but with various attempts by others to derive ethical (and unethical) implications from *The Origin of Species by Means of Natural Selection*. Flew's wry refutation of divers philosophical and ideological misappropriations of Darwin's revolutionary work makes for an amusing, as well as an illuminating, read. He skewers Herbert Spencer and "Social Darwinism," Julian Huxley and his notion that evolution is happily progressive (in sharp contrast to the pessimistic views of his grandfather), along with various notorious ideologues invoking Darwin's *Origin* for support—among them Petr Kropotkin, the arch anarchist; Karl Marx and Friedrich Engels, the arch communists; and Adolf Hitler, the arch fascist.

But all that is largely beside the point of the themes of the previous and present chapters. In this chapter, I trace the development of the science of ethics after the rise and fall of sociobiology, followed by its quiet rehabilitation under a new name—perhaps for security reasons—"evolutionary psychology," which, integrated with the study of ethics in developmental psychology, has become "moral psychology." (In order not to put too fine a point on it, throughout the remainder of this discussion, I will elide "evolutionary psychology" and "moral psychology" to form "evolutionary moral psychology.") Jonathan Haidt, the leading contemporary voice in the field of evolutionary moral psychology offers this paean to E. O. Wilson and confirms the ancestral relationship of sociobiology to the current state of the art in the science of ethics:

> Prophets challenge the status quo, often earning the hatred of those in power. Wilson therefore deserves to be called a prophet of moral psychology. He was harassed and excoriated in print and in public. He was called a fascist, which justified (for some) the charge that he was a racist, which justified (for some) the attempts to stop him from speaking in public....

In 1995 ... [m]oral psychology was still devoted to the study of moral reasoning [in the tradition of Lawrence Kohlberg, as detailed and documented in 4.8]. But if you looked beyond developmental psychology, Wilson's new synthesis was beginning. A few economists, philosophers, and neuroscientists were quietly constructing an alternative approach to morality, one whose foundation was the emotions, and the emotions were assumed to be shaped by evolution. These synthesizers were assisted by the rebirth of sociobiology in 1992 under a new name—evolutionary psychology.[2]

The contribution of contemporary professional philosophers, however, to the quiet construction of "an alternative approach to morality" is not very evident in Haidt's discussion. In the bibliography of his *The Righteous Mind*, works by very few contemporary philosophers (philosophers living in the twenty-first century) are listed—namely, one each by Kwame Anthony Appiah, Daniel Dennett, Jerry Fodor, Martha Nussbaum, Peter Singer, Elliot Sober, and Robert Solomon. Of these academic philosophers only the names of Dennett, Singer, and Sober are indexed. On the whole, contemporary professional philosophers have been resistant to an approach to morality that is alternative to a rationalist approach. After 1975, the uproar and outrage provoked by the advent of sociobiology did bait a few philosophers to take a renewed interest in the current state of the science of ethics—some to denounce the hubristic and politically incorrect turn it had taken, some to point out its problematic assumptions and reasoning, and some to offer qualified support.[3] Not only would E. O. Wilson shrink the social sciences to specialized branches of biology, he insists that "the time has come for ethics to be removed temporarily from the hands of philosophers and biologisized."[4] As Peter Singer notes, "Most of my colleagues in university departments of philosophy regard Wilson's invasion of their territory as too absurd to merit a considered response."[5] Two able philosophers, however, did give the sociobiological science of ethics patient and sustained attention: Singer himself and Daniel Dennett. In addition, James Rachels—also an able philosopher—joined Singer in attempting to draw ethical conclusions, not from sociobiology (become evolutionary moral psychology), but from a more general evolutionary worldview.

5.1 SINGER'S RESPONSE TO THE EVOLUTIONARY ACCOUNT OF ETHICS

At bottom, Singer sides with T. H. Huxley in grounding ethics proper in reason and opposing it to genetically (under)determined emotionally motivated behavior, whether altruistic or selfish. Singer does not dispute the sociobiological account of the origin of other-regarding feelings, but thinks that it accounts only for what one might call proto-ethics, not ethics proper. With the advent of language, emotionally motivated altruistic behavior was channeled into distinct customs or mores, which varied, sometimes diametrically, from culture to culture. So far, sociobiologists, such as Wilson, and contemporary evolutionary moral psychologists, such as Haidt, would agree.[6] But neither customs nor mores are ethics proper, according to Singer. True ethics was foreshadowed, he argues, by Socrates, only some two and a half millennia ago, who submitted the customs of his culture to rational interrogation. Nor was even that enough to qualify as actual ethics, because Socrates professed nothing positive, according to Singer; he only exposed the potential contradictions inherent in the customs of his time and place. Ethics proper rests, Singer asserts, solely on a principle of impartiality, according to which equal weight is given to the like interests of all those whom the actions of a moral agent may affect. Such a principle is generated by reason, not sentiment, because it is *self-contradictory* for one to give unequal weight to equal interests, to render "different ethical judgments in apparently identical situations."[7] Or, mindful that Hume persuasively argued that reason alone could never motivate action, the one genuinely moral passion that Singer would recognize is an aversion to self-contradiction.

To make ethics proper turn exclusively on the principle of impartiality is to make ethics altogether impracticable, indeed, altogether inhuman. Consider the following extreme and ridiculous conclusion:

> [T]he standard of impartiality means that I ought to give as much weight to the interests of people in Chad or Cambodia as I do to the interests of *my family* or neighbors; and this means that if people in those countries are suffering from famine and my money can help, I ought to give and go on giving until the sacrifices that I *and my family* are making begin to match the benefits recipients obtain from my gifts.[8]

Not only should ethical people give as much weight to the interests of distant strangers as to their own family members and neighbors, Singer insists, but we must also acknowledge that many other sentient animals also have interests, and thus we must "give equal weight to the interests of the human and the mouse."[9] That, of course, Singer is quick to point out, does not imply treating "the human and the mouse" equally—equally, that is, in the sense of treating the human and the mouse the same way. Mice have no interest in getting a good education or in voting, so we have no obligation to send them to college along with our children and extend them suffrage. But they do have an interest in a pain-free, comfortable existence, so the principle of impartiality would entail no less self-and-family sacrifice by genuinely ethical agents on behalf of satisfying the similar needs of mice than on behalf of satisfying the needs of people in Chad and Cambodia!

The title of Singer's engagement with sociobiology is *The Expanding Circle.* Compare the following figure (Figure 5.1) with Figure 2.3 in Chapter 2.

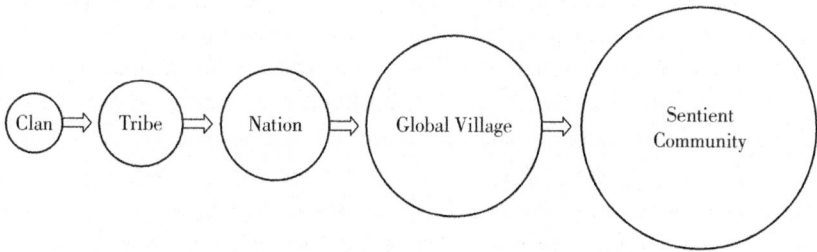

Figure 5.1 Singer's expanding circle of ethics.

For Singer, as the ethical circle expands, no trace of more intimate and more venerable community boundaries remain—*for the purposes of ethics*. But, of course, for many other purposes they do remain. That's one way of indicating why Singer's cardinal principle of impartiality is literally inhuman as well as wildly impracticable; it ignores the complex, hierarchically nested structure of contemporary human society and the fact that ethics must be equally complex and nuanced so as to reflect and conserve that structure. Finally, Singer's conception of true ethics is both absolutistic and imperialistic. According to Singer, "The principle of impartial consideration of interests…alone remains a rational basis for ethics"—and therefore is the moral absolute.[10] And because it devolves from the tradition of thinking about ethics flowing from Socrates, it is Western in provenance. Other cultural traditions may have their customs and mores, but, lacking a Socrates to put them on the path to ethics proper, they remain in a pre-ethical state of cultural development—unless and until, of course, in a spirit of noblesse oblige Western civilization cognitively colonizes those cultures with genuine ethics.

5.2 RACHELS'S RESPONSE TO THE EVOLUTIONARY ACCOUNT OF ETHICS

Like Singer, James Rachels begins by noting the sniffy disregard of what he calls "Darwinism" evinced by most twentieth-century academic philosophers. Darwin's "theory is discussed of course in works devoted narrowly to the philosophy of science. But in philosophical works of more general interest, and particularly in books about ethics, it is largely ignored."[11] It is therefore surprising to discover that Rachels himself ignores—not just largely, but totally—Darwin's own account of the origin and evolution of ethics in the *Descent of Man*; and he discusses its successor in evolutionary thought, sociobiology, only to dismiss it as irrelevant to ethics. That we do in fact have certain feelings—say heartfelt sentiments of care for family and friends or passionate impulses to heroic self-sacrifice—has nothing whatever to do with whether or not such feelings and the behavior they motivate are morally right. In short, *is* does not imply *ought*. Rachels insists that "particular ethical issues…are to be determined by rational methods, and standards of criticism and justification, that are internal to ethics itself."[12] Thus one might conclude that twentieth-century academic moral philosophers were entirely justified in ignoring Darwin's natural history of ethics and its sociobiological successor. Ethics, it seems, is an autonomous discipline, completely independent of any scientific account of its origins or development.

Rather, the interest that Rachels takes in "Darwinism" is that it undermines the metaphysical anthropocentrism of "traditional ethics" founded on some putative unique essence that humans possess, such as the image of God or quasi-divine rationality, which is altogether lacking in other animals and that entitles humans—and thus humans alone—to moral consideration. Basically, for Rachels as for Singer, the relevance of evolutionary theory to ethics is that it can be conscripted on behalf of their case for animal liberation. Darwin blurred, if he did not erase, the erstwhile metaphysical divide between humans and animals. Except for terminological and rhetorical differences, Rachels's theory of ethics—which he denominates "moral individualism"—is identical to Singer's theory: "where relevant differences between individuals exist, they may be treated differently; otherwise, the comparable interests of individuals, whether human or non-human, should be given equal weight."[13] The "principle of equality" and the "principle of rationality" are one and the same: "like cases should be treated alike and unlike cases should be treated differently."[14] And, just as for Singer, so also for Rachels, what makes the principle of equality identical with the principle of *rationality* is that it is an application of the logical law of non-contradiction or, more positively put, the moral law of self-consistency: in sum, "Moral individualism is, therefore, nothing but the *consistent* application of the principle of equality to decisions about what should be done, in light of what Darwinism taught us about our nature and about our relation to the other creatures that inhabit the earth."[15]

5.3 DARWIN'S ALTERNATIVE TO ANIMAL ETHICS À LA SINGER AND RACHELS

Twentieth-century neo-Scholastic philosophy so narrowed the very conception of ethics that it seems impossible for twentieth-century Anglo-American philosophers to have conceived of a non-anthropocentric ethic except in the hybrid form of some ahistorical blend of utilitarian sentientism and Kantian rationalism. If a being is *sentient*—capable of experiencing pleasure and pain, happiness and misery, à la Bentham—it should be included in the "expanding circle" of morally considerable moral *patients*. And a *rational* moral *agent* should be consistently impartial—the Kantian criterion of non-contradiction—in giving equal consideration to the interests of all equally sentient beings. But why should we accept with such alacrity what "Darwinism taught us about our nature and about our relation to the other creatures that inhabit the earth"—that we are not metaphysically set apart from other sentient beings—and discount or ignore what Darwin taught us about the very nature of human ethics, its origins and development? The answer cannot be because a Darwinian conception of ethics cannot provide support for animal liberation. As noted in 2.6, Darwin himself anticipated the eventual advent of animal-welfare ethics. As quoted there and once more here, he writes,

> Sympathy beyond the confines of man, that is, *humanity* to the lower animals, seems to be one of the latest moral acquisitions....This virtue, one of the noblest with which man is endowed, seems to arise incidentally from our sympathies becoming more tender and more widely diffused. As soon as this virtue is honored and practiced by some few men, it spreads through instruction and example to the young, and eventually becomes incorporated in public opinion.[16]

"In addition to being human," writes Frans de Waal, "we pride ourselves on being *humane*. What a brilliant way of establishing morality as the hallmark of human nature—by adopting our species name for charitable tendencies."[17] However, instead of more tender and more widely diffused sympathies, which can be spread through instruction and example to the young, and instead of charitable tendencies, Singer and Rachels prefer to try to compel us coldly to give equal consideration to the interests of all sentient beings—on pain of self-contradiction. I ask you this: Practically speaking, is the more powerful *motivator* for the ethical treatment of sentient beings on the part of most moral agents humane, charitable sympathy for their suffering or a self-centered aversion to self-contradiction? (See 10.7 for a distinction between the theoretical and motivational inadequacies of Rational Individualism.) Which (rhetorical) question leads me to the following point.

A perfectly plausible and practicable animal-welfare ethics can be built on Darwin's natural history of ethics in a way analogous to the way that Leopold builds the land ethic on it. Central to Darwin's natural-history account of ethics—as oft-repeated in this book—is the idea that ethics evolved correlative to the evolution of society or community. Thus our moral duties and obligations are generated by our community memberships—how and why, I have explained 2.5–2.7—which are multiple and varied. In "The Land Ethic," Leopold points out that we are members not only of many and varied human communities but also of a biotic community. Membership in that community thus generates unique land-ethical duties and obligations to "fellow-members," as well as to the community as such. Mary Midgley has shown the way to build a plausible and practicable animal-welfare ethics on Darwin's natural history of ethics in a way analogous to the way that Leopold builds the land ethic on it.

5.4 MIDGLEY'S ALTERNATIVE TO ANIMAL ETHICS À LA SINGER AND RACHELS

Midgley points out that human beings have, from time immemorial, been members not only of biotic communities but also of *mixed* human-animal communities.[18] Membership in these "mixed communities" also generates particular correlative duties to fellow-members and to those communities as such. As in all our intraspecies (human) community memberships, the duties and obligations to fellow-members differ from community to community. We owe different duties and obligations to family members and family than we do to fellow-citizens and country. So also we owe different duties and obligations to fellow-members of one kind of mixed community and to that community per se than we do to fellow members of another kind of mixed community and to that other kind of community per se.

Pets, for example, are ersatz family members. We treat them as second-class children, obliged to provide them food, shelter, medical care, affection, and even, in the case of dogs, a rudimentary education in proper habits of hygene and proper social behavior (both with proximate members of our species and with their own); oft-times we even educate them to perform various "tricks." (Well, perhaps one should say "train" rather than "educate"; but then one is reminded that academic philosophers often boast of their "training" in analytic methods—which would seem to foster, among philosophers especially, a sense of membership in a mixed community, *sensu* Midgley. We are trained in the proper methods of philosophy; dogs are trained to heel, sit, and shake. Speaking only for myself, I have, therefore, always preferred to say that I received an *education* in philosophy, not *training* in it, a form of learning that seems to me be to be more liberal and less constraining.) But when canine and feline "family members" get old or gravely ill, it is permissible to euthanize them—"put them down," as we say—something that is not permissible to do to actual family members.

Barnyard animals are members with us of a different kind of mixed community; and our duties and obligations to them differ accordingly. We are obliged to feed, shelter, and medicate them and fend off wild animals that might prey on them, but not to shower them with affection. Some—such as cattle, pigs, and various fowl—we may kill and eat, but we are obliged to do so humanely, that is, as skillfully, quickly, and painlessly as possible. Others, such as horses, who were bred to be our associates in various forms of work—pulling wagons and plows, for example—or that have been our comrades in arms, we may not kill and eat; but we may buy and sell them, as if they were slaves, and we may euthanize them. I am certainly not opposed to animal-welfare ethics, just to some impracticable one-size-fits-all version of such, based on a principle of impartial, equal consideration of equal interests irrespective of our highly nuanced social relationships, including those with animals, and irrespective of the correlative nuances of our moral sentiments.

So what of Singer's mouse on a Humean/Darwinian/Leopoldian/Midgleyan account of ethics? Some mice occupy a gray borderland between fellow-members of our biotic communities and fellow-members of our domiciles, though they are certainly not pets. I can only speak for what duties I myself have felt in regard to the mice of my acquaintance. When I lived in Wisconsin, I had a Waldenesque shack near Riley Lake in Portage County, twenty miles southeast of Stevens Point—my own "weekend refuge from too much modernity."[19] During winter weekend sojourns, I shared my shack with a colony of meadow mice, who had moved in for the season. At night, before falling asleep, I would hear them scurrying around on and in the walls and rafters and sometimes see them at their scurryings by candlelight or by the light of the moon. I felt a duty, in regard to these mice, simply "to live and let live."[20] Because I spent, at most, only two or three winter nights out of seven at my shack, I was a visitor in their demesne. My occasional human companions sometimes felt the same as I and sometimes differently. Some worried that a mouse might run across her face as she slept—a legitimate concern—but others found them to be, though a small nuisance, as harmless as I did. Some even thought they were cute. But, pace Singer, I never thought that I had a duty actively to give *equal* consideration to their interests as to those of my human companions. Had the mice significantly interfered with our own interests—say, for example, posed a threat of hantavirus infection—my weekend companions would have included a hungry cat or two.

Further to this brief digression, applying the method of resolving conflicts between the duties and obligations generated by our many community memberships set out in 2.15, in one notable instance I allowed my duties to the fellow members of my biotic community—plants, animals, soils, and waters—and to that community as such to take precedence over my duties to a rural neighbor. That neighbor asked permission to graze his dairy cows on my eighty acres, seeing that, from his perspective, my land was going to "waste." I politely but firmly refused. He was a member of a small-scale human community of mine and I certainly would have allowed his cattle to graze on my land had it been a matter of life and death for him, which clearly it was not. The health of my biotic community was pitted against his marginal economic interest (and probably more importantly, albeit more subliminally, his Lockean ideology of use and property and property rights); and my land-ethical duties clearly outweighed my neighborly duties—in this particular instance, in my judgment.[21] As to mixed-community duties versus professional-community duties, I often decline an invitation to have a late-afternoon beer with colleagues and sometimes I leave a committee meeting before it adjourns because I feel a duty to get home and walk and feed my loyal dog at her accustomed hour.

5.5 A COMMUNITY-BASED ANALYSIS OF ETHICAL PARTIALITY

There is a further irony in Rachels's evolutionary demystification of what he calls "traditional ethics." Rachels certainly exposes its unjustified anthropocentrism. But far from challenging what Jacques Derrida called the phallogocentrism of traditional (Western) ethics, Rachels warmly endorses it.[22] The existential ontology and moral sensibilities of the typically male, consistent-at-all-costs, Western individual is universalized as the paradigmatic ethical being. As elaborated in 11.1, ontologically, such a being conceives of himself as essentially rational; externally related; and motivated, so far as he is ethical, only by his reason in its most fundamental logical manifestation—the law of non-contradiction. His aversion to inconsistency trumps all other feelings, and especially those evoked by relationship—to spouse and kin, friend and neighbor. Rachels writes as if Carol Gilligan had never deconstructed the phallogocentrism of ethics centered exclusively on impartiality (detailed and documented in 4.9).

To expose what he thinks is the immorality of partiality, Rachels evokes the bugbear of racism. According to good ethical common sense,

> one is justified in giving special weight to the interests of one's family or neighbors.... The problem with this way of thinking is that there are lots of groups to which one naturally belongs, and these group memberships are not always (if they are ever) morally significant.... Suppose it were suggested that we were justified in giving the interests of our own race greater weight than the interests of other races.[23]

To avoid racism—and to be consistent in avoiding it—we must, Rachels argues, altogether abjure "this way of thinking." That is, thinking that our social relationships are morally significant—any and all of them. We now know what was not widely known when Rachels was writing: that "one *naturally* belongs" to no race at all—because racially sorting *Homo sapiens* has no foundation in the human genome.[24] Race is not a natural—that is, not a biological—kind of grouping. But what is the relevance to ethics of "groups to which one *naturally* belongs"? Indeed, qua naturally, none at all. Ethics is not correlative to *natural* groupings, except incidentally, but to *social* groupings (as detailed in 2.5–2.6). For example, we might sort *Homo sapiens* into groups to which they *naturally* belong according to handedness—left-handed, right-handed, and ambidextrous. Everyone with two hands naturally belongs to one of these three groups, but none of them are societies and thus none generate duties and obligations peculiar to themselves. Indeed, it would be ridiculous to say that one felt an obligation to give greater weight to the interests of one's right-handed fellows than to members of the left-handed and ambidextrous minority groups. Some morally significant relationships are natural, but their moral significance derives not from the fact that they are natural but that they are also social or communal relationships. Being a member of a family is a natural relationship and also a social relationship, the moral significance of which Hume implicitly recognizes with his odd phrase, "family society" (documented in 2.11). There are, furthermore, some duty-generating social relationships that are not natural in this sense either, such as citizenship in a nation-state.

In short, in the first place, one's race is not a "group to which one naturally belongs," but even if it were, that would be beside the point. Rather, the point is that the racial group to which one belongs is not a society or community; and thus, there are no duties and obligations to which one is subject generated by one's membership in a racial group. Therefore, one must conclude that "giving special weight to the interests of one's family and neighbors" does not imply that, by parity of reasoning, we might also justifiably give special weight to "the interests of our own race" (that is, to the interests of the *members* of our own race, which is what, one must suppose, Rachels means to convey by this infelicitous phrase). Furthermore, in contemporary cosmopolitan societies, members of morally significant societies (including families) often include people of different racial identity. Hence if race had any moral significance at all—and it does not, because a racial group is not a society—its slight significance would be swamped by the overarching significance of membership in other, genuine social groups, such as extended families, neighborhoods, municipalities, and nation states. According to the *analysis of ethics* offered in 2.15, moral duties and obligations are generated by our various social memberships. And, according to the *method of ethics* outlined in 2.16, one can appropriately choose among them when those duties and obligations come into conflict as just illustrated (5.4) in the case of my duties and obligations to my rural Wisconsin neighbor and to the fellow members of my rural Wisconsin biotic community and to that community as such.

5.6 A COMMUNITY-BASED ANALYSIS OF ETHICAL IMPARTIALITY

Let me hasten to note that "giving special weight to the interests of one's family and neighbors" is not always justifiable. If, for example, one is a member of a university search committee seeking to fill an academic position, it would be unethical (and probably illegal) for one to cajole the other committee members into offering the job to one's lesser-qualified nephew or friend than to a better-qualified stranger. But that's not because doing so would fall afoul of Singer's cardinal principle of impartiality or Rachels's cardinal principle of equality. Rather, as just noted and illustrated, duties and obligations generated by our multiple community memberships often come into conflict. And the impropriety of nepotism can be explained in terms of such conflicts. The academic community and other professional communities generate duties and obligations peculiar to themselves. Nepotism violates those duties and obligations and, in the case of filling a professional position, professional duties and obligations trump familial and amiable duties and obligations. The matter becomes more complicated if the academic job on offer is at a public institution. Such institutions often specify that lesser-qualified candidates who are citizens should be given preference over better-qualified candidates from other countries for citizen-supported and citizen-serving jobs. (US citizens rarely bother even to apply for an academic job at a Canadian university because of the favoritism toward Canadian citizens mandated by the Canadian government for academic hiring. And the US Citizenship and Immigration Services requires an accounting of academic hiring procedures before issuing an extended visa for a non-citizen to join the faculty of an American institution of higher learning.) But such complications arise for the same reason: peculiar duties and obligations are generated by community membership—and nation-states are paradigmatic contemporary communities generating correspondingly paradigmatic and often preemptive duties and obligations. Nepotism, a species of partiality, in filling professional positions is wrong; but nationalism, also a species of partiality, in filling professional positions, may sometimes be right. Therefore, nepotism is often immoral not because it involves partiality per se, but because it improperly prioritizes one set of community-generated duties and obligations over another. (For further discussion of ethically mandated and ethically impermissible partiality and discrimination, see 11.1).

We are most strongly obligated morally to be impartial in the application of statutory law. Impartiality in the application of statutory law is almost a sacred duty of law enforcement officers, such as policemen and -women, and court functionaries, such as judges, jurors, and prosecutors. Why? Once again, because of the nature of the communities that enact statutory laws: hierarchically structured, pluralistic, liberal, democratic nation-states. In the United States, the political hierarchies run from villages and municipalities, to counties, states, and the federal nation-state—each with its cops, courts, and judiciary. A cardinal organizing principle of such hierarchically organized communities is equality before the law and equality of participation in the processes of self-government, such as universal adult suffrage and the equal opportunity to stand for public office. But unless we are willing to follow social-contract theorists, such as Protagoras, among the ancients, Thomas Hobbes, among the moderns, and John Rawls, among our near contemporaries, and privilege one virtue among many—justice—and conflate all ethics with legislation, then we must allow that while impartiality is preemptive in legal and many other public domains, it is not preemptive in all moral domains. Once again, I recommend the method set out in 2.16 for deciding what moral domain—what duties and obligations generated by what community memberships—should take precedence in what circumstances. And indeed a commonly recognized principle of jurisprudence is that a spouse cannot be compelled to testify against his or her spouse in a court of law. That practice quite generally privileges familial duties and obligations over the duties and obligations generated by civil communities, and, *eo ipso*, makes partiality a more fundamental moral principle than the principle of impartiality, the latter raised beyond the status of a cardinal principle to the status of a papal principle by Singer and Rachels.

5.7 DENNETT, SINGER, AND ARNHART ON THE PHILOSOPHICAL IMPLICATIONS OF DARWINISM

Darwin's Dangerous Idea by Daniel Dennett is far more wide-ranging than the narrow focus evinced by Singer on deploying the theory of evolution in service of the deconstruction of metaphysical anthropocentrism in support of animal liberation.[25] Rachels's discussion, like Dennett's, is wide-ranging, including a warm portrait of Darwin and his contemporaries, but his purpose, shared with Singer, is single-minded: to build a case for animal liberation. However wide-ranging, Dennett's discussion is unified by an overarching general theme: Darwin disabuses us of some cherished illusions; and among them is the kind of true and absolute ethics propounded by Singer and Rachels. In respect to traditional Western belief in God, belief in quasi-divine human reason as an instrument for discovering the unvarnished truth, belief in a providential human destiny, and so on and so forth, Darwin is like a mischievous bachelor uncle who tells his five-year-old nephew and three-year-old niece that there is no Santa Claus. Ultimately, Dennett thinks that while for young children to believe in Santa Claus is appropriate, for adults to do so is certainly not appropriate. Thus we have Darwin to thank for our culturally mature intellectual liberation. As to ethics, more especially, neo-Darwinian sociobiologists and evolutionary psychologists may explain why we think that certain things are right and others wrong, but because *ought* does not follow logically from *is*—the sledgehammer in the analytic philosopher's tool kit—we are left, according to Dennett, to wonder if those things really are right and the others wrong. Thus, in practical ethics, all we can do is muddle through and hope for the best. In this domain as in all the others, there are no "skyhooks," as Dennett calls them—no transcendent truths—that will satisfy the vain human craving for certainty.

One development in the philosophical response to what Wilson styled the "biologization" of ethics brings the history of that response full circle back to the question: what political agenda does an evolutionary science of ethics support?—the question taken up by Spencer, Marx, Engels, Kropotkin, and Hitler, among others. In the last year of the twentieth century, Peter Singer put out a little book—only seventy pages in length—titled *A Darwinian Left* that tries to convince Leftists that sociobiology is the not the bête noire they feared and loathed. Singer insightfully puts his finger on the core concern of Leftists: "the malleability of human nature."[26] The Left embraces the "Standard Social Science Model," as Dennett calls it, according to which "animals are controlled by their biology, [but] human behavior is determined by culture, an autonomous system of symbols and values. Free from biological constraints, cultures can vary from one another arbitrarily without limit."[27] According to Singer, "From this it follows that education in the broadest sense is the great panacea, with the potential to mold human beings into perfect citizens" or for that matter into any kind of human beings that reformers would like for them to become: non-racists, non-sexists, non-materialists—whatever.[28] Sociobiology is the skunk at the Leftist garden party, proclaiming, as does Wilson, that "The genes hold culture on a leash. The leash is long, but inevitably values will be constrained in accordance with...the human gene pool."[29] Singer divides the various features of human nature into three categories from most to least malleable. That human beings naturally are xenophobic and tend to form male-dominated social hierarchies does not imply that these human characteristics are good—invoking once again the lacuna between fact and value, *is* and *ought*—and they can be countered if not altogether extinguished by education and cultural reform. While sexual orientation itself is recalcitrant to education and social pressure, *attitudes* toward alternative sexual orientation are highly malleable. Rather it behooves Leftist social reformers to know the material with which they work—human nature—and the challenges and limitations they face in shaping it to their liking.

Despite the best efforts of Marx, Engels, Kropotkin, and, more recently, Singer, the Right seeks and still finds more succor in evolutionary ethics than does the Left. Spencerian Social Darwinism was warmly embraced by both John D. Rockefeller and Andrew Carnegie.[30] Presently, Larry Arnhart argues that the biologization of ethics supports the political/cultural agenda of the Republican Party: husband-headed nuclear families; a gender-based division of labor, with the husband off in the concrete jungle stalking the bacon and the wife staying home baking the bread, while caring for the children; limitless accumulation of private property; territoriality; an aversion to immigrants (especially if their surnames end with a vowel, they appear to be of non-European descent, or they speak a language other than English).[31] Long since the days of Rockefeller and Carnegie, however, the Republican Party has allied itself with Christian Fundamentalists for whom Darwin is the incarnation of the devil who undermines human dignity and the sanctity of human life and the literal truth of the account of creation in the Bible—never mind that there are two mutually inconsistent ones to be found there. Patrick Cohen reports that Arnhart and his "Darwinian Conservatism" has opened up a rift in the GOP.[32]

Jonathan Haidt has entered the debate about which political persuasion is better supported by evolutionary moral psychology.[33] His analysis accords more with that of Arnhart than that of Singer. According to Haidt, our Humean moral sentiments are modular and fall into the following clusters: (1) care/harm, (2) liberty/oppression, (3) fairness/cheating, (4) loyalty/betrayal, (5) authority/subversion, (6) sanctity/degradation. The corresponding moral sentiments might be (1) sympathy, (2) outrage, (3) indignation, (4) patriotism, (5) respect, (6) awe. Haidt believes that the ethical sensibilities of Leftists, are narrowly confined to (1) care/harm and (2) liberty/oppression, while those of Right-wingers range more evenly across the spectrum from 1 to 6. Thus, Haidt believes that Leftists are inclined to (1) care deeply about harm to vulnerable persons (which may include animal persons) and (2) to think that people should be free to do what they want to do as long as what they do substantively harms no one else. The ethical sensibilities of Right-wingers also incline them (1) to care about harm and (2) about freedom, but they also are inclined (3) to resent and punish cheaters; (4) to put a premium on loyalty to family, country, and God; (5) to respect authority in the persons of bosses and police; and (6) to be deeply disgusted by the violation of various taboos, especially those regarding sex and food. As Haidt sees it, "conservatives" exhibit the full spectrum of human moral sensibilities, while the moral sensibilities of "liberals" are constricted. In Haidt's view, one might say that conservatives exhibit a richer and fuller humanity than do liberals.

More fully human, perhaps, but also, it seems, less humane to those who occupy a lower status in the social hierarchies to which they are inclined to be loyal and to the sexual "deviants" that elicit their self-righteous disgust. Surely a case can be made that liberals resent and would like to punish predatory banksters, would like for gays and lesbians to enjoy equal rights with straights, feel loyalty to labor unions, and think that snowmobiles and all-terrain vehicles violate the sanctity of wilderness areas. The difference between conservatives and liberals lies more in how the moral sentiments are cognitively stimulated and less in the balance among them. Haidt seems to be especially tone deaf when it comes to the way liberal or left-leaning environmentalists manifest their outrage not only about violations of the sanctity of wilderness areas by motorized recreationalists but also by mineral miners and by the degradation of biotic communities by developers. (See 9.9 for a discussion of the way environmental ethics might be better served by an emphasis on Haidt's sanctity/degradation module than on the care/harm module as argued by Antoine Dussault.)

5.8 GROUP SELECTION REVISITED

So much for a review of twentieth-century philosophical responses, such as they are, to twentieth-century approaches to the science of ethics, which was dominated first by developmental psychology, then by sociobiology.[34] As the century waned, sociobiology morphed into evolutionary psychology and, wed to the further study of ethics in developmental psychology, spawned evolutionary moral psychology. So what has become of the science of ethics in the early twenty-first century and what implications do recent science-of-ethics developments have for the conceptual foundations of the Leopold land ethic? (The Darwinian political musings of Arnhart and Haidt, I should note, were published in the twenty-first century and so my foregoing review of them gets a little ahead of the unfolding story told in this chapter.)

First, group selection has been resurrected from the dead, due in large measure to the collaborative work of Elliot Sober, a philosopher of biology, and David Sloan Wilson, an evolutionary biologist.[35] Until very recently, most evolutionary biologists thought that the concept of group selection should be relegated to the dustbin of discarded scientific ideas, along with phlogiston and the luminiferous ether. But presently, even E. O. Wilson has come around to embrace "multi-level selection theory," as it is now called.[36] Indeed E. O. has teamed with D. S. Wilson (no relation) and together they have made multi-level selection not only respectable but pretty much now widely accepted.[37] For example, in *Moral Minds: The Evolution of Virtue, Altruism, and Shame*, Christopher Boehm employs group selection with as much alacrity as he employs kin selection to explain the origin and evolution of human ethics—as if group selection were a well-accepted standard explanatory device in the tool kit of evolutionary moral psychology.[38] For another example, in *A Cooperative Species: Human Reciprocity and Its Evolution*, Samuel Bowls and Herbert Gintis are both forthright and emphatic: "Two approaches inspired by *standard biological models* have constituted the workhorses of our explanation, multi-level selection and gene-culture coeveolution."[39] (Gene-culture coevolution is the idea that just as the capacity for enculturation is a heritable human trait, culture is among the environmental conditions exerting selective pressure on the human genome.[40]) According to Bowles and Gintis, the workhorses of twentieth-century sociobiology,

> the kin-based and reciprocal altruism models, operating alone or in tandem, are peculiarly ill-suited to explain the distinctive aspects of human cooperation.... [T]he nature of preferences revealed in behavioral experiments and other observations of human behavior is consistent with the view that genuine altruism, a willingness to sacrifice one's own interest to help others, including those who are not family members, and not simply in return for reciprocation in the future, provides the proximate explanation of much of human cooperation. These ethical and other-regarding group-beneficial social preferences are the most likely psychological consequence of the gene-culture coevolutionary and multi-level selection process.[41]

Human *groups*, like human individuals (some of whom are tall, blue-eyed, and blonde; others short, brown-eyed, and brunette) exhibit "phenotypic variation," according to Sober and Wilson (if not genotypic variation).[42] Think, for example, of the stark contrasts between a street scene in, say, Riyadh, Saudi Arabia, and one in Honolulu, Hawai'i. In the former, one sees a public society of mostly men fully clothed in long, loose, white garments and the occasional veiled woman, escorted by a male relative, draped from head to foot in black; in the latter, one sees a public society of roughly equal numbers of men and women, the men more fully clothed than the women, some of whom wear only three tiny patches of thin cloth bound on by strings, and who paint, tattoo, and bejewel their bodies in ways calculated to maximally arouse the sexual interest of most of the men (and some of the women) around them. The scenes differ in respect to the ear as well as the eye: the differences in language and music are especially great.

Human *groups*, unlike human individuals, have no DNA. Nevertheless, according to Sober and Wilson, the phenotypic characters of groups are "heritable," that is, they are passed down from one generation to the next.[43] And they are persistent, remaining constant over many generations. Certainly this is true not only for various "mother tongues"—languages—but also for the massive and intricate cultural content stored and transmitted in those languages, especially the religious and moral content. Finally, according to Sober and Wilson, the heritable phenotypic variation between groups confers more or less "fitness" on them when they compete, as groups, for territory or other resources, such that one group can displace another.[44] When that happens, *that* is group selection. One group can displace another, nota bene, even when the individuals composing the displaced group are not themselves displaced qua individuals. If enough individuals culturally migrate from one group to another—assimilate—then the abandoned group disappears, even though its erstwhile members survive and flourish. When that happens, *that* too is group selection.

Group-level viability and fitness depend in part on limiting within-group competition. They depend on a reduction of the relative fitness of individuals within groups, who are required to make concessions and even sacrifices on behalf of others; this enables cooperation among individuals, which, in turn, enables the group to function as a unit. Neo-Darwinians, such as G. C. Williams, just could not imagine how it were possible for individuals to defer and sacrifice on behalf of others, given the blind impulses orchestrated by "selfish" genes "competing" to represent themselves in greater and greater numbers of individuals. According to Sloan and Wilson, "social norms" are the low-cost means groups have evolved to suppress all-out struggles between individual members that render the groups dysfunctional and ultimately disintegrative.[45] These norms reward such behaviors as sharing resources and deference to consensus and punish such behaviors as hoarding and boastful self-assertion. These rewards and punishments can be preeminently powerful and yet be as immaterial as public praise and censure.

Sharing and deference are altruistic *behaviors* as evolutionary biologists understand altruism—increasing the individual survival and reproductive success of other organisms at some risk or at some cost to the altruist. Psychologically, one might insist that, because altruistic behaviors are encouraged by a social system of rewards and punishments, they are not motivated by altruistic *sentiments* but by a kind of enlightened self-interest, especially if "noble" behavior attracts more desirable mates and social esteem, while "vicious" behavior attracts sanctions that in some cases can be as severe as ostracism, imprisonment, and even execution. Sober and Wilson argue that genuine psychological altruism evolved to foster the inclusive fitness of mammals—the survival not only of the individual, considered alone, but of her offspring as well. Parental care for offspring is motivated by many feelings and passions, pleasure in being suckled, for example, but also viscerally felt self-sacrifice in defending offspring against attack. They call this diversity of motives for parental care "motivational pluralism."[46] Thus they implicitly follow Darwin whose account of the evolution of ethics begins with "the parental and filial affections" as the psychological raw material for more widely cast altruistic sentiments. Sober and Wilson appear to be too close to the moment in which kin selection, as a more reductive alternative, had all but vanquished group selection, which they so stoutly defend. Thus they explicitly grant kin selection *by name* no role at all in the evolution of ethics. But their account of the evolution of psychological altruism, with its extended focus on parental care, implicitly involves a combination of kin selection and group selection as well as a principal role for culture in explaining the extremely varied forms that human ethics take. In *Moral Origins*,

Boehm is more comfortable employing kin selection and group selection in tandem to explain both the origins and diversity of human ethics.

In an important and influential state-of-the-art review of the science of ethics in *Science*, Jonathan Haidt anticipates Bowles and Gintis in pointing out that the classic twin pillars of the sociobiological account of ethics, kin selection and reciprocal altruism, cannot account for the phenomenon, requiring group selection to fill the theoretical breach. "The unifying principle" of morality, Haidt suggests, is

> that morality binds and builds; it constrains individuals and ties them to each other to create groups that are emergent entities with new properties....Psychological mechanisms that promote uniformity within groups and maintain differences across groups create conditions in which group selection can occur, both for cultural traits and for genes. Even if groups vary little or not at all genetically, groups that develop norms, practices, and institutions that elicit more group-beneficial behavior can grow, attract new members, and replace less cooperative groups....Humans attain their extreme group solidarity by forming moral communities within which selfishness is punished and virtue rewarded.[47]

Further support for group selection has emerged from an unexpected quarter: endo-symbiotic evolutionary biology. In addition to an organism's own cells, all multi-celled organisms consist of a wide variety of microbes that are vital to their developmental, metabolic, physiological, and immunological processes. According to Gilbert et al.,

> This symbiotic relationship appears to fulfill the criteria for group selection: alleles can spread throughout a population because of the benefits they bestow on groups, irrespective of the alleles' effect on the fitness of individuals within that group. Except, in this case the beneficial alleles are genetic variations in bacterial symbionts, which provide their hosts with a second source of inherited selectable variation; and if there is no "individual organism," what remains of classic notions of individual selection.[48]

There are two arguments in this short paragraph, one technical, the other purely conceptual.

The first is that "alleles can spread through a population [of "holobionts" as Gilbert et al. call multi-celled organisms] because of the benefits they bestow on groups [the populations of holobionts], irrespective of the effect of the fitness of individuals within that group. Gilbert et al. initially provide examples of pea aphids and two of their bacterial symbionts. In the first example, a parasitoid wasp that threatens them is chemically warded off by a particular species of bacteria inhabiting some aphids, but that bacterium also reduces the fertility of those aphids in comparison with aphids lacking that microbial species. In the second example, the same species of aphid is enabled by another species of bacteria to tolerate more heat than those that do not harbor that microbial species, but that bacterium carries with it a similar cost in aphid reproductive prowess. Thus bacterially biodiverse populations of pea aphids come through episodes of high wasp parasitism and heat waves.

The second argument is not only conceptual but also quite general. Multi-celled organisms are not individuals; they are, rather, super-ecosystems (as detailed and documented in 11.2) or holobionts. And so, if there are no individual multi-celled organisms, how can G. C. Williams and his ilk natter on coherently about "individual selection"? All selection is group selection, for what is selected is not, say, the human genotype, but the human genotype together with all its vital microbial symbionts—a group if there ever was one.

5.9 THE ANALOGY BETWEEN LANGUAGE AND ETHICS

As the science of ethics is taking shape in the twenty-first century, both the evolutionary and philosophical foundations of the Leopold land ethic are more strongly affirmed than ever. With the work first of Sober and Wilson, later Wilson and Wilson, now Haidt, Boehm, Bowles and Gintis, and others too numerous to name, Darwin's basic account of the origin and evolution of ethics—on which Leopold based the land ethic—has been fully vindicated, including its reliance on group selection (or, more precisely, multi-level selection). Further, and more fundamentally, as it has ripened in the twenty-first century, the science of ethics has been thoroughly Humean. It has been Humean in the conception of a proper science of ethics as inductive and descriptive rather than deductive and prescriptive; and it has also been Humean in regarding ethics as ultimately grounded in emotion with reason playing a supportive role, as opposed to the Kantian conception of ethics as ultimately grounded in reason overcoming all human emotions, whether they be self-regarding or other-regarding.[49] In the playfully but significantly titled "The Emotional Dog and Its Rational Tale," Jonathan Haidt traces the contemporary state-of-the-art of the science of ethics back to David Hume.[50] And in "The New Synthesis in Moral Psychology," Haidt affirms that

> Evolutionary approaches to morality generally suggest affective primacy. Most propose that the building blocks of human morality are emotional (e.g., sympathy in response to suffering, anger at nonreciprocators, affection for kin and allies) and that some early forms of these building blocks were already in place before the hominid line split off from that of *Pan* 5 to 7 million years ago. Language and the ability to engage in conscious moral reasoning came much later, perhaps only in the past 100 thousand years, so it is implausible that the neural mechanisms that control human [moral] judgment and behavior were suddenly rewired to hand control of the organism over to this new deliberative faculty.[51]

More implausible still is Singer's suggestion that ethics proper emerged only 2,500 years ago with the application of the logical principle of non-contradiction to moral reasoning. If the primary function of "morality" is—as Haidt suggests, following Darwin—that "it constrains individuals and ties them to each other to create groups that are emergent entities with new properties," then morality must have been around much much longer than two and half millennia. Furthermore, the sharp Kantian distinction between reason and "inclination" has been blurred in the recently elaborated concept of "emotional intelligence" (EI)—or EQ, by parity of acronym with IQ—in contemporary evolutionary moral psychology.[52]

One recent and comprehensive theory of human morality in evolutionary moral psychology more fully develops my analogy (in 4.17), between culturally variable ethics and culturally variable languages. Marc D. Hauser endorses the theory of language espoused by Noam Chomsky and Steven Pinker—that all languages, however different and mutually unintelligible, evince a common, underlying structure, "a deep grammar."[53] Just as both the capacity for language and its underlying structure are genetically inherited and universal in our species, so the capacity for ethics and its "moral grammar" are genetically inherited and universal in our species, according to Hauser.[54]

Hauser and his associates have tested this hypothesis empirically by means of a web-based survey, asking respondents to make moral judgments regarding several permutations of the "trolley problem" first developed by Phillipa Foot.[55] The problem is this: imagine that a runaway trolley will kill five people walking ahead on its track unless a bystander throws a switch diverting it onto a sidetrack where one person is walking; that person will be killed by the bystander's action; but by the same action the bystander will have saved the lives of five people. Sixty thousand subjects—children and adults; old people and young people; male and female, educated and uneducated people—from 120 countries and ethnicities responded during the first year. Ninety percent thought that the bystander should throw the switch and save five people and kill one. Now imagine that the bystander is on a bridge above the tracks and can prevent the trolley from killing five people only by pushing a large man off the bridge onto the tracks stopping the trolley, thereby killing the large man. A comparable number of respondents to Hauser's survey thought that the bystander should not push the large man onto the tracks and thus save five people and kill only one.

Why is there such general agreement that throwing the switch to divert the trolley onto the sidetrack is morally permissible, indeed obligatory, but that pushing the large man onto the track to stop the trolley is morally impermissible? In both cases the agent chooses to sacrifice one person's life to save that of five. To bring out the difference intuitively, imagine that in an emergency room there are five accident victims, two with irreparably lacerated kidneys, one with an irreparably lacerated liver, one with crushed lungs, and one with a pierced heart. Would it be permissible for a physician to mine the healthy body of a living hospital orderly to harvest his five corresponding organs to save the five accident victims? Surely all would say: Certainly not! But why? Again we would be sacrificing the life of one person to save that of five. The reason is this, according to Hauser: in the case of throwing the switch to divert the trolley onto the sidetrack, saving five lives *and* killing one, the killing of the one is an unintended, albeit foreseen, consequence of a low-cost altruistic action. In the alternative case, the agent stops the trolley, and thus saves the lives of five people walking ahead on the track, *by* pushing the large man off the bridge. Harm to the large man and the emergency-room orderly is an intended, as well as a foreseen, consequence of the agent's action.

According to Hauser, few survey respondents, however, were able to analyze the difference between the two kill-one/save-five permutations of the trolley problem, nor did the absence of any such analysis prevent them from rendering confident moral judgments regarding those cases. Hauser takes this to indicate that such judgments flow from a natural moral sense, analogous to our natural grammatical sense. We make grammatical statements and judge the grammaticality or lack thereof of our own statements and those of others almost altogether in the absence of any grammatical analysis or conscious application of any grammatical rules, as Steven Pinker notes in *The Language Instinct*. In a subsequent study, *The Better Angles of Our Nature*, Pinker finds that the "moral sense" also has a "moral grammar" of its own.[56] Hauser's trolley-problem research also provides evidence for another central contention of this book. Throwing the switch and pushing the large man onto the tracks are *rationally equivalent*—kill one to save five in both cases. The fact that there is general agreement that to do the former is morally obligatory, but to do the latter is morally impermissible strongly indicates, if it does not prove, that the Singer-Rachels principle of treating identical interests in identical ways—kill one to save five in both cases—is not a correct guiding principle of *human* ethics.

5.10 HUME ON NATURE AND NURTURE IN ETHICS

Setting aside the linguistic analogy, which Hume himself did not draw, twenty-first-century science of ethics is distinctly Humean in two further particulars. Hume implicitly draws a distinction between moral *action* and moral *judgment*. Moral actions are motivated by such other-regarding sentiments as sympathy and benevolence. Moral judgment is based on a "moral sense," a faculty distinct from the moral sentiments. And while both the moral sentiments and the moral sense are universal features of human nature, like Haidt, Pinker, and most other contemporary researchers in the science of ethics, Hume provides for wide cultural variation. *An Enquiry Concerning the Principles of Morals* ends with a part simply titled "A Dialogue." There, Hume regales the reader with a droll fictional conversation between himself and one Palamedes who essays to get Hume to admit that "fashion, vogue, custom, and law, were the chief foundation of all moral determinations"—*nurture*, in a word—not some universal faculty of human *nature*.[57] Palamedes sets Hume up by describing the morals of the strange country of Fourli, which are "diametrically opposite ours"— among them the elevation of male homosexuality to the highest measure of manly virtue and the practice of infanticide.[58]

Of course, this strange country turns out to be ancient Athens—with a bit of ancient Rome thrown in for good measure—which, we think, despite these and other alien peculiarities of their morals, to be the crown jewels of ancient civilizations and the secular wellsprings of modern Western civilization. Palamedes generalizes and concludes his argument as follows: "What wide difference, therefore, in the sentiments of morals, must be found between civilized nations and Barbarians, or between nations whose characters have little in common. How shall we pretend to fix a standard for judgments of this nature?"[59] This is Hume's rejoinder:

> By tracing matters, replied I, a little higher, and examining the first principles, which each nation establishes, of blame or censure. The Rhine flows north, the Rhone south; yet both spring from the *same* mountain, and are also actuated, in their opposite directions, by the *same* principle of gravity. The different inclinations of the ground, on which they run, cause all the difference in their courses....Very well, I am willing to comply with you; and shall endeavor to account for these [moral] differences [between the ancient Athenian/Roman and the modern English societies] from the most universal, established principles of morals.[60]

Hume's account of the Athenian practice of infanticide is typical: "Had you asked a parent at Athens, why he bereaved his child of that life, which he had so lately given it, It is because I love it, he would reply; and regard the poverty which it must inherit from me, as a greater evil than death, which it is not capable of dreading, feeling, or resenting."[61] Hume attributes the wide cultural variation in ethics to differently reasoning out conclusions about what is right and wrong in accordance with the humanly universal moral sentiments and sense; to different cultural and political circumstances, such as that between republican and monarchical forms of government; and to chance—that is, to what we might think of as initially small differences magnified over time by memetic drift. Pinker provides a similar account for something so foreign and so diametrically opposed to contemporary Western ethics as honor killings in some Middle Eastern countries: violence in response to offenses against honor are typical of cultures with a herding heritage in which property (in the form of livestock and women) is easily stolen and legal recourse is unavailable. Honor killing may persist long after industrialization has replaced pastoralism as a culture's economy, due to memetic inertia.[62]

Hume's understanding of the workings of the moral sense, however, differs from that of contemporary exponents of a science of ethics. The latter focus on a subtle deep moral grammar so basic as to be inaccessible to its "speakers" by means of reflection or introspection. Hume regards the discrimination between virtue and vice to be a universal human capacity well understood, well articulated, and well theorized by the ancient moral philosophers. Continuing his reply to Palamedes, Hume says, "Good sense, knowledge, wit, eloquence, humanity, fidelity, truth, justice, courage, temperance, constancy, dignity of mind. These [universally approved virtues] you have all omitted; in order to insist only on the points in which they may by accident differ."[63]

5.11 POST-POSITIVIST ETHICAL ABSOLUTISM

After Logical Positivism, the science of ethics has remained the domain of the social and biological sciences, now combined as evolutionary moral psychology. Moral philosophers, however, did not altogether give up the hope of discovering absolute moral truths. After Positivism, philosophers were convinced that statements describing what people do in fact *assert* or what their actions and judgments indicate that they *believe* to be right and wrong, permissible and impermissible, good and bad, could be empirically true or false and thus meaningful. And the job of formulating hypotheses about what people do in fact assert or what their actions and judgments indicate that they believe to be right and wrong, permissible and impermissible, good and bad, and testing them empirically was the job of developmental psychologists, later sociobiologists, and now evolutionary moral psychologists. But—as the foregoing discussion of this chapter amply indicates—many philosophers still insist that regardless of what people assert or what they apparently believe, the question of what really and truly is right and wrong, permissible and impermissible, good and bad remains open. The Athenian father imagined by Hume may act on the assumption that infanticide is permissible and defend its permissibility if challenged in the way Hume indicates he might, but is it really and truly permissible? We may adamantly insist that it is impermissible for an emergency room surgeon to mine the organs of a healthy living orderly to save five critically injured accident victims, but is it really and truly impermissible?

A.J. Ayer himself implicitly embraced both a radical (or individualistic) and cultural relativism: "All that one can legitimately inquire in this connection is, What are the moral habits of a *given person* or *group of people*, and what causes them to have precisely those habits and feelings? And this inquiry falls wholly within the scope of the existing social [and biological] sciences."[64] The moral habits of a serial killer and of a society that practices "female circumcision" and approves of "honor killing" women who are unfortunate enough to be raped are describable and explainable by the methods of the existing social and biological sciences. But, according to Ayer, both the values of individual serial killers and genital-mutilating, honor-killing cultures are beyond the pale of meaningful criticism: "It is plain that the conclusion that it is impossible to dispute about questions of value follows from our theory also."[65] Hume and evolutionary psychologists disagree. They posit the existence of a universally human moral sense—*relative to which* serial killing is certainly wrong and bad and genital mutilation and honor killing of female family members who may be willingly or even unwillingly sexually active outside of marriage are arguably wrong and bad.

That, however, does not satisfy the age-old philosophical thirst for absolute moral truth—a moral truth relative to nothing, including a universally human moral sense. And it is just here that the Is/Ought dichotomy is routinely invoked by heavy-handed moral philosophers. The human moral sense may, for example, be inveterately partial, as contemporary moral science seems to confirm. Suppose that is the case? But is judicious and limited partiality really, truly right? We can still fairly ask, Ought we to be probatively and circumspectly partial or unwaveringly and absolutely impartial? For, from what *is* the case, we cannot deduce what *ought* to be the case, as Hume is supposed to have pointed out, once and for all, in the eighteenth century. But how can we discover what is really, truly right and good under the severe aegis of Logical Positivism?

As noted in 4.6, Positivism allowed two species of meaningful statements: statements of fact that could be empirically verified or falsified; and analytic statements, such as those of logic and mathematics, that were true or false by virtue of the meaning of their terms. If the *truth* of moral discourse cannot be verified and falsified empirically, by appeal to objective moral facts, then perhaps it can be by appeal to the other meaningful species of discourse allowed by Positivism, the analytic statements of logic and mathematics. This historically Kantian gambit is exemplified by Singer and Rachels in the late twentieth century; true morality is derived from the logical law of non-contradiction. The law of non-contradiction requires that we give equal weight to equal interests, according to Singer; and thus judicious and limited partiality, however deeply imbued in human nature, is wrong, absolutely wrong. Rachels provides an even clearer appeal to logic: "If we think it is wrong to treat a human in a certain way, because the human has certain characteristics, and a particular non-human animal also has those characteristics, then *consistency* requires that we also object to treating the non-human in that way."[66] And thus we ought never to be partial—to family and neighbors over distant strangers, to humans over other sentient animals—however judicious and limited our partiality may be.

5.12 WHEREFORE POST-POSITIVIST ETHICAL RATIONALISM AND EXCLUSIONISM?

Perhaps now it should be clear why, in neo-Scholastic Anglo-American moral philosophy, the very conception of ethics has been narrowed to an essentially Kantian modality. Logical Positivism precluded the possibility of *empirical* moral certainty. The only alternative that Positivism left open was analytic moral certainty—that is, logico-mathematical moral certainty. And the prototype of logic-based moral certainty is Kant's ethics. This exceedingly narrow conception of ethics is even taken for granted in the work of Sober and Wilson. Indeed, they go so far as to endorse an essentially Kantian *science* of ethics: "Moral principles," they write, "like all principles, properly so called, are *general.*...In this respect, *moral principles formally resemble scientific laws of nature.*"[67] Sober and Wilson do not go so far as to label general moral principles "the laws of freedom," as Kant does, but they implicitly follow Kant to the letter in stating that "Moral principles, if they are general in just the way described, conform to an abstract universality criterion."[68] Then, in exactly the same vein as Singer and Rachels (severally), Sober and Wilson (collectively) claim that moral principles "entail [*entail!*] that if it is right for one individual to perform an action in a given circumstance, then it is right for anyone else who is relevantly similar to perform the same action in the same circumstance....Moral principles involve a kind of impersonal [impartial] assessment that differs from the personal [partial] perspective that frequently accompanies our emotions and desires."[69]

These remarks come in a section titled "Altruism and Morality." The mantra of neo-Scholastic Anglo-American philosophy might well be, *There is no ethics except the rational ethics of universality and impartiality and Kant is its prophet.* There is no such thing as Humean ethics because Hume's "ethics" is based on "emotions and desires," which have nothing to do with morality. There is no such thing as Aristotelian "ethics" because Aristotle thought that it was a mark of virtue to treat different people in similar circumstances differently depending on one's relationship with them. Basically, mainstream twentieth-century moral philosophers have simply stipulated that the terms "ethics" and "morality" be limited in their application to a logic-based system of universal, impartial principles. Any other conception of ethics found in non-Western traditions of thought, in the history of Western philosophy, in other contemporary schools of Western philosophy, such as environmental philosophy and feminist philosophy, or in contemporary evolutionary moral psychology are not conceptions of *ethics* at all.

5.13 MORAL NORMS IN HUMEAN ETHICS ANALOGOUS TO MEDICAL NORMS

As already noted (5.1 and 5.2), however, the conclusions of a logic-based ethics, followed out quite rigorously and unflinchingly by Singer and Rachels, are so inhuman and impracticable as to be idiotic. The Is/Ought dichotomy was roundly discussed and obviated 3.1–3.5. But an ancillary problem still remains: How can an inductive, descriptive science of ethics, in the manner of Hume's, also be prescriptive? To be *ethics*, ethics must be normative, prescriptive. If moral philosophy in the tradition of Hume cannot underwrite prescriptive norms, then we must concede that neo-Scholastic Anglo-American philosophers have a point. A Humean science of ethics can never be demonstrative in the manner of Hobbes's science of ethics, modeled on geometry. It can never be normative in the manner of Kant's science of ethics, modeled on logic. But it can be prescriptive and normative in the manner of medicine.

In medical discourse, the statement, "A human body temperature of 98.6^0 is normal," at once states a physiological fact about human nature and makes a normative claim. A healthy human body does in fact maintain a temperature of 98.6°; and a human body indeed ought to maintain a temperature of 98.6°; and when it departs from that norm, corrective medical intervention is mandated. Moral science—as presently understood, in the manner of Hume and Darwin—is not medical science, but moral science is analogous to medical science. There are anatomical and physiological facts about human nature, which become *medical norms*; and there are socio-psychological facts about human nature that become *moral norms*. It is not morally wrong to be medically abnormal. It is not morally wrong, for example, due to a genetic defect, to be born with a crooked spine or a withered limb. Nor is it morally wrong to be genetically normal but to be sick and running a fever, due to an environmental cause such as a pathogen like *Plasmodium malariae*. But if, due to a genetic defect, someone lacks a normally human moral sense or normally human other-regarding feelings, or has had that sense corrupted or those feeling extinguished by a psychological trauma or a bad education, then we are right to morally judge that person to be ethically disabled. And, as in medical science, wherein deviation from anatomical and physiological norms mandates corrective *medical* intervention, so in moral science, deviation from socio-psychological moral norms also mandates corrective *moral* intervention.

The normative and prescriptive implications of contemporary evolutionary moral psychology—a science of ethics in the manner of Hume and Darwin—is most evident in the emotional-intelligence literature. Following Hume, Smith, and Darwin, Frans de Waal regards sympathy or empathy as the quintessential moral sentiment.[70] In contemporary evolutionary moral psychology, by the way, empathy is distinguished from sympathy. Sober and Wilson, for example, define *empathy* as "sharing the emotion of another," feeling their pain, as it were, even though the empathetic person has not been exposed to the stimulus of the pained person's pain, as when one whose child is well and safe grieves along with another parent whose child has died.[71] *Sympathy* is defined as feeling an emotion on behalf of someone else—say, feeling sorry for him or her—without feeling the same emotion as the displayer feels, as when one feels sorry for the demonstrably grief-stricken parent of a dead child without actually feeling any grief oneself. Lack of empathy is a hallmark of psychopaths. They exhibit "an unparalleled egoism, supported by a lack of empathy that most of us find foreign and frightening."[72] Pinker notes, however, that the word *empathy* entered the English language only as late as the first decade of the twentieth century, originally coined to express an aesthetic concept, different from, but not altogether unlike the aesthetic meaning of *sublime*. Later it took on "a new meaning, one that is closer to 'sympathy' or 'compassion.'"[73] Pinker himself finds that at least four distinct senses of *empathy* are currently ambient in English. The word *empathy*, it might be worth noting, was not available to Hume, Smith, and Darwin, and any distinction between *sympathy* and *empathy* drawn by twentieth-century and contemporary moral philosophers is largely stipulative.

Daniel Goleman, perfectly illustrating the analogy between medical norms and moral norms, notes that "This utter lack of empathy for their victims is one of the main focuses of new treatments being devised for child molesters and other such offenders."[74] In the case of child molesters and rapists, corrective medical intervention and corrective moral intervention are hardly distinguishable. On the other hand, "While there may be some small hope for instilling a sense of empathy in offenders such as child molesters, there is much less for another criminal type, the psychopath."[75] In which case, though Goleman doesn't say so, medical and moral intervention part company. We isolate incurable psychopaths, when we catch them, from the rest of society—nowadays either by imprisonment or execution. Nor do we hesitate to condemn their murderous behavior in the strongest ethical terms—as wrong, bad, evil, depraved, and heinous.

Precedent for an analogy between medical science and moral science comes from an unexpected source, Plato's *Republic*. In contrast to ancient social-contract theorists, such as Protagoras, who, anticipating Hobbes and now Rawls, thought that morals were an artificial imposition on egoistic human nature, Plato regarded human nature to be irreducibly social and morality (virtue) to be a natural condition of the soul. After establishing these facts, Socrates says, "Virtue, then, as it seems, would be a kind of health and beauty and good condition of the soul, and vice would be disease, ugliness, and weakness."[76] (Actually, Plato here collapses my medical-science/moral-science analogy into a metaphor.) Socrates next asks whether or not a person would prefer to live in accordance with virtue or its opposite, the fundamental question of the whole dialogue. And Glaucon replies,

> I think that from this point on our inquiry becomes an absurdity—if, while life is admittedly intolerable with a ruined constitution of body, even if accompanied by all the food and drink and wealth and power in the world, we are yet to suppose that, when the very nature and constitution of that whereby we live is disordered, life is going to be worth living, if a man can only do as he pleases, and pleases to do anything save that which will rid him of evil and injustice and make him possessed of justice and virtue—now that the two have been shown to be as we have described them.[77]

5.14 CRITICALLY APPRAISING MORAL NORMS IN TERMS OF INTRASOCIAL FUNCTIONALITY AND INTERSOCIAL HARMONY

But what actions and patterns of behavior are virtuous? Plato thought he knew. So did Hume. Our latter-day cosmopolitanism, however, makes us keenly and often painfully aware that different groups of people, different societies, different cultures often have very different views about what is right and wrong, permissible and impermissible, good and bad. How do we adjudicate among them? We can hardly argue that whole groups who espouse what we would regard as abnormal values are composed of abnormal individuals, whole societies of psychopaths. In 2.9, I suggested employing a hierarchically organized criterion of social functionality—confirmed in this chapter by this review of the current state-of-the-art of the science of ethics—to distinguish right from wrong, permissible from impermissible, good from bad. Ethics exist to maintain the integrity of groups; they evolved to hold human societies together, as Darwin first observed, and as the work of Sober and Wilson, Haidt, Bowles and Gintis, Boehm, and many other evolutionary moral psychologists now confirms. Thus, one reason that conceptions of virtue differ from one group to another is that human societies have radiated out into many different forms (hunting-gathering, pastoral, horticultural, agricultural, industrial) adapted to many different natural environments and ecosystems (tropical rainforests, temperate savannahs, steppes, deserts, arctic tundras). The values and virtues fostering these different kinds of societies, adapted to different environments, differ from society to society, within the constraints of universal human nature. Thus, some fairly wide degree of cultural relativism is consistent with the current state-of-the-art of the science of ethics. On the other hand, cultural notions and practices are subject to the memetic analogs of genetic drift and inbreeding depression, which can lead to social morbidity. And so "the moral habits," as Ayer calls them of different groups *are* liable to criticism; we can, pace Ayer, meaningfully "dispute about questions of value" even though various "groups of people"—various cultures—espouse mutually opposed values. We can meaningfully and conclusively dispute about questions of value in two ways.

First, we can ask if a society's values, its conceptions of virtue and vice, its moral notions and habits are functional or dysfunctional, adaptive or maladaptive. Do they serve the purpose for which ethics evolved—to hold the group together and to enable its members to pursue life's struggle collectively and cooperatively, thus to flourish and to prosper? If the answer is No, then the ethical system in question should be replaced by one that better serves the primary evolved function of ethics.

Second, if the answer is Yes, or even Maybe, we can ask further if a society's values, its conceptions of virtue and vice, its moral notions and habits, while functioning well enough to foster and sustain that society, tolerably fit into the hierarchically ordered congeries of societies that make up the global village. Here, by way of clarification, I can borrow a bit from Kant's conception of a "Kingdom of Ends." According to Kant, each autonomous rational being is not only subject to the universal laws flowing from its rational (logical) essence, each autonomous rational being is the legislator of those laws. Hence, Kant argues, the laws generated by each individual legislator must be harmonized or made mutually compatible in an idealized Kingdom of Ends. Various human groups, according to the current state-of-the-art of the science of ethics, not various individuals, generate systems of ethics. Whereas formerly such groups may have existed in relative isolation and have interacted competitively, now they are inextricably interdigitated by a network of communication and transportation technologies. If a society's values, its conceptions of virtue and vice, its moral notions and habits are jarringly dissonant with others—not in the Kantian Kingdom of Ends, but in the Darwinian Global Consortium of Societies—then its ethical system should be replaced by one that is. Furthermore, contemporary mid-scaled human societies or communities are not only parts of larger societies—regional super-nations like the European Union, the global village, and the biotic community—they are composed of smaller societies, among them, extended families. Their systems of ethics must tolerably harmonize with those of their components as well.

Here are two examples of disharmony, one in respect to the larger global village, the other in respect to the smaller extended—nay, rather, the nuclear—family. As more extensively argued in 2.15, the "virtue" and "moral habit" of female circumcision is not in harmony with the human-rights ethic of the global village.[78] Thus one can legitimately criticize it and work to rid the world of that practice. Similarly the "virtue" and "moral habit" of honor killings—in which the father or brother of a girl merely suspected of sexual impropriety is obliged to kill her to preserve their own and their family's honor—abrogates the very parental and filial affections that (according to Darwin, followed by Sober and Wilson and, latterly, by Boehm) are the affective material on which natural selection worked ultimately to evolve ethics.[79] As female circumcision is a violation of the global village's ethic of universal human rights, honor killings are an affront, one might well say, to family flourishing and the inclusive fitness of its members.

5.15 A HUMEAN-DARWINIAN SCIENCE OF ETHICS AND CONSTRAINED CULTURAL RELATIVISM

So, to conclude this chapter, an inductive and descriptive science of human ethics, in the manner of Hume and Darwin, can also be normative and prescriptive, just as an inductive and descriptive science of human medicine is also normative and prescriptive. Hence, radical relativism—the dogma of Logical Positivism that the perverse values of psychologically abnormal human individuals are beyond the pale of criticism or dispute—is not the price one pays for accepting an inductive and descriptive science of ethics as the only possible science of ethics. An inductive and descriptive science of ethics does, however, justify what might be called a constrained cultural relativism. The biologically underdetermined universal human moral sense or deep moral grammar can take as many protean expressions as the universal human deep linguistic grammar may take.

Despite the great diversity of human languages, all are nevertheless constrained by the universal human deep linguistic grammar, if Chomsky's and Pinker's science of linguistics is generally correct. Similarly, the many and culturally diverse systems of human ethics are constrained by the universal human deep moral grammar, by the general contours of the universal human moral sense, if Hume's and Haidt's science of ethics is generally correct. Further, because ethics were naturally selected since they foster and sustain the integrity and functionality of the societies of which they are the ethics, then they may be fairly criticized and replaced if they fail to do so tolerably well. Further still, culture-scaled systems of ethics may be fairly criticized and replaced if they do not tolerably harmonize with the systems of ethics of the societies or communities that both compose them and are composed by them, most especially if they do not tolerably harmonize with both family values and the human-rights ethic of the global village.

5.16 THE PHILOSOPHICAL FOUNDATIONS OF THE LAND ETHIC VINDICATED BY THE CONTEMPORARY SCIENCE OF ETHICS, BUT LIMITED TO ECOLOGICAL SPATIAL AND TEMPORAL SCALES

Because the Leopold land ethic is based on a conception of ethics in the scientific vein of Hume and Darwin, and because the general science of ethics sketched by Hume and Darwin has been fully vindicated by state-of-the-art twenty-first-century evolutionary biology and evolutionary moral psychology, the philosophical and evolutionary foundations of the Leopold land ethic, far from being undermined by subsequent developments in that tradition of the science of ethics, have only been reinforced by those developments.

The land ethic, however, is ecologically scaled, both temporally and spatially. That is, it directs the holistic human (Humean) moral sentiments that we feel for our hierarchically nested human communities toward our hierarchically nested biotic communities and associated ecosystems. In *A Sand County Almanac*, Leopold asks us to think like a mountain (detailed and documented in 1.10). A mountain is a big, old thing, but what does it think? This, according to Leopold: "I now suspect that just as a deer lives in mortal fear of its wolves, so does a mountain live in mortal fear of its deer. And perhaps with better cause, for while a buck pulled down by wolves can be replaced in two or three years, a range pulled down by too many deer may fail of replacement in as many decades." The land ethic is spatially scaled to biotic communities and ecosystems. Relative to us, a mountain is big and so is its associated montane biotic community, but any given mountain and indeed any given mountain range and associated biotic communities cover only a minuscule fraction of the Earth's surface. Relative to the whole Earth, a mountain, or even a mountain range, is small. And, relative to us, mountains are old, but relative to the biography of the whole Earth they are ephemeral. And their thinking is temporally scaled in decades, if this remark by Leopold is any indication. Here in the first quarter of the twenty-first century our most pressing environmental concern is *global* climate change, the full effects of which may not be visited on us for another quarter century or more and a full recovery from its untoward environmental effects may not be possible before many centuries pass, perhaps not before several millennia pass. We must therefore now think ethically on a much larger temporal scale than Leopold thinks that mountains think—we must think like a planet.

The land ethic, in short, is inappropriately scaled to meet the challenge posed by global climate change. The summary moral maxim of the original land ethic— "A thing is right when it tends to preserve the integrity, stability, and beauty of the *biotic community*. It is wrong when it tends otherwise"—ignores the major objects of contemporary concern, the *global* atmosphere and the *global* ocean. In Leopold's day, these objects seemed as far beyond the reach of significant human impact as is the moon. Leopold was indeed a prophet, but he did not foresee that a human would walk on the moon and leave a bit of earthly litter on it two decades after he penned "The Land Ethic" or that half a century afterward anthropogenic global warming would be a looming reality, accompanied by rising sea levels and an altered chemistry of the atmosphere and hydrosphere. The revised summary moral maxim for the land ethic that I recommend at the end of Chapter 3—"A thing is right when it tends to preserve the beauty of the *biotic community* and to disturb it only at normal spatial and temporal scales; it is wrong when it tends otherwise"—in light of the paradigm shift that occurred in ecology after Leopold's death in 1948, seems no more adequate than the original to address the anthropogenic changes now befalling the *global* atmosphere and *global* ocean and for the same reason.

5.17 LOOKING FORWARD TO THE LEOPOLD EARTH ETHIC

Fortunately, Leopold left us at least a point of departure for constructing an environmental ethic that is globally scaled spatially and millennially scaled temporally—an Earth ethic—to complement the land ethic. Don't get me wrong; we still need a land ethic as badly as ever to provide us the ethical wherewithal to morally criticize and dispute everything from overgrazed, eroding mountains in the US southwest to clear-cut rainforests in the Neotropics to the ravages of invasive species practically everywhere. But the land ethic is only derivatively or indirectly relevant to the anthropogenic increase of carbon dioxide in the global atmosphere and the effects that that will have on the global ocean.

In other words, to the extent that global climate change will have an adverse effect on biotic communities and their members and the health of ecosystems—and it certainly will—then the human actions causing global climate change are land-ethically wrong. But to argue that therefore the land ethic is perfectly capable of providing the ethical wherewithal to criticize and dispute the human values and the actions they motivate that are causing global climate change is analogous to the argument of moral anthropocentrists that we do not need a land ethic. Harm to the integrity, stability, and beauty of biotic communities almost always entails harm to humans—so we don't need a new-fangled non-anthropocentric land ethic; our old human-centered ethics will do, thank you very much. I shall thus only conclude that if we do in fact need a land ethic—and I made the case that we do in 2.17—then we also need an Earth ethic for precisely analogous reasons. Morally anthropocentric concern about the adverse effect of human actions on biotic communities and their members and the health of ecosystems—say, concern for the impairment or loss of ecosystem services and aesthetic gratification—complements morally non-anthropocentric land-ethical concern for biotic communities and their members and the health of ecosystems. Anthropocentric environmental ethics and the non-anthropocentric land ethic are mutually reinforcing, not mutually canceling. In like manner, morally non-anthropocentric land-ethical concern about global climate change complements Earth-ethical concern about global climate change. The land ethic is fully engaged with and applicable to the moral challenge of global climate change, but that moral challenge brings forth new concerns for which the land ethic has no conceptual resources. Collective human activities seem to be threatening to alter the Earth itself and the very biosphere at scales that exceed those to which the land ethic is geared.

Part Two is devoted to an exposition of the Leopold Earth Ethic and the exposition of the Earth ethic in Part Two parallels the exposition of the land ethic in Part One. In Chapter 6, I provide a close reading, analysis, and interpretation of the relevant parts of the posthumously published essay "Some Fundamentals of Conservation in the Southwest," in which Aldo Leopold broached the possibility of an Earth ethic and hinted at its philosophical and scientific foundations. Chapter 6 thus mirrors Chapter 2, in which I provide a close reading, analysis, and interpretation of the relevant parts of "The Land Ethic." And just as I elaborate the philosophical and scientific foundations of the Leopold land ethic and trace and evaluate their subsequent developments in the form of ecosystem ecology, neo-Darwinian evolutionary theory, sociobiology, and evolutionary moral psychology in Chapters 3–5, so in the several chapters following Chapter 6, I elaborate and trace the subsequent development of the philosophical and scientific foundations of the Leopold Earth ethic in the form of biogeochemistry, the Gaia hypothesis, and Earth systems science. It is one thing for the land ethic and the Earth ethic to be complementary; it is quite another and much better thing if they may be erected on the same philosophical foundations. In Chapters 8 and 9, I explore the various philosophical foundations—virtue ethics, consequentialism, deontology—at which Leopold hints in "Some Fundamentals." In Chapter 10,

I criticize the shopworn conventional philosophical foundations of "climate ethics" in contemporary mainstream moral philosophy. In the eleventh and final chapter of this book, I argue that to base a metaphysically non-anthropocentric but morally anthropocentric Earth ethic on the same philosophical foundations as the land ethic, reaching back through Darwin to Hume, turns out to be the only philosophical foundations that give us any hope of adequately addressing the spatial and temporal scales of moral concern regarding global climate change. Thus the land ethic and the Earth ethic, while differently scaled and informed by different natural sciences, turn out to rest on the same philosophical foundations. They therefore represent not only complementary environmental ethics, but also ethical branches diverging from the same conceptual root system.

Part Two
The Earth Ethic

6

The Earth Ethic: A Critical Account of
Its Philosophical Foundations

In "Some Fundamentals of Conservation in the Southwest," Aldo Leopold made his first sustained sortie into ethical territory. He begins the essay with a list of five kinds of economic resources existing in the region: mineral, organic, climatic, historic, and geographic. Leopold immediately confines his discussion to the first two; and of those, he devotes but one paragraph to the mineral and concentrates almost exclusively on the organic resources. Still more focused, his overriding concern is with soil, as a foundational organic resource, and its alarming rate of erosion. He concludes the first section of the essay as follows: "[T]he deterioration of our fundamental resources—land and water—is in the nature of permanent destruction, and the process is cumulative and gaining momentum every year."[1]

Part of the deterioration of water resources is proximately caused by the deterioration of land resources, because eroded soil winds up, year in and year out, as silt in reservoirs, shortening their life span. But Leopold believes that the ultimate cause of the deterioration of both land and water resources is overgrazing. Living plant roots anchor the soil of stream banks. Cattle denude stream banks of their vegetation and loosen the soil with their hooves, thus making stream banks vulnerable to widening by the scouring action of sand and rocks washed off the increasingly grassless uplands that cattle also graze. And without grass to slow runoff and allow rainwater to percolate into the soil, wherethrough it flows into the streams more slowly and steadily, the streams become "flashy," surging after a storm and drying up a short while later—rather than, as formerly, running narrow, deep, clear, and 24-7-52. Further, without grass to carry ground fires, woody brush establishes itself, tipping the xeric biome from one domain of ecological attraction to another.[2]

The second and longest section of "Some Fundamentals," titled "Erosion and Aridity," is devoted to a fuller argument that overgrazing—and not regional climate change—is responsible for the "intricate" ecological changes that spelled ruin for the land and water resources of the Southwest. Leopold's main reason for discounting climate change as the culprit in flipping the ecosystem from grass to brush is based on temporal scale—while weather varies on annual to decadal periodicities, climate change occurs on decadal and centennial periodicities. The dramatic ecological transmogrification of the Southwest occurred over only a forty-year period. While there were significant climate shifts in the past—most recently the "Great Drought" of the thirteenth century, which led to the collapse of the Anasazi civilization—no such climate change was indicated by weather records and tree-ring analysis between 1880 and 1920.[3]

In "Some Fundamentals," Leopold adumbrates several concepts that figure large in this book. Two of them, the concepts of ecological equilibria and disturbance regimes (here a drought cycle), figure large in 3.12 and 3.16. Two more, the concept of temporal scale (and the boundaries between temporal scales) and, of course, the concept of climate change, figure large in subsequent chapters. In this chapter, I critically examine and interpret the third section of the essay, titled "Conservation as a Moral Issue." And, in the course of that interpretation, I engage in a polemic with Bryan G. Norton—a fellow philosopher and self-styled "environmental pragmatist"—who has interpreted that text very differently. Which of our radically differing interpretations is the more plausible will turn on a feature of Leopold's style—his frequent use of irony to drive home a point (see also 1.15). Thus, I here also devote some discussion to the rhetorical function of irony in general, as well as to Leopold's particular use of it.

6.1 LEOPOLD AND BIBLICAL TROPES

Exactly ten years after writing "Some Fundamentals," Leopold will turn to a classic text, the *Odyssey*, to launch his second sustained sortie, "The Conservation Ethic," into the terra incognita of environmental ethics (and he will incorporate the Odysseus vignette of "The Conservation Ethic" into his third sustained venture into the domain of ethics, "The Land Ethic," as noted in 2.4). In "Some Fundamentals," Leopold launches his first-ever systematic discussion of the "moral aspects" of conservation by way of reference to another classic text, the Bible, more particularly the Book of Ezekiel (34:18): "Seemeth it a small thing unto you to have fed upon [eaten up] good pasture, but ye must tread down the residue of your pasture[s]. And to have drunk of the clear [deep] waters, but ye must foul the residue with your feet."[4] (The material in brackets indicates the words of the more familiar King James Version.)[5]

During this period of his life, Leopold was giving extensive study to the Bible (detailed and documented in 1.15)—apparently, however, this was by no means devotional study, but study more of the Bible as literature, one of the West's great books.[6] In "The Forestry of the Prophets," he attests to "the intensely interesting reading on a multitude of subjects to be found in the Old Testament."[7] In that article, a playful, irreverent piece, published in the *Journal of Forestry* three years before he wrote "Some Fundamentals," Leopold critically compared and evaluated the knowledge evinced by various Old Testament writers about trees, woods, and forests. In addition to their forestry lore, Leopold indicates that he paid close attention to the stylistic techniques of the Bible's authors, noting, for example, "the frequency with which they use similes based on forest phenomena" and how "impersonization [*sic*; i.e., personification] of trees is characteristic of Biblical writers."[8] Further, he praises "Jesus the son of Sirach" as "a master of the epigram."[9] Indeed, the lasting influence of the Bible on Leopold appears to be literary, not doctrinal. One key to understanding the remarkable impact of his prose is its subtly biblical phrasing and use of biblical tropes and literary devices, as John Tallmadge has convincingly argued (documented and detailed in 1.15).[10] Leopold's experimentation with a biblical style occurs, as a matter of fact, in the climactic concluding paragraph of the second section of "Some Fundamentals": "Erosion eats into our hills like a contagion, and floods bring down the loosened soil like a scourge."[11]

Leopold finds "[i]n these two sentences" of Ezekiel "an epitome of the moral question involved." Indeed, the quotation from Ezekiel is perfectly selected to address morally the central themes of the foregoing discussion: the despoliation of soil, by overgrazing, and of waters, ultimately due to the same cause. Because Leopold was acutely sensitive to the way biblical writers use similes and similar literary tropes, he must have realized that the material he quotes from Ezekiel is entirely metaphorical. The "Shepherds of Israel" (34:2) that Ezekiel is taking to task are shepherds of the people—their errant, exploitative, exclusively self-interested leaders, whom Ezekiel (34:23) prophesizes will be succeeded by David, "and he shall be their shepherd." Leopold chooses, nevertheless, to quote the passage out of its metaphorical context, as if Ezekiel were making a case for ecological conservation rather than for political reform. At any rate, there follow three possible foundations on which to build an Earth ethic, all different and mutually inconsistent theoretically.

6.2 EZEKIEL AND VIRTUE ETHICS–BOTH INDIVIDUALISTC AND HOLISTIC

The first is a kind of three-pronged version of virtue ethics: "Ezekiel seems to scorn waste, pollution, and unnecessary damage as something unworthy—as something damaging not only to the reputation of the waster, but to the self-respect of the craft and the society of which he is a member."[12] Virtue ethics is all about character, reputation, and *self*-respect. It is "agent-based" rather than patient-based.[13] A virtuous person chooses to be just, for example, primarily to exemplify excellence of character and only secondarily to give fair consideration to the interests of others. A virtuous person also chooses to be just primarily to earn his or her own *self*-respect and only secondarily the respect of others. Nor should self-*respect* be confused with self-*interest*—as usually (and narrowly) understood—with which it is often in conflict.

One prong of Leopold's three-pronged virtue ethics is the environmental virtue (or lack thereof) on the part of individuals—personally and severally—that is, on the part of the "waster."

A second prong—less personally, more abstractly—is the self-respect of the craft, of pasture management per se, in this case. Presently, this is a nearly forgotten kind of virtue. The individual waster represents a guild, a profession, and casts aspersions on it, as such, when performing in a way that exhibits poor workmanship. I remember once being impatient with an old truck mechanic whom I tasked with retrofitting seat belts on an antique vehicle and asked him to achieve the practical end I envisioned in a way that he regarded as improper and inelegant. He was insulted and replied that he had no intention of "jerry-rigging it" to save time and labor. That would not only violate his own integrity as a craftsman but would also sully the spirit of the mechanic's trade. The Leopold family business was a desk-making company and the company motto was "Built on Honor to Endure."[14] So Aldo well knew firsthand the pride of craftsmanship and the kind of virtue associated with it.

A third prong—even less individually and more holistically—is the way the despoliation of lands and waters reflects badly on the society, collectively, that tolerates it.

Here we see an early example of the ethical holism (fully discussed in 2.13–2.15), which is so evident in "The Land Ethic." An individual person who presumes to own other persons—a slave owner, in short—is reprehensible. A society that condones slavery is also reprehensible—not aggregatively, as a sum of more or less reprehensible individuals, but corporately as a second-order entity with an emergent character of its own (see Figure 6.1). (I provide a more extensive discussion of virtue ethics as a possible theoretical support for an Earth ethic in 9.10–9.17.)

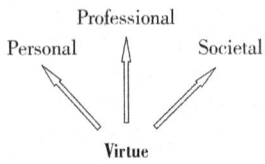

Figure 6.1 Leopold's three-pronged version of virtue ethics.

6.3 EZEKIEL AND RESPONSIBILITY TO FUTURE GENERATIONS

The second possible rationale for an Earth ethic that Leopold broaches in "Conservation as a Moral Issue" of "Some Fundamentals of Conservation in the Southwest" is responsibility to future generations: "We might even draw from his [Ezekiel's] words a broader concept—that the privilege of possessing the earth entails the responsibility of passing it on, the better for our use, not only to immediate posterity, but to the Unknown Future, the nature of which is not given to us to know."[15]

Why does Leopold characterize responsibility to future generations as "a broader concept?" One cannot say for sure what he meant, but the context suggests an interpretation. The foregoing order of presentation—personal virtue, professional virtue, and societal virtue—form a kind of progressive series of inclusion. The individual land user is a member of a guild or trade—farmer, rancher, forester—and the guild or trade is one element of a political economy, a society. Responsibility to future generations is even more inclusive because it embraces not just the current society, but the persons, professions, and societies that will succeed our own—hence, it is "a broader concept."

Note too that there is a shift from a noble self-regard, characteristic of virtue ethics, to *responsibility to* future *others* and to future societies. Note further that Leopold expressly introduces a temporal-scale parameter into the way we might conceive of the future, distinguishing between "immediate posterity" and an apparently indefinite, deep future time. And he seems confident that a sense of moral responsibility can actually extend to the "Unknown Future." While responsibility to immediate posterity might be individualistic—to sons, daughters, grandchildren, and so on severally—responsibility to distant future generations would necessarily be holistic, precisely because the individuals composing those generations are presently "unknown" and also arguably *indeterminate*. I provide a more extensive discussion of responsibility to future generations in 10.10 and 11.4–11.5 (see Figure 6.2).

Personal Virtue (Individualistic)	<	Professional Virtue (Abstract)	<	Societal Virtue (Holistic)	<	Responsibility to Immediate Posterity (Individualistic)	<	Responsibility to the Unknown Future (Holistic)	<	Respect for the Earth (Holistic and Non-anthropocentric)

Figure 6.2 Leopold's series of "broader [ethical] concepts."

6.4 EZEKIEL AND DEONTOLOGICAL RESPECT FOR THE EARTH AS A LIVING THING

The third possible foundation for an Earth ethic that Leopold broaches in "Conservation as a Moral Issue" of "Some Fundamentals" is not only broader still, and not only holistic, it is also non-anthropocentric: "It is possible that Ezekiel respected the soil, not only as a craftsman respects his material, but as a moral being respects a living thing."[16] Here again we see a shift in the operative ethical modality: first Leopold moves from a virtue-ethic modality—personal, professional, and societal *self-regard*—to responsibility to future *others* individually and collectively; then he moves from that essentially consequentialist modality to *respect* for the "soil" as a living being, which immediately in the next paragraph becomes the "earth."

Responsibility is a concept more at home in the context of consequentialist ethics—because it implies a concern for the interests of others and how the consequences of an agent's actions affect those interests. Respect is a concept more at home in the context of deontological ethics—involving less the interests of others and how the consequences of an agent's actions bear on those interests, than regard for their dignity. We may have a responsibility to future generations even if we can have no respect for them—because we cannot know whether they are worthy of our respect. And we can have respect for the Earth, even if it has no interests that the consequences of our actions may impact.

Leopold broaches these three possible foundations for an Earth ethic all in one paragraph (Table 6.1). Of the remaining eleven paragraphs of the essay, all but the final two—which return to the virtue-ethic modality—are devoted to an elaboration of the third possible foundation of an Earth ethic: respect for the Earth as a living being. The first five of the remaining eleven paragraphs are devoted to considerations in favor of the proposition that the Earth itself is indeed a living being; the next four are devoted to the possibility of according *non-anthropocentric* "respect as such" for the living Earth.

Table 6.1 The Three Ethical Modalities That Leopold Broaches as Foundations of an Earth Ethic

Ethics Type	Characteristic Features
Virtue	Individual, professional, and societal self-respect
Consequentialist	Responsibility to future generations, individually, and holistically
Deontological	Respect for the Earth as a living being

6.5 LEOPOLD DIMLY ENVISIONS HIERARCHY
THEORY IN "SOME FUNDAMENTALS"

Leopold begins this relatively extensive excursion into a deontological, non-anthropocentric Earth ethic by claiming that "Many of the most penetrating minds…have felt intuitively" that the Earth is a "living thing."[17] Purportedly among them is "the Russian philosopher [P. D.] Ouspensky," whom Leopold both twice quotes and otherwise putatively paraphrases.[18] In modern times, especially under the influence of modern science, "the mechanistic conception of the earth" predominates.[19] The classic alternative is that of "an organized animate nature."[20] The difference between the two, according to Leopold (following, he thinks, Ouspensky) is perspectival. As noted in 3.13, hierarchy theory resolves the perennial mereological-versus-holological and mechanistic-versus-organismic dichotomies in ecology. The downscale set of objects constitutes the mechanism for the upscale object of interest, which exhibits such organismic characteristics as functional, emergent, and systemic properties. Hierarchy theory was not articulated until the late twentieth century, nor in 1923 had Leopold's personal journey into the science of ecology gone nearly as far as it eventually would. Thus Leopold can only dimly envision a hierarchical resolution to the age-old tension between a mechanistic and an organismic conception of the Earth and struggle to find the right words to express it.

Despite these limitations—that formal hierarchy theory was half a century off in the future and that Leopold had not yet himself become deeply immersed in ecology—he expresses a scale-sensitive, hierarchical reconciliation of the modern mechanistic and the venerable organismic conceptions of the Earth quite effectively. He begins by quoting Ouspensky: "Were we to observe, from the inside, one cubic centimeter of the human body, knowing nothing of the existence of the entire body and of man himself, then the phenomena going on in this little cube of flesh would seem like elemental phenomena in inanimate nature."[21] Imagine yourself to be a microbially scaled scientist having been unknowingly injected into a living human being to study the phenomena you find going on there. It would all be, so far as you could tell, biochemistry. Nor would you believe that the "environment" in which you found yourself was a unified macro-scaled organism, despite the constant temperature and various patterns of fluid and electromagnetic dynamics that you observe and measure. Now, Leopold suggests, relative to the Earth, we are as microbially scaled scientists and all the phenomena we observe are either physical and chemical in nature; or, I might add, when biological, all the organisms we encounter are at the same scales as ourselves or even smaller. But,

> [i]f we could see this whole [the Earth], *as a whole, through a great period of time*, we might perceive not only organs with coordinated functions, but possibly also that process of consumption and replacement which in biology we call metabolism, or growth. In such a case we would have all the attributes of a living thing, which we do not now realize to be such because it is *too big*, and its life processes *too slow*.[22]

6.6 HOW LEOPOLD INTERPRETS P. D. OUSPENSKY AND HIS BOOK *TERTIUM ORGANUM*

Doubtless, all these reflections on temporal and spatial scale and hierarchical organization were *inspired* by Ouspensky, but Leopold too generously *attributes* them to "the Russian philosopher": "He [Ouspensky] then states," according to Leopold, "that it is at least not impossible to regard the earth's parts—soil, mountains, rivers, atmosphere, etc.—as organs, or parts of organs, of a coordinated whole, each part with a definite function."[23] But when we take a look at the book from which Leopold quotes, we find nothing like this that actually follows. Ouspensky goes on instead to discuss the difference between a stone and a snail (about which more in 6.8). Immediately *preceding* the passage that Leopold quotes, Ouspensky does write, "The degree of the activity of life can be determined from the standpoint of its power of reproducing itself. In inorganic, mineral nature, this activity is so insignificant that units of this nature accessible to our observation do not reproduce themselves, although it may only seem so to us because of the narrowness of our view in time and space. *Perhaps if that view embraced hundreds of thousands of years and our entire planet simultaneously*, we might then see the growth of minerals and metals."[24]

The italicized words may well have set Leopold to thinking about planetary temporal and spatial scale and hierarchy, but they only serve Ouspensky's narrow and jejune focus on the absence of observable growth (and reproduction) of minerals and metals. There is an irony in this regard: Ouspensky's fellow-Russian contemporary, Vladimir Vernadsky, who pioneered the science of biogeochemistry (the history of which is traced out in 7.2–7.6) began his scientific career as a mineralogist, specializing, more particularly, in crystallography; and crystals grow and, after a fashion, reproduce; and they do so in ways that are, in fact, "accessible to our observation."[25]

I mean to cast no aspersions on Leopold's scholarly integrity or intellectual taste. To the contrary, Leopold is making very good sense of Ouspensky's eclectic (ranging over everything from Riemannian geometry to Kantian transcendental philosophy to Theosophy) and undisciplined metaphysical blather—which Leopold was probably reading because it was then all the rage with the American intelligentsia. The title of Ouspensky's book, *Tertium Organum*, together with Leopold's references to it in "Some Fundamentals," might suggest—as in fact it first did to me—that *Tertium Organum* was all about a *third* order of biological *organization*: single-celled organisms eventually united into multi-celled organisms finally united into the whole Earth organism—similar to Clements's super-organism concept (detailed and documented in the Introduction and in 3.11–3.13). But that's not the sense to be made of the title (which, if I were as good a student of ancient Greek philosophy, the Latin language, and the history of science as I wish I were, I should have guessed). Rather, Ouspensky imagined himself to be creating a new kind of tool—in Greek, an οργανου—for discovering (esoteric) knowledge. First there was "The *Organon* of Aristotle, [then] the *Novum Organum* of Bacon and [now the] *Tertium Organum*" of Ouspensky.[26] The book as a whole is not at all about what Leopold made of it—which is something wonderful indeed—but rather positions itself as the epistemological successor to Bacon, just as Bacon positioned his epistemology as the successor to Aristotle's!

Pyotr Demianovich Ouspensky was born in 1878, nine years prior to Leopold's birth in 1887; he died in 1947, a year before Leopold's death in 1948; he earned no credentials as an academic philosopher; and, as a young man, he worked as a journalist.[27] *Tertium Organum* was published in Russia in 1912. The English translation was first published in 1920 by Manas Press in Rochester, New York. Apparently it was such a popular sensation that it was republished by Knopf in 1922, probably the edition Leopold read.[28] Surprisingly—to me, anyway—it remained sufficiently popular to warrant a new (and more readable) translation, which Ouspensky himself assisted, published in 1947, also by Knopf, and republished as recently as 1981. Shortly after the Russian edition of *Tertium Organum* came out, Ouspensky fell under the influence of Georges Ivanovich Gurdjieff (1866–1949), a Russian-speaking Greek-Armenian charlatan, whom Ouspensky served as an acolyte from 1915 to 1918.[29] Both left Russia after the Bolshevik revolution, Gurdjieff eventually settling in Paris and Ouspensky in London. Gurdjieff pioneered what eventually became the New-Age self-help industry—utilizing such disparate techniques as meditation, dance, work teams, and encounter groups—promising his followers that they would achieve a higher form of consciousness, enabling them to become super-human beings.[30] Ouspensky's authorized account of Gurdjieff's doctrines was published, posthumously, in 1949, by Routledge in London and Harcourt Brace in New York under the title *In Search of the Miraculous: Fragments of an Unknown Teaching*. That same year, *A Sand County Almanac and Sketches Here and There* was also published, posthumously.

In *Sand County*'s "Guacamaja," Leopold alludes to Ouspensky's pervasive distinction—ultimately derived of course from Kant—between noumena and phenomena: "A philosopher [Ouspensky] has called this imponderable essence the noumenon of material things.... The grouse is the noumenon of the north woods, the blue jay of the hickory groves, the whiskey-jack of the muskegs, the piñonero of the juniper foothills."[31] Here, however, is how Ouspensky introduces the distinction in *Tertium Organum*:

> *Noumenal* means apprehended by the mind; and the characteristic property of the things of the noumenal world is the fact that they cannot be comprehended by the same method as things of the phenomenal world are comprehended. We may speculate about the things of the noumenal world; we may discover them by a process of reasoning, and by means of analogy; we may feel them, and enter into some sort of communion with them; but we can neither see, hear, touch, weigh, measure them; nor can we photograph them or decompose them into chemical elements or number their vibrations.[32]

According to Kant, more severely, noumena cannot be comprehended by any means whatsoever. In any case, by Ouspensky's account, let alone Kant's, grouse, blue jays, whiskey-jacks, piñoneros, and thick-billed parrots are, one and all, things of the phenomenal world, comprehended by the same method—our five senses and taxonomical minds—as everything else in the north woods, the hickory groves, the muskegs, the juniper foothills, and the Sierra Madre. To his great credit and unfailing charm, Leopold stays grounded in the phenomenal world—the only real world, I might add—*despite* reading and admiring P. D. Ouspensky, whose amateur "philosophy" only serves to give philosophy a bad name, and who, for that reason, is not counted among our number by any of us credentialed philosophers (however much we may cavil, quarrel, and dispute with one another about what counts as philosophy and what does not).

A more generous and positive portrayal of Ouspensky's influence on Leopold is provided by Ashley Pryor.[33]

6.7 THE EARTH'S SOUL OR CONSCIOUSNESS

Leopold concludes this essentially scale-sensitive argument for a living whole Earth by taking a more speculative turn himself: "And there would also follow that invisible attribute—a soul or consciousness—which not only Ouspensky, but many philosophers of all ages, ascribe to all living things and aggregations thereof, including the 'dead' earth."[34] The Earth is either dead (that is, non-living) or living depending on the spatial and temporal scale in accordance with which it is observed. At local human spatial and temporal scales—at most, areas that we can see from horizon to horizon and times measured by comprehensible multiples of our own lifetimes—the earth is not living. At *geological* spatial and temporal scales, the earth exhibits organic attributes—characteristics of living beings: "a coordinated whole, each part with a definite function." At that scale—the planetary—the Earth may have a psyche. And indeed many philosophers of all ages have thought so—Leopold got that right. For example, Plato—the greatest of the ancient philosophers, arguably the greatest philosopher of all time—provides a detailed account of a world soul in the *Timaeus*.

Again, Leopold's reading of Ouspensky is too charitable. Leopold seems to be hewing to his own scalar-hierarchical analogy between downscaled organisms (plants and animals) and upscaled (putative) organisms—that is, our planet and perhaps others in the universe. Animal consciousness is an emergent phenomenon. Our own animal consciousness emerges from the dynamic neural processes of our brains, but individual neurons are not conscious, nor is the consciousness of the whole animal an aggregate of the several consciousnesses of our brain cells.[35] So Earth might be supposed to have a similar consciousness, emergent upon the dynamic processes internal to it—manifest, perhaps, in its surrounding polarized magnetic field. Ouspensky, on the other hand, appears to be more a panpsychist and idealist—if any coherent view at all can be discerned in his pontifications. "There can be nothing dead or mechanical in nature," he declares. "If, in general, life and feeling exist, they must exist in all. Life and rationality make up the world." [36] According to Ouspensky, we believe most things lack consciousness because such "'beings' whose psyche does not manifest itself to us in the three dimensional section of the world are inaccessible to us"—whatever that means. As Ouspensky then raves on, "A mountain, a tree, a river, the fish within the river, dew and rain, planet, fire—each separately must possess a psyche of its own."[37] The planet is included in this apparently random list of things with a psyche, but that's only because Ouspensky thinks that *everything* has one. Incidentally, the title of *Sand County*'s "Thinking Like a Mountain" may have also been inspired by Leopold's recollection of *Tertium Organum*, for there, Ouspensky cryptically writes, "Between the psyche of a mountain and the psyche of a man there must be the same difference as between a mountain and a man."[38] Ashley Prior, for one, argues that the title of Leopold's confessional, epiphanic wolf essay was inspired by Ouspensky's attribution of a psyche specifically to a mountain—among other things both animate and those usually regarded as inanimate.[39]

6.8 A SCALAR RESOLUTION OF A "DEAD" EARTH VERSUS THE EARTH AS A "LIVING BEING"

Leopold mentions Ouspensky in three consecutive paragraphs of "Conservation as a Moral Issue" in "Some Fundamentals of Conservation in the Southwest." He begins the third by repeating once again his own central insight that the difference between "this conception of a living earth, and the conception of a dead earth" is a matter of temporal and spatial scale and hierarchy.[40] From the downscale spatial and temporal perspective of physics, chemistry—and, I might add, organismic biology and ecology—the Earth *itself* is "dead" (an unfortunate word choice, for which Ouspensky is to blame); life may teem on the earth's surface, but the whole Earth, per se, does not seem to be alive. From the upscale temporal and spatial perspective of geoscience, the Earth might seem to be alive—and possibly conscious. Further, the downscale physical, chemical, and biological phenomena are appropriately regarded as the mechanisms for the upscale processes going on in the (putative) super super-organism—the Earth. So, as Leopold notes, "there is not much discrepancy, except in language, between" these two conceptions of the Earth.[41] That is, we have two universes of discourse—the reductive-mechanical and the holistic-organic—describing one thing, the Earth. And while they seem to produce inconsistent—if not contradictory—descriptions, there is in fact no discrepancy between them, as long as we specify the spatial and temporal scales to which either appropriately applies.

Leopold notes, however, a conception common to both types of description: "The essential thing for present purposes is that both admit the interdependent functions of the elements." Certainly in ecology, a downscale science, the elements—plants, animals, soils, and waters—are interdependent and may be seen to be functionally interrelated. And just as certainly the elements eventually to be studied by the upscale geosciences—the Earth's core and mantle, its continents, ocean, and atmosphere—are interdependent. Then Leopold exclaims, "'But anything indivisible is a living being,' says Ouspensky." Indeed he does.[42] To illustrate his point, Ouspensky notes that when we split a stone in two, we get two stones, but when we cut a snail in two we get one dead snail, not two snails. So apparently the reasoning is this: because snails are indivisible—in this sense—and they are alive, then anything indivisible is alive. But such reasoning is seriously flawed—for, obviously, there are many counterexamples. When we cut an automobile in two we do not get two automobiles, and automobiles are not alive (although Ouspensky may well have thought they were—I don't know). Ouspensky also thought that the cells of organisms, such as snails, were also indivisible—never mind that cell division (mitosis) is the means by which cells reproduce—and thus alive and (therefore) "must have a certain psychic life."[43]

Just as there are many counterexamples of indivisible things that are dead, so there are many other (than cells) counterexamples of living things that are divisible. For instance, if one takes a cutting from a shrub and roots it in water and then replants it in soil, the cutting goes on living and growing and reproducing on its own, as does the shrub from which the cutting was taken. Thus we have a living thing that is divisible: when we divide a shrub in this way, we get not one dead shrub, but two living shrubs. Clearly, Leopold would have been well advised to delete this quote and move on. In any case, he brings this part of his argument—devoted to the proposition that the Earth is a living being, possibly with a soul or consciousness, and thus an appropriate non-human object of respect—to a conclusion with the following poetic coda, climaxing with biblical allusions (to Job 38:7 and to 2 Kings 22:20):

> Possibly, in our intuitive perceptions, which may be truer than our science and less impeded by words than our philosophies, we realize the indivisibility of the earth—its soil, mountains, rivers, forests, climate, plants, and animals, and respect it collectively not only as a useful servant, but as a living being, vastly less alive than ourselves in degree, but vastly greater than ourselves in time and space—a being that was old when the morning stars sang together, and, when the last of us has been gathered unto our fathers, will still be young.[44]

6.9 RESPECT FOR LIFE AS SUCH

Having argued that the Earth is a living being when apprehended at planetary spatial and temporal scales, Leopold next turns to a discussion of the possibility of a non-anthropocentric, deontological Earth ethic. He seems to take for granted—and states without argument—that respect for life is universal: "Philosophy, then"—apparently epitomized by Ouspensky, in Leopold's estimation—"suggests one reason why we cannot destroy the earth with moral impunity; namely, that the 'dead' earth is an organism possessing a certain kind and degree of life, *which we intuitively respect as such.*"[45]

But do we really respect life as such—intuitively or otherwise? In the current political discourse surrounding the legality of abortion and the use of human embryonic stem cells for biomedical research, we do indeed hear a lot of zealous rhetoric concerning a "right to life" and "respect for life." But those who bandy these phrases about are not talking about life "*as such.*" In all that rhetoric, there are two adjectives missing: "innocent" and "human." Far from universal, respect for life as such appears to be limited to a few out-of-the-box thinkers, most notably Albert Schweitzer, who passionately advocates "reverence for life," and Paul W. Taylor, who almost as passionately advocates a "life-centered system of ethical principles."[46] (I discuss their biocentric moral philosophies in 8.4–8.5 and 8.11–8.13, respectively.)

Among those most strident about what *they* call the right to life, only pre-natal human life seems to be the object of respect, as they are often the same people who also advocate reduced funding for post-natal medical care for indigent children, elective wars that kill tens of thousands of people, and capital punishment. I am not sure, but the reason for this radical narrowing of respect for life among many Right-wing "conservatives" may be theological. *Human* life—for them, it seems, the existence of other forms of life are of so little significance as to be not worth even indirectly acknowledging with an adjectival qualification—begins at conception, so the doctrine seems to go, and until birth, a fetus remains "innocent"; after birth, all humans are tainted with original sin. Maybe that explains it. Or maybe it's just a matter of obfuscating mean-spiritedness: they have no genuine concern for fetuses; they just want to make sure that women who indulge in sex, but do not want to bear children—the only religious justification for having sex—pay the wages of sin and, once that debt is paid, why should a self-righteous person care if their accidental offspring suffer from or even die of malnutrition or preventable disease?[47]

6.10 LEOPOLD'S CHARGE THAT BOTH RELIGION AND SCIENCE ARE ANTHROPOCENTRIC

In any case, Leopold appears to realize that his foregoing advocacy of an Earth ethic—based on the sanguine assumption of a universal respect for life as such and a very speculative, albeit sophisticated, argument that the whole Earth is itself an instance of life—is pretty unlikely to play in Peoria: "Possibly to most men of affairs, this reason is too intangible to either accept or reject as a guide to conduct."[48] That being not just "possibly" but almost certainly correct, Leopold takes aim at popular anthropocentrism. If his foregoing affirmative argument for a life-respecting deontological Earth ethic is too abstract and sophisticated to appeal to ordinary people, perhaps he can cast doubt on metaphysical anthropocentrism and thus get his reader to come around to the precept with which he began—respect for the Earth—if not as a living being, at least as a more-than-instrumentally valuable thing. "[W]as the earth made for man's use," Leopold asks, "or has man merely the privilege of temporarily possessing an earth made for other and inscrutable purposes?"[49] This, he claims, is a "more easily debatable question."[50]

"Most religions," states Leopold, "are premised squarely on the assumption that man is the end or purpose of creation, and not only the dead earth, but all creatures thereon, exist solely for his use."[51] He also thinks that "the mechanistic or scientific philosophy" is also anthropocentric.[52]

On a worldwide cultural scale, that most religions are anthropocentric, metaphysically speaking, is probably not true. It is not true, for example, of Buddhism or Daoism.[53] It is true of most of the protean *sects*—Catholic, Protestant, Evangelical, Pentecostal Christianity; Orthodox, Conservative, and Reformed Judaism; Sunni and Shiite Islam—of the Abrahamic religions. It is worth noting that the Judeo-Christian stewardship environmental ethic artfully combines metaphysical anthropocentrism with moral non-anthropocentrism.[54] In that interpretation of Genesis, God first confers intrinsic value on the non-human creation, by declaring it to be "good." Afterward God creates "man" in His own image to have "dominion" over the creation, which dominion, God later explains, means to "dress and keep" the intrinsically valuable creation. Human beings enjoy a unique metaphysical status, which at once confers on us unique privilege but also unique moral responsibility. But the Judeo-Christian stewardship environmental ethic had not been developed in 1923 and so the Abrahamic religions were not only metaphysically anthropocentric; they were, in general, morally anthropocentric as well.

"The mechanistic or scientific philosophy," Leopold says, "does not start with this [anthropocentrism] as a premise, but ends with it as a conclusion." Frankly, I am not sure what Leopold may be referring to by *premise* and *conclusion*. I can offer only a guess. The mechanistic or scientific philosophy is not anthropocentric in its metaphysical foundations (premises?)—in sharp contrast to the Abrahamic religions—but is put to use or technologically applied for purely anthropocentric ends or purposes (conclusions?). Thus it is morally anthropocentric. Anthropocentric applications were, after all, the express rationale for the development of a mechanistic or scientific philosophy by its first advocates and architects—especially by René Descartes and Francis Bacon.[55]

Leopold then documents the implicit claim that anthropocentrism is prevalent in our culture—characteristic, he believes, of both Western religion and science—by quoting three authors. The first two of those authors, Jeanette (*sic*) Marks and John Muir, reinforce Leopold's own disdain for anthropocentrism, while the third, William Cullen Bryant, provides what Leopold thinks "is the noblest expression of this anthropomorphism."[56] *Anthropocentrism* is a term that became common only after Leopold's death and especially common in the academic environmental-philosophy literature, which dates only to the mid-1970s. Nor is it a term that he himself uses. Leopold uses the term *anthropomorphism*. By *anthropomorphism*, however, Leopold seems to mean what contemporary environmental philosophers mean by *anthropocentrism*. The ancient Greek gods are anthropomorphic; that is, they are depicted in human form. The god of Abraham might also be arguably anthropomorphic—because he is said to have created man in his own image. That god too is sometimes depicted in human form, perhaps most memorably by Michelangelo on the ceiling of the Sistine Chapel in Rome. Thus, when Leopold goes on to characterize the Abrahamic religions, which he evidently has in mind, as "anthropomorphic," he just might really mean *anthropomorphic*, not *anthropocentric*. But if the concept also characterizes "the scientific school of thought" as Leopold says that it does, then by *anthropomorphic*, Leopold could only mean *anthropocentric*. Further to the same point, by *anthropomorphism* Leopold refers back to his own definition—"the assumption that man is the end and purpose of creation"—which is latterly called *anthropocentrism*—*metaphysical* anthropocentrism, more particularly, which is often posited to justify *moral* anthropocentrism.

As noted in the Introduction to this book, the distinction between metaphysical and moral anthropocentrism is very important for a proper understanding and interpretation of both the land ethic and the Earth ethic. In Leopold's terms, metaphysical anthropocentrism is the doctrine that human beings, humanity collectively, and perhaps human institutions (such as religions or sovereign states) have "a special nobility...a special cosmic value, distinctive from and superior to all other life" or that "man is the end or purpose of creation."[57] Moral anthropocentrism—the claim that human beings, humanity collectively, or human institutions should be the only beneficiaries of ethics—is often premised on metaphysical anthropocentrism, but it need not be. Indeed, the anthropocentric Earth ethic developed in Chapters 9, 10, and 11 is premised precisely on a firm and unequivocal rejection of metaphysical anthropocentrism. Advocates of militant moral anthropocentrism *premised on metaphysical anthropocentrism* (whether the metaphysical premises are religious or philosophical) are hostile to any species of moral non-anthropocentrism. But moral anthropocentrism and moral non-anthropocentrism need not be mutually exclusive. As indicated in 2.17, the land ethic is both anthropocentric and non-anthropocentric, depending on whether one's perspective is experiential or analytical. In Chapter 11, I develop and commend a new anthropocentric Earth ethic. And in the final section of the final chapter of this book, 11.6, I indicate how the morally non-anthropocentric land ethic and the morally anthropocentric Earth ethic rest on both the same non-anthropocentric metaphysical premises and the same moral philosophy originating with David Hume, naturalized by Charles Darwin, ecologized by Aldo Leopold, and experimentally validated by contemporary moral scientists. In 9.2, I once more revisit the complicated and vexed issue of anthropocentric versus non-anthropocentric environmental ethics and their anthropocentric or non-anthropocentric metaphysical foundations.

6.11 HOW LEOPOLD RIDICULES METAPHYSICAL ANTHROPOCENTRISM

Jeannette Augustus Marks (1874–1964) was a poet, playwright, scholar, and English professor at Mount Holyoke College—and a suffragette with socialist sympathies—who, according to Leopold, characterized metaphysical anthropocentrism as "'the great human impertinence.'"[58] Leopold provides no clue about where he found these words, but the phrase appears in an essay she wrote for the 1919–1920 volume of the *Yale Review*, to which Leopold must have subscribed as an alumnus of the university. The phrase reminds me of the title of David Ehrenfeld's blistering denunciation of metaphysically grounded moral anthropocentrism, *The Arrogance of Humanism*. In "Swinburne: A Study in Pathology," Marks, in any case, wrote: "The whole mediaeval superstitious fearing of knowledge is nonsense. Every truth is but further conviction that God is—perhaps not in the way we want God to be. But that we should standardize God according to our human limitations is the great human impertinence!"[59]

Next, Leopold quotes a little more extensively from Muir than from Marks: "as if nothing that does not obviously make for the benefit of man had any right to exist; as if our ways were God's ways."[60] That phrase occurs in the second chapter of Muir's *Our National Parks*. I do not know if Leopold had also read *A Thousand-Mile Walk to the Gulf*, but in that book, published posthumously in 1916, Muir provides more sustained eco-theological commentary in much the same vein. There, this time in regard to alligators, he exclaims, "How narrow we selfish and conceited creatures are! how blind to rights of all the rest of creation!"[61] To my knowledge, Muir was the first precursor of environmental philosophy to attribute rights—a concept most at home in a deontological ethical mode—to nature. The theme common both to the Marks and Muir quotes seems to be the arrogation to themselves by modern humans of the perspectives and powers properly belonging to God.

Finally, Bryant's "Thanatopsis" is, as the title suggests (literally translating the Greek: "a look at death"), a poetic meditation on personal mortality and more generally, human mortality. I cannot agree that its anthropocentrism is, as Leopold claims, noble, but it is certainly spectacular, for, according to Bryant (1794–1878), Earth's "hills," "vales," "woods," and "rivers," "Are"—one and all—"*but* the solemn decorations / Of the great tomb of man."[62] Leopold quotes nine consecutive lines of the poem and underscores these last two so that his reader cannot fail to miss the impertinence and arrogance of the outlandish metaphysical anthropocentrism evinced by Bryant.

Having introduced the question of anthropocentrism as "a more easily debatable one"—compared with the question of whether the Earth is living or "dead"—it is initially surprising to find that Leopold immediately follows the quotation from "Thanatopsis" by stating that because most of his contemporaries "profess either one of the anthropomorphic religions or the scientific school of thought which is likewise anthropomorphic" he "will not dispute the point."[63] Reading on, however, we find that while indeed Leopold does not dispute the point, neither does he concede it. Rather, Leopold refuses to dignify the prevailing anthropocentrism of both the Abrahamic religions and scientific mechanism with discursive disputation. Instead, he ridicules it. Simply underscoring Bryant's claim that Earth's mountains, valleys, forests, and streams are "but [but!] decorations" is enough to show its ridiculousness, as is the insinuation that the Earth itself is *but* "the great tomb of man."

Then Leopold continues his ridiculing dismissal of anthropocentrism with the following comment, dripping with irony:

> It just occurs to me in answer to the scientists that God started his show a good many million years before he had any men for audience—a sad waste of actors and music—and in answer to both, that it is just barely possible that God

himself likes to hear birds sing and see flowers grow. But here again we encounter the insufficiency of words as symbols for reality.[64]

In what sense are these words insufficient as symbols for reality? First, it is doubtful that Leopold believes that, in reality, God is responsible for all the things that Bryant reduces to decorations of the tomb of man—the Earth and all its topographical features. And second it is doubtful that Leopold believes that, in reality, God has preferences—things he "likes to hear…and see"—or indeed that God has animal sensory modalities, such as vision and hearing, which require eyes and ears. Finally, third, it is doubtful that Leopold believes that any actual, objective entity corresponds to the conventional concept of God at all—in "reality." Rather, more literally, given the immense age of the Earth and its evolutionary biography, the proposition that its *telos*, its end or purpose, is to serve as a pool of resources for a late-coming anthropoid ape or serve as that ape's well-decorated tomb, when that ape goes extinct, is as preposterous as it is hubristic. Putting it in theological terms, following Marks and Muir, gets Leopold's point across, but he warns his reader not to take him literally. However insufficient as "symbols for reality," Leopold's words certainly do effectively achieve their purpose of ridiculing metaphysical anthropocentrism and the moral anthropocentrism that it undergirds—and making perfectly clear just why metaphysical anthropocentrism is in fact so ridiculous.

6.12 LEOPOLD'S USE OF IRONY AS AN INSTRUMENT OF RIDICULE

In what sense are these words ironic? If we take the statement that "God started his show a good many million years before he had any men for audience" as a *symbol* for the reality that Leopold has in mind, then we cannot possibly think that Leopold himself believes that the millions of years before the arrival of *Homo sapiens* were a "waste." The statement that he sets off in dashes is ironic because its literal meaning is the opposite of the actual meaning that Leopold intends his reader to garner. In addition to biblical phrasing and tropes, one of the literary devices that makes *A Sand County Almanac* so powerfully persuasive is Leopold's liberal use of irony throughout the book. As noted in 1.15, according to John Tallmadge, Leopold employs two basic "techniques of compression": (1) concentration—"eliminating whatever does not advance" his point; and (2) "engagement"—"whereby the text invites the reader to supply vital information at which it can only hint."[65] The suite of means that Leopold employs to achieve the engagement that Tallmadge finds in *Sand County* are synecdoche, allusion, understatement, rhetorical questions, and irony. An excellent example of irony, noted by Tallmadge, comes in "Good Oak":

> The oak laid on wood just the same, even in 1915, when the [Wisconsin] Supreme Court abolished state forests and Governor Phillip pontificated that "state forestry is not a good business proposition." (… It did not occur to him

that while the courts were writing one definition of goodness in the law books, fires were writing quite another one on the face of the land. *Perhaps, to be a governor, one must be free from doubt on such matters.*)[66]

Of course, I am assuming, as does Leopold, that readers can *hear* the irony in the final sentence of this extract from "Good Oak." Surely, Leopold does not believe—nor, surely, does he want his readers to think that he actually believes—that freedom from doubt about environmental policy is a proper qualification for being a governor. So, just as Leopold experiments in "Some Fundamentals" with biblical phrasing and tropes (as noted and illustrated in 6.1 and 6.8), there he also liberally experiments with the rhetorical power of irony. The next full paragraph continues in the same sardonically ironic vein as its predecessor. "Granting," writes Leopold, evidently for the sake of his coup de grace, his final lethal stroke of irony, that "the earth is for man—there is still a question: what man?"[67]

Did not the cliff dwellers who tilled and irrigated these our valleys think that they were the pinnacle of creation—that these valleys were made for them? Undoubtedly. And then the Pueblos? Yes. And then the Spaniards? Not only thought so, but said so. And now we Americans? Ours beyond a doubt! (*How happy a definition is that one of Hadley's which states, "Truth is that which prevails in the long run"!*)[68]

Here, Leopold mocks anthropocentrism by comparing it with ethnocentrism. Each of the successive possessors of the Southwest believed that it was created specially for them. The Anasazi, the Pueblos, the Spanish, and the Americans each believed that they were "the pinnacle of creation" and that the Southwest was "made for them." But they cannot all be right. Leopold also exposes—with the perfect irony, in this context—the absurdity of Hadley's definition of truth as "that which prevails in the long run." Ethnocentrism doggedly persists in each successive culture and thus prevails in the long run. Hence, the mutually contradictory belief, prevailing in each successive people, that *they and they alone* were the pinnacle of creation and that the Southwest was made for *them and them alone* and not for another people is, by Hadley's definition of truth, *true*—albeit logically contradictory!

6.13 NORTON'S READING OF LEOPOLD AS AN ANTHROPOCENTRIC PRAGMATIST

Thanks to the scholarly diligence of Bryan G. Norton, we can be confident that Leopold here refers to Arthur Twining Hadley, who was president of Yale University when Leopold was a student there.[69] But Norton reads Leopold with a deaf ear to his irony, which is not an uncommon sensory affliction. Many years ago, shortly after I began teaching the world's first philosophy course in environmental ethics at the University of Wisconsin-Stevens Point, a student quoted the following passage from "The Land Ethic" during a presentation to the class: "obey the law, vote right, join some organizations, and practice what conservation is profitable on your own land; the government will do the rest."[70] The student thought that Leopold was endorsing, not ridiculing, this caricature of the then-popular understanding of conservation. After all, Leopold does not come right out and declare this understanding of conservation to be inadequate. Instead, he follows it with a rhetorical question, another one of his methods of "engagement" identified by Tallmadge: "Is not this formula too easy to accomplish anything worthwhile?"[71] Similarly, Norton thinks that Leopold is endorsing, not mocking, Hadley's definition of truth. And he has constructed an elaborate interpretation of "Conservation as a Moral Issue" based on this assumption, torturing Leopold's text to shoehorn it into conformity with his own brand of environmental ethics in the anthropocentric tradition of American Pragmatism.[72]

I agree with Norton that Hadley's putative definition of *truth* "clearly derives from American [P]ragmatism."[73] Hadley himself was not, however, an American Pragmatist, nor was he at all a credentialed philosopher. Rather, he was a credentialed political economist who developed an enthusiasm for the philosophy of William James late in his academic career during his tenure as president of Yale. Further, Hadley defines *right*, not *truth*, in terms of "that which prevails in the long run." Norton acknowledges the discrepancy in a footnote but downplays its importance, claiming that Pragmatists "treated 'true' and 'right' as largely interchangeable."[74] Perhaps, but *truth* does not have the same epistemological/moral ambiguity as does *right*. And Hadley appears to be defining *right* more as a moral than an epistemological concept. For example, Hadley avers that "Whereas previous generations said, 'Right must prevail in the long run'; and held it as somewhat an article of religious faith, the present generation sets out to discover what is going to prevail in the long run, in the full confidence that if this can be found it will be right."[75] Whatever. We are concerned here with what Leopold thought of Hadley's definition—whether of *right* or of *truth*—not what Hadley thought. And because Leopold himself misremembers Hadley's definition of *right* as a definition of *truth*, having noted the discrepancy, I join Norton in ignoring it.

Norton informs us that Hadley was Yale's first *lay* president. Under that circumstance, he may have had to establish his conservative religious bona fides. In any case, according to Hadley, "We hold the beliefs that have preserved our fathers. It is not far from the truth to say that we hold them because they have preserved our fathers."[76] Because Christian beliefs were "the beliefs that have preserved our fathers" and those beliefs have "prevailed in the long run"—some two thousand years—then Christian beliefs, by Hadley's definition of *truth*, must be true. According to Norton, because he is a faithful disciple of Hadley, Leopold must also agree with Hadley that the long-prevailing, father-preserving metaphysically anthropocentric beliefs of Christianity are true and his opening quotation from the Bible proves it: "When Leopold invoked Ezekiel, he was invoking the 'beliefs that have preserved our fathers.' As understood by Hadley, the [P]ragmatists' notion of truth amounted to a recommendation to respect the wisdom of our ancestors"—who were of course both militantly ethnocentric (originally God's chosen people and, in their latest Christian incarnation, the agents of Manifest Destiny) as well as militantly anthropocentric (created in the image of God and charged with the task of subduing the Earth).[77]

6.14 OUSPENSKY, LEOPOLD, AND "LINGUISTIC PLURALISM"—ACCORDING TO NORTON

According to Norton, Ouspensky too is something of a Pragmatist, espousing "linguistic pluralism." In support of this contention, Norton cites the translation of *Tertium Organum* that first appeared in 1947, not the translation that was available to Leopold in 1923. In any case, it would be far more accurate to say that Ouspensky was a *logical* pluralist, for, on the pages of the later translation that Norton cites, he writes:

> we should be prepared to find that all attempts to express *super-logical* relations in our language will appear absurd, and actually will only *hint* at what we wish to convey....Having begun to understand this we shall begin to grasp separate ideas concerning the essence of the "noumenal world" or *the world of many dimensions* in which we actually live. In such a case the *higher logic*, even with the imperfect formulae—crude as they may appear in our language of concepts—represents a powerful instrument of cognition of the world, the only means of preserving us from illusions.[78]

This, by the way, is exactly what Ouspensky meant by *"tertium organum,"* the new higher logic he envisioned himself to be announcing. On the basis of this misunderstanding—or misrepresentation—of what Ouspensky was up to, Norton claims that Leopold follows Ouspensky, not by positing two logics—as in fact did Ouspensky: logic as we know it and a light-headed, unspecified "higher logic"—but two "second-order" beliefs about the world, the one mechanistic and the other organismic. According to Norton, these are just two different ways of conceptually organizing "first-order" beliefs, which are "the facts of physics, chemistry, and geology."[79] And the difference between the two second-order beliefs, according to Norton, is really only a matter of language: just "two differing linguistic approaches to the same 'earth.'"[80]

This seems meant to evoke the way William James famously settled a "ferocious metaphysical dispute" among his friends about whether a man chasing a squirrel around a tree went around the squirrel or not, as well as around the tree, by making it all turn on a choice of language—what we mean by *around*.[81] Because the first-order facts remain the same, however we choose to describe them, the metaphysical dispute, for all its ferocity, is trivial. Similarly, Norton seems to suggest, the choice between the organismic and mechanistic descriptions of the Earth, which Leopold tries to reconcile in "Some Fundamentals," is no less trivial, reducible to a mere choice of language. With this essentially Jamesian interpretation, Norton can minimize the importance of Leopold's suggestion that the Earth is a living being—with, possibly, a soul or consciousness—and thus a proper object of *non-anthropocentric* respect. But, as a close and careful reading of Leopold's essay clearly shows, Leopold considered the appropriateness of either a mechanistic or an organismic description of the Earth to turn not merely on a comme-ci-comme-ça choice of language, but on a choice of temporal and spatial scale. Or better put, one's choice of language is not free; it is constrained by one's choice of scale. At local temporal and spatial scales, once more, a mechanistic description of the phenomena is appropriate; at global temporal and spatial scales an organismic description of the phenomena is more appropriate. Or so Leopold claims.

I of course agree that the difference between the mechanistic and organismic conceptions of the Earth are alternative descriptions of the same entity. But the correct description, Leopold thought, is, as I say, determined by our choice of scale, not, as Norton demeans it, a matter of "arbitrary choice"—each according to his or her metaphysical tastes.[82] Thus Norton concludes, "By applying Hadley's definition of truth"— which Leopold lampoons, as any reader with an ear for irony can tell—"to the cultural practices that were causing deterioration of the land in the Southwest, Leopold could sidestep the issue of anthropocentrism and declare those practices 'false.' He relied not upon Ouspensky"—to whose thought Leopold devotes the three longest paragraphs of the section—"but upon Ezekiel buttressed by Hadley's definition of truth," which definition Leopold mentions but once, in parentheses, ironically, in order to ridicule ethnocentrism and by implication anthropocentrism, and, not least, in order to ridicule that very definition of truth itself.[83]

6.15 LEOPOLD'S RETURN TO VIRTUE ETHICS

After disparagingly comparing anthropocentrism to ethnocentrism and lampooning, in passing, Hadley's definition of truth, Leopold continues: "Five races—five cultures—have flourished here."[84] He had just identified, however, only four: the cliff dwellers, the Pueblos, the Spaniards, and the Americans. Perhaps he realized that he had neglected to mention the Mexicans. The region was, after all, a part of Mexico from 1821, when Mexico won independence from Spain, until 1848, when Mexico lost its war with the United States and with it what remained in its possession (after losing Texas in 1836) of the northern half of the county.[85] Nor does it seem worthwhile to dwell on whether Leopold was distinguishing race from culture or conflating them. By the common understanding of race, then and now, the Anasazi and the Pueblos belong to the same race, as do the Spaniards and the Americans, while many Mexicans are mestizos—a mixture of both races.[86] He goes on, "We may truthfully say of our four predecessors that they left the earth alive, undamaged. Is it possibly a proper question for us to consider what the sixth will say about us?"[87] With this question, it seems to me that Leopold shifts back, momentarily, to a virtue-ethics modality. And, Leopold answers, "If we are logically anthropomorphic, yes."[88]

There are two ways to interpret the phrase "logically anthropomorphic," one in line with Norton's reading of this text, the other in line with mine.

In one sense, we are *necessarily* anthropocentric, for all our values and attitudes are *human* values and attitudes. In the Introduction, I identified this species of anthropocentrism as *tautological anthropocentrism*. We may respect the Earth as a living being and agree with Muir that other creatures, including rattlesnakes and alligators, have a right to life, but, because respect is a human attitude and the concept of rights is a human concept, in so doing we are, nevertheless, try as we might to transcend it, still logically—that is, necessarily—anthropocentric. In this sense, anthropocentrism is inescapable, nor is there an alternative to being anthropocentric. That we are anthropocentric is thus a matter of logic; that is, the proposition that we are anthropocentric is *analytically* true; it is a tautology. But, for the same reason, it is also trivially true. To bother to say that we are anthropocentric, to characterize "most religions" and "the mechanistic or scientific philosophy" as anthropocentric—as if there were any alternative—is pointless.

A second interpretation of what Leopold means by "logically anthropocentric" is "consistently anthropocentric." Why is "consistently" a synonym for "logically?" Because the most fundamental law of logic, as noted in 5.2, is the law of non-contradiction. So, what I think Leopold means is this: if we are self-consistent in our metaphysical anthropocentrism—that is, in the belief that "the earth was made for man's use," that "man is the end and purpose of creation," "the pinnacle of creation," and that "not only the...earth, but all creatures thereon, exist solely for [our] use"—then we should be concerned about what our human successors will think of us. And we should want to live up to our high opinion of ourselves.

There follows immediately a quotation of another ten lines from "Thanatopsis," the sole point of which seems to be that we Americans, collectively, as a race or culture, are no less mortal than those who preceded us. The last three lines that Leopold quotes from the poem read: "And millions in those solitudes, since first / The flight of years began, have laid them down / In their last sleep."[89] Following which, Leopold simply notes, "And so, in time, shall we."[90] But, back to the question of being logically—that is, consistently—anthropocentric: What form should a self-consistent metaphysical anthropocentrism take? Paradoxically, it should take the form of moral non-anthropocentrism—a proper respect, as a "moral being," for our fellow denizens of the Earth and for the Earth itself: "And if there be, indeed, a special nobility inherent in the human race—a special cosmic value, distinctive from and superior to all other life—by what token," Leopold asks, "shall it be manifest?"[91] He answers that question with two more: "By a society decently *respectful of* its own and *all other life*, capable of inhabiting the earth without defiling it? Or by a society like that of John Burroughs' potato bug, which exterminated the potato, *and thereby exterminated itself?*"[92]

6.16 LEOPOLD'S NON-ANTHROPOCENTRIC ANTHROPOCENTRISM

The title of the article in which Norton develops his interpretation of "Some Fundamentals" is "The Constancy of Leopold's Land Ethic." There was no major shift in Leopold's moral philosophy between the early 1920s and the late 1940s, Norton argues. Leopold's constant moral philosophy was "derived from American [P]ragmatism" and remained true to "a philosophical approach borrowed from Arthur Twining Hadley."[93] Norton reiterates this claim, if anything more dogmatically, nearly two decades later in his book, *Sustainability*.[94] But, as noted, there is scant evidence to support Norton's baroque revisionist reading of "Some Fundamentals." Nonetheless, when all the learned dust has settled, I would certainly agree with Norton that Leopold was a lifelong pragmatist—not, however, in the philosophical sense of the term but rather in the vernacular sense.[95] He was focused on practical outcomes, and not a stubborn adherent to inflexible principles, whether they worked or not; he strove for sustainable land use; and he was concerned about the environmental legacy that he and his generation would bequeath to future generations. I think that there was, however, a significant shift in Leopold's moral *philosophy* from the 1923 Earth ethic to the 1948 land ethic—the exploration of which is the central burden of this entire book, considered, however, in reverse order—and it had little to do with Hadley or American Pragmatism as a school of philosophy.

In Leopold's moral philosophy, however, there is certainly one salient constant on which I think Norton and I would further agree, at least in part. Leopold believed that there is indeed, but only potentially, "a special nobility in the human race—a special cosmic value, distinctive from *and superior to* all other life." And what is that? Perhaps Norton would not agree with me about this, but clearly for Leopold, it is our capacity to value other forms of life intrinsically, to respect them and the Earth that we share with them—our capacity, in short, to transcend moral anthropocentrism. If we are able to realize our potential for *moral* non-anthropocentrism, in other words, we can stake a defensible claim to *metaphysical* anthropocentrism. In addition to the many expressions of a non-anthropocentric moral attitude in "The Land Ethic," documented in Chapter 2, a passage in the *Almanac*'s "On a Monument to the Pigeon" directly articulates the same paradoxical morally non-anthropocentric metaphysical anthropocentrism that we find in "Some Fundamentals":

> For one species to mourn the death of another is a new thing under the sun. The Cro-Magnon who slew the last mammoth thought only of steaks. The sportsman who shot the last pigeon thought only of his prowess. The sailor who clubbed the last auk thought of nothing at all. Had the funeral been ours, the pigeons would hardly have mourned us. In this fact, rather than in Mr DuPont's nylons or Mr. Vannevar Bush's bombs, *lies our superiority over the beasts.*[96]

But, as I say, that superiority is a fragile potential that we may or may not realize. The Cro-Magnon who slew the last mammoth did not "manifest" it; nor did the sportsman who shot the last pigeon, nor the sailor who clubbed the last auk. Nor, for that matter, did Abraham, if Leopold understands him aright, because "Abraham knew exactly what the land was for: it was to drip milk and honey into Abraham's mouth."[97] (So much for Norton's insistence that Leopold was a Hadleyan who evinced respect for "the wisdom of our ancestors" and the *truth* (!) of the "beliefs that preserved our fathers.") Further, to "manifest" our "superiority over the beasts" by being respectful of them and of the Earth is, still more paradoxically, the ultimate key to our own lasting success as a species. For if we go on exterminating other species, like Burroughs's potato bug, we risk exterminating ourselves. This permutation of non-anthropocentric anthropocentrism was fully discussed in 2.17, as it is also a feature of the land ethic. The choice is ours, "As one or the other shall we be judged in 'the derisive silence of eternity.'"[98] And thus, does "Some Fundamentals of Conservation in the Southwest" end.

6.17 THE LEOPOLD EARTH
ETHIC: A SUMMARY AND A PREVIEW

In comparison with the twenty-five-page-long "The Land Ethic," the three-and-a-half-page-long section "Conservation as a Moral Issue" in the essay "Some Fundamentals of Conservation in the Southwest" is a spare sketch. Further, "The Land Ethic" is supported by the two hundred pages of *A Sand County Almanac* that precede it, while "Conservation as a Moral Issue" is only supported by the eight pages of the two preceding sections of "Some Fundamentals." In "Conservation as a Moral Issue," Leopold offers two central suggestions: (1) that—regarded from the perspective of planetary temporal and spatial scales—the Earth itself, as a whole, may be a living being; and (2) that we need an Earth-oriented ethic to "round out a real understanding" of conservation.[99]

The first of these suggestions anticipates the Gaia hypothesis, which was not developed as such until the 1970s. However, unbeknownst to Leopold the science that anticipates the Gaia hypothesis was being conceived by Vladimir Vernadsky as Leopold was writing "Some Fundamentals" and was made public, albeit only in Russian, just shortly thereafter. In Chapter 7, I trace the development of that science.

As to the second of these suggestions, Leopold broached several modalities that an Earth-oriented ethic might take in "Conservation as a Moral Issue": virtue ethics; consequentialist responsibility to future generations; and deontological respect for the Earth itself, as a moral being respects a fellow living being. Of the three, he gives most attention to the third. In Chapter 8, I explore a variety of theoretical foundations for a non-anthropocentric, deontological Earth ethic.

In Chapter 9, I look for theoretical support in the robust new subfield of contemporary environmental virtue ethics for the opening and closing gestures that Leopold himself makes toward environmental virtue ethics in "Some Fundamentals." Having traced, in Chapter 7, the development of the Gaia hypothesis that Leopold anticipates in 1923, some recent remarks by James Lovelock, one of its contemporary architects, lead me to explore, also in Chapter 9, Michel Serres's "natural-contract" theory for an Earth ethic (based on an analogy to classical social-contract theory, especially as developed by Jean-Jacques Rousseau).

In the context of our own time of global climate change and the disproportionate harms that it inflicts on different human populations across the planet and throughout the foreseeable future, considerations of intragenerational international justice and of intergenerational justice seem imperative. In Chapter 10, I indicate how conventional *rationalistic and individualistic theories* of intragenerational international justice and intergenerational justice are overwhelmed by the spatial and (especially) temporal scales of global climate change. The temporal and spatial scales of global climate change, which is the overarching environmental concern of the first century of the third millennium, require a thorough rethinking of ethical theory and moral philosophy. Accordingly, in Chapter 11, I explore an Earth ethic grounded in the same Humean-Darwinian foundations as the land ethic—thus achieving a cognitive consonance between the Leopold land ethic and a Leopold Earth ethic. Humean-Darwinian foundations for an Earth ethic also render it consonant with the current state of the art in the *science* of ethics, reviewed in Chapter 5. The Leopold land ethic and the most viable form of a Leopold Earth ethic may thus be seen to be not only complementary environmental ethics, but theoretically integrated environmental ethics.

7

The Earth Ethic: A Critical Account of
Its Scientific Metaphysical Foundations

Before the ascendance of Logical Positivism in the 1930s, the first quarter of the twentieth century was rife with metaphysical speculation, often of an undisciplined and amateurish kind. The anti-metaphysical wind that would sweep through twentieth-century philosophy, however, had already begun to blow from the quarter of Pragmatism.[1] If two apparently different, even contradictory, formulations of belief issue in the same course of action or policy, then those stated beliefs are Pragmatically equivalent in meaning—to reduce the Pragmatic theory of meaning to its bare bones.[2] Further, if the actions or policies based on a belief prove to be successful, measured by some specified criterion of success, then that belief is true—to reduce the Pragmatic theory of truth to its marrow.[3] In effect, *post hoc ergo propter hoc*, the fallaciousness of which is finessed because the meaning of the belief (the *propter hoc*) is just the action or policy expression of it (the *post hoc*). These two cornerstones of the Pragmatic epistemology, especially the former, undermined metaphysical speculation. The *cognitive content* of metaphysical speculation is as devoid of meaning in the Pragmatist tradition as it would be in the Positivist tradition, albeit for a different reason. For the Positivist, only logico-mathematical and empirically verifiable propositions are meaningful; for the Pragmatist, the meaning of metaphysical speculation has less to do with its cognitive content than with the way it translates into the actions or policies of the speculators or those in their thrall.

These Pragmatic theories of meaning and truth underlie Bryan G. Norton's interpretation (6.13–6.15) of "Conservation as a Moral Issue" in Aldo Leopold's "Some Fundamentals of Conservation in the Southwest."[4] As to meaning, the seemingly different, even apparently contradictory organismic and mechanistic conceptions of the Earth differ, according to Norton, only in choice of language because they both lead to soil conservation—Leopold's main concern in "Some Fundamentals"—provided the mechanistic conception includes a recognition of the "intricate and interrelated functions among [the Earth's] parts."[5] As to truth, according to Norton, from a Pragmatic point of view, "the [biblical] beliefs which have preserved our fathers" are true for that reason—because they have preserved our fathers, a plausible criterion of success.[6]

Norton finds Leopold affirming the Pragmatic theory of meaning by his several comments on language. For example, Leopold writes, "In discussing such matters [organicism versus mechanicalism] we are beset on all sides with the pitfalls of language. The very words *living thing* have an inherited and arbitrary meaning derived not from reality, but from human perceptions of human affairs. But we must use them for better or worse." (In 6.8, and 6.11, I quoted Leopold's three other comments in "Some Fundamentals" on the limitations of "language" and "words" to convey his meaning.) As I read Leopold, he is not, with these comments, endorsing the Pragmatic theory of meaning; rather, he is simply making the observation that because human languages are humanly scaled, to express thoughts about phenomena going on at planetary spatial and especially temporal scales is difficult.

Norton also finds Leopold affirming the Pragmatic theory of truth on two occasions in "Some Fundamentals." First, Leopold quotes Ezekiel, thus affirming the truth of the biblical beliefs that have preserved our fathers; and, second, Leopold (mis)quotes A. T. Hadley, a disciple of William James, to the effect that "Truth is that which prevails in the long run!"[7] As detailed in 6.13 and 6.14, in addition to disagreeing with Norton that Leopold manifests the Pragmatic theory of meaning, I also disagree with him that Leopold is invoking such a grotesque version of the Pragmatic theory of truth that he allegedly garnered from a reading of Hadley. To the contrary, I argue that he is ridiculing both biblical anthropocentrism and what he represents to be Hadley's dictum and, along with it, the Pragmatic theory of truth.[8]

In any case, my present point is that in "Some Fundamentals of Conservation in the Southwest" Leopold is engaged in what might be called science-inspired metaphysics and, despite the chill wind blowing from the philosophical quarter of Pragmatism, he was not out of step with his contemporaries in waxing metaphysical in 1923. In this chapter, I begin by contextualizing the metaphysical speculations in which Leopold indulges in "Some Fundamentals"—speculations that were inspired, however improbably, by his reading of P. D. Ouspensky. Apparently unbeknownst to Leopold, at about the same time, another Russian, Vladimir Vernadsky, was thinking more deeply along lines similar to those along which Leopold himself was thinking in the 1920s. This line of thinking—apparently dropped by Leopold by the time he was composing "The Land Ethic," perhaps because metaphysics in post-Positivist philosophical and scientific circles had become so malodorous—migrated from Russia to the United States in attenuated form in the 1940s, with the help of G. Evelyn Hutchinson. It resurfaced, full throated, in the 1970s culminating at the end of that decade with *Gaia: A New Look at Life on Earth* by James Lovelock, and has been further developed since then by Lovelock, Lynn Margulis, and others as the "Gaia hypothesis."

7.1 OUSPENSKY'S METAPHYSICS AND THE FOUR-DIMENSIONAL SPACE-TIME CONTINUUM

The kind of speculative metaphysics, typified by Absolute Idealism—the kind that so disgusted the Logical Positivists—was not inspired by science. It had evolved dialectically from the eighteenth-century philosophy of Immanuel Kant and reached its fatuous zenith in the nineteenth century in German and British philosophy. It too carried over into the early twentieth century before it was finally pilloried and drawn and quartered by the Positivists. Bernard Bosanquet, at Oxford, for example, was a twentieth-century Absolute Idealist as was Josiah Royce—who was, incidentally, a member of the same Harvard philosophy faculty as William James. Another kind of speculative metaphysics was inspired by the second scientific revolution, led by Albert Einstein, which occurred during the first decade and a half of the twentieth century. Indeed, the second scientific revolution really should have inspired speculative metaphysics by credentialed philosophers. After all, following the first scientific revolution in the sixteenth century, the metaphysical worldview of Western civilization was thoroughly reorganized by Hobbes, Descartes, Spinoza, and Leibniz, to name only the most notable metaphysicists of the seventeenth century.[9] Actually, that Pragmatism and Positivism so effectively discouraged speculative metaphysics in the philosophical community is a crying shame. The great need and opportunity for it offered up by the second scientific revolution went begging among those most talented and best prepared to pursue it. Nevertheless, whether the Pragmatists and the Positivists approved or not, many of the scientific revolutionaries themselves—the natural philosophers of the twentieth century—advanced science-inspired metaphysics. The best of it was articulated by the principal contributors to the second scientific revolution—first by Einstein himself, followed by Niels Bohr, Erwin Schrödinger, Werner Heisenberg, and others.[10]

Unfortunately, Leopold was reading the worst of it in the early1920s—Ouspensky's *Tertium Organum*. To his credit, Leopold made the best use of the worst of the science-inspired metaphysics to be had in the early years following the second scientific revolution—which occurred between 1905, the year Einstein published his paper on the special theory of relativity, and 1916, the year he published his paper on the general theory of relativity.[11] Einstein himself had popularized his revolutionary physics almost immediately in *Relativity: The Special and General Theory*, published in London in 1916 and in the United States in 1920.[12] Among the most arresting aspects of the theories of relativity was a revised geometry for the cosmos. One implication of the special theory of relativity, first expressed mathematically by Hermann Minkowski, was the unification of space and time into a four-dimensional space-time continuum.[13] And one implication of the general theory of relativity was that the four-dimensional space-time continuum was non-Euclidean. Space-time is "curved" and Einstein adapted the geometry worked out in the nineteenth century by G. F. Bernhard Riemann to map it.[14]

The notion that space(-time) has four dimensions is a central motif of *Tertium Organum*. Ouspensky's speculations about the "fourth dimension" are rooted in Kant—in this respect, his metaphysics has something in common with that of the Absolute Idealists—as well as in the new physics. Kant had idealized or psychologized space and time as the "forms of intuition"; and beyond the spatially and temporally presented "phenomena," he posited the existence of inaccessible and incomprehensible "noumena."[15] Ouspensky seemed to think (there is hardly any way of knowing for sure) that the "fourth dimension" was a realm apart, a realm of possible experience or consciousness in which the Kantian noumena resided and were actually accessible and comprehensible.[16] His "*tertium organon*" was just the ticket to transport one's mind to the Fourth Dimension.

7.2 VERNADSKY'S METAPHYSICS AND THE FOUR-DIMENSIONAL SPACE-TIME CONTINUUM: SPACE

It was actually not Ouspensky but Vladimir Vernadsky—a far more astute Russian thinker, a credentialed scientist, and more disciplined metaphysicist—whose thought was mirrored, as in a glass, faintly, by Leopold's in 1923.

According to George S. Levit, at the metaphysical foundations of Vernadsky's thought about a living Earth is his own theory of space and time.[17] Einstein had only paved the way for Vernadsky's geometrical metaphysics. According to Vernadsky, "Prior to our century, in scientifically studied phenomena, one reckoned only with Euclidean geometry of three dimensions. In the new scientific-philosophical conceptions which follow from Einstein's work one deals with a space of four dimensions, and that space, in the opinion of some, corresponds to the space not of Euclid's but of Riemann's geometry."[18] Vernadsky thought that the Einsteinean space-time revolution was incomplete because it did not take account of biological as well as of physical phenomena: "Theoretical physical thought rightly seeks here new paths but it does not conclude its analysis as required by logic."[19]

In 1860, Louis Pasteur discovered that organic tartaric acid (found in wine) was "optically active"—that is, it rotates the plane of polarized light—while synthetic tartrate was optically inactive.[20] The cause, he also discovered, was that the crystals of organic tartrate all have the same asymmetric orientation, while in synthetic tartrate the crystals are also asymmetric, but exhibit both dextral (right-handed) and sinistral (left-handed) orientations, mutually canceling any overall optical effects.[21] From this discovery, Pasteur reached a general conclusion: that preferential molecular asymmetry was a characteristic of organically synthesized molecules. Or, as Vernadsky himself put it, "As a result of the influence of living matter, only one isomer, either left or right, is obtained and the other is not produced.... Pasteur rightly saw here a sharp violation of the law of crystal symmetry."[22] Later, Pierre Curie postulated a General Dissymmetry Principle: an asymmetrical effect must have a cause that is similarly asymmetrical.[23] Or, as Vernadsky put it: "a phenomenon connected with some form of dissymmetry must have a cause possessing the same form of dissymmetry. This conclusion may be conveniently called Curie's principle."[24] Vernadsky regarded physical spaces (as opposed to idealized mathematical spaces) to be asymmetrical. The physical space-state we normally experience, for example, is made asymmetrical by the presence of Earth's gravitational field, which biases movement toward the downward direction on the up-down axis of the three-dimensional space of our experience. In addition to the gravitational asymmetry of physical space near the Earth's mass, the space of living matter is enantiomorphically (handedly) asymmetrical: many complex organic molecules and complex multi-cellular structures orient either to the right or to the left. Applying Curie's principle, Vernadsky concluded that the cause of the molecular asymmetry of living matter was the enantiomorphic geometrical asymmetry of the physical space occupied by living matter.

7.3 VERNADSKY'S METAPHYSICS AND
THE FOUR-DIMENSIONAL SPACE-TIME
CONTINUUM: TIME

Furthermore, many natural processes are reversible—and thus temporally symmetrical—but the life histories of living things are not; nor is the unfolding of biological evolution. The temporal dimension of the four-dimensional space of living matter is, thus, also asymmetrical, running inexorably from the past to the future. One might conceive of biological time as analogous to gravitational space. We are falling inexorably futureward, as it were, along the temporal axis of the four-dimensional space-time continuum. "These peculiarities [and more] of the spatial [and temporal] organization of living matter...make it possible [for Vernadsky] to propose that the space[-time] of living natural bodies differs principally from the space[-time] of their inert environments."[25] Or, as Vernadsky himself put it, "the space inside living matter is different from that inside the inert natural bodies of the biosphere. The state of the former space is not confined within the limits of Euclidean geometry. Time may be expressed in this space by a polar vector."[26] Moreover, "The conspicuous absence in living organisms of flat surfaces and straight lines is characteristic; the symmetry of living organisms is marked by curved lines and curved surfaces, characteristic of Riemann's geometries. Another characteristic of Riemann's geometries is that they deal with space which is finite, closed, sharply differing from its environment. This corresponds to the aloofness of living organisms."[27] By the "aloofness" of living organisms, Vernadsky seems to refer to the fact that they establish and defend a boundary between themselves and their environments and maintain chemical, thermal, and other equilibria within themselves and disequilibria between themselves and their environments.

In other words, Vernadsky, *like Ouspensky*, suggests that two parallel realms co-exist and interface, but they occupy different physical spaces with different space-state geometries. Inert matter occupies a locally Euclidean physical space with a reversible Newtonian time vector with only gravitational and electromagnetic asymmetries, while living matter occupies a four-dimensional space-time continuum, which is temporally asymmetrical, enantiomorphically asymmetrical, and curvilinear—characterized by a locally Riemannian geometry. Vernadsky thought that only atoms—of hydrogen, oxygen, nitrogen, carbon, calcium, iron, phosphorous, and so on—flow across the spatio-temporal boundary between these two realms.[28] Because atomic matter is common to both living matter and inert matter, the two realms must differ, qua matter, not only in their geometries but also in their chemistries. The *molecular structure* of living matter differs, in other words, from that of inert matter. However strange they appear to us—and certainly they do to me— Vernadsky, *unlike Ouspensky*, is offering up subtle and scientifically informed metaphysical speculations, based on his observations of the real living world, not on wild speculations about an occult world conjured up in a perfervid and undisciplined imagination such as Ouspensky's.

7.4 VERNADSKY'S DOCTRINE OF THE NON-GENESIS OF LIFE ON EARTH

Vladimir Vernadsky did not coin the word "biosphere"; Eduard Suess, a Viennese geologist, whom Vernadsky visited in 1910, coined it.[29] In the winter of 1922–23, Vernadsky delivered two lectures in Paris. They were subsequently published in 1926 as a book in Russia, *Biosfera*, and in France, *La Biosphère*, in 1929. Vernadsky's *The Biosphere*, translated from the Russian original, remained unavailable in English until 1998, except for a severely redacted translation—characterized by Lynn Margulis et al. as "bowdlerized"—of the French translation in 1986.[30] Suess developed the geological concept of the planet Earth as a series of nested spheres. The biosphere is the thin film of biota at the interface of the lithosphere, hydrosphere, and atmosphere. The biosphere goes down as deep in the Earth's lithosphere and hydrosphere as living organisms penetrate into the depths of the ocean, subterranean caves, and the Earth's crust and as high up in Earth's atmosphere as living organisms rise into the heights of the air. For Vernadsky, the living matter of this thinnest and most diaphanous of geospheres is a titanic geological force, profoundly affecting the chemical constitution of the atmosphere, the hydrosphere, even the lithosphere.[31] Indeed, according to Margulis et al., for Vernadsky, "Life is not merely *a* geological force, it is *the* geological force"—at least "at Earth's surface."[32]

Vernadsky's notion that living matter occupies a space-time continuum different from and parallel to the space-time continuum of inert matter is not found in *The Biosphere*. We find it, rather, in one of the few things he published in English during his lifetime.[33] But the notion that life exists in its own spatio-temporal habitus is consonant with and supportive of another claim that Vernadsky makes and makes prominently and repeatedly in *The Biosphere*. In the Preface, Vernadsky dismisses the "assumption," prevailing in twentieth-century geology, "of the existence of a beginning of life—life genesis or biogenesis at a certain stage in the geological past"—as having illegitimately "penetrated science in the form of religious and philosophical speculation."[34] He thought that belief in the genesis of living matter from inert matter was a legacy of the biblical myth(s) in which living beings are called into existence at a moment of time in the past, before which time they did not exist. Mark McMenamin, the editor of the English translation of *The Biosphere*, confirms that in fact "Vernadsky sees Earth as a planet on which life has always been present."[35] Vernadsky reiterates and elaborates this doctrine throughout *The Biosphere* in a way that is so obdurate and defensive that one suspects that he knew, in his heart of hearts, that the non-genesis of life was a lost cause.

The reason, I conjecture, for this seemingly strange and unscientific dogma was Vernadsky's belief that living matter is not just a titanic *geological* force, but a primitive *cosmic* force, no less fundamental than radiant energy and inert matter. To prove his point, he appealed to Louis Pasteur's experiments debunking the Aristotelian concept of the "spontaneous generation" of molds and other such organisms from purely material substrates.[36] This, of course, confuses two senses of the "generation" of living matter from inert matter; it conflates an *original* (and possibly unique) moment of spontaneous generation, with a *routine* process of spontaneous generation. The fact that the latter does not occur is no proof—indeed, no indication at all—that the former did not occur. When the evidence that the early Earth was devoid of life became too massive to ignore, Vernadsky then subscribed to the doctrine of "panspermia"— that living matter had inseminated the Earth, having migrated from somewhere else in the cosmos.[37] If the Earth was originally devoid of life, but life colonized Earth from elsewhere in the universe, Vernadsky could salvage his core belief—which itself was certainly a product of his own religious and philosophical speculation—that living matter (a term be preferred to *life*) is an *eternal* cosmic phenomenon no less primitive than inert matter and energy.

7.5 VERNADSKY'S ANTI-VITALISM

To his credit, Vernadsky resisted the temptation to make of life a force oppositional to the second law of thermodynamics. Arguably the two greatest scientific achievements of the nineteenth century were Charles Darwin's theory of evolution and William (Lord Kelvin) Thomson's laws of thermodynamics.[38] At first blush, Darwin's science and Thomson's appeared to contradict one another, the former accounting for a progressive order and organization in the realm of living matter, the latter accounting for a progressive disorder and disorganization—entropy—in the realm of inert matter and energy. Such an apparent contradiction led Henri Bergson to posit an *élan vital*, a vital impetus or force, responsible for the negentropy apparently manifest in living matter.[39] But Vernadsky realized that

> The biosphere is at least as much a *creation of the sun* as a result of terrestrial processes.... The action of solar radiation on earth-processes provides a precise basis for viewing the biosphere as both a terrestrial and a cosmic mechanism. The sun has completely transformed the face of the earth by penetrating the biosphere, which has changed the history and destiny of our planet by converting rays from the sun into new and varied forms of energy. At the same time the biosphere is largely a product of this radiation.[40]

Vernadsky's understanding of life is purely thermodynamical, not anti-thermodynamical. Living matter converts radiant solar energy into potential chemical energy by photoreducing elements (basically hydrogen and carbon) found in molecules of inert matter (basically water and carbon dioxide) and photosynthesizing them into organic compounds (basically sugar) and releasing the excess oxygen as a waste gas. Other forms of living matter then "burn" (re-oxidize) those compounds, using the energy thus released to power their own metabolic, physiological, and locomotive processes and activities. How this thermodynamical understanding of the relationship of solar radiation to Earth's self-organized biosphere could be consistent with Vernadsky's resistance to the genesis of life on Earth is a mystery to me. McMenamin characterizes this apparent contradiction in Vernadsky's thinking as a paradox: "Inert matter...represents the raw materials of life. Although Vernadsky emphasizes his view that living organisms have never been produced by inert matter, he paradoxically implies that nonliving stuff...at least has latent life....He was examining the idea that life has special properties, as old as matter itself, that somehow separated it from ordinary matter (into which it can by dying, be transformed)." Further, "[l]ife can expand its realm into inert matter but it was not formed from [it]."[41]

This would lead one to expect that Vernadsky would have found an ally in Bergson, whom he met during his sojourn in France. The difference between inert matter and living matter, one would expect Vernadsky to agree, is the presence of the *élan vital* in the latter. By embracing vitalism, Verrnadsky could obviate the paradox that, though existing in different spatio-temporal matrices and being coeval and eternal, living matter (matter animated by the *élan vital*) colonized inert matter (matter devoid of the *élan vital*). Vernadsky's opposition to vitalism, however, is just as clear and emphatic as his opposition to the genesis of life on Earth. Like Leopold, he steers a course between "the vitalistic and mechanistic representations of life."[42] Thus, to his credit, Vernadsky did not let his quasi-religious veneration of living matter trump his scientific acuity—in this case his acute grasp of the purely thermodynamic understanding of biological organization.

7.6 VERNADSKY'S LASTING CONTRIBUTION TO BIOGEOCHEMISTRY AND GAIAN SCIENCE

The idea that living matter is an ungenerated, *eternal* (!) cosmic phenomenon—co-equal and coeval with inert matter and energy in duration and force—existing in a separate and distinct parallel space-time continuum ultimately proved, of course, to be a scientific wind egg. By now, the evolutionary conception of the universe from a moment of inception in a Big Bang down to the present is so ingrained in our cosmological outlook that Vernadsky's belief that the cosmos, and with it living matter, is of infinite duration seems preposterous. Even as late as the mid-twentieth century, however, astronomer Fred Hoyle could plausibly hold out for a steady-state cosmology, a universe eternal without a beginning in time.[43] Nonetheless, Vernadsky's bad pet metaphysical speculations do not diminish his lasting insights. Indeed, reading *The Biosphere* one even gets the sense that the whole work is a paean to the wonder and power of living matter. It would not be hyperbolic to say that Vernadsky was intoxicated by the transformative force of "living matter"—something seemingly so delicate and fragile, yet something that exists not just tenuously clinging to Earth's surface, but something that has transformed the Earth from what it otherwise would be—a dead planet like its neighbors Venus and Mars, a carbon-dioxide smothered naked mass of inert rock—to the dynamic and vibrant jewel of the solar system. Whatever motivated Vernadsky—whether it was his own metaphysical passions or his disinterested pursuit of scientific knowledge—his *The Biosphere* does contribute both foundationally and enduringly to biogeochemistry.

Vernadsky clearly represents autotrophic organisms as transformers of radiant solar energy into potential chemical energy. He also clearly represents a consequence of that photosynthetic process—the accumulation of free oxygen, especially, and other biogenic gases in the atmosphere. Vernadsky clearly recognizes that therefore the Earth's atmosphere is highly reactive and far from chemical equilibrium. He attempts, furthermore, to calculate the quantities of energy and matter involved in these biospheric processes. For example, he calculates the quantity of free oxygen in the atmosphere to be 1.5×10^{21} grams.[44] Regarding this figure, McMenamin comments that "Vernadsky's value is too low by at least three orders of magnitude" and estimates that the correct figure is closer to 1.143×10^{24}.[45] Indeed, most of Vernadsky's calculations in *The Biosphere* are erroneous in retrospect, but my point here is that he is at least pioneering a quantificational Gaian science.

Vernadsky got so many facts and figures wrong and indeed so many fundamentals of biospheric processes wrong that it is easy to overlook his great achievements. I just gave an example of a wrong figure. As to facts, he asserts that the quantity of solar radiation reaching the Earth has been constant through time, while it is now believed to have increased by some 25 percent since life first emerged on Earth—as indeed *first* it once did.[46] This claim is driven by his essentially metaphysical insistence that the biomass of living matter has remained constant on Earth…forever.[47] For Vernadsky, evolution on Earth consists only in "morphological changes," changes in the forms of organic life (speciation), not in the functions of organic life—which are converting radiant solar energy into terrestrial chemical energy, chemically reorganizing the atoms of inert matter into the compounds of living matter, cycling atoms across the spatio-temporal boundary between inert and living matter, and radically transforming its planetary habitat to create conditions more favorable to itself.[48] Evolutionary development consists, for Vernadsky, in the increased efficiency and stability of those functions.

As to both facts and fundamentals, Vernadsky's obsession with the idea of life or living matter being ungenerated—cosmically co-equal and coeval with radiant energy and inert matter, even eternal—blinded him to the "oxygen crisis" in the biosphere's biography some two and a half billion years ago. In *The Biosphere*, he comments on banded oxidized iron formations in the Earth's crust, but fails to grasp the key they hold to an understanding of the evolution of the atmosphere.[49] Reduced iron near the Earth's surface was a sink for the oxygen produced as a waste product of photosynthesizing cyanobacteria, to form ferric oxides. But after the Great Rusting, when the available iron in the biosphere became saturated with oxygen, the gas began to build up in the atmosphere and hydrosphere.[50] For Earth's first microbial life forms, oxygen was a poisonous pollutant. Afterward, photosynthetic organisms evolved to tolerate it and respiring organisms evolved to exploit it.

While many aspects of Vernadsky's materialistic dualism—of living matter, on the one hand, and inert matter, on the other—are now metaphysical curiosities, that the chemistry of the one greatly differs from that of the other is of profound lasting significance. What Vernadsky got right is the starring role that living matter plays in the chemical composition of the Earth's atmosphere, hydrosphere, and even the Earth's crusty lithosphere. Limestone, for example, formed as a result of the calcium in the shells of marine organisms raining down through the water column and settling on the ocean floor. Then, under increasing pressure, sedimentary limestone became travertine and via metamorphosis marble.[51] But limestone and iron ores are just the poster-children of biogenic rock and, more generally, of mineral formation. Before the advent of life on Earth, there were some 1,500 species of minerals.[52] Life processes added another 3,600—more than double that of the pre-life total—to make up the present nearly trebled total of about 4,300.[53] Vernadsky clearly understood the biogenesis of much of the Earth's crust. From life processes, the ocean floor receives "millions of tons per year of calcium and magnesium carbonates (limestones and dolomites), silica (opals), hydrated iron oxides (limonites), hydrated manganese compounds (pyrolucite and psilomelane), and complex phosphates of calcium (phosphorites)," notes Vernadsky. [54] *Biosfera* and *La Biosphère* preceded by several decades the advent of plate techtonics in geology. Thus Vernadsky could not have been aware of the forceful role that biogenic rock formation plays—along with convection currents in the molten mantle—in the Earth's rock cycle.[55] In addition to the oxygen-rich air and the salty seas, not only the soil we stand on but the rock beneath it is biogenic. Vernadsky got that right! And if we count the Earth's biogenic crust—albeit inert matter, as Vernadsky conceived it, but born of living matter—as part of the biosphere, Vernadsky's biosphere is much more extensive than Suess's. In his own estimation, it included the whole of the granitic crust: "the biogenic rocks constitute part of its [the biosphere's] mass, and go far beyond the boundaries of the biosphere. Subject to the phenomenon of metamorphism, they are converted, losing all traces of life, into the granitic envelope...the area of former biospheres."[56]

In my opinion, Vernadsky's lasting contribution to Gaian science lies not in the details—wherein resides the devil of error—that is, not in the facts, figures, and even fundamentals that fill *The Biosphere*. Rather, three foundational conceptual features stand out. First, the two just noted, (1) that the solar-radiation-powered chemistry of living matter is radically different from that of inert matter, and (2) that life is, as a result, a titanic force driving the chemical composition of the Earth's atmosphere, hydrosphere, and even crusty lithosphere. Third, the temporal and spatial scales of Vernadsky's thinking about *life* on Earth are newly planetary. As Vernadsky says, life *"must be a planetary phenomenon."*[57] From our Protagorean perspective, we perceive the myriads of macroscopic organisms partially constituting the biosphere—being one of them ourselves—as a collection of individuals, each, like ourselves, self-absorbed and engaged in its own struggle for existence. From the same Protagorean perspective, we perceive the myriads of microscopic organisms with which we share the planet not as individuals, but—if and when we perceive them at all—we perceive them only collectively as mats or scums or slimes. Likewise, from Vernadsky's planetary spatio-temporal perspective, all living organisms—ourselves included—merge into "thin films" of living matter completely covering the land surface of the earth and forming an "envelope" enclosing the hydrosphere, one such film at its upper surface, another at its benthos. We think of a mature tree as a single living organism, although by far the greatest bulk of it is biogenic inert matter—wood. Its living matter is the thin cambium between the bark and the wood. The woody inert matter itself forms strata from the pith at the very core, surrounded by the heartwood, and then the sapwood—the area of former cambiums.[58] In a similar way, does Vernadsky conceive of the entire Earth as a single living planet, although the vast bulk of it is composed of inert matter.

7.7 TEILHARD'S CONCEPT OF THE NOÖSPHERE

In "Some Fundamentals of Conservation in the Southwest," Aldo Leopold imagines that the Earth itself, as a whole, might be a "living thing" with "a soul or consciousness"— a fugitive thought that Leopold finds in Ouspensky's *Tertium Organum*. Vernadsky engages in similar speculations under the rubric of the "noösphere." As noted (7.4), Vernadsky did not coin the word *biosphere*. Nor did he coin the word *noösphere*. He borrowed the former from Suess and the latter from Edouard Le Roy.[59] Vernadsky has nothing to say about the noösphere in *The Biosphere*. Le Roy, a disciple of Bergson and a friend of Pierre Teihard de Chardin and, like Teilhard, a devout Catholic, coined the term after that book was written. A mathematician, Le Roy was keen to reconcile evolutionary science with his religion, a project he shared with the metaphysically more talented Teilhard.

In my opinion, the roots of Teilhard's concept of the noösphere reach back to Gottfried Leibniz's monadology, whose roots also sprout off into Alfred North Whitehead's science-inspired metaphysics.[60] The most glaring metaphysical problem left by Descartes's radical mind-body dualism was the causal interaction between mind and body, more generally between the *res cogitans* and the *res extensa*, between the purely mental and the purely physical. Descartes had categorically separated the one from the other, defining them oppositionally: beings in the *res cogitans* are thinking and unextended; things in the *res extensa* are extended and unthinking.[61] Thus, how can a wish, a mental event in the *res cogitans,* cause an arm movement, a physical event in the *res extensa*? And how can a blow to the body, a physical event in the *res extensa,* cause a pain, a mental event in the *res cogitans*? Descartes provides no satisfactory solution to that problem. Leibniz solves the problem by endowing each geometrical point in the *res extensa*—of which there are infinitely many—with mind.[62] A geometrical point is in the *res extensa*, but it is dimensionless and thus itself unextended. Leibniz must have thought somewhat as follows: if unextended in the *res extensa*, of what does a point's very being consist? Descartes had allowed only two modes of being: to be extended or to be thinking. Further, to be unextended is a defining characteristic of beings in the Cartesian *res cogitans*. Thus for it to be at all, a point must be a thinking thing. Each point in space has, as it were, a spatial and a psychological aspect. Its spatial aspect is to be a *point*; its psychological aspect is to be an unextended unit of consciousness, a *monad*. That consciousness is an indivisible unity was a fact stressed by Leibniz, additional evidence that he associated it with indivisible points in space.[63] A point/monad is at once an indivisible physical thing in the *res extensa* and an indivisible thinking thing in the *res cogitans*; and while most monads are but infinitesimally conscious, some are self-aware and rational. All monads have what Leibniz understood as "perception," while some have "apperception." There are bare monads; there are souls; and there are spirits—but only the latter rise to apperceptive, reflective, rational consciousness.[64]

Both Descartes and Leibniz were first and foremost mathematicians; and so, not surprisingly, they developed, each in his own way, a physico-mathematical ontology in the same vein as Plato's construction of the elements in the *Timaeus* ultimately from triangles.[65] The very essence of a Cartesian physical body is to be extended in space. Thus a purely mathematical (geometrical) description of nature, such as we find in Descartes's physics as in Plato's, is exhaustive—no aspect of the cosmos is beyond the reach of mathematical physics. Isaac Newton, however, opted for a Democritean ontology of material—as opposed to mathematical—bodies existing *in* space but not composed *of* delimited space; and that left a lasting imprint on science-inspired metaphysics.[66] Thus, in the science-inspired metaphysics as developed by Teilhard, not monads but matter is ensouled—even individual atoms have an interior psychological as well as an exterior physical aspect. Teilhard viewed evolution as a cosmic process in which elemental interiority—the rudimentary consciousness within all matter— becomes increasingly developed and eventually dominant over the external, material aspect of the cosmos.[67] Cosmic evolution will, Teilhard believed, reach an "Omega Point," whereat evolution achieves its goal (Teilhard's evolutionary metaphysics was teleological) and consciousness becomes liberated from matter altogether. All of this was, of course, expressed in Christian theological terms—in thanks for which the Vatican hierarchy branded Teilhard a heretic, put his writings on the *Index Librorum Prohibitorum*, and exiled him to China.[68]

The evolutionary march to the Omega Point on Earth, for Teilhard, has so far achieved reflective human consciousness. Self-aware consciousness or consciousness proper (apperception) first begins to emerge with the evolution of central nervous systems or the biological process of "cephalization," first remarked by James D. Dana.[69] The noösphere will fully emerge when human consciousness becomes integrated— via such phenomena as the internet, contemporary Teilhardians enthuse—into a kind of unified planetary super-consciousness.[70] We can, perhaps, imagine electronically linked individual human minds to be, in relationship to the emerging mind of the whole planet, what synapsally linked brain cells are to our individual human minds. Just as mind, as we know it, is an emergent epiphenomenon of an integrated central nervous system, so the planetary mind may be an emergent epiphenomenon of a wired (and/or wireless) humanity. Such, more or less, is what Teilhard thought the noösphere would be—the virtual film of mind stuff layered over the actual film of the biosphere—the penultimate condition of consciousness before its ultimate liberation at the Omega Point.

7.8 VERNADSKY'S CONCEPT OF THE NOÖSPHERE

Vernadsky was also a dualist, but of another kind; unlike Teilhard, he was not a mind-body dualist in the tradition of Descartes and Leibniz. Rather, he was a matter-matter dualist in no tradition at all—his dualism, as far as I am aware, being unique. Vernadsky regards himself, however, to be in a short nineteenth-century lineage of thinkers at the head of which is Dana, followed by another American, Joseph Le Conte, a geologist who identified a "psychozoic era" in biological evolution on planet Earth.[71] For Vernadsky, there is inert matter and living matter, both existing from here to eternity—both being primal, coeval, and co-equal. Living matter colonizes inert matter and expands its domain (and that domain's associated peculiar space with its enantiomorphically asymmetrical locally Riemannian geometry) at the expense of inert matter. As living matter evolves it becomes more efficient at converting radiant solar energy into terrestrial chemical energy, by means of more complex organisms, and it becomes more and more established on its planetary platform of inert matter and maintains more and more stable biogeochemical conditions favorable to itself. Vernadsky believed that scientific knowledge was a biogeochemical phenomenon—whose evolutionary origins were traceable to cephalization, à la Dana, and which is now advancing and accumulating as Le Conte's psychozoic era reaches its zenith.[72] After enumerating a few of the indicators of the global scope of "man's" physical and mental colonization of the planet—penetrating all continents and permanently residing on all but one, mapping the entire world, flying all over it in airplanes, communicating instantaneously by radio around the world—Vernadsky reveals his evolutionary materialism by attributing these accomplishments not to the human mind, but to the human *brain*: "All this is the result of 'cephalization,' the growth of man's brain and the work directed by his brain."[73] The corpus of scientific knowledge presently accumulating in the biosphere, its technological application, and the way human technology is uniting humankind and transforming the biosphere is Vernadsky's nascent noösphere.

For Vernadsky, the noösphere is the latest and greatest morphological development in the evolution of living matter. What living matter does changes not one iota: it transforms radiant solar energy into terrestrial chemical energy; it recruits atoms from inert matter and chemically reorganizes them into itself; it chemically transforms the atmosphere, hydrosphere, and lithosphere—better to accommodate itself. As it evolves it just does what it does more and more efficiently and secures its hold on and control over the planet. None of that changes with the advent of the noösphere; it all only gets elaborated and accelerated. In the noösphere "native" (reduced) iron and aluminum are being produced in smelters; "artificial chemical combinations (biogenic 'cultural' minerals) [are being] newly created on our planet." Indeed, "[c]hemically, the face of our planet, the biosphere, is being sharply changed by man, consciously, and even more so, unconsciously.... Besides this, new species and races of plants and animals are being created by man."[74]

7.9 SCIENTIFIC KNOWLEDGE AS A PLANETARY PHENOMENON

In "The Biosphere and the Noösphere," Vernadsky exudes a spirit of technological optimism. He was a Russian; and he was also a loyal citizen of the Soviet Union, although he did not approve of the oppressive political methods of its rulers. With the Soviet authorities he did agree that religion impedes scientific enlightenment and should be discouraged. And by at least one measure, the Soviet Union was superior to the West in fostering the birth of the noösphere, which advances the age-old work of living matter via scientifically informed technology. The putatively rational Soviet-style command and control economic system keeps a firm hand on the tiller of evolutionary progress. To his credit, Vernadsky sounds a note of caution: to wit, that the birth of the noösphere is fraught with danger and pain. As he writes, World War II is raging; and Vernadsky opens the noösphere section of the essay with a reference to the war, refers to it several more times as he proceeds, and closes the essay by returning to reflections on the war. The belligerents, we must remember, employ cultural minerals (gun powder, for example) and native iron and aluminum for destructive purposes, proving that rational, scientifically informed means can be employed to serve retrogressive and destructive ends. Vernadsky anticipates the "tragedy of the commons" when he cautions that "Man now must take more and more measures to preserve for future generations the wealth of the seas which have so far belonged to nobody."[75] He also notes that change to the face of our planet is being effected by "man" more unconsciously than consciously. That is certainly a sobering thought. Vernadsky may have believed that only atoms cross the spatio-temporal boundary between inert matter and living matter, but if that were true, we would have nothing to fear from the "artificial chemical combinations" being created by "man"—such as dichlorodiphenyltrichloroethane (DDT) and polychlorinated dibenzodioxins. Vernadsky could have learned as much about the "side effects" of twentieth-century technologies from Leopold (and Rachel Carson) as Leopold could have learned about biogeochemistry from him.

Vernadsky's technological optimism and his optimism about the noöspherical future is principled, not pollyannaish. While religious "knowledge" (or, better, religious cognition) is sectarian and thus divisive, scientific knowledge is universal and unifying in two principal ways.[76] Theravada Buddhism, for example, originated in India and differs fundamentally with and contradicts Roman Catholic Christianity, but there is no such thing as, say, a distinctly Chinese science that differs fundamentally from and contradicts, say, French science. There is simply international science, though sometimes it is accented, as it were (which is very evident in reading Vernadsky). Religious epistemology, moreover, leads to conflict. In religious epistemology, propositional belief is a matter of choice and will, not evidence and rational compulsion. One person chooses to believe that Jesus Christ is the Son of God and his personal Savior, while another chooses to believe that there is no god but Allah and Mohammed is His Prophet. No evidence is sought to decisively adjudicate between these conflicting beliefs; rather, conflicting religious beliefs often erupt into violent conflicts between mutually contradicting believers. One scientist, on the other hand, may believe that light is propagated through a fluid-like luminiferous ether and another that it moves through space as quantized photons. When an experiment like that performed by Michelson and Morley (detailed and documented in 4.3) provides decisive evidence that there is no luminiferous either in which light propagates, as waves do in water or sound does in air, then most scientists abandon the one belief in favor of the other (and when those scientists who refuse to abandon their pet falsified theory die off, a discredited belief, such as that in a luminiferous ether, disappears from science universally).

Second, science has shown that there is but one human species, *Homo sapiens*, and that racial distinctions have little basis in human biology. As Vernadsky notes, "The geological evolutionary process shows the biological unity and equality of all men …; their progeny in the mixed white, red, yellow, and black races evolves ceaselessly in enumerable generations" and combinations.[77] He then states the principal reason for his optimism: "In a historical context, as for instance in a war of such magnitude as the present one, he finally wins who follows … the principle of the unity of all men as a law of nature."[78] The German and Japanese fascists prosecuted the war motivated largely by racist ideologies. And they lost.

The noösphere, in the form of scientific knowledge and its technological application, is—like its parent stock, living matter—a planetary phenomenon.[79] In sharp contrast both to speculative philosophies, which bear the stamp of their individual excogitators (Platonism, Aristotelianism, Cartesianism, Hegelianism, etc.), and to dogmatic, sectarian religions, which are tethered to a founder (Confucius, Buddha, Moses, Jesus, Mohammed, etc.), science is a collective cognitive corpus distributed throughout the network of human brains scattered over the entire planet and connected by all the various means of scientific communication—conferences, journals, books, now the internet. For Vernadsky, because scientific cognition is the only kind of cognition that is independent, impersonal, distributed, self-organizing, self-correcting, and planetary in form and scope, it is the only kind of cognition that constitutes the noösphere.

7.10 THE BIOSPHERE CROSSES THE ATLANTIC

The biosphere idea was born of Suess in Austria in the late nineteenth century and migrated to Russia in the early twentieth. It reappeared in Western Europe, greatly elaborated by Vernadsky, in his lectures at the Sorbonne in 1922–23, followed, in France, by the publication of his *La Biosphère* in 1929.[80] Le Roy and Teilhard attended those lectures and befriended Vernadsky, but they were more interested in developing the metaphysics of the noösphere than the biogeochemistry of the biosphere. The biosphere idea crossed the Atlantic in the 1940s due to a fortunate coincidence of academic collegiality. Vernadsky's son, George, was a professor of Russian history at Yale University and introduced his father's work to a leading Anglo-American ecologist, G. Evelyn Hutchinson, who was also a member of the Yale faculty.

Hutchinson facilitated the publication of two short but synoptic works by Vernadsky in English in 1944 and 1945—"Problems of Biogeochemistry, II" and "The Biosphere and the Noösphere," respectively. In the former, Vernadsky elaborates his theory, inspired by Einstein, that the space in which living matter exists is describable by an enantiomorphically asymmetrical Riemannian geometry, which is different from the space and its correlative geometry occupied by inert matter (as detailed and documented in 7.2 and 7.3). In the same year that Vernadsky's "Problems of Biogeochemistry, II" was published, Hutchinson first broached his conception of an ecological niche as "a region of n-dimensional hyperspace comparable to the phase-space of statistical mechanics" (detailed in 3.14).[81] It is possible that Vernadsky's metaphysical speculations about the peculiar four-dimensional space-time continuum occupied by living matter inspired Hutchinson's development of his n-dimensional-hyperspace niche theory in ecology, which he eventually elaborated more than a decade later.[82] Hutchinson's ecological hyperspace bears no closer resemblance to Vernadsky's living-matter space than Vernadsky's living-matter space bears to Einstein's general-relativity cosmic space. In the nineteenth century, Riemann (and also Nikolai Lobachevsky) liberated geometry from its classical Euclidean confines.[83] In the twentieth century, Einstein demonstrated that non-Euclidean geometries were more than recreational mathematics; they might have physical manifestations. Einstein's application of Riemannian geometry to cosmic space freed Vernadsky to apply it locally and with added asymmetries to the space of living matter. Vernadsky's speculations about the geometry of the space inside living matter may have inspired Hutchinson to think about ecological niche theory in a geometrical mode. One cannot know for sure, however, for, as far as I am aware, Hutchinson does not credit Vernadsky for his inspiration as Vernadsky credits Einstein for his own.

Be that as it may, the biosphere idea lay dormant in the West for a quarter century—until 1970, after which time it experienced a period of intense interest and publicity. What brought the biosphere idea out of the shadows and shone both popular and scientific attention on it were the stunningly beautiful photographs of the Earth—actually perceptible for the first time as a whole living planet—taken from the moon by the Apollo 8, 10, and 11 astronauts in 1968 and 1969. In 1970, *Scientific American* devoted its September issue to "the biosphere." In the "Foreword" to the publication of its articles in book form, the editors' first words—"Photographs of the earth..."—implicitly acknowledge the debt of the biosphere concept, for its revival, to those images.[84]

Fittingly, Hutchinson wrote the introductory article, "The Biosphere," for the *Scientific American* special issue (and book) and begins with a short history of the biosphere idea, highlighting the centrality of Vernadsky to its development. Hutchinson emphasized the cyclical nature of biogeochemical processes.[85] Most of the rest of the articles (chapters) focus on one or another biospheric cycle in more detail. A ubiquitous theme running throughout is the dire threat to the biosphere and its biogeochemical equilibria posed by industrialized humanity. Hutchinson sets the tone. He ends by contrasting Vernadsky's giddy techno-optimism about the advent of the noösphere with his own apocalyptic pessimism that *Homo sapiens* may lately have become a more destructive than creative biogeochemical development in the biosphere.

7.11 THE ADVENT OF THE GAIA HYPOTHESIS

By his own account, James Lovelock "first put forward the Gaia hypothesis at a scientific meeting about the origins of life on Earth which took place in Princeton, New Jersey, in 1969."[86] At that conference, he met Lynn Margulis and they began "a most rewarding collaboration" in advancing the hypothesis.[87] Margulis and Lovelock elaborated the Gaia hypothesis in several co-authored publications over the course of the 1970s.[88]

The link between Lovelock and Verndasky was indirect, but only by one degree of separation. Lovelock first introduced Gaia, by that name, to the community of atmospheric scientists and environmentalists in a two-page letter to the editors of *Atmospheric Environment* in 1972.[89] In that letter, Lovelock simply bestows a proper name on the biosphere: "The Biosphere," [note both the capital "T" and the capital "B"] he writes, being "such a large creature, even if only hypothetical,...needs a name; I am indebted to Mr. William Golding [a novelist and Nobel laureate, author of *Lord of the Flies*, and a neighbor of Lovelock's] for suggesting the use of the Greek personification of mother Earth, 'Gaia.'"[90] In his introductory article, "The Biosphere," in the *Scientific American* special issue and book (titled *The Biosphere*), Hutchinson credited Vernadsky with articulating "the concept of the biosphere...that we accept today."[91] Lovelock does not cite that article, but he does cite a more technical work by Hutchinson on the biochemistry of the atmosphere published in 1954.[92] There, Hutchinson does not cite Vernadsky, although his prominent use of the phrases "living matter," which Vernadsky preferred to "life," and "the biosphere" indicates his debt to the Russian biogeochemist and natural philosopher. Lovelock thus rhetorically connects his Gaia hypothesis with Vernadsky's concept of the biosphere—which had come into scientific vogue, thanks in large part to Hutchinson, by the early 1970s—although he seems to do so less deliberately than subconsciously. Indeed, as Lovelock later confesses, "When I first formulated the Gaia hypothesis, I was entirely ignorant of the related ideas of these earlier scientists, especially...Vernadsky."[93]

Because the revival of the biosphere concept followed closely on the heels of the appearance of the extraterrestrial photographs of the Earth, it is fitting that the Gaia hypothesis, closely associated by Lovelock with the biosphere idea, would emerge from the planetary perspective of the nascent Space Age. In the 1960s, Lovelock was consulted by the US National Aeronautics and Space Administration (NASA) to help it devise instruments to detect life on Mars, if any there might be. The thought was to equip a vehicle to be landed on Mars with instruments to dig around on the Martian surface to discover any microbial organisms that might be living there or traces of biogenic chemicals that presently extinct organisms might have left behind. Lovelock and a NASA colleague, Dian Hitchcock, however, suggested a cheaper way to determine if there were life on Mars, without having to send a robot there. Just spectroscopically examine the composition of the Martian atmosphere; if only signatures of inert gases at chemical equilibrium are seen, that would be a sign that the tell-tale reactive by-products of living matter—such as oxygen and methane—were not being constantly replenished on Mars as they are on Earth.[94] Lovelock concluded that the predominance of carbon dioxide in the Martian atmosphere indicated that it was lifeless—unwelcome news to his rocket-crazed clients, but news that set him to thinking less about Mars than about the living Earth.[95] He was led to "the development of the hypothesis that the entire range of living matter on Earth, from whales to viruses, and from oaks to algae, could be regarded as constituting a single living entity, capable of manipulating the Earth's atmosphere to suit its overall needs and endowed with faculties and powers far beyond those of its constituent parts."[96]

Although Lovelock and Margulis closely collaborated in developing the Gaia hypothesis and co-authored a number of seminal papers about Gaia, their conceptions of Gaia eventually diverged on (at least) one crucial point. They both understand life in thermodynamic terms and they both agree that the biosphere is self-organizing and self-regulating. While Lovelock conceives the biosphere to be a "single living organism," Margulis disagrees—indeed quite pointedly: "I reject Jim's statement: 'The Earth is alive.'…I do not agree with the formulation that says 'Gaia is an organism.'…Rather, Gaia is an extremely complex system with identifiable regulatory properties which are very specific to the lower atmosphere."[97]

7.12 THE BIOSPHERE AND GAIA ECOLOGIZED

Hutchinson and the other contributors to the *Scientific American* special issue (and book) implicitly ecologize, as it were, the biosphere concept—which is somewhat foreign to the way Vernadsky presented it. Vernadsky was educated to be a crystallographer, mineralogist, and geologist, not an ecologist. Lovelock became acquainted with the biosphere concept not by reading Vernadsky's book, as he confesses in *The Ages of Gaia* (even though it had long been available in French), but via the representation of it by Hutchinson in the 1954 article that Lovelock cites in his 1972 letter to the editors. In 1972, moreover, he could hardly have been ignorant of the articles by Hutchinson and the other authors, many of whom were also ecologists, in the *Scientific American* special issue and book, *The Biosphere*, published in 1970.[98] Not surprisingly then, Lovelock, though no more an ecologist himself than was Vernadsky, ecologizes the biosphere idea: "'The Biosphere,' *like other associations in biology* is an entity with properties greater than the simple sum of the parts."[99] The biosphere was conceived by Hutchinson—and also, it seems, by Lovelock—as the ecosystem of ecosystems. But, in the early 1970s, ecosystems (prominent among the other "associations" in biology) were thought to be hierarchically nested organismic or quasi-organismic entities (as detailed in 3.12).[100] In 1970, accordingly, Hutchinson and the other authors of Scientific American's *The Biosphere*, implicitly followed by Lovelock, took the biosphere to be the largest and most comprehensive of Earth's organism-like ecosystems, an organismic ecosystem of planetary proportions. Because Lovelock introduced Gaia as "The Biosphere" by another, more personal name, she acquired this essentially ecological identity.

Margulis, in step with the post-1970s paradigm shift in ecology (as detailed in 3.16), would eventually "reject" the *organismic interpretation* of Gaia. For Margulis, as for Lovelock, Gaia, the biosphere by another name, is a homeostatic planetary ecosystem, but she, unlike he, appears to understand ecosystems more as neo-Gleasonian networks of symbiotic organisms than as neo-Clementsian super-organisms. In her own words, "Less a single entity than a huge set of interacting ecosystems, the Earth, as Gaian regulatory physiology, transcends all individual organisms….Gaia is the series of interacting ecosystems that compose a single huge ecosystem at the Earth's surface. Period….Gaia is the sum of these growing, interacting, dying populations; a multispecies planetary covering, composed of myriad very different beings, Gaia is the largest ecosystem on Earth."[101]

At the core of Gaia's thermodynamic identity is that she has a metabolism; at the core of her ecological identity is that she has a physiology. When ecology was coalescing as a distinct, "self-conscious" science, some of the first ecologists—among them Ernst Haeckel who coined the term *œcology* in the late nineteenth century, F. E. Clements, the dean of American ecology during the first quarter of the twentieth century, and H. C. Cowles, a lauded contemporary of Clements—characterized it as a branch or as a species of physiology.[102] On first hearing, I was puzzled by this characterization, because as I understood physiology, it is the study of the function of the *internal* organs of an organism—a study of the functions of the kidneys and livers in animals, of the stomata and chloroplasts in plants. How could ecology—which studies not just whole organisms, but the relations among organisms and with their inorganic environments—be thought to be a branch of physiology? Finally it dawned on me. More generally, physiology is a study of the functional components of living systems. And the first paradigm in ecology, most forcefully articulated by Clements, was that multi-organismic biological associations were super-organisms.[103] Ecology was initially conceived to be the study of the functional components, the "organs," of the living systems that were later dubbed "ecosystems." Ecosystem ecology, especially, represents organisms as the functional components in the processes of energy transformation and flux and the cycling of "nutrients"—atoms, such as carbon, oxygen, nitrogen, phosphorous, iron, calcium, and so on. Ecosystem ecology is thus, quintessentially, a species of physiology. If Gaia is the biosphere personified and the biosphere is the highest-order ecosystem in the nested hierarchy of ecosystems, then planetary biogeochemistry is the study of Gaia's physiology.

7.13 VERNADSKY'S BIOSPHERE AND LOVELOCK'S GAIA: SIMILARITIES AND DIFFERENCES

After reading Vernadsky, the Gaia-hypothesis literature from the mid-1970s seems a bit redundant and to some extent serves to undermine confidence in Vernadsky's idea that scientific knowledge is a planetary phenomenon. The nearly universal ignorance of Vernadsky in the Anglophone world bespeaks two things: first, the intellectual isolation of the Soviet Union, even before the postwar descent of the Iron Curtain, and, second, the monolingual provincialism of the Anglophone scientific community. If it is too much to expect that British and American biologists, geologists, and chemists might read Vernadsky's epic masterpiece, *Biosfera*, in the Russian original, surely it would not be too much to expect that some might read *La Biosphère* in French and build a biospheric biogeochemical Anglophone literature on that foundation. Whatever. The independent emergence of biospheric biogeochemistry in the Russo-French scientific community in the early twentieth century, on the one hand, and, on the other, in the Anglo-American scientific community half a century later affords the opportunity for comparing differences in scientific foci and in their correlative science-inspired metaphysics.

Common to Vernadsky's biospheric biogeochemistry and Lovelock's is the idea that life must be understood in thermodynamic terms, that living organisms are *thermodynamically* far-from-equilibrium systems—little energy-consuming and energy-dissipating nodules of negentropy, as it were. The autotrophs use solar energy to assemble themselves and, in doing so, convert radiant energy into potential chemical energy; the heterotrophs dissipate that chemical energy and recycle the elements from which the autotrophs again assemble themselves. Also common is the understanding that the thermodynamical processes characteristic of living matter create a *chemically* far-from-equilibrium planetary atmosphere and hydrosphere. While Vernadsky focused on the *self-creating* chemical transformation of the Earth by living matter—the chemical transformation of the atmosphere, the hydrosphere, and even the lithosphere—Lovelock focused on the cybernetic *self-regulating* function of living matter. Because Lovelock was a member of a generation of scientists disabused of any ideas that the cosmos and the Earth in it existed in an eternal steady state, he was keenly aware that the Earth's cosmic environment had significantly changed, but that, after the Oxygen Crisis, the environmental conditions on Earth favorable to life had remained relatively constant. Therefore, Gaia appeared to be self-regulating as well as self-organizing, "a biological cybernetic system able to homeostat the planet for an optimum physical and chemical state appropriate to its current biosphere."[104]

7.14 LEOPOLD'S LIVING THING, VERNADSKY'S BIOSPHERE, AND LOVELOCK'S GAIA

As noted at the beginning of this chapter, Aldo Leopold and Vladimir Vernadsky were thinking along similar lines in the 1920s, the latter far more deeply and extensively than the former. As also noted (7.12), Vernadsky's concept of the biosphere is informed less by ecology than by biogeochemistry, the science that Vernadsky pioneered, springing forth from his background in crystallography, mineralogy, and geology. So, to recap, Vernadsky's biosphere crossed the Atlantic in the 1940s and was ecologized by G. E. Hutchinson. Led by Hutchinson, the ecologized biosphere concept gave scientific substance to the Space-Age realization of the 1970s that the Earth is a living planet—the only living planet in the solar system, in stark contrast with all the others. The biosphere was conceived to be the universal ecosystem of ecosystems, an ecosystem of planetary proportions and scale. Ecosystems were then conceived in neo-Clementsian organismic terms. Lovelock conferred a personal identity, Gaia, on the biospheric planetary eco-organism. Foundational to the gestation of ecology is physiology, so much so that, at its inception, ecology was thought to be a subfield of physiology—the study of the functional components of super-organisms à la Clements.

Thus in the person of Gaia, Vernadsky's biosphere harked back to the faint sketch that Leopold drew of her at about the same time that Vernadsky was painting his far richer and more detailed portrait. Here again is the central figure of Leopold's sketch. "A good expression of this conception of organized animate nature is given by the

Russian philosopher."[105] Of course, Leopold identifies that philosopher as Ouspensky, but, as here oft insisted, Leopold's true contemporary on this intellectual venture was another Russian, a bona fide philosopher and scientist, Vladimir Vernadsky. Of course, it would have been impossible for Leopold to have been aware of Vernadsky's biospheric science and philosophy in 1923, short of attending Vernadsky's Parisian lectures in 1922–23, because *Biosfera* did not appear until 1926 in Russia and again in 1929, as *La Biosphère* in France. That the inferior "philosophy" of the one Russian was then available in English and the far superior philosophy of the other did not fully appear in English until 1998 (!) is a telling irony. As Leopold goes on, however, he might as well have been referring to Vernadsky's philosophy—at least as Vernadsky's thought was filtered through the mind of Hutchinson and unwittingly channeled by Lovelock a quarter century after Vernadsky's death:

> He then states that it is at least not impossible to regard the earth's parts—soil, mountains, rivers, atmosphere, etc.—as organs or parts of organs, of a coordinated whole, each part with a definite function. And if we could see this whole, as a whole, through a great period of time, we might perceive not only organs with coordinated functions, but possibly also that process of consumption and replacement which in biology we call metabolism or growth. In such a case we would have all the visible attributes of a living thing, which we do not realize to be such because it is too big, and its life processes too slow. And there would also follow that invisible attribute—a soul or consciousness—which…many philosophers of all ages ascribe to all living things and aggregations thereof including the "dead" earth.[106]

Leopold here captures the two most fundamental features of Gaia's identity. She exhibits both physiological (functional parts) and metabolic (transformative) attributes. In light of this review of Vernadsky's insights into the titanic force represented by living *matter*, Leopold appears prescient in identifying not plants and animals as the organs of the Earth organism, but "soil, mountains, rivers, atmosphere." Plants and animals—and the monera, the protoctista, and the fungi, Margulis would be quick to add—are the functional components of smaller-scale ecosystems in the hierarchy of ecosystems.[107] Along with the ocean, the biogenic soil, mountains, rivers, and atmosphere are plausibly regarded as the macro-organs of the living Earth. In addition to "organs with coordinated functions" Leopold speculates that this big living thing with slow life processes might also have a metabolism. While Leopold's emphasis on physiology—on organs with coordinated functions—comports with the ecological spin given the biosphere idea by Hutchinson, the idea that the living Earth has a metabolism is at the heart of Vernadsky's conception of the biosphere. Metabolism—from the Greek, μεταβολισμός, meaning change or transformation—is the universal process by which living beings ingest and chemically transform external materials and energy to organize and maintain themselves.[108] For Vernadsky, life is a planetary phenomenon, the essence of which is the transformation of solar radiation into potential chemical energy by living matter incorporating and transforming inert matter into itself.

The distinctly Lovelockean feature of Leopold's big, slow planetary living thing is its soul or consciousness, which is also the most controversial aspect of Lovelock's Gaia hypothesis. It is a short step from speculation about an autopoietic or *self-organizing* and cybernetic or *self-regulating* living Earth—which is also animate and conscious—to speculation about a living Earth that is *self-designing*. That, however, would be tantamount to teleology, the Earth consciously envisioning and pursuing ends, purposes, or goals. And explanations of natural phenomena in terms of final causes is a scientific anathema. In the preface to his first book-length summary and consolidation of the Gaia hypothesis, Lovelock is aware of the danger: "there are passages and sentences which may read as if infected with the twin blights of anthropomorphism and teleology." He goes on,

> I have frequently used the word Gaia as a shorthand for the hypothesis itself, namely that the biosphere is a self-regulating entity with the capacity to keep our planet healthy by controlling the chemical and physical environment. Occasionally it has been difficult, without excessive circumlocution, to avoid talking as if she were known to be sentient. This is meant no more seriously than is the appellation "she" when given to a ship by those who sail in her, as a recognition that pieces of wood and metal when specifically designed and assembled may achieve a composite identity with its own characteristic signature, as distinct from the mere sum of its parts.[109]

The ship analogy, however, only serves to undermine the "shorthand"-to-avoid-"circumlocution" caveat. The functional components and internal environment of a ship are, as Lovelock says, "specifically *designed* and assembled." If the ship comparison is apt, then Gaia has a designer. Lovelock is hardly doing natural theology in the creationist tradition; he never so much as hints at the existence of an *external* Designer—no biblical Creator, no Platonic demiurge. Thus the only Designer we are left to suppose might be orchestrating things is Gaia herself. His very disclaimer infects Lovelock's Gaia hypothesis with those "twin blights of anthropomorphism and teleology." This is the more inexplicable because in his 1972 introduction of Gaia to the world, Lovelock contemptuously denounced a version of the ship analogy—the metaphor of "Space Ship Earth"—as being both hubristically and dangerously anthropo*centric* if not maladroitly anthropo*morphic*.[110]

7.15 IS THE GAIA HYPOTHESIS NECESSARILY TELEOLOGICAL AND ANTHROPOMORPHIC?

Lovelock's *Gaia: A New Look at Life on Earth* was immediately criticized by his fellow scientists, especially by neo-Darwinian evolutionary biologists, as being infected by the twin blights of anthropomorphism and teleology. Among the first to firmly but temperately level such a criticism was the distinguished ecologist Herb Bormann, a colleague of Hutchinson's at Yale.[111] Less temperately, molecular biologist Ford Doolittle leveled the same charges in the pages of *Co-Evolution Quarterly*, where, to much fanfare, Lovelock and Margulis had broached the Gaia hypothesis in 1975.[112] Also notable was a critique by Richard Dawkins, famed author of the *Selfish Gene*.[113]

I can only say that these critics must not have read Lovelock's book carefully and sympathetically. True, he appears at points to drag Gaia in as a deus ex machina (regular employment for Greek goddesses, one must suppose) when it seems that the planet would, without her intervention, be at risk of some lethal runaway accumulation of some substance, such as too much salt in the sea or too much oxygen or too much carbon dioxide in the atmosphere. For example,

> If Gaia regulates carbon dioxide, it is probably by the indirect method of assist-
> ing the attainment of equilibrium rather than opposing it....With the situa-
> tion so well in hand, is there any need for Gaia's intervention? There certainly
> may be a need, if the attainment of equilibrium is not rapid enough for the
> biosphere as a whole....There are many signs of Gaian impatience with the
> leisurely progress towards natural equilibrium in the case of carbon dioxide.[114]

But such language is, as Lovelock announced in the preface, only a "shorthand" to avoid "excessive circumlocution" in explaining planetary cybernetics in non-teleological and impersonal terms. We accept teleological locutions in physiological discourse all the time and without exception. The *purpose* of the heart is to pump blood through the circulatory system and the *purpose* of the kidneys is to remove wastes and excess water from the blood. No scientist supposes that evolutionary physiologists are suggesting that the heart and kidney have been thoughtfully designed to serve those purposes as have, say, the fuel pump and catalytic converter in an automobile. Rather, through many millions of years, such organs have blindly evolved through chance variation and natural selection, their "functions" originally having resulted from fortuitous muta-tions of some other cellular structure or fortuitous side effects of some other bio-chemical process. Lovelock is simply asking his readers to allow him similar liberties for expository convenience.

So much for the teleological blight, what about the blight of anthropomorphism? As Lovelock himself hints, there is a delicious irony in the charge of anthropomorphism coming from an evolutionary biologist like Richard Dawkins, who popularized the concept of the "*selfish* gene," an idea first proffered by W. D. Hamilton.[115] Selfishness is a conscious state of mind and disposition. Genes have no states of mind nor any dis-positions. In the very pages in which Dawkins excoriates Lovelock for anthropomor-phizing the biosphere, he himself anthropomorphizes plants. As Dawkins understands Lovelock, "plants are supposed to make oxygen for the good of the biosphere"; but he insists that "the scientific world accepts" his own anthropomorphic view "that oxygen production is a by-product of something that plants do for their own selfish good."[116] As Lovelock later gently noted, "We all know that the selfish gene is a metaphor as prone to misinterpretation as any in science. But it was produced in a world where, at least, in scientific circles, it faced paltry opposition, and so its proponents were spared endless debates on whether or not a gene could be truly selfish....Gaia was not so lucky."[117]

The "selfish gene" is by no means the only pass that neo-Darwinian evolutionary biologists are given in scientific circles. The neo-Darwinian evolutionary biology literature is rife with anthropomorphic and teleological locutions (as both noted and quoted in 4.15). To various organisms are attributed not only such intentions as to maximize their reproductive potential but also to them are attributed complicated "strategies" for accomplishing their goals, based on exact statistical knowledge of the behavior of such things as sperm, eggs, and genes. Orthodox evolutionary biologists attribute selfishness to genes and goals and sophisticated strategies for achieving them to brute beasts and even unconscious organisms, such as plants, without being accused of teleology and anthropomorphism. But only the tiny fraction of the human population that is biologically literate has any awareness at all of such things, much less brute beasts and dumb plants. We understand—and hope that the neo-Darwinians do as well—that such locutions are a form of metaphorical shorthand. But when unorthodox scientists, such as Lovelock, use a similar shorthand—despite explicit warnings not to take it literally—they are accused, it seems inevitably, of teleology and anthropomorphism.

Why the difference? Margulis and other exponents of the Gaia hypothesis suggest that the difference can be found by reference to the prevailing models of economics, politics, and analytic philosophy.[118] The idea of *selfish* genes figuring out ingenious ways to achieve their single-minded goal of increased phenotypic representation chimes well with capitalism and liberalism in political economics. And the selfish-*gene* metaphor chimes well with reductionism—underwritten and celebrated by mainstream philosophers of science—in the so-called hard and rigorous sciences. One thus uncovers an invidious "hermeneutic circle" in which evolutionary biology, as a social phenomenon, reflects and is validated by its cultural context and, in turn, reinforces and validates the cultural context that it reflects. The Gaia hypothesis breaks out of this hermeneutic circle and is thus met with the kind of furious persecution reserved for heresy.

7.16 VARIETIES OF THE EARTH'S SOUL OR CONSCIOUSNESS

Unfairly held to a higher standard than his neo-Darwinian critics, Lovelock and his associates created an ingenious model to purge the Gaia hypothesis of the twin blights of anthropomorphism and teleology—Daisyworld.[119] The simplest and most familiar cybernetic system known to man is a thermostat in a heated box of some sort—a house in winter or an oven in a kitchen. Lovelock painstakingly explains the workings of a thermostat in *Gaia* (the 1979 book) and indeed one of the self-regulating functions of Gaia is temperature equilibrium in the face of ever-increasing solar radiation. Daisyworld is what philosophers call a thought experiment, enhanced by computer modeling and scenario running. The black and white daisies of that model planet constitute an organic thermostat. The planet's star, like the sun, gradually increases its radiation output. When incoming energy is low, black daisies predominate, capture heat, and warm the planet's surface. As the incoming energy increases, the black daisies wilt from the surface-heat beneath them; and the white ones, which reflect solar radiation back to space—the albedo effect—take their place and the surface cools. If there is too much cooling the black daisies increase their population at the expense of the white ones and so on—just like the way the thermostat in one's house or oven operates to oscillate the internal temperature closely about a set point. No need for teleology, no need for an anthropomorphic mind to manipulate the machinery of control. Daisyworld passes the strictest test of neo-Darwinian evolutionary dogma; the black and white daisies evolved by chance mutation and natural selection and each specimen of each species is "selfish," competing with specimens of the other species for a place in the sunshine.

So, have we come all this way to just to cave in to evolutionary orthodoxy and reduce Gaia to an entity no more mysterious and no more alive and soulful than a thermostat? Again, we might turn to Leopold for some insightful guidance: "There is not much discrepancy, except in language, between [the] conception of a living earth, and the conception of a dead earth, with enormously slow, intricate, and interrelated functions among its parts, as given us by physics, chemistry, and geology."[120] The task is to find suitable language (and language is, above all, the vehicle of thought) to express the "conception of a living earth" with "that invisible attribute—a soul or consciousness—which" Leopold thought would inspire an Earth ethic. But there is a paramount constraint on that language, which all our scientific metaphysicists—Leopold, Vernadsky, Lovelock, Margulis—either explicitly or implicitly endorse. It must be consistent with "the conception of…[E]arth…given us by physics, chemistry, and geology." Gaia cannot be supposed to work miracles—to contravene the workings of the laws of nature—in order to effect some optimization of the earthly environment in the interest of organic life on Earth. Gaia is constrained by the laws of thermodynamics, by the conservation laws of physics and chemistry, by the law of competitive exclusion in evolutionary biology and ecology. And she is constrained by a law of science, if not of nature—the law of ateleology. We can no more plausibly suppose that Gaia plans her ontogeny or deliberately controls her own physiology and metabolism than do us mindful reference organisms to which Gaia is compared.

A good reason for thinking that Lovelock's critics did not read him closely is that he speculates quite soberly about Gaian psychology at the very end of his 1979 book-length exposition of the Gaia hypothesis. As an opening gambit, he defines intelligence quite broadly as a pragmatic response to information, so that even the simplest of cybernetica, such as the domestic thermostat, would be "intelligent" in some minimal sense. "There is a spectrum of intelligence," Lovelock avers, "ranging from the most rudimentary…to our own conscious and unconscious thoughts during the solving of a difficult problem."[121] Where Gaia falls on that spectrum—if anywhere at all on it—Lovelock does not speculate. From that observation he moves on to his own version of noöspheric metaphysics: "If we [humans] are a part of Gaia it becomes interesting to ask: 'To what extent is our collective intelligence also a part of Gaia? Do we as a species constitute a Gaian nervous system and a brain which can consciously anticipate environmental changes?'"[122] Gaia, we must suppose, has heretofore not been an anthropomorphic teleological system but may become one through networked, integrated, scientific human intelligence. For example, astronomers might predict a catastrophic asteroid impact and rocket scientists and nuclear physicists might devise a means of averting it, all to the good of life on Earth. Lovelock's is pretty much Vernadsky's concept of the noösphere redux. Going a bit further than Vernadsky, but not as far as Teilhard, Lovelock suggests that Gaia "is now through us awake and aware of herself."[123]

Margulis is even more conservative than the Dawkins-chastened post-1970s Lovelock. To Gaia, Margulis attributes only "proprioceptive" sensibility—a kind of pre-consciousness. Proprioception is the unawares processing of information regarding spatial orientation and locomotion. Continuously, we—that is, our bodies—maintain upright posture and balance while sitting, standing, walking, and riding on moving vehicles that change speed and direction. "Analogous to proprioception," Margulis writes, "Gaian patterns appear to be planned...." That is, they appear to be teleologically determined,

> but occur in the absence of any central "head" or "brain." Proprioception, as self-awareness, evolved long before animals evolved, and long before their brains did. Sensitivity, awareness, and responses of plants, protoctists, fungi, bacteria, and animals, each in its local environment, constitute the repeating pattern that ultimately underlies global sensitivity and the response of Gaia "herself."[124]

Consistent with her more neo-Gleasonian ecological understanding of Gaia, Margulis is loath to think that there is a unified planetary soul or consciousness—because there is no single planetary organism to which it belongs. Rather, the billions upon billions of contemporaneous proprioceptive organisms, in repeating the same proprioceptive pattern, in the manner of fractal geometry, produce the same proprioceptive pattern scaled up to planetary proportions. Hers is a subtle conception of Gaian cybernetics, but it differs little in principle from thermostats and daisyworlds and therefore differs greatly from Leopold's speculations about the whole Earth as a *living being with a soul or consciousness*. Nor does Margulis follow Vernadsky and Lovelock in making of wired (and wireless) *Homo sapiens sapiens* an awakening planetary central nervous system that is becoming self-aware and soon capable of forethoughtfully refining the self-regulation and optimization of its internal biogeochemical states and of foreseeing and planning to avoid extraterrestrial threats. Quite the contrary, Margulis appears to be downright misanthropic. "We need to be free of our species-specific arrogance....Our tenacious illusion of special dispensation belies our true status as upright mammalian weeds."[125] So much, then, for her thoughts about any emerging anthropic noösphere.

7.17 PERSONAL SPECULATIONS ON THE EARTH'S SOUL OR CONSCIOUSNESS

Let me conclude this chapter with an account of my own experience upon first reading "Some Fundamentals of Conservation in the Southwest" and of my own quasi-scientific metaphysical speculations to which that experience led. Leopold's article was published in the same year as Lovelock's book, *Gaia: A New Look at Life on Earth*—1979. Familiar then only with *A Sand County Almanac* and "The Land Ethic," here was something wholly unexpected from Leopold's pen. I was transfixed both by the Space-Age spatio-temporal scales of Leopold's thinking in 1923 and by the bold metaphysical speculation in which he indulged. I wandered outside in a state of dazed wonderment. Amazingly, the night sky was aglow with the northern lights. I was then living in Stevens Point, Wisconsin, at just about 45° north latitude. So active was the aurora borealis on that particular evening that the dancing green streaks of light extended beyond the zenith—almost as far into the southern sky, as seen from my position on the planet, as the ecliptic.

My own consciousness biochemically enhanced (I admit) by tetrahydrocannabinol, it came to me literally in a flash. The activity of the soul or consciousness of the living Earth was occasionally visible as the northern lights. For what causes the aurora borealis is the concentration by the Earth's magnetic field of charged particles from cosmic sources, primarily the solar wind.[126] Our own chordate central nervous systems also generate electromagnetic fields that can be detected and measured by electroencephalography and other medical technologies, such as magnetic resonance imaging. The physics of consciousness is electrodynamics. The electromagnetic activity of the Earth, excited by cosmic radiation, might therefore be the physical basis of Gaia's soul or consciousness. The relationship of a unified consciousness to its physical basis—to nerve cells, brain cells, synapses, and the electromagnetic fields generated by their coordinated and orchestrated activity—remains an unsolved mystery of science and philosophy. But the evidence for the existence of consciousness is unimpeachable—our own vivid experience of it. True, as Margulis points out, the Earth has no head or brain, but the Earth does have an electromagnetic field of planetary proportions. And the exciting radiation received from the sun and other cosmic sources might be received and processed by the Earth as information.

Would Gaia's soul or consciousness, so conceived, be anthropomorphic? Perhaps. Would it be teleological? Not if it were truly anthropomorphic. As conscious humans we may plan on what to have for dinner of an evening; we may plan for retirement. We set all sorts of goals and devise means to achieve them—sometimes successfully, sometimes not. But we do not consciously plan our own ontogeny, our growth and development; we do not consciously control our internal temperature, metabolism, and bodily functions. Gaia may well be conscious, just as we are, but not be the kind of teleological agent that Lovelock was accused of imagining and invoking. Does Gaia have a soul or consciousness of the same general kind, though vastly different in degree and content, as our own human soul or consciousness? Who can know for sure? Some philosophers, Descartes most notably, doubt that other animals have souls or consciousnesses. The occasional solipsist impregnably doubts that other humans have a soul or consciousness. The Earth? Gaia? The humility befitting an upright mammalian weed requires us to agree with Hamlet that "There are more things in heaven and earth, Horatio,/Than are dreamt of in your philosophy."

8

The Earth Ethic: A Critical Account
of Its Biocentric Deontological
Foundations

As amply documented in Chapter 7, scientific metaphysics in the Gaian mode of thought—a mode of thought that includes the thinking of Aldo Leopold and Vladimir Verndasky as well as of James Lovelock and Lynn Margulis—involves speculation about some kind of "soul or consciousness" (in Leopold's words) associated with planet Earth.[1] We have no clue what Leopold might have thought about the nature of that consciousness; he never elaborated a Gaian psychology. For purposes, however, of grounding a non-anthropocentric Leopold Earth ethic, whether the Earth has or has not a soul or consciousness matters little. Several times in the section titled "Conservation as a Moral Issue" of "Some Fundamentals of Conservation in the Southwest," Leopold suggests that if the Earth is a "living thing," it would, "as such," merit and indeed would receive our "respect." A non-anthropocentric Earth ethic, as Leopold envisions it, turns on the question, Is the Earth a living being? not Does the Earth have a soul or consciousness? Other-oriented respect—for life or for anything else—is a moral category most at home in the Kantian deontological tradition of ethics (as detailed in 6.4).[2] Accordingly, I here explore the variety of biocentric (or life-centered) ethical theories, associated—some more explicitly than others—with that tradition, which might support, more particularly, a *deontological* non-anthropocentric Earth ethic such as Leopold adumbrated in 1923.

Leopold also suggests that an Earth ethic might be grounded in virtue ethics as he also invokes the moral category of "*self*-respect"—which is at the heart of virtue ethics (6.2). Virtue ethics has enjoyed a robust revival in recent moral philosophy generally, and environmental philosophers have not failed to enrich recent environmental ethics with the fruits of this revival. Leopold indicates, further, a third foundation for an Earth ethic, near- and long-term duties to future generations or, in his words, "responsibility...not only to immediate posterity but also to the Unknown Future" (6.3).[3] Virtue ethics and responsibility to posterity—presumably future human generations—are anthropocentric in their ethical orientation. The possibility of erecting an Earth ethic on the anthropocentric foundations that Leopold suggests—(1) personal, professional, and social virtue and (2) concern for and/or responsibility to future generations—is the central focus of the final three chapters of this book.

8.1 LEOPOLD'S BIOCENTRIC EARTH ETHIC AND THE LIVING EARTH

However intriguing may be the previous chapter's (7.16–7.17) speculations about Gaia's soul or consciousness—noöspheric, cybernetic, proprioceptive, electromagnetic, whatever—they seem to be beside the point of an Earth ethic as Leopold has prefigured it. According to Leopold, the Earth possesses "a certain kind and degree of life," and *life*, he thinks, is that "which we intuitively respect as such."[4] Gaia may not have any kind of soul or consciousness at all, but there most certainly is life on Earth—in sharp contrast to the lifelessness of Earth's neighboring planets. Moreover, as comparison with Mars and Venus reveals, life is certainly a planetary phenomenon.[5] That is, living organisms do not inhabit the Earth piecemeal. Nor, according to Lovelock, could life inhabit any other planet in a spotty way.[6] Thus there could not, for example, be a little self-sustaining isolated colony of life on Mars, either native to Mars or sent there from Earth (thus, foreclosing the possibility of establishing a *self-sustaining* human colony on Mars in some sort of enclosed capsule). Whether or not the Earth—the only living planet we know—is a *single organism* (a perennially mooted question), living matter constitutes an integrated whole at a planetary scale. In other words—and in any case—on Earth there exists a biosphere no less palpably and indubitably than there exists a lithosphere, a hydrosphere, and an atmosphere. Therefore, not only is there life *on* Earth, the Earth is, as a whole, a living planet.

Further, and just as certainly, the biosphere and its living matter have profoundly transformed the face of the Earth—its atmosphere, its hydrosphere, and even its lithosphere. Further still, life certainly sustains—if not maintains—conditions on Earth favorable to the flourishing and proliferation of the various and myriads of forms that living matter takes. These considerations too lead to the same conclusion: Earth is, therefore, undoubtedly a living planet. Margulis might quibble with Leopold's characterization of the Earth as "*an organism* possessing a certain kind and degree of life" (as she does with Lovelock's similar characterization of it), but that the Earth possesses a certain kind and degree of integrated or unified life is beyond all doubt and dispute among all those who (1) breathe biogenic oxygen and (2) are biologically literate. And once more, according to Leopold, *life* is that "which we intuitively respect as such." Thus, whether or not the Earth has a soul or consciousness or even whether or not she is a single organism, the Earth, possessing a certain kind and degree of life, should be the beneficiary of the respect that life demands. Or so Leopold thinks.

Thus there falls to this chapter the task of considering the prospects for Leopold's then novel suggestion in 1923 that we might respect the Earth "as a moral being respects a living thing."[7] Most of the thinkers who took up the task of developing an environmental ethic based on the concept of respect for life as such were concerned only about putatively "individual" living things, macro-organisms proper, not the whole Earth—nor any other super-organismic or quasi-organismic wholes, for that matter. One pioneering biocentric ethicist, however, Kenneth Goodpaster, hints at the possibility of scaling up respect-for-life ethics to planetary proportions. Goodpaster's biocentrism may, therefore, prove to be the best theory, among available alternatives, for grounding a non-anthropocentric Leopold Earth ethic.

8.2 GAIAN ONTOLOGY

A biocentric Earth ethic will be most plausible, most immune to criticism—and thus most secure—if it can be based on the least speculative assumptions, including the least speculative ontological assumptions. Most speculative is Gaian psychology—speculation that a planetary soul or consciousness exists and, if it does, speculation about the form it might take. Less speculative, but speculative nonetheless, is the claim that the Earth is a single organism. As detailed in the previous chapter (7.11–7.12), Lynn Margulis prefers to think that the Earth is a "huge ecosystem." While cogently to question the proposition that the Earth is a single organism is certainly possible, as Margulis effectively demonstrates, that the Earth exhibits ecosystemic character-istics seems to be as indubitable as that the Earth is a living planet. Certainly, ecosys-temic processes—generally, materials cycling and energy flows, carried out by various organisms—occur at a planetary scale. Margulis's conception of Gaia—not as a single organism, but as a comprehensive ecosystem—would therefore seem to be the least speculative Gaian ontological assumption.

To conceive of Gaia as a huge, planetary-scaled, comprehensive ecosystem may be the least speculative ontology for a philosophically secure Earth ethic, but it is not an unproblematic ontology. As noted in 3.15, ecosystems, as conventionally conceived in ecology, are not very robust ontologically. They have porous and fuzzy boundaries; indeed, their boundaries are partly artificial—partly determined by the interests of the ecologists who interrogate them. As also noted in 3.15, however, all natural *systems* are subject to similar ontological challenges. Can the solar system be precisely bounded by astronomers? Perhaps, but different astronomers bound it differently depending on the different scientific questions they pose of it?[8] One astronomer studying the plane-tary bodies of the solar system, for example, might draw the solar system's boundary at the edge of the Kuiper belt or at the orbit of the farthest dwarf planet, Eris, enthralled by the sun's gravitational field.[9] A second astronomer, interested in the highly eccentric orbits of long-period comets, might draw it at the limits of the Oort cloud, from which such comets emanate.[10] A third astronomer interested in the solar wind might draw the solar system's boundary at the heliopause, the distance from the sun at which solar wind merges with the interstellar medium and is no longer detectable.[11] A fourth astronomer, interested in solar/stellar gravitational fields, might draw it at the dis-tance from the sun at which the sun's gravitational influence is no greater than that of neighboring stars.

Generally speaking, ecosystems and solar/stellar systems are ontologically less robust than their *constitutive objects*—organisms and stars and planets, respectively. Even so, as dissipative structures, capturing chemical energy and cycling through organic mate-rials, proper organisms too are living *systems*—indeed they are living ecosystems host to and dependent on billions of microbes representing thousands of species—and while many are bounded by skin or a membrane of some sort, their boundaries too are porous if not fuzzy.[12] Regarded as a huge ecosystem, the living planet Earth, Gaia, is *more robust* ontologically than its *constitutive ecosystems*. Photographs of the Earth taken from the moon certainly show it to be a clearly identifiable thing, an object. A nearer view shows Gaia's atmospheric boundary to be no less distinct, proportionate to the planet's spatial scale, than is the skin boundary of mammals, such as bears or badgers, and might actually be less fuzzy (taking into account the hairy, wooly, or furry skins of mammals). Like skin or a cell membrane, Gaia's atmospheric boundary is open to some things and closed to others; it is transparent to visible solar radiation, but it excludes much ultraviolet radiation, and incinerates much of the ambient solar-system debris it encounters. But it is not nearly as porous as the boundaries—to the extent that they may be determined—of its downscale ecosystems into and out of which move a variety of materials and organisms.

The foregoing comparison of the Earth's atmospheric boundary to the epidermis boundary of organisms or of the enclosing membranes of cells is not intended to suggest that Leopold and Lovelock are right to conceive of the Earth as a single organism and that Margulis is wrong to prefer to conceive of it as a huge ecosystem. As noted, she declares, "I cannot stress strongly enough that Gaia is not a single organism," but in the same breath Margulis also declares that "Just as the human body is sharply bounded by skin, temperature differences, blood chemistry and a calcium phosphate skeleton, so is Earth distinguished from its surroundings by its persistently anomalous atmosphere, its steady temperature, and unusual limestone and granitic rocks."[13] My main point—and that of Margulis—is to indicate that the Earth, qua ecosystem, is as robust an object as an organism proper, with a clear and natural (as opposed to artificial) boundary. But an ancillary insight is forthcoming from the comparison of the Earth's atmospheric boundary to the epidermal boundary of organisms: when Gaia is conceived not only as a huge but also as a comprehensive ecosystem, her constitutive ecosystems appear to be less robust ontologically and to be partly artificial precisely because they are virtually sliced and diced, as it were, from the planetary whole—mentally cut out for manageable study by ecologists.

For purposes of a biocentric Earth ethic, the ontological problem might be put this way. The Earth cannot be an object of human respect if it is not an object at all. We may well wonder if downscale ecosystems are actual objects. But the Earth—indubitably a living planet and indubitably a planetary ecosystem—is certainly an ontologically robust *object*. To that extent, therefore, the Earth is capable of being the object of respect.

8.3 GAIAN NORMS

There must exist an actual object of respect for an Earth ethic such as Leopold envisions—respect for the Earth as a living thing—to be intelligible. There must also exist norms against which respect or lack thereof may be assessed. In just what would respect consist? How can we determine what would constitute respect and what would not? To leave "the earth alive, undamaged," Leopold answers, "to be capable of inhabiting the earth without defiling it."[14] All right, but we are left to wonder of what damage to and defilement of the Earth might consist. In 1923, Leopold himself was mainly concerned about soil erosion in the North American Southwest. In the meantime, other serious environmental problems have captured our attention. In any case, ethics, when philosophically developed, does not consist of a laundry list of dos and don'ts—do preserve biodiversity; do not cause the soil to erode; do not pollute fresh waters; do not deplete and stagnate the ocean, and so on and so forth. By the time Leopold composed the land ethic, he was philosophically sophisticated enough to provide it with a very general summary moral maxim: "A thing is right when it tends to preserve the integrity, stability, and beauty of the biotic community. It is wrong, when it tends otherwise."[15] Given the state of ecological science in the 1940s, ecologists would have little trouble in determining what would and what would not tend to preserve the integrity, stability, and beauty of the biotic community. For purposes of developing an Earth ethic, we need to identify equally definite criteria—commensurate with *global* ecological processes and parameters—of respecting Gaia as a living being. How can we inhabit the global, comprehensive ecosystem without defiling it and leave it alive and undamaged?

The least speculative Gaian ontology—the conception of the Earth as a huge ecosystem, à la Margulis—presents yet another Earth-ethic challenge. Downscale ecosystems do not evince the clear norms that an Earth ethic would ideally require. The ecosystems that ecologists historically recognized and studied were once conceived to develop predictably until they reached a mature, climax state, thereafter to remain in that state until exogenously disturbed.[16] They were conceived to be relatively closed, to be self-regulated, and to oscillate closely about stable equilibria.[17] Now such ecosystems are conceived to develop along no set successional pathway toward no determinate goal. They are open to ingressing and egressing organisms and various fluxes of materials and are often significantly influenced, sometimes in periodic ways—and thereby are often regulated—by distant phenomena (such as the El Niño/La Niña oscillation in the southern Pacific Ocean).[18] Ecosystems are subject to local disturbances (by fire, pestilence, wind, and such) that are so natural, frequent, periodic, and incorporated that ecologists style them "disturbance regimes."[19] And human influence has been ubiquitous and long-standing.[20] As detailed in 3.16, the paradigm shift in ecology from the "balance of nature" to the "flux of nature" undermined the land ethic because it rendered otiose two of Leopold's criteria for the rightness of things—integrity and stability—thus necessitating its revision (as detailed in 3.17).

Gaia, considered as a huge ecosystem, is also dynamic and has developed along no set pathway toward no determinate goal or *telos*. Not only do current Gaia theorists assiduously avoid teleology, consistent both with evolutionary biology and the flux of nature paradigm in ecology, they also assiduously avoid a static conception of the planetary ecosystem—which is consistent also with the paleontological facts. The editors of *Gaia in Turmoil* note in their introductory essay that as Gaian science matured during the past forty years, Lovelock's original attribution to Gaia of

> homeostasis has come to be seen as too static a paradigm to deliver the essence of a dynamic planet that has exhibited extremely varied physiochemical states and biota types over geologic time. Homeostasis gave way to *homeorrhesis*, an

idea cognate to the evolutionary model proposed by Niles Eldridge and Stephen J. Gould: long periods of stable parameters (e.g. of temperature, atmospheric composition, and elemental cycling) are punctuated by planetary shifts, instigated by strong internal or external forcings, into new stable states.[21]

Hierarchy theory in ecology is largely about scale—temporal as well as spatial scale.[22] To conceive of Gaia as a *huge* planetary ecosystem is to conceive of it in terms of *spatial scale*. To conceive of it as a *comprehensive* ecosystem, from the perspective of hierarchy theory, is to conceive of it as comprehending various levels of spatially downscale ecosystems—everything from the Greater Yellowstone Ecosystem, spatially defined by the home ranges of its resident large mammals (such as bison, wolves, and grizzly bears), to the micro-ecosystems in the Yellowstone's geyser pools composed of thermophilic bacteria.[23] Not only do ecosystems vary in terms of spatial scale; they also vary in terms of *temporal scale*; and processes in smaller ecosystems often proceed faster than those in larger ecosystems. For example, canopy closure after a catastrophic fire or clearcut covering many hectares in a temperate forest requires decades to achieve, while the decomposition of organic detritus in a tropical soil ecosystem of a few square meters requires only days.[24]

From the perspective of temporally downscale processes, the slower dynamics of temporally upscale processes can be ignored; that is, they may be regarded as static.[25] For example, the Canadian Laurentian shield is moving northwest with the North American plate at a rate of about three centimeters per year and is gaining elevation at a rate of about ten millimeters per year as it rebounds from the last glaciation.[26] Its latitude, longitude, and elevation may, however, be regarded as stable, static, by an ecologist studying the predator-prey dynamics of lynx and snowshoe hare. For another example, the dynamics of forest succession can be ignored—that is, the composition of the vascular plant and vertebrate animal community can be regarded as unchanging—if one's spatio-temporal focus of interest is on the decomposition of organic detritus in a small-scale soil ecosystem. Although the Earth's temperature, atmospheric composition, sea level, oceanic pH, and other parameters in the planetary ecosystem have changed, sometimes profoundly, the temporal scales of such changes in the planet's past are measured in centuries, millennia, and eons.[27] Because the temporal scales of changes in Gaian ecosystem parameters dwarf the temporal scales of the matters of human concern, they may be ignored—that is, regarded as static—when we humans concern ourselves with such matters. For example, if our focus of concern is on dynamic downscale ecological parameters—such as non-erosive land use, water quality, biotic community composition, and biodiversity—we may regard the fact that free oxygen composes about 21 percent of the Earth's atmosphere as a constant, although at one time in the distant past, there was little free oxygen in the Earth's atmosphere.[28] For a synoptic overview of the homeorrhetic life-supporting conditions on planet Earth, see *The Goldilocks Planet: The Four Billion Year Story of Earth's Climate* by Jan Zalasiewicz and Mark Williams.[29]

Therefore, to come to the point of this section, such things as the Earth's average temperature, the composition of the Earth's atmosphere (including the parts per million of carbon dioxide), sea level, the pH of the global ocean—although they have changed over time in a homeorrhetic manner—may serve as norms for an Earth ethic. In this sense, then, we can adapt the notions of integrity and stability that are key features of the original summary moral maxim of the Leopold land ethic for purposes of formulating an Earth ethic. At planetary spatial and temporal scales such variables as the Earth's average temperature, the composition of the Earth's atmosphere (including the parts per million of carbon dioxide), sea level, the pH of the global ocean would be relatively stable—except for human activities. Or at least they have been *relatively stable* for the duration of the entire Holocene. The over-arching principle to which Leopold devotes most of his discussion in "Conservation as a Moral Issue" in "Some Fundamentals of Conservation in the Southwest" is respect for the Earth as a living thing. Yes, but in just what would respect consist? To inhabit the Earth without defiling it and to leave it alive and undamaged, Leopold answers. Yes, but again, in just what would that consist? To preserve the integrity, stability, and beauty of the dynamic equilibria of the comprehensive global ecosystem would seem to be the right way to show respect for Gaia as a living thing.

Or perhaps not. In the next chapter (9.1), I discuss reasons that a biocentric Earth ethic may be a philosophical wind egg, precisely because the temporal scales of Gaian ecological dynamics and those of human concerns are so out of phase with one another. Ethics may have scalar limits. Can we respect the sun? Certainly we can. Anyone who does not risks severe consequences from sun exposure. But would a solar ethic be intelligible? Hardly, because the sun is too big (to say nothing of its being too far away) to be the object of respect *and* right treatment. We can and many of us do respect the Earth, often manifest in our aesthetic experience of the sublime. But perhaps the Earth is also too big to be the object of respect and *right treatment* as well. And even if one decides that the Earth is not too big to be the object of respect and right treatment, perhaps it is too long-lived—"a being that was old when the morning stars sang together, and, when the last of us has been gathered unto his fathers, will still be young"—for that to make sense.[30] The spatial and temporal scales of the Earth did not, however, discourage Leopold from faintly sketching a biocentric Earth ethic in "Some Fundamentals." In the remainder of this chapter, I explore various ethical theories that might round out a proper picture.

8.4 SCHWEITZER'S REVERENCE-FOR-LIFE ETHIC

The first person to explore the possibility that we might have a "reverence"—if not respect—for life as such is Albert Schweitzer in the penultimate chapter of *The Philosophy of Civilization*. The German edition of that book was published in 1923, the same year in which Leopold wrote "Some Fundamentals"; the English translation first appeared in 1949, the same year in which *A Sand County Almanac* was published (posthumously, as noted in 1.2, in the year following Leopold's death). According to Schweitzer, "Ethics consist . . . in my experiencing the compulsion to show to all will-to-live the same reverence as I do my own. There we have given us that basic principle of the moral [*sic*] which is a necessity of thought. It is good to maintain and to encourage life; it is bad to destroy life or obstruct it."[31] But what is life? Schweitzer provides no general definition of *life*, contenting himself with ostensively defining it. So, by *life* to what does Schweitzer refer or verbally point? Schweitzer goes on to mention a "leaf from a tree," a "flower," an "insect" and an "earthworm," unspecified "tiny creatures," a "mouse" and, collectively, "plants and animals."[32] These are all macroscopic organisms. In addition he mentions "bacteria."[33] Nowhere does he mention the Earth. So a Leopold Earth ethic finds little *direct* support from Schweitzer. It might, however, find *indirect* support from him.

Schweitzer was no more a credentialed philosopher than was Ouspensky, but Schweitzer's thinking is much more organized, coherent, disciplined, and historically grounded than is Ouspensky's. In *The Philosophy of Civilization*, Schweitzer devotes much intelligent and critical discussion to ancient and modern European philosophy, going all the way back to the pre-Socratics. He extensively discusses post-Kantian German metaphysics, which (as noted in 4.6) was largely given over to what Schweitzer soberly judged to be "presumptuous speculation."[34] Schweitzer especially admires Goethe who, though living "in a time of abstract and speculative thought, he has the courage to remain elemental."[35] Nevertheless, Schweitzer is most deeply influenced by the metaphysics of Schopenhauer, whom he thought to "pursue no abstract cosmic speculations."[36] Whether that is true or not, Schopenhauer's metaphysics is at least grounded in something palpable and was very well informed by biology.

8.5 SCHWEITZER'S REVERENCE-FOR-LIFE ETHIC ROOTED IN THE METAPHYSICS OF SCHOPENHAUER

As with most post-Kantian German metaphysics, Schopenhauer's starts with Kant's distinction between phenomena and noumena. Disappointingly, Kant is skeptical about the possibility of ever knowing noumenal things-in-themselves, both noumenal subjects and noumenal objects, as they are in themselves. Au contraire, we can and do most intimately and immediately know the inner essence of noumena, Schopenhauer thinks. Just let someone put a pillow over your face and try to suffocate you. The will-to-live springs to the fore and presents itself to you in its pure, naked noumenal reality.[37] Schweitzer correctly summarizes the vital kernel of Schopenhauer's philosophy as follows: "The world, he says, I can understand only by analogy with myself. Myself, looked at from outside, I conceive as a physical phenomenon in time and space, but looked at from within as will-to-live. Everything, accordingly, which meets me in the world of phenomena is a manifestation of the will-to-live."[38] And by "everything" Schopenhauer means absolutely *every* thing.

Schopenhauer was influenced by South Asian metaphysics—"Indian philosophy," as Schweitzer calls it—in which Brahman was the one Being or Reality manifest in everything, including the Atman (roughly equivalent to Kant's Transcendental Ego) in oneself.[39] In Schopenhauer's rendition, Will is the one reality, which then becomes divided and pitted against itself. And, as Schweitzer recognizes, Schopenhauer shares a world-denying pessimism with classical South Asian philosophy:

> [C]ountless individualities which are rooted in the universal will-to-live are continually seeking satisfaction, which is never gratified, in aims which they set before themselves in obedience to an inward impulse. Again and again they...have to struggle against hindrances; their own will-to-live continually comes into conflict with other wills-to-live. The world is meaningless and all existence is suffering. The knowledge of this is attained by the will-to-live in the highest living creatures, who are gifted with the power of remaining always conscious that the totality of what is around them, outside themselves, is merely a world of appearance [phenomena, in post-Kantian metaphysics; *maya* in Vedantan metaphysics].[40]

As to ethics, Schopenhauer believes that in every act of violence perpetrated by one phenomenal manifestation of the will-to-live on another, there was perfect and precise retributive justice—"eternal justice"—because the will-to-live manifest in the victim is the self-same will-to-live manifest in the perpetrator. "[T]he difference between him who inflicts the suffering and him who must bear it is only the phenomenon, and does not concern the thing itself [the noumenon], for this is the Will living in both....The inflictor of suffering and the sufferer are one."[41] For Schopenhauer, to revolt against it—"the denial of the will-to-live"—is the only appropriate moral response to knowledge of the universality and ubiquity of the will-to-live.[42] Schweitzer, in contrast to Schopenhauer, takes a more Buddhist approach. Those of us who are among the "highest living creatures" can indeed become enlightened about the phenomenal charade that is the world, but instead of withdrawing from it in abhorrence and disgust, we can dedicate ourselves to treating other manifestations of the will-to-live with loving kindness.

That may all be well and good, but what philosophical support for an Earth ethic, such as Leopold broaches, can be indirectly derived from Schweitzer and his intellectual forebear, Schopenhauer? When Schweitzer comes to detail his reverence-for-life ethic, he seems to forget that—according to the Schopenhauerian metaphysics on which it is based—not just organisms, but every phenomenal thing, is a manifestation of the will-to-live. Even "elemental" forces like inertia and gravity are phenomenal expressions of the Will's essential striving. Because the Earth is a phenomenal thing—whether a super-scaled organism with a soul or consciousness or just a lifeless gravitational mass inertially careering through space-time, on which individual organisms severally happen to live—it also would be a manifestation of the will-to-live. Schweitzer's reverence-for-life ethic may, however, be too bound up with Schopenhauer's metaphysics to be coherently integrated with the directions in which Leopold's thinking runs. To be sure, Leopold is also thinking metaphysically, but his is a scientific metaphysics. That is, he is thinking about the Earth in terms of metabolic processes and physiologic functions, not in terms of an Atman-Brahman essence merged with Kantian noumena.

Put it this way: for Leopold, phenomenal life, he sanguinely thought, is what we respect as such; for Schweitzer—thoroughly informed metaphysically by Schopenhauer—the noumenal essence of living things is the true object of concern and compassion.

8.6 FEINBERG'S CONATIVISM

Joel Feinberg contributed an influential paper, "The Rights of Animals and Unborn Generations," to *Philosophy and Environmental Crisis*, the first volume of collected papers on environmental ethics—published in 1974—that included essays written (mostly) by professional philosophers (Eugene P. Odum, an ecologist, being the single exception). "To have a right," Feinberg begins, "is to have a claim *to* something and *against* someone, the recognition of which is called for by legal rules or, in the case of moral rights, by the principles of enlightened conscience."[43] To have legal and especially moral rights is to enjoy a rather elevated moral status, although Feinberg is, in this essay, rather less strict and more expansive about the application of the concept of rights than is usual. Both Kenneth E. Goodpaster and Paul W. Taylor eschew the concept of rights—because it usually does indicate a very strong moral claim—in favor of other, weaker moral notions, as detailed in subsequent sections of this chapter (8.8 and 8.11, respectively).

After some erudite ruminating about the concept of rights, Feinberg allows that H. J. McClosky achieved "a very important insight expressed in the requirement that a being have interests if he is to be a logically proper subject of rights. This can be appreciated if we consider just why it is that mere things cannot have rights."[44] Feinberg's example of a rightless mere thing is the Taj Mahal (the mausoleum in India, not the African American blues musician). Regarding the Taj Mahal, per se, one cannot "help or hurt it, benefit or aid it, succor or relieve it"; it has no "sake," no "welfare," no "well-being," which a moral agent might morally consider or take account of.[45] Thus it has no interests. In general, that is because "mere things have no conative life: no conscious wishes, desires, and hopes; or urges and impulses; or unconscious drives, aims, and goals; or latent tendencies, direction of growth, and natural fulfillments. Interests must be compounded somehow out of conations; hence mere things have no interests."[46] And therefore mere things can have no rights.

By this account, clearly, animals *can* have rights—whether they actually do have rights or not depends, in the case of legal rights, on "recognition…by legal rules or, in the case of moral rights, by the principles of enlightened conscience." (As Goodpaster subtly notes, Feinberg is discussing "questions of intelligibility" not "questions of normative substance"—"what sorts of beings can logically be said to deserve moral consideration" not "what sorts of beings do, as a matter of 'ethical fact,' deserve moral consideration.")[47] Feinberg thinks that distant "unborn [human] generations" can also have rights (a matter for further discussion in 10.10–10.11 and 11.4–11.5). As Feinberg points out, however, between paradigmatic rights holders—fully competent human beings—and mere things, there is arrayed a wide spectrum of other things or beings. Feinberg thinks that the title characters of his essay (animals and unborn generations), which fall somewhere along that spectrum, can intelligibly have rights. But what about plants?

Feinberg's discussion of the possibility that plants can have rights is sorely vexed. Ultimately, he decides that they cannot. He concedes, however, that "[p]lants, after all, are not 'mere things'; they are vital objects with inherited biological propensities determining their natural growth....An owner may need a plant (say, for its commercial value or as a potential meal), but the plant itself...needs nutrition and cultivation....Plants no less than animals are said to have needs of their own."[48] Yes, but don't we also say that "[a]n automobile needs gas and oil in order to function"?[49] We do, but "[t]he needs of plants might well seem closer to the needs of animals than to the pseudo-needs of mere things," such as automobiles.[50] Why then can plants not have rights like animals can? The reason is that, despite being vital objects with inherited biological propensities and needs of their own, plants do not have interests, Feinberg decides. He declares that "an interest...presupposes at least rudimentary cognitive equipment" and plants have "no *conscious* wants or goals of their own....Interests are compounded out of *desires* and *aims*, both of which presuppose something like *belief* or cognitive awareness."[51] Gary Varner—a self-described "biocentric individualist"—"distinguishes between two kinds of interests, those that are relativized to the beliefs of an individual (such as the desire to marry someone) and those that are not (such as the need to maintain functional lungs or the need for ascorbic acid)."[52] According to Varner, we share the latter kind with plants and, moreover, they are the kinds of interests that are morally relevant. In apparently conflating the two kinds of interests, Feinberg is guilty of the informal logical fallacy of equivocation.

The fallacy of equivocation aside, Feinberg is guilty of an even more egregious violation of logical thinking. Clearly he contradicts himself for he had previously declared that interests must be compounded out of conations and the conation concept includes *unconscious* drives, aims, and goals and *latent* tendencies, directions of growth, and natural fulfillments, as well as conscious wishes, desires, and hopes. Plants are conative if not conscious beings and, once more, if interests are somehow compounded out of conations, then plants have interests and therefore plants too can have rights. In short, if Feinberg is correct about both (1) interests being somehow compounded out of conations and (2) having interests is the sine qua non of qualifying for rights, then plants can have rights.[53] The glaring contradiction that Feinberg evinces reveals the psychocentric bias endemic to modern moral philosophy.

8.7 FEINBERG'S CONATIVISM AS A FOUNDATION FOR A BIOCENTRIC EARTH ETHIC?

So much for individual plants, what about the whole Earth? Granted the Earth is alive, but is Gaia conative? This is a question that appears not to have occurred to Feinberg, nor may he have then ever even heard of Gaia, writing, as he was, before *Gaia: A New Look at Life on Earth* came out and only a couple of years after Lovelock quietly introduced Gaia in a letter to the editors of a specialized (if not obscure) applied science journal.

Feinberg's version of conativism is conceptually tangential to Leopold's nascent Earth ethic in two ways. Leopold thinks that *life,* as such, is an appropriate object of *respect.* First, Feinberg is concerned with grounding *rights,* usually taken to be a much stronger moral concept than respect (as noted in 8.6); and second, Feinberg connects rights with interests and interests with *conations* not with life as such. Despite being conceptually tangential to Leopold's thoughts about an Earth ethic and despite his backsliding toward the psychocentrism of modern Western moral philosophy, Feinberg's bold suggestion that rights might ultimately be grounded in conativity, represents an important step in the direction of an Earth ethic. Perhaps all living beings are conative. If so, then because the Earth is a living being—and (as indicated in 8.2) there can be no doubt about that—the Earth too is conative.

But are all living beings conative? The uncommon English word "conation" is derived from the Latin verb *conari,* meaning to attempt. Meaning impetus, impulse, effort, endeavor, and especially striving, *conatus,* the past participle of *conari,* has had a long career in ancient—the equivalent word in Greek is ὀρμη—medieval, and modern natural philosophy.[54] With the possible exception of Democritus, the ancients thought of locomotion in quasi-animate terms. Objects move due to an inner impetus—a ὀρμη or *conatus.* The first locomotive causes identified by the ancient Greeks were Love and Strife (by Empedocles) and Mind (by Anaxagoras).[55] Contemporary scholars often anachronistically characterize these putative causes of motion as "forces," analogous to gravity or magnetism, operating externally on inanimate objects.[56] But the Greek natural philosophers who posited them—judging from the psychological names they gave them—thought that objects moved because of an internal impetus: that is, a ὀρμη or *conatus.*

Anticipating Newton's first law of motion, Descartes used the term *conatus* in his *Principia Philosophiae* to refer to a moving object's inertial state—despite the residues of animism, as he must have realized, lingering in the word.[57] Spinoza appropriated the term from Descartes's physics to articulate an important metaphysical concept in his own philosophy, attributing *conatus*—striving or persevering—to every natural thing, whether conscious or not.[58] By doing so, Spinoza, in attempting to overcome Descartes's problematic dualism, intended to integrate psychology and physics by assimilating subjective motives and objective locomotions. Whether intentionally or not, by doing so, he also espoused a philosophy of psychology and physics closer to that of the ancients than to that of his fellow moderns.

Spinoza's naturalization of *conscious* striving or persevering by use of the term *conatus*—which had long been used in the context of physical motion—is reinforced by Hobbes's use of the term in his Latin translation of the *Leviathan* to render "endeavor"—the physical or physiological basis of human desire and aversion.[59] Spinoza's *conatus* is universal; all finite "modes" of both the humanly experienced "attributes" of the one "substance" are conative—whether conscious or not, indeed whether living or not. Most important, Spinoza's *conatus* carries no teleological overtones, which Gaian scientists have striven mightily to avoid. For while "striving" may implicitly introduce the notion of a goal—striving for or toward something, whether consciously or not—persevering may be understood homeostatically or inertially: the impetus, whether conscious or not, to continue or remain in an existing state or condition. In this Spinozistic sense, therefore, the living Earth may be conative, irrespective of the question of the Earth's soul or consciousness or of the teleological question.

Feinberg does not identify the *locus classicus* for his own appropriation of the concept of conativity. Whether he appropriated it from Spinoza and/or Hobbes, the most likely sources, he does not say. For purposes of grounding a Leopold Earth ethic, Feinberg's conativism is compromised by his own inconsistency and equivocation and by the vagaries of the meaning of its venerable parent concept, *conatus*, in the long history of philosophy. Feinberg's conations include "conscious wishes, desires, and hopes"—which seem too personal and anthropomorphic even for those who attribute a soul or consciousness to Gaia. Feinberg's conations also include "unconscious drives, aims, and goals"—which would seem to veer off the hard-won straight and narrow ateleological path of latter-day Gaian theory. Even "latent tendencies, direction of growth, and natural fulfillments," which Feinberg includes in the conation concept, while clearly attributable to plants may themselves be a tad too telelological for comfortable attribution to Gaia. Moreover, the focus of Feinberg's discussion is on rights, while Leopold's is on respect. As Goodpaster notes, however, Feinberg's discussion of rights can be transposed to a discussion of respect because Feinberg's notion of rights is looser or wider than the stricter or narrower notion that one often encounters in philosophical discourse. From all these considerations, I submit that Feinberg's conativism thus might provide *buttressing philosophical support* for a biocentric Earth ethic—respect for the Earth as a certainly living and possibly conative thing—such as Leopold envisioned, but not a very sound *foundation* for it.

8.8 GOODPASTER'S BIOCENTRISM

In my opinion, "On Being Morally Considerable," by Kenneth E. Goodpaster is among the finest papers ever written on environmental philosophy. It is clear, concise, linearly organized, elegantly written, creative, thoughtful, insightful, visionary, and intellectually honest. It was published in 1978 in the *Journal of Philosophy*, which is to be commended for publishing an essay so radically departing—in its conclusions, not in its style—from mainstream Anglo-American moral philosophy. Goodpaster's uncharacteristically elegant analytic style—replete with logical symbols and numbered propositions—and his self-positioning in respect to the work of "several respected philosophers" may have been redeeming features in the eyes of the journal's editors.[60] Goodpaster contributed only one other paper to environmental ethics, "From Egoism to Environmentalism," published in 1979, which is also a very fine piece of work (discussed in 10.4).[61] Unfortunately, he abandoned environmental ethics for the more pedestrian (but both more lucrative and professionally respectable) field of business ethics in 1980, when he joined the faculty of the Harvard Business School—after having been denied tenure at Notre Dame. (Peer punishment for doing non-anthropocentric environmental ethics in the previous century could be very severe.) After a decade in Cambridge, Massachusetts, he moved on to the University of St. Thomas in St. Paul, Minnesota, where he holds the David and Barbara Koch Chair in Business Ethics.

Goodpaster extends the trail blazed by G. J. Warnock and Peter Singer much further into the *terra incognita* of moral philosophy.[62] A fundamental assumption of this line of thinking is that possessing a certain property or characteristic entitles the beings that possess it to "moral standing"; in other words, possessing that property or characteristic renders them "morally considerable." What is that property? In classical Western ethics—and Kant's more especially—it was reason.[63] Classically (going back to Aristotle), reason was also man's essential, species-specific property—the property that distinguishes human beings from the other animals. But if we think of reason not as some non-empirical metaphysical essence, like the image of God, but as some empirical and measurable capacity for mental activities like simple arithmetic and logical thinking, then, as a matter of fact, not all human beings are rational. The "marginal cases"—as Tom Regan labeled them—are pre-rational human infants, sub-rational mentally enfeebled human children and adults, and post-rational elderly humans who suffer from dementia.[64] If we apply the rationality criterion of moral considerability rigorously and fairly, non-rational humans have no moral standing—they are not morally considerable—and so may be treated as any other unfortunate being who falls beyond the pale of ethics. We might perform painful medical experiments on orphaned infants, just as we do on laboratory rats; we might use the institutionalized mentally enfeebled as game for sport hunting, just as we do white-tailed deer; we might send the demented elderly to abattoirs and make dog food out of them, just as we do dairy cattle at the end of their careers as milk producers. Thus ethical rationalists confront a trilemma: (1) advocate treating the marginal cases like other beings that do not qualify for moral consideration are treated; (2) admit to an unjustified prejudice, speciesism, analogous to racism and sexism; or (3) select another criterion for moral considerability.

The third choice seems to be the only justifiable one. The first is repugnant and the second is philosophically indefensible. So what alternative criterion of moral considerablility should be selected? Sentience, answer Warnock and Singer. Why? Because it would bring into the moral fold the otherwise excluded marginal human cases—who may not be rational but certainly are sentient—and it seems eminently relevant to ethics because only sentient beings can be harmed in ways that they themselves care about or that matter to them. But of course not only are all humans—including the marginal cases—to be numbered among the sentient, so are many many other kinds of animals. While that is the conceptual point to which Warnock and Singer cheerfully arrive, that is the conceptual point from which Goodpaster bravely departs. Interestingly, Goodpaster challenges the appropriateness of sentience as a criterion for moral considerability on evolutionary grounds. "Biologically, it appears that sentience is an adaptive characteristic of living organisms that provides them with a better capacity to anticipate and so avoid threats to life. This at least suggests...that the capacities to suffer and to enjoy are ancillary to something more important rather than tickets to considerability in their own right."[65] In short, sentience is not an end in itself; it is a means to a more basic end—life. Thus the end—life—to which sentience is a means should be the criterion of moral considerability. Or so Goodpaster reasons.

Goodpaster buttresses his case for a biocentric ethic by soliciting help from the paper by Joel Feinberg, reviewed in the previous sections of this chapter (8.6–8.7). Feinberg too is engaged in the search for the proper property by means of which to accord a being moral standing or "moral considerability" as Goodpaster labels it. For Feinberg that property is not sentience but having interests and, for him, interests are compounded out of conations. As noted (in 8.7), Feinberg inconsistently conflates and confuses conativity with sentience, but the concept of sentience does not jibe at all well with the concept of interests. Sentient beings have an interest in not suffering, to be sure, but their interests can be ill-served in ways from which they do not palpably suffer or in ways about which they do not care—indeed in ways in which they may be voluntarily complicit. For example, to smoke cigarettes is not in what Varner identifies as the morally central "persistent" and "biological" interest of teenagers; and the adult who enables their cigarette smoking ill-serves the true interests of cigarette-smoking teenagers, even though they take pleasure in smoking cigarettes and are complicit in acting contrary to their own best interests.[66] And sentient beings can palpably suffer from things done to them that are in their interest to have done to them. My dog palpably suffers from veterinary treatment, but to receive veterinary treatment is in her interest. To eat spinach and other vegetables is in the interest of children, but they may palpably suffer from being made to do so. These considerations reinforce Goodpaster's argument that being sentient is not the proper criterion for moral considerability and they reinforce Feinberg's point that having interests is a better one. Other things being equal in this deontological line of thinking about ethics, the right thing to do for a being that has interests is to at least respect if not actively foster those interests and the wrong thing to do is to abrogate those interests—whether in the process the beneficiary experiences pleasure or pain does not matter. Neither does it matter, a fortiori, whether the beneficiary can experience any pleasure and pain at all, whether the beneficiary is at all sentient. Or so Feinberg's interest principle would imply.

All living beings, Goodpaster contends, have interests, including plants, and, one would assume, all other unconscious organisms do as well. Goodpaster ridicules Feinberg's self-contradictory argument to the contrary as patently disingenuous:

> There is no absurdity in imagining the representation of the needs of a tree for sun and water in the face of a proposal to cut it down or pave its immediate radius for a parking lot....
>
> Nor will it do to suggest, as Feinberg does, that the needs (interests) of living things like trees are not really their own but implicitly ours: "Plants may need things to discharge their functions, but their functions are assigned by human interests, not their own...." As if it were human interests that assigned to trees the tasks of growth or maintenance! The interests at stake are clearly those of the living things themselves, not simply those of the owners or users or other human persons involved.[67]

Thus the two most defensible properties or characteristics that may serve as criteria for moral considerability—being alive and having interests—closely overlap though the set of entities each defines may not be precisely the same.

8.9 GOODPASTER'S HOLISTIC BIOCENTRISM AS A FOUNDATION FOR A BIOCENTRIC EARTH ETHIC?

Interestingly, Goodpaster chooses the summary moral maxim, the golden rule, of the Leopold land ethic—"A thing is right when it tends to preserve the integrity, stability, and beauty of the biotic community. It is wrong when it tends otherwise"—to be the epigraph of his article. Goodpaster attributes these now famous words to "Aldo Leopold," but he cites neither "The Land Ethic" nor *A Sand County Almanac* as the source of the quotation. Evidently, Goodpaster does not consider Leopold to be among those "several respected philosophers" in relation to whose work he positions his own. Nor can I fault him for that. For while Leopold is certainly respected—and indeed principally for his philosophy—he was by no stretch of the imagination a professional or academic philosopher and exclusively with the work of such does Goodpaster essay to engage.

Goodpaster has nothing further to say about "the biotic community"; wisely, because by no stretch of the imagination can biotic communities as such be thought to be either alive or to have interests (or, for that matter, to be conative). In beginning, he boldly declares that "Neither rationality nor the capacity to experience pleasure and pain seem to me to be necessary (even though they may be sufficient) conditions on moral considerability. Nothing short of the condition of being alive seems to me to be a plausible and nonarbitrary condition."[68] Most of his discussion concerns non-rational and insentient organisms typified by plants. But he suggests, in passing, that

> this criterion, if taken seriously, could admit of application to entities and systems of entities heretofore unimagined as claimants on our moral attention (such as the biosystem itself). Some may be inclined to take such implications as a *reductio [ad absurdum]* of the move "beyond humanism." I am beginning to be persuaded, however, that such implications may provide both a meaningful ethical vision and the hope of a more adequate action guide for the long-term future.[69]

One must suppose that by "the biosystem," Goodpaster refers to the biosphere, which had by then (1978) been given the name Gaia by Lovelock. Remarkably, Goodpaster returns to the possibility that the biosphere might itself be a claimant on our moral attention at the end of his essay. Pressed by the anticipated objection that "life" is a vague and ill-defined concept and thus unserviceable as a criterion for moral considerability, Goodpaster points out that the leading alternatives—rationality, sentience, and having interests—are hardly less vague and ill-defined. He then quotes what appears to him to be both a defensible and serviceable characterization of living beings: "The typifying mark of a living system...appears to be its persistent state of low entropy, sustained by metabolic processes for accumulating energy, and maintained in equilibrium with its environment by homeostatic feedback processes."[70] (Actually a living system, such as an organism proper, maintains itself in a state far from equilibrium *with its environment*; rather it maintains internal equilibria, such as body temperature, in the face of environmental fluxes.)

Goodpaster anticipates another objection surely forthcoming from the community of "respected philosophers" whom he is principally addressing: "If life, as understood in the previous response, is really taken as the key to moral considerability, then it is possible that larger systems besides our ordinarily understood 'linear' extrapolations from human beings (e.g., animals, plants, etc.) might satisfy the conditions, such as the biosystem [the biosphere, one may suppose he means] as a whole. This surely would be a *reductio* [*ad absurdum*] of the life principle."[71] To which he first replies: "At best, it would be a *reductio* [*ad absurdum*] of the life principle in this form or without qualification."[72] It is not clear to what "this form" refers. Goodpaster probably means the life principle in the form of the biosphere (or "biosystem") and the qualification of the life principle he has in mind would probably be to restrict it, such that it applies only to individual organisms. Goodpaster, however, goes on quite clearly and very boldly to embrace the extrapolation of the life principle to larger systems, including the biosphere (or "biosystem").

> But it seems to me that such (perhaps surprising) implications if true should be taken seriously. There is some evidence that the biosystem as a whole exhibits behavior approximating to the definition [of life] sketched above, and I see no reason to deny it moral considerability on that account. Why should the universe of moral considerability map neatly onto our medium-sized framework of organisms?[73]

To document this claim, he cites an article by Lovelock (and Lovelock's co-author).[74] As a philosophical foundation for Leopold's embryonic non-anthropocentric Earth ethic, Goodpaster's version of biocentrism appears to be perfect. Goodpaster provides a well-conceived argument on behalf of respect for life as such or, what comes to the same thing, the moral considerability of any and every living thing, including the Earth, understood as "the biosystem" (the biosphere), personified by Lovelock as Gaia. The living Earth—the biosphere, Gaia—exhibits the defining characteristics of life that Goodpaster endorses: a persistent state of low entropy (that is, contrapositively, a high degree of organization), sustained by metabolic processes for accumulating energy (and transforming inert into living matter), maintained in (a state far-from) equilibrium with its environment by homeostatic feedback processes.

Goodpaster poses the question with which he ends this reply as a rhetorical question, but I think that it should be treated as a question deserving an answer: "Why should the universe of moral considerability map neatly onto our medium-sized framework of organisms?" Perhaps because the universe of moral considerabilty (and ethics more generally) is scale-sensitive. Perhaps a biocentric Earth ethic such as Leopold envisions and such as Goodpaster fleshes out ultimately evaporates when the wave of argument crashes on the shoals of the spatial and temporal scalar limits of ethics. I return to these essentially scalar questions in Chapters 10 and 11.

8.10 FEINBERG—THE TIE THAT BINDS SCHWEITZER AND GOODPASTER

A non-philosopher once remarked to me—after accompanying me to a session of analytic philosophy at the Eastern Division meetings of the American Philosophical Association—that philosophers seemed, among all academics, to be the most obstreperous and combative of the lot. In reply, I agreed with her and supplied what I hoped was an apt image. Presenting a thesis to a roomful of analytic philosophers is like jumping into a tank of water with a school of hungry barracuda. If you do, you want to make sure that you are well armed and not bleeding. Thus Goodpaster ends "On Being Morally Considerable" by anticipating a series of objections and offering replies, surely in the hopes of fending off his potential attackers—circling about, looking for a weakness—before they have a chance to wound him or devour him completely.

A couple of these objections and replies, I have already reviewed in the previous section (8.9). The very first objection that Goodpaster anticipates would be the most fatal to an analytic philosopher, among whom "rigor" is prized above all other intellectual virtues—cleverness being a close second—and who most despise and contemn soft-mindedness among all other intellectual vices. Thus to be philosophically associated with the "reverence-for-life" ethic of Albert Schweitzer would be as damaging to Goodpaster's analytic-philosophy street cred as to be associated with the "metaphysics" of Shirley MacLaine, the "objectivism" of Ayn Rand, or, for that matter, P. D. Ouspensky's third kind of "logic." Here is the way Goodpaster imagines an aggressive barracuda might lunge at that perceived vulnerability of his argument: "A principle of moral respect or consideration for life in all its forms is mere Schweitzerian romanticism, even if it [Schweitzerian romanticism] does not involve, as it probably does, the projection of mental or psychological categories beyond their responsible boundaries into the realms of plants, insects, and microbes."[75] To actually consult *The Philosophy of Civilization* to determine whether in fact Schweitzer projects mental or psychological categories into the realms of plants, insects, and microbes is, of course, beneath an analytic philosopher's dignity. A careful reading of Schweitzer and of his philosophical muse, Schopenhauer, would reveal that he does not. The will-to-live is the essential noumenal reality of all phenomena absolutely, according to Schopenhauer. It is a noumenal thing, neither a mental nor psychological thing, although in some of its phenomenal forms the will-to-live is consciously experienced. Goodpaster, however, is content to concede that Schweitzer is "probably" guilty of such a projection and leave it at that.

Whatever; this is Goodpaster's reply: "This objection misses the central thrust [a noun both virile and combative] of my discussion, which is not that the sentience criterion is necessary, but applicable to all life forms—rather the point is that the possession of sentience is not necessary for moral considerability. Schweitzer himself may have held the former view—and so have been 'romantic'—but this is beside the point."[76] Schweitzer's works—unlike those of, say, Pythagoras—are not irretrievably lost, so that we can never certainly know what views he actually held. Thus Goodpaster might easily have been able to set that record straight, Schweitzer's writings being not only extant but conveniently available in English translation—had he deigned to do so. Goodpaster's point, in any case, is that his own respect-for-life ethic is not vitiated by the idea that plants (and other organisms) have an acute or even, for that matter, a dull consciousness of some sort.[77] Having life as such—living, being alive—is the criterion of moral considerability, not some distinctly psychological capacity or property.

I should not complain. Given the prevailing climate in Anglo-American philosophy, Goodpaster's desire to distance his own proposed environmental ethic from Schweitzer's is understandable. Nonetheless, Goodpaster links himself to Schweitzer by the way he associates his own arguments with those of Feinberg, who was indeed a respected Anglo-American philosopher. Schweitzer acknowledges borrowing the concept of the will-to-live from Schopenhauer and Schopenhauer in turn acknowledges being informed by the long philosophical legacy of the *conatus* concept, especially as it was developed by Spinoza and Hobbes.[78] Indeed the Schweitzerian will-to-live is just the Spinozistic *conatus* by another name, mediated, as it were, by the metaphysics of Schopenhauer. The *conatus* concept shows up again in Feinberg's claim that interests must somehow be compounded out of conations, an idea that Goodpaster uses to buttress his own claim that being alive is the best criterion for moral considerability. So, analytically respectable or not, Goodpaster's biocentrism is thus linked with that of Schweitzer, albeit Goodpaster's careful philosophical exposition of a biocentric environmental ethic is far superior to Schweitzer's—and to Feinberg's, for that matter, as well.

8.11 TAYLOR'S INDIVIDUALISTIC BIOCENTRISM AND REGAN'S CASE FOR ANIMAL RIGHTS

Goodpaster contributed to environmental ethics briefly in 1978 and 1979, but very substantially and very importantly, at the beginning of an illustrious career as a professional philosopher. Paul W. Taylor contributed to environmental ethics also briefly—with five papers and a book between 1981 and 1987—at the end of an illustrious career as a professional philosopher.[79] Taylor's contribution is also very substantial and very influential. Indeed, Taylor changed the meaning of the term "biocentrism," which had originally been associated with Deep Ecology as first sketched by Arne Naess and later popularized by George Sessions and Bill Devall.[80] In the Deep-Ecology literature and in the conservation-biology literature it influenced, "biocentrism" was used more comprehensively to refer to non-anthropocentric environmental ethics in general and would often be used more particularly to characterize the Leopold land ethic—even by me in casual conversation.[81] Taylor appropriated it for his own more narrowly cir-cumscribed theory of non-anthropocentric environmental ethics.[82] The term "bio-centrism"—life-centered—actually does better fit Taylor's environmental ethic than Leopold's and for that reason I eventually conceded it to him and began to use "eco-centrism" to characterize the land ethic. I apply "biocentrism" here to Goodpaster's sketch of a non-anthropocentric environmental ethic anachronistically—or perhaps better retrospectively—as Goodpaster himself did not use that term. Ditto, regarding Schweitzer and Feinberg.

Based on the "evidence that the biosystem [the biosphere] as a whole exhibits behav-ior" characteristic of life, supplied by Lovelock and his fellow travelers, Goodpaster is willing to entertain the possibility that "entities and systems of entities heretofore unimagined as claimants on our moral attention (such as the biosystem itself)" might deserve the kind of respect that the early Leopold thought that life as such both mer-ited and actually received. Taylor seems to be carrying that vision forward when he writes, "If we were to accept a life-centered theory of environmental ethics, a profound reordering of our moral universe would take place. We would begin to look at the whole of the Earth's biosphere in a new light."[83] Alas, he is only expressing himself imprecisely. Taylor, disappointingly, instead retreats from Goodpaster's more generous holistic biocentrism to a niggardly biocentric individualism:

> When the basic characteristics of the attitude of respect for nature are made clear, it will be seen that a life-centered system of environmental ethics need not be holistic or organicist in its conception of the kinds of entities that are deemed appropriate objects of moral concern and consideration. Nor does such a system require that the concepts of ecological homeostasis, equilibrium, and integrity provide us with normative principles from which could be derived (with the addition of factual knowledge) our obligations with regard to natural ecosystems....I argue that finally it is the good (well-being, welfare) of *indi-vidual organisms*, considered as entities having inherent worth, that determines our moral relations with the earth's wild communities of life.[84]

Ironically, I myself may be indirectly but ultimately responsible for Taylor's retreat from Goodpaster's expansive holistic biocentrism—with its explicit, if only program-matic, embrace of the biosphere—and for Taylor's militant anti-holism and fervent espousal of ethical individualism. I had aggressively criticized the individualism of animal liberation and animal rights, from the point of view of environmental ethics, and defended the holism of the Leopold land ethic in a notorious paper published in 1980.[85] Tom Regan, the principal exponent of animal rights, responded by accusing the land ethic, as I had represented it, of "environmental fascism." In 2.15, I review the environmental-fascism indictment against the land ethic and indicate why the land ethic is not guilty as charged. However the land ethic, *as I had represented it in the 1980 paper*, was fairly susceptible to the charge of environmental fascism. I thank Regan and the other ethical individualists who joined him as plaintiffs in his case against the land ethic (the relevant literature is cited in Chapter 2, n. 76) for unwittingly pointing out the error of my representation and I revised it in all subsequent iterations (including that in Chapter 2 of this book). But, back to my present point, in the fall semester of 1982, Regan was Distinguished Visiting Professor at Brooklyn College, where Taylor had long been a member of the philosophy department. Regan's magnum opus, *The Case for Animal Rights*, was then in production by the University of California Press.[86] According to Taylor, during his visit, Regan "kindly read the last chapter of the book [Taylor's book, *Respect for Nature*] and made extensive comments on it. I benefited greatly from this, as well as from discussions with him concerning various matters related to other parts of the book."[87] Prominent among those matters, I surmise, was the specter of environmental fascism that then haunted holism in environmental ethics—thanks to my initial erroneous representation of the land ethic—an evil spirit that Taylor was determined to drive away from his biocentrism.

The chronology of their relevant publications suggest that Taylor's philosophy was also influenced in other ways by Regan's. Regan's trail-blazing paper, "Animal Rights, Human Wrongs," was published in 1980; Taylor's "The Ethics of Respect for Nature" was published in 1981—both in *Environmental Ethics* (the journal). Regan's book-length treatment of animal rights was published in 1983; Taylor's book-length treatment of biocentrism was published in 1986. The similarities are unmistakable. For reasons too technical (and too insignificant) to rehearse here, both Regan and Taylor prefer the term "inherent" to "intrinsic" as an adjective modifying "value" (Regan) and "worth" (Taylor).[88] For Regan, a being's inherent value is the platform supporting its claim to moral rights, while, for Taylor, a being's inherent worth is the platform supporting its claim to be respected morally. What gives a being inherent value, according to Regan, is that it is the "subject of a life," while what gives a being inherent worth, according to Taylor, is that it is a "teleological center of life." These structural and even sonorous similarities between Taylor's philosophy and Regan's suggest that, just as Goodpaster is taking the next step beyond Peter Singer's sentience-based animal-liberation ethic, Taylor is taking the next step beyond Tom Regan's deontological animal-rights ethic.

8.12 TAYLOR'S DEONTOLOGY AND TELEOLOGICAL CENTERS OF LIFE

Tom Regan is explicit about the Kantian deontological affinities of his case for animal rights.

> [W]e can explain, in general terms reminiscent of Kant, what is involved in mistreating human beings. Humans are mistreated if they are treated as valuable only if they forward the interests of other beings. To treat a human being thus is to show a lack of proper respect for the sort of value humans have. In Kant's terms, what has value in itself must always be treated as an end, never merely as a means.[89]

So much for proper respect. Regan goes on immediately to ground rights on inherent value. But on what does inherent value rest? "[H]uman beings not only are alive," Regan points out, "*they have a life*. What is more, we are subjects of a life that is better or worse for us, logically independently of anyone else's valuing us or finding us useful."[90] Those animals that are also subjects of a life have inherent value, are ends in themselves and, as such, merit proper respect, and their rights should be recognized.

While Regan is clearly adapting the second formulation of Kant's categorical imperative to his theory of animal rights, Taylor adapts the first formulation as well as the second:[91]

> To put it in a Kantian way, to adopt the attitude of respect for nature is to take a stance that one wills to be a universal law of nature for all rational beings. It is to hold that stance categorically, as being validly applicable to every moral agent without exception, irrespective of whatever personal feelings toward nature such an agent might have or might lack.[92]

Taylor regards his biocentric theory of ethics as "symmetrical with a theory of ethics grounded on respect for persons." The theory of respect for persons that he has in mind is Kant's as Taylor soon indicates when he writes, "This is what Kant meant by conceiving of persons as ends in themselves"—which refers to the second formulation of the categorical imperative.[93] Kant's third formulation of the categorical imperative, incidentally, would be impossible to adapt either to an animal-rights ethic or to a respect-for-life ethic, as the third formulation requires moral agents to think of themselves not only as obedient to universal moral laws but as the authors of those laws, as legislators in the kingdom of ends. Beings who lack reason cannot formulate categorical imperatives and thus could not universalize the maxims of their actions, either as subjects or as legislators of moral laws. Thus the symmetry with a Kantian ethics of respect for persons that Taylor claims for his ethics of respect for nature is imperfect. But I suppose that it is as permissible for twentieth-century ethicists to take liberties with Kant's ethics as it was for nineteenth-century metaphysicists to take liberties with his metaphysics.

Much more perfect is the symmetry between Taylor's non-anthropocentric ethical theory and Regan's. As Regan rests rights on inherent value, Taylor rests respect on inherent worth. As Regan rests inherent value on being the subject of a life, Taylor rests inherent worth on being a teleological center of life. What is it to be a teleological center of life?, one might fairly ask. Taylor is not all that forthcoming. As a first (and in his original paper, his last) stab at a definition Taylor offers the following: "when we conceive of individual plants and animals...as teleological centers of life...[w]e need not...consider them to have consciousness...[rather] all are equally teleological centers of life in the sense that each is a unified system of goal-oriented activities directed toward their preservation and well-being."[94] In his book, and final statement on the subject, he is only a little more prolix:

We conceive of the organism as a teleological center of life, striving to preserve itself and realize its good in its own way. To say it is a teleological center of life is to say that its internal functioning as well as its external activities are all goal-oriented, having the constant tendency to maintain an organism's existence through time and to enable it successfully to perform those biological operations whereby it reproduces its kind and continually adapts to changing environmental events and conditions.[95]

8.13 TAYLOR'S BIOCENTRISM AS A FOUNDATION FOR A LEOPOLD EARTH ETHIC?

Taylor's biocentrism is hopeless as a foundation for the Leopold Earth ethic. Taylor is militantly anti-holistic, while a biocentric Leopold Earth ethic is necessarily holistic with a vengeance—according, as it does, respect for the whole Earth as a living being. There are other disqualifying peculiarities of Taylor's biocentrism. For one, preposterously, he insists that inherent worth does not come in degrees. If a being has inherent worth, because it is a teleological center of life, it has it absolutely and independently. Which means that it has it equally with all other beings that have inherent worth. That, in turn, implies that all teleological centers of life command equal respect. Yes, it's true. In Taylor's biocentric environmental ethic, a human being and a cockroach have the same inherent worth and warrant the same respect; a human being and a cockroach—indeed a human being and a bacterium—are moral equals. But as Goodpaster notes,

> the clearest and most decisive refutation of the principle of respect for life is that one cannot *live* according to it, nor is there any indication in nature that we were intended to. We must eat, experiment to gain knowledge, protect ourselves from predation (macroscopic and microscopic), and in general deal with the overwhelming complexities of the moral life while remaining psychologically intact. To take seriously the criterion of considerability being defended, all these things must be seen as somehow morally wrong. [96]

For Taylor, all these things are morally wrong. They can, however, be justified in the same way that we sometimes justify killing other human beings—by appeal to self-defense.[97] Building on this concept, Taylor justifies human activities involving the consumption and destruction of other organisms in terms of "defending" our own lives in the process of satisfying our "basic interests," such as to eat.[98] The satisfaction of our "nonbasic interests"—the kinds of examples Taylor offers are wearing fur garments and owning artifacts made from ivory—are not justifiable.[99] Of course, these and the other extravagant non-basic interests that Taylor enumerates are hardly the only non-basic interests that make of our human lives more than just a bare existence. The ethic that Taylor develops in theory, if actually practiced, would entail a lifestyle that would make the lifestyle of the strictest Jain mendicant appear luxurious by comparison.

8.14 ROLSTON'S BIOCENTRISM AS A FOUNDATION FOR A LEOPOLD EARTH ETHIC?

Goodpaster carefully and reasonably distinguishes between "*a criterion of moral considerability* and *a criterion of moral significance.*"[100] All living beings are morally considerable—yes, cockroaches and bacteria included—but some may be more considerable than others. Goodpaster's own examples are trees, dogs, and humans. He eschews the philosophical task of exploring criteria of moral significance, confining his discussion to a criterion of moral considerability, but his examples suggest a certain hierarchy of moral significance, such that humans are more significant than dogs and dogs more than trees.

Holmes Rolston III does not characterize himself as a biocentrist; nor, as an environmental philosopher, does he focus on the problem of identifying the property that confers moral standing. Rather, he focuses on the related problem of intrinsic value in nature. Rolston claims to defend a resolutely objectivist theory of intrinsic value in nature. That is, the value of natural beings is neither their instrumental value in relation to human interests, nor do they have intrinsic value because they are intrinsically valued by human subjects, in Rolston's view. Rather, their intrinsic value is independent of human valuation of any kind.

Apparently, Rolston builds his theory of objective intrinsic value in nature on the paradigm of intrinsic value provided by Kant. According to Kant, "an end in itself does not have mere relative worth, i.e., a price, but an intrinsic worth, i.e., *dignity.*"[101] According to Kant, the intrinsic value of ends-in-themselves is objective:

> Man necessarily thinks of his existence in this way: thus far it is a subjective principle of human actions. Also every other rational being thinks of his existence by means of the same ground which holds also for myself; thus it is at the same time an objective principle from which, as a supreme practical ground, it must be possible to derive all laws of the will.[102]

Two senses of "objectivity" seem to be a play in this passage. Subject/object dualism is at the heart of Kant's ethics, serving as the basis of his account of human freedom and moral autonomy. Fully subscribing to the distinction between subjects and objects, Kant must regard all value as subjectively conferred. Thus, an object's value cannot be objective in the same way that its mass or shape is objective. The value of an object is the value conferred on it by a valuing subject. If there existed no valuing subjects, objects would be devoid of value. We valuing subjects value all sorts of objects instrumentally as means to our various ends—our houses for shelter, our cars for transportation, and so on and so forth. We valuing subjects value ourselves intrinsically, as ends in ourselves. That kind of value too is subjectively conferred, as Kant notes. But because every other rational being values himself or herself intrinsically as an end in himself or herself, that makes the intrinsic value of rational beings somehow "objective." But how, exactly? Not in the same way that the mass and shape of the physical bodies of rational beings are objective. The mass and shape of the physical bodies of rational beings exist independently of any subjective acts, whether acts of valuing or knowing or any other mental or emotional condition (except the very general and universal conditions specified in the *Critique of Pure Reason*). The intrinsic value of rational beings depends on their self-valuing, a subjective act, but their intrinsic value becomes—or should become—objective in another sense. We describe an act of judgment—say as a referee of an academic paper or a basketball game—as objective if it is unbiased. The academic paper may have been written by a friend or colleague; my son may be a player on one of the basketball teams; I am an objective referee in either case if I do not allow my affections to sway my judgment of the publishability of the paper in question or the rule-conforming play on the court.

So this is what Kant means by objective intrinsic value: because self-valuing is common to all rational beings—is universal among all rational beings—we should not allow our own self-valuing to becloud our recognition of everyone else's self-valuing. When we distance ourselves from our own personal inclinations (desires, passions, emotions, preferences) and regard others with disinterested attention, we recognize that they value themselves in exactly the same way that we value ourselves—intrinsically. The intrinsic value subjectively conferred by each rational being on himself or herself is not objective, as Kant notes, but, due to its universality, it is the ground of an "objective" *principle*—that is, a principle unconditioned by the vagaries of personal "inclinations." Kant's senses of *subjective* and *objective* are therefore equivocal. All value is ontologically subjective but can and ought to become epistemologically objective if unbiased. My judgment of the artistic merits of a ballerina's performance is "objective"—in the sense of unbiased—if the fact that she is exceptionally attractive (or unattractive) or the fact that she is my niece (or my daughter's rival) is ignored. Clearly, Kant is asserting that a rational being's intrinsic value is *epistemologically objective* while remaining *ontologically subjective*—to invoke a distinction formally drawn by John Searle.[103]

Countering the way Kant limits "objective" intrinsic value to rational human beings, Rolston wryly remarks, "No doubt the lemurs will take a dim view of such a theory, since lemurs...value their own lives intrinsically for what they are in themselves....Lemurs cannot self-consciously evaluate...but they can behaviorally demonstrate what they value."[104] Beginning with lemurs, Rolston sets up a slippery slope from self-valuing rational humans to self-valuing plants. Next after lemurs (with humans, members of the primate order) come warblers, fellow members of the chordate phylum: "A warbler eats insects instrumentally as a food resource; the warbler defends her own life as an end in itself and makes more warblers as she can. A life is defended intrinsically."[105] What about plants? Plants compete with other plants for space and light and they defend themselves against plant competitors and animal predators with allelopathic chemicals. Thus, in the case of plants and other unconscious organisms devoid of subjectivity, "A life is defended for what it is in itself, without further contributory reference....That is *ipso facto* value in both the biological and philosophical senses, intrinsic because it inheres in, has focus within, the organism itself."[106]

Because the intrinsic self-valuing of primates (lemurs), vertebrates (warblers), and plants does not depend on other subjects valuing them intrinsically and such non-human intrinsically self-valuing beings exist objectively in nature, intrinsic value exists objectively in nature. Or so Rolston appears to argue. To his baseline biocentrism, Rolston adds a value premium for sentience and an additional value premium for rationality. Thus, humans (rational beings) have more intrinsic value than dogs (sentient beings) and dogs have more intrinsic value than trees (unconscious, albeit self-valuing because self-defending, beings).[107]

Because humans have the greatest intrinsic value and thus the greatest moral significance—followed by animals, such as other primates and mammals that have a rich conscious life, then by barely sentient animals, and last by plants and other unconscious organisms—Rolston's biocentrism is not tortured by the same intellectual contortions to which Taylor's egalitarian biocentrism drives him in order to justify a tolerably livable human lifestyle. Rolston also provides moral standing or moral considerability for various biological wholes. Species are "the kinds" which individual organisms "defend" and "re-present" as a "good kind."[108] Ecosystems are the ecological theater in which the evolutionary play unfolds, which "projects" the good kinds (species) that are defended and re-presented by individual organisms.[109] Unfortunately, for purposes of a biocentric Earth ethic, Rolston provides no intrinsic value nor any moral considerability for the biosphere, for Gaia.

8.15 GOODPASTER'S BIOCENTRISM PROVIDES THE BEST THEORETICAL SUPPORT FOR A NON-ANTHROPOCENTRIC EARTH ETHIC

With the single exception of Goodpaster, biocentrist theories in academic environmental ethics provide poor foundations for a biocentric Earth ethic, such as Leopold adumbrated in 1923. The main problem with the biocentrism of Feinberg, Taylor, and Rolston is the subjective, if not the psychological, orientation of the way they conceive of life. The common ancestor of their various conceptions of life is the *conatus* concept, an ancestor that their conceptions of life also share with Schweitzer's. By all except Goodpaster, life is understood in terms of some sort of inner impetus toward a goal. It is clearest in Schweitzer's concept of the will-to-live, which he appropriates from Schopenhauer. The *conatus* concept is identified by its Anglicized name, "conation," and elaborately characterized disjunctively by Feinberg as "conscious wishes, desires, and hopes; *or* urges and impulses; *or* unconscious drives, aims, and goals; *or* latent tendencies, directions of growth, and natural fulfillments." Taylor's characterization of his notion of a "teleological center of life" prominently includes a "striving...tendency." Rolston's organisms defend their lives—each such life is an *end* in itself—and they *strive* to reproduce.

Goodpaster is the only biocentrist who provides less a conative characterization of life and more of a thermodynamic characterization of it—in terms of "low entropy," "metabolic processes," and "homeostatic feedback processes"—which is consistent not only with Leopold's characterization of life in terms of metabolic processes and physiological functions, but also with the thermodynamical and biogeochemical characterization of life by Vernadsky, Lovelock, and all the other contemporary Gaia theorists. The essentially conative characterization of life common to Schweitzer, Feinberg, Taylor, and Rolston is not just beside the point, it is antithetical to the ateleological commitment of contemporary Gaia theory, which is necessary to maintain in order to ensure the consilience of Gaian science with evolutionary biology and indeed with the spirit of science itself. And Goodpaster is the only biocentrist to explicitly include the biosphere (or "biosystem") among the living things that deserve to be morally considerable.

Two other features of Goodpaster's biocentrism recommend it.

One has already been noted. Goodpaster provides a distinction between moral considerability and moral significance, but leaves the question of moral significance open. Rolston takes advantage of the opening Goodpaster provides and distributes moral significance differentially among different orders of living beings. I am not moved to consider whether Gaia has greater moral significance than an individual organism, including an individual human organism, and if so, how conflicts between human rights and Gaia's well-being and dignity might be resolved. In anticipation of the scalar issues discussed in Chapters 10 and 11 that question turns out to be purely, as we sometimes say, "academic." However that may be, Goodpaster's biocentrism, like Rolston's, is both reasonable and practicable.

The other feature of Goodpaster's biocentrism that recommends it is the way Goodpaster deals with a closely related practical problem facing any biocentric ethic, any plea to respect life itself in all its protean manifestations—from the microbial to the biospheric. As Goodpaster soberly observes,

> It seems to me that there clearly are limits to the operational character of respect for living things. We must eat, and usually this involves killing (though not always). We must have knowledge, and sometimes this involves experimentation with living things and killing (though not always). We must protect ourselves from predation and disease, and sometimes this involves killing (though not always).[110]

As any good analytic philosopher would, Goodpaster has a distinction for that: the distinction between "regulative and operative moral consideration." We may be convinced, that is, by Goodpaster's argument and grant that *all* living things deserve moral consideration, but we may not be able, due to ethical overload and psychological incapacity, to actually consider them all morally. "[W]e are subject to thresholds of moral sensitivity just as we are subject to thresholds of cognitive or perceptual sensitivity."[111] Hence biocentrism may be regulative but not operative. Doesn't that astute and candid observation about thresholds of moral sensitivity and the distinction between regulative and operative moral consideration make of biocentrism little more than recreational moral philosophy? What's the practical point? There is a practical point to biocentrism—perhaps not at the biospheric scale, but there is certainly a practical point to biocentric individualism as Goodpaster indicates:

> The regulative character of the moral consideration due to all living things asks, as far as I can see, for sensitivity and awareness, not for suicide (psychic or otherwise). But it is not vacuous, in that it does provide a *ceteris paribus* encouragement in the direction of nutritional, scientific, and medical practices of a genuinely life-respecting sort.[112]

At the very least, such a ceteris paribus or other-things-being-equal encouragement toward life-respecting practices would lead a biocentrist to avoid the wanton and gratuitous destruction of living things. Schweitzer, although an arch conativist, and thus in regard to biocentric metaphysics not in agreement with Goodpaster, does implicitly anticipate Goodpaster's regulative/operative distinction and his ceteris paribus solution to the practicability problem facing biocentrism. Biocentrism would seem to be impracticable because of the psychologically intolerable burden it would impose on us human—indeed, all-too-human—moral agents. We have to do what we have to do. Nevertheless, "The farmer," Schweitzer declares, "who has mown down a thousand flowers in his meadow as fodder for his cows, must be careful on his way home not to strike off *in wanton pastime* the head of a single flower by the roadside, for he thereby commits a wrong against life without being under the pressure of necessity."[113] Goodpaster's ceteris paribus biocentrism is by no means vacuous; the cultural institutionalization of ceteris paribus biocentrism would entrain significant improvements in the lot of most living beings in the more-than-human world. Whether or not it would entrain significant improvements in Gaia's lot in life is the first question that I address in the next chapter.

9

The Earth Ethic: A Critical Account of Its Anthropocentric Foundations—The Natural Contract and Environmental Virtue Ethics

Lynn Margulis thinks that human worries about destroying or even seriously damaging life on Earth—the living Earth, the biosphere, Gaia—are exaggerated. "Gaia, a tough bitch," she writes, "is not at all threatened by humans."[1] Indeed, Margulis thinks that we humans could not destroy or even seriously damage the biosphere if we actually set out to do just that:

> No human culture despite its inventiveness, can kill life on this planet, were it even to try.... Fossil evidence records that Earth life in its 3,000-million-year history has withstood numerous impacts equal to or greater than the total detonation of all [twenty-]five-thousand stockpiled nuclear bombs.... The notion that we can destroy all life, including bacteria thriving in the water tanks of nuclear power plants or boiling hot vents, is ludicrous."[2]

According to Margulis, "We cannot put an end to nature; we can only pose a threat to ourselves."[3] The Earth is too big and even more immensely too long-lived to be the credible beneficiary of a holistic biocentric Earth ethic. While I agree with Margulis that we can and do pose a threat to ourselves, we also pose a threat to organic nature, *as we know it*. The Leopold land ethic (detailed in Chapter 2) remains credible and operative because it is certainly possible to destroy, seriously to damage, and significantly to harm the fellow-members of our biotic communities and those communities as such, and to violate the "biotic rights" of extant non-human species to continuance—our "fellow voyagers in the odyssey of evolution." Suppose we take the referent of *the biotic community* in the summary moral maxim of the land ethic—"A thing is right when it tends to preserve the integrity, stability, and beauty of the biotic community"—in its widest possible sense to refer to the extant global complement of species collectively. Certainly, global climate change threatens to compromise the integrity, stability, and beauty of the global biotic community as presently constituted. To that extent, the land ethic is *spatially* scalable and, therefore, it remains, as I say, credible and operative. It is temporally scalable to the normal pace of normal evolutionary processes of extinction and speciation as indicated in the dynamized land ethic developed in 3.16 and 3.17. But it is not scalable to the *temporal dimensions* of the Earth's biography stretching back more than three billion years and forward for perhaps half as long into the future.[4] Such immense temporal scales vastly exceed the temporal parameters of ethics—any ethic.

Rather, what we need—and need desperately—is an *anthropocentric* Earth ethic in this time of imminent global climate change to complement the non-anthropocentric land ethic. Ours is a time of existential threat. Not to the Earth and probably not to the species *Homo sapiens*, specimens of which would probably survive a climatic apocalypse in much fewer numbers and in scattered populations on continents reshaped by risen sea levels and expanded deserts and ravaged by violent weather and extreme seasons. Nor is there presently an existential threat to the more privileged of us humans alive today (among whom I count myself). Rather, ours is a time of immediate existential threat to the most vulnerable humans alive today; ours is also a time in which the existential threat to future human generations, whether privileged or not, looms on the temporal horizon if we do nothing to avert radical climate change; and, ultimately, ours is, as well, a time of existential threat to the global human civilization whose roots descend several thousand years into the humus of past time.

Therefore, the final three chapters of this book provide critical accounts of the two possible types of anthropocentric Earth ethic broached by Leopold in "Conservation as a Moral Issue" in "Some Fundamentals of Conservation in the Southwest": environmental virtue ethics and responsibility to future generations. Environmental virtue ethics is considered in this chapter and responsibility to future generations is considered in the next two chapters of the book.

In addition to a critical account of contemporary environmental virtue ethics, this chapter also provides a critical account of another type of anthropocentric Earth ethic that seems never to have occurred to Leopold—the "natural contract." The "natural contract" was first proposed by Michel Serres and latterly endorsed by Bruno Latour and, implicitly, by James Lovelock himself. The natural contract is an adaptation of the classic social contract theories of the origin and nature of ethics to contemporary environmental concerns, just as environmental virtue ethics is a similar adaptation of the classic theories of virtue ethics. The ur-theories of both the social contract and of virtue ethics originated in ancient Greek moral philosophy. And those two theories of ethics—social-contract and virtue—are dialectically linked, the latter originating in the philosophies of Plato and Aristotle as their responses to the inaccuracies and inadequacies that they perceived in the former. Before critically accounting for the natural contract and environmental virtue ethics, I begin this chapter by (1) elaborating and documenting Margulis's portrait of Gaia as a "tough bitch" and a "mother of invention" and (2) revisiting the concept of anthropocentrism, previously visited in the Introduction, in 1.11, 2.17, and 6.10–6.16.

In addition to a critical account of theories of responsibility to future generations, Chapter 10 also provides a critical account of inter*national* justice, which is the preoccupation of most contemporary climate-change ethicists. Responsibility to future generations is often represented by the same ethicists as inter*generational* justice and may, thus, be regarded as apposite to inter*national* justice. More abstractly, international and intergenerational justice are linked by the concept of scale—an unprecedented global spatial scale in regard to the former and an unprecedented planetary temporal scale (as well as a global spatial scale) in regard to the latter. However symmetrical spatial and temporal scale may at first appear, there are significant asymmetries that render extrapolations from the one to the other problematic.

9.1 NO NEED TO PATRONIZE GAIA WITH BIOCENTRIC MORAL CONSIDERABILITY

Of all the "impacts" that Earth's life has withstood, perhaps the severest was the Great Oxygenation Event (GOE)—the "oxygen crisis"—that occurred about 2,400 million years ago, an eon or so after the autopoiesis of life on Earth. When iron and other minerals that combined with the poisonous waste oxygen produced by photosynthetic cyanobacteria during the Great Rusting became saturated, and highly reactive oxygen began to accumulate in the atmosphere, microbes that were adapted to an anaerobic environment either got killed off or driven into oxygen-free refugia.[5]

Methane, a powerful greenhouse gas, was abundant in infant Gaia's oxygen-poor atmosphere. After the GOE, methane was greatly depleted by reacting with oxygen, in the presence of ultraviolet radiation, to produce water and carbon dioxide—also a greenhouse gas, to be sure, but a much less effective one than methane.[6] With 25 percent less solar radiation reaching the Earth then in comparison with now, a diminished greenhouse effect led to a second great challenge to Earth's life, global cooling.[7] The Earth froze. The Huronian Glaciation—a planetary ice sheet extending from both poles almost to the equator—lasted some 300 million years.[8] Nor was this early ultra-freezing unique; it was followed by several near-total glaciations in Gaia's Precambrian childhood and adolescence.[9] Through these temporally protracted episodes of atmospheric-chemistry fluctuation and glaciation, life not only persisted but diversified.

The Earth has also experienced catastrophic asteroid impacts, the one occurring sixty-five million years ago at the Cretaceous-Tertiary boundary being only the most notorious.[10] After the Cambrian explosion of biodiversity some 530 million years ago, there have been four other mass extinction events: at the Ordovician-Silurian transition, about 445 million years ago; during the Late Devonian period, about 370 million years ago; at the Permian-Triassic transition, the worst one of all, 251 million years ago; and at the Triassic-Jurassic transition, about 205 million years ago.[11] For a synoptic discussion of the extreme environmental fluctuations through which life endured, and after which it flourished, see *Revolutions that Made the Earth* by Tim Lenton and Andrew Watson. (Lenton and Watson also affirm that the Gaia hypothesis become Gaia theory has now become Earth systems science.[12] The Gaia hypothesis has thus migrated from the New-Age margins of science, whereto it was shunted in the 1970s, to a respectable place among twenty-first-century integrative sciences. One can only hope that *eventually* environmental philosophy and ethics will rise to a similar status among the humanities and in the discipline of philosophy more particularly.)

After each of the "revolutions" in Earth's biography, life speciated anew—more prolifically than ever.[13] As Margulis notes, "Life, especially bacterial life, is resilient. It has fed on disaster and destruction from the beginning. Gaia incorporates the ecologic crises of her components, responds brilliantly, and in her new necessity becomes the mother of invention."[14] Our unstinted burning of fossil fuels may elevate CO_2 and other greenhouse gases—attended by compounding positive-feedback biospheric processes, such as a decreased albedo resulting from retreating glaciers and increased methane from melting tundra—and may thus accelerate an increase in warming and with it a reduction of biodiversity so great as to mark a sixth mass extinction event. If Earth's past life history is any indication, afterward, new species will evolve, biodiversity will gradually recover, and Gaia will live on stronger and richer than ever. Indeed, without the anthropogenic revolution in Earth's biography now emerging, the Earth would be headed for another glaciation and trending toward one of Huronian magnitude.[15] From a Gaian perspective, by recycling sequestered carbon *Homo petroleumus* (as we might be renamed by some future beneficiary) may be just what the doctor ordered to keep the Earth from eventually freezing over.

The ultimate expression of human arrogance and self-importance is to think that we need a biocentric Earth ethic to restrain ourselves from destroying or even significantly harming the biosphere. About this Margulis is typically blunt: "To me, the human move to take responsibility for the living Earth is laughable—the rhetoric of the powerless. The planet takes care of us, not we of it. Our self-inflated moral imperative to guide a wayward Earth or heal our sick planet is evidence of our immense capacity for self-delusion. Rather, we need to protect us from ourselves."[16] Ethics, as we see, is scale dependent. To justify our current orgy of fossil-fuel exhumation, combustion, and CO_2 dumping, by invoking its potential benefits for some state of the biosphere millions of years in the future, would be morally irresponsible. Within the window of time that is ethically relevant, climate change is predicted to have few, if any, beneficial effects on our species, to say nothing of our non-human shipmates in the odyssey of evolution. What Margulis avers needs repeating: we need a climate ethic to protect us from ourselves. We need an anthropocentric Earth ethic.

9.2 THE CONCEPT OF ANTHROPOCENTRISM REVISITED

After going on and on in 6.11 about how, in "Some Fundamentals of Conservation in the Southwest," Leopold ridicules anthropocentrism, one may wonder how I can here explore, with neither prejudice nor effrontery, an anthropocentric Earth ethic. First in the Introduction and reiterated in 6.11, I explicitly draw a distinction between *metaphysical* and *moral* anthropocentrism. The anthropocentrism that Leopold ridicules in the section of "Some Fundamentals" titled "Conservation as a Moral Issue" is *metaphysical* anthropocentrism—"the assumption," in Leopold's words, "that man is the end and purpose of creation."[17] It is the metaphysical anthropocentrist's "high opinion of his own importance in the universe" that Leopold ridicules—and justly so—in "Some Fundamentals."[18]

What I call *moral anthropocentrism*—that humans and humans alone deserve moral consideration and ethical treatment—is traditionally based on metaphysical anthropocentrism. In the Western tradition of thought, human moral exceptionalism has been based on claims that "man" has been uniquely created in the image of God or that "man" is uniquely rational. *Because* humans alone are uniquely created in the image of God or are uniquely rational, humans alone uniquely deserve moral treatment—or so goes the move from metaphysical to moral anthropocentrism. The *moral* anthropocentrism implicit in Margulis's foregoing remarks and explicit in those of Lovelock and Serres, which follow, is based precisely—however paradoxically—on the firm and unequivocal rejection of *metaphysical* anthropocentrism. There is nothing to be found in *Homo sapiens* that justifies claims of a privileged place in the cosmos on behalf of the species as a whole or of its members severally. To believe otherwise, they think, is not just a delusion; it is a very dangerous delusion. Certainly the cosmos, expansively, and Gaia, more locally, care not a fig whether we humans exist or not, much less—if that is possible—whether we flourish individually and as a species or not. We humans have to look out for ourselves in the face of an indifferent universe and a biosphere "that was old when the morning stars sang together and, when the last of us has been gathered unto our fathers, will still be young."[19]

While ridiculing metaphysical anthropocentrism as traditionally conceived—that "man is the end and purpose of creation" and a being of great "importance in the universe"—Leopold himself suggests (as noted in 6.16) the possibility of an alternative kind of metaphysical anthropocentrism centered (also paradoxically) on the human capacity for ethical *non*-anthropocentrism:

> And if [—IF—] there be, indeed, a special nobility in the human race—a special cosmic value distinctive from and superior to all other life—by what token shall it be manifest?
>
> By a society decently respectful of its own and all other life, capable of inhabiting the earth without defiling it? Or by a society like that of John Burrough's potato bug, which exterminated the potato, and thereby exterminated itself? By one or the other shall we be judged in "the derisive silence of eternity."[20]

In any case, the kinds of anthropocentric Earth ethics considered in this chapter and the next are not based on metaphysical anthropocentrism of any sort, either traditional metaphysical anthropocentrism or the alternative dialectical sort suggested by Leopold. Nor must a philosophically well-crafted anthropocentric Earth ethic be cognitively dissonant with the non-anthropocentric land ethic. That is, a philosophically well-crafted anthropocentric Earth ethic need not confer moral status *exclusively* on human beings and/or on the human species, on all *and only* human beings and/or *Homo sapiens*. Indeed, a philosophically well-crafted anthropocentric Earth ethic, inspired by Aldo Leopold's polytheoretical (or "pluralistic") sketch of such in "Some Fundamentals," should be compatible with and a companion to his by now well-theorized non-anthropocentric land ethic (detailed in 11.6).

9.3 WAR AND PEACE

James Lovelock (twenty-first-century iteration) agrees with his longtime fellow Gaia theorist, Lynn Margulis, that we need to protect us from ourselves. But he more carefully indicates that we are not a direct threat to ourselves—as we would be if, say, fundamentalist Christian Americans managed to elect End-Times politicians determined to stage a nuclear Armageddon, the horrors of which they imagine that they and their ilk would be spared by the Rapture. We are, rather, an indirect threat to ourselves as the agents of global climate change. Complacent Americans and complacent citizens of other industrialized democracies elect politicians who either deny the existence of global climate change outright or accept the fact that global climate change is happening, but deny that it is anthropogenic. Or they accept the fact that anthropogenic global climate change is happening, but lack the courage and political will to try to stanch it. Thus we are, despite ourselves, radically altering the environmental conditions of our planet; and the planet will, as it were, retaliate against us by no longer being a habitat hospitable to *Homo sapiens*: "By changing the environment we have," in Lovelock's estimation, "unknowingly declared war on Gaia...and made it our greatest enemy."[21] A declaration of war is symmetrical; if we make war on Gaia, Gaia will retaliate and make war on us. Lovelock thinks that such a belligerent relationship with the planet is sheer folly—for "the ineluctable forces of Gaia marshal against us."[22]

Lovelock is less (but only a little less) sanguine than Margulis, about Gaia's resilience. Human industrial activities have incubated "Earth's disease, the fever brought on by a plague of people."[23] But Gaia is not likely to succumb to that anthropogenic illness: "What we are doing has weakened her, but is unlikely to destroy her."[24] Rather, more likely, Gaia is being driven to a new stable state, a new climatic equilibrium at a higher average temperature and with all the other changes in planetary conditions that that entrains: risen sea levels and diminished continents; less productive, acidified oceans; expanded deserts and shrunken forests—to name but a few such changes that are confidently predictable. And who knows what else might follow in a world ten or fifteen Celsius degrees warmer, on average, than at present? Ironically, just those anthropogenic changes constitute Gaia's "revenge"—per the title of Lovelock's 2006 book. He thinks that we face "an imminent shift in our climate towards one that could easily be described as Hell."[25] Our Mother Earth has turned against us: "she acts as a mother who is nurturing but ruthlessly cruel towards transgressors, even when they are her progeny."[26]

According to Lovelock, Gaia is using the best methods of a crafty general—turning our short-sighted machinations against us—in her retaliatory counter-war. Our only hope against such an implacable and overwhelming enemy is to sue for peace. "In several ways," he avers, "we are unintentionally at war with Gaia, and to survive with our civilization intact we urgently need to make a just peace with Gaia while strong enough to negotiate and not a defeated and broken rabble on the way to extinction."[27] The theme of war and peace frames *The Revenge of Gaia*, introduced in the book's first chapter and reiterated in its last. The motive for framing environmental policy in such terms is to unify and mobilize us humans—to make of us a true *us* as opposed to a collection of self-absorbed and complacent egos clustered into fractious and contentious tribes haphazardly and often imperfectly organized into mutually competitive and truculent polities, preoccupied with power and advantage, obdurately ignoring the global commonweal. The microcosm is Britain in 1938 (or 1939).[28] Our only hope is to form a political leviathan and surrender our liberties to an absolute sovereign power:

> Can the present-day democracies, with their noisy media and special-interest lobbies, act fast enough for an effective defense against Gaia? We may need restrictions, rationing and a call to service that were familiar in wartime and in addition to suffer for a while a loss of freedom. We will need a small permanent group of strategists who, as in wartime, will try to outthink our Earthly enemy and be ready for the surprises bound to come.[29]

9.4 THE SOCIAL CONTRACT: THE ANCIENT AND MODERN THEORIES

A philosophical underpinning for the anthropocentric Earth ethic adumbrated by Lovelock was first developed by Michel Serres in *Le Contrat Naturel*.[30] Serres's title echoes Jean-Jacques Rousseau's *Du Contrat Social* and thus situates this approach to an anthropocentric Earth ethic as a trope on the social-contract theory of the origin and nature of ethics.

The social-contract theory of the origin and nature of ethics actually appears to be the very first moral philosophy in the Western tradition. Among the Greek moral philosophers of the fifth century BCE—maligned and dismissed by Plato as "sophists"—only Socrates, if we may trust Plato, appears not to have advocated some version of the social contract. The vagaries of imperial Roman politics and Christian piety apparently caused to be destroyed the writings of the moral philosophers who were Socrates's contemporaries in the collection of the Royal Library of Alexandria, established by the Ptolemys. (Part of the library was burned accidentally in 48 BCE by Julius Caesar, who, allied with Egypt's Queen Cleopatra, defended the city against an insurrection by deposed King Ptolemy XIII; and what survived that fire was piously burned deliberately by Theophilus, Bishop of Alexandria, in 391 CE.)[31] Thus our best source, unfortunately, for the ancient social-contract theory of the origin and nature of ethics is Plato, who, apparently like Socrates, was hostile to it. If portrayed truly in Plato's dialogue named for him, Protagoras proffered a very wholesome variation on the social-contract theme; if portrayed truly in the first book of the *Republic*, Thrasymachus proffered a very cynical one. Glaucon, in the second book of the *Republic*, provides a terse summary:

> By nature, they say, to commit injustice is good and to suffer it is evil, but that the excess of evil in being wronged is greater than the excess of good in doing wrong. So that when men do wrong and are wronged by one another and taste of both, those who lack the power to avoid the one and take the other determine that it is for their profit to make a compact with one another neither to commit nor to suffer injustice; and that is the beginning of legislation and covenants

between men, and that they name the commandment of the law the lawful and the just, and that this is the genesis and the essential nature of justice—a compromise between the best, which is to do wrong with impunity, and the worst, which is to be wronged and to be impotent to get one's revenge.[32]

Glaucon adds that "in reality a true man (αληθως ανδρα) would never make a compact with anybody neither to wrong nor to be wronged"—because such a compact would deprive such a man, a predator by nature, of his natural prey.[33] Lions might as well make such a compact with lambs. To counter the typically Greek inegalitarian assumption that "by nature" there exist the few, the elite, the strong, on the one hand, and, on the other, "hoi polloi," the many, the cowering weak, Thomas Hobbes, the first modern contractarian, strenuously insisted that all humans were equal—or at least sufficiently so that no one could win the war of each against all, which characterizes the "state of nature":

Nature hath made men so equal in the faculties of body and mind as that, though there be found one man sometimes manifestly stronger in body or of quicker mind than another, yet when all is reckoned together the difference between man and man is not so considerable that no man can thereupon claim to himself any benefit to which another may not pretend as well as he.[34]

Famously, according to Hobbes, in the state of nature, humans live in "that condition which is called war; and such a war as is of every man, against every man…and the life of man [is] solitary, poor, nasty, brutish, and short."[35] The first "Law of Nature," according to Hobbes is, therefore, "to seek peace and follow it" as the only means of having a long, secure, and prosperous life.[36] The social contract, as conceived by both the ancient theorists (if we can rely on Plato) and by Hobbes (at least) among the moderns is a peace treaty (see Table 9.1).

Table 9.1 Ancient and Modern Social-Contract Theory of the Origin and Nature of Ethics

Social-Contract	Reductive	Holistic	Egalitarian	Inegalitarian
Ancient "Sophists"	X			X
Modern 17th century Hobbes	X		X	
Modern 18th century Rousseau		X	X	

While there are many differences between Hobbes's theory of the *social* contract and Rousseau's, the salient one, for Serres's purposes of theorizing the *natural* contract is that Hobbes is a reductionist and Rousseau a holist. For Hobbes, humans are social atoms and remain so even after becoming signatories to the social contract. There is, thus, an irony in the title of Hobbes's great work, *Leviathan*—the name of one huge being constituted by many small ones. The Hobbesean body politic is no true leviathan. It is not a unified super-organism. Rather, it is a collection of individuals, each unstintedly endeavoring, conating, ever striving for whatever—no less after contracting than before—motivated by personal, self-seeking desire and aversion. Each refrains from forcibly taking the lives and property of their fellows only because each is "over-awed" by an absolute sovereign, who enforces the covenants of the social contract. Hobbes, indeed, could scarcely conceive of that sovereign in terms other than social atomism—a monarch, himself an all-powerful individual, a monad supreme. For Rousseau, by contrast, individual social electrons (to mix metaphors only slightly) make a quantum leap into a new orbit of political ontology when they sign on to the social contract:

> If, then, we eliminate from the social pact everything that is not essential to it, we find it comes down to this: "Each one of us puts into the community his person and all his powers under the supreme direction of the general will; and, as a body, we incorporate every member as an indivisible part of the whole."
>
> Immediately, in the place of the individual person of each contracting party, this act of association creates an artificial and corporate body composed of…many members…, and by this same act that body acquires its unity, its common *ego*, its life and will.[37]

9.5 DU CONTRAT SOCIAL AU CONTRAT NATUREL

Michel Serres's *Le Contrat Naturel* is truly remarkable—if for no other reason than its date of publication, 1990. Serres is perhaps the first philosopher (along with Dale Jamieson—see 10.1) to respond to the second wave of the environmental crisis, which washed ashore of the collective mind of the common ego in the late 1980s. Chainsaws and bulldozers had by then so ravaged the Earth's tropical forests that a precipitous erosion of biodiversity, on a planetary scale, and the horrible prospect of a sixth mass extinction event ominously dawned in the collective consciousness.[38] A thinning of the Earth's protective ozone membrane had been noticed since the 1970s, but in 1985 an alarming "hole" in the stratospheric ozone layer was detected during the austral summer over the Antarctic pole and surrounding latitudes.[39] And the boreal summer of 1988—the same summer in which massive wildfires raged out of control in Yellowstone National Park—was, as I personally recall, so palpably hot and dry that "global warming" became, for the first time, a subject of alarmed discussion in the mass media.[40] A member of the French philosophical community—in which, until then, environmental ethics had no representation whatever—Serres offered up an environmental ethic on the cutting edge of the field: the natural contract. It has, however, been little appreciated in the Anglophone community of environmental philosophers nor given its rightful, honored place in the largely Anglophone field. I suspect that that is because it appears—among those of us environmental philosophers in the biophilial tradition of Thoreau, Muir, and Leopold—to be perverse. Serres portrays Nature as humanity's implacable foe, not, as we grew accustomed to think, humanity's succor and savior. For Serres, in wildness is not the preservation of the world; going to the mountains is not going home; we are not plain members and citizens of the biotic community. Until very recently, according to Serres, nature was but a "stage theater" for "the interesting spectacle we [French] call cultural." But "all those things that never interested anyone [that is, never interested any true Parisian], from now on thrust themselves brutally and without warning into our schemes and maneuvers. They burst in on our [French] culture, which had never formed anything but a local, vague, and cosmetic idea of them: nature."[41]

Serres puts his finger on one defining feature of the second wave of the twentieth-century environmental crisis—its globality, its global spatial scale: "Global history enters nature; global nature enters history: this is something utterly new in philosophy."[42] He anticipates Lovelock in imagining that the new threat, on a global scale, posed by Nature will unify global humanity to defend itself against a common enemy: "'General mobilization!' I purposely use the term employed at the beginning of wars. 'Air raid warning!' I deliberately use the alert given in land and sea combat."[43] (Air raid warning indeed!—as the perceived threat is principally forthcoming from the changed chemical composition of the air.) Like Lovelock, Serres experienced World War II firsthand and vividly remembers the way it brought about national unity (at least among the British if not among the Franch), single-minded purpose, and strengthened governmental authority. Serres's rhetorical motive for portraying the post-industrial human-nature relationship as one of belligerence is precisely, I think, a device to foster international unity, single-minded purpose, and strengthened governing authority. As to the governing authority, Serres is of one mind with Lovelock: "Scientific groups…are preparing to take the helm of the worldly world."[44]

9.6 WAR OR PEACE?

Serres's concept of war follows that of Rousseau and is more subtle than that of Hobbes. War is not a fact of life in the state of nature; rather, "objective violence" is. War is itself a contract, something declared, something mutually agreed to, governed by "Geneva conventions" and having "rules of engagement." Until recently, the human relationship with Nature was one of unreflective violence—running in both directions, with humans eventually gaining the upper hand, thanks to the Industrial Revolution. So the first stage of the natural contract is to *declare* a war against Nature, which will enable "general mobilization" and establish the conventions and rules of engagement in that war. We live during "a time when the old social contract ought to be joined by a natural contract. In a situation of objective violence, there is no way out but to sign it. At the very least, war; ideally, peace."[45]

More than two decades after Serres's *Le Contrat Naturel*, we can perhaps see more clearly the difference between war and peace with nature. Ideally, we could have seized the opportunity to "mitigate" climate change through a concerted effort significantly to reduce greenhouse gases emitted into the atmosphere—and thus make peace with

Gaia by ceasing our aggression. Serres imports into *Le Contrat Naturel* a trope that he had elaborated in another book—humanity as a planetary parasite.[46] If the parasite itself is to survive the morbidity it inflicts on its host, parasite and host must co-evolve a mutualistic relationship. (Unfortunately, Serres offers no concrete suggestions about how post-industrial human culture can achieve a mutualistic relationship with its planetary host. All he offers is a hollow bromide: "We must then change direction and abandon the heading imposed by Descartes' philosophy.")[47] The United States government, however, refused to heed the call for general mobilization following the Kyoto [climate-change] Protocol in 1997; the Copenhagen Summit on climate change ended, in the waning days of 2009, with no agreement; and the Durban climate conference of 2011 ended with only a "roadmap" to show the global community of nations the way to future agreements, binding, if ever they will be, only by 2020; and the Rio + 20 Earth Summit of June 2012 "accomplished nothing," according to climate activist Bill McKibben, nor did the Doha Climate Change Conference of November–December 2012 reach any agreement to take immediate and effective action.[48] Thus the window of opportunity for a peace treaty with a provoked and aroused Nature appears now to be all but closed; so peace, it would seem, is no longer a viable option.

War remains an option; and there appear to be but two strategies of war: (1) national defense in the form of "adaptation" (such as building sea walls to protect coastal cities, migrating or modifying agricultural crops and methods to fit with a changed climate, and so on); and (2) geo-engineering to cancel the heat-trapping effects of greenhouse gases with countermeasures (such as giant sun-screens orbiting the Earth or the ferrous fertilization of pelagic phytoplankton, which suck carbon out of the atmosphere and send it to the bottom of the ocean, there to be buried in the abyssal sediments).[49] Being a matter of *national* defense, the former strategy—adaptation—will effectively abandon the most vulnerable and poorest peoples in "developing" nations to their several fates. The latter—geo-engineering—while benefiting everyone if successful, will also harm everyone if such unprecedented schemes should gang agley, as aft do even the best-laid of them. Geo-engineering is, in short, a desperate and reckless gambit. There is a third alternative—the ostrich strategy. It seems to be the default posture in the United States, wherein obdurate denial of the scientific consensus that climate change is both real and anthropogenic is not merely politically tolerated but it is, apparently, politically viable. The ultimate consequence of "climate denial" would be to continue to dump ever increasing amounts of greenhouse gases into the atmosphere thus to ever intensify and ever accelerate the pace of global climate change. Having created an environment to which it is no longer adapted, global human civilization will almost certainly collapse. And Nature doesn't have a Marshall Plan ready for its reconstruction. The ostrich strategy will be followed by an interminable age of barbarism, a new and everlasting Dark Age.

9.7 THE FRENCH CONNECTION: LARRÈRE

According to Catherine Larrère, "From a French point of view, the putative ethical dimension of environmental problems is actually a political dimension."[50] I can only guess why. Perhaps the French proclivity to prefer a political to an ethical mode of engaging environmental problems is a legacy handed down from Rousseau and his post-contract submergence of the "individual person" (the conventional moral agent) into the "common ego" and the "general will"—into the body politic, the state. Accordingly—whatever the source—Serres devotes much discussion to the integration of two rational discourses that he calls the "scientific" and the "juridical" (political). Serres observes that "Morality is written in the imperative and [scientific] knowledge in the indicative."[51] In the domain of the *political*—in contrast to that of both the ethical and the scientific—"Law never gives orders and rarely writes or speaks in the imperative, nor does it designate, that is, write or speak in the indicative. It uses the performative. The performative makes speaking an efficacious act, a sort of fiat."[52] Science describes and declares; ethics prescribes and proscribes; the juridical judges and arbitrates. Setting ethics aside as uninteresting, from a French point of view, both the juridical and the scientific discourses are, also from the French point of view, socially embedded *human* discourses. As all social contractarians—ancient, modern, and contemporary—agree, civil law (and with it juridical discourse) is a creation of the social contract. However, as Larrère astutely notes, "Science is also a contract between men, because science is not the activity of isolated individuals, but of a cooperative community.... Science is a social activity. Whether it entails examining competences, producing knowledge, or getting that knowledge recognized by the rest of society, social relations are in play and the contract can model them. But the originality of the scientific contract lies in the fact that it not only establishes relations among men, but also between men and natural objects."[53]

With but a couple more bits of French cooking, we can solve the problem of how to take the step from the social to the natural contract. To the amazement and con-sternation of one American environmental philosopher in the tradition of Thoreau, Muir, and Leopold, Larrère blithely avers that "Nature is only the name given to a certain state of science."[54] The "state of science" regarding climate change is now one of near universal consensus. Climate scientists now speak, practically unanimously, regarding the nature of Nature—global climate change is happening; it's real. And climate scientists now speak nearly unanimously about the relations between men and Nature—global climate change is anthropogenic; it's man made. How do we respond? What are we to do? "Science provides the discourse to formulate the alternatives. But it is the responsibility of politics to make a judgment and take a decision."[55] This cooperative but well-compartmentalized relationship between the discourse of science and that of politics is, of course, very familiar to Anglophone environmental scientists who struggle with the bugbear of "advocacy."[56]

Herself drawing as much on the social-contract theory of Hobbes as on that of Rousseau, Larrère reminds us that, according to Hobbes, while we humans cannot contract with God, we can with His representatives—the clergy. By the same token, neither can we can contract with Nature, namely Gaia, but we can contract with Her representatives—the community of scientists. Indeed, "Anything can be personi-fied—that is, represented—and become a subject, because somebody can speak in its name."[57] Via the discourse of science, Nature now has a voice in the political arena. "In this way," according to Larrère, "Serres makes nature a legal subject. The question then becomes Who should represent nature? Who should speak in its name? It is for science to speak for nature."[58] As Larrère notes, "legal subject" is ambiguous. Nature may be a subject *in* law, but, by no stretch of the imagination can Nature be subject *to* law. It would be absurd to suppose that we can make a law "which forbids nature to grow warmer, another to rain acid, and so on."[59] As Larrère reads Serres, in law, Nature is like a legally incompetent person, who needs a guardian ad litem to represent it. That guardian advocate is the scientific community, which acquires a kind of fictive personhood of its own to the extent that a scientific consensus—unanimity—is reached within the scientific community.

9.8 THE FRENCH CONNECTION: LATOUR

As I do here (9.5), Bruno Latour acknowledges and celebrates Michel Serres for "the argument he had made, many years ago and before everyone else, in his *Natural Contract*," advocating that Nature be granted the status of a legal subject with a political voice articulated by the discourse of science.[60] According to Latour, "Serres' solution was to take the language, rituals, and practices of politics—good at representing humans—and the language procedures, and rituals of science—good at representing facts—and *join them together*."[61] Serres's solution is, however, futile, Latour thinks, because it assumes a false dichotomy—the subject (*res cogitans*)/ object (*res extensa*) distinction—which is the bedrock of modernism, in Latour's view. Larrère characterizes this dichotomy less in Cartesian terms than in Galilean. Galileo's telescope-aided astronomical observations and the conclusions favorable to Copernican astronomy that he drew from them landed him in political trouble. A century after the "Galileo Affair" there emerged what Larrère styles "the Galilean armistice"—which "came about by dividing the law into two domains: …the prescriptive law-commandments of man's world [and] the descriptive law-relations of the natural world."[62] Of course, Galileo was the architect of the allied distinction between primary and secondary qualities, which Latour singles out for particular ridicule: "primary qualities (real, speechless, yet somehow speaking by themselves, but, alas, devoid of any meaning and value) went one way, while secondary qualities (subjective, meaningful, able to talk, full of values, but, alas, empty of any reality) went another."[63]

Being French himself, Latour, with more authority than have I, puts his finger on the typically French proclivity to embrace authoritarian collectivism: "What [Serres] dreamed of…was in effect a government of scientists." Latour thinks that this is "A very French temptation, from the '*gouvernement des savants*' during the Revolution all the way to our atomic program and our love affair with the '*corps techniques de l'Etat*,' the close-knit clique of engineers-cum-bureaucrats that oversee national scientific and industrial policy."[64] Too much can be made of such an alleged "French temptation," because it can hardly explain Lovelock's almost identical longing for a government of scientists. But by simply bringing the discourse of science into politics and thus giving Nature political expression "we have not moved an inch," Latour thinks, because doing so insidiously validates "the great Bifurcation" of subject and object and of real value-free primary qualities and illusory value-laden secondary qualities.[65]

Latour attacks Modernism and its core foundation—the great Bifurcation, the subject/object Dichotomy—from but one flank: the pretense of science to provide an "objective" description of nature. That is consistent with his career-long deconstruction of scientific pretenses, as the founder of the discipline of sociological/anthropological/philosophical science studies, the antithesis of the Anglophone hagiography of science called the "philosophy of science." Taking a step beyond Larrère's reduction of Nature to a "certain state of science," Latour proclaims "the end of nature"—nor does he mean by that phrase what Bill McKibben meant by it in his book by that title.[66] McKibben meant that pristine, virgin Nature (bequeathed by Thoreau and Muir to the American imaginary) was everywhere violated, sullied by the human stain of pollution. Humans and their offal have invaded and thoroughly occupied Nature, ending its independence and autonomy, lamented McKibben. By contrast, Latour means "the total dissolution of various *notions* of nature."[67] Science does not mirror Nature; rather the dirty little secret is that science "composes"—or constructs—"Nature." Thus what is really at an end is the notion of an objective, independent, and autonomous Nature.

Latour provides an anecdote—about "climategate"—to illustrate his point. On the eve of the 2009 Climate Summit in Copenhagen, purloined emails revealed

That the scientific facts of the matter [of anthropogenic climate change] had to be constructed....What I found so ironic in the hysterical reaction of scientists and the press was the almost complete agreement of both opponents and proponents of the anthropogenic origin of climate change. They all seemed to share the idealistic view of Science (capital S): "If it slowly composed, it cannot be true," said the skeptics; "if we reveal how it is composed," said the proponents, "it will be discussed, thus disputable, thus it cannot be true either!"...After thirty years or so of work in science studies, it is more than embarrassing to see that scientists had no better epistemology with which to rebut their adversaries. They kept using the old opposition between what is constructed and what is not constructed, instead of the slight but crucial difference between what is *well* and what is *badly* constructed (or composed).[68]

Unlike Serres, Latour does not *join* the language, rituals, and practices of politics and the language, rituals, and practices of science. Instead, he assimilates the latter to the former and thus reduces the one to the other: "This [climategate] was the ideal moment to connect the disputability of politics with the disputability of science (small s)—instead of trying to maintain, despite the evidence to the contrary, the usual gap between, on the one hand, what is politics and what can be discussed, and, on the other hand, a Science of what is beyond dispute."[69] That moment may not have been epistemically decisive, but it only dramatizes a trend that must end, Latour hopes, in a new scientific epistemology, for "Rare now are topics among scientists where you do not see scientists publicly disagreeing among themselves on what they are, how they should be studied, financed, portrayed, distributed, understood, cast. Facts have become *issues*....I hope to have made it clear why I stated earlier that between nature and politics one has to choose."[70]

The politicization of facts—facts become issues—is now a mainstay of American politics. And the consequences are not reassuring. Just as Big Tobacco did in the 1950s, now Big Coal and Big Oil are taking advantage of scientific uncertainty and internecine controversy to sell their own manufactured facts to the electorate.[71] Yes, there is the "crucial distinction"—in the new scientific epistemology recommended by Latour—between what is well and what is badly constructed, but that distinction is not only crucial, it is also, according to Latour himself, "slight." Slight and subtle differences, however, have no place in "the language, rituals, and practices of politics"— at least not in American politics, in which the sound bite, the ephemeral image, and the thirty-second attack ad are what is (dare I put it so) *in fact* crucial. Replacing the old Modernist epistemology, in American politics, is not a new and refined scientific compositionistic epistemology, à la Latour, but an essentially religious epistemology. Members of the electorate and their elected representatives seem to feel entitled freely to choose to believe or not to believe in evolution, in Keynesian economics, in anthropogenic climate change—just as one might choose to believe or not to believe in God or Jesus or Heaven and Hell. Religious beliefs, and now their political counterparts, are intractable to evidence and experience to the contrary. Like matters of sectarian religious dogma, matters amenable to scientific investigation and resolution, may, in the contemporary state of American politics, be unapologetically affirmed or denied as articles of partisan faith.

According to Latour, Serres's *le contrat naturel* is vitiated by Serres's failure to remark and discard the "great Bifurcation" and with it the radical distinction between "the language, rituals, and practices of politics" and those of science. Latour thoroughly rejects that distinction, but ultimately shows himself to be an idealist in both senses of the word. He is a *metaphysical idealist*, thoroughly deconstructing the object side of the subject/object dichotomy, but leaving the subject side unscathed. For Latour, reality is just as it is socially constructed in the Rousseauian "common ego," in the collective consciousness. In a word, the formerly objective world is but a skein of rapidly evolving and changing constellations of scientific ideas. According to Latour, science constructs—composes—Nature. The proof of that pudding is in the "increase of disputability—the amazing extension of scientific and technical controversies."[72] And "while somewhat terrifying at first"—and as I just noted it has certainly cast a terrifying pall over American politics—this increase of disputability in science "is also the best path to finally taking seriously the political task of establishing the continuity of all entities that make up the common world."[73] Thus does Latour also reveal himself to be a *political idealist*, indeed a utopianist. Analogous to the way in which the natural world is self-organizing and self-composing—as increasingly reflected in science—his utopian fantasy envisions a self-organizing or self-composing global polity. Hence, his "Compositionist Manifesto":

> compositionism takes up the task of searching for universality but without believing that this universality is already there, waiting to be discovered....From

universalism it takes the task of building a common world [which] has to be built up from utterly heterogeneous parts that will not make a whole, but at best a fragile, revisable, and diverse composite material.[74]

Those heterogeneous parts include not only "billions of people" but also "their trillions of affiliates and commensals."[75] In other words, non-human beings also have a seat in the parliament of this Latourian Erehwon. Already, "animals, plants, soils, and chemicals are indeed acknowledged to have their friends and their enemies, their assemblies and their websites, their blogs and their demonstrators."[76] Thus does sprawling Nature (fragmented now into its heterogeneous parts) have a voice in politics. But unlike Serres and Larrère, Latour does not restrict their guardians ad litem to the magisterium of science (see Table 9.2).

Table 9.2 The French Reduction of Environmental Ethics to Environmental Politics

Natural Contract Theorists	Subject/Object Dichotomy	Anti-Objective Idealism	Scientific-Authoritarian Scientocracy	Science Speaks for Nature	Utopian Politics of Nature
Serres	X		X		
Larrére	X			X	
Latour		X			X

9.9 THE FRENCH-CANADIAN CONNECTION: DUSSAULT

Without directly referencing the work of Serres, Larrère, and Lovelock, Canadian philosopher Antoine Dussault offers another way of understanding their idea of a war between humans and Nature (personified as Gaia by Lovelock) to be resolved by a natural contract enforced by a scientocratic sovereign. Dussault draws on the twenty-first-century science of ethics (reviewed in Chapter 5), which has identified several relatively independent ethical domains or modules. Exactly how many such domains or modules exist differs depending on which evolutionary moral psychologist is consulted. Richard Shweder and co-authors and Paul Rozin and co-authors (among them Jonathan Haidt) identified three such domains: community, autonomy, and divinity.[77] Haidt and Craig Joseph, evolutionary moral psychologists, went on first to identify four such domains (suffering, hierarchy, reciprocity, and purity), then five (harm/care, fairness/reciprocity, in-group/loyalty, authority/respect, and purity/sanctity).[78] At last count (2012), Haidt has identified six moral domains (care/harm, liberty/oppression, fairness/cheating, loyalty/betrayal, authority/subversion, sanctity/degradation—discussed and associated with corresponding Humean moral sentiments in 5.7).[79] Common to all such sets—whether three, four, five, or six of them—is the last, variously codified as divinity, purity, purity/sanctity, or sanctity/degradation. Dussault argues that the best way to ground environmental ethics is not, as I have done in regard to the land ethic, on the community module and in-group loyalty, but on the divinity-purity-sanctity module, in which Nature replaces God or divinity as the object of awe and reverence.[80] In support of Dussault, one might note that "pollution" was a religious not an environmental concept among the ancient Greeks. Oedipus's unwitting sins of patricide and incest so polluted Thebes that Apollo visited a plague on the whole city and Plato's Euthyphro is concerned that his father's negligent homicide of a murderous slave might pollute the whole family and incur the wrath of the gods. Further, to Dussault's point, conservationists often bemoan ecological "degradation."

One might cast the moral response of Serres and Lovelock to the prospect of global climate change in these terms as well. Locating the excessive rhetoric of Serres (full of bombast and violence, as Larrère notes) and Lovelock in this domain of moral consciousness reveals its genre—prophesy and apocalypse. Through the lens that Dussault has ground we can easily see that Gaia—named, after all, for a Greek goddess, Mother of the Titans—stands in for the wrathful God of Abraham punishing the defilement of Her being by a hubristic humanity. Serres and Lovelock look to Nature/Gaia's high priests—the community of scientists in possession of an esoteric knowledge, and wielding a mysterious powerful wisdom—to intercede on our behalf. If, under their authority, we purify ourselves by practicing severe austerities (in the form of "restrictions" and "rationing") and by "sacrificing" some of our freedom, She may be appeased and stay Her mighty sword and spare us a hellish retribution.

In Kantian terms, the contractarian Earth ethic of Serres (and, by extension, Lovelock) is a classic case of moral heteronomy. Nature/Gaia sets the terms—the imperatives—of our human salvation from Her own wrath. We are motivated not by pure reason to act on those imperatives—precisely because they do not flow from pure reason—but by collective self-interested "inclinations." We desire not to suffer the "Hell," as Lovelock revealingly characterizes it, of an Earth forced into a more energetic state by our own collective industrial self-indulgence. There is a curious mix of anthropocentrism and non-anthropocentrism going on here. Gaia both deserves and demands our respect—the hallmark of non-anthropocentrism—but remains beyond our power to actually harm. To be sure, we can push her into an excited state, but at our own peril not hers. This way of thinking is very familiar and typifies the moral psychology of the Abrahamic-religions—Juadaism, Christianity, and Islam.

9.10 VIRTUE ETHICS

In "Conservation as a Moral Issue," in "Some Fundamentals of Conservation in the Southwest," Aldo Leopold suggests that "waste, pollution, and unnecessary damage" is "something unworthy…something damaging not only to the reputation of the waster, but to the self-respect of the craft and the society of which he is a member."[81] In 6.2, I declared that this way of characterizing conservation as a moral issue is to express it in terms of virtue ethics—because virtue ethics is primarily concerned with *self*-respect. Note well, however, that virtue ethics does not share the egoism characteristic of the Anglophone tradition of social-contract theory going back to Hobbes—and beyond Hobbes, even, to the so-called sophists. In the tradition of virtue ethics, which also originates among the ancient Greek philosophers, a virtuous person does not single-mindedly pursue his or her own *interests*, while remaining entirely indifferent to the interests of others. On the contrary, respect for others and a concern for their interests is itself a virtue, a quality of character the possession of which is essential to the virtuous person's self-*respect*. Rather, self-respect for one's own humanity is the fundamental motive, and being human is to feel sympathy for others and solidarity with them. The performance of virtuous actions includes actions respectful of others and expressive of concern for their interests as well as for one's own.

From the late eighteenth century through most of the twentieth, Western moral philosophy was dominated, almost exclusively, by two paradigms: utilitarianism and deontology. Jeremy Bentham is the fountainhead of utilitarianism, Immanuel Kant of deontology. Thanks to G. E. Moore's *Principia Ethica*, intuitionism—the view that good, bad, right, wrong and other moral "properties" are non-natural qualities of actions that we directly apprehend—enjoyed some fifteen minutes of fame (actually, more like fifteen years, to be less flippant and more precise, of popularity) among British philosophers, during the early twentieth century (detailed and documented in 3.1). Intuitionism, however, was soon enough tossed onto the rubbish heap of trendy but vapid philosophical theories because, obviously, fully competent intuitors often disagree about good, bad, right, wrong and other simple putatively non-natural moral properties, while few competent observers disagree about simple natural properties, such as whether an object is rectilinear or curved. Further, positing the existence of non-natural properties available only to intuition is no less metaphysical than positing the existence of any other unobservable property and thus fell afoul of the Logical-Positivism tidal wave, the next trendy philosophical movement to sweep over the Anglo-American philosophical community.

Utilitarianism and deontology are still dominant in Western moral philosophy, but one sign that the prevailing bicameral governance of moral philosophy is weakening is the robust revival of virtue ethics in the late twentieth century and the early twenty-first. G. E. M. Anscombe is generally credited with identifying the shortcomings of the dominant paradigms and reintroducing virtue ethics, in the 1950s.[82] Her stature and influence in the Anglo-American philosophical community was such that a few other notable members of that community followed her sally into the domain of virtue ethics.[83] Thus the seed that Anscombe planted began to sprout. Virtue ethics became a vigorous growth area in moral philosophy with the publication of *After Virtue*, by Alasdair MacIntyre in 1981.[84] After *After Virtue*, virtue ethics made its way into environmental ethics, perhaps better represented there than in moral philosophy generally or in any other of its subfields.[85]

It would, however, be a mistake to think of virtue ethics as merely an ethical paradigm. It is that, but it is also, more generally, a distinct modality of moral thought. Western civilization has two taproots, one descending deeply into the Greco-Roman cognitive substrate, the other into the Judeo-Christian—iconically characterized by some as "Athens" and "Jerusalem," respectively.[86] Each had its distinctive and very different way of thinking about morality—as also about many other things. In addition to modalities of moral thought, the difference between Greco-Roman and Judeo-Christian modes of epistemology is especially noteworthy—reason being the primary source of knowledge and truth in the former tradition, divine revelation in the latter.

The Judeo-Christian mode of moral thought is legalistic. In the sacred texts of the Judeo-Christian tradition, the Ten *Commandments* and the Golden *Rule* are revealed. In this mode of moral thought, to be a morally good person is to obey a set of rules (or one single overarching rule). Both historically and presently one also finds, in this tradition, various *codes* of conduct—bodies of law, such as the Napoleonic Code, or specific sets of rules governing deportment, such as high-school dress codes. Of the two currently dominant moral paradigms, Kantian deontology is unequivocally legalistic. Kant characterizes morality as respect for the principle of *law*; which takes the general form of an apodictic categorical *imperative*; which, in turn, may be given concrete expression in terms of the universalization of the *maxim* of the action that one contemplates performing.[87] For its part, so-called act utilitarianism seeks to discover an algorithm—a rule by another name—to guide the action of individual moral agents, on a case-by-case basis, toward the goal of maximum aggregate utility. Bentham himself developed one such crude algorithm, dubbed the "hedonic calculus."[88] So-called rule utilitarianism is based on the premise that inherited moral *rules*, such as those found in the Ten Commandments—in particular, Honor Thy Father and Thy Mother, Thou Shalt Not Murder, Thou Shalt Not Commit Adultery, Thou Shalt Not Steal, Thou Shalt Not Bear False Witness, and Thou Shalt Not Covet a Neighbor's Property (including his house, wife, servants of both sexes, ox, ass, or anything else)—are good guides, "rules of thumb," which if habitually followed tend to produce aggregate maximum utility.[89]

The Greco-Roman mode of moral thought is aretaic (from αρετη, most often translated as *virtue*). To be a morally good person is to actively manifest, in one's demeanor and behavior, certain qualities of character. In the biblical context (Exodus 20 ff.) in which the Ten Commandments are revealed, one also finds many, many other divinely mandated rules—for example, to whom one may or may not sell one's daughter; what the owners of an ox owe the owner of an ass if their ox should gore his ass; and so on. Likewise, while the Greeks recognized many, many virtues, they also recognized a smaller set of "cardinal virtues." And just as the Bible is not entirely clear about how the Ten Commandments should be parsed out and numbered, so the Greeks were not entirely unanimous about the exact number and identity of the cardinal virtues. But on practically everyone's list would be found Justice (first and foremost, universally ordained by Zeus himself, according to Hesiod), Wisdom (which Zeus himself acquired by swallowing his sister, Metis, according to the same source), Temperance, Courage, Piety, and Liberality (Table 9.3). Plato devoted an entire dialogue to an exploration (taking the form of an enigmatic search for a Socratic definition) of four of these six cardinal virtues.[90] In the fourth-century BCE, Plato and Aristotle were the principal ancient theorists of virtue ethics, which arose as a dialectical response to fifth-century contractarian ethics (as more fully explained in 9.14 and 9.15).

Table 9.3 The Judeo-Christian and Greco-Roman Moral Modalities and Their Six Respective Cardinal Commandments and Virtues (The two columns are not to be understood as correlated in any way)

Judeo-Christian Legalistic Moral Modality	Greco-Roman Aretaic Moral Modality
Honor thy father and thy mother	Justice
Thou shalt not murder	Temperance
Thou shalt not commit adultery	Courage
Thou shalt not steal	Wisdom
Thou shalt not bear false witness (lie)	Piety (filial and religious)
Thou shalt not covet	Generosity

9.11 ARISTOTELIAN VIRTUE ETHICS

Most contemporary theories of virtue ethics may be traced back to Aristotle's *Nichomachean Ethics* as the source from which they spring. According to Aristotle, the ultimate *telos*—the overall end, purpose, or goal—of human action is to realize *eudaimonia* (ενδαιμονια), an ancient Greek word with no adequate equivalent in English.[91] Its literal, etymological sense is "well-spirited," which could be understood in two basic ways (which are not necessarily exclusive of one another). (1) To be well-spirited might mean that a person's spirit, soul…or character (if you prefer, so as not rhetorically to hypostatize the thing that is well) is in a good state or condition. Or (2) it might mean—and more likely did mean among Aristotle's superstitious contemporaries—that a *eudaimonious* or well-spirited person has a benign spiritual protector, a guardian angel. (Let us not forget, in this context, that Socrates famously claimed to have a personal δαιμων watching over him, which never bade him do anything, but only forbade his doing something he was about to do. And, though unjustly condemned to death, Socrates died a happy [eudaimonious] man.)[92] In which case, the best English translation of the ordinary Greek meaning of *eudaimonia* might be "blessed."

The most common (and probably the worst) English translation of *eudaimonia* is "happiness," from happy, derived from the Middle English *hap* (as in *happen, hapless* and *happenstance*) meaning fortune, chance, or luck. Happiness just happens to befall a person—which suggests a state of being that is entirely too passive—especially for the sense that Aristotle gives the term. For, as he repeatedly emphasizes, Aristotle conceives *eudaimonia* to be an active state of being. As philosophers always have, Aristotle appropriated a common word in ordinary language and tailored its definition to suit his philosophical purposes. He defined it as an *activity* of soul in accordance with *aretē*.[93] But neither is there an adequate English equivalent for that Greek word. The Latinate *virtue*—the most common translation of *aretē*—is equally opaque. Its contemporary utility as a moral concept is confounded by its etymological derivation from the Latin root *vir*—meaning (male) "man"—and the fact that it is cognate with *virile*. Aristotle (perhaps deliberately, we cannot know for sure) elided two senses of "good" (αγαθος)—namely, morally good and good of its kind. In effect, Aristotle suggests that the person who attains *eudaimonia* is a very good or excellent human being—that is, a human being who fully realizes the potential of human nature. Such a person excels at being human, just as the racehorse, Secretariat, excelled at being a horse. Contemporary virtue ethicists have, accordingly, settled on "flourishing" as a way of rendering *eudaimonia* and "excellence" as a way of rendering *aretē*, while retaining "virtue" as the rubric for the general ethical paradigm in which they are working.[94]

According to Aristotle, all living beings—plants as well as animals—are ensouled.[95] But for Aristotle, the souls of living beings are not independent or "separable" entities—in sharp contrast to the views of both Pythagoras and Plato, in this regard, and also to those of Descartes among modern philosophers.[96] In other words, Aristotle does not hypostatize or reify the soul. Rather, the soul is to the whole organism what sight is to the eye. Sight is the actualization of the potentiality of the organ of sight; the soul is the actualization of the potentiality of the organism as a whole.[97] Sessile plants nourish themselves on soil, water, and air—thus do they grow—and they reproduce themselves. Responsible for the actualization of these potentialities is the nutritive/reproductive soul. Motile animals also nourish themselves; they grow as well; and they too reproduce—thus they share the nutritive/reproductive soul with plants. Because they move locally from place to place, animals have an appetitive and sensitive soul—desires and aversions to motivate and sensations to guide their movements. Humans are animals, but we humans are uniquely rational animals (ζῷοι λογίκοι).[98] Thus, a virtuous or excellent human being, one who fully actualizes the potential of human nature, lives his or her animal life—the life of appetites and sensations—but governed by a rational principle. The usual Latinate rendition of λογικός as "rational" is confirmed as better than the other alternative, "logical," by Aristotle's analysis of the virtues in quasi-mathematical terms—as the mean between the extremes of excess (too much) and defect (too little): "In everything that is continuous and divisible it is possible to take more, less, or an equal amount, and that either in terms of the thing itself or relatively to us; and the equal is intermediate between the excess and the defect."[99]

Among the cardinal virtues, temperance and courage are paradigmatic for Aristotle's exposition of his general theory of moral virtue as the mean between the extremes of excess and defect. In regard to the animal appetites, the excess is the over-indulgence of the desires for food, intoxicating drink, and sex—leading to the vices of gluttony, drunkenness, and debauchery, respectively. The defect is the under-indulgence of those desires leading to the vices of abstemiousness and prudery, respectively. Temperance is the virtuous mean between the vicious extremes. In regard to the flip side of the passionate coin—fear or aversion—courage is the virtuous mean between the vices of cowardice (the defect) and rashness (the excess). In Books II and III of the *Nichomachean Ethics*, Aristotle analyzes many other commonly recognized virtues in exactly the same way—as the virtuous means between the vicious extremes of excess and defect. Salient among them are generosity (the mean between prodigality and miserliness), magnificence (the mean between vulgarity and chintziness), pride (the mean between vanity and diffidence), wit (the mean between buffoonery and stodginess), modesty (the mean bashfulness and shamelessness), and friendliness (the mean between obsequiousness and churlishness) (Table 9.4).

Table 9.4 Aristotle's Analysis of Virtue as the Mean Between the Extremes of Excess and Defect

Defect	Mean (relative to us)	Excess
Abstemiousness	Temperance	Gluttony, Debauchery
Cowardice	Courage	Rashness
Miserliness	Generosity	Prodigality
Chintziness	Magnificence	Vulgarity
Diffidence	Pride	Vanity
Boorishness	Wit	Buffoonery
Bashfulness	Modesty	Shamelessness
Churlishness	Friendliness	Obsequiousness

In addition to the moral virtues, which emerge from the good governance of the animal appetites and passions by the rational faculty of the soul, Aristotle also identifies a class of intellectual virtues or excellences. Some are the leisurely actualization of the potential of the rational faculty working in its own right, when free of the burden of managing the animal aspect of human life. Others concern the moral life—the life of the whole rational animal—but have to do not with disciplining immediately felt animal appetites and passions, but with the ultimate ends of action and with deliberation and judgment in the choice of actions instrumental to achieving those ends. Among the former are science (διανοια), intuitive reason (νους), and philosophic wisdom (σοφια). Principal among the latter is practical wisdom (φρονησις) while art (τεχνη) is also practical, but it is concerned with making, not doing.

9.12 ENVIRONMENTAL VIRTUE ETHICS

In 6.2, I also observed that the virtue ethics at which Leopold hints by means of a single sentence in "Some Fundamentals" is "three-pronged." At issue is (1) individual virtue, but also holistic forms of virtue pertaining to (2) crafts and (3) societies. The self-respect of a craft is besmirched if it tolerates the shoddy workmanship of its apprentices, journeymen, and masters. And the self-respect of a society is besmirched if it tolerates violations of human rights *and*, Leopold would add, environmentally vicious individuals and environmentally vicious crafts. *Virtuous crafts* organize professional guilds—of plumbers, electricians, carpenters, and so on—to certify competency in various "trades" (as they are often called) and to sanction or to decertify and expel practitioners of vicious craftsmanship. *Self-respecting societies* enact laws against human trafficking, inhuman working conditions, *and*, Leopold would add, waste, pollution, and unnecessary environmental damage—and it would punish those who violate both human rights and environmental integrity, stability, and beauty. Thus the latter two prongs may be characterized as *holistic* environmental virtue ethics. The Aristotelian cast of the contemporary revival of virtue ethics, consistent with the hyper-individualism of Modern moral philosophy, renders contemporary environmental virtue ethics supportive of the first prong of the virtue ethics at which Leopold hints, the self-respect of the individual. Aristotle himself provides a clue as to how his approach to virtue ethics might be extended to account for the self-respect of the craft, but we shall have to repair to Plato's virtue ethics to find theoretical support for Leopold's implicit allegation that the self-respect of a society as a whole is impugned by its tolerance of "waste, pollution, and unnecessary damage" (Figure 9.1).

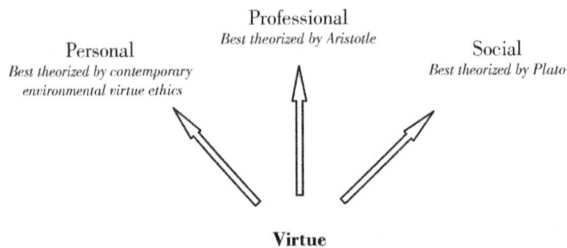

Figure 9.1 Leopold's three-pronged version of environmental virtue ethics and the theorist(s) of each.

The most straightforward (but also the most simplistic) extension of virtue ethics to the environmental domain is to add environmental virtues to the catalogue of those virtues that are already commonly recognized. Louke van Wensveen combed through popular and scholarly environmental literature and discovered no fewer than 189 environmental virtues and 174 environmental vices therein.[100] In addition to such commonly recognized virtues as frugality and gratitude, she catalogued attunement and earthiness among environmental (or "ecological" in the loose, European sense of the term) virtues. Sue P. Stafford has extended the intellectual virtues, first mapped by Aristotle, into the environmental domain by adding "thoroughness, patience, perseverance, carefulness...open-mindedness...and flexibility" to the catalogue of environmental virtues.[101]

Though Aristotle is the ancient source of contemporary environmental virtue ethics, if van Wensveen and Stafford are representative, the highly systematic theoretical foundations of Aristotelian virtue ethics are hard to find in contemporary environmental virtue ethics. Most of van Wensveen's environmental virtues are hardly (quasi-mathematical) means between any recognizable extremes of excess and defect, nor are they tied to the psychological faculties of reason, on the one hand, and the animal appetites and passions, on the other. Stafford, for her part, provides no clear principle for distinguishing between moral and intellectual virtues, listing courage among the latter, while for Aristotle courage is a moral virtue par excellence. Among the intellectual virtues, she also lists self-sufficiency, which is neither a moral nor an intellectual virtue in Aristotle's system of ethics, but a criterion that any adequate conception of *eudaimonia* must meet. I am not suggesting that contemporary environmental virtue ethicists should be slavishly bound to the particulars of Aristotle's virtue-ethics theory. Rather, I am lamenting that the environmental virtue ethics of van Wensveen and Stafford provide little if any *theoretical* support—Aristotelian or otherwise—for the kind of environmental virtue ethics at which Leopold hints in "Some Fundamentals."

Philip Cafaro identifies "four books [that] have been particularly influential in the development of environmental virtue ethics."[102] In addition to van Wensveen's pioneering work in the field, Cafaro cites John O'Neill's *Ecology, Policy, and Politics*, Ronald Sandler's *Character and Environment*, and Cafaro's own *Thoreau's Living Ethics*.[103] Sandler and Cafaro also edited an influential collection of papers titled *Environmental Virtue Ethics*.[104] Van Wensveen's account of what she paradoxically called "dirty virtues" (one would think that it would be the correlative vices that were dirty) was criticized for lacking a clear theoretical underpinning, such as Aristotle supplied for the catalogue of commonly recognized virtues among his Greek contemporaries. She responded that acquiring and practicing environmental virtues is warranted as means (no pun intended) to the end of ecological sustainability—the end, in this case, providing justification for the means.[105] John O'Neill is faithful to Aristotle in at least one particular—positing human flourishing (the preferred contemporary rendition of *eudaimonia*) as the touchstone for his approach to environmental virtue ethics. Sandler's development of environmental virtue ethics is, so far, the most theoretically articulate and comprehensive system of environmental virtue ethics. While grounding environmental virtue in human flourishing, he also advocates pluralism by espousing "noneudaimonistic" virtue "that allows considerations unrelated to agent flourishing," such as the flourishing of both human and non-human moral patients.[106] Thus, Sandler opens up the possibility of non-anthropocentric virtue ethics. He also opens up the possibility that some environmental "collectives," might be moral patients, concluding that

> Living organisms and some environmental collectives have inherent worth, which is the basis for a noneudaimonistic end that is part of the pluralistic teleological account of what makes a character trait a virtue. This end justifies virtues of respect for nature, including care, compassion and restitutive justice, and reinforces several virtues of sustainability, virtues of environmental activism, and virtues of environmental stewardship. The land virtues are those character traits that make human beings good "citizens" of the biotic "community." Ecosystems and species [however] do not have inherent worth.[107]

Cafaro's treatment of Thoreau as a paragon of environmental virtue dramatizes the way in which the hyper-individualism of post-Enlightenment moral philosophy also infects environmental virtue ethics. For Thoreau, environmental care and concern was certainly a virtue. Thoreau's austere lifestyle and opulent writing style (beautifully merged in the autobiographical *Walden*) also illustrate how close attention to nature and the systematic study of natural history, participation in nature's rhythms, and interaction with nature's other denizens can be integral to human flourishing. But the man who declared that "in Wildness is the preservation of the World" is also the one who suggested that "If a man does not keep pace with his companions perhaps it is because he hears a different drummer."[108] As much as he is celebrated for his environmentalism, Thoreau is even more celebrated for his rugged individualism and social contrarianism. The first prong of the three-pronged environmental virtue ethic adumbrated by Leopold—individual self-respect—may find ample theoretical support in contemporary environmental virtue ethics. In it, however, one finds little if any theoretical support for the other two—especially if Thoreau is the exemplar.

Here I must tread carefully. Thoreau was among the first practitioners of civil disobedience and certainly its earliest eloquent advocate. Both Mohandas Gandhi and Martin Luther King Jr.—themselves eloquent advocates and supremely effective practitioners of civil disobedience—acknowledge their respective debts to Thoreau.[109] For both of them, the purpose of civil disobedience is not disobedience for its own sake, certainly, nor for the sake of personal virtue, but for the sake of social change—reformation of policy and law, which exist as social, not individual attributes. Thoreau, however, is hard to pin down on this score as on many others. He actually flirts with anarchism and radical individualism, opening his essay, "Civil Disobedience," with the following declaration: "I heartily accept the motto,—'That government is best which governs least'; and when 'Carried out [to its logical conclusion] finally amounts to this, which also I believe,—'That government is best which governs not all.'"[110] Thoreau follows that opening with an antigovernment-pro-individual-agent rant that would outdo a twenty-first-century Tea-Party Republican demagogue. But then he remarks, "I ask for, not at once no government, but *at once* a better government. Let every man make known what kind of government would command his respect, that will be one step toward obtaining it."[111] The repeated and, in the second instance, italicized phrase "at once" suggests that while anarchy remains the distant goal, a better government is a more nearly attainable goal. While he allows that a better government can command an individual's respect, Thoreau does not broach the possibility that a better government might also be self-respecting. On the other hand, he attributes agency to the American government of the mid-nineteenth century, which, he thinks, reduces docile and compliant individual citizens, especially citizen soldiers, to will-sapped "machines"—the tools of government agency. But, taken as a whole, the decided emphasis of the essay is on individual conscience—that, when heeded, results in individual virtue.

9.13 HOLISTIC VIRTUE ETHICS: SELF-RESPECTING CRAFTS

Although Sandler provides for non-anthropocentric and for a limited holistic environmental virtue ethics, the limited holism he provides for is for moral patients, not agents. Leopold appears to broach the possibility that collectives can also themselves be virtuous moral agents. His father ran the Leopold Desk Company in Burlington, Iowa, the motto of which was "Built on Honor to Endure" (as noted in 6.2).[112] Leopold thus had, from childhood, a keen sense of the virtue of craftsmanship. But how to theorize that? Aristotle himself provides some theoretical support. Indeed, Aristotle models human virtue on virtuous craftsmanship or artisanship:

Now if the function of man is an activity of soul which follows or implies a rational principle, and if we say a "so-and-so" and "a good so-and-so" have a function which is the same in kind, e. g., a lyre-player and a good lyre-player, and so without qualification in all cases, eminence in respect of goodness being added to the name of the function (for the function of the lyre-player is to play the lyre, and that of a good lyre-player is to do so well): if this is the case…human good turns out to be activity of soul in accordance with virtue [*aretē*, excellence], and if there be more than one virtue, in accordance with the best and most complete.[113]

Not infrequently does Aristotle illustrate the nature of the whole by analogy with a part. The soul, as noted (in 9.11), is to the whole organism what sight is to the eye. Similarly, human virtue—human excellence—is analogous to the virtue of a craftsman or artisan. And what is the virtue of an artisan or craftsman but to perform the work of the art or craft well? Thus, human virtue or excellence is to perform the work of a human being well. And what is the work of a human being? As in the illustrative case of a lyre-player, the answer follows from a consideration of the nature of the beast. The nature of a lyre-player is—as Aristotle says tautologically but not uninformatively—to play the lyre. So, what is a human being and what is the work of a human being? A human being is a rational animal. Therefore, to govern the animal life of sensation, desire, and passion by the rational faculty of the soul, while guiding one's life prudently and wisely is the work of a human being. Poor artisanship or craftsmanship is an insult to the self-respect of the art or craft itself. And poor exemplification or manifestation of humanity is an insult to the self-respect of the art of being human.

9.14 HOLISTIC VIRTUE ETHICS: THE POLIS AS A SOCIAL WHOLE

After beginning "Conservation as a Moral Issue" in "Some Fundamentals of Conservation in the Southwest" by indignantly observing that "waste, pollution, and unnecessary damage [are] something unworthy—…something damaging not only to the reputation of the [individual] waster, but to the self-respect of the craft and the society of which he is a member," Leopold returns to the theme of environmental virtue ethics at the conclusion of the section and of the essay. Worth quoting again, Leopold writes,

And if there be, indeed, a special nobility inherent in the *human race*—a special cosmic value, distinctive from and superior to all other life—by what token shall it be manifest?
By a *society* decently respectful of its own and all other life, capable of inhabiting the earth without defiling it? Or by a *society* like that of John Burroughs' potato bug, which exterminated the potato, and thereby exterminated itself? As one or the other shall we be judged by "the derisive silence of eternity."[114]

Aristotle's virtue ethic—as is evident from the quotation from the *Nichomachean Ethics* in the previous section (9.12)—assumes that there is, at least potentially, a nobility inherent in the human race, the human species. The realization or actualization of the potentiality represented by human nature—rational animality—is *eudaimonia,* "the best, noblest, and most pleasant thing in the world."[115] We know that Leopold had read the *Nichomachean Ethics* because he samples a phrase from it in the opening line of "The Geese Return" (analyzed in 1.6), one of *Sand County's* shack sketches: "One swallow does not make a summer, but one skein of geese, cleaving the murk of a March thaw, is the spring."[116] For inclusion in the *Almanac,* Leopold redacted an essay previously written for and published in the *Wisconsin Agriculturist and Farmer* in 1940, "When the Geese Return." In it too, Leopold opens with the same sample from the *Nichomachean Ethics:* "One swallow does not make a summer, but one flock of honkers, winging northward through a murky March thaw, make a spring, come later blizzards to the contrary notwithstanding."[117] Aristotle writes, "For one swallow does not make a summer, nor does one fine day; and so too one day, or a short time, does not make a man blessed and happy."[118] We can only wonder if Leopold had read the *Nichomachean Ethics* by the time he wrote "Some Fundamentals" in 1923, but it is not unlikely that he encountered it as a student at Yale some time between 1904 and 1909.

Aristotle positions the *Nichomachean Ethics* as an extended propaedeutic to the *Politics.*[119] Aristotle regards the *polis* or city-state—in his own time the apex of the social hierarchy—to be the most evolved and complete social whole. Beneath it and emerging before it were families, households, and villages.[120] Following Plato, in this regard, and contrary to the contractarian contemporaries of Socrates, Aristotle regards this social hierarchy as existing by nature, not by artifice, *and* as ontologically prior to the existence of *human* individuals: "The proof that the state is a creation of nature and prior to the individual is that the individual, when isolated, is not self-sufficing; and therefore he is like a part in relation to the whole."[121] Typically, Aristotle illustrates the part-whole relationship of the individual to the *polis* by way of the part-whole relationship of an organ to the organism of which it is a part. For "if the whole body be destroyed, there will be no foot or hand, except in an equivocal sense, as we might speak of a stone hand; for when [the whole body is] destroyed the hand will be no better than that."[122] A "human individual" not living as a part of a social whole is, Aristotle indicates, no more really a *human* individual than a stone hand or the severed hand of a dead body is really a hand.

Aristotle certainly provides the moral ontology for making sense of Leopold's suggestion that a society is the sort of thing to which we might attribute virtue and its attendant self-respect. Although providing the ontological platform for doing so—that social wholes exist by nature and are ontologically prior to their individual parts—Aristotle attributes neither virtue nor its attendant self-respect to the society on which he focuses, the *polis.* Rather, the *polis* exists, Aristotle thinks, as the necessary social matrix for the cultivation of individual *aretē* and personal *eudaimonia:*

> It is clear then that a state (*polis*) is not a mere society, having a common place, established for the prevention of mutual crime and for the sake of exchange. These are conditions without which a state cannot exist.... The end (*telos*) of the state is the good life, and these the means towards it. And the state is the

union of families and villages in a perfect and self-sufficing life, by which we mean a happy (*eudaimoniac*) and honourable (*aretaic*) life.[123]

Plato, by contrast, considers, most unequivocally, that both *aretē* and *eudaimonia* are attributable to social wholes—states or *polises*, principally, for Plato no less than for Aristotle—as well as to their individual parts or constituents. Aristotle disagrees with much of Plato's politics (as expressed both in the *Republic* and the *Laws*), just as he disagrees with much of Plato's metaphysics, psychology, and epistemology. Despite his well- and oft-stated disagreements with Plato, Aristotle's philosophy and Plato's nonetheless have much in common in regard to politics if not to metaphysics, psychology, and epistemology. One of the many things that their political philosophies have in common is their rejection of social-contract theory and its fundamental assumption that morality is a human invention in conflict with human nature. Plato and Aristotle both opposed the contractarian axiom that morality, born of convention, exists not only unnaturally but anti-naturally, that it exists in opposition to and in defiance of nature.

9.15 HOLISTIC VIRTUE ETHICS: *NOMOS* VERSUS *PHUSIS*

Following the death of the Olympian gods, slain by Greek natural philosophy, the origin and nature of ethics suddenly became problematic. Formerly, Zeus was the source and sanction of justice. Zeus, as Aristophanes confirms in the *Clouds*, was supplanted by the "Aerial Whirlwind"—the cosmic vortex of Anaxagoras, Anaximenes, Anaximander, and several other pre-Socratic physicists.[124] But if there is no Zeus, who or what is the source of justice and by whom or what is it sanctioned? According to the majority of fifth-century moral philosophers (the sophists), it is a human creation; justice exists by convention (νομος), not by nature (φυσις). In Greek, νομος has several senses, but the principal classical ones are *custom* and *law*. The English word *convention* is equally rich in meaning—principally an agreement (as in the Geneva Conventions) and the assembly or meeting (as in the National Nominating Conventions of the two principal US political parties) in which agreements are made. From the Great Original Convention (assembly), whereat the social contract was negotiated, came various conventions (agreements). Further, the language of ethics in social-contract theory is nominal—justice is but the *name* given to the keeping of the conventions. In the state of nature, prior to the social contract, while there exist good (according to Hobbes, what is desired) and evil (according to Hobbes, what is averted), there do not exist right and wrong, justice and injustice.

Plato finds fatal problems with both the source and sanction aspects of the social contract theory. As to the former, because it pits ethics against nature, to act ethically one must overcome one's natural proclivities. Morality therefore is unstable, a constant struggle against natural inclinations, always liable to be overcome by human nature. As to the latter, morality is enforced not by divine but by purely human and, therefore, imperfect devices. Public disapprobation and retribution can be avoided by concealing unethical behavior from public notice. Legal sanctions are only as effective as the police and the judiciary. From Zeus, you can run but you cannot hide. From the law, you can both hide and run if you must. *Republic* II is largely devoted to cataloging the many possible ways of avoiding the external sanctions on which the social contract relies for enforcing its covenants. (Traditional Greek religion is hardly any better, Plato notes, because it too portrays injustice as easy and pleasant, while portraying justice as hard and onerous; and it portrays the gods, including Zeus, as open to bribery in lieu of a just payment of the true wages of sin.)

Plato offers a natural theory of the origin and nature of ethics. In the state of nature as characterized by Hobbes, human life is solitary as well as poor, nasty, brutish, and short. Plato, in effect, challenges that characterization of the original condition of humanity. There are indeed solitary species of animals—including bears, badgers, cougars, and many others—but the human species can, by no stretch of the imagination, be numbered among them. How could solitary humans have acquired language and with it the capacity to reason about their condition, except in an intensely social environment? To imagine solitary but fully rational human beings calling a convention and hammering out a contract, expressed in language, with new names invented for compliance ("justice" and "right") and violation ("injustice" and "wrong") is patently absurd, as Plato clearly recognized. Rather than supposing that humans originally lived as solitaries in the state of nature—each at war with all—he suggests that humans are by nature social animals. We humans necessarily live in cooperative societies because alone we cannot supply our own basic needs of food, shelter, and clothing—to say nothing of security. Aristotle follows Plato in treating human society as both natural and primal.

9.16 HOLISTIC VIRTUE
ETHICS: SELF-RESPECTING SOCIETIES

In Book II, Adeimantus assigns the fundamental task of the *Republic* to Socrates: "show us what it is that each [justice and injustice] does to its possessor—whether he does or does not escape the eyes of gods and men—whereby the one is good and the other is evil."[125] To show the nature of each—justice and injustice—Socrates constructs the fundamental structural analogy of the dialogue:

> "there is a justice of one man, we say, and, I suppose, also of an entire [or whole] city (ὅλης πόλεως)?" "Assuredly," said he. "Is not the city larger than the man?" "It is larger," he said. "Then, perhaps, there would be more justice in the larger object and more easy to apprehend. If it pleases you then, let us look for its quality in states (πόλεσι), and then only examine it in the individual, looking for the likeness of the greater in the form of the less."[126]

For Plato, "the state is the soul writ large"—as every doctoral student of philosophy learns in graduate school. Immediately, Socrates begins to construct a rudimentary state, based on the premise that solitary individuals cannot supply all their own needs. Correlatively, the organizational principle of states is a division of labor, according to natural proclivities, capacities, and talents, thus maximizing productive efficiency. There are two republics in the *Republic*—the healthy rustic state and the fevered luxurious state, the former egalitarian and the latter hierarchical.

Plato's conception of justice amplifies the mythopoeic notion of justice implicit in Hesiod's *Theogony*. The kind of justice Zeus established was first distributive and only secondarily retributive. He and his male siblings drew lots for hegemony over territory: to Zeus went the sky; to Poseidon the ocean; to Hades the underworld; the earth remained a commons for all. Plato's similarly tripartite theory of justice allots not territorial hegemony but political functions to the three classes in the originally luxuriant, but gradually chastened and disciplined, state. The best and wisest members of society should rule; the bravest and most loyal should execute the orders of the ruling junta; and the producing and consuming members of society should drive its economic engine. Justice is found in the state when each of its classes minds its own business, when each performs its natural function. Injustice is found in the state when one class meddles with the business proper to another—when, for example, rulers seek wealth (the business of the economic class) or when the military/civil-servant class seeks to rule (the business of the philosophers kings). In the one circumstance a true meritocracy (government by the best) degenerates into a corrupt plutocracy; in the other circumstance a true meritocracy degenerates into a brutal military dictatorship. Similarly, justice is found in the soul when each of its three parts does its proper business—reason ruling, the spirited element executing the orders of the rational faculty, and the other passions and myriad appetites submitting to the discipline imposed by reason and executed by the will.

Much more could be said about Plato's theory of the cardinal virtue of justice, elaborated in the *Republic*, as it pertains to the individual as well as to the state. But more said about that would digress from the present point, which is to validate, philosophically, Leopold's assumption that a society as a whole can manifest virtue and, if so, be self-respecting. More generally put, is a holistic virtue ethic intelligible? Leopold seems to suppose so when he speaks of the "self-respect of the craft [of land management] and of the society," in addition to the self-respect of individual craftspersons and individual members of society. Contemporary virtue ethics and more particularly contemporary environmental virtue ethics seem to share the post-Enlightenment hyper-individualism of mainstream utilitarianism and deontology, at least where moral agents are concerned. But the philosophical lineage of contemporary virtue ethics goes directly back to ancient Greek moral philosophy, more especially to the moral philosophy of Aristotle. (The moral philosophy of Plato seems to have been less a source of inspiration for contemporary virtue ethicists—perhaps because Plato's moral philosophy is more difficult to extract from his dialogues, while Aristotle established the form of communication, the treatise, ever after canonical in philosophy.) When, then, we trace contemporary virtue ethics back to its source in ancient Greek moral philosophy we find clear and unambiguous theoretical support for the holistic dimensions of the environmental virtue ethics toward which Leopold gestures in

"Some Fundamentals." Indeed, in my opinion, it seems hardly possible to find a more venerable and authoritative *locus classicus* for holistic virtue ethics than Aristotle's *Nichomachean Ethics* and Plato's *Republic*. The former philosophically validates the intelligibility of holistic virtue ethics pertaining to crafts (such as lyre playing) and the latter philosophically validates the intelligibility of virtue ethics pertaining to societies (such as city-states or *polises*).

9.17 THE DIALECTIC OF SOCIAL-CONTRACT THEORY AND VIRTUE ETHICS

Leopold himself does not suggest grounding an anthropocentric Earth ethic in social-contract theory. But because James Lovelock suggests it, this chapter reviews (9.5–9.8) a strain of anthropocentric social-contract theory that has recently sprung up in French environmental philosophy beginning with Michel Serres's *Le Contrat Naturel*. In it too we find a (perhaps unexpected and therefore surprising) holism. According to Jean-Jacques Rousseau—from whom Serres derives his inspiration and to whose *Du Contrat Social* Serres alludes with his own title—the social contract submerges the individual into the collective life of the corporate body with a common ego and a general will. Lovelock and Serres both hope that, upon confronting the common Earth enemy—facing the revenge of Gaia—and collectively recognizing the indiscriminate threat of global climate change, something like a Rousseauian unity of purpose will emerge, governed from the top down by a scientific junta. Latour is certainly skeptical about the possibility of a global scientocracy emerging—and indeed about the wisdom of fostering any such—but he is no less faithful to Rousseau's holism than is Serres. Indeed one might even go so far as to say that Latour is even more faithful to Rousseau's holism and even to Rousseau's romaticism because he envisions a common, universal world built from the bottom up out of heterogeneous parts that will come together to form a composite material, if not a social whole.

When traced to their classical origins in ancient Greek moral philosophy, one finds a dialectical relationship between social-contract theory and virtue ethics.

The former was the first theory of the origin and nature of ethics in Western philosophy. Thomas Hobbes was much more in tune with the individualistic moral ontology of ancient social-contract theory than was Rousseau. The ontology of ancient social contract theory mirrored the ontology of the atomic theory of matter and motion in pre-Socratic natural philosophy.[127] Human individuals are the analogs in moral philosophy of the externally related atoms in natural philosophy. Both are driven by simple inertial forces on collision courses with one another—the one in the natural void, the other in the social void of the "state of nature." The social contract comes into being to bring a modicum of order (*nomos*) to the otherwise violent and chaotic conditions that exist by nature (*physis*). In sharp contrast to modern social-contract theorists, especially Hobbes, ancient Greek social contract theorists assumed that just as some physical atoms were bigger and denser (had more mass, put in later Newtonian terms) than others, so some social atoms were stronger and more powerful than others. For those ancient social-contract theorists—most notably Thrasymachus, if Plato's portrait of him does justice (no pun intended) to the man himself—the social contract was disadvantageous to the "stronger."

Plato and Aristotle found the tension between *physis* and *nomos* to be both ethically maladroit and anthropologically implausible. Humans are by nature social animals, not solitaries, inconceivable, qua human, outside a social context. For Plato, virtue is the natural condition of both the human soul and human society. In *Republic* Book IV, Plato develops a three-tiered body-soul-polis analogy to characterize the nature of virtue. Virtue is to the soul as health is to the body (its natural condition) just as the virtue of the city-state is analogous to that of the soul—for the *polis* is the *psyche* writ large. For Aristotle, as for Plato, the rational animal is also a social animal. The goal of life is *eudaimonia* achieved by the cultivation of the perfection of human nature in the social matrix of the *polis* culminating in *aretē* or excellence at being a rational animal.

There remains to be considered an anthropocentric Earth ethic based on responsibility to future human generations—both to "immediate posterity" and to the "Unknown Future"—that Leopold also mentions in "Conservation as a Moral Issue" in "Some Fundamentals of Conservation in the Southwest." In Chapter 10, I show that the prevailing über-paradigm in mainstream moral philosophy, Rational Individualism, is not up to the task, especially not in regard to the Unknown Future (distant human generations). In Chapter 11, I provide an alternative ethical paradigm that can coherently account for responsibility to future human generations both to "immediate posterity" and to the "Unknown Future"—a relational moral ontology, a sentiment-based moral psychology, and a holistic communitarian theory of moral duties and obligations.

10

The Earth Ethic: A Critical Account of Its Anthropocentric Foundations—The Limits of Rational Individualism

Global climate change is the most urgent environmental concern of the first century of the third millennium. Its immense magnitude overshadows all the others. From the first decade of the twentieth century to the second decade of the twenty-first the concentration of CO_2, the most abundant if not the most powerful greenhouse gas in the Earth's atmosphere, increased by fifty percent—from 300 to 400 parts per million, which was achieved in May 2013.[1] In the Introduction to this book, I identified two "waves" of the environmental crisis. The environmental concerns of the first wave, which crested in the 1960s, are local—urban smog here, oil spills on beaches there, pesticide-polluted groundwater yonder.[2] The second wave of the environmental crisis is global in scope (although some regions of the globe will be impacted more severely than others by higher ambient energies and altered atmospheric and oceanic chemistries). And global climate change, its signature phenomenon, is potentially catastrophic, portending more powerful storms; more severe episodes of floods and droughts; higher sea levels (and with that, submerged island nations and coastal metropolises); increased acidification and possibly stagnation of the ocean.[3] On top of its catastrophic severity, global climate change is protracted in time to an even greater extent than it is extensive in space: the changes in the global climate induced by accumulated greenhouse gases—higher average temperatures and all that goes with that—are expected to last for thousands of years.[4]

The temporal and spatial scales of global climate change eclipse all other environmental concerns: as the vanishing point of our perspective on environmental problems recedes in both space and time, it shifts our perspective of concern as well. Over the duration of my lifetime, for instance, I have visited the Willamette Valley of Oregon on many occasions. During those in the twentieth century, I vividly recall my despair and outrage at the sight of clearcuts scarring and disfiguring the magnificent old-growth forests of the mountains—the Cascades and Coastal Range—framing the Valley. On a recent visit (2011), as I walked through a grove of Douglas fir trees—some five hundred years old, seventy meters tall, and two meters in diameter—in the McKenzie River watershed, I began to wonder what is "old" growth, after all?[5] To be sure, I was duly humbled and diminished as I compared the scale of my human being to the being of those trees; but when I compared the being of those trees to the scale and duration of the global Holocene climate—concern with which I am now preoccupied—and how that climatic regime is about to change and remain changed for a duration comparable to that of the Holocene (about ten thousand years), the being of those trees was duly diminished.

My concern for the old-growth forest was not only eclipsed by my concern for the Holocene climate, it was entrained. When the new greenhouse global climate stabilizes sometime in the future—and god only knows when that will be (which is to say that no one knows)—Douglas fir may no longer be adapted to the eventual climatic conditions of the Pacific Northwest.[6] I perceived the value of the now seemingly ephemeral—relatively speaking—forest less intrinsically and more as a carbon sink and microclimate modulator, precious as not only a product of but also a preserver of the Holocene climate and a mitigator of climate change. And what of biodiversity?—to which one's thoughts are inevitably led in such a place, which is habitat for the Northern spotted owl, among the most iconic and charismatic of endangered species in North America.[7] Global climate change will only exacerbate biodiversity loss and make the sixth mass extinction almost certain to occur. For the onslaught of global climate change is predicted to be relatively sudden, happening so fast that many species cannot adapt to the new local climates of the places in which they currently reside and, indeed, perhaps so fast that many species cannot migrate to the places at which their preferred climates will have turned up, if any such currently existing regional climates will continue to exist in any place at all.[8]

If this personal anecdote seems unconvincing—I may be losing my environmental-ethical edge—consider the anecdote related by Aldo Leopold in "Thinking Like a Mountain." What does it mean to think like a mountain? The title of Leopold's essay clearly invokes—albeit in his masterly style of indirection—temporal scale: "Only the mountain has *lived long enough* to listen objectively to the howl of a wolf."[9] But just how long is long enough? Leopold doesn't tell us that, but he does tell us at what temporal scale a mountain thinks: "I now suspect that just as a deer herd lives in mortal fear of its wolves, so does a mountain live in mortal fear of its deer. And perhaps with better cause, for while a buck pulled down by wolves can be replaced in *two or three years*, a range pulled down by deer may fail of replacement *in as many decades*."[10] In the late 1940s, when that essay was written, Leopold was embroiled in a dispiriting public controversy over his policy recommendation for reducing the Northern Wisconsin deer herd.[11] The temporal scale of the thinking of the up-in-arms nimrods, who were marshaled against him, was measured in years and counted on the fingers of one hand, while the *ecologically relevant* scale—determined by vegetative succession—was measured in units greater by an order of magnitude. The temporal scale relative to global climate change is measured in units that are one or two orders of magnitude more—centuries or millennia (depending on what aspect of climate change one has in mind).

In short, global climate change is an environmental issue of potentially catastrophic consequence and colossal spatial and temporal scale. And it is indeed a *moral* issue as insists every intellectually honest person of substance—from true statespersons, such as Al Gore, to thoughtful environmental philosophers, such as Stephen Gardiner, to activists, such as Bill McKibben.[12] What we of the present generation are doing to the

Earth will *adversely* affect not the fate of the Earth per se (see 9.1), but that of future generations for many centuries to come. And while the process of biological evolution per se is in no more jeopardy than is the Earth per se, global climate change will also affect the fates of our "fellow-voyagers…in the odyssey of evolution" and affect the course of evolution.[13] In other words, the global biotic community, *as presently constituted*, and the *trajectory* of its evolutionary development is also in jeopardy. It is my contention that we need to think up a moral philosophy that is commensurate with the spatial and temporal scales of the wholly novel, utterly (and literally) unprecedented ethical issues with which we are now confronted. The moral philosophies that we have inherited from the past are woefully inadequate to the task—as I demonstrate in this chapter. Clinging to them, as many climate ethicists still do, leads to moral impotence and despair.

10.1 THE YEAR WAS 1988 AND SERRES AND JAMIESON WERE THE FIRST PHILOSOPHICAL RESPONDERS

Dale Jamieson deserves equal credit with Michel Serres (acknowledged in 9.5 and 9.8) for being the first thinkers to recognize the distinct and novel *philosophical* challenge presented by global climate change. If there were an annual Nobel Prize for philosophy, Serres and Jamieson should share one for their discovery of the radical transformation of moral (and, in Serres's case, political) philosophy that is necessary if we are to mount an appropriate ethical response to the threat.

As I mentioned in the Introduction, it was in the summer of 1988 that I became palpably aware that a new, second wave of the environmental crisis had swept over us, characterized by its globality. That same year, so did both Serres and Jamieson; and both immediately responded philosophically—Serres with *Le Contrat Naturel* and Jamieson, a bit less spectacularly, with a seminal journal article. Toward the beginning of his book, published in 1990, Serres writes, "Let us propose two equally plausible interpretations of the stable high-pressure zones over North America and Europe in *1988* and 1989."[14] (That they only signify temporally local and soon-to-be-passing *weather anomalies* is one interpretation; that they signify the advent of *climate change* is the other interpretation, the one favored by Serres.) And toward the beginning of his article, based on a conference paper delivered in 1989 and published in 1992, Jamieson writes, "The emerging consensus about climate change was brought home to the American public on June 23rd *1988*, a sweltering day in Washington, D. C., in the middle of a severe drought, when James Hansen testified to the US Senate Committee on Energy and Natural Resources that it was 99% probable that global warming had begun."[15]

Aldo Leopold, the "prophet," anticipated the first wave of the environmental crisis with his book *A Sand County Almanac*, published in 1949. By the early 1960s, industrial air and water pollution were evident to the senses. Validation of our collective environmental experience was afforded by Rachel Carson with her book *Silent Spring*, published in 1962, and by Stewart Udall with his book, *The Quiet Crisis*, published in 1963. They mark the popular advent of the first wave of the environmental crisis. A decade later, Arne Naess, Richard Routley, Holmes Rolston III, and I responded philosophically. Roger Revelle, also something of a prophet, anticipated the advent of global warming in 1957, with a paper published in *Tellus*.[16] The heat and drought of the summer of 1988 were evident to the senses; and Bill McKibben with his *The End of Nature*, published in 1989, validated a sense that the environmental crisis had entered a new phase and become a planetary phenomenon. Serres and Jamieson were the first philosophical responders. So just as Naess, Routley, Rolston, and I are widely acknowledged to be the founders of environmental ethics, Serres and Jamieson should be widely acknowledged to be the founders of climate ethics. Alas, it has taken me nearly a quarter century to catch up, but with this book I am confident that my slower response goes much further down the path of ethical reformation than either Serres or Jamieson has managed to go. Indeed, Jamieson, meanwhile, seems to have gradually retreated from the program of radical philosophical reform that he initially broached, as I document shortly (10.3).

What I characterize here as a currently prevailing "moral philosophy," Jamieson characterizes as a currently prevailing "value system" that is "a relatively recent construction, coincident with the rise of capitalism and modern science, and expressed in the writings of such philosophers as Francis Bacon, John Locke, and Bernard Mandeville."[17] Whether one calls it a value system or a moral philosophy, it "presupposes," according to Jamieson, "that harms and their causes are individual, that they can be readily identified, and that they are local in space and time."[18] In my opinion, the coincidence of an individualistic moral ontology with the rise of modern science is of greater explanatory power than its coincidence with the rise of capitalism, enabling, indeed, a deeper understanding of the rise of capitalism as well as of the emergence of modern modes of thinking about ethics.

To Jamieson's list of philosophers who express the individualistic ontology of modern ethics (if the satirist Mandeville can be called a philosopher), I would add Thomas Hobbes. In the moral and political philosophy of Hobbes, the atomistic ontology of modern science and modern ethics are perfectly entwined (detailed in 9.4 and 9.17). Hobbes begins the *Leviathan* with a *literal* reduction of organisms and their organs to mechanical automata—quite in concert with Descartes, in this regard.[19] But unlike Descartes, a mind-matter (or soul-body) dualist, Hobbes is a thoroughgoing materialist, thus effectively reducing ethics to a branch of physics. Literally mechanical automata, human individuals are—analogically or metaphorically considered—social atoms, driven on a collision course with other social atoms by a bivalent psycho-physical force, "endeavor" (*conatus* in the Latin translation of the *Leviathan*, as noted in 8.7). When toward an object, it is called *appetite* or *desire*; and when fromward, *aversion*. All other feelings, emotions, and passions are reducible to this bivalent force of attraction and repulsion. Hope, for example, is nothing but desire while believing its object is obtainable; despair is nothing but desire while believing that its object is unobtainable; and so forth and so on.[20]

10.2 JAMIESON FRAMES THE THEORETICAL PROBLEM: THE LEGACY OF SMITH-AND-JONES ETHICAL THEORY

But whatever the historical coincidences and origins of the individualistic ontology of modern moral philosophy, conceived in the seventeenth century and nurtured into maturity in the eighteenth, it is an ineffective resource for addressing the moral issue of global climate change. Contemporary ethicists who assume that the moral aspects of global climate change can be accounted for without reconfiguring moral philosophy from its foundations are like engineers proposing to design a system of air transport using steam propulsion or like ecologists proposing to model biocomplexity using a slide rule. No one, in my opinion, has better and more succinctly expressed the reason that the individualistic ontology of modern moral philosophy is an ineffective resource for addressing the moral issue of global climate change than Dale Jamieson:

> Consider an example of the sort of case with which our value system [moral philosophy] deals best. Jones breaks into Smith's house and steals Smith's television set. Jones's intent is clear:…Smith suffers a clear harm;…Jones is responsible for Smith's loss,…
>
> We know how to identify the harms and to assign responsibility. We respond…by punishing Jones in order to prevent her from doing it again and to deter others from such acts, or we require compensation from Jones so that Smith may be restored to his former position.
>
> It is my contention that this paradigm *collapses* when we try to apply it to global environmental problems, such as those associated with human-induced global climate change….
>
> There are three important dimensions along which global environmental problems such as those involved with climate change vary from the paradigm: [1] apparently innocent acts can have devastating consequences, [2] causes and harms may be diffuse, and [3] causes and harms may be remote in space and time. (Other important dimensions may concern non-linear causation, threshold effects, and the relative unimportance of political boundaries.)[21]

People who (1) innocently use energy generated by fossil fuels—daily, as they illuminate, heat, and air-condition their homes and offices, run their household appliances and office equipment, drive their cars; or occasionally, as they fly from city to city and continent to continent in airplanes; operate heavy machinery; and so on—did not know, until relatively recently, that their actions were contributing to global climate change and that a changed climate would adversely affect presently existing distant persons, immediate posterity, unknown future generations, and the fellow-members of their biotic communities and those communities per se. Certainly they intended no harm. Further (2), while the single and well-defined action of a single and well-defined individual who steals a television set is the single and well-defined cause of significant harm to another single and well-defined individual, the contribution to global climate change and the resulting harm that can be attributed to a single and well-defined action of a single and well-defined individual is infinitesimal. Even (3) when all the energy-consuming, greenhouse-gas-emitting actions of a single well-defined individual over the course of a year—nay, even over the course of a lifetime—are aggregated, that individual's contribution to future global climate change is still negligible.

After October 2011, each of us is now one of some seven billion humans on the planet (and counting).[22] At the coarsest level of analysis, our individual share of responsibility for the causes and remedies of global climate change is one seven-billionth. Of course, individual humans do not all emit the same amount of CO_2 and other greenhouse gases into the atmosphere. The quantitative spectrum of individual emissions ranges from those of persons who do little more than breathe to those who travel among their many energy-consuming and greenhouse-gas-emitting mansions on their energy-consuming and greenhouse-gas-emitting private jets and luxury yachts. As far as I know, there is no way to determine how much CO_2 I or any other person emits into the atmosphere, personally. But the Average American emits about one three-hundred millionth *of the total US emissions*, which, in 2012, the latest year for which figures are available at this writing (July 2013), amounted to almost six gigatons (continuing to trend down from a 2007 high, due mainly to power plants switching to cheap hydro-fractured natural gas, which emits half as much CO_2 per kilowatt as does coal).[23] The Average American's fraction of annual *global greenhouse-gas emissions* (which are still steeply trending up, infortunately) of about 31.6 gigatons would be much smaller than one three-hundred millionth, but, of course, much greater than one seven billionth.[24] James Garvey has done some research and arithmetic and calculated his share, as a Better-Than-Average Brit, of global CO_2 emissions:

> There are…7 billion people on the planet. Together we emit 28.4 gigatons of CO_2 each year. A gigaton is one billion tons [and one billion tons is one thousand million tons]. I am responsible for about 4 tons of CO_2 each year. Am I to see myself as responsible for 4/28.4 x 1,000,000,000 or 0.000000000141% of the harm done to our planet this year? Should I try to do better and aim for 4/28,399,999,999?[25]

As noted in the introductory comments of this chapter and in 9.1, the *planet* (pace Garvey) is suffering no anthropogenic harm this year or any other. Rather, human and other-than-human beings are suffering climate-related harm this year and will suffer even more climate-related harm in future years. I cannot vouch for Garvey's data or arithmetic—his book was published in 2011, perhaps accounting for the 3.2 Gt discrepency between the latest totals I find and those he found—but his point is the same as mine. Individual responsibility for causing global climate change and the ensuing harm to presently existing distant persons, immediate posterity, unknown future generations, and our fellow-voyagers in the odyssey of evolution is "so impossibly teeny that it can't figure into a real motivation for green action"—that is, action aimed at mitigating climate change.[26] The Average American emits roughly twice the tonnage of CO_2 into the atmosphere as the Average Brit.[27] But to whatever the Average American's fraction of the total works out, the individual responsibility of an Average American for causing the harms that will be visited on presently existing distant persons, immediate posterity, unknown future generations, and fellow-voyagers in the odyssey of evolution is still so "teeny" as to be negligible. On the flip side of that coin, if a morally scrupulous individual Average Brit or Average American reduced his or her annual carbon footprint by 75 percent—no mean feat of lifestyle change—the annual *global total* of greenhouse-gas emissions would not be *measurably* reduced.

While the prorated individual responsibility for causing and for remedying the harms that will be visited on presently existing distant persons, immediate posterity, unknown future generations, and fellow-voyagers in the odyssey of evolution are both negligible, the harms themselves will hardly be negligible. Nor will they be sliced into similar micro-fractions of suffering. The full brunt of sea-level rise, for example, will be visited on *each one* of those that it harms—the wealthy gentry of Charleston living south of Broad Street on the North American East Coast as well as the impoverished denizens of Dhaka, on the Bay of Bengal, although the former will be far better able to cope with storm surges in the near future and dispossession by the sea a bit further down the road than will the latter. Therefore, as Jamieson bluntly puts it, the Jones-Smith ethical paradigm "collapses" in the face of the moral quandary presented by global climate change.

10.3 JAMIESON SUGGESTS AN ALTERNATIVE MORAL PHILOSOPHY–VIRTUE ETHICS

Is this Jones-Smith individualistic paradigm the only possible way that we can conceptualize our responsibilities to presently existing distant persons, immediate posterity, unknown future generations, and fellow members of our biotic communities? If so, is it any wonder that climate ethicists have been unable to convince decent, morally upright individuals that they are no less obliged to refrain from individually using so much carbon-based energy than they are obliged to refrain from individually stealing television sets? Their individual actions simply have no significant effect, one way or another, on total greenhouse gas emissions or on the eventual global climate change that ever-greater accumulations of greenhouse gases in the atmosphere will eventually bring about.

Accordingly, Jamieson suggests that as we try to mount an effective ethical response to the moral quandary presented by global climate change, philosophers, in the role of public intellectuals, shift paradigms from one centered on *individual agents, individual patients*, and the harmful or beneficial *consequences* of the individual actions of individual agents on individual patients to one focused on character. That would amount to a paradigm shift from utilitarianism to virtue ethics—indeed as indicated in 9.10, it would be tantamount to a shift from one way of conceiving of ethics to another, from the legalistic/consequentialist mode of thinking about ethics to the aretaic mode:

[W]e should focus more on character and less on calculating probable outcomes [consequences, in other words]....[W]e need to nurture and give new content to some old virtues such as humility, courage, and moderation and perhaps develop such new virtues as those of simplicity and conservatism. But whatever the best candidates are for twenty-first century virtues, what is important to recognize is the importance and centrality of the virtues in bringing about value change.[28]

Like many of the environmental virtue ethicists reviewed in 9.11, Jamieson's initial discussion of climate-change virtue ethics is theory poor. He basically just evokes virtue ethics, identifies some currently relevant old virtues, and adds a couple of new ones to the list. Be that as it may, his practical point is more complex and more insightful. However we might theorize environmental virtue ethics, a focus on individual *virtue* is more likely to achieve positive results than a focus on calculating the *consequences* of well-meaning individual actions. With the full knowledge that being moderate in one's habits of consumption, simple in one's needs and wants, conservative of the resources at one's command, and respectful of one's environment will result in no appreciable reduction in the accumulation of greenhouse gases in the atmosphere, one may at least enjoy self-respect. One may take pride in the knowledge that if everyone—and that's what it would take, if not absolutely everyone then almost everyone—were as environmentally virtuous as oneself, future climate change could be mitigated. Ronald Sandler has recently joined Jamieson in recommending a paradigm shift from consequentialist to virtue ethics in response to the moral challenge of global climate change.[29]

Nonetheless, as Garvey notes, changing prognosticated *outcomes*—avoiding the catastrophic *consequences* of global climate change—is the whole practical point of climate-change ethics. There may be a consequentialist paradox related to climate-change ethics analogous to the old pursuit-of-happiness paradox (when happiness is conceived in terms of pleasure as did the classical utilitarians).[30] Paradoxically, one can never attain happiness (or pleasure) by pursuing that goal per se but only by pursuing and achieving more specific goals. (As a celebrated hedonist once lamented in song, "I can't get no satisfaction," but soon thereafter discovered that "you can't always get what you want, but if you try sometime, you just might find, that you get what you need.") Similarly, by concerning oneself less with the negligible climate consequences of one's actions and concerning oneself instead with cultivating and manifesting environmental virtues, positive climate consequences may follow indirectly. How so? One's virtuous lifestyle may become a model for other self-respecting individuals to emulate. Virtue, one would like to think, is contagious. A growing sub-population of environmentally virtuous people might become large enough to self-organize—especially in the era of internet-enabled social media—into a political force that might begin to affect national and international environmental policy and law. Changes in policy and law would in turn either externally induce (by means of incentives) or externally coerce (by means of disincentives and penalties) changes in the behavior of those who are not internally motivated to be environmentally virtuous. This is what I think Jamieson has in mind when he observes that "our values permeate our institutions and practices. Reforming our values is part of constructing new moral, political, and legal concepts."[31]

In a subsequent discussion, Jamieson, anticipating Garvey on this head, reaffirms the centrality of consequences to climate ethics—the whole point is to "bring something about," namely, to avoid a climate holocaust.[32] That requires, Jamieson thinks, a commitment to utilitarianism, the quintessential expression of consequentialism—a commitment to utilitarianism in principle, if not exactly in any of its classical expressions. But because there are no appreciable climate consequences, at least not directly, of individual actions, utilitarianism might be leavened with virtue ethics, Jamieson suggests. Though Jamieson does not note it, Mill provides an unimpeachable precedent for doing just that in *Utilitarianism*—there devoting extensive discussion to virtue. In "When Utilitarians Should Be Virtue Theorists," while Jamieson's discussion of utilitarianism is richly theoretical, it is less so in regard to virtue ethics. As to the consequences of the actions of individuals who conceive of their climate-conscious behavior in terms of personal virtue, Jamieson is, at last, quite explicit: although he has previously given the same reasons as Garvey gives for thinking otherwise, Jamieson declares that "One's behavior in producing and consuming is important for its immediate environmental impacts."[33] Actually, not in regard to the immediate impacts of one's behavior on climate. I would agree, however, that one's behavior in producing and consuming *is* important "for the example-setting and role-modeling dimensions of the behavior....Even if in the end, one's values do not prevail, there is comfort and satisfaction in living in accordance with one's ideals."[34]

10.4 THE MORAL ONTOLOGY AND LOGIC OF SMITH-AND-JONES ETHICAL THINKING

Let me autopsy the individualistic paradigm of moral thought that Jamieson so nicely captures in his little ditty about Jones stealing a television set from Smith. First, Smith and Jones are *externally related* to one another. That is, the identity of neither is bound up with or defined by the other. For mind-body dualists in the tradition of Descartes, Smith and Jones are isolated psychic monads inhabiting mechanical bodies—ghosts in machines. This ghost-in-the-machine ontology is a legacy of both the Greco-Roman philosophical tradition, going back to Pythagoras and Plato, and the Judeo-Christian tradition, particularly its Hellenistic Christian aspect. Aristotle complained that the Pythagorean-Platonic doctrine of transmigration absurdly assumes that any *psyche* can inhabit any *soma*, without considering the bodily infrastructure, as it were, that psychological functions require: "they all join the soul to a body, or place it in a body, without adding any specification of the reason of their union or the bodily conditions required for it...as if it were possible, as in the Pythagorean myths, that any soul could be clothed upon with any body—an absurd view."[35] And among the first verses that little Christian American children learn is "Now I lay me down to sleep / I pray the Lord my soul to keep / If I should die before I wake / I pray the Lord my soul to take."[36] For materialists in the tradition of Hobbes, individuals are nothing but mechanical bodies—machines sans ghosts—existing in and separated by empty social space, moved by endeavor (or *conatus*), an internal force, like that of a wound-up spring. However conceived—either dualistically or materialistically—human monads or social atoms are rational: by which is meant that they (1) pursue only their own self-interest exclusively and (2) they do so in a calculating way in order to serve their own interests—that is, to satisfy their own desires (or preferences)—to the maximum extent possible.[37] According to Kenneth Goodpaster,

> the two major foundational accounts of morality [utilitarianism and Kantian deontology] share, both in their classical formulations and in their contemporary interpretations, a fixation on egoism and a consequent loyalty to a model of moral...reason which in essence generalizes or universalizes that very egoism....Perhaps we are supposed to believe that self-interest so clearly provides a paradigm of practical rationality that only by working off its persuasive power (only by tying our carts to its automotive [horse]) can we hope to ground an adequate set of moral principles.[38]

Given this moral ontology of externally related egoistic but rational individuals, ethics may be understood in one or the other of two ways.

In the seventeenth-century tradition of Hobbes, self-interest is rationally *enlightened* by the frustrating experience of the universal blind pursuit of immediate desires. It is thus rational to restrain the pursuit of one's own desires, just to the extent prescribed by law or convention (*nomos*), in exchange for others doing the same. Mutual restraint allows for the aggregate satisfaction of desires—one's own and those of other contracting rational egoists—to increase to the greatest extent possible. The "normative force" of the classical seventeenth-century-individualistic paradigm of ethics— that which compels compliance—is an external physical force imposed by a sovereign power, whether monarchical (as Hobbes thought necessary), republican, or some other form of legitimate power. That's one way to understand ethics under the aegis of a moral ontology of externally related egoistic and rational individuals.

In the eighteenth century, Immanuel Kant and Jeremy Bentham came up with another way. Reason discloses a common essence in all the individual members of the class defined by the inhering of that essence in those individuals. This common essence entitles the members of that class to moral regard and ethical treatment by the other members of that class. The moral regard and ethical treatment of one individual by another do not rest on mutual sympathy or concern for others, but on what might be called an argument of mutual entitlement—on a kind of moral *logic*. That argument runs as follows. I demand moral regard and ethical treatment from others on the basis of my claim to possess or manifest a putative moral essence; classically, that essence was reason (according to Kant) or sentience (according to Bentham). *To be consistent*, I must extend moral regard and ethical treatment to all (and only) those who also possess or manifest the same putative moral essence. The "normative force" of the classical eighteenth-century-individualistic paradigm of ethics—that which compels compliance—is internal logical necessity, not, as in its seventeenth-century antecedent, external physical or causal necessity. Kant provides the clearest possible exposition:

> Some actions are so constituted that their maxims cannot *without contradiction* even be thought of as a universal law of nature, much less be willed as what

should become one. In the case of others this internal impossibility is indeed not found, but there is still no possibility of willing that their maxim should be raised to the universality of a law of nature, because such a will would *contradict itself....*Consequently, if we weighed up everything from one and the same standpoint, namely, that of reason, we would find a *contradiction in our own will*, viz., that of reason, that a certain principle should be objectively necessary as a universal law, and yet subjectively not hold universally, but admit of exceptions.[39]

10.5 THE ESSENCE-AND-ACCIDENT MORAL ONTOLOGY OF RATIONAL INDIVIDUALISM

Well, so what?—one might reply to Kant. As a moral agent, I may be caught in a contradiction...AND? Why should that bother me? Though rarely understood in just these terms, the ontology of Rational Individualism, as we may now label the über-paradigm of modern (inclusive of both Kantian deontology and utilitarianism) moral philosophy, is of the venerable essence-accident sort, originating with Aristotle. "The essence of each thing," according to Aristotle, "is what it is said to be *propter se*. For being you is not being musical. What then you are by your very nature is your essence."[40] And Aristotle declares that "'Accident' means that which attaches to something and can be truly asserted, but neither of necessity nor usually."[41] He gives an example, "it is an accident that a man is pale...but it is not by accident that he is an animal."[42] Nor is it by accident that a man is a *rational* animal as Aristotle subsequently insists.[43] That a human being is a rational animal is an essential attribute; that he or she is white, or (fe)male, or Christian is an accidental attribute. Aristotle always allows, however, for what might be called controlled or disciplined ambiguity and relativity: "There are several senses in which a thing may be said to 'be'...; for in one sense the 'being' meant is 'what a thing is' or a 'this,' and in another sense it means a quality or quantity or one of the other things that are predicated as these are."[44] There is being qua being and being qua this or that.

Accordingly, paradigmatic modern moral philosophers seek to identify the essence of a being qua *moral* being, all other attributes of such beings being *morally irrelevant* accidents. The classical Kantian tradition is true to Aristotle's identification of "man" as the rational animal in making rationality the essence of a moral being as well as the *propter-se* essence of a human being, only differing from Aristotle in holding open the possibility that there may be other-than-human rational beings (angels or extraterrestrials, we must assume that Kant has in mind). In the classical utilitarian tradition, rationality is an essential attribute of moral *agents*, but not of moral patients. The essential attribute of moral *patients* is sentience, the capacity to experience pleasure and pain, to enjoy and suffer. Quoted ad nauseam by animal liberationists, of animals Bentham wrote, "the question is not, Can they reason? nor Can they talk? but, Can they suffer?"[45]

From this ontology of externally related individuals, defined as a class of moral patients by virtue of the possession of a common moral essence, there follows the principle of equality or impartiality: an individual moral agent should give equal consideration and accommodation to the equal interests of those individual moral patients who equally possess the identified moral essence, irrespective of differences in their morally accidental attributes. If the identified moral essence is coextensive with the essence of humankind, as those who identified it in terms of rationality assumed it to be, then a moral agent must give equal consideration and accommodation to the equal interests of *all* human beings, irrespective of such morally accidental attributes as race, gender, sexual orientation, religious affiliation, nationality, intelligence quotient, familial or social relationship...or else. Or else what? Or else a rational moral agent would be guilty of inconsistency. And that—to answer the question at the beginning of this section (10.5)—would betray his or her very essence as a rational moral *agent*.

If sentience is identified as the essence of moral *patients*, then species membership must be added to the list of morally accidental attributes that a moral agent must ignore in considering and accommodating the equal interests of moral patients—as classically articulated by Peter Singer.[46] Now that the effects of the actions of consistent-at-all-costs rational moral agents can be felt on the other side of the planet and far into the future, spatial and temporal *distance* must be added to the list of morally irrelevant accidental attributes of moral patients. Or so the contemporary exponents of this eighteenth-century über-paradigm insist. Peter Singer, for example, specifically accidentalizes, so to speak, spatial distance:

> It makes no moral difference whether the person I can help is a neighbor's child ten yards from me or a Bengali, whose name I shall never know, ten thousand miles away....If we accept any principle of impartiality, universality, equality, or whatever, we cannot discriminate against someone merely because he is far away from us (or we are far away from him)....There would seem therefore to be no possible justification for discriminating on geographical grounds.[47]

These declamations were published in 1972 (see 5.1 for similar declamations published in 1981) and concerned famine relief, well before any philosophers considered the moral issues raised by anthropogenic climate change. But now that philosophers are considering the moral issues raised by anthropogenic climate change, we find that adamant adherents of the eighteenth-century über-paradigm draw a perfect analogy between spatial distance and temporal "distance." James Garvey could hardly be more succinct and blunt: "If spatial distance does not make a moral difference, it is hard to see how temporal distance could matter to what we ought to do."[48] It seems that we tend to think of time by way of analogy to space. We readily speak of the "near" and "far-flung" future. Our very language (English at least) tempts us to theorize responsibilities to temporally distant persons by analogy with responsibility to spatially distant persons. The temptation to do so seems to be irresistible to conventional ethicists in the context of global climate change, the most urgent environmental concern of the first century of the third millennium. For we affluent members of the present generation—collectively the agents of global climate change—adversely affect both spatially and temporally distant persons. But when the temporal distance between the present and future generations reaches a certain magnitude, the moral analogy breaks down. Spatially distant persons are determinate; they actually exist. If we project far enough into the future—actually, not all that far—temporally distant persons are indeterminate. Not only do they not presently exist, whether they will exist or not, qua *individual* persons, is entirely contingent—contingent partly on the actions that we presently exiting persons choose to undertake—as I shortly explain in more detail (10.10).

10.6 *HOMO ECONOMICUS* AND *HOMO ETHICUS*–TWO SIDES OF THE SAME RATIONAL COIN

Let me be clear about the state of play to which Rational Individualism leads us in the context of global climate change. Every rational moral agent is ethically required to give equal consideration and accommodation to the equal or like interests of every moral patient, irrespective of their morally inessential (that is, accidental) attributes. Hence, distance must be added to the more usual litany of accidents (gender, race, and religion)—not only regarding those actually (spatially) distant moral patients existing now, but also regarding those that will exist in the "distant" future. If the status of moral patiency is limited to human beings—the charge of speciesism or human chauvinism notwithstanding—the following is implied. Presented with an array of possible actions, every moral agent at every moment of their moral lives should choose to perform the action that will most greatly benefit and least harm the greatest number of moral patients. The number of moral patients—each, in virtue of his or her moral essence, having exactly the same moral standing and therefore being perfectly equal in his or her desert of moral consideration and accommodation—is staggering. That number now exceeds seven billion. If temporal "distance" is as accidental an attribute as spatial distance the number swells by orders of magnitude and becomes literally astronomical. But then, orthodox utilitarians demand that we heed Bentham's dictum: "The French have already discovered that the blackness of skin is no reason why a human being should be abandoned without redress to the caprice of a tormentor. It may come one day to be recognized, that the number of legs, the villosity of the skin, or the termination of the *os sacrum*, are reasons equally insufficient for abandoning a sensitive being to the same fate."[49] Reason therefore demands that species membership be added to the list of accidental attributes of moral patients and, accordingly, that the set of moral patients be expanded to include not only all human but also all sentient beings now and forever after. Stated so baldly, consequentilist Rational Individualism leads to an absurdly impracticable extreme.

Eighteenth-century moral philosophy has given birth to a new species of *Homo* that befuddles our thinking about climate-change ethics—*Homo ethicus*, the good twin of *Homo economicus*. *Homo economicus* is the descendent of Hobbes's enlightened egoistic social atom, specimens of which satisfy their own desires (now become preferences) limited only by their opportunities and capacities and by the legally instituted constraints that they and the other members of the species have agreed to be bound by—in utter indifference to the interests, desires, or preferences of their fellow specimens.[50] Every specimen of *Homo ethicus* demands that every other specimen of the species give due consideration to his or her interests, when their actions affect him or her. To be consistent, to avoid self-contradiction, to be, in short, perfectly rational—because rationality is his or her essential attribute as a moral agent—every specimen of *Homo ethicus* is obliged to give due and equal consideration to the like interests of all the other specimens of the species that his or her actions affect. And if the class of moral agents is but a subset of the class of moral patients, then every specimen of *Homo ethicus* is obliged to give due and equal consideration to the like interests of all other moral patients (irrespective of species membership) as well.

10.7 SAVING RATIONAL INDIVIDUALISM: MORAL MATHEMATICS

As noted, Jamieson and Garvey think that because an individual's greenhouse gas emissions are so tiny a fraction of the total as to be negligible, an individual can therefore bear no personal responsibility for the harms that anyone will suffer from climate change. Derek Parfit argues that such thinking is one of several "mistakes of moral mathematics."[51] Parfit does not perform a moral mathematical analysis of climate change, but John Nolt does. After carefully disclosing all the assumptions involved in his calculations and with the caveat that the resulting figures are "crude," Nolt arrives at the following conclusion: "the average American is responsible for about one two-billionth of current and near-term emissions....If over the next millennium as few as four billion people (about 4%) are harmed (that is suffer and/or die) as a result of current or near-term global emissions, then the average American causes through his or her greenhouse gas emissions the suffering and/or deaths of two future people."[52]

Grant that Nolt's calculations, however crude, are in the ballpark; what practical conclusion is to be drawn from them? Is the obverse of this calculation also plausible? Suppose that Nolt, but only Nolt, cut his greenhouse emissions by half at considerable trouble and expense to himself. Would one person among the one hundred billion people that Nolt estimates to live over the next one thousand years be spared suffering and/or death attributable to global climate change? If Nolt decided that it was his duty to stop breathing and so cut his greenhouse gas emissions to zero, would two people over the next one thousand years be spared? How do Nolt's calculations compare with alternative utilities that an Average American might realize by devoting an equivalent amount of trouble and expense to alleviating the suffering and preventing the deaths of presently existing people who otherwise might suffer and die from causes other than climate change? I am not disposed to attempt a comparative calculation, but I would bet that an Average American might spare many more presently existing people from suffering and dying from famine by giving to Oxfam the money that he or she might spend on insulation, solar-voltaic panels, and the like, in an effort voluntarily and individually to spare a single person living in the Unknown Future from suffering and/

or dying from global climate change. And he or she might spare many more presently existing people from suffering and dying from human trafficking by taking the time and trouble to open and operate a shelter for liberated labor- and sex-slaves than devoting an equal amount of time and trouble to bike instead of drive, to shop for locally produced foods and clothing, and so on.

The burden of my argument is not, however, comparative utilities, but the utility of Rational Individualism—the Smith-Jones paradigm of ethics—that Nolt and others cling to in addressing the very real, the very urgent, and the very grave *moral* problem of global climate change. Basically, moral mathematics aggregates the minuscule consequences of the acts of a large number of individual moral agents ($Jones_1$, $Jones_2$, $Jones_3$, ... $Jones_n$) into a gargantuan totality that adversely affects a gargantuan number of individual moral patients ($Smith_1$, $Smith_2$, $Smith_3$ ... $Smith_n$). It then arbitrarily assigns responsibility for the harms suffered by say, $Smith_x$, $Smith_y$, and $Smith_z$ to $Jones_x$. $Jones_x$ has an individual identity as a moral agent but can never, in principle, ascertain the individual identity of the moral patients for whose suffering and/or death he bears personal responsibility. But so what? All moral patients are *essentially* the same; any distinguishing characteristic is an accident.

Grant, for the sake of argument, that the moral mathematics of Rational Individualism is conceptually coherent. One wonders how motivating mathematically massaged Rational Individualism can be? When pressed to such extremes by moral mathematics, its bloodlessness is exposed. Further, another consideration—the non-identity problem—raised, ironically, by Derek Parfit undermines moral mathematics when the large number of individual moral patients is protracted into Leopold's "Unkown Future," as subsequently detailed in 10.10.

10.8 SAVING RATIONAL INDIVIDUALISM: PROXIMATE ETHICAL HOLISM

Let's get back to basics. The end in view is to drastically reduce the emission of greenhouse gases in order to prevent or, because that is no longer possible, to mitigate global climate change—that is, to postpone its advent as long as possible, to stabilize the concentration of greenhouse gases in the atmosphere, and thus to diminish the magnitude of change. Mistakes in moral mathematics notwithstanding, *voluntary individual* reduction of fossil-fuels consumption—the major source of greenhouse-gas emissions—will not achieve that end for all sorts of reasons: ignorance, disinformation, apathy, free-rider resentment, miscasting *Homo sapiens* in the role of the mythical *Homo ethicus*. If the end of drastically reducing the emission of greenhouse gases is to be achieved, individuals must act collectively so that the effects of their combined actions are coordinated and aggregated to add up to something significant. The familiar way that individuals act collectively is through their governments, which can realize ends—such as building networks of roads and sewers or fleets of warships—unattainable by individuals acting individually. Governments, then, in effect, become agents undertaking complex coordinated actions on a grand scale. Significantly reducing greenhouse gas emissions will require governments to act forcefully and decisively. But that requires exponents of Rational Individualism to embrace a proximate ethical holism. It is a form of ethical holism because supra-individual entities—governments—are treated as moral agents; it is proximate because the sacrifices demanded of morally responsible governments are ultimately distributed among their individual constituents.

As to moral holism, in the introductory chapter to his book, *One World*, Peter Singer, for example, challenges the concept of sovereign nation-states and the associated idea of "internationalization" and instead espouses the idea of "globalization": "we are moving beyond the era of growing ties between nations and are beginning to contemplate something beyond the existing conception of the nation-state."[53] But in the very next chapter, "One Atmosphere," nations are hypostatized, so much so, that they are equated, at a global scale, with "people": "So, to put it in terms a child could understand, as far as the atmosphere is concerned, the developed nations broke it. If we believe that *people* should contribute to fixing something in proportion to their responsibility for breaking it, then the developed *nations* owe it to the rest of the world to fix the problem with the atmosphere."[54] In a comprehensive review of climate-change ethics up until 2004, Stephen Gardiner indicates that Singer's proximate holism is representative: "We have seen that there is a great deal of convergence on the issue of *who* has primary responsibility to act on climate change. The most defensible accounts of fairness and climate change suggest that the rich countries [that's "who"] should bear the brunt and perhaps even the entirety of the costs."[55] In addition to Singer's, notable among convergent accounts of fairness and climate change are those by Henry Shue and (after Gardiner's review article was published) those by Simon Caney.[56]

The conventional way that governments obtain the means to achieve large, collective goals is through taxation, which distributes the costs of government actions to individual constituents. And if taxation is progressive—the rich paying not only more in taxes than the poor but also a higher percentage of their income in taxes—then the same principles of fairness among nation-states will obtain among their individual constituents, the rich presumably laying down a bigger carbon footprint than the poor. Taxation is often conventionally used for purposes other than financing projects such as roads, sewers, and navies. It can be used as a means of changing and orchestrating the behavior of individuals. So-called sin taxes, for example, are used to discourage the collective consumption of alcohol and tobacco. Similarly carbon taxes could be used as a means of discouraging the consumption of fossil fuels by individuals. Further, revenues generated by carbon taxes might fund public investment in alternative-energy research and development. Other governmental policies than taxation, such as regulating greenhouse-gas emissions and instituting cap-and-trade carbon markets, might also increase the cost to individuals of consuming fossil fuels and thus significantly reduce their collective consumption and thus also reduce the attendant emission of greenhouse gases. Such policies might also incentivize private investment in alternative energy research and development.

All that comes at a steep price, leaving individuals much less discretionary income to spend on such things as dining out, drinking fine wine, collecting fine art, watching cable television, and enjoying other luxuries. Adding to the price is the moral obligation to compensate moral patients living in other, poorer, less-developed countries who have emitted relatively small amounts of greenhouse gases into the atmosphere and are more vulnerable to the many harmful facets of global climate change, some of which are now kicking in. The governments of affluent countries might create a fund, upon which the governments of poor countries might draw, with which to invest in such adaptive measures as sea walls, buildings able to withstand hurricane-force winds, and drought-resistant cultivars, and so on and so forth. Despite a series of international negotiations—Rio (1992), Kyoto (1997), Copenhagen (2010), Durban (2011), Rio + 20 and Doha (2012)—aimed at achieving collective action on a global scale to reduce greenhouse gas emissions, the response has been anemic and the results elusive. There are many explanations for failure. Salient among them, powerful corporate entities ("Big Coal," "Big Oil")—which find anthropogenic climate change to be an "inconvenient truth" threatening their profits—use every means at their disposal, including intensive lobbying and bribing politicians with campaign contributions, to frustrate the enactment of policy changes that would result in reduced consumption of fossil fuels.[57] Because most of the governments of affluent counties are democratically constituted, climate-oriented tax and regulation policies require the support of the electorate. To sew seeds of doubt and confusion in the minds of the electorate, disinformation campaigns—aimed at undermining public confidence in the scientific consensus that global climate change is actually happening, that it will rapidly accelerate in magnitude and intensity, and that its causes are anthropogenic—are conducted. As a result, fewer than 40 percent of the American electorate believe that anthropogenic climate change is occurring.[58]

10.9 THE FAILURE OF RATIONAL INDIVIDUALISM: PROTRACTED SPATIAL SCALE

No small part of the explanation for the failure to achieve collective action on a global scale to reduce greenhouse gas emissions may be the particular way in which prominent ethicists have framed the moral task that global climate change sets upon us. Giving equal consideration to the equal interests of billions of spatially and temporally distant moral patients appears to be absurd to all but a few moral philosophers willing to embrace the implications, carried to their logical extremes, of a moral paradigm, constructed in a time when people lived in actual villages, not a global village.

Derek Parfit and Peter Singer are perhaps the most loyal and certainly among the most prominent exponents of consequentialist utilitarianism among contemporary ethicists. And both seem keenly aware that the radically different spatial scales of the worlds inhabited by eighteenth-century moral agents and patients and those of the twenty-first century present an existential challenge to *Homo ethicus*. Writes Parfit, "Until this century [the twentieth], most of mankind lived in small communities. What each did could affect only a few others. But conditions have now changed....We can have real though small effects on thousands or millions of people. When those effects are widely dispersed, they may be either trivial or imperceptible."[59] Similarly, Peter Singer observes that "For most of the eons [*sic*] of human existence, people living only short distances apart might as well, for all the difference they made to each other's lives, have been living in separate worlds....Over the past few centuries the isolation has dwindled, slowly at first, then with increasing rapidity. Now people are linked in ways previously unimaginable."[60]

It would seem to me that the most cogent response of a moral philosopher would be to abandon the ethical paradigm that made sense in bygone days when people lived in small communities and could affect only a few others. Surely these present conditions, now so radically changed, demand radical change in our moral philosophy. Surely we should rethink ethical theory from the ground up and come up with a way of thinking about ethics that makes sense in a global village of seven billion people (and counting), and when our present collective actions reverberate centuries and millennia into the future. But Parfit can only stick with the Smith-and-Jones individual agent-patient paradigm and complicate it with mind-boggling moral mathematics, which make rocket science look easy and straightforward by comparison. Singer opts for a simpler response to the protracted spatial scale of the most urgent moral problem of the present century, but at the cost of abandoning a pure form of Rational *Individualism* and embracing Proximate Ethical Holism. That is, he scales up moral agents to supra-individual entities—to nation-states. He effects this philosophically significant ontological move cryptically, however—that is, without specifically confessing that he is making it—simply by a rhetorical shift from referring to "people" severally and individually to whole hypostatized "nations." To quote but one typical example, Singer writes, "For the rich nations not to take a global viewpoint has long been seriously morally wrong."[61] This shift is of the greatest significance. Surely he owes us some explanation of how nations per se can take a viewpoint—any viewpoint at all—and can themselves be moral agents.

10.10 THE FAILURE OF RATIONAL INDIVIDUALISM: PROTRACTED TEMPORAL SCALE

The coup de grace for Rational Individualism is delivered by consideration of the moral obligations of the present generation to the uncountable generations that will follow, which Aldo Leopold aptly refers to as the "Unknown Future." Derek Parfit first sketched the "non-identity problem" regarding unborn future generations in 1976.[62] Parfit begins with a parable. Consider "a woman who intends to become pregnant as soon as possible." But

She learns that she has an illness which would give to any child she conceives now a certain handicap. If she waits for two months the illness will have passed, and she would then conceive a normal child.

Suppose she decides not to wait—suppose she knowingly conceives a handicapped rather than normal child. Has she thereby harmed her child, or affected him for the worse?...When her child grows up, could he truly say, "If my mother had waited, I would have been born later, and been a normal child?" No. If she had waited, he would not have been born at all; she would have had a different child....It seems then, that the handicapped child is not worse off than he would have been—for he *wouldn't* otherwise have been.[63]

Parfit then applies this parable to choices between public policies that impact future generations.

Suppose we have a choice between two social policies....The effects of one policy would, in the short term, be slightly better, but in the long term, be *much* worse for several later generations....[O]n the "Short-Term Policy," the quality of life would be slightly higher for (say) the next three generations, but be lower for the fourth generation, and be *much* lower for several later generations.[64]

However, "The particular members of the fourth and later generations, on the Short-Term Policy, would not have been born at all if instead we had pursued the Long-Term Policy."[65] The more austere Long-Term Policy would change the behavior of the members of the present generation and of the next three generations: couples might delay (or hasten) marriage and pregnancy; different men and women would meet, marry, and conceive different children. The demographic effects of the Long-Term Policy would multiply, over time, until, by the fourth generation, few if any of the same individuals would exist had the Short-Term Policy been pursued. "So," Parfit concludes, "if we pursue the Short-Term Policy there will never be anyone who is worse off than he would otherwise have been. The Short-Term Policy harms no one. Since it benefits certain people (those who now exist), it is the policy chosen by our principle"—the "person-affecting" principle, as Parfit calls it, the Rational Individualism paradigm as I call it.[66] Parfit's point is this: consider the *members* of the fourth and subsequent generations following us. We members of the present generation are acting in accordance with do-nothing (or, at best, do-little) climate-change policies. No *members* of the fourth generation, nor those of any generation thereafter could *truly* say that *they*, personally and individually, lived in a world made worse *for them* by the policies (or non-policies) pursued by the members of the present generation. For if we pursued effective policies to radically reduce our greenhouse emissions, *they, individually and particularly*, would not exist.

Though a digression from the argument of this section, I should note that perhaps more consistent with classical utilitarianism is not the person regarding principle, but the utility maximizing principle—which leads to what Parfit called the Repugnant

Conclusion.[67] The non-identity problem leads Parfit to reject the person-regarding principle in favor of the utility-maximizing principle. And the utility-maximizing principle leads to the repugnant conclusion, which was first noticed by Henry Sidgwick, who writes, "the point up to which, on utilitarian principles, the [human] population ought to be encouraged to increase, is not that at which the average happiness is greatest—as assumed often by political economists of the school of Malthus—but that at which the happiness reaches its maximum."[68] Suppose with the Malthusians that the Earth's resources for producing human (or sentient being) happiness is limited. For convenience, let us quantize happiness; that is, an individual's happiness increases or decreases in indivisible units, H. Let us stipulate that a point of fully diminished returns is reached at 100H, such that no matter how much additional consumption and desire gratification one gets, one's H quotient does not increase. And let us stipulate that the point at which the average happiness is greatest, under Earth's resource limits, would be reached with a population of N individuals x 50H. The Repugnant Conclusion is that global utility maximizes at N x 1H; and that thus no N x <1H state of affairs satisfies the utility-maximizing principle. If utilitarianism leads to the Repugnant Conclusion—and I trust that Sidgwick, Parfit, and the legions of twentieth-century neo-Scholastics who have puzzled over it are right that it does—then that is yet another reason to consign utilitarianism to the dust bin of obsolete moral philosophies.

The Parfit Paradox—as I like to call the non-identity problem, in honor of its inventor, our own Zeno—is not specifically about climate policy or even, necessarily, about environmental policy more generally. Parfit does not identify any particular kind of policy at all, for, as he observes, "Since there clearly could be such a difference between two policies, we need not specify details."[69] But certainly the demographic effects of the policy differences he sketches characterize climate policy options to a tee. The currently prevailing do-nothing (or, at best, do-little) climate policies make the present generation "better off"—or so most people seem to think. Nor does it make any *individuals* who will exist several generations out into the future worse off, unless it would be better for them not to exist at all than to cope with the unpleasant effects of a more energetic biosphere.

To drive home Parfit's point, his paradox can be retrofitted to the present, so that those of us presently existing can personally test the force of the argument. Anthropogenic global climate change was discovered in the mid-twentieth century, but began in the eighteenth century with the coal-powered Industrial Revolution. Suppose the climate-changing effects of fossil-fuel burning alarmed the public in 1788 instead of in 1988. And suppose that policies to industrialize more slowly, using non-carbon-based sources of energy, were decreed by autocratic eighteenth-century monarchs who didn't have to worry about getting reelected. In which case, few if any of the seven billion people alive today would be alive today. To wish that the industrial history of the world had unfolded differently would entail the wish that oneself and some seven billion other people in one's present cohort were not to have lived. It may have seemed extremely insensitive of me to even suggest (10.7) that John Nolt might choose to stop breathing in order not to be responsible for the death of two indeterminate future persons (by his reckoning). Is it any less insensitive of me to implicitly wish that I had never lived and, in addition to that, to implicitly wish that everyone living today had never lived?

I am not for a moment suggesting that either (1) the prevailing do-nothing (or, at best, do-little) climate policies are the most ethical policy choice or (2) that we have no moral obligations regarding the Unknown Future. What the Parfit Paradox shows, rather, is that Rational Individualism is a bankrupt moral philosophy for theorizing our moral obligations regarding distant future generations. Our moral obligations to the Unknown Future must be conceived collectively, holistically—they must be somehow conceived to be to those generations "as such" or "per se," not to the individual members of those generations. Ethical holism has a long history in environmental ethics, going back to Aldo Leopold and the land ethic: "In short, a land ethic changes the role of *Homo sapiens* from conqueror of the land community to plain member and citizen of it. It implies respect for his fellow members *and also respect for the community as such.*"[70] As Edward A. Page concludes, after carefully considering the Parfit Paradox, ethical holism is the only way that we can coherently conceive of moral obligations to distant future generations.[71]

10.11 THE ROLE OF "THEORETICAL INEPTITUDE" IN GARDINER'S PERFECT MORAL STORM

With his 2004 comprehensive review of climate-change ethics followed by his 2011 magisterial 489-page monograph, *A Perfect Moral Storm*, Stephen Gardiner has perhaps succeeded Dale Jamieson as the leading climate ethicist. Clinging to the prevailing moral paradigm, however, leads Gardiner to despair and to broadcast accusations of "moral corruption," making Gardiner a good candidate also to succeed the disgraced William Bennett as the National Scold.[72] Even so ready a finger-pointing scold as Peter Singer is appalled by Gardiner's analysis: "Given how bad the conduct of the [hypostatized supra-individual] United States (and, for that matter, Australia) is, Steve Gardiner's account of the ways in which the nature of the situation enhances the risk that these [reified] nations will continue to shirk their responsibilities [as holistic moral agents] suggests that the only rational response is extreme pessimism."[73] According to Gardiner, climate change involves a convergence of three features that combine to form "the perfect moral storm": (1) it is global in spatial extent with no corresponding global governance to enforce cooperation to mitigate it; (2) it is intergenerational and the interests of future generations have (a) weak representation in present policy decisions and (b) no power to retaliate against the present generation if it defects; and (3) we moral philosophers who attempt to confront it do so with "theoretical ineptitude."[74]

Thus Gardiner follows Jamieson in partially blaming the theoretical inadequacies of contemporary moral philosophy for inaction on the impending climate crisis. After initially suggesting a wholesale paradigm shift to virtue ethics, Jamieson winds up, less boldly, settling on a virtue-leavened utilitarianism as the best ethical theory for engaging the colossal moral problem of global climate change (as detailed in 10.3). Gardiner, for his part, criticizes Jamieson's embrace of utilitarianism, but not because Jamieson embraces utilitarianism. Rather, because Jamieson does so in so general a way that his virtue-leavened utilitarian theory is vacuous and probably incoherent, Gardiner insinuates. Gardiner professes to be "making only minimal ethical claims" himself and to be neither a "partisan" nor certainly a "zealot" in regard to any particular theory.[75] Rather, any adequate theory—be it utilitarian, Kantian, libertarian (the only ones Gardiner mentions by name)—should be detailed enough for us to test it decisively in regard to its capacity to clearly mandate and specify proactive climate-change policy. Gardiner does, however, seem biased toward developing a more detailed utilitarianism. Nor is there any evidence that he is himself willing to venture deeply into the metaphysics of morals and hold the prevailing individualistic moral ontology and rationalistic moral psychology up for critical scrutiny.

Gardiner does provide an example of an adequate ethical theory by way of analogy to feminist philosophy which

> has progressed beyond the stage of initial diagnosis to serious deep analysis and proposals for redemptive measures.... [I]n the case of the global environmental tragedy, and the perfect moral storm in particular, the relevant moral and political philosophy is much closer to the stage of initial diagnosis than this. We are still largely at the stage of saying, for example, that climate change is seriously unjust to the global poor, future generations, and nature, rather than at the stage of offering deep analysis of what exactly has gone wrong and what it would take to get it right.[76]

In the next and final chapter of this book, I go where neither Gardiner himself, nor, if he is right, any other climate ethicist—Dale Jamieson, Peter Singer, Henry Shue, prominent among them—has so far gone. I undertake a "deep analysis" of what has gone wrong in our *thinking* about the colossal moral problem of global climate change—what has gone wrong in *theorizing* climate change ethics—and what it would take to get it right.

11

The Earth Ethic: A Critical Account of Its Anthropocentric Foundations— Responsibility *to* Future Generations and *for* Global Human Civilization

We now live in the first century of the third millennium. We face unprecedented social and environmental challenges, the greatest of which is global climate change. To meet these challenges requires bold leadership guided by bold new thinking. But as the previous chapter reveals, those from whom we might expect the most systematic bold new thinking—moral and social philosophers—seem most reticent to provide it. After announcing the *collapse* of the prevailing über-paradigm in moral philosophy—Rational Individualism—in 1992, the only alternative that Dale Jamieson could think of to recommend in its stead was classical virtue ethics, originally theorized by Plato and Aristotle before the advent of the first millennium (as noted in 10.2). And by 2007, Jamieson had retreated and was recommending utilitarianism cross-pollinated with virtue ethics (as noted in 10.3)—the theoretical coherence of any such hybrid Stephen Gardiner sagely questions (as noted in 10.11). The conceptual foundations of the still prevailing über-paradigm in moral philosophy were formulated by Jeremy Bentham and Immanuel Kant in the late eighteenth century, when—as two of its leading contemporary exponents, Derek Parfit and Peter Singer, both candidly attest—the moral universe was much, much smaller than it presently is (as noted in 10.9). Meanwhile a vigorous science of ethics—pioneered by Charles Darwin in the late nineteenth century, updated in the late twentieth century under the rubric of sociobiology, and presently pursued with great vigor and great success under the rubric of evolutionary moral psychology—has matured. But the triumphant science of ethics has been largely ignored, if not contemptuously dismissed, by mainstream moral philosophers (as noted at the beginning of Chapter 5 and in 5.2).

It has not been ignored in the strain of environmental ethics that developed over the last quarter of the twentieth century in the tradition of the Aldo Leopold land ethic. Leopold's thinking was rooted in the same great tradition of scientific natural history as was Darwin's; and so it is not surprising that Leopold's thinking about ethics was more influenced by Darwin than by Darwin's philosophical contemporaries, most notably John Stuart Mill and Henry Sidgwick, both utilitarians. The spatial and temporal scales of the Leopold land ethic, however, are incommensurate with the spatial and temporal scales of global climate change. In the third section of "Some Fundamentals of Conservation in the Southwest," titled "Conservation as a Moral Issue," Leopold faintly sketched a fittingly scaled Earth ethic in a paper written in 1923 and eventually published in 1979 that, in effect, anticipated the Gaia hypothesis. In it, he hinted at various conceptual foundations for such an Earth ethic, among them an essentially Kantian non-anthropocentric respect for the Earth as a living being (with possibly a soul or consciousness of its own) and both individualistic and holistic versions of virtue ethics. He also insisted on concern for future generations. The theoretical grounding of non-anthropocentric respect for a living Earth was explored in Chapter 9. The theoretical grounding of the kind of personal, professional, and social virtue that Leopold adumbrates was explored in Chapter 10. There remains for this chapter an exploration of the theoretical grounding for intergenerational ethics.

Leopold declares that "the privilege of possessing the earth entails the responsibility of passing it on, the better for our use, not only to immediate posterity, but to the Unknown Future, the nature of which is not given us to know."[1] Leopold here draws an important distinction between two sets or classes of future generations—"immediate posterity" and the "Unknown Future." That distinction is of the greatest moment for intergenerational ethics. Leopold does not, however, clearly indicate exactly (or even roughly) how far into the future immediate posterity reaches, beyond which there lies the Unknown Future. In this chapter, I try to figure that out. I also try to show that, however the boundary between them is determined, responsibilities to immediate posterity and to unknown—and, more especially, indeterminate—future generations must rest on different, though not incompatible, theoretical foundations.

In this chapter, I also provide supporting theories for those future-oriented concerns. I also try to show that, at a deeper conceptual level, the Leopold land and the Leopold Earth ethics may be theoretically unified. I take up Stephen Gardiner's call for a "deep analysis" of what has gone wrong in our *thinking* about the colossal moral problem of global climate change—what has gone wrong in *theorizing* climate-change ethics—and what it would take to get it right. But, unlike what Gardiner seems to expect, I do so in a way that leaves the prevailing über-paradigm in moral philosophy where it belongs: in the history of philosophy. In so doing, I try to take moral philosophy at last not only into the new century but into the new millennium.

11.1 MORAL ONTOLOGY: RELATIONALLY DEFINED AND CONSTITUTED MORAL BEINGS

The atomic or monadic essence-accident moral ontology of Rational Individualism is arguably its most fundamental feature—so fundamental that the exponents of Rational Individualism take it for granted. Indeed, they rarely if ever even seem to notice it, and thus it escapes critical scrutiny. A monadic essence-accident moral ontology is, rather, a background assumption of Rational Individualism. So a deep analysis of what exactly has gone wrong with moral philosophy and what it would take to get it right should start with the ontological question: What is a moral being? A moral being is not a "ghost in a machine"; not an "ego enclosed in a bag of skin"; not a calculating, endeavor-driven, preference-satisfying "social atom."[2] As prefigured by Carol Gilligan (detailed and documented in 4.9), to be a moral being is to be a unique node in or nexus of a multi-dimensional web of relationships. One is the son or daughter of a particular mother and father; possibly the brother or sister of particular siblings, possibly the father or mother of particular children; a neighbor of particular persons, a fellow-worker or colleague of other particular persons; a citizen of a township, village, municipality, county/parish, state/province/prefecture, nation. All such relationships are superimposed on one's biological endowments and cultural conditioning and coalesce to make one the particular and unique person that one is. These relationships are what generate our moral duties and obligations and they do so in a nuanced way that makes "any principle of impartiality, universality, equality, or whatever," to quote Singer once more, appear to be ridiculously ham-handed. Remember (see 10.5), Singer claims that

> It makes no moral difference whether the person I can help is a neighbor's child ten yards from me or a Bengali, whose name I shall never know, ten thousand miles away....If we accept any principle of impartiality, universality, equality, or whatever, we cannot *discriminate* against someone merely because he is far away from us (or we are far away from him)....There would seem therefore to be no possible justification for *discriminating* on geographical grounds.[3]

By parity of reasoning, we must suppose, neither does it make any moral difference if I were to take the mother of the same unknown Bengali into my home and care for her in her old age instead of my own mother. To lodge and care for my own mother instead would be to *discriminate* against the aged Bengali mother merely because of an inessential accident of a morally entitled being—the lack of a familial relationship to me. And if we accept any principle of impartiality, universality, equality, or whatever, we cannot *discriminate* against someone merely because he or she is not familially related to us. So, we now confront a choice: we can either embrace the conclusion that there is no possible justification for *discriminating* on accidental familial grounds or we can reject the principle of impartiality, universality, equality, or whatever, among beings who equally possess the essential property of a moral patient. When the quaint essence-accident metaphysical foundation of that principle is exposed, it proves to be a wraith from the philosophical crypt scaring off our natural moral sentiments. Indeed, any Average American (or any Average Australian, for that matter) who randomly selected a stranger (say via a lottery with his mother in the pool) to bring into his home to care for in his or her old age and ignored the like needs of his own mother (who unfortunately was not selected by lot) would be regarded as a moral idiot. Why? Because familial relationships generate peculiar duties and obligations. And so do other palpable but less intimate relationships, such as neighborly relationships.

Contrary to Singer's declamation, it does make a moral difference whether the person I can help is a neighbor's child ten yards from me or a Bengali, whose name I shall never know, ten thousand miles away. Nor is the difference it makes a matter of spatial distance, but of the nature of the relationship—it's a *neighbor's* child, we're talking about here. Suppose the neighbor's child were spatially distant—ten thousand miles away, kidnapped by Somali pirates, and held hostage for ransom. And suppose my poor, distraught neighbor is scouring the neighborhood for donors in order to collect enough money to pay the ransom needed to free his child and perhaps to save his child from being murdered. And suppose I can help. Of course, I should contribute as much money as I can. Suppose, for the sake of comparison, that, simultaneously, I receive an appeal for exactly the same help via email from a Bengali, whose name I had never heard before and whose child has also been kidnapped and held for ransom by Indonesian pirates. First, I would check to see if I were a victim of attempted phishing, then I would consider that my means are limited, so I would ask myself to whom *should* I give—morally *ought* to give—all I can? To my neighbor or to the Bengali stranger? Am I guilty of *unjustified* discrimination if I give the money to my neighbor and ignore the Bengali stranger? I hardly think so! (For a similar critique see Stephen T. Asma, *Against Fairness*.[4])

Notice Singer's politically charged rhetoric. The US civil rights movement turned "discrimination" into an epithet—and surely it *is* wrong to discriminate against someone on the basis of race *in regard to civil rights*. We have many kinds of morally infused social relationships, in regard to some of which some forms of discrimination are morally reprehensible and, in regard to others, some forms of discrimination are morally laudatory (see 5.5). As noted in 5.6, our professional relationships require that we not discriminate in hiring on the basis of anything except professional qualifications. Indeed, it is an especial breach of professional ethics to discriminate on the basis of familial relationship in hiring—so much so that the associated violation of professional ethics has a name: nepotism (cognate with *nephew*). As also noted in 5.6, every citizen is equal before the "law of the land," however broadly "land" is determined—city, county, state, nation in the case of American citizens. But every suitor is not equal in a romantic relationship, where discrimination on the basis of gender, race, age, size, wit, and any number of other attributes is not only acceptable but required. It would be absurd of someone to claim that a woman to whom he (or she) was attracted was guilty of *unethical* discrimination on the basis of gender, affectional orientation, race, age, or size because she spurned his (or her) advances. Such spurning would indeed be "discrimination," but such discrimination would emphatically not be morally censurable. In such circumstances to be "discriminating" is a virtue not a vice. Furthermore, the person with whom a discriminating woman enters into a romantic relationship assumes certain mutual duties and obligations generated by that relationship, prominent among them fidelity. In short, discrimination is right in regard to some ethically charged relationships and wrong in regard to others.

Here it would be beside the point to try to catalogue all the variously weighted and nuanced duties and obligations imposed by all the relationships entered into by relationally defined and constituted moral beings. Because relationally defined and constituted moral beings are actually and richly individuated—as opposed to metaphysically and merely numerically individuated—no two moral beings have the same suite of relationships and thus no two moral beings have the same suite of duties and obligations imposed on them by those relationships. Even the *kinds* of relationships defining relationally defined and constituted moral beings vary widely. All moral beings have duties and obligations associated with familial relationships (at least during some substantial and significant part of their lives), but not all moral beings have duties and obligations associated with professional relationships. And among professional relationships, duties and obligations vary widely with profession. Physician-to-physician and physician-to-patient moral duties and obligations differ from lawyer-to-lawyer and lawyer-to-client duties and obligations, both of which also differ from professor-to-professor and professor-to-student duties and obligations. Thus any catalogue of variously weighted and nuanced duties and obligations imposed by all the relationships entered into by relationally defined and constituted moral beings would be impossible to draft, especially on a global scale, considering the cultural diversity of the world's peoples and the fact that social relationships are culturally embedded. The point, rather, is to remind ourselves of what it is to be a morally encumbered specimen of *Homo sapiens*, not a specimen of a morally overburdened *Homo ethicus* (characterized in 10.6). If *Homo economicus* may be fairly characterized as a "rational fool," *Homo ethicus* might just as fairly be characterized by the same epithet.[5] Only a rational fool would actually believe and act on the proposition that his duties and obligations to a neighbor and to an unknown person on the other side of the planet were indistinguishable. Only a rational fool would think that discriminating between a neighbor and an unknown person on the other side of the planet in matters of assistance was equivalent to racial discrimination in matters of civil rights, public accommodations, hiring, and housing. Both mythical species of *Homo* lack what has recently been called "emotional intelligence."[6]

11.2 MORAL ONTOLOGY: ETHICAL HOLISM

The relationally defined and constituted alternative to the essence-accident ontology of a moral being leads naturally to ethical holism. If a moral being is a unique node in or nexus of a multi-dimensional web of relationships, the web of relationships is ontologically prior to the nodes or nexuses therein. Or, if not ontologically prior, a web of relationships is no less real than the nodes or nexuses within it. If we conceive of moral beings as ghosts in machines, egos enclosed in bags of skin, or social atoms, then we must conceive of social wholes as mere aggregates of individuals—in which case, the status of such aggregates as moral beings is problematic. We are left to wonder, for example, how the United States per se can be personally responsible for anything? If, instead, one adopts a relational ontology, to be an Average American, implies that one's very identity as a person is determined by one's native landscape, ecosystem, and biotic community; by one's mother tongue; by one's formal and informal education, customs, historical legacy, citizenship, and so on.

Reflecting on what it is to be an Average American, one begins to trace longer strands of the relationships that constitute one's being first into the wider cognitive and material civilization that has determined one's most intimate self, right down to one's Cartesian reflections on one's very existence and Sartrean reflections on personal authenticity. To think is to be, perhaps, but the thought that to think is to be is not one's own thought but a legacy of the cognitive culture that one inhales as if it were an ambient cognitive ether. To suppose that existence precedes essence is to affirm an idea—the concept, essence—that is scarcely intelligible in isolation from the long history of Western thought going back to Aristotle.

And the thought of the ambient cognitive ether that one continuously breathes leads one to think of the ambient physical atmosphere, inhaled many times a minute, uniting one's bio-physical being with the bio-physical being of the Earth and its myriads of other denizens. When one considers these and all the other relationships that define and constitute one's physical and psychological being as an Average American, there is nothing of oneself left over. There is no core self. Yes, one is a real being and, indeed, a moral being, but the wholes in which one's being is embedded are even more real. The Earth as a whole, the biomes, the landscapes, the biotic communities within it; the cultures, the languages, the civilizations, the nation-states and their political subdivisions—they too are all moral beings. Certainly most such entities are moral patients—proper objects of concern and care—and some are proper moral agents.

Furthermore, our vaunted individuality disappears into a swarm of micro-ecosystemic relationships when looking inward, literally, as well as when looking outward. Each one of one's own billions of cells is inhabited by other organelles called mitochondria, with their own deoxyribonucleic acid (DNA) and enclosing membranes—and thus their own organismic identities and phylogenies. They are symbionts—more precisely mutualists, not parasites—that supply our cells with adenosine triphosphate, the source of our cellular energy; and they also provide many other functional biochemical services.[7] The endogenous human gut microbial community is composed of a bewildering biodiversity of bacteria—up to 250 known phylotypes, yet unresolved into narrower Linnaean taxa; and the sheer number of the bacteria residing in the roughly ten-meter-long human intestine exceeds the number of human cells in the whole human organism by an order of magnitude.[8] In a healthy human micro-ecosystem—for that is what we are when we are in fact healthy—many of the resident intestinal microbes are mutualists aiding in the digestion of food, while others are commensals, and still others parasites. Healthy human skin is colonized by bacteria belonging to nineteen different phyla, 205 genera, and some 1,000 species.[9] And the whole microbial community is constantly repelling invasive pathogens.[10] Nearly forty years ago, cell biologist Lewis Thomas presciently observed that all "[t]his is, when you think about it, really amazing. The whole dear notion of one's own Self—marvelous old free-willed, free-enterprising, autonomous, independent, isolated island of a Self—is a myth."[11]

In 2008, the US National Institutes of Health (NIH) launched the Human Microbiome Project to study in depth the organisms that inhabit the human body, including both classification (taxonomy) and genetic sequencing on five bodily sites vitally interacting with the environment: mouth, alimentary tract, nasal/lung tract, urinary/reproductive tract, and skin.[12] As Thomas noted, "A good case can be made for our nonexistence as entities. We are not made up, as we always supposed, of successively enriched packets of our own parts. We are shared, rented, occupied."[13]

There is an irony in this development: one hundred years before, F. E. Clements (as noted and documented in the Introduction and in 1.16 and 3.10) represented what a quarter century later came to be called ecosystems as super-organisms.

Now we recognize that organisms, including the human organism, are actually super-ecosystems. They exhibit all the characteristics that Clements and later Odum (discussed and documented in 3.12) mistakenly attributed to ecosystems in the conventional sense of the term. These super-ecosystems that we are are homeostatic and self-regulating, maintaining a constant internal body temperature, a relatively narrow blood-pressure gradient, a constant abundance and balance of electrolytes in the blood, a constant blood pH and salinity, a constant resting heart rate that elevates with exercise within a relatively narrow gradient, and so on.[14] These super-ecosystems, as noted in the previous paragraph, resist and repel invasive organisms that attempt to establish populations in them (us). They (we) are spatially well defined with clear boundaries. They (we) develop in a determinate and predictable way. While most species of super-ecosystems do not attempt to control their environments, we do, but all resist the tendency of inert matter toward entropic equilibrium with their environments. These super-ecosystems exhibit low entropy and high information content.

The consequences for moral ontology of this twenty-first-century ecological representation of the nature of the human being have been expressed by Scott F. Gilbert, Jan Sapp, and Alfred I. Tauber in a paper published in the *Quarterly Review of Biology*; its title, which alludes to Bruno Latour's provocative book, *We Have Never Been Modern*, is "A Symbiotic View of Life: We Have Never Been Individuals":

New technologies...continue to transform our conceptions of the planet's biosphere. They have not only revealed a microbial world of much deeper diversity than previously imagined, but also a world of complex and intermingled *relationships*—not only among microbes, but also between microscopic and macroscopic life. These discoveries have profoundly challenged the generally accepted view of "individuals." Symbiosis is becoming a core principle of contemporary biology, and it is replacing an essentialist conception of "individuality" with a conception congruent with the larger systems approach now pushing the life sciences in different directions. These findings lead us into directions that transcend the self/non-self, subject/object dichotomies that have characterized Western thought....Animals cannot be considered individuals by anatomical or physiological criteria because a diversity of symbionts are both present and functional in completing metabolic pathways and serving other physiological functions. Similarly these new studies have shown that animal development is incomplete without symbionts. Symbionts also constitute a second mode of genetic inheritance, providing selectable genetic variation for natural selection. The immune system develops, in part, in dialogue with symbionts and thereby functions as a mechanism for integrating microbes into the animal-cell community.[15]

Gilbert et al. suggest replacing the concept of a human individual with the concept of a human "holobiont."[16] This is an apt characterization capturing both the holism of our internal relationality in its outward modality, both socio-culturally and biospherically, and in its inward modality, both with our microbial symbionts and would-be pathogens.

11.3 MORAL PSYCHOLOGY: THE MORAL SENTIMENTS

So much for the deconstruction of the individual aspect of Rational Individualism; now on to the deconstruction of the rational aspect. Ethical holism leads naturally to a Humean moral psychology, in which ethical actions are motivated not directly by reason but by the moral sentiments. There is no common moral essence shared by one's holobionic self, one's native landscape, ecosystem, and biotic community; one's inherited culture and civilization, one's nation-state and its political subdivisions. Thus one cannot be found guilty of self-contradiction if one fails to morally consider any of these very real entities while demanding moral consideration for oneself from them. Most such wholes have no interests to consider, although they are of supreme value. They are instrumentally valuable as the defining and constitutive web of relationships that make oneself the moral being that one is. And they are intrinsically valuable. As a moral being, one is, oneself, relatively ephemeral. But a truly moral being would act to sustain one's native landscape, ecosystem, and biotic community; one's inherited culture and civilization; one's nation-state and its political subdivisions after one's own personal life is over. For they are what make one the person one is. They are as constitutive of oneself as are one's microbial symbionts. If there is no soul to live on after bodily death, the extended self, shared by many others, lives on. So one *can* care about the future of one's native landscape, ecosystem, and biotic community; one's inherited culture and civilization; one's nation-state and its political subdivisions after one's own personal life is over. Many people *do* care about all such things. And everyone *should* care about them lest one be judged by oneself as well as by others to be an emotionally deficient human being.

David Hume argued that reason alone can never motivate specimens of *Homo sapiens* to act. As the very name indicates, *emotions* (e-motions) motivate. They are what set self-moving beings in motion. And, Hume would add, *only* emotions (inclusive of feelings, sentiments, passions, and desires) motivate. Immanuel Kant argued, to the contrary, that reason—in its most basic form, the law of non-contradiction—could also motivate *Homo sapiens* to act. The human will, he thought, stands at the "crossroads," faced with the choice of succumbing to the "material" tug of the irrational "inclinations" (emotions, feelings, sentiments, passions, and desires) or acceding to the "formal principle" of reason (the law of non-contradiction).[17] A will free of any association with material inclinations—in short, a "divine will" or "holy will"—would act "completely [in] accord with reason," according to Kant.[18] Toward the end of the *Grounding for the Metaphysics of Morals*, however, Kant ultimately concedes that Hume is right after all: there must be "an interest which man can take in moral laws"; otherwise he would never act upon them.[19] Indeed, just as Hume himself would insist, so also does Kant: "In order to will what reason alone prescribes as an *ought* for sensuously affected rational beings, there certainly must be a power of reason to infuse a *feeling* of pleasure or satisfaction in the fulfillment of duty."[20] There is a lively debate in contemporary neo-Scholastic philosophy concerning whether reason alone can be a motive to action as Kant is thought to have believed by those who did not read the *Grounding* all the way through to the end.[21] I shall not enter it.

So even Kant, the most stalwart paragon of ethical rationalism concedes that reason by itself cannot motivate moral beings to act morally. In sharp contrast to *Homo ethicus*, *Homo sapiens* can only be motivated by affective interests—interest in the interests of others as well as self-interest—and by feelings of pleasure and satisfaction in the fulfillment of duties and in the exercise of virtues. For *Homo sapiens*, as just noted (11.1), a suite of variously weighted and nuanced duties are generated by the relationships that constitute a human being. And human beings are moved to fulfill those duties not only by an affective interest associated merely with formal self-consistency and by feelings of pleasure and satisfaction in the fulfillment of those duties, but by the emotions, feelings, sentiments, and passions associated with the relationships that define and constitute a moral being.

Why care for one's aged mother and not some aged stranger? Why send one's son or daughter to college and not some other equally deserving and more needy young man or woman? Because we have filial duties and obligations *and* because we love our parents and children. Why serve one's country? Dutifully, because one's country has served oneself *and* because one has patriotic feelings for one's country. And, indeed, why contribute to Oxfam and other globally oriented charities? Not because of any rationally dictated duty to all other equally qualified moral patients severally, but because one is a dutiful citizen of the worldwide cosmopolis and a denizen of the global village *and* one has beneficent feelings for one's fellow citizens and denizens.

11.4 RESPONSIBILITY TO IMMEDIATE POSTERITY

The Parfit Paradox (10.10) applies only to unborn future generations, to the "Unknown Future" in Leopold's terms. Some members of future generations are presently existing and thus determinate persons. How many future generations coexist with oneself is relative to one's age and how far into the future immediate posterity extends is relative to the moral being who carefully considers them. I am around seventy years old; my son is around forty-five years old; and his son is around twenty years old. If we stipulate that a generation consists of the interval between the birth of a child and that child's child, a new generation comes along every twenty-five years for the Average American, every twenty years or even every fifteen years depending on the fertility demographics of various cultures and societies.[22] However much the interval between generations is relative to the fertility demographics of various cultures and societies, what counts as a new generation is relative to individual persons in societies. Average Americans are born every year and so the twenty-five-, and/or fifty-, and/or seventy-five-year generational intervals roll around every year for a sizable fraction of the total American population. Relative to me, two future generations are my contemporaries and I have a good chance of sharing the world with a yet a third generation beyond my own—that of my great-grandchildren, if my grandson reproduces like an Average American.

I love my son and my grandson. I care deeply about them and I have and I will continue to make sacrifices in terms of my own comfort, time, and money for their sakes—educating them, traveling to visit them, helping them to buy houses and other big-ticket items. A very big part of caring for them is caring what kind of world they will have to live in as they progress through their lifetimes. By the mid-twenty-first century, I will almost certainly be dead, but my son will probably be alive at about age seventy-five and my grandson will almost surely be alive at age fifty, and his sons or daughters, my great-grandchildren, whom I expect to live to see born, will be about twenty-five, possibly with sons or daughters of their own. By the end of the twenty-first century, my great-grandchildren may well still be living. What kind of world will they be living in? I have a deeply personal stake in the answer to that question. And no matter what I can bequeath to them as a relatively affluent member of an affluent nation-state, no personal resources will insulate them from all or even most of the dire effects of a more energetic biosphere. I can bequeath to them and to them alone a trust fund, but I cannot bequeath to them and to them alone a livable and pleasant climate. But surely I am not alone in caring deeply for my children, grandchildren, and great-grandchildren. So do most other Average Americans and, for that matter of course, so do most other Average Global Villagers—and that irrespective of affluence or poverty, religious affiliation, political ideology, race, ethnic identity, nationality and all the other things that divide us and frustrate cooperative collection action. If moral philosophers put the ethical case for responsibility to future generations in terms of the moral sentiments—and not in terms of game-theoretical enlightened self-interest or rational coercion, guilt-tripping, and accusations of moral corruption—cooperative collective action on internationally coordinated climate policy might just be possible.

11.5 RESPONSIBILITY TO THE UNKNOWN FUTURE EQUALS RESPONSIBILITY FOR GLOBAL HUMAN CIVILIZATION

After about a century, my personal stake in the state of the world begins to fade and its demographic composition is presently indeterminate. No one who now exists and for whom I do care will exist very far into the twenty-second century. And, as Derek Parfit has demonstrated (see 10.10 for the full demonstration), by doing nothing now to mitigate global climate change we can make no individuals who will exist in the distant future worse off than they would be had we pursued an aggressive policy of climate mitigation unless they determine that it would have been better not to exist at all. That's because the climate policy we presently implement (or do not implement) will determine who exists in the distant future. Therefore, any concern that we can have for the Unknown Future must have, as the object of care, some supra-individual entity. In short, ethical concern for the Unknown Future must necessarily be holistic.

What supra-individual entity is threatened by climate change? I believe that there are two principal ones.

First, the Earth itself, the planet, the biosphere, Gaia—all various terms for the same being—is in no mortal danger (as noted in 10.1). What does appear to be threatened by global climate change is the Holocene climate and the biota that is adapted to it. Global climate change threatens to exacerbate the mass extinction event already in progress and to alter familiar ecosystems and biotic communities. The more-than-human world that we know and love is at risk of being so radically changed as to be altered beyond recognition. We need look no further than the Leopold land ethic to find the moral wherewithal for motivating concern for preserving the Holocene climate and thus the biota that is adapted to it—the manifest (in the nautical sense of the word) of our "fellow voyagers in the odyssey of evolution."

Second, the human species, *Homo sapiens*, is probably not at risk of extinction. Even if the world population in the twenty-second century is decimated by climate-exacerbated disease epidemics, drought-and-heat-related crop failure and famine, resource wars, and other disasters, small bands of *Homo sapiens* will probably survive. What is at serious risk of extinction is not the human species, but human civilization. Severe global climate change may be followed by an impoverished biota and dysfunctional ecosystems and a new and irreversible Dark Age, a new and permanent state of barbarism. Currently failed states—the Somalias, the Libyas, the Malis, the Afghanistans—provide a window into what the socio-cultural-political-economic reality of the whole world might well be by 2150. Think of the magnificent achievements of global human civilization—its architecture, its literature, its graphic arts and music, its sciences, its technology, its philosophy. One can—and should—care about all these things per se, as such. Personally, I am motivated to head off the ruin and loss of all that the term *civilization* connotes. I am motivated to try to help sustain global human civilization into the Unknown Future. I would hope that any reflective moral being would share my concern and motivation.

But for how long into the Unknown Future can we care about global human civilization or anything else? All things, good and bad, will eventually come to an end. All things, bad as well as good, pass. Ethics is scale sensitive. There is a temporal limit to care. Can one care that in about 7.5 billion years the sun will become a red giant and incinerate the Earth?[23] Hardly. Long before that happens geomorphological changes may render the Earth inhospitable to life.[24] Can one care about that? Perhaps, but there is no conceivable moral response that one can have to such a distant prospect. Can one really care that in about a million years the human species will, one way or another, become extinct?—evolved into another species, done in by an asteroid strike, incinerated by a nuclear holocaust, whatever. The past and potential future duration of the global human civilization is in the goldilocks interval of the temporal reach of the moral sentiments. It is also commensurate with the temporal scale of global climate change.

At the very beginning of "The Land Ethic," Aldo Leopold invokes the past duration of Western civilization in the opening vignette from Homer's *Odyssey*: "During the three-thousand years which have since elapsed" after "god-like Odysseus returned from the wars in Troy."[25] The *Iliad* and the *Odyssey* are the oldest extant literature in the Western canon. The Greeks themselves regarded their civilization to be young in comparison with that of the Egyptians. And we know that the civilizations to the east of the Mediterranean Basin were older still. So to put a round number on it, global human civilization has been a continuously going concern for about five thousand years. Thus we can well imagine that it might continue to be a going concern for about another five thousand years. And that about reaches the limit, by my own register anyway, of the human capacity to care, the limit of the moral sentiments. We can also calibrate the most persistent consequences of past, present, and near-term future emissions of greenhouse gases in terms of millennia—up to about five thousand years out.

Therefore, global human civilization is the perfect candidate for the supra-individual anthropocentric object of concern for the Unknown Future. It is fragile and at grave risk of extinction from the combined environmental and social disruptions of climate change. It is something about which we presently care and care deeply for its own sake—at least so it seems to me, if my own feelings are at all representative. The temporal scale of its existence, calibrated in millennia, spans what appears to me to be the farthest temporal reach of the moral sentiments. And the temporal scale of its potential future existence coincides with the temporal scale of global climate change.[26]

11.6 SUMMARY AND CONCLUSION

The conceptual foundations of the land ethic are traceable first to Charles Darwin's account of the origin and evolution of ethics in *The Descent of Man*. Darwin in turn drew heavily on the moral philosophy of David Hume, who located ethics in human nature and especially in a class of feelings called the moral sentiments. Darwin indicates how those sentiments might have evolved, by means of descent with modification and natural selection, from primitive filial affections bonding mammalian parents and offspring into "family societies" (as Hume tellingly calls them) and how those feelings might have spread to other more distant blood relatives bonding them all into an extended-family society. And as Hume notes, such family societies must have rudimentary ethics to keep them whole and intact. Darwin speculates that such kinship groups eventually merged to form larger, less-closely related societies because, being larger and more complex, they were advantaged in competition with smaller, simpler societies. And Darwin observes that such group selection drove the selection of morally better-endowed individual members of society—because the subordination of individual advantage to the coordinated function of the social whole, as every team-sport coach well knows, confers a competitive advantage on the group. And if a group thrives and flourishes so, on average, will its several members. At each step in the evolution of larger, more complex societies, the moral sentiments were thus broadcast ever more widely and personal morality became ever more refined.

The larger and more complex societies, however, did not replace the smaller, simpler societies of an earlier stage of social evolution; rather the former were layered over the latter and the latter were incorporated into the former. The nuclear- and extended-family societies and the special moral sentiments and the reciprocal duties and obligations that hold them together remained robust, as did those of the larger societies following them in the order of social evolution. Today, we exist in a hierarchically scaled social order including the family society at its core and the global village at its periphery. Each level of the social hierarchy is attended by its own peculiar kind of moral sentiment—everything from filial affections to patriotism to general beneficence. And each level generates its own peculiar duties and obligations—from family duties obliging us to love and educate the young and care for the old to serving our countries to respect for universal human rights.

Onto this Humean-Darwinian account of ethics, Aldo Leopold layered the land ethic, pointing out that we are no less members of a land or biotic community than we are members of various hierarchically ordered human communities. And no less than are our various human community memberships, so also our membership in the biotic community is attended by peculiar moral sentiments—which Leopold cultivates in his readers throughout the whole of *A Sand County Almanac*. And that membership generates its own peculiar duties and obligations, which are, however, very different from those of our human social ethics—different to the same extent that the multi-species biotic community and its economy is different from all the hierarchically ordered single-species societies of which we are members.

Most of our daily moral quandaries do not involve a choice between doing the right thing or doing the wrong; rather, most involve a choice between fulfilling duties generated by membership in one social order and fulfilling those generated by membership in another—as when, for example, a working parent must choose between staying home and nursing a child sick with a cold and attending a critical meeting at the office.

These Humean-Darwinian foundations of the land ethic are increasingly validated by contemporary evolutionary moral psychology and neurobiological studies of ethics—that is, by the contemporary science of ethics. The land ethic, however, is spatially scaled to local and regional more-than-human societies—biotic communities and ecosystems. It is designed to address potential threats—from otherwise ethically unconstrained human actions—to the integrity, stability, and beauty of those local and regional more-than-human societies. It is temporally scaled to be proportionate to the dynamics internal to biotic communities and ecosystems—especially to ecological succession and, more recently, to disturbance regimes—which are calibrated in decades. The spatial scale of global climate change is planetary and its temporal scale is calibrated in centuries and millennia. The land ethic is, therefore, a poor fit with the most urgent and dire environmental concern of our time. To have some chance of confronting global climate change successfully, we need to be equipped with an environmental ethic that is commensurate with its spatio-temporal scale.

Fortunately, Leopold also very faintly sketched an Earth ethic in a 1923 essay that he never succeeded in publishing during his own lifetime. In it he portrays the Earth as itself a living being with, possibly, a soul or consciousness. The living Earth, he thought, should command our respect, if not affection. In that essay, Leopold anticipates the Gaia hypothesis, which made its popular debut in a book by James Lovelock the same year, 1979, in which Leopold's Earth-ethic essay was finally published. Following up on Leopold's hints, a theoretically coherent non-anthropocentric Earth ehic might be constructed on philosophical foundations originating with Kant not Hume. I do not wish to foreclose the appeal to anyone else of a Kantian non-anthropocentric Earth ethic, but I myself am convinced that the leap from the spatial and temporal scales of biotic communities and the attendant land ethic to the spatial and temporal scales of the whole Earth is a leap too far—a leap beyond both the spatial and temporal limits of ethics and the spatial and temporal scales of anthropogenic global climate change. The Earth is too big and, more especially, too long-lived for us humans to be able to adversely affect it. A non-anthropocentric deontological Earth ethic is, in my opinion, no more needed than a non-anthropocentric deontological Jupiter ethic.

But it is not at all beyond our collective capacity to radically change the conditions for life on Earth to which we humans and our fellow-voyagers in the odyssey of evolution are precisely and exquisitely adapted. Global climate change will adversely affect existing biotic communities and ecosystems and it threatens to accelerate the already wildly abnormal rate of species extinction. Therefore, we still need the land ethic— now more than ever. We also, I think, need an *anthropocentric* Earth ethic, because now global climate change poses an existential threat probably not to the human species, but almost certainly to human civilization. We cannot ground an effective anthropocentric Earth ethic on Rational Individualism (on either its Kantian or utilitarian expressions) because of its radically individualistic moral ontology and a purely rational principle of "impartiality, universality, equality, or whatever." Such a principle cannot reach out and touch the presently indeterminate individual members of Unknown Future generations and its inhuman demands overwhelm our capacity for a genuine and effective moral response. Rational Individualism itself is what has created a perfect moral storm and produced moral corruption.

Leopold suggested two theoretical foundations for an anthropocentric Earth ethic: personal, professional, and societal virtue ("self-respect") and two distinct kinds of responsibility to future generations—to immediate posterity and to the Unknown Future. Fortunately, the same—now scientifically well confirmed—Humean and Darwinian foundations grounding the land ethic can also perfectly ground all three versions of an anthropocentric Earth ethic—(1) personal, professional, and societal virtue; (2) responsibility to immediate posterity; and (3) responsibility to unknown (and indeterminate) future generations.

Anyone familiar with Hume's writings on ethics well knows that he is quite at home speaking the language of virtue. Michael Slote, notably, argues (rather awkwardly but not ineffectively) that "Moral sentimentalism offers virtue ethics some splendid opportunities it has previously to a large extent neglected," among them embracing and theoretically supporting "the so-called feminine ethic of caring" which is "at least best understood or best defended as a form of agent-based virtue ethics."[27] Slote goes on to say that

> [P]artiality toward near and dear is quite compatible with substantial concern for all human beings, whether known to one or not, and...the morality of caring can and should take in a concern not just for those one intimately knows or may come to know, but for those who one cannot ever really become

acquainted with and whom one may learn about only as members of some group or nation one has heard of.[28]

While Slote does not reach beyond "agent-based" virtue ethics—that is, beyond personal virtue to the more holistic professional and societal virtue ethics that Leopold hints at—he does tie virtue ethics to the Humean (if not the Darwinian) roots of the land ethic. We can care and care passionately about the climatic conditions of the world in which immediate posterity at large will live. That is because our own kith and kin (or "near and dear" in Slote's terms), for whom we care passionately and partially—appropriately so—are members of that cohort. And each and every one of the billions of members of that cohort will suffer—albeit some more and others less—the full brunt of global climate change. We cannot care at all about the *individual* members of Unknown Future generations because they are presently indeterminate. Continue with business as usual and those born in the future cannot lament our inaction and indifference unless they also lament their very existence. For had we vigorously implemented effective climate-change mitigation policies those individuals would not in fact exist. We cannot benefit individuals who would not exist because they would not exist precisely because of our benign intentions toward them. And we cannot have harmed the individuals who only will exist because we were inconsiderate of their welfare. We can, however—and many of us actually do—care for Unknown Future generations holistically or collectively.

As to immediate posterity, for whom we can care individually and do care passionately for some select few (our kith and kin, our near and dear), their lives are not of a duration equal to that of the climatic effects of our present actions. But how can we cash out care for something so abstract as indeterminate distant future generations considered holistically or collectively? I suggest a palpable surrogate for that abstraction: there is something palpable, precious and fragile—global civilization—that presently exists; something we can care about and many of us do care about passionately. It can serve as a surrogate for Unknown Future generations because it is scaled proportionately to the effects of our present actions on the global climate—a fortuitous coincidence. Human civilization has endured and evolved for five thousand years. It may well endure and evolve for another five thousand—but only if we can preserve some semblance of the Holocene climate that permitted it to emerge, enabled it to endure, and afforded ideal conditions for its evolution.

Appendix

Some Fundamentals of Conservation in the Southwest[1]

Aldo Leopold

Introduction

The future development of the Southwest must depend largely on the following resources and advantages:

Minerals: chiefly copper and coal.
Organic: farms, ranges, forests, waters and water powers.
Climatic: chiefly health and winter resort possibilities.
Historic: archaeological and historical interest.
Geographic: on route to California and Mexico.

This discussion is confined to the two first named. While the last three are of great value, the Southwest should hardly be satisfied to build its future upon them. They are what might be termed unearned advantages.

Excluding these, it is apparent that all of the remaining economic resources are of such a nature that their permanent usefulness is affected more or less by that idea or method of development broadly called conservation. It is the purpose of this paper to discuss the extent to which this is true, and the extent to which unskillful or nonconservative methods of exploitation threaten to limit or destroy their permanent usefulness.

A brief statement of some of the salient facts about each of these resources is first necessary as a background:

Minerals. Of six of the leading Arizona copper mines, the average life in sight is twenty-two years. This is a short life. Undoubtedly, our mineral wealth will be expanded from time to time by new processes, better transportation, discovery of additional ore bodies, demand for rare minerals, exploitation of gross minerals such as sulphur and salt, and possible discovery of oil. But the fact remains that, with the exception of coal, the mineral wealth of the Southwest, from the standpoint of an economic foundation for society, is exhaustible. Our coal will probably always be handicapped by long hauls and absence of water transport.

Farms & waters must be considered together. The late drouth ought to have sufficiently redemonstrated that generally speaking, dry farming, as a sole dependence for a livelihood, is a broken reed.[2] The outstanding fact that we can never change is that we have roughly twenty million acres of water-producing or mountain area and fifty million acres of area waiting for water. Most of the latter is tillable. But, it takes say four feet of water per year to till it, whereas less than two feet falls on the mountains, of which only a very small percent runs off in streams in usable form. Therefore, if we impounded all the non-flood runoff and had no evaporation (both

303

impossibilities), we should still have scores of times more land than water to till it. This is partially offset by underground storage of part of the water which does not run off, but, nevertheless, we still have an overwhelming shortage of water as compared with land. Therefore, the term *irrigable land* actually represents a combination of natural resources which is really very rare and accordingly vital to our future. By artificially impounding water we are steadily adding to our irrigated area, but these gains are being offset by erosion losses in the smaller valleys, where water was easily available simply through diversion. Broadly speaking, no net gain is resulting. We are losing the easily irrigable land and "replacing" it by land reclaimed at great expense. The significant fact that is not understood is that this "replacement" is no replacement at all, but rather slicing at one end of our loaf while the other end sloughs away in waste. Some day the slicing and sloughing will meet. Then we shall realize that we needed the whole loaf.

Water powers. Erosion and silting are likewise deteriorating our water powers, though the silting of a reservoir is not so destructive to its power possibilities as to its use for irrigation. Also, the water powers not dependent upon storage are not yet badly damaged. It is obvious, however, that anything which damages the regularity of stream flow and interferes with storage of waters is depreciating the value of our power resources.

Forests. While _____ percent of our area bears trees, only _____ of this bears saw timber, of which the present stand is thirty-five billion feet. Most of this sawtimber land is in the national forests. The management plans of the Forest Service indicate that if handled under proper methods these sawtimber lands will sustain indefinitely a cut of 300 million feet per year. A larger cut will be possible temporarily because of the excess proportion of mature stands.

New Mexico and Arizona now consume about 450 million feet per year. The salient fact about our forests, therefore, is this: that in the long run the timber yield will only partly suffice to sustain our own agriculture, cities, and mines. Its conservation for these purposes is, of course, absolutely essential in order that we may not have to depend on expensive importations. But, even with good forestry, the Southwest cannot figure on timber export as a future source of wealth.

Ranges. Arizona and New Mexico are carrying about three million sheep and two million cattle. About one-fourth of these are on the national forests. It would not mean anything to try to state in figures the original carrying capacity of the two states because much of the virgin range was without water. Great progress has been made in developing water, but a wholesale deterioration in both the quality and quantity of forage has also taken place. On certain areas of national forests and privately owned range this deterioration has been checked and the productiveness of the forage partially restored through range improvements and conservative methods of handling stock. The remainder continues to deteriorate under the system of competitive destruction inherited from frontier days but now perpetuated by the archaic land policy of the government and some of the several states. It is safe to state that the condition of our range forage has depreciated 50 percent and is still going down-hill.

This overgrazing of our ranges is chiefly responsible for the erosion which is tearing out our smaller valleys and dumping them into the reservoirs on which our larger valleys are dependent. The significant element in this situation is that cessation of overgrazing will usually not check this erosion.

Summary. All of our organic resources are in a rundown condition. Under existing methods of management our forests may be expected to improve, but our total possible farm areas are dwindling and our waters and ranges are still deteriorating. In the case of our ranges, deterioration could be easily checked by conservative handling, and the original productiveness regained and restored. But the deterioration of our fundamental resources—land and water—is in the nature of permanent destruction, and the process is cumulative and gaining momentum every year.

Erosion and Aridity

The task of checking the ravages of erosion and restoring our organic resources to a productive condition is so intricate and difficult a problem that we must know something about causes before we can well consider remedies.

Is our climate changing? The very first thing to know about causes is whether we are dealing with an "act of God," or merely with the consequences of unwise use by man. If this collapse of stable equilibrium in our soil and its cover is being caused or aggravated by a change in climate, the possible beneficial results of conservation might be very limited. On the other hand, if there is no change of climate going on, the possible results of conservation are limited only by the technical skill which we can train upon the problem and the public backing available to get it applied.

In discussing climatic changes, a clear differentiation between the geological and historical viewpoints is essential. The status of our climate from the geological viewpoint has nothing to do with the question in hand. Any such changes that may be taking place would be too slow to have any bearing on human problems.

Historically speaking, our climate has recently been checked back with considerable accuracy to 1390 A.D. through study of the growth rings of yellow pine in Arizona, and to 1220 B.C. through the growth rings of sequoia in California. These studies, conducted by Douglas and Huntington, demonstrate convincingly that there has been no great increase or decrease in aridity of the Southwest during the last 3,000 years.[3]

Yellow pines recently excavated at Flagstaff show very large growth rings, indicating a wetter climate during some recent geological epoch, but, as previously stated, that has a merely academic bearing on our problem.

Ancient Indian ditches and ruins in localities now apparently too dry for either irrigation or dry farming would seem to contradict the conclusion derived from tree rings, but little is known of the age of these relics or the habits of the people who left them. Archaeologists predict that we may soon know more about the age of the cliff culture through possible discoveries connecting it with the now accurately determined chronology of the Maya culture in Central America.[4]

Long straight cedar timbers found in some Southwestern ruins likewise might be taken to indicate a process of dessication, but other and unknown factors are involved, such as the effect of fire on our forests and the distances from which the timbers were transported.[5]

Changes in the distribution of forest types likewise might be interpreted to throw a little light on the recent tendency of our climate. In the brush forests of southern Arizona there is strong evidence of an uphill recession, such as would accompany dessication, former woodland now being occupied by brush species and former yellow pine by woodland and brush. At the same time, in the region of the Prescott and Tusayan Forests, there is an indisputable encroachment of juniper downward into former open parks. A similar encroachment of yellow pine is taking place in the Sitgreaves and Apache Forests. Most of these changes, however, can be accounted for through purely local causes such as fire and grazing. This fact, and the fact that any attempt at a climatic theory of causation would result in contradictory conclusions, makes it seem logical to regard these phenomena either as shedding no light on the question of climate, or as possibly somewhat substantiating the conclusion derived from tree rings.

In general, there thus far appears to be no clear evidence of dessication during any recent unit of time small enough to be considered from an economic standpoint, but at least one line of pretty clear evidence as to the general stability of our climate during the last 3,000 years.

Drouth cycles and their effect. While science has shown that there is no general trend in our climate either for better or for worse, it has shown most conclusively that there are periodic fluctuations which vitally effect our prosperity and the methods of handling our resources. The same tree rings which assure us that Southwestern climate has been stable for 3,000 years warn us plainly that it has been decidedly unstable from year to year, and that the drouth now so strongly impressed on every mind and pocketbook is not an isolated or an accidental bit of hard luck, but a periodic phenomenon the occurrence of which may be anticipated with almost the same certainty as we anticipate the days and the seasons. It is cause for astonishment that our attitude toward these drouths which wreck whole industries, cause huge wastes of wealth and resources, and even empty the treasures of commonwealths should still be that of the Arkansan toward his roof—in fair weather no need to worry, and in foul weather too wet to work.

The tree rings show, in short, that about every eleven years we have a drouth.[6] Every couple of centuries this eleven-year interval lengthens or shortens rather abruptly, running as low as nine and as high as fourteen. The drouths vary a little in length and intensity, and usually there is a "double crest" to both the high and low points, i.e., a better or worse year interlarded between the bad or good extremes. But always, and as sure as sunrise, "dust and a bitter wind shall come."[7]

In addition to the eleven-year cycle, there is a curious chop or "zigzag" (two-year cycle), and probably a long or low groundswell measured in centuries, but the amplitude of all these is too low to have any great practical present economic significance. The eleven-year wave is the one that swamps the boats.

If there be those who doubt whether the tree rings tell a true story, let them be reminded that history supports their testimony. The great flood of the Rio Grande in 1680 is recorded in the trees. The famines of 1680–90 are there—possibly the drouth that produced them had something to do with the Pueblo Rebellion that sent De Vargas to Santa Fe. The great drouths of 1748, 1780, and 1820–23 are all concurrently reported by trees and historians. And in the last century came the weather records, which likewise concur. Douglas has tied in the eleven-year cycle of tree rings with sunspots. Munns has tied in the sunspots with lightning, and with forest fires as recorded in old scars.[8] The chain of evidence as to the existence of the drouth cycle is very complete, and its bearing on economic and conservation problems is obvious. But like much other scientific truth, it may remain "embalmed in books, which are interred in university libraries, and then, long after, worked out by rule of thumb, by practical politicians and businessmen."[9]

The point is that, if every eleven years we may expect a drouth, why not manage our ranges accordingly? This means either stocking them to only their drouth capacity, or arranging to move the stock or feed it when the drouth appears. But instead, we stock them to their normal capacity, and, when drouth comes, the stock eat up the range, ruin the watershed, ruin the stockman, wreck the banks, get credits from the treasury of the United States, and then die. And the silt of their dying moves on down into our reservoirs to someday dry up the irrigated valleys—the only live thing left!

Equilibrium of arid countries. To complete a background for the understanding of natural laws and their operation on our resources it is necessary to consider briefly the so-called "balance of nature."

There appears to be a natural law which governs the resistance of nature to human abuse. Broadly speaking, the law is this: the degree of stability varies inversely to the aridity.

Of course, this concept of a "balance of nature" compresses into three words an enormously complex chain of phenomena. But history bears out the law as given. Woolsey says that decadence has followed deforestation in Palestine, Assyria, Arabia, Greece, Tunisia, Algeria, Italy, Spain, Persia, Sardinia, and Dalmatia.[10] Note that these are all arid or semi-arid. What well watered country has ever suffered serious permanent damage to all its organic resources from human abuse? None that I know of except China. It might be reasonable to ascribe this one exception to the degree of abuse received. Sheer pressure of millions exerted through uncounted centuries was simply too much.

A definite causal relation has long been believed to exist between deforestation and decline in productiveness of nations and their lands. But it strikes me as very curious that a similar causal relation between overgrazing and decadence has never to my knowledge been positively asserted. All our existing knowledge in forestry indicates very strongly that overgrazing has done far more damage to the Southwest than fires or cuttings, serious as the latter have been. Even the reproduction of forests has now been found to be impossible under some conditions without the careful regulation of grazing, whereas fire was formerly considered the only enemy.

The relative seriousness of destructive agencies may be illustrated by an example. Take the Sapello watershed, which forms a major part of the GOS range in the Gila National Forest. Old settlers state that when they came to the country the Sapello was a beautiful trout stream lined with willows. Yet old burned stumps show beyond a doubt that great fires burned in the watershed of the Sapello for at least a century previous to settlement. These fires spoiled the timber, but they did not spoil the land. Since then we have kept the fires out, but livestock has come in. And now the watercourse of the Sapello is a pile of boulders. In short, a century of fires without grazing did not spoil the Sapello, but a decade of grazing without fires ruined it, as far as the watercourses are concerned.

Now the remarkable thing about the Sapello is that it has not been overgrazed. The GOS range is pointed to with pride as a shining example of range conservation. The lesson is that under our peculiar Southwestern conditions, any grazing at all, no matter how moderate, is liable to overgraze and ruin the watercourses. And the wholesale tearing out of watercourses is sufficient to silt our irrigation reservoirs, whether or not it is followed by wholesale erosion of the range itself.

Of course, this one example does not prove that grazing is the outstanding factor in upsetting the equilibrium of the Southwest. It is rapidly becoming the opinion of conservationists, however, that such is the case, and that erosion-control works of some kind are the price we will have to pay if we wish to utilize our ranges without ruining our agriculture.

Examples of destruction. The effect of unwise range use on the range industry, or of unwise farming on the land, are all too obvious to require illustration. What we need to appreciate is how abuses in one of these industries in one place may unwittingly injure another industry in another place.

A census of thirty typical agricultural mountain valleys in the national forests of the Southwest shows four ruined, eight partly ruined, fifteen starting to erode, and only three undamaged. Of the twenty-seven valleys damaged, every case may be ascribed to grazing or overgrazing, supplemented more or less by the clearing of cover from stream banks, fire, and the starting of washes along roads or trails.

A detailed survey of one mountain valley (Blue River, Arizona) shows 3,500 acres of farm land washed out, population reduced two-thirds, and half a million paid for a road over the hills because there was no longer any place to put a road in the valley. This entire loss may be ascribed to overgrazing of creek bottoms and unnecessary clearing of banks.

A special study of one cattle ranch showed that the loss of sixty acres of farm land through erosion imposed a permanent tax of $6 per head on the cost of production. This was a herd of 860 head.

Data on reservoirs shows that Elephant Butte and Roosevelt Lake must probably be raised prematurely because of silting. One of the big Pecos dams (Lake MacMillan) is said to have silted up 60 percent in fifteen years. A detailed report on the Zuni Reservoir, which may be considered typical of a smaller class, shows that its life will be twenty-one years, twelve of which have passed.[11] Silting is forcing the amortization of this half-million dollar investment at the rate of $7 per irrigated acre per year. Raising the dam is necessary to extend its life. In all these cases the silting seems to have been faster than was calculated, and is tending to force the amortization of the investments during alarmingly short periods. Inexpensive desilting methods have not yet been devised. What will be left of the Southwest if silting cuts down our already meager facilities for storage of an already meager water flow?

Here are some typical flood figures: Cave Creek, which flooded Phoenix in 1921, destroyed $150,000 in property and forced construction of a dam costing $500,000. The Pueblo flood of 1921 cost $17,000,000. A little flood in Taos Canyon in 19____ destroyed a new road costing $15,000. Every year it costs $40,000 to clear the diversion plants below Elephant Butte of silt from side washes. These are merely random examples. Undoubtedly we always had floods, but all the evidence indicates that they usually spent themselves without damage while our watercourses were protected by plenty of vegetation, and such damage as occurred was quickly healed up by the roots remaining in the ground.

Summary. Our organic resources are not only in a rundown condition, but in our climate bear a delicately balanced interrelation to each other. Any upsetting of this balance causes a progressive deterioration that may not only be felt hundreds of miles away, but may continue after the original disturbance is removed and affect populations and resources wholly unconnected with the original cause. Erosion eats into our hills like a contagion, and floods bring down the loosened soil upon our valleys like a scourge. Water, soil, animals, and plants—the very fabric of prosperity—react to destroy each other and us. Science can and must unravel those reactions, and government must enforce the findings of science. This is the economic bearing of conservation on the future of the Southwest.

Conservation as a Moral Issue

Thus far we have considered the problem of conservation of land purely as an economic issue. A false front of exclusively economic determinism is so habitual to Americans in discussing public questions that one must speak in the language of compound interest to get a hearing. In my opinion, however, one can not round out a real understanding of the situation in the Southwest without likewise considering its moral aspects.

In past and more outspoken days conservation was put in terms of decency rather than dollars. Who can not feel the moral scorn and contempt for poor craftsmanship in the voice of Ezekiel when he asks: *Seemeth it a small thing unto you to have fed upon good pasture, but ye must tread down with your feet the residue of your pasture? And to have drunk of the clear waters, but ye must foul the residue with your feet?*[12]

In these two sentences may be found an epitome of the moral question involved. Ezekiel seems to scorn waste, pollution, and unnecessary damage as something unworthy—as something damaging not only to the reputation of the waster, but to the self-respect of the craft and the society of which he is a member. We might even draw from his words a broader concept— that the privilege of possessing the earth entails the responsibility of passing it on, the better for our use, not only to immediate posterity, but to the Unknown Future, the nature of which is not given us to know. It is possible that Ezekiel respected the soil, not only as a craftsman respects his material, but as a moral being respects a living thing.

Many of the world's most penetrating minds have regarded our so-called "inanimate nature" as a living thing, and probably many of us who have neither the time nor the ability to reason out conclusions on such matters by logical processes have felt intuitively that there existed between man and the earth a closer and deeper relation than would necessarily follow the mechanistic conception of the earth as our physical provider and abiding place.

Of course, in discussing such matters we are beset on all sides with the pitfalls of language. The very words *living thing* have an inherited and arbitrary meaning derived not from reality, but from human perceptions of human affairs. But we must use them for better or for worse.

A good expression of this conception of an organized animate nature is given by the Russian philosopher Ouspensky, who presents the following analogy:

> Were we to observe, from the inside, one cubic centimetre of the human body, knowing nothing of the existence of the entire body and of man himself, then the phenomena going on in this little cube of flesh would seem like elemental phenomena in inanimate nature.[13]

He then states that it is at least not impossible to regard the earth's parts—soil, mountains, rivers, atmosphere, etc.—as organs, of parts of organs, or a coordinated whole, each part with a definite function. And, if we could see this whole, as a whole, through a great period of time, we might perceive not only organs with coordinated functions, but possibly also that process of consumption and replacement which in biology we call the metabolism, or growth. In such a case we would have all the visible attributes of a living thing, which we do not now realize to be such because it is too big, and its life processes too slow. And there would also follow that invisible attribute—a soul, or consciousness—which not only Ouspensky, but many philosophers of all ages, ascribe to all living things and aggregations thereof, including the "dead" earth.

There is not much discrepancy, except in language, between this conception of a living earth, and the conception of a dead earth, with enormously slow, intricate, and interrelated functions among its parts, as given us by physics, chemistry, and geology. The essential thing for present purposes is that both admit the interdependent functions of the elements. But "anything indivisible is a living being," says Ouspensky. Possibly, in our intuitive perceptions, which may be truer than our science and less impeded by words than our philosophies, we realize the indivisibility of the earth—its soil, mountains, rivers, forests, climate, plants, and animals, and respect it collectively not only as a useful servant but as a living being, vastly less alive than ourselves in degree, but vastly greater than ourselves in time and space—a being that was old when the morning stars sang together, and, when the last of us has been gathered unto his fathers, will still be young.[14]

Philosophy, then, suggests one reason why we can not destroy the earth with moral impunity; namely, that the "dead" earth is an organism possessing a certain kind and degree of life, which we intuitively respect as such. Possibly, to most men of affairs, this reason is too intangible to either accept or reject as a guide to human conduct. But philosophy also offers another and more easily debatable question: was the earth made for man's use, or has man merely the privilege of temporarily possessing an earth made for other and inscrutable purposes? The question of what he can properly do with it must necessarily be affected by this question.

Most religions, insofar as I know, are premised squarely on the assumption that man is the end and purpose of creation, and that not only the dead earth, but all creatures thereon, exist solely for his use. The mechanistic or scientific philosophy does not start with this as a premise, but ends with it as a conclusion, and hence may be placed in the same category for the purpose in hand. This high opinion of his own importance in the universe Jeanette Marks stigmatizes as "the great human impertinence."[15] John Muir, in defense of rattlesnakes, protests: "...as if nothing that does not obviously make for the benefit of man had any right to exist; as if our ways were God's ways."[16] But the noblest expression of this anthropomorphism is Bryant's "Thanatopsis":

> ...The hills
> Rock-ribbed and ancient as the sun,—the vales
> Stretching in pensive quietness between;
> The venerable woods—rivers that move
> In majesty, and the complaining brooks
> That make the meadows green, and, poured round all
> Old oceans gray and melancholy waste,—
> *Are but the solemn decorations all*
> *Of the great tomb of man.*[17]

Since most of mankind today profess either one of the anthropomorphic religions or the scientific school of thought which is likewise anthropomorphic, I will not dispute the point. It just occurs to me, however, in answer to the scientists, that God started his show a good many million years before he had any men for audience—a sad waste of both actors and music— and in answer to both, that it is just barely possible that God himself likes to hear birds sing and see flowers grow. But here again we encounter the insufficiency of words as symbols for realities.

Granting that the earth is for man—there is still a question: what man? Did not the cliff dwellers who tilled and irrigated these our valleys think that they were the pinnacle of creation—that these valleys were made for them? Undoubtedly. And then the Pueblos? Yes. And then the Spaniards? Not only thought so, but said so. And now we Americans? Ours beyond a doubt! (How happy a definition is that one of Hadley's which states, "Truth is that which prevails in the long run"!)[18]

Five races—five cultures—have flourished here. We may truthfully say of our four predecessors that they left the earth alive, undamaged. Is it possibly a proper question for us to consider what the sixth shall say about us? If we are logically anthropomorphic, yes. We and

> ...all that tread
> The globe are but a handful to the tribes
> That slumber in its bosom. Take the wings
> Of morning; pierce the Barcan wilderness
> Or lose thyself in the continuous woods

Where rolls the Oregon, and hears no sound
Save his own dashings—yet the dead are there,
And millions in those solitudes, since first
The flight of years began, have laid them down
In their last sleep.[19]

And so, in time, shall we. And if there be, indeed, a special nobility inherent in the human race—a special cosmic value, distinctive from and superior to all other life—by what token shall it be manifest?

By a society decently respectful of its own and all other life, capable of inhabiting the earth without defiling it? Or by a society like that of John Burrough's potato bug, which exterminated the potato, and thereby exterminated itself?[20] As one or the other shall we be judged in "the derisive silence of eternity."[21]

Notes

Introduction

The following abbreviations are used in the Notes:

AL, *ASCA*   A. Leopold, *A Sand County Almanac and Sketches Here and There*

AL, "SFCS"   A. Leopold, "Some Fundamentals of Conservation in the Southwest"

CD, *DM*   C. Darwin, *The Descent of Man and Selection in Relation to Sex*

CM, *AL*   C. Meine, *Aldo Leopold: His Life and Work*

DH, *ATHN*   D. Hume, *A Treatise of Human Nature*

DH, *ICPM*   D. Hume, *An Inquiry Concerning the Principles of Morals*

F&C, *RMG*   S. L. Flader and J. B. Callicott, eds., *The River of the Mother of God and Other Essays by Aldo Leopold*

IK, *FMM*   I. Kant, *Foundations of the Metaphysics of Morals*

IPCC 2007   S. Solomon et al., Intergovernmental Panel on Climate Change, 2007

JBC, *CASCA*   J. B. Calicott, ed., *Companion to* A Sand County Almanac

1. J. B. Callicott, *Earth's Insights: A Multicultural Survey of Ecological Ethics From the Mediterranean Basin to the Australian Outback* (Berkeley: University of California Press, 1994).
2. J. B. Callicott, "The New New (Buddhist?) Ecology," *Journal for the Study of Religion, Nature, and Culture* 2 (2008): 166–182.
3. E. P. Odum, *Fundamentals of Ecology*, Third Edition (Philadelphia: W. B. Saunders, 1971). The first and second editions were published in 1953 and 1959, respectively. "The Odum" as it was called by ecology students and professors dominated the field for twenty years or more.
4. In addition to "the Odum," two of Odum's prominently published papers were also widely influential: E. P. Odum, "The New Ecology," *BioScience* 14 (1964): 14–16; E. P. Odum, "The Strategy of Ecosystem Development," *Science* 164 (1969): 260–270. (The title of my paper cited in n. 3, "The New New (Buddhist?) Ecology," riffs on Odum's title, "The New Ecology"—because his new ecology is no longer new and has been super-seded by a new new ecology.)
5. F. E. Clements, *Research Methods in Ecology* (Lincoln, Neb.: University Publishing, 1905).
6. J. B. Hagen, *An Entangled Bank: The Origins of Ecosystem Ecology* (New Brunswick, N. J.: Rutgers University Press, 1992) agrees that Odum's characterization of ecosystems is an extension of Clements's characterization of super-organisms.
7. A. G. Tansley, "The Use and Abuse of Vegetational Concepts and Terms," *Ecology* 16 (1935): 284–307.

8. H. A. Gleason, "The Structure and Development of the Plant Association," *Bulletin of the Torrey Botanical Club* 43 (1917): 463–481; H. A. Gleason "The Individualistic Concept of the Plant Association," *Bulletin of the Torrey Botanical Club* 53 (1926): 1–20.

9. R. P. McIntosh, "H. A. Gleason, 'Individualistic Ecologist,' 1882–1975: His Contributions to Ecological Theory," *Bulletin of the Torrey Botanical Club* 102 (1975): 253–273.

10. J. T. Curtis and R. P. McIntosh, "An Upland Forest Continuum in the Prairie-Forest Border Region of Wisconsin," *Ecology* 32 (1951): 434–455; R. H. Whittaker, "Gradient Analysis of Vegetation," *Biological Reviews* 42 (1967): 207–264.

11. L. Brubaker, "Vegetation History and Anticipating Future Vegetation Change," in J. K. Agee and D. R. Johnson, eds., *Ecosystem Management for Parks and Wilderness* (Seattle: University of Washington Press): 41–61.

12. F. E. Clements, *Plant Succession: An Analysis of the Development of Vegetation* (Washington: Carnegie Institution, Publication No. 242, 1916); E. P. Odum, "The Strategy of Ecosystem Development."

13. S. T. A. Pickett and P. S. White, eds., *The Ecology of Natural Disturbance and Patch Dynamics* (San Diego, Cal.: Academic Press, 1985).

14. Ibid.

15. W. Denevan, ed., *The Native Population of the Americas in 1492* (Madison: University of Wisconsin Press, 1992).

16. D. Botkin, *Discordant Harmonies: A New Ecology for the Twenty-first Century* (New York: Oxford University Press, 1990).

17. A particularly bold discussion of the evolution of competing biotic communities by natural selection is the famous paper by G. E. Hutchinson, "Homage to Santa Rosalia; or Why Are There So Many Kinds of Animals?," *American Naturalist* 93 (1959): 145–159.

18. G. C. Williams, *Adaptation and Natural Selection: A Critique of Some Evolutionary Thought* (Princeton, N. J.: Princeton University Press, 1966).

19. Indeed, when Arthur Tansley first introduced the ecosystem idea he made this point. In "The Use and Abuse of Vegetational Concepts and Terms" (p. 300), he wrote, "the systems we isolate mentally are not only included as parts of larger ones, but they also overlap, interlock, and interact with one another. The isolation is partly artificial, but is the only possible way in which we can proceed."

20. See their "Chapter 3, The Ecosystem Criterion," in T. F. H. Allen and T. W. Hoekstra, *Toward a Unified Ecology* (New York: Columbia University Press, 1992) for a particularly clear and emphatic discussion of how ecosystem ontology is driven by ecological epistemology.

21. See, for example, J. B. Callicott, *In Defense of the Land Ethic: Essays in Environmental Philosophy* (Albany: State University of New York Press, 1989) and J. B. Callicott, *Beyond the Land Ethic: More Essays in Environmental Philosophy*. Albany: State University of New York Press, 1999).

22. A. Leopold, *A Sand County Almanac and Sketches Here and There* (New York: Oxford University Press, 1949), pp. 224–225.

23. M. B. McElroy, "Humans as a Force for Global Environmental Change." See M. B. McElroy, *The Atmospheric Environment: Effects of Human Activity* (Princeton, N. J.: Princeton University Press, 2002).

24. For example, J. B. Callicott, "Do Deconstructive Ecology and Sociobiology Undermine the Leopold Land Ethic?," *Environmental Ethics* 18 (1996): 353–371; J. B. Callicott, "From the Balance of Nature to the Flux of Nature: The Land Ethic in a Time of Change," in R. L. Knight, ed., *Aldo Leopold: An Ecological Conscience* (Lanham, Md.: Rowman and

Littlefield, 2002), pp. 91–104; J. B. Callicott, "Chapter 4: Conservation Values and Ethics," in M. J. Groom, G. K. Meffe, C. R. Carrol, and Contributors, *Principles of Conservation Biology*, Third Edition (Sunderland, Mass.: Sinauer Associates, 2006): 111–135.

25. See, for example, J. B. Callicott, "Principal Traditions in American Environmental Ethics: A Survey of Moral Values for Framing an American Ocean Policy," *Ocean and Shoreline Management* 17 (1992): 299–308; J. B. Callicott, "Whaling in Sand County: A Dialectical Hunt for Land-ethical Answers to Questions Concerning the Morality of Norwegian Minke-Whale Catching," *Colorado Journal of International Environmental Law and Policy* 8 (1997): 1–30; J. B. Callicott and E. Back, "The Conceptual Foundations of Rachel Carson's Sea Ethic," in L. Sideris and K. D. Moore, eds., *On Nature's Terms: The Legacy and Challenge of Rachel Carson* (Albany: State University of New York Press, 2007): 94–117.

26. A. D. Barnosky, E. A. Hadly, J. Bascompte, E. L. Berlow, J. H. Brown, M. Fortelius, et al., "Approaching a State Shift in Earth's Biosphere," *Nature* 486 (June 7, 2012): 52–58.

27. Ibid.

28. A. Leopold, "Some Fundamentals of Conservation in the Southwest," *Environmental Ethics* 1 (1979): 131–141; republished in S. L. Flader and J. B. Callicott, eds., *The River of the Mother of God and Other Essays by Aldo Leopold* (Madison: University of Wisconsin Press, 1991): 86–97. The republication of "Some Fundamentals" in *River of the Mother of God* (*RMG*) includes a few editorial changes from the "original" in *Environmental Ethics* (*EE*). In the *EE* version, Ouspensky's name is rendered as "Onspensky," which faithfully follows the typescript found among the Leopold papers in University of Wisconsin archives. Leopold typically wrote with a pencil and had his manuscripts typed by a secretary. I suspected that Leopold's secretary misinterpreted his tight script, mistaking his "u" for an "n" and, accordingly, I corrected it for republication in *RMG*, along with a few other incidentals. In this book all references to, and quotations from "Some Fundamentals" will be to the *RMG* version.

29. G. S. Levit, *Biogeochemistry—Biosphere—Noosphere* (Berlin: Verlag für Wissenschaft und Bildung, 2001) provides a "scientific biography" of Vernadsky. Also see the Foreword by L. Margulis et al. in V. I. Vernadsky, *The Biosphere*, tr. D. B. Langmuir (New York: Copernicus/Springer Verlag, 1998).

30. W. [V.] I. Vernadsky, "Problems of Biogeochemistry, II," tr. George Vernadsky; ed. G. E. Hutchinson, *Transactions of the Connecticut Academy of Arts and Sciences* 35 (1944): 483–517; W. [V.] I. Vernadsky, "The Biosphere and the Noösphere," tr. George Vernadsky; ed. G. E. Hutchinson, *American Scientist* 33 (1945): 1–12.

31. J. Lovelock, *Gaia: A New Look at Life on Earth* (Oxford: Oxford University Press, 1979); J. Lovelock, *Ages of Gaia* (New York: W. W. Norton, 1988); L. Margulis and D. Sagan, *Slanted Truths: Essays on Gaia, Symbiosis and Evolution* (New York: Coperncus/Springer Verlag, 1997).

32. A. Schweitzer, *Civilization and Ethics* (London: A. & C. Black, 1923); P. W. Taylor, *Respect for Nature: A Theory of Environmental Ethics* (Princeton, N. J.: Princeton University Press, 1986); J. P. Sterba, "From Biocentric Individualism to Biocentric Pluralism," *Environmental Ethics* 17 (1995): 361–376; G. E. Varner, *In Nature's Interests: Interests, Animal Rights, and Environmental Ethics* (New York: Oxford University Press, 1998).

33. K. E. Goodpaster, "On Being Morally Considerable," *Journal of Philosophy* 75 (1978): 308–325.

34. P. D. Ouspensky, *Tertium Organum: The Third Canon of Thought, A Key to the Enigmas of the World*, tr. N. Besseraboff and C. Bragdon (Rochester, N.Y.: Manas Press, 1920).

35. J. C. Smuts, *Holism and Evolution* (London: Macmillan, 1920); P. Teilhard de Chardin, *Le Phenomene Humain* (Paris: Éditions du Seuil, 1955).

36. R. Routley, "Is There a Need for a New, an Environmental Ethic," Bulgarian Organizing Committee, eds., *Proceedings of the XVth World Congress of Philosophy*, Volume 1 (Varna: Sophia Press, 1973): 205–210.

37. Leopold, *Sand County*, pp. 210–211.

38. R. Leakey and R. Lewin, *The Sixth Extinction: Patterns of Life and the Future of Humankind* (New York: Anchor Books, 1996).

39. D. M. Raup and J. J. Sepkoski Jr., "Periodicity of Extinctions in the Geologic Past," *Proceedings of the National Academy of Sciences of the United States of America* 81 (1984): 801–805.

40. A. L. Melott and R. K. Bambach, "A Ubiquitous ~62-Myr Periodic Fluctuation Superimposed on General Trends in Fossil Biodiversity. I. Documentation," *Paleobiology* 37 (2011): 92–112.

41. B. G. Norton, *Toward Unity Among Environmentalists* (New York: Oxford University Press, 1991).

42. The oft-repeated characterization of Leopold as a prophet appears traceable to R. Mann, "Aldo Leopold: Priest and Prophet," *American Forests* 60, no. 8 (August, 1954): 23, 42–43; it was picked up by E. Swift, "Aldo Leopold: Wisconsin's Conservation Prophet," *Wisconsin Tales and Trails* 2, no. 2 (September 1961): 2–5; R. Nash institutionalized it in his chapter, "Aldo Leopold Prophet" in *Wilderness and the American Mind* (New Haven, Conn.: Yale University Press, 1967); after that the characterization spread so wide so fast that it is impossible to document fully. According to C. Meine, *Aldo Leopold: His Life and Work* (Madison: University of Wisconsin Press, 1988), Leopold was a serious student of the Bible, as his playful 1920 essay "The Forestry of the Prophets" (*Journal of Forestry* 18: 412–419) documents. As "Some Fundamentals" documents, Leopold was more interested in discovering and incorporating into his own writing the Bible's rhetorical power. Not only is Leopold routinely called a prophet, *Sand County* is often called the "bible" of the contemporary conservation movement (by, for example, W. Stegner, "Living on Our Principal," *Living Wilderness* 49 (Spring 1985): 5–21), probably in part because Leopold's style sometimes has a biblical flavor.

Chapter 1

1. A. Pryor, "Thinking Like a Mystic: The Legacy of P. D. Ouspensky's *Tertium Organum* on the Development of Leopold's 'Thinking Like a Mountain,'" *Journal for the Study of Religion, Nature, and Culture* 5 (2011): 465–490, p. 466.

2. See C. Meine, *Aldo Leopold: His Life and Work* (Madison: University of Wisconsin Press, 1988/2010)—hereafter CM, *AL*.

3. See, for example, "To the Forest Officers of the Carson" (1913) in S. L. Flader and J. B. Callicott, eds., *The River of the Mother of God and Other Essays by Aldo Leopold* (Madison: University of Wisconsin Press, 1991): 41–46—hereafter F&C, *RMG*.

4. See, for example, "The Conservation Ethic" (1933) in F&C, *RMG*: 181–208.

5. See, especially, "Grass, Brush, Timber, and Fire in Southern Arizona" (1924) in F&C, *RMG*: 114–122.

6. CM, *AL*.

7. CM, *AL*.

8. D. Ribbens, "The Making of *A Sand County Almanac*" in J. B. Callicott, ed., *Companion to* A Sand County Almanac: *Interpretive and Critical Essays* (Madison: University of Wisconsin Press, 1987): 91–109, pp. 92–93—hereafter JBC, *CASCA*.

9. Ibid., p. 99.

10. Ibid., p. 93.

11. The 1947 Foreword may be found in JBC, *CASCA*, pp. 281–288.

12. CM, *AL*.

13. Both Meine, *Aldo Leopold*, and Ribbens, "The Making," provide accounts of the posthumous publication process.

14. A. Leopold, *A Sand County Almanac and Sketches Here and There* (New York: Oxford University Press, 1949), p. viii—hereafter AL, *ASCA*.

15. Ribbens, "The Making," p. 102.

16. Ibid.

17. AL, *ASCA*, p. viii.

18. J. Tallmadge, "Anatomy of a Classic," in JBC, *CASC*, pp. 110–127.

19. AL, *ASCA*, p. viii.

20. Ibid., pp. 204–205.

21. L. White Jr., "The Historical Roots of Our Ecologic Crisis," *Science* 155 (1967): 1203–1207.

22. AL, *ASCA*, p. ix.

23. Ibid., p. viii.

24. H. D. Thoreau, *Walden or Life in the Woods* (Boston: Ticknor and Fields, 1854).

25. AL, *ASCA*, pp. viii–ix.

26. Ibid., p. ix.

27. Leopold, Aldo/Correspondence: L-S. Mann, Roberts, through 1948, pp. [651]–[742]. http://digicoll.library.wisc.edu/cgi-bin/AldoLeopold/AldoLeopold-idx?type=turn&entity=AldoLeopold.ALCorresLS.p0658&id=AldoLeopold.ALCorresLS&isize=XL. I thank Curt Meine for alerting me to this "gem" (personal communication, January 21, 2012).

28. AL, *ASCA*, p. ix, emphasis added.

29. Ibid., p. 3, emphasis added.

30. Ibid., p. 4, emphasis added.

31. Ibid., emphasis added.

32. Ibid., emphasis added.

33. C. Elton, *Animal Ecology* (London: Sidgwick and Jackson, 1927).

34. AL, *ASCA*, p. 18, emphasis added.

35. Ibid.

36. Ibid., pp. 18–19.

37. Ibid., p. 19, emphasis added.

38. Ibid., p. 20, emphasis added.

39. Ibid., emphasis added.

40. Ibid.

41. Ibid., pp. 20–21.

42. See W. D. Oliver, "A Sober Look at Solipsism," *American Philosophical Quarterly*, Monograph Series 4 (1970), 30 pages.

43. AL, *ASCA*, p. 65.

44. R. Vincent, *Funk: The Music, the People, and the Rhythm of the One* (New York: St. Martins Press, 1996).

45. AL, *ASCA*, p. 95.

46. Ibid., p. 96.

47. W. Allen, *The Insanity Defense: The Complete Prose* (New York: Random House, 2007).

48. AL, *ASCA*, p. 96.

49. P. Fritzell, "The Conflicts of Ecological Conscience" in JBC, *CASCA*: 128–153, p. 147.

50. M. Arnold, "From the Hymn of Empedocles," Arthur Quiller-Couch, ed., *Oxford Book of English Verse*, 1250–1900 (Oxford: Clarendon Press, 1919), p. 754.

51. AL, *ASCA*, p. 66.

52. Ibid., p. 108, emphasis added.

53. Ibid.

54. Ibid., pp. 107–108.

55. A. Tansley, "The Use and Abuse of Vegetational Concepts and Terms," *Ecology* 16 (1935): 284–307.

56. Ibid., p. 299.

57. R. L. Lindeman, "The Trophic Dynamic Aspect of Ecology," *Ecology* 23 (1942): 399–418.

58. A. Leopold, "A Biotic View of Land," *Journal of Forestry* 37 (1939): 727–730; A. Leopold, "Odyssey," *Audubon* 44 (May–June, 1942): 133–135.

59. AL, *ASCA*, p. 149.

60. Ibid.

61. Ibid., emphasis added.

62. Ibid., p. 130.

63. Ibid.

64. Ibid.

65. Ibid., pp. 130–132.

66. B. G. Norton, *Sustainability: A Philosophy of Adaptive Ecosystem Management* (Chicago: University of Chicago Press, 2005), p. 222.

67. AL, *ASCA*, p. 132.

68. Norton, *Sustainability*, p. 222.

69. For the date and place of the event, see CM, *AL*.

70. Ribbens, "The Making," p. 96.

71. Ibid.

72. G. Van Horn, "Fire on the Mountain," *Journal for the Study of Religion, Nature, and Culture* 5 (2011): 437–464, p. 447; H. D. Thoreau, *Excursions* (New York: Corinth Books, 1962), p. 185.

73. AL, *ASCA*, p. 133, emphasis added.

74. Van Horn, "Fire," pp. 449–450, emphasis in original.

75. Norton, *Sustainability*, p. 224, emphasis added.

76. A. Leopold, "The State of the Profession" (1940) in F&C, *RMG*: 276–280, p. 280— originally published in *Journal of Wildlife Management* 4 (1940): 343–346, p. 346, emphasis added.

77. The evidence for this claim is overwhelming. Van Horn, "Fire," points out that former US Secretary of the Interior Bruce Babbitt and the US Fish and Wildlife Service Mexican wolf recovery team coordinator were both inspired by the "fierce green fire." J. Caputi, "Feeding Green Fire," *Journal for the Study of Religion, Nature, and Culture* 5 (2011): 410–436, notes the following: P. Shabecoff, *A Fierce Green Fire: The American Environmental Movement* (Washington: Island Press, 2003); "A Fierce Green Fire at 100," the title of an NEH 2009 Summer Institute devoted to Aldo Leopold's philosophy; *The*

Green Fire Times, an alternative media source offering "news and views from the sustainable Southwest." B. Taylor notes in "Editor's Introduction: Encountering Leopold," *Journal for the Study of Religion, Nature, and Culture* 5 (2011): 393–395, pp. 393–394, that Leopold's story of receiving an epiphany as the "green fire" died in the eyes of the wolf that he shot had become for Earth First! activists "a mythic, moral fable in which the wolf communicates with human beings, stressing inter-species kinship."

78. Norton, *Sustainability*, p. 225.
79. AL *ASCA*, p. 225, emphasis added.
80. Ibid., p. 204.
81. Ibid.
82. Ibid, pp. 173–174.
83. See A. J. Ayer, *Language, Truth, and Logic* (London: Victor Gallantz,1936).
84. M. Black, "The Gap Between 'Is' and 'Should,'" *Philosophical Review* 73 (1964): 165–181.
85. I. Kant, *Grounding for the Metaphysics of Morals*, tr. James W. Ellington (Indianapolis, Ind.: Hackett, 1993), p. 40.
86. AL, *ASCA*, p. 223.
87. For a full discussion see J. B. Callicott, "The Philosophical Value of Wildlife," in D. J. Decker and G. Goff, eds., *Economic and Social Values of Wildlife* (Boulder, Colo: Westview Press, 1987): 214–221.
88. Plato, *Republic*, Bk I.
89. Elton, *Animal Ecology*.
90. F. F. Darling, *A Naturalist on Rona: Essays of a Biologist in Isolation* (Oxford: Clarendon Press, 1939); W. Vogt, *Road to Survival* (New York: William Sloan, 1948).
91. Rick Bass, "Introduction by Rick Bass." in R. Bedicheck, *Adventures with a Texas Naturalist* (Austin: University of Texas Press, 1947/1994): v–xvii, p. vi.
92. Tallmadge, "Anatomy," p. 115.
93. Ibid., p. 116.
94. Ibid., p. 115.
95. Ibid., p. 116.
96. Ibid.
97. Ibid., p. 119.
98. Ibid., p. 123.
99. CM, *AL*.
100. A. Leopold, "The Forestry of the Prophets" in F&C, *RMG*: 71–77, p. 71—originally published in *Journal of Forestry* 18 (1920): 412–419, p. 412.
101. A. Leopold, "Some Fundamentals of Conservation in the Southwest," in F&C, RMG: 86–97, p. 93—originally published in *Environmental Ethics* 1 (1979):131–141, p. 139.
102. Tallmadge, "Anatomy," p. 116.
103. See the Introduction, n. 42, for relevant citations.
104. Elton, *Animal Ecology*.
105. J. T. Curtis, *The Vegetation of Wisconsin* (Madison: University of Wisconsin Press, 1959); R. P. McIntosh, "The Continuum Concept of Vegetation," *Botanical Review* (1967) 33: 130–187; R. H. Whittaker, "A Criticism of the Plant Association and Climatic Climax Concepts," *Northwest Science* 25 (1951): 18–31.
106. Tansley, "Use and Abuse," p. 300, emphasis added.
107. A. Leopold, "The Arboretum and the University," *Parks and Recreation* 18, no. 2 (1934): 59–60, p. 59.

108. F. E. Clements, *Research Methods in Ecology* (Lincoln, Neb.: University Publishing, 1905); F. E. Clements, *Plant Succession: The Analysis of the Development of Vegetation* (Washington: Carnegie Institution; Publication no. 242, 1916).

109. See especially D. Worster, *Nature's Economy: A History of Ecological Ideas* (Cambridge: Cambridge University Press, 1977).

110. Tansley, "Use and Abuse," pp. 289, 291, 300.

111. E. P. Odum, "The Strategy of Ecosystem Development," *Science* 164 (1969): 260–270.

112. Elton, *Animal Ecology*; A. Leopold, "A Biotic View of Land," *Journal of Forestry* 37 (1939): 727–730; AL, *ASCA*; Lindeman, "Trophic-Dynamic Aspect"; Tansley, "Use and Abuse."

113. AL, *ASCA*, p. 221.

114. Ibid., p. 223.

115. Ibid., p. 214.

116. R. V. O'Neill, D. L. DeAngelis, J. B. Waide, and T. F. H. Allen, *A Hierarchical Concept of Ecosystems* (Princeton, N.J.: Princeton University Press, 1986).

117. T. F. H. Allen, and T. W. Hoekstra, *Toward a Unified Ecology* (New York: Columbia University Press, 1992).

118. H. A. Gleason, "The Individualistic Concept of the Plant Association," *Bulletin of the Torrey Botanical Club* 53 (1926): 1–20; R. H. Whittaker, "Gradient Analysis of Vegetation," *Biological Review* 28 (1967): 207–264; R. P. McIntosh, "H. A. Gleason, 'Individualistic Ecologist,' 1882–1975," *Bulletin of the Torrey Botanical Club* 102 (1975): 253–273.

119. S. T. A. Pickett and P. S. White, *The Ecology of Natural Disturbance and Patch Dynamics* (Orlando, Fla.: Academic Press, 1995).

120. S. T. A. Pickett and R. S. Ostfeld, "The Shifting Paradigm in Ecology," in R. L. Knight and S. F. Bates, eds., *A New Century for Natural Resources Management* (Washington: Island Press, 1995): 261–278.

121. I. Douglas, D. Goode, M. Houk, and R. Wang, *The Routledge Handbook of Urban Ecology* (New York: Routledge, 2011).

122. J. B. Callicott, *Beyond the Land Ethic: More Essays in Environmental Philosophy* (Albany: State University of New York Press, 1999).

123. L. Margulis, *Symbiotic Planet: A New Look at Evolution* (New York: Basic Books, 1998).

124. L. Margulis and K. Schwartz, *Five Kingdoms: An Illustrated Guide to the Phyla of Life on Earth* (New York: W. H. Freeman, 1982); C. R. Woese, O. Kandler, and M. L. Wheelis, "Towards a Natural System of Organisms: Proposal for the Domains Archaea, Bacteria, and Eucarya," *Proceedings of the National Academy of Science* 87 (1990): 4576–4579.

125. White, "Historical Roots"; I. McHarg, *Design with Nature* (New York: Natural History Press, 1969); R. Dawkins, *The God Delusion* (London: Bantam Press, 2006); Daniel Dennet, *Darwin's Dangerous Idea: Evolution and the Meanings of Life* (New York: Simon and Schuster, 1995).

126. T. Berry, *The Sacred Universe: Earth, Spirituality and Religion in the 21st Century*, ed. M. E. Tucker (New York: Columbia University Press, 2009); B. Swimme and T. Berry, *The Universe Story From the Primordial Flaring Forth to the Ecozoic Era—A Celebration of the Unfolding of the Cosmos* (New York: HarperCollins, 1992).

Chapter 2

1. A. Leopold, *A Sand County Almanac and Sketches Here and There* (New York: Oxford University Press, 1949), pp. 201–202—hereafter AL, *ASCA*.

2. See J. Bell, "To the Tenth Generation: Homer's Odyssey as Environmental Ethics," *Environmental Ethics* 32 (2010): 51–66.

3. See M. D. Yaffe, "Introduction" in M. D. Yaffe, ed., *Judaism and Environmental Ethics* (Lanham, Md.: Lexington Books, 2001): 1–70, for a thorough critical discussion of Leopold's rendition and interpretation of the *Odyssey*.

4. The best-known and most compelling case that gender oppression is central to environmental ethics is made by K. J. Warren, "The Power and the Promise of Ecological Feminism," *Environmental Ethics* 12 (1990): 125–146.

5. AL, *ASCA*, p. 203.

6. Ibid., p. 202.

7. Ibid.

8. For a thorough discussion of moral regress and progress see S. Pinker, *The Better Angles of Our Nature: Why Violence Has Declined* (New York: Viking, 2011).

9. AL, *ASCA*, p. 209.

10. Ibid., p. 202.

11. Ibid.

12. A. Leopold, "The Conservation Ethic," *Journal of Forestry* 31 (1933): 634–643; reprinted in S. L. Flader and J. B. Callicott, eds., *The River of the Mother of God and Other Essays by Aldo Leopold* (Madison: University of Wisconsin Press, 1991): 181–192. One emendation was made by the editors of *RMG* that is worth noting. Apparently, either Leopold's secretary or the editor of the *Journal of Forestry* was not familiar with the word "pogrom," for in "The Conservation Ethic," as it appeared in the *Journal of Forestry*, there one finds the following nonsensical sentence: "For example, his sense of right and wrong may be aroused quite as strongly by the desecration of a nearby woodlot as by a famine in China or a near-program in Germany, or the murder of the slave-girls in ancient Greece." We changed "near-program" to "near-pogrom." Leopold visited Germany—he himself was of German ancestry—in 1935. Hitler was then in power and had been since 1933, the year that Leopold wrote "The Conservation Ethic."

13. The definitive biography is C. Meine, *Aldo Leopold: His Life and Work* (Madison: University of Wisconsin Press, 1988, revised edition 2010); a lite biography is provided by M. Lorbiecki, *A Fierce Green Fire: An Illustrated Biography* (Helena, Mt.: Falcon, 1996, republished by Oxford University Press, 1999).

14. C. Darwin, *The Descent of Man and Selection in Relation to Sex*, Second Edition (London: Murray, 1874), p. 100—hereafter CD, *DM*.

15. CD, *DM*, p. 120.

16. Ibid., p. 101.

17. Ibid., p. 120.

18. See S. M. Di Scala, *Italy: From Revolution to Republic, 1700 to the Present* (Boulder, Colo.: Westview Press, 1998); R. J. Evans, *Rereading German History: From Unification to Reunification, 1800–1996* (London: Routledge, 1997).

19. CD, *DM*, pp. 126–127.

20. Ibid., p. 126.

21. Most notably, for P. Singer, *Animal Liberation: A New Ethic for Our Treatment of Animals* (New York: Avon, 1977).

22. See especially K. Goodpaster, "On Being Morally Considerable," *Journal of Philosophy* 75 (1978): 308–325.

23. Of course, some sentient beings do form a community with man—domestic animals. M. Midgley, *Animals and Why They Matter* (Athens: University of Georgia Press, 1983),

calls such human-domestic animal communities "mixed communities." See 5.3 for a discussion.

24. For a comprehensive discussion, see R. P. McIntosh, *Background of Ecology* (Cambridge: Cambridge University Press, 1988).
25. Meine, *Aldo Leopold.*
26. C. Elton, *Animal Ecology* (London: Methuen, 1927), p. 64.
27. AL, *ASCA*, p. 203.
28. Ibid., p. 204.
29. Ibid.
30. D. Hume, *An Inquiry Concerning the Principles of Morals* (New York: Liberal Arts Press, 1957), first published as *An Enquiry Concerning the Principles of Morals* in 1751—hereafter DH, *ICPM.*
31. CD, *DM*, pp. 112, 109, 100, 101and 124, 102 and 124, respectively.
32. Ibid., p. 109.
33. Indeed Darwin seems to directly repudiate utilitarianism; see CD, *DM*, p. 124.
34. DH, *ICPM*, p. 8
35. Ibid., p. 6.
36. D. Hume, *Dialogues and Natural History of Religion*, ed. J. A. C. Gaskin (New York: Oxford University Press, 1993).
37. See M. Mauss, *The Gift: The Form and Reason for Exchange in Archaic Societies*, tr. W. D. Halls (New York: W. W. Norton, 2000).
38. See R. B. Lee and I. DeVore, eds., *Man the Hunter* (Chicago: University of Chicago Press, 1968).
39. See A. E. Komter, ed., *The Gift: An Interdisciplinary Perspective* (Amsterdam: Amsterdam University Press, 1996).
40. See D. J. Kennet and B. Winterhalder, eds., *Behavioral Ecology and the Transition to Agriculture* (Berkeley: University of California Press, 2006).
41. CD, *DM*, p. 118.
42. Ibid.
43. DH, *ICPM*, p. 23.
44. AL, *ASCA*, p. 202.
45. T. Hobbes, *Leviathan [with Selected Variants From the Latin Edition of 1668]* (Indianapolis, Ind.: Hackett, 1994), p. 76, emphasis added. *Leviathan* was first published in 1651.
46. DH, *ICPM*, p. 21.
47. Ibid., p. 47, emphasis added.
48. AL, *ASCA*, p. 202.
49. Ibid., pp. 202–203.
50. CD, *DM*, p. 123.
51. AL, *ASCA*, p. 203.
52. See W. E. Adams, *Memoir of a Social Atom* (London: Hutchinson's University Library, 1903) for the "social atom" characterization of materialistic Hobbesian individualism.
53. J. Bentham, *An Introduction to the Principles of Morals and Legislation* (Oxford: Clarendon Press), pp. 2–3.
54. Ibid., p. 3.
55. M. Slote, *Morals from Motives* (New York: Oxford University Press, 2001).
56. G. E. Varner, "No Holism without Pluralism," *Environmental Ethics* 13 (1991): 175–179, p. 179.

57. A. Carter, "Humean Nature," *Environmental Values* 9 (2000): 3–37.

58. Y. S. Lo, "Non-Humean Holism, Un-Humean Holism," *Environmental Values* 10 (2003): 113–123, p. 113.

59. *Fide* C. W. Hendel, "Introduction" to D. Hume, *An Inquiry Concerning the Principles of Morals* (New York: Liberal Arts Press, 1957), p. vii.

60. DH, *ICPM*, p. 11.

61. Ibid., p. 14.

62. Ibid., p. 53.

63. Ibid., p. 58.

64. Ibid., p. 97.

65. Ibid., pp. 122–123.

66. Ibid., p. 127.

67. AL, *ASCA*, p. 203.

68. Ibid., p. 210.

69. Ibid., p. 211.

70. Ibid., p. 212, emphasis added.

71. Ibid.

72. Ibid., pp. 224–225.

73. Elton, *Animal Ecology*, pp. 63, 56, 52.

74. See, for example, M. Kheel, "The Liberation of Nature: A Circular Affair," *Environmental Ethics* 7 (1985): 135–149.

75. See, for example, R. B. Primack, *Essentials of Conservation Biology* (Sunderland, Mass.: Sinauer Associates, 1993).

76. For the environmental-fascism charge against the land ethic as I have interpreted it, see T. Regan, *The Case for Animal Rights* (Berkeley: University of California Press, 1983); W. Aiken, "Ethical Issues in Agriculture," in T. Regan, ed., *Earthbound: New Introductory Essays in Environmental Ethics* (New York: Random House, 1984): 247–288; F. Ferré, "Persons in Nature: Toward an Applicable and Unified Environmental Ethics," *Ethics and the Environment* 1 (1996): 15–25; K. Shrader-Frechette, "Individualism, Holism, and Environmental Ethics," *Ethics and the Environment* 1 (1996): 55–69; M. E. Zimmerman, "Ecofascism: An Enduring Temptation," in M. E. Zimmerman, J. B. Callicott, K. J. Warrren, I. J. Klaver, and J. Clark, eds., *Environmental Philosophy: From Animal Rights to Radical Ecology* (Upper Saddle River, N. J.: Prentice Hall, 2005), pp. 390–408. For my reply, see "4. Holistic Environmental Ethics and the Problem of Ecofascism," in J. B. Callicott, *Beyond the Land Ethic: More Essays in Environmental Philosophy* (Albany: State University of New York Press, 1999), pp. 59–76.

77. AL, *ASCA*, pp. 202–203.

78. *Merriam-Webster's Collegiate Dictionary*, Eleventh Edition (Springfield, Mass: Merriam-Webster, 2004), p. 9.

79. See my "Holistic Environmental Ethics and the Problem of Ecofascism" for a fuller discussion of these second-order principles.

80. I am indebted to Y. S. Lo, "The Land Ethic and Callicott's Ethical System (1980–2001): An Overview and Critique," *Inquiry* 44 (2001): 331–358 for identifying the otherwise cryptic TOP.

81. H. Rolston III, "Duties to Endangered Species," *BioScience* 35 (1985): 718–726.

82. See M. Faber, *Naturalism and Subjectivism* (Springfield, Ill.: Charles C. Thomas, 1959).

83. AL, *ASCA*, p. 203, emphasis added.

84. S. Lehmann, "Do Wildernesses Have Rights?," *Environmental Ethics* 3 (1981): 129–146, p. 131.

Chapter 3

1. G. E. Moore, *Principia Ethica* (Cambridge: Cambridge University Press, 1903).
2. See Sprigge, "Naturalistic Fallacy," in L. C. Becker and C. B. Becker, eds., *Encyclopedia of Ethics*, Second Edition, Volume II (New York: Routledge, 2001): 1215–1217.
3. D. Hume, *A Treatise of Human Nature* (Oxford: Clarendon Press, 1888), p. 469—originally published in 1739 and 1740—hereafter DH, *ATHN*.
4. C. Darwin, *The Descent of Man*, Second Edition (London: Murray, 1874), p. 126.
5. R. M. Hare, "Universalizability," *Proceedings of the Aristotelian Society* 55 (1954/1955): 295–312.
6. M. Black, "The Gap Between 'Is' and 'Should,'" in W. D. Hudson, ed., *The Is-Ought Question* (London: Macmillan, 1969): 99–113, p. 100.
7. D. C. Gerould, *Guillotine: Its Legend and Lore* (New York: Blast Books, 1992).
8. S. Farrell and J. Sutherland, *Madame Guillotine: The French Revolution* (London: HarperCollins, 1986).
9. A. Leopold, *A Sand County Almanac and Sketches Here and There* (New York: Oxford University Press), p. 211—hereafter AL, *ASCA*. For confirmation that *should* may be a verbal stand-in for *ought,* note the title of Black's paper cited in note 6, supra.
10. A. Leopold, "The Conservation Ethic" in S. L. Flader and J. B. Callicott, eds., *The River of the Mother of God and Other Essays by Aldo Leopold* (Madison: University of Wisconsin Press, 1991): 181–192, p. 182—originally published in *Journal of Forestry* 31 (1933): 634–643.
11. A. C. MacIntyre, "Hume on 'Is' and 'Ought,'" in W. D. Hudson, ed., *The Is-Ought Question* (London: Macmillan, 1969): 35–50, p. 43.
12. Ibid.
13. Ibid., p. 44.
14. DH, *ATHN*, pp. 468–469.
15. Ibid., pp. 469–470.
16. MacIntyre, "Hume on," pp. 47–48. MacIntyre cites A. N. Prior, *Logic and the Basis of Ethics* (Oxford: Oxford University Press, 1949).
17. I. Kant, *Prolegomena to Any Future Metaphysic*, tr. Lewis White Beck (New York: Library of Liberal Arts, 1950), p. 8—originally published as *Prolegomena zu einer jeden künftigen Metaphysik* in 1783. It was Hume's critique of cause and effect relationships in the *Treatise* that drew Kant's attention and set him off on his project to effect a Copernican revolution in philosophy. I only wish to note that Kant was a close student of Hume and may have also been stimulated by Hume to think equally deeply about the Is/Ought Dichotomy.
18. I. Kant, *Foundations of the Metaphysics of Morals*, tr. Lewis White Beck (Indianapolis, Ind.: Library of Liberal Arts, 1959), pp. 30–31—originally published as *Grundlegung zur Metaphysik der Sitten* in 1785—hereafter IK, *FMM*.
19. IK, *FMM*, pp. 34–35.
20. MacIntyre, "Hume on," pp. 36, 46.
21. Y. S. Lo, "A Humean Argument for the Land Ethic?," *Environmental Values* 10 (2001): 523–539, pp. 528–529.
22. Ibid., p. 32.

23. D. Hume, *An Inquiry Concerning the Principles of Morals* (New York: Liberal Arts Press, 1957), pp. 92–93, emphasis in original—first published as *An Enquiry Concerning the Principles of Morals* in 1751—hereafter DH, *ICPM*.

24. DH, *ATHN*, p. 459.

25. AL, *ASCA*, p. 206.

26. DH, *ICPM*, p. 6.

27. MacIntye, "Hume on," p. 48.

28. A. Leopold, "Grass, Brush, Timber, and Fire in Southern Arizona," *Journal of Forestry* 22 (1924): 1–10.

29. Ibid.

30. AL, *ASCA*, p. 207.

31. Ibid., pp. 205 and 219.

32. Ibid., p. 109.

33. Most notably, S. J. Gould, *The Structure of Evolutionary Theory* (Cambridge, Mass.: Belknap Press of Harvard University, 2002).

34. Gould's revisionist evolutionary theory is popularized in S. J. Gould, *Wonderful Life: The Burgess Shale and the Nature of History* (New York: W. W. Norton, 1989).

35. L. Margulis and R. Fester, *Symbiosis as a Source of Evolutionary Innovation: Speciation and Morphogenesis* (Cambridge, Mass.: MIT Press, 1991), popularized in L. Margulis, *Symbiotic Planet: A New Look at Evolution* (New York: Basic Books, 1998); for the mainstreaming of endosymbiotic evolutionary theory, see S. F. Gilbert, J. Sapp, and A. I Tauber, "A Symbiotic View of Life: We Have Never Been Individuals," *Quarterly Review of Biology* 87 (2012): 325–341.

36. AL, *ASCA*, p. 109.

37. Ibid.

38. Ibid., p. 110.

39. Ibid., p. 109.

40. Ibid.

41. C. Elton, *Animal Ecology* (London: Sidgwick & Jackson, 1927).

42. A. Leopold, "A Biotic View of Land," *Journal of Forestry* 37 (1939): 727–730.

43. R. Lindeman, "The Trophic-Dynamic Aspect of Ecology," *Ecology* 23 (1942): 399–418.

44. A. G. Tansley, "The Use and Abuse of Vegetational Concepts and Terms," *Ecology* 16 (1935): 284–307.

45. Ibid., p. 297.

46. Ibid., p. 299.

47. D. Worster, *Nature's Economy: A History of Ecological Ideas*, Second Edition (Cambridge: Cambridge University Press, 1994).

48. Tansley, "Use and Abuse," p. 285.

49. Elton, *Animal Ecology*, p. 63.

50. AL, *ASCA*, p. 215.

51. Ibid.

52. Ibid., p. 216.

53. Ibid.

54. Lindeman, "Trophic-Dynamic Aspect," p. 408.

55. A. Leopold, "Odyssey," *Audubon Magazine* 44, no. 3 (May–June 1942): 133–135.

56. F. E. Clements, *Research Methods in Ecology* (Lincoln, Neb.: University Publishing Company, 1905); F. E. Clements, *Plant Succession: An Analysis of the Development of Vegetation*, Publication no. 242 (Washington: Carnegie Institution, 1916).

57. AL, *ASCA*, p. 221.

58. Ibid., p. 223, emphasis on "versus" in original; emphasis on "collective organism" added.

59. A. Leopold, *Game Management* (New York: Charles Scribner's Sons, 1933); for a discussion, see S. L. Flader, *Thinking Like a Mountain: Aldo Leopold and the Evolution of an Ecological Attitude Toward Deer, Wolves, and Forests* (Columbia: University of Missouri Press, 1974).

60. See Flader, *Thinking Like a Mountain*.

61. Leopold, *Game Management*.

62. A. Leopold, "Wilderness as a Land Laboratory," *The Living Wilderness* 6 (July 1941): 3, p. 3.

63. AL, *ASCA*, p. 194.

64. A. Leopold, "Biotic Land-Use," in J. B. Callicott and E. T. Freyfogle, eds., *For the Health of the Land: Previously Unpublished Essays and Other Writings* (Washington: Island Press, 1999): 198–207; A. Leopold, "The Land-Health Concept and Conservation," in J. B. Callicott and E. T. Freyfogle, eds., *For the Health of the Land: Previously Unpublished Essays and Other Writings* (Washington: Island Press, 1999): 218–226.

65. AL, *ASCA*, p. 202.

66. Ibid., p. 204.

67. Ibid., p. 205.

68. Ibid.

69. Ibid., p. 209.

70. Ibid., p. 214.

71. Ibid.

72. Worster, *Nature's Economy*, p. 290.

73. R. P. McIntosh, *The Background of Ecology: Concept and Theory* (Cambridge: Cambridge University Press, 1985), p. 194

74. Ibid., p. 228.

75. J. B. Hagen, *An Entangled Bank: The Origins of Ecosystem Ecology* (New Brunswick, N.J.: Rutgers University Press, 1992), pp. 128, 136.

76. Tansley, "Use and Abuse," pp. 289–290; 334.

77. See W. M. Wheeler, *Emergent Evolution and the Development of Societies* (New York: W. W. Norton, 1928); and É. Durkheim, *The Division of Labor in Society; Being a Translation of His La Division du Travail Social* [1893] (New York: Macmillan, 1933).

78. See T. F. H. Allen and T. B. Starr, *Hierarchy: Perspectives for Ecological Integrity* (Chicago: University of Chicago Press, 1982).

79. R. V. O'Neil, D. L. DeAngelis, J. B. Waide, and T. F. H. Allen, *A Hierarchical Concept of Ecosystems* (Princeton, N. J.: Princeton University Press, 1986).

80. H. A. Gleason, "The Structure and Development of the Plant Association," *Bulletin of the Torrey Botanical Club* 43 (1917): 463–481 and H. A. Gleason, "The Individualistic Concept of the Plant Association," *Bulletin of the Torrey Botanical Club* 53 (1926): 7–26.

81. See, I. Prigogine and I. Stengers, *Order Out of Chaos: Man's New Dialogue with Nature* (New York: Bantam Books, 1984).

82. G. E. Hutchinson, "The Lacustrine Microcosm Reconsidered," *American Scientist* 52 (1964): 334–341.

83. Gleason, "Individualistic Concept," p. 26.

84. S. Strogatz, *Sync: The Emerging Science of Spontaneous Order* (New York: Theia Press, 2004).

85. *Merriam-Webster's Collegiate Dictionary*, Eleventh Edition (Springfield, Mass.: Merriam-Webster, 2004), p. 836.

86. G. E. Hutchinson, "Concluding Remarks," *Population Studies: Animal Ecology and Demography/Cold Spring Harbor Studies on Quantitative Biology* 22 (1957): 415–427.

87. G. E. Hutchinson, *The Ecological Theater and the Evolutionary Play* (New Haven, Conn.: Yale University Press, 1965).

88. Tansley, "Use and Abuse," p. 299.

89. Ibid., p. 300.

90. Ibid.

91. H. Morowitz, "Biology as a Cosmological Science," *Main Currents in Modern Thought* 28 (1972): 151–157.

92. Tansley, "Use and Abuse," p. 299.

93. Ibid., p. 300.

94. Gleason, "Individualistic Concept," p. 9.

95. AL, *ASCA*, pp. 216–217.

96. Ibid., p. 217.

97. Ibid.

98. Ibid.

99. Ibid.

100. C. Elton, *The Ecology of Invasions by Animals and Plants* (London: Methuen, 1958).

101. AL, *ASCA*, p. 217.

102. E. R. Boose, D. R. Foster, and M. Fluet, "Hurricane Impacts to Tropical and Temperate Forest Landscapes," *Ecological Mongraphs* 64 (1994): 369–400.

103. See E. S. Blake, E. N. Rappaport, and C. W. Landsea, *The Deadliest, Costliest, and Most Intense United States Tropical Cyclones From 1851 to 2006: And Other Frequently Requested Hurricane Facts*, NOAA Technical Memorandum NWS TPC-5 (Miami, Fla.: National Weather Service, National Hurricane Center, 2007).

104. Ibid.

105. M. S. Ross, M. Carrington, L. J. Flynn, and P. L. Ruiz, "Forest Succession in Tropical Hardwood Hammocks in the Florida Keys: Effects of Direct Mortality From Hurricane Andrew," *Biotropica* 33 (2001): 23–33.

106. S. J. Pyne, *World Fire: The Culture of Fire on Earth* (Seattle: University of Washington Press, 1999).

107. F. A. Albini, "Estimating Wildfire Behavior and Effects," General Technical Report INT-30 (Ogden, Utah: U.S. Forest Service, 1976).

108. T. P. Duncan, D. A. Harpman, M. I. Voita, and T. J. Randall, "A Managed Flood on the Colorado River: Background, Objectives, Design, and Implementation," *Ecological Applications* 11 (2001): 635–643.

109. AL, *ASCA*, pp. 224–225.

110. A. Leopold, "Land Pathology" in S. L. Flader and J. B. Callicott, eds., *The River of the Mother of God and Other Essays by Aldo Leopold* (Madison: University of Wisconsin Press, 1991): 212–217; Leopold, "The Land Health Concept and Conservation".

Chapter 4

1. R. Descartes, *The Philosophical Works of Descartes*, ed. and tr. E. S. Haldane and G. R. T. Ross (Cambridge: Cambridge University Press, 1911).

2. See E. A. Burtt, *The Metaphysical Foundations of Modern Science* (Garden City, N.Y.: Doubleday, 1954).

3. T. Hobbes, *Leviathan with Selected Variants From the Latin Edition of 1668*; ed. E. Curley (Indianapolis, Ind.: Hackett, 1994). Hobbes writes (p. 7), "when a thing lies still, unless somewhat else stir it, it will lie still forever...[and] when a thing is in motion, it will eternally be in motion, unless somewhat else stay it"—this is Hobbes's anticipation of Newton's first law of motion. His anticipation of Newton's third law of motion is less general, restricted to the impact of external bodies on the internal organs of animals (p. 6): "the external body...presseth the organ proper to each sense...; which pressure, by the mediation of nerves and other strings and membranes of the body, causeth there a resistance or counter-pressure."

4. J. L. Heilbron, *Geometry Civilized: History, Culture, Technique* (New York: Oxford University Press, 1998).

5. Leviathan Chapter XIV is titled "Of the First and Second Natural Laws and of Contracts" and Chapter XV is titled "Of Other Laws of Nature." At the end of the latter, however, Hobbes writes (p. 100, emphasis added): "These dictates of reason men use to call by the name of laws, but improperly; for they are but conclusions or *theorems* concerning what conduceth to the conservation and defense of themselves, whereas law, properly, is the word of him that by right hath command over others. But yet if we consider the same *theorems*, as delivered in the word of God, that by right commandeth all things, then they are properly called laws."

6. See Hobbes, *Leviathan*, Chapter I, "Of Sense."

7. See Hobbes, *Leviathan*, Chapters II, "Of Imagination" and V, "Of Reason, and Science."

8. Hobbes, *Leviathan*, p. 25.

9. See Hobbes, *Leviathan*, Chapter VI, "Of the Interior Beginnings of Voluntary Motions, Commonly Called the Passions, and the Speeches by which They Are Expressed."

10. Hobbes, *Leviathan*, pp. 28, 30.

11. Ibid., p. 76.

12. See See Hobbes, *Leviathan*, Chapter XIII, "Of the Natural Condition of Mankind, as Concerning Their Felicity and Misery."

13. J. Locke, *An Essay Concerning Human Understanding*, Volume I, ed. J. Y. Yolton (New York: E. P. Dutton, 1961), p. xxxiv.

14. Ibid., p. 5.

15. Ibid.

16. J. Locke, *Essay*, p. 155.

17. Ibid. p. 157.

18. Ibid., p. 242.

19. Ibid.

20. Ibid., p. 156.

21. D. Hume, *An Inquiry Concerning the Principles of Morals*, ed. C. W. Hendel (New York: Liberal Arts Press, 1957), p. 8.

22. The *locus classicus* for the term "*experimentum crucis*" is I. Newton, "A Letter of Mr. Isaac Newton, Mathematick Professor in the University of Cambridge, containing his New Theory about Light and Colors," *Philosophical Transactions* 6 (1671): 75–87.

23. See, K. Popper, *The Logic of Scientific Discovery* (New York: Harper and Row, 1968).

24. S. G. Brush, "Why Was Relativity Accepted?," *Physics in Perspective* 1 (1999): 184–214.

25. A. A. Michelson and E. W. Morley, "On the Relative Motion of the Earth and the Luminiferous Ether," *American Journal of Science* 34 (1887): 333–345.

26. H. E. Múnera, "The Effect of Solar Motion upon the Fringe-shifts in a Michelson-Morley Interferometer à la Miller," *Annals de la Fondation Louis de Brogli* 27 (2002): 463–483.

27. Hume, *Inquiry*, p 8.

28. Popper, *Logic*.

29. Hume, *Inquiry*, p. 46.

30. Ibid., p. 8.

31. Ibid.

32. Ibid.

33. Ibid, p. 34.

34. I. Newton, *The Mathematical Principles of Natural Philosophy*, ed. S. Hawking, tr. A. Motte (Philadelphia: Running Press, 2005), p. 308.

35. Ibid.

36. B. Greene, *The Elegant Universe: Superstrings, Hidden Dimensions, and the Quest for the Ultimate Theory* (New York: W. W. Norton, 2003).

37. J. D. Barrow, ed., *Routledge Companion to the New Cosmology* (London: Routledge, 2001).

38. Newton, *Mathematical Principles*, p. 309.

39. I. Kant, *Foundations of the Metaphysics of Morals*, tr. L. W. Beck (Indianapolis, Ind.: Library of Liberal Arts, 1959), p. 4—originally published as *Grundlegung zur Metaphysik der Sitten* in 1785.

40. D. Hume, *An Enquiry Concerning the Principles of Morals*, ed. C. W. Hendel (New York: Liberal Arts Press, 1957), p. 99, emphasis added.

41. Kant, *Foundations*, p. 3, emphasis added.

42. Ibid., emphasis added.

43. Ibid., p. 4.

44. Ibid., p. 39.

45. Ibid., p. 42.

46. J. Bentham, *An Introduction to the Principles of Morals and Legislation* (online: Batoche Books, 2000), p. 14.

47. Ibid., pp. 14–15.

48. See J. S. Mill, *Utilitarianism* (London: Longmans, 1907).

49. Attributed to Bentham by J. S. Mill, "Bentham" *London and Westminster Review* (1838), revised and reprinted in John Stuart Mill, *Dissertations and Discussions* (London: G. Routledge, 1905). Bentham indeed wrote something to this effect in *The Rationale of Reward* (London: John and H. L. Hunt, 1825).

50. See, P. A. Samuelson, *Foundations of Economic Analysis* (Cambridge, Mass.: Harvard University Press, 1947).

51. P. C. Fishburn, *Utility Theory for Decision Making* (Huntington, N.Y.: Robert E. Kreiger, 1970).

52. A. Randall, "Cost-Benefit Analysis," in J. B. Callicott and R. Frodeman, eds., *Encyclopedia of Environmental Ethics and Philosophy* (New York: Macmillan, 2009): 189–193.

53. See I. Kant, *Critique of Pure Reason*, tr. M. Müller (New York: Doubleday, 1961).

54. See M. Baur and D. O. Dahlstrom, eds., *The Emergence of German Idealism* (Washington: Catholic University of America Press, 1999).

55. See R. C. Solomon and K. M. Higgins, eds., *The Age of German Idealism* (New York: Routledge, 2003).

56. See K. Ameriks, *The Cambridge Companion to German Idealism* (Cambridge: Cambridge University Press, 2000).

57. See D. Boucher, ed., *The British Idealists* (Cambridge: Cambridge University Press, 1997).

58. See A. J. Ayer, ed., *Logical Positivism* (New York: Free Press, 1959).

59. L. Wittgenstein, "A Lecture on Ethics," *Philosophical Review* 74 (1965): 3–12, pp. 7, 11–12, emphasis in original. The text of this lecture delivered in 1929 or 1930 was published posthumously and is of uncertain provenance.

60. By "proposition" Ayer meant what is asserted by a statement, allowing that there were alternative ways of stating a proposition. Thus in the two sample propositions here stated, the words "absolutely" and "intrinsically" might be swapped for one other, altering the statements, but not the propositions.

61. A. J. Ayer, *Language, Truth, and Logic* (New York: Dover, 1946), p. 103—first published in 1936 in London by V. Gollancz.

62. Ibid.

63. Ibid., pp. 103–104.

64. Ibid., pp. 112–113.

65. Ibid., p. 113.

66. Ibid., p. 112.

67. See L. Kohlberg, *The Psychology of Moral Development: The Nature and Validity of Moral Stages* (San Francisco: Harper and Row, 1984).

68. See J. Piaget, *Biology and Knowledge: An Essay on the Relations between Organic Regulations and Cognitive Processes*, tr. B. Walsh (Chicago: University of Chicago Press, 1971); and J. Piaget, *Behavior and Evolution*, tr. D. Nicholson-Smith (New York: Pantheon Books 1978).

69. See J. Piaget, *The Development of Thought: Equilibration of Cognitive Structures*, tr. A. Rosin (New York: Viking Press, 1977).

70. See L. Kohlberg, *Essays on Moral Development* (San Francisco: Harper and Row, 1981).

71. The concept of justice was central to the *telos* of Kohlberg's moral development process. See L. Kohlberg, *The Philosophy of Moral Development: Moral Stages and the Idea of Justice* (San Francisco: Harper and Row, 1981).

72. See C. Gilligan, *In a Different Voice: Psychological Theory and Women's Development* (Cambridge, Mass.: Harvard University Press, 1982). See also E. F. Kittay and D. T. Myers, eds., *Women and Moral Theory* (Totowa, N. J.: Rowman and Littlefield, 1987).

73. Hesiod, *Theogony*, tr. N. O. Brown (New York: Liberal Arts Press, 1953).

74. J. Rawls, *Justice as Fairness: A Restatement* (Cambridge, Mass.: Belknap Press of Harvard University, 2001).

75. For discussion, see Kittay and Myers, *Women and Moral Theory*.

76. Gilligan, *In a Different Voice*.

77. C. Darwin, *The Descent of Man*, Second Edition (London: Murray, 1874), p. 137, emphasis added.

78. V. C. Wynne-Edwards, *Animal Dispersion in Relation to Social Behavior* (London: Oliver & Boyd, 1962).

79. Ibid., p. 18.

80. G. F. Gause, *The Struggle for Existence* (Baltimore: Williams and Wilkins, 1934); G. Hardin, "The Competitive Exclusion Principle," *Science* 131 (1960): 1292–1297.

81. Ibid., p. 20.

82. See, for example, W. M. Wheeler, *The Social Insects: Their Origin and Evolution* (New York: Harcourt, Brace, 1928) and W. M. Wheeler, *Essays in Philosophical Biology* (Cambridge, Mass.: Harvard University Press, 1939).

83. See, for example, R. C. Miller, "The Mind of the Flock," *Condor* 21, no. 6 (1921): 183–186.

84. See T. Dobzhansky, *Genetics and the Origin of Species* (New York: Columbia University Press, 1937); J. B. S. Haldane, *The Causes of Evolution* (London: Longman, Green, 1932); J. S. Huxley, *Evolution: The Modern Synthesis* (London: Allen and Unwin, 1942).

85. G. C. Williams, *Adaptation and Natural Selection: A Critique of Some Current Evolutionary Thought* (Princeton, N. J.: Princeton University Press, 1966), p. 19.

86. Ibid., p. 243.

87. F. de Waal, *Good Natured: The Origins of Right and Wrong in Humans and Other Animals* (Cambridge, Mass.: Harvard University Press, 1996), p. 18.

88. T. H. Huxley, *Evolution and Ethics* (London: Macmillan, 1894), p. 11.

89. Ibid., p. 12.

90. Ibid., p. 59; G. C. Williams, "A Sociobiological Expansion of *Evolution and Ethics*," in J. Paradis and G. C. Williams, eds., *T. H. Huxley's Evolution and Ethics with New Essays on Its Victorian and Sociobiological Context* (Princeton, N.J.: Princeton University Press, 1989): 179–214; p. 180.

91. Ibid., p. 208.

92. R. Dawkins, "The Ontogeny of a Pecking Preference in Domestic Chicks," *Zeitschrift für Tierppsychologie* 25 (1968): 170–186; See also R. Dawkins, *The Extended Phenotype: The Gene as the Unit of Selection* (Oxford: W. H. Freeman, 1982).

93. E. O. Wilson, *The Insect Societies* (Cambridge, Mass.: Belknap Press of Harvard University, 1971).

94. E. O. Wilson, *Sociobiology: The New Synthesis* (Cambridge, Mass.: Belknap Press of Harvard University, 1975), p. 3.

95. Ibid., pp. 3–4.

96. J. Maynard Smith, "Group Selection and Kin Selection," *Nature* 201 (1964): 1145–1147; W. D. Hamilton, "The Genetical Evolution of Social Behavior," *Journal of Theoretical Biology* 7 (1964): 1–52.

97. R. L. Trivers, "The Evolution of Reciprocal Altruism," *Quarterly Review of Biology* 46 (1971): 35–57.

98. Wilson, *Sociobiology*, p. 120.

99. R. Axelrod and W. D. Hamilton, "The Evolution of Cooperation," *Science* 211 (1981): 1390–1396.

100. A similar point is made by M. Midgley, "Gene Juggling," *Philosophy* 54 (1976): 439–458.

101. Wilson, *Sociobiology*, p. 3.

102. Ibid.

103. Ibid.

104. Williams, "A Sociobiological Expansion," p. 198.

105. de Waal, *Good Natured*, pp. 16–17.

106. See, for an early and particularly incisive example, M. Sahlins, *The Use and Abuse of Biology: An Anthropological Critique of Sociobiology* (Ann Arbor: University of Michigan Press, 1976).

107. Wilson, *Sociobiology*, p. 547.

108. See, for example, E. Allen, B. Beckwith, J. Beckwith, S. Chorover, D. Culver, M. Duncan, et al., "Against 'Sociobiology'" *New York Review of Books*, November 13, 1975; and Sociobiology Study Group of Science for the People, "Sociobiology—Another Biological

Determinism," *BioScience* 26, no. 3 (1976): 182, 184–186—among these authors are also R. Lewontin and S. J. Gould.

109. E. O. Wilson, *On Human Nature* (Cambridge, Mass.: Belknap Press of Harvard University, 1978), p. 36.

110. Wilson, *Sociobiology*, p. 559.

111. S. Pinker, *The Language Instinct: How the Mind Creates Language* (New York: HarperCollins, 1995).

Chapter 5

1. A. G. N. Flew, *Evolutionary Ethics* (London: Macmillan, 1967).

2. J. Haidt, *The Righteous Mind: Why Good People Are Divided by Politics and Religion* (New York: Pantheon Boooks, 2012), pp. 33 and 35.

3. For example, all the following collections of papers include contributions by academic philosophers: M. S. Gregory, A. Silvers, and D. Sutch, eds., *Sociobiology and Human Nature* (San Francisco: Josey-Bass Publishers, 1978)—by D. L. Hull, J. R. Searle, J. B. Schneewind, and M. Grene; A. L. Caplan, ed., *The Sociobiology Debate* (New York: Harper & Row, 1978)—by A. Flew, M. Ruse, and A. L. Caplan; G. W. Barlow and J. Silverberg, eds., *Sociobiology: Beyond Nature/Nurture?* (Boulder, Col.: Westview Press, 1980)—by D. L. Hull and A. L. Caplan; Ashley Montague, ed., *Sociobiology Examined* (New York: Oxford University Press, 1980)—two papers by M. Midgley.

4. E. O. Wilson, *Sociobiology: The New Synthesis* (Cambridge, Mass.: Belknap Press of Harvard University, 1975), p. 562.

5. P. Singer, *The Expanding Circle: Ethics and Sociobiology* (New York: Farrar, Straus and Giroux, 1981), p. xi.

6. Wilson, *Sociobiology*; J. Haidt, "The Moral Emotions," in R. J. Davidson, K. R. Scherer, and H. H. Goldsmith, eds., *Handbook of Affective Sciences* (New York: Oxford University Press, 2002).

7. Singer, *Expanding Circle*, p. 93.

8. Ibid., p. 153.

9. Ibid., p. 121.

10. Ibid., p. 109.

11. J. Rachels, *Created From Animals: The Moral Implications of Darwinism* (New York: Oxford University Press, 1990), p. 1.

12. Ibid., p. 79.

13. Ibid., p. 194.

14. Ibid., p. 196.

15. Ibid., p. 197, emphasis added.

16. C. Darwin, *The Descent of Man and Selection in Relation to Sex*, Second Edition (London: Murray, 1874), p. 127.

17. F. de Waal, *Good Natured* (Cambridge, Mass.: Harvard University Press, 1996), p. 1.

18. M. Midgley, *Animals and Why They Matter* (Athens: University of Georgia Press, 1983).

19. A. Leopold, *A Sand County Almanac and Sketches Here and There* (New York: Oxford University Press, 1949), p. viii.

20. Ibid., p. 109.

21. For implicitly Lockean land-use-property-and-property-rights prevailing assumptions in rural American communities, see E. C. Hargrove, "Anglo-American Land Use Attitudes," *Environmental Ethics* 2 (1980): 121–148.

22. J. Derrida, *Politiques de l'Amitié* (Paris: Galileé, 1994); J. Derrida, *Pregnaces: The Wash Paintings by Collette Deblé* (Mont-de-Marsan: L'Atelier des Brisants, 2004).

23. Rachels, *Created From Animals*, p. 184.

24. A. Smedley and B. D. Smedley, "Race as Biology Is Fiction, Racism as a Social Problem Is Real," *American Psychologist* 60 (2005): 16–26.

25. D. Dennet, *Darwin's Dangerous Idea: Evolution and the Meanings of Life* (New York: Simon and Schuster, 1995).

26. P. Singer, *A Darwinian Left: Politics, Evolution, and Cooperation* (New Haven, Conn.: Yale University Press, 1999), p. 32.

27. Dennet, *Darwin's*, p. 490; Dennet quotes and cites, S. Pinker, *The Language Instinct* (New York: Morrow, 1994), p. 406.

28. Singer, *Darwnian Left*, pp. 32–33.

29. Wilson, *On Human Nature*, p. 167.

30. As noted by Flew, *Evolutionary Ethics*; Dennet, *Darwin's*; and Singer, *Darwnian Left*.

31. L. Arnhart, *Darwinian Natural Right: The Biological Ethics of Human Nature* (Albany: State University of New York Press, 1998); L. Arnhart, *Darwinian Conservatism* (Charlottesville, Va.: Imprint Academic, 2005).

32. P. Cohen, "A Split Emerges as Republicans Discuss Darwin," *New York Times*, Saturday, May 5, 2007.

33. Haidt, *The Righteous Mind*.

34. For a synoptic history see J. Haidt, "The New Synthesis in Moral Psychology," *Science* 316 (2007): 998–1002.

35. E. Sober and D. S. Wilson, *Unto Others: The Evolution and Psychology of Unselfish Behavior* (Cambridge, Mass.: Harvard University Press, 1998).

36. E. O. Wilson, "Ken Selection as the Key to Altruism: Its Rise and Fall," *Social Research* 72 (2005): 159–166; M. A. Novak, C. E. Tarnita, and E. O. Wilson, "The Evolution of Eusociality," *Nature* 466 (2010): 1057–1062.

37. D. S. Wilson and E. O. Wilson, "Rethinking the Theoretical Foundations of Sociobiology," *Quarterly Review of Biology* 82 (2007): 327–348; D. S. Wilson and E. O. Wilson, "Evolution 'for the Good of the Group,'" *American Scientist* 96 (2008): 380–389.

38. C. Boehm, *Moral Origins: The Evolution of Virtue, Altruism, and Shame* (New York: Basic Books, 2012).

39. S. Bowles and H. Gintis, *A Cooperative Species: Human Reciprocity and Its Evolution* (Princeton, N. J.: Princeton University Press, 2011), p. 198, emphasis added.

40. For a summary, see R. McElreath and J. Henrich, "Dual Inheritance Theory: The Evolution of Human Cultural Capacities and Cultural Evolution," in R. Dunbar and L. Barrett, eds., *Oxford Handbook of Evolutionary Psychology* (New York: Oxford University Press, 2007).

41. Ibid., pp. 198–199.

42. Sober and Wilson, *Unto Others*, p.107.

43. Ibid., p. 111.

44. Ibid., p. 189.

45. Ibid., p. 150.

46. Ibid., p. 308.

47. Haidt, "The New Synthesis," pp. 1000–1001.

48. S. F. Gilbert, J. Sapp, and A. I. Tauber, "A Symbiotic View of Life: We Have Never Been Individuals," *Quarterly Review of Biology* 87 (2012): 325–341, p. 331.

49. See, for example, P. S Churchland, *Braintrust: What Neuroscience Tells Us about Morality* (Princeton, N.J.: Princeton University Press, 2011); M. S. Gazzaniga, *The Ethical Brain: The Science of Our Moral Dilemmas* (New York: Dana Press, 2005); J. J. Prinz, *The Emotional Construction of Morals* (New York: Oxford University Press, 2007).

50. J. Haidt, "The Emotional Dog and Its Rational Tail: A Social Intuitionist Approach to Moral Judgment," *Psychological Review* 108 (2001): 814–834.

51. Haidt, "The New Synthesis," p. 998.

52. See, for example, J. D. Meyer, P. Salovey, and D. R. Caruso, "Models of Emotional Intelligence," in R. J. Sternberg, ed., *Handbook of Intelligence* (Cambridge: Cambridge University Press, 2000).

53. See N. Chomsky, *Knowledge of Language: Its Nature, Origin, and Use* (New York: Praeger, 1986); S. Pinker, *The Language Instinct: How the Mind Creates Language* (New York: HarperCollins, 1995).

54. M. D. Hauser, *Moral Minds: How Nature Designed Our Universal Sense of Right and Wrong* (New York: HarperCollins, 2006).

55. P. Foot, "The Problem of Abortion and the Doctrine of Double Effect," *Oxford Review* 5 (1967): 5–15.

56. S. Pinker, *The Better Angels of Our Nature: Why Violence Has Declined* (New York: Viking, 2011), pp. 622 and 628.

57. Hume, *Inquiry*, p. 149.

58. Ibid., p. 141.

59. Ibid., p. 149.

60. Ibid., pp. 149–150.

61. Ibid., p. 150.

62. Pinker, *Better Angels.*

63. Hume, *Inquiry*, p. 150.

64. Ayer, *Language, Truth, and Logic*, p. 112.

65. Ibid., p. 110.

66. Rachels, *Created From Animals*, p. 175.

67. Sober and Wilson, *Unto Others*, pp. 237–238, emphasis in original.

68. Ibid., p. 238.

69. Ibid., pp, 238–239.

70. de Waal, *Good Natured.*

71. Sober and Wilson, *Unto Others*, p. 233.

72. Ibid., p. 234.

73. Pinker, *Better Angles*, p. 574.

74. Goleman, *Emotional Intelligence*, p. 107.

75. Ibid.

76. Plato, *The Republic* 444e, tr. Paul Shorey, Loeb Classical Library (London: William Heineman Ltd., 1963), p. 418.

77. Ibid.

78. For details see D. Gollaher, "Female Circumcision," *Circumcision: A History of the World's Most Controversial Surgery* (New York: Basic Books, 2001), pp. 187–207.

79. P. Chesler, "Are Honor Killings Simply Domestic Violence?," *Middle East Quarterly* 16 (2009): 61–69. Chesler's answer to the title question is an emphatic "No." Honor killings are regarded as virtuous in some cultures.

Chapter 6

1. A. Leopold, "Some Fundamentals of Conservation in the Southwest," *Environmental Ethics* 1 (1979): 131–141, reprinted in S. L. Flader and J. B. Callicott, eds., *The River of the Mother of God and Other Essays by Aldo Leopold* (Madison: University of Wisconsin Press, 1991): 86–97, p. 88—hereafter AL, "SFCS." Because the reprinted version corrects some errors that appear in the original typescript that survived in the 1979 publication—most notably the spelling of Ouspensky's name as "Onspensky," which was probably due to a misreading of Leopold's handwriting by his secretary—I will refer to the reprinted essay here.

2. See A. Leopold, "Grass, Brush, Timber, and Fire in Southern Arizona," *Journal of Forestry* 22, no. 6 (1924): 1–10 reprinted in S. L. Flader and J. B. Callicott, eds., *The River of the Mother of God and Other Essays by Aldo Leopold* (Madison: University of Wisconsin Press, 1991): 114–132, for a detailed analysis.

3. W. deBuys, *A Great Aridness: Climate Change and the Future of the Southwest* (New York: Oxford University Press, 2011).

4. AL, "SFCS," p. 94.

5. Leopold quotes the same passage from the Book of Ezekiel in "The Forestry of the Prophets" (cited in note 7) and there cites his source as "*Moulton's Reader's Bible*." See R. G. Moulton, *Modern Reader's Bible* (New York: Macmillan, 1907).

6. According to C. Meine, *Aldo Leopold: His Life and Work* (Madison: University of Wisconsin Press, 1988), p. 183: "Leopold's love of literature focused during this period on the Bible...[with] a particular fondness for the Old Testament prophets, proverbs, and psalms." The editor and translator of Leopold's Bible, R. G. Moulton, was also author of *The Literary Study of the Bible: An Account of the Leading Forms of Literature Represented in the Sacred Writings* (Lexington, Mass.: D. C. Heath, 1899).

7. A. Leopold, "The Forestry of the Prophets," *Journal of Forestry* 18 (1920): 412–419, reprinted in S. L. Flader and J. B. Callicott, eds., *The River of the Mother of God and Other Essays by Aldo Leopold* (Madison: University of Wisconsin Press, 1991): 71–77, p. 77.

8. Ibid., pp. 71 and 76.

9. Ibid., p. 72. Jesus the Son of Sirach is a late Old Testament author whose book is canonized in some, but not all bibles depending on the sect.

10. J. Tallmadge, "Anatomy of a Classic," in J. B. Callicott, ed., *Companion to A Sand County Almanac: Interpretive and Critical Essays* (Madison: University of Wisconsin Press, 1987): 110–127.

11. AL, "SFCS," p. 93.

12. Ibid., p. 94.

13. Virtue ethics is characterized as "agent-based" by M. Slote, *Morals from Motives* (New York: Oxford University Press, 2001).

14. Meine, *Aldo Leopold*, p. 17.

15. AL, "SFCS," 94.

16. Ibid.

17. Ibid.

18. Ibid., pp. 94–95.

19. Ibid., p. 94.

20. Ibid.

21. Ibid. Leopold accurately quotes from P. D. Ouspensky, *Tertium Organum: The Third Canon of Thought; A Key to the Enigmas of the World*, tr. N. Bessaraboff and C. Bragdon (New York: Knopf, 1922), p. 200.

22. AL, "SFCA," p. 95, emphasis added.

23. Ibid.

24. Ouspensky, *Tertium Organum*, p. 200, emphasis added; emphasis in original on "accessible to our observation" and "the growth" removed.

25. J. W. Cahn, "Theory of Crystal Growth and Interface Motion in Crystalline Materials," *Acta Metallurgica* 8 (1960): 554–562.

26. Ouspensky, *Tertium Organum*, p. xiii.

27. See, C. Freemantle, "Ouspensky" in *Man, Myth, and Magic: An Illustrated Encyclopedia of the Supernatural*, 12 vols. (London: Pinell, 1972): 2092–2093.

28. S. L. Flader, "Leopold's Some Fundamentals of Conservation: A Commentary," *Environmental Ethics* 1 (1979): 143–148, notes that the copy she found in Leopold's library was published by Knopf and dated 1925, two years *after* the composition of "Some Fundamentals"—which was "early in 1923," according to Flader, p. 144.

29. See G. Munson, "Black Sheep Philosophers: Gurdieff—Ouspensky—Orage," *Tomorrow* 6 (1950): 20–25.

30. See J. Shirley, *Gurdjieff: An Introduction to His Life and Ideas* (New York: J. P. Tracher/Penquin, 2004).

31. A. Leopold, *A Sand County Almanac and Sketches Here and There* (New York: Oxford University Press, 1949), p. 138.

32. Ouspensky, *Tertium Organum*, p. 177.

33. A. Pryor, "Thinking Like a Mystic: The Legacy of P. D. Ouspensky's *Tertium Organum* on the Development of Aldo Leopold's 'Thinking Like a Mountain,'" *Journal of Religion, Nature, and Culture* 5 (2011): 465–490.

34. AL, "SFCS," p. 95.

35. See A. Clark, *Being There: Putting Brain, Body, and World Together Again* (Cambridge: MIT Press, 1997); S. Blackmore, *Consciousness: An Introduction* (New York: Oxford University Press, 2004).

36. Ouspensky, *Tertium Organum*, p. 200.

37. Ibid., p. 199.

38. Ibid.

39. Pryor, "Thinking."

40. AL, "SFCS," p. 95.

41. Ibid.

42. Ibid. Leopold accurately quotes Ouspensky, *Tertium Organum*, p. 201.

43. Ouspensky, *Tertium Organum*, p. 201.

44. Al, "SFCS," p. 95, emphasis added.

45. Ibid.

46. See A. Schweitzer, *The Philosophy of Civilization* (New York: Macmillan, 1951) and P. W. Taylor, *Respect for Nature: A Theory of Environmental Ethics* (Princeton, N.J.: Princeton University Press, 1986).

47. See J. Dudley, *Broken Words: The Abuse of Science and Faith in American Politics* (New York: Random House, 2011).

48. AL, "SFCS," p. 95.

49. Ibid.

50. Ibid.

51. Ibid.

52. Ibid.

53. See, J. B. Callicott and R. T. Ames, eds., *Nature in Asian Traditions of Thought* (Albany: State University of New York Press, 1989).

54. B. Horwood, "Stewardship as an Environmental Ethic," *Pathways* 3, no. 4 (1991): 5–10.

55. See C. Merchant, *The Death of Nature: Women, Ecology, and the Scientific Revolution* (New York: Harper and Row, 1983).

56. AL, "SFCS," p. 96.

57. Ibid., pp. 97 and 95.

58. Ibid., p. 95. Leopold probably refers to Jeannette Augustus Marks, "Swinburne: A Study in Pathology," *Yale Review* 9 (January 1920): 349–365.

59. Marks, "Swinburne," p. 353. D. Ehrenfeld, *The Arrogance of Humanism* (New York: Oxford University Press, 1978).

60. AL, "SFCS," pp. 95–96. See J. Muir, *Our National Parks* (Boston: Houghton Mifflin, 1901), p. 57.

61. J. Muir, *A Thousand-Mile Walk to the Gulf* (Boston: Houghton Mifflin, 1916), p. 98. The book was edited by W. F. Badè from the original journal Muir kept on his trek from Indiana to Florida in 1867–1868 and a typed transcription which Muir himself had caused to be made.

62. AL, "SFCS," p. 96, emphasis in original. "Thantopsis" was written in 1811, when Bryant was only seventeen years old and first published in the *North American Review* in 1817. See P. Godwin, ed., *The Poetical Works of William Cullen Bryant*, Volume First (New York: Russell and Russell, 1883), pp. 17–20.

63. AL, "SFCS," p. 96.

64. Ibid.

65. Tallmadge, "Anatomy of a Classic," pp. 117–118. The numbers in parentheses refer to pages in the Oxford edition of *A Sand County Almanac*.

66. Leopold, *Sand County*, p. 10.

67. AL, "SFCS," p. 96.

68. Ibid., emphasis added.

69. See B. G. Norton, "The Constancy of Leopold's Land Ethic," *Conservation Biology* 2 (1988): 93–102.

70. Leopold, *Sand County*, p. 207.

71. Ibid.

72. For a full discussion, see J. B. Callicott, W. Grove-Fanning, J. Rowland, D. Baskind, R. H. French, and K. Walker, "Was Aldo Leopold a Pragmatist? Rescuing Leopold from the Imagination of Bryan Norton," *Environmental Values* 18 (2009): 453–486.

73. I capitalize "Pragmatism" and "Pragmatist" thus throughout, when the former is the proper name of a particular school of philosophy and the latter the proper name of its exponents; I reserve "pragmatism" and "pragmatist" thus, with a lower-case "p" to refer, respectively, to an experimental approach to problem solving and to those who approach problem solving experimentally.

74. Norton, "Constancy," p. 101.

75. A. T. Hadley, *Some Influences in Modern Philosophic Thought* (New Haven, Conn.: Yale University Press, 1913), p. 98.

76. Ibid., p. 73.
77. Norton, "Constancy," p. 95.
78. P. D. Ouspensky, *The Third Canon of Thought: A Key to the Enigmas of the World*, tr. E. Kadloubovsky and P. D. Ouspensky (New York: Alfred A. Knopf, 1947). By the time he assisted in the retranslation of *Tertium Organum*, Ouspensky had been long under the influence of Gurdjieff's thought.
79. Norton, "Constancy," p. 96.
80. Ibid., p. 97.
81. W. James, "Lecture 2. What Pragmatism Means," in W. James, *Pragmatism: A New Name for Some Old Ways of Thinking* (New York: Longman Green, 1907): 17–32, p. 17.
82. Norton, "Constancy," p. 97.
83. Ibid.
84. AL, "SFCS," p. 96.
85. P. S. Ybarra, "Erasure by U.S. Legislation: Ruiz de Burton's Nineteenth Century Novels and the Lost Archive of Mexican American Environmental Knowledge," in S. LeMenager, T. Shewry, and Ken Hiltner, eds., *Environmental Criticism for the Twenty-First Century* (New York: Routledge, 2011): 135–147; W. C. Davis, *Lone Star Rising: The Revolutionary Birth of the Texas Republic* (New York: Free Press, 2004).
86. M. Menchaca, *Recovering History, Constructing Race: The Indian, Black, and White Roots of Mexican Americans* (Austin: University of Texas Press, 2001).
87. AL, "SFCS," p. 96.
88. Ibid.
89. Ibid., pp. 96–97. Leopold quotes from Bryant, "Thanatopsis" p. 19, with only some slight emendation in punctuation.
90. Ibid, p. 97.
91. Ibid.
92. Ibid, p. 97, emphasis added. Burroughs's potato bug that exterminates the potato and thereby exterminates itself was a favorite trope of Leopold's, which he deploys in other essays, for example, in "Wilderness as a Form of Land Use," *Journal of Land and Public Utility Economics* 1 (1925): 398–404, reprinted in S. L. Flader and J. B. Callicott, eds., *The River of the Mother of God and Other Essays by Aldo Leopold* (Madison: University of Wisconsin Press, 1991): 134–142. In none of these places does Leopold cite his source in Burroughs's large corpus. Leopold probably alludes to J. Burroughs, "Each for Its Own Sake," in J. Burroughs, *Accepting the Universe: Essays in Naturalism* (Boston: Houghton Mifflin, 1920): 30–53. On p. 35 these words are found: "The potato bug, if left alone would exterminate the potato and so exterminate itself." The entire essay is a blistering attack on anthropocentrism.
93. Norton, "Constancy," p. 94.
94. B. G. Norton, *Sustainability: A Philosophy of Adaptive Ecosystem Management* (Chicago: University of Chicago Press, 2005).
95. For a full discussion, see Callicott et al., "Was Aldo Leopold a Pragmatist?"
96. Leopold, *Sand County*, p. 110.
97. Ibid., pp. 204–205.
98. AL, "SFCS," p. 97. Leopold does not identify the author of the line he quotes. It seems concordant with "Thanatopsis," but it is not to be found there; rather, it is a fragment from R. L. Stevenson, *Virginibus Puerisque* (Teddington: Echo Library, 2006), p. 80.
99. AL, "SFCS," p. 94.

Chapter 7

1. I capitalize *Pragmatism* as the proper name of a philosophical school (and also of its grammatical variants *Pragmatic*, *Pragmatist* and so on) to avoid confusion with and assimilation to *pragmatism* (*pragmatic*, *pragmatist* and so on), which is the common name of a flexible and adaptive stance toward problem solving. There were many pragmatists before Pragmatism came on the philosophical scene and the pragmatism of many pragmatists who came after Pragmatism was not influenced by the philosophies of such Pragmatists as Charles Sanders Peirce, William James, and John Dewey.

2. W. James, *Pragmatism, A New Name for Some Old Ways of Thinking, Popular Lectures on Philosophy* (New York: Longmans, Green, 1907).

3. Ibid.

4. B. G. Norton, "The Constancy of Leopold's Land Ethic," *Conservation Biology* 2 (1988): 93–102.

5. A. Leopold, "Some Fundamentals of Conservation in the Southwest," *Environmental Ethics* 1 (1979): 131–141, reprinted in S. L. Flader and J. B. Callicott, eds., *The River of the Mother of God and Other Essays by Aldo Leopold* (Madison: University of Wisconsin Press, 1991): 86–97, p. 95.

6. Norton, "Constancy," p. 95.

7. Leopold, "Some Fundamentals," p. 96.

8. In addition to the discussion in Chapter 6, see J. B. Callicott, W. Grove-Fanning, J. Rowland, D. Baskind, R. H. French, and K. Walker, "Was Aldo Leopold a Pragmatist? Rescuing Leopold from the Imagination of Bryan Norton," *Environmental Values* 18 (2009): 453–486.

9. For an excellent discussion, see E. A. Burtt, *The Metaphysical Foundations of Modern Physical Science*, Second Edition (Garden City, N.Y.: Doubleday, 1954).

10. See, for example, N. Bohr, *Atomic Physics and Human Knowledge* (New York: John Wiley, 1958); E. Schrödinger, *What Is Life?* and *Mind and Matter* (Cambridge: Cambridge University Press, 1944 and 1958, respectively); W. Heisenberg, *Philosophical Problems of Quantum Physics*, tr. F. C. Hayes (Woodbridge, Conn.: Ox Bow Press, 1952) and *Physics and Philosophy: The Revolution in Modern Science* (New York: Prometheus Books, 1958).

11. A. Einstein, "Zur Elektrodynamik Bewegter Körper," *Annalen der Physik* 17 (1905): 891–921; A. Einstein, "Die Grundlage der Allgemeinen Relativitaetstheorie," *Annalen der Physik* 49 (1916): 769–822.

12. A. Einstein, *Relativity: The Special and General Theory*, tr. R. W. Lawson (London: Methuen, 1916; New York: Henry Holt, 1920).

13. H. Minkowski, "Raum und Zeit," *Physikalische Zeitschrift* 10 (1909): 104–111.

14. See M. Monastyrsky, *Riemann, Topology, and Physics* (Boston: Birkhäuser, 1999).

15. I. Kant, *Critique of Pure Reason*, tr. J. M. D. Meikeljohn (London: Henry G. Bohn, 1855).

16. P. D. Ouspensky, *Tertium Organum: The Third Canon of Thought; A Key to the Enigmas of the World*, tr. N. Bessaraboff and C. Bragdon (New York: Knopf, 1920).

17. G. S. Levit, *Biogeochemistry—Biosphere—Noosphere: The Growth of the Theoretical System of Vladimir Ivanovich Vernadsky* (Berlin: VWB—Verlag für Wissenschaft und Bildung, 2001).

18. V. I. Vernadsky, "Problems of Biogeochemistry, II," tr. G. Vernadsky; ed. G. E. Hutchinson, *Transactions of the Connecticut Academy of Arts and Sciences* 35 (1944): 487–517, p. 510.

19. Ibid.

20. L. Pastuer, "On the Asymmetry of Naturally Occurring Organic Compounds," in G. M. Richardson, ed., tr., *The Foundations of Stereochemistry* (New York: American Book Company, 1901).

21. P. Debré, *Louis Pasteur*, tr. E. Forster (Baltimore: Johns Hopkins University Press, 1998).

22. Vernadsky, "Problems," p. 495.

23. P. Curie, "Sur la symétrie dans les phénomènes physiques: Symétrie d' un champ électrique et d'un champ magnétique," *Journal de Physique*, 3rd series, Volume 3 (1894): 393–417; see A. F. Chalmers, "Currie's Principle," *British Journal for the Philosophy of Science* 21 (1970): 133–148.

24. Vernadsky, "Problems," p. 496.

25. Levit, *Biogeochemistry*, p. 21.

26. Vernadsky, "Problems," p. 512.

27. Ibid.

28. V. I. Vernadsky, *The Biosphere*, tr. D. B. Langmuir; ed. M. A. S. McMenamin (New York: Copernicus, 1998); see also Levit, *Biogeochemistry*.

29. In E. Suess, *Das Antlitz der Erde* (Wien: F. Tempsky, 1892); E. Suess, *The Face of the Earth*, tr. H. B. C. Sollas (Oxford: Clarendon Press, 1904).

30. V. I. Venrnadsky, *The Biosphere*, ed. Tango Snyder Parrish (Oracle, Ariz.: Synergetic Press, 1986). For the story behind this evisceration and mutilation of *The Biosphere*, see L. Margulis, M. Ceruti, S. Golubic, R. Guerrero, N. Ikeda, N. Ikezawa, et al., "Foreword to the English Edition," in V. I. Vernadsky, *The Biosphere*.

31. Vernadsky, *Biosphere*.

32. Margulis et al., "Foreword."

33. Vernadsky, "Problems."

34. Vernadsky, *Biosphere*, p. 40.

35. Ibid., p. 41, n. 3.

36. Ibid., p. 54, n. 49; p. 89, n. 170.

37. Ibid.

38. See M. Goldstein and F. Inge, *The Refrigerator and the Universe* (Cambridge, Mass.: Harvard University Press, 1993), for a history of thermodynamics.

39. H. Bergson, L'Évolution créatrice (Paris: PUF, 1907).

40. Vernadsky, *Biosphere*, p. 48 (emphasis in original).

41. Ibid., p. 53, n. 45.

42. Ibid. p. 51.

43. F. Hoyle, "A New Model for the Expanding Universe," *Monthly Notices of the Royal Astronomical Society* 108 (1948): 372.

44. Vernadsky, *Biosphere*, p. 70.

45. Ibid., p. 71, n. 105. An authoritative figure is 5.1480×10^{18} kg. See K. E. Trenberth and L. Smith, "The Mass of the Atmosphere: A Constraint on Global Analyses," *Journal of Climate* 18 (2005): 864–875.

46. Ibid., p. 149; K. J. H. Phillips, *Guide to the Sun* (New York: Cambridge University Press, 1995).

47. Vernadsky, *Biosphere*, p. 55.

48. Ibid., p. 141.

49. Ibid., p. 139.

50. R. A. Berner, "Atmospheric Oxygen Over Phanerozoic Time," *Proceedings of the National Academy of Sciences of the United States of America* 96 (1999): 10955–10957.

51. H. Blatt, G. Middleton, and R. Murray, *Origin of Sedimentary Rocks* (Englewood Cliffs, N.J.: Prentice Hall, 1980); H. Blatt and R. J. Tracy, *Petrology; Igneous, Sedimentary, and Metamorphic*, Second Edition (New York: W. H. Freeman).

52. R. M. Hazen, D. Papineau, W. Bleeker, R. T. Downs, J. M. Ferry, T. J. McCoy, et al., "Mineral Evolution," *American Mineralogist* 93 (2008): 1693–1720.

53. Ibid.

54. Vernadsky, *Biosphere*, p. 144.

55. P. Lowman, *Exploring Space, Exploring Earth: New Understanding of the Earth From Space Research* (Cambridge; Cambridge University Press, 2002); C. Plummer, D. McGeary, and D. Carlson, *Physical Geology* (New York: McGraw Hill, 2005).

56. V. I. Vernadsky, "The Biosphere and the Noösphere," *American Scientist* 33 (1945): 1–12, p. 6.

57. Vernadsky, *Biosphere*, p. 70 (emphasis in original).

58. See D. Wells, *Lives of a Tree: An Uncommon History* (Chapel Hill, N.C.: Algonquin Books, 2010).

59. E. Le Roy, *Les Origines Humaines et l'Évolution de l'Intelligence* (Paris: Bolvin & Cie, 1928).

60. A. N. Whitehead, *Process and Reality* (New York: Macmillan, 1929).

61. R. Descartes, *Meditations on First Philosophy with Selected Objections and Replies*, ed. J. Cottingham (Cambridge: Cambridge University Press, 1986).

62. G. W. Leibniz, *Monadology and Other Philosophical Essays*, ed. and tr. P. Schrecker and A. M. Schrecker (New York: Bobbs-Merrill, 1965).

63. Ibid.

64. See R. Gennaro, "Leibniz on Consciousness and Self-Consciousness," in R. Gennaro and C. Huenemann, eds., *New Essays on the Rationalists* (Oxford: Oxford University Press, 1999): 353–371; M. Kulstad, *Leibniz on Apperception, Consciousness, and Reflection* (München: Philosophia, 1991); R. McRae, *Leibniz: Perception, Apperception, and Thought* (Toronto: Toronto University Press, 1976).

65. See Burtt, *Metaphysical Foundations*.

66. See Burtt, *Metaphysical Foundations*.

67. P. Teilhard de Chardin, *Le phénomène de l'homme* (Paris: Seuil, 1955); P. Teilhard de Chardin, *The Phenomenon of Man*, tr. B. Wall (New York: Harper and Row, 1959).

68. See R. Speaight, *The Life of Teilhard de Chardin* (New York: Fordham University Press, 1967).

69. J. D. Dana, "The Classification of Animals Based on the Principle of Cephalization," *American Journal of Science* 37 (1864): 10–35.

70. See, for example, A. Judith, "Teilhard de Chardin 1881–1955," http://www.gaiamind.com/Teilhard.html.

71. J. Le Conte, *Elements of Geology* (New York: D. Appleton, 1878).

72. W. [*sic*] I. Vernadsky, "The Biosphere and the Noösphere," tr. George Vernadsky, *American Scientist* 33 (1945): 1–12; V. I. Vernadsky, *Scientific Thought as a Planetary Phenomenon*, tr. B. A. Starostin (Moscow: Vernadsky Ecological Institute, 1977). See Levit, *Biogeochemistry*, for a discussion.

73. Vernadsky, "The Biosphere and the Noösphere," p. 8.

74. Ibid., p. 9

75. Ibid., pp. 9–10.
76. Vernadsky, *Scientific Thought*.
77. Vernadsky, "The Biosphere and the Noösphere," p. 8.
78. Ibid.
79. Vernadsky, *Scientific Thought*.
80. V. I. Vernadsky, *La Biosphère* (Paris: Félix Alcan, 1929).
81. G. E. Hutchinson, "Limnological Studies in Connecticut. VII. A Critical Examination of the Supposed Relationship Between Phytoplankton Periodicity and Chemical Changes in Lake Water," *Ecology* 25 (1944): 3–26, p. 20, n. 5.
82. G. E. Hutchinson, "Concluding Remarks," *Cold Harbor Symposium on Quantitative Biology* 22 (1957): 415–427 (in which he does not cite Vernadsky).
83. See R. Bonola, *Non-Euclidean Geometries with a Supplement Containing "The Theory of Parallels" by Nicholas Lobachevski and "The Science of Absolute Space" by John Bolyai*, tr. H. S. Carslaw and J. B. Halsted (Mineola, N.Y.: Dover, 1955).
84. G. Piel, D. Flanagan, F. Bello, P. Morrison, J. B. Piel, J. Purcell, et al., eds., *The Biosphere* (San Francisco: W. H. Freeman, 1970).
85. G. E. Hutchinson, "The Biosphere," in G. Piel et al., eds., *The Biosphere* (San Francisco: W. H. Freeman, 1970): 1–11.
86. J. E. Lovelock, *Gaia: A New Look at Life on Earth* (New York: Oxford University Press, 1979), p. 11.
87. Ibid.
88. J. E. Lovelock and L. Margulis, "Atmospheric Homeostasis by and for the Biosphere: The Gaia Hypothesis," *Tellus* 26 (1974): 2–10; L. Margulis and J. E. Lovelock, "Biological Modulation of the Earth's Atmosphere," *Icarus* 21 (1974): 471–489; J. E. Lovelock and L. Margulis, "Homeostatic Tendencies of Earth's Atmosphere," *Origins of Life* 5 (1974): 93–103; L. Margulis and J. E. Lovelock, "The Atmosphere as Circulatory System of the Biosphere," *Co-Evolution Quarterly* 6 (Summer 1975): 30–41; L. Margulis and J. E. Lovelock, "The View from Mars and Venus," *The Sciences* (March–April 1977): 10–13; J. E. Lovelock and L. Margulis, "The Biota as Ancient and Modern Modulator of the Earth's Atmosphere," *Pure and Applied Geophysics* 116 (1978): 239–243.
89. J. E. Lovelock, "Gaia as Seen Through the Atmosphere," *Atmospheric Environment* 6 (1972): 579–580.
90. Ibid., p. 579.
91. Hutchinson, "The Biosphere," p. 1.
92. G. E. Hutchinson, "The Biochemistry of the Terrestrial Atmosphere," in G. P. Kuiper, ed., *The Earth as a Planet* (Chicago: University of Chicago Press, 1954): 371–433.
93. J. E. Lovelock, *The Ages of Gaia: A Biography of Our Living Earth* (New York: W. W. Norton, 1988), p. 11.
94. D. R. Hitchcock and J. E. Lovelock, "Life Detection by Atmospheric Analysis," *Icarus* 7 (1967): 149–159.
95. J. E. Lovelock and C. E. Griffin, "Planetary Atmospheres: Compositional and Other Changes Associated with Life," *Advances in the Astronautical Sciences*, 25 (1969): 179–193.
96. Lovelock, *Gaia*.
97. L. Margulis, "Jim Lovelock's Gaia," in P. Bunyard, ed., *Gaia in Action* (Edinburgh: Floris Books, 1996): 54–64, p. 54.
98. Lovelock, *Ages of Gaia*.
99. Lovelock, "Gaia as Seen," p. 579, emphasis added.

100. See E. P. Odum, *Fundamentals of Ecology*, Third Edition (Philadelphia: W. B. Saunders, 1971), the standard, field-defining textbook in ecology for two decades—from the mid-1950s to the mid-1970s.

101. L. Margulis, *Symbiotic Planet: A New Look at Evolution* (New York: Basic Books, 1998), pp. 120–121.

102. McIntosh, *Background*.

103. Ibid.

104. Lovelock, "Gaia as Seen," p. 579.

105. Leopold, "Some Fundamentals," p. 94.

106. Ibid., p. 95.

107. L. Margulis and K. V. Schwartz, *Five Kingdoms: An Illustrated Guide to the Phyla of Life on Earth* (W. H. Freeman, 1997).

108. See N. R. Pace, "The Universal Nature of Biochemistry," *Proceedings of the National Academy of Science U.S.A.* 98 (2001): 805–808; E. Smith and H. Morowitz, "Universality in Intermediary Metabolism," *Proceedings of the National Academy of Science USA* 101 (2004): 13168–13173

109. Lovelock, *Gaia*, pp. ix–x.

110. Lovelock, "Gaia as Seen," p. 179.

111. F. H. Bormann, "The Gaia Hypothesis [review of *Gaia: A New Look at Life on Earth*, by James Lovelock]," *Ecology* 62 (1981): 502.

112. W. F. Doolittle, "Is Nature Really Motherly?" *Co-Evolution Quarterly* 30 (Spring, 1981): 58–63.

113. R. Dawkins, *The Extended Phenotype: The Gene as the Unit of Selection* (Oxford: W. H. Freeman, 1983).

114. Lovelock, *Gaia*, p. 81.

115. R. Dawkins, *The Selfish Gene* (New York: Oxford University Press, 1976); W. D. Hamilton, "The Genetical Theory of Social Behaviour, I, II," *Journal of Theoretical Biology* 7 (1964): 1–52.

116. Dawkins, *Extended Phenotype*, p. 236.

117. J. Lovelock, "Reflections on Gaia," in S. H. Schneider, J. R. Miller, E. Crist, and P. J. Boston, eds., *Scientists Debate Gaia: The Next Century* (Cambridge, Mass.: MIT Press, 2004), p. 3.

118. L. Margulis, "Gaia by Any Other Name," in S. H. Schneider, J. R. Miller, E. Crist, and P. J. Boston, eds., *Scientists Debate Gaia: The Next Century* (Cambridge, Mass.: MIT Press, 2004): 7–12; T. M. Lenton and H. T. P. Williams, "Gaia and Evolution," in E. Crist and H. B. Rinker, eds., *Gaia in Turmoil: Climate Change, Biodepletion, and Earth Ethics in an Age of Crisis* (Cambridge, Mass.: MIT Press, 2010): 61–83.

119. A. J. Watson and J. E. Lovelock, "Biological Homeostasis of the Global Environment: the Parable of Daisyworld," *Tellus* 35 (1983): 286–289; T. M. Lenton and J. E. Lovelock, "Daisyworld Revisited: Quantifying Biological Effects on Planetary Self-Regulation," *Tellus* 53 (2001): 288–305.

120. Leopold, "Some Fundamentals," p. 94.

121. Lovelock, *Gaia*, p. 146.

122. Ibid., p. 147.

123. Ibid., p. 148.

124. Margulis, *Symbiotic Planet*, p. 126.

125. Ibid., p. 119.

126. B. Hultqvist, "The Aurora," in Y. Kamide and A. Chian, eds., *Handbook of the Solar-Terrestrial Environment* (Heidelberg: Springer-Verlag, 2007): 331–354.

Chapter 8

1. A. Leopold, "Some Fundamentals of Conservation in the Southwest," *Environmental Ethics* 1 (1979): 131–141, reprinted in S. L. Flader and J. B. Callicott, eds., *The River of the Mother of God and Other Essays by Aldo Leopold* (Madison: University of Wisconsin Press, 1991): 86–97, p. 95.
2. Ibid., pp. 94 and 95, respectively.
3. Ibid., p. 94.
4. Ibid., p. 95
5. V. I. Vernadsky, *The Biosphere* (New York: Copernicus, 1998).
6. J. E. Lovelock, *Gaia: A New Look at Life on Earth* (New York: Oxford University Press, 1979).
7. Ibid., p. 94.
8. See M. Woolfson, "The Origin and Evolution of the Solar System," *Astronomy and Geophysics* 41 (2000): 1.12–1.19.
9. F. Bertoldi, W. Altenhoff, A. Weiss, K. M. Menten, and C. Thum, "The Trans-Neptunian Object UB313 Is Larger Than Pluto," *Nature* 439 (2006): 563–564.
10. V. V. Emel'yanenko, D. J. Asher, and M. E. Bailey, "The Fundamental Role of the Oort Cloud in Determining the Flux of Comets through the Planetary System," *Monthly Notices of the Royal Astronomical Society* 381 (2007): 779–789.
11. R. A. Kerr, "Tying Up the Solar System with a Ribbon of Charged Particles," *Science* 326, no. 5951 (2009): 350–351.
12. See S. F. Gilbert, J. Sapp, and A. I Tauber, "A Symbiotic View of Life: We Have Never Been Individuals," *Quarterly Review of Biology* 87 (2012): 325–341 and J. B. Callicott, "Ecology and Moral Ontology," in D. Bergandi, ed., *The Structural Links Between Ecology, Evolution and Ethics/Boston Studies in the Philosophy of Science* 296 (Dordrecht: Springer, 2013): 101–116.
13. L. Margulis, *Symbiotic Planet: A New Look at Evolution* (Amherst, Mass.: Basic Books, 1998), p. 123.
14. Leopold, "Some Fundamentals," pp. 96–97.
15. A. Leopold, *A Sand County Almanac and Sketches Here and There* (New York: Oxford University Press, 1949), pp. 224–225.
16. E. P. Odum, "The Strategy of Ecosystem Development," *Science* 164 (1969): 262–270.
17. S. T. A. Pickett and R. S. Ostfeld, "The Shifting Paradigm in Ecology," in R. L. Knight and S. E. Bates, eds., *A New Century for Natural Resources Management* (Washington: Island Press, 1995): 261–278.
18. Ibid.
19. S. T. A. Pickett and P. S. White, eds., *The Ecology of Natural Disturbance and Patch Dynamics* (San Diego, Calif.: Academic Press, 1995).
20. M. J. McDonnell and S. T. A. Pickett, eds., *Humans as Components of Ecosystems: The Ecology of Subtle Human Effects and Populated Areas* (New York: Springer Verlag, 1993).
21. E. Crist and H. B. Rinker, *Gaia in Turmoil: Climate Change, Biodepletion, and Earth Ethics in an Age of Crisis* (Cambridge, Mass.: MIT Press, 2010). Crist and Rinker cite N. Eldridge and S. J. Gould, "Punctuated Equilibria: An Alternative to Phyletic

Gradualism," in T. J. M. Schopf, ed., *Models of Paleontology* (San Francisco: Freeman Cooper, 1985): 82–115.

22. T. F. H. Allen and T. B. Starr, *Hierarchy Perspectives for Ecological Complexity* (Chicago: University of Chicago Press, 1982).

23. R. B. Keiter and M. S. Boyce, eds., *Greater Yellowstone Ecosystem: Redefining America's Wilderness Heritage* (New Haven, Conn.: Yale University Press, 1991); J. Wiegel and M. W. W. Adams, eds., *Thermophiles: The Keys to Molecular Evolution and the Origins of Life* (Philadelphia: Taylor and Francis, 1998).

24. M. Boyce and A. Haney, eds., *Ecosystem Management: Applications for Sustainable Forest and Wildlife Management* (New Haven, Conn.: Yale University Press, 1997); D. C. Coleman, D. A. Crossley, and P. F. Hendrix, eds., *Fundamentals of Soil Ecology*, Second Edition (San Diego, Calif.: Elsevier Academic Press, 2004).

25. R. V. O'Neill, D. L. DeAngelis, J. B. Waide, and T. F. H. Allen, *A Hierarchical Concept of Ecosystems* (Princeton, N. J.: Princeton University Press, 1986).

26. W. J. Kious and R. I. Tilling, *This Dynamic Earth: The Story of Plate Tectonics* (Washington: US Geological Service, 1996); W.Van der Wal, P. Wu, M. G. Sideris, and C. K. Shum, "Glacial Isostatic Adjustment at the Laurentide Ice Sheet Margin: Models and Observations in the Great Lakes Region," *Journal of Geodynamics* 48 (2008): 165–173.

27. E. Bryant, *Climate Process and Change* (Cambridge: Cambridge University Press, 2002); W. J. Burroughs, *Climate Change* (Cambridge: Cambridge University Press, 2001).

28. H. D. Holland, "Early Proterozoic Atmosphere Change," in S. Bengston, ed., *Early Life on Earth* (New York: Columbia University Press, 1994): 237–244; L. Margulis, *Environmental Evolution: Effects of the Origin and Evolution of Life on Earth* (Cambridge, Mass.: MIT, 2000).

29. J. Zalasiewicz and M. Williams, *The Goldilocks Planet: The Four Billion Year Story of Earth's Climate* (New York: Oxford University Press, 2012).

30. Leopold, "Some Fundamentals," p. 95.

31. A. Schweitzer, *The Philosophy of Civilization*, tr. C. T. Campion (New York: Macmillan, 1949), p. 309.

32. Ibid., p. 310.

33. Ibid., p. 317

34. Ibid., p. 209.

35. Ibid.

36. Ibid., p. 235.

37. See A. Schopenhauer, *The World as Will and Idea*, tr. R. B. Haldane and J. Kemp (Garden City, NY: Doubleday, 1961).

38. Schweitzer, *Philosophy of Civilization*, p. 237.

39. See F. Edgerton, *The Beginnings of Indian Philosophy* (Cambridge, Mass.: Harvard University Press, 1965) and A. T. Embree, *The Hindu Tradition* (New York: Modern Library, 1966).

40. Schweitzer, *Philosophy of Civilization*, p. 237.

41. Schopenhauer, *The World as Will and Idea*, p. 364.

42. Ibid., p. 297.

43. J. Feinberg, "The Rights of Animals and Unborn Generations," in W. T. Blackstone, ed., *Philosophy and Environmental Crisis* (Athens: University of Georgia Press, 1974): 43–68, p. 43, emphasis in original.

44. Feinberg, "Rights," p. 49. Feinberg cites H. J. McCloskey, "Rights," *Philosophical Quarterly* 15 (1965): 115–127.

45. Ibid., p. 49.
46. Ibid., pp. 49–50.
47. K. E. Goodpaster, "On Being Morally Considerable," *Journal of Philosophy* 75 (1978): 308–325, p. 312.
48. Feinberg, "Rights," pp. 50–51.
49. Ibid., p. 52.
50. Ibid., p. 51
51. Ibid., p. 52.
52. G. Varner, *In Nature's Interests? Interests, Animal Rights and Environmental Ethics* (New York: Oxford University Press, 1998), p. 73.
53. For a similar critique, see P. W. Taylor, "Frankena on Environmental Ethics," *The Monist* 60 (1981): 313–324.
54. R. Sorabji, *Matter, Space, and Motion: Theories in Antiquity and Their Sequel* (London: Duckworth, 1988).
55. See W. K. C. Guthrie, *A History of Greek Philosophy*, Volume II, *The Presocratic Tradition from Parmenides to Democritus* (Cambridge: Cambridge University Press, 1965).
56. Ibid.
57. R. Descartes, *Principles of Philosophy*, Part II, Principle XXXVII, Part III, Principles LVI and LVIII.
58. B. Spinoza, *Ethics*, Part III, Proposition VI. For a discussion see D. Garrett, "Spinoza's *Conatus* Argument," in O. Koistinen and J. Biro, eds., *Spinoza: Metaphysical Themes* (Oxford: Oxford University Press, 2002): 127–158; and M. Schrijvers, "The Conatus and the Mutual Relationship Between Active and Passive Affects in Spinoza," in Y. Yovel, ed., *Desire and Affect: Spinoza as Psychologist* (New York: Little Room Press, 1999): 63–80.
59. T. Hobbes, *Leviathan with Selected Variants from the Latin Edition of 1688*, ed. Edwin Curley (Indianapolis, Ind.: Hackett, 1994), Part I, Chapter VI.
60. Goodpaster, "On Being," p. 310.
61. K. E. Goodpaster, "From Egoism to Environmentalism," in K. E. Goodpaster and K. M. Sayre, eds., *Ethics and Problems of the 21st Century* (Notre Dame: University of Notre Dame Press, 1979): 21–35.
62. Goodpaster cites G. J. Warnock, *The Object of Morality* (New York: Methuen, 1971) and P. Singer, "All Animals Are Equal," in T. Regan and P. Singer, eds., *Animal Rights and Human Obligations* (Englewood Cliffs, N.J.: Prentice Hall, 1976): 148–162.
63. I. Kant, *Foundations of the Metaphysics of Morals*, tr. L. W. Beck (Indianapolis, Ind.: Bobbs-Merrill, 1959).
64. T. Regan, "An Examination and Defense of One Argument Concerning Animal Rights," *Inquiry* 22 (1978): 189–219.
65. Goodpaster, "On Being," p. 316.
66. Varner, *Nature's Interests*, p. 83.
67. Goodpaster, "On Being," p. 319. Goodpaster quotes Feinberg, "Rights," p. 54.
68. Ibid., p. 310.
69. Ibid.
70. Ibid., p. 323; Goodpaster cites K. M. Sayer, *Cybernetcs and the Philosophy of Mind* (New York: Humanities Press, 1976), p. 91.
71. Ibid.
72. Ibid.
73. Ibid.

74. Ibid. Goodpaster cites J. Lovelock and S. Epton, "The Quest for Gaia," *The New Scientist* 65 (1975): 304–309.

75. Ibid., p. 322.

76. Ibid.

77. See P. Tompkins and C. Bird, *The Secret Life of Plants* (New York: Harper and Row, 1973). The claims in that book were almost immediately debunked; see K. A. Horowitz, D. C. Lewis, and E. L. Gasteiger, "Plant 'Primary Perception': Electrophysiological Unresponsiveness to Brine Shrimp Killing," *Science* 189 (1975): 478–480.

78. Schopenhauer, *The World as Will and Idea*.

79. P. W. Taylor, "The Ethics of Respect for Nature," *Environmental Ethics* 3 (1981): 197–218; P. W. Taylor, "Frankena on Environmental Ethics," *The Monist* 63 (1981): 313–324; P. W. Taylor, "In Defense of Biocentrism," *Environmental Ethics* 5 (1983): 237–243; P. W. Taylor, "Are Humans Superior to Animals and Plants?" *Environmental Ethics* 6 (1984): 149–160; P. W. Taylor, *Respect for Nature: A Theory of Environmental Ethics* (Princeton, N.J.: Princeton University Press, 1986); P. W. Taylor, "Inherent Value and Moral Rights," *The Monist* 70 (1987): 15–30.

80. A. Naess, "The Shallow and the Deep, Long-Range Ecology Movements: A Summary," *Inquiry* 16 (1973): 95–100; B. Devall and G. Sessions, *Deep Ecology: Living as if Nature Mattered* (Salt Lake City: Gibbs M. Smith, 1985).

81. See, for example, M. L. Hunter, *Fundamentals of Conservation Biology*, Second Edition (Malden, Mass.: Blackwell Science, 2002).

82. See especially, Taylor, "In Defense of Biocentrism."

83. Taylor, "The Ethics of Respect," p. 198.

84. Ibid., pp. 197–198, emphasis added.

85. J. B. Callicott, "Animal Liberation: A Triangular Affair," *Environmental Ethics* 2 (1980): 311–338.

86. T. Regan, *The Case for Animal Rights* (Berkeley: University of California Press, 1983).

87. Taylor, *Respect for Nature*, p. ix.

88. T. Regan, "Animal Rights, Human Wrongs," *Environmental Ethics* 2 (1980): 99–120; Taylor, "The Ethics of Respect."

89. Regan, "Animal Rights," p. 115.

90. Ibid., p. 116, emphasis in original.

91. Kant, *Foundations*.

92. Taylor, "The Ethics of Respect," p. 203.

93. Ibid., p. 206; Kant, *Foundations*.

94. Ibid., pp. 210–211.

95. Taylor, *Respect for Nature*, pp. 121–122.

96. Goodpaster, "On Being," p. 324, emphasis in original.

97. Taylor, "In Defense of Biocentrism."

98. Taylor, *Respect for Nature*, p. 263.

99. Ibid., p. 270.

100. Goodpaster, "On Being," p. 311, emphasis in original.

101. Kant, *Foundations*, p. 53, emphasis in original.

102. Ibid., p. 47.

103. J. R. Searle, *Consciousness and Language* (Cambridge: Cambridge University Press, 2002).

104. H. Rolston III, *Conserving Natural Value* (New York: Columbia University Press, 1994), p. 160.

105. Ibid. p. 177.

106. Ibid., p. 173.

107. H. Rolston III, "Challenges in Environmental Ethics," in M. J. Zimmerman, J. B. Callicott, G. Sessions, K. J. Warren, and J. Clark, eds., *Environmental Philosophy: From Animal Liberation to Radical Ecology* (Englewood Cliffs, N. J.: Prentice Hall, 1993): 135–157.

108. H. Rolston III, *Environmental Ethics: Duties to and Values in the Natural World* (Philadelphia: Temple University Press, 1988), p. 101.

109. Rolston, "Challenges," p. 152.

110. Goodpaster, "On Being," p. 324.

111. Ibid., p. 313.

112. Ibid., p. 324.

113. Schweitzer, *Philosophy of Civilization*, p. 318, emphasis added.

Chapter 9

1. L. Margulis, *Symbiotic Planet: A New Look at Evolution* (Amherst, Mass.: Basic Books, 1998), p. 119.

2. Ibid., pp. 120 and 128. R. S. Norris and H. M. Kristensen, "Global Nuclear Weapons Inventories 1945–2010," *Bulletin of Atomic Scientists* 66 (2010): 77–84 give a figure of ~23,000, down from a high of ~70,000 in 1986.

3. Ibid., p. 128.

4. D. E. Brownlee, "Planetary Habitability on Astronomical Time Scales," in C. J. Schrijver and G. L. Siscoe, eds., *Heliophysics: Evolving Solar Activity and the Climates of Space and Earth* (Cambridge: Cambridge University Press, 2010).

5. D. A. Sverjensky and N. Lee, "The Great Oxidation Event and Mineral Diversification," *Elements* 6 (2010): 31–36.

6. J. Lovelock, *The Revenge of Gaia: Earth's Climate Crisis and the Fate of Humanity* (New York: Basic Books, 2006), p. 39, claims that methane is twenty-four times more powerful a greenhouse gas than carbon dioxide. See D. T. Shindell, G. Faluvegi, D. M. Koch, G. A. Schmidt, N. Unger, and S. E. Bauer, "Improved Attribution of Climate Forcing to Emissions," *Science* 326 (2009): 716–718.

7. D. Palmer, *Prehistoric Past Revealed: The Four Billion Year History of Life on Earth* (Berkeley: University of California Press, 2003).

8. R. E. Kopp, J. L. Kirschvink, I. A. Hilburn, and C. Z. Nash, "The Paleoproterozoic Snowball Earth: A Climate Disaster Triggered by the Evolution of Oxygenic Photosynthesis," *Proceedings of the National Academy of Science, U.S.A.* 102 (2005): 11131–11136.

9. B. Bodiselitsch, C. Koeberl, S. Mastrer, and W. U. Reimold, "Estimating Duration and Intensity of Neoproterozoic Snowball Glaciations From Ir Anomalies," *Science* 308 (2005): 239–242; A. G. Smith, "Neoproterozoic Timescales and Stratigraphy," *Geological Society, London, Special Publications* 326 (2009): 27–54.

10. A. Shukolyukov and G. W. Lugmair, "Isotopic Evidence for the Cretaceous-Tertiary Impactor and Its Type," *Science* 282 (1998): 927–929.

11. J. Alroy "Colloquium Paper: Dynamics of Origination and Extinction in the Marine Fossil Record," *Proceedings of the National Academy of Sciences of the United States of America* 105, Suppl. 1 (2008): 11536–11542; D. M. Raup and J. J. Sepkoski Jr., "Mass Extinctions in the Marine Fossil Record," *Science* 215 (1982): 1501–1503.

12. T. Lenton and A. Watson, *Revolutions That Made the Earth* (New York: Oxford University Press, 2011).

13. A. Markov and A. Korotayev, "Hyperbolic Growth of Marine and Continental Biodiversity Through the Phanerozoic and Community Evolution," *Journal of General Biology* 69 (2008): 175–194.

14. Margulis, *Symbiotic Planet*, p. 120. Margulis cleverly alludes to the 1960s and 1970s rock band, The Mothers of Invention, fronted by Frank Zappa.

15. Lenton and Watson, *Revolutions*.

16. Ibid., p. 115.

17. A. Leopold, "Some Fundamentals of Conservation in the Southwest," *Environmental Ethics* 1 (1979): 131–141, reprinted in S. L. Flader and J. B. Callicott, eds., *The River of the Mother of God and Other Essays by Aldo Leopold* (Madison: University of Wisconsin Press, 1991): 86–97, p. 95. The allusion is probably to J. Burroughs, "Each for Its Own Sake," in J. Burroughs, *Accepting the Universe: Essays in Naturalism* (Boston: Houghton Mifflin, 1920): 30–53. The quoted phrase is from R. L. Stevenson, "Walking Tours," of *Virginibus Peurique,* found in *The Works of Robert Louis Stevenson*, Swanston Edition (London: Chatto and Windus, 1911), p. 413.

18. Ibid.

19. Ibid.

20. Ibid., p. 96.

21. J. Lovelock, *Revenge of Gaia*, pp. 10 and 17.

22. Ibid., p. 10.

23. Ibid., p. 3.

24. Ibid., p. 60.

25. Ibid., p. 147.

26. Ibid.

27. Ibid., p. 153.

28. Ibid., pp. 10 (1938) and 13 (1939).

29. Ibid., p. 153.

30. M. Serres, *Le Contrat Naturel* (Paris: Éditions François Bourin, 1990).

31. L. Canfora, *The Vanished Library: A Wonder of the Ancient World* (Los Angeles: University of California Press, 1990).

32. Plato, *Republic* (358 E-359 A), tr. P. Shorey, Loeb Classical Library (London: William Heineman, 1963), p. 115.

33. Ibid.

34. T. Hobbes, *Leviathan with Selected Variants from the Latin Edition of 1668*, Part I, ch. xii (Indianapolis, Ind.: Hackett, 1994), p. 74.

35. T. Hobbes, *Leviathan or the Matter, Forme and Power of a Commonwealth Ecclesiasticall and Civil* (New York: Collier Books, 1962), p. 100. The phrase "state of nature" does not occur in *Leviathan*, but *"l'état de nature"* is common enough in Rousseau's *Du Contrat Social.*

36. Ibid., p. 104.

37. J. J. Rousseau, *The Social Contract*, tr. Maurice Cranston (New York: Penguin Books, 1968).

38. R. Leakey and R. Lewin, *The Sixth Extinction: Patterns of Life and the Future of Humankind* (New York; Anchor Books, 1996).

39. F. S. Rowland, "Stratospheric Ozone Depletion," *Philosophical Transactions of the Royal Society B* 361 (2006): 769–790; S. C. Zehr, "Accounting for the Ozone Hole: Scientific Representations of the Anomaly and Prior Incorrect Claims in Public Settings," *Sociological Quarterly* 35 (1994): 603–619.

40. See M. Serres, *The Natural Contract* (Ann Arbor: University of Michigan Press, 1995), p. 3, for indication that Serres is deliberately responding to the alarming heat of 1988.
41. Ibid., p. 3.
42. Ibid., p. 4.
43. Ibid., p. 6.
44. Ibid., p. 23.
45. Ibid., p. 20.
46. Ibid., p. 27; See M. Serres, *Le Parasite* (Paris: Grasset, 1980).
47. Serres, *Natural Contract.*, p. 34.
48. See "Outcome of the Work of the Ad Hoc Working Group on Long-term Cooperative Action Under the Convention," *United Nations Framework on Climate Change* http://unfccc.int/meetings/durban_nov_2011/meeting/6245.php., January 2012; and B. McKibben, "The Reckoning," *Rolling Stone* (August 2, 2012): 52–58, p. 52.
49. W. N. Adger, I. Lorenzoni, and K. L. O'Brian, eds., *Adapting to Climate Change: Thresholds, Values, and Governance* (New York: Cambridge University Press, 2009); T. M. L. Wigley, "A Combined Mitigation/Geoengineering Approach to Climate Stabilization," *Science* 314 (2006): 452–454.
50. C. Larrère, "Ethics, Politics, Science, and the Environment," tr. J. B. Callicott, in J. B. Callicott and F. J. R. da Rocha, eds., *Earth Summit Ethics: Toward a Reconstructive Postmodern Philosophy of Environmental Education* (Albany: State University of New York Press, 1996), p. 117.
51. Serres, *Contract*, p. 78.
52. Ibid., p. 75.
53. Larrère, "Ethics, Politics, Science," pp. 123–124.
54. Ibid., p. 122; see H. Rolston III, "Nature for Real: Is Nature a Social Construct?" in T. D. J. Chappel, ed., *The Philosophy of the Environment* (Edinburgh: University of Edinburgh Press, 1997): 38–64.
55. Ibid., p. 129.
56. For a recent discussion, see J. M. Scott and J. L. Ranchlo, "Refocusing the Debate about Advocacy," *Conservation Biology* 25 (2011): 1–3.
57. Larrère, "Ethics, Politics, Science," p. 132.
58. Ibid.
59. Ibid., p. 130.
60. B. Latour, "An Attempt at a 'Compositionist Manifesto,'" *New Literary History* 41 (2010): 471–490, p. 479.
61. Ibid.
62. Larrère, "Ethics, Politics, Science," p. 126; see M. Artigas, R. Matinez, and W. R. Shea, "New Light on the Galileo Affair," in E. McMullin, ed., *The Church and Galileo* (South Bend, Ind.: Notre Dame University Press, 2005), pp. 213–233.
63. Latour, "Attempt," p. 481.
64. Ibid., p. 479.
65. Ibid.
66. Ibid., p. 476. See W. McKibben, *The End of Nature* (New York: Random House, 1989).
67. Ibid.
68. Ibid., p. 478.
69. Ibid.
70. Ibid., p. 485.

71. See J. Goodell, *Big Coal: The Dirty Secret Behind America's Energy Future* (New York: Houghton Mifflin, 2006) and McKibben, "The Reckoning."

72. Latour, "Attempt," p. 485.

73. Ibid.

74. Ibid., p. 474.

75. Ibid., p. 477.

76. Ibid., p. 480.

77. P. Rozin, L. Lowrery, S. Imada, and J. Haidt, "The CAD Triad Hypothesis: A Mapping Between Three Moral Emotions (Contempt, Anger, Disgust) and Three Moral Codes (Community, Autonomy, Divinity)," *Journal of Personality and Social Psychology* 76 (1999): 547–586; R. A. Shweder, N. Much, L. Park, and M. M. Mahapatra, "The 'Big Three' of Morality (Autonomy, Community, Divinity)," in A. Brant and P. Rozin, eds., *Morality and Health* (New York: Routledge, 1997): 119–169.

78. Jonathan Haidt and Craig Joseph, "Intuitive Ethics: How Innately Prepared Intuitions Generate Culturally Variable Virtues," *Daedalus* 133, no. 4 (2004): 55–66; J. Haidt, and C. Joseph, "The Moral Mind: How 5 Sets of Innate Moral Intuitions Guide the Development of Many Culture-specific Virtues, and Perhaps Even Modules," in P. Carruthers, S. Laurence, and S. Stich, eds., *The Innate Mind*, Volume 3 (New York: Oxford University Press, 2007): 367–391.

79. J. Haidt, *The Righteous Mind: Why Good People Are Divided by Politics and Religion* (New York: Pantheon Books, 2012).

80. A. Dussault, "In Search of Ecocentric Sentiments: Insights from the CAD Model of Moral Psychology," *Environmental Ethics* 35 (2013): forthcoming.

81. A. Leopold, "Some Fundamentals of Conservation in the Southwest," in S. L. Flader and J. B. Callicott, eds., *The River of the Mother of God and Other Essays by Aldo Leopold* (Madison: University of Wisconsin Press, 1991), p. 94.

82. G. E. M. Anscombe, "Modern Moral Philosophy," *Philosophy* 33 (1958): 1–19.

83. See, for example, P. Foot, *Virtues and Vices* (Oxford: Blackwell, 1978); P. Geach, *The Virtues* (Cambridge: Cambridge University Press, 1977).

84. J. MacIntyre, *After Virtue* (London: Duckworth, 1981); see also M. Slote, *From Morality to Virtue* (New York: Oxford University Press, 1992); R. Hursthouse, *On Virtue Ethics* (Aukland: Oxford University Press, 1999); Philippa Foot, *Natural Goodness* (New York: Oxford University Press, 2001).

85. E. Katz, *The Moral Justification for Environmentalism*, Ph.D. dissertation, Boston University, 1983, written under the supervision of Alasdair MacIntyre, appears to be among the first migrations of virtue ethics into environmental philosophy.

86. See, for example, L. Strauss, *Jewish Philosophy and the Crisis of Modernity, Athens and Jerusalem* (Albany: State University of New York Press, 1997).

87. I. Kant, *Grounding for the Metaphysics of Morals*, Second Edition, tr. J. Ellington (Indianapolis, Ind.: Hackett, 1981).

88. J. Bentham, *Principles of Morals and Legislation* (Oxford: Clarendon Press, 1789).

89. For an early expression of rule utilitarianism, see J. S. Mill, *Utilitarianism* (London: Parker, Son, and Bourn, 1863).

90. See Hesiod, *Theogony*, for the association of Justice and Wisdom with Zeus; as to Plato's dialogues devoted to one or another of the cardinal virtues, see *Republic* (Justice), *Charmides* (Temperance), *Laches* (Courage), *Euthyphro* (Piety). In addition, the *Meno* is devoted to the topic of virtue as a whole and might well be interpreted to support the Socratic doctrine that all the virtues are reducible to Wisdom.

91. Aristotle, *Nichomachean Ethics*, Book I, ch. 4, 1095a, 20.

92. See, Plato, *Apology* and *Phaedrus* for especially significant references to Socrates's δαιμων and its critical function.

93. Aristotle, *Nichomachean Ethics*, Book I, ch. 7, 1098a, 15.

94. See J. Annas, *Intelligent Virtue* (New York; Oxford University Press, 2011).

95. See Aristotle, *De Anima (On the Soul)*.

96. Ibid.

97. Ibid., Book II, ch. 1, 412b, 20.

98. Aristotle, *Metaphysics* Z (VII), ch. 12.

99. Aristotle, *Nichomachean Ethics*, Book II, ch. 6, 1106a, 25–30, tr. W. D. Ross, in R. McKeon, ed., *The Basic Works of Aristotle* (New York: Random House, 1941).

100. L. v. Wensween, *Dirty Virtues: The Emergence of Ecological Virtue Ethics* (Amherst, N.Y.: Humanity Books, 2000).

101. S. P. Stafford, "Intellectual Virtue in Environmental Virtue Ethics," *Environmental Ethics* 32 (2010): 339–352, p. 341.

102. P. Cafaro, "Virtue Ethics," in J. B. Callicott and R. Frodeman, eds., *Encyclopedia of Environmental Ethics and Philosophy*, Volume 2 (New York: Macmillan, 2009), p. 375.

103. P. Cafaro, *Thoreau's Living Ethics: Walden and the Pursuit of Virtue* (Athens: University of Georgia Press, 2001); J. O'Neill, *Ecology, Policy, and Politics: Human Well-Being and the Natural World* (London: Routledge, 1993); R. L. Sandler, *Character and Environment: A Virtue-Oriented Approach to Environmental Ethics* (New York: Columbia University Press, 2007).

104. R. L. Sandler and P. Cafaro, eds., *Environmental Virtue Ethics* (Lanham, Md.: Rowman and Littlefield, 2005).

105. L. v. Wensveen, "Ecosystem Sustainability as a Criterion for Genuine Virtue," *Environmental Ethics* 23 (Fall 2001): 227–241.

106. Sandler, *Character and Environment*, p. 28.

107. Ibid., p. 83.

108. H. D. Thoreau, *Walking* (Rockville, Md.: Arc Manor, 2007), p. 26; H. D. Thoreau, *Walden* (New York: Thomas Y. Crowell, 1910) p. 430.

109. H. A. Bedau, ed., *Civil Disobedience in Focus* (London: Routledge, 1999), provides an excellent introduction to classic texts, historical relationships, extensive bibliographic notes, and a bibliography.

110. H. D. Thoreau, "Civil Disobedience," in P. Smith, ed., *Civil Disobedience and Other Essays* (Mineola, N.Y.: Dover, 1993), p. 1.

111. Ibid., p. 2.

112. C. Meine, *Aldo Leopold: His Life and Work* (Madison: University of Wisconsin Press, 1988), p. 17; University of Iowa Special Collections and University Archives, Papers of the Leopold Desk Company, 1886–1964, MsC 209.

113. Aristotle, *Nichomachean Ethics*, Book I, ch. 7, 1098a, 8–18.

114. Leopold, "Some Fundamentals," p. 97.

115. Aristotle, *Nichomachean Ethics*, Book I, ch. 8, 1099a, 24–25.

116. A. Leopold, *A Sand County Almanac and Sketches Here and There* (New York: Oxford University Press, 1949), p. 18.

117. A. Leopold, "When the Geese Return Spring Is Here," *Wisconsin Agriculturist and Farmer* 67 (April 6, 1940), p. 15, reprinted as A. Leopold, "When the Geese Return," in J. B. Callicott and E. T. Freyfogle, eds., *For the Health of the Land: Previously Unpublished Essays and Other Writings* (Washington: Island Press, 1999): 109–110, p. 109.

118. Aristotle, *Nichomachean Ethics*, Book I, ch. 7, 1098a, 18–19. Leopold does more than allude to the *Nichomachean Ethics*, but one cannot say that he quotes Aristotle; so I use the current hip-hop term: he "samples" Aristotle's *Nichomachean Ethics*.

119. See ibid., Book X, ch. 9.

120. See Aristotle, *Politics*, Book I.

121. Aristotle, *Politics*, Book I, ch. 2, 1253a, 25–23, tr. B. Jowett, in R. McKeon, ed., *The Basic Works of Aristotle* (New York: Random House, 1941).

122. Ibid., 20–23.

123. Ibid., Book III, 1280b, 30–33, 39–42.

124. Aristophanes, *Clouds*, tr. J. Henderson (New York: Focus, 1993); W. K. C. Guthrie, *A History of Greek Philosophy*, Volume 1, *The Earlier Presocratics and the Pythagoreans* (Cambridge: Cambridge University Press, 1962).

125. Plato, *Republic*, Book II, 367E, tr. P. Shorey, Loeb Classical Library (London: William Heineman, 1937).

126. Ibid., 368E.

127. For a development and discussion of this relationship between physical atomism and social individualism, see J. B. Callicott, "Primauté de la Philosophie Naturelle sur la Philosophie Morale: Le Forme des Choses à Venir," tr. Adeline Caute, in a special issue devoted to Naturalismes d'Aujourd'hui of *Cahiers Philosophique* 27 (2011): 41–62.

Chapter 10

1. R. Priddle, ed., *Redrawing the Energy-Climate Map: World Energy Outlook Special Report* (Paris: International Energy Agency, 2013).

2. See, for example, G. de Bell, ed., *The Environmental Handbook: Prepared for the First National Environmental Teach-in* (New York: Ballentine, 1970).

3. S. Solomon, D. Qin, M. Manning, Z. Chen, M. Marquis, K. B. Averyt, et al., eds., *Climate Change 2007: The Physical Science Basis. Contribution of Working Group I to the Fourth Assessment Report of the Intergovernmental Panel on Climate Change* (Cambridge: Cambridge University Press, 2007); hereafter cited as IPCC 2007.

4. Ibid.

5. R. Van Pelt, *Forest Giants of the Pacific Coast* (Seattle: University of Washington Press, 2001).

6. Ibid.

7. A. B. Franklin, D. R. Anderson, R. J. Guttiérez, and K. P. Burnham, "Climate, Habitat, Fitness in Northern Spotted Owl Populations in Northwestern California," *Ecological Monographs* 70 (2000): 539–590.

8. E. Newton, "Can Vulnerable Species Outrun Climate Change?" *Environment* 360 (Nov. 3, 2011): http://e360.yale.edu/content/feature.msp?id=2460; R. G. Pearson and T. P. Dawson, "Predicting the Impacts of Climate Change on Species Migrations: Are Bioclimate Impact Models Useful," *Global Ecology and Biogeography* 12 (2003): 361–371.

9. A. Leopold, *A Sand County Almanac and Sketches Here and There* (New York: Oxford University Press, 1949), p. 132.

10. Ibid.

11. See S. L. Flader, *Thinking Like a Mountain: Aldo Leopold and the Evolution of an Ecological Attitude Toward Deer, Wolves, and Forests* (Madison: University of Wisconsin Press, 1974).

12. S. M. Gardiner, *A Perfect Moral Storm: The Ethical Tragedy of Climate Change* (New York: Oxford University Press, 2011); A. Gore, *Earth in the Balance: Ecology and the Human Spirit* (Boston: Houghton Mifflin, 1992); B. McKibben, ed., *The Global Warming Reader: A Century of Writing About Climate Change* (New York: Penguin Books, 2012).

13. I quote Leopold, *Sand County*, p. 109.

14. M. Serres, *The Natural Contract* (Ann Arbor: University of Michigan Press, 1995), p. 3.

15. D. Jamieson, "Ethics, Public Policy, and Global Warming," *Science, Technology, and Human Values* 12 (1992): 139–153, p. 140. In an "author's note," Jamieson writes, "This material was discussed with an audience at the 1989 AAAS [American Association for the Advancement of Science] meetings in New Orleans" and in other venues that year.

16. R. Revelle and H. E. Suess, "Carbon Dioxide Exchange Between Atmosphere and Ocean and the Question of an Increase of Atmospheric CO2 During the Past Decades," *Tellus* 9 (1957): 18–27.

17. Jamieson, "Ethics," p. 148.

18. Ibid.

19. T. Hobbes, *Leviathan with Selected Variants from the Latin Edition of 1688*, ed. Edwin Curley (Indianapolis, Ind.: Hackett, 1994).

20. Ibid.

21. Jamieson, "Ethics," p. 149, emphasis added. Jamieson later changed the names of Smith and Jones to Jack and Jill, without much change in his basic point, in D. Jamieson, "The Moral and Political Challenges of Climate Change," in S. Moser and L. Dilling, eds., *Creating a Climate for Change: Communicating Climate Change and Facilitating Social Change* (Cambridge: Cambridge University Press, 2007): 475–484, and in several other subsequent papers.

22. S. Roberts, "U. N. Says 7 Billion Now Share the World," *New York Times*, October 31, 2011, p. 1.

23. US Energy Information Administration, *Annual Energy Outlook 2013 with Projections to 2040* (Washington: US Department of Energy, 2012); US Environmental Protection Agency, *Inventory of U. S. Greenhouse Gas Emissions and Sinks 1990–2010* (Washington: US Environmental Protection Agency, 2012).

24. R. Priddle, *Redrawing*.

25. J. Garvey, "Climate Change and Causal Inefficacy," in Anthony O'Hear, ed., *Philosophy and the Environment: Royal Institute of Philosophy Supplement: 69* (Cambridge: Cambridge University Press, 2011): 157–174, p. 166.

26. Ibid.

27. See Priddle, *Redrawing*. Per capita CO_2 emissiona are now also trending down in the US and UK from ~19 to ~17 and ~9 to ~7 tons, respectively; Garvey believes himself to be more conservative by about half than the Average Brit in 2011.

28. Jamieson, "Ethics," pp. 150–151.

29. Ronald Sandler, "Ethical Theory and the Problem of Inconsequentialism: Why Environmental Ethicists Should Be Virtue-oriented Ethicists," *Journal of Agricultural and Environmental Ethics* 23 (2010): 167–183.

30. First noticed by Henry Sidgwick, *The Methods of Ethics* (Indianapolis, Ind.: Hackett, 1981).

31. Jamieson, "Ethics," p. 150.

32. D. Jamieson, "When Utilitarians Should Be Virtue Theorists," *Utilitas* 19 (2007): 160–183, p. 161.

33. Ibid., p. 181.

34. Ibid.

35. Aristotle, *De Anima (On the Soul)*, Book I, ch. 3, 407b, 15, 23; tr. J. A. Smith.

36. See D. T. O'Neal and N. Munger, *Now I Lay Me Down to Sleep: Action Prayers, Poems, and Songs for Bedtime* (Minneapolis: Augsburg Books, 1994).

37. K. Arrow, "Economic Theory and the Hypothesis of Rationality," in J. Eatwell, M. Milgate, and P. Newman, eds., *The New Palgrave: Utility and Probability* (New York: W. W. Norton, 1990): 25–37.

38. K. E. Goodpaster, "From Egoism to Environmentalism," in K. E. Goodpaster and K. M. Sayre, eds., *Ethics and Problems of the 21st Century* (Notre Dame, Ind.: Notre Dame University Press, 1979): 21–35, pp. 28 and 25.

39. I. Kant, *Grounding for the Metaphysics of Morals*, tr. J. W. Ellington (Indianapolis, Ind.: Hackforth, 1981).

40. Aristotle, *Metaphysics* Z (VII), chapter 4, 1029b, 14–15; tr. W. D. Ross.

41. Ibid., Bk. Δ (V), ch. 30, 1025a, 14–15.

42. Ibid., Bk. E (VI), ch. 2, 1026b, 36–37.

43. Ibid., Bk. Z (VII), ch. 12.

44. Ibid., Bk. Z (VII), ch. 1, 1028a, 10–13.

45. J. Bentham, *An Introduction to the Principles of Morals and Legislation* (Oxford: Clarendon Press, 1789), Chapter XVII, footnote 122.

46. P. Singer, *Animal Liberation: A New Ethics for Our Treatment of Animals* (New York: Avon, 1977).

47. P. Singer, "Famine, Affluence, and Morality," *Philosophy and Public Affairs* 1 (1972): 229–243, p. 30.

48. J. Garvey, *The Ethics of Climate Change: Right and Wrong in a Warming World* (New York: Continuum International, 2008).

49. Bentham, *Principles*, Chapter XVII, footnote 122.

50. See J. Persky, "Retrospectives: The Ethology of Homo Economicus," *Journal of Economic Perspectives* (1995) 9: 221–231.

51. D. Parfit, *Reasons and Persons* (New York: Oxford University Press, 1984); see Chapter 3, "Five Mistakes of Moral Mathematics," pp. 67–87.

52. J. Nolt, "How Harmful Are the Average American's Greenhouse Gas Emissions," *Ethics, Policy, and Environment* 14 (2011): 3–10.

53. P. Singer, *One World: The Ethics of Globalization*, Second Edition (New Haven, Conn.: Yale University Press, 2004), p. 8.

54. Ibid., p. 34.

55. S. M. Gardiner, "Ethics and Global Climate Change," *Ethics* 114 (2004): 555–600, p. 590.

56. S. Caney, "Cosmopolitan Justice, Responsibility, and Global Climate Change," *Leiden Journal of International Law* 18 (2005): 747–775; H. Shue, "Subsistence Emissions and Luxury Emissions," *Law and Policy* 15 (1993): 39–59.

57. J. Goodell, *Big Coal: The Dirty Secret Behind America's Energy Future* (New York: Houghton Mifflin 2006); B. Walsh, "Who's Bankrolling the Climate-change Deniers," *Time*, Oct. 4, 2011; B. McKibben, "The Reckoning," *Rolling Stone* (August 2, 2012): 52–58.

58. A. Leiserowitz, E. Maibach, C. Roser-Renouf, and J. D. Hmielowski, *Climate Change in the American Mind: Americans' Global Warming Beliefs and Attitudes in March 2012* (New Haven, Conn.: Yale University and George Mason University Project on Climate Change Communication, 2012).

59. Parfit, *Reasons and Persons*, p. 86.

60. Singer, *One World*, p. 9.

61. Ibid., p. 13.

62. D. Parfit, "On Doing the Best for Our Children," in M. Bayles, ed., *Ethics and Population* (Cambridge, Mass.: Schenkman, 1976): 100–115.

63. D. Parfit, "On Doing the Best for Our Children," reprinted in J. S. Fishkin and R. E. Goodin, eds., *Population and Political Theory: Philosophy, Politics, and Society 8* (Malden, Mass.: Wiley-Blackwell, 2010): 68–80, pp. 69–70 (emphasis in original).

64. Ibid., p. 71.

65. Ibid.

66. Ibid.

67. Parfit, *Reasons and Persons*.

68. H. Sidgwick, *The Methods of Ethics*, Seventh Edition (London: Macmillan, 1907), p. 418.

69. Ibid.

70. A. Leopold, *A Sand County Almanac and Sketches Here and There* (New York: Oxford University Press, 1949), p. 204.

71. E. A. Page, *Climate Change, Justice, and Future Generations* (Northhampton, Mass.: Edward Elgar, 2006).

72. For William Bennett's title to be the National Scold, see Keith Olberman, *The Worst Person in the World and 202 Strong Contenders* (Hoboken, N.J.: John Wiley, 2006).

73. P. Singer, "Ethics and Climate Change: Commentary," *Environmental Values* 15 (2006): 415–422, p. 421.

74. S. M. Gardiner, "A Perfect Moral Storm," *Environmental Values* 15 (2006): 397–413, p. 407.

75. Gardiner, *Perfect Moral Storm*, p. 243.

76. Ibid., p. 244.

Chapter 11

1. A. Leopold, "Some Fundamentals of Conservation in the Southwest," *Environmental Ethics* 1 (1979): 131–141, reprinted in S. L. Flader and J. B. Callicott, eds., *The River of the Mother of God and Other Essays by Aldo Leopold* (Madison: University of Wisconsin Press, 1991): 86–97, p. 94.

2. We are indebted to G. Ryle, *The Concept of Mind* (London: Hutchinson's University Library, 1949) for the "ghost-in-the-machine" characterization of dualistic individualism; and to A. Watts, *The Book on the Taboo Against Knowing Who You Are* (New York: Random House, 1966) for the "ego-enclosed-in-a-bag-of-skin" characterization of the same; and to W. E. Adams, *Memoir of a Social Atom* (London: Hutchinson's University Library, 1903) for the "social atom" characterization of materialistic Hobbesian individualism.

3. Emphasis added.

4. S. T. Asma, *Against Fairness* (Chicago: University of Chicago Press, 2013).

5. See A. Sen, "Rational Fools: A Critique of the Behavioral Foundations of Economic Theory," *Philosophy and Public Affairs* 6 (1977): 317–344.

6. P. Salovey and D. Sluyter, "What Is Emotional Intelligence?," in P. Salovey and D. Sluyter, eds., *Emotional Development and Emotional Intelligence: Implications for Educators* (New York: Basic Books, 1997): 3–31.

7. H. M. McBride, M. Neuspiel, and S. Wasiak, "Mitochondria: More Than Just a Power-house," *Current Biology* 16 (2006): R551–R560.

8. C. L. Sears, "A Dynamic Partnership: Celebrating Our Gut Flora," *Anaerobe* 11 (2005): 247–251.

9. E. A. Grice, H. H. Kong, S. Conlan, C. B. Deming, J. Davis, A. C. Young, et al., "Topographical and Temporal Biodiversity of the Human Skin Microbiome," *Science* 324 (2009): 1190–1192.

10. A. I. Tauber, "The Immune System and Its Ecology," *Philosophy of Science* 75 (2008): 224–245.

11. L. Thomas, *Lives of a Cell: Notes of a Biology Watcher* (New York: Viking Press, 1974), p. 142.

12. P. J. Turnbaugh, R. E. Ley, M. Hamady, C. M. Fraser-Liggett, R. Knight, and J. I. Gordon, "The Human Microbiome Project," *Nature* 449 (2007): 804–810.

13. Thomas, *Lives of a Cell*, pp. 4–5.

14. T. G. Buchman, "The Community of the Self," *Nature* 420 (2002): 246–251.

15. S. F. Gilbert, J. Sapp, and A. I. Tauber, "A Symbiotic View of Life: We Have Never Been Individuals," *Quarterly Review of Biology* 87 (2012): 325–341, pp. 325–326, emphasis in original.

16. Ibid., p. 327.

17. I. Kant, *Grounding for the Metaphysics of Morals*, tr. J. W. Ellington (Indianapolis, Ind.: Hackforth, 1981) p. 13.

18. Ibid., p. 24.

19. Ibid., p. 59.

20. Ibid.

21. See, for a sampling, K. Setiya and H. Paakkunainen, *Internal Reasons: Contemporary Readings* (Cambridge, Mass.: MIT Press, 2012).

22. G. Livingston and D. V. Cohn, *The New Demography of American Motherhood* (Washington: Pew Research Center Social and Demographic Trends Report, May 2010, Revised August 2010).

23. I. J. Sackmann, A. I. Boothroid, and K. E. Kraemer, "Our Sun. III.: Present and Future," *Astrophysical Journal* 418 (1993): 457.

24. D. E. Brownlee, "Planetary Habitability on Astronomical Time Scales," in C. J. Schrijver and G. L. Siscoe, eds., *Heliophysics: Evolving Solar Activity and the Climates of Space and Earth* (Cambridge: Cambridge University Press, 2010).

25. A. Leopold, *A Sand County Almanac and Sketches Here and There* (New York: Oxford University Press, 1949, pp. 202, 201.

26. A.-S. B. Cochelin, L. A. Mysak, Z. Wang, and Zhaomin, "Simulation of Long-Term Future Climate Changes with the Green McGill Paleoclimate Model: The Next Glacial Inception," *Climatic Change* 79 (2006): 381–401.

27. M. Slote, *Morals from Motives* (New York: Oxford University Press, 2001), pp. viii–ix.

28. Ibid., ix.

Appendix

1. A. L., "Some Fundamentals of Conservation in the Southwest," *Environmental Ethics* 1 (1979): 131–141, reprinted in S. L. Flader and J. B. Callicott, eds., *The River of the Mother of God and Other Essays by Aldo Leopold* (Madison: University of Wisconsin Press, 1991): 86–97. The essay was written in 1923. Leopold did not succeed in publishing it during his lifetime. Eugene C. Hargrove found it among Leopold's papers in the University of Wisconsin archives as he was gathering material for the inaugural volume of his new journal. Because the reprinted version corrects some errors that appear in the original typescript that survived in the 1979 publication in *Environmental Ethics*—most

notably the spelling of Ouspensky's name as "Onspensky," which was probably due to a misreading of Leopold's handwriting by his secretary—the anthologized version of 1991 is reprinted here. J. Baird Callicott annotated this iteration, which had not been done for the two previous iterations. The blanks that Leopold left to fill in later have been retained.

2. The word *drouth* is an alternative spelling (and pronunciation) of *drought* that has fallen out of common usage.

3. Leopold may be informed by, if not referring here to, A. E. Douglass, "Evidence of Climatic Effects in the Annual Rings of Trees," *Ecology* 1 (1920): 24–32. Douglass refers to E. Huntington, *The Climatic Factor in Arid America* (Washington: Carnegie Institute, Publication 192, 1914), a book that Leopold may have read or relied on Douglass faithfully to summarize. One wonders whether Leopold had meant to write 300 rather than 3,000, as the evidence noted in the previous sentence provides a climate record going back only 500 years for "yellow pine" identified by Douglass as *Pinus ponderosa* in the Southwest. For Sequoia in California, Douglass (p. 27) gives "1087 B. C., 1122 B. C., and 1305 B. C.," as the farthest back the tree-rings took him—which does go back 3,000 years more or less—so Leopold's citing evidence for climate change, or the lack thereof, in northern California as evidence for climate change or the lack thereof in Arizona and New Mexico appears to be a lapse of logic. The claim that there had been no great increase or decrease in aridity over the past 300 years would put it on the conservative side of the evidence he cites for the Southwest. Better resolution of tree-ring data indicates that in fact there were both significant—if not "great"—increases and decreases in precipitation in the region, the latter representing periods of persistent drought lasting up to half a century. See H. Grassino-Mayer, "A 2129-year Reconstruction of Precipitation for Northwestern New Mexico, USA," in J. S. Dean, D. M. Meko, and T. W. Swetnam, eds., *Tree Rings, Environment, and Humanity: Proceedings of an International Conference* (Tucson, Ariz.: Radiocarbon, 1996): 191–204.

4. Leopold probably refers here to the Anasazi who settled Chaco Canyon in what is now northwestern New Mexico in about the sixth century CE and later Mesa Verde, in what is now southwestern Colorado and abandoned their settlements between the twelfth and thirteenth centuries because of a series of prolonged droughts. See P. F. Reed, *The Puebloan Society of Chaco Canyon* (Westport, Conn.: Greenwood Publishing Group, 2004, and D. D. Roberts, *In Search of the Old Ones: Exploring the Anasazi World of the Southwest* (New York: Simon & Schuster, 1996).

5. Leopold's spelling, "dessication" is an alternative spelling of "desiccation" that has fallen out of common usage.

6. This pattern is clearly visible in the afore-cited paper by A. E. Douglass who provides a graph (Figure 2) tracking rainfall measured at Prescott, Arizona, for the years 1865–1910—further evidence that the "Douglas" whom Leopold mentions is A. E. Douglass and the paper he has in mind was Douglass's paper published in volume 1, number 1 of *Ecology*.

7. The quotation is from a poem by C. Sandburg, "The Windy City," in A. McLeish, ed., *The Complete Poems of Carl Sandburg*, Revised and Expanded Edition (New York: Harcourt, 1969): 271–281, p. 275.

8. The reference is probably to Edward Norfolk Munns, like Leopold a forester, but the work of Munns to which Leopold refers is not traceable.

9. The quotation is from C. H. Rowell, "The Press as an Intermediator Between the Investigator and the Public," *Science* 50 (1919): 146–150, p. 150.

10. Here Leopold himself cites "Studies in French Forestry" by T. S. Woolsey. He refers to T. S. Woolsey Jr., *Studies in French Forestry* (New York: John Wiley, 1920).

11. Here Leopold cites Silt Problem of the Zuni Reservoir, H. F. Robinson, Amer. Soc. C. E., Vol. 83, p. 868, 1920. He refers to H. F. Robinson, "Silt Problem of the Zuni Reservoir," *Transactions of the American Society of Civil Engineers* 83 (1919–20): 868–893.

12. Ezekiel 34:18.

13. Leopold quotes P. D. Ouspensky, *Tertium Organum: The Third Canon of Thought; A Key to the Enigmas of the World*, tr. N. Bessaraboff and C. Bragdon (New York: Knopf, 1920), p. 200.

14. Leopold alludes to Job 38.7 and to 2 Kings 22:20.

15. Leopold probably refers to Jeannette Augustus Marks, "Swinburne: A Study in Pathology," *Yale Review* 9 (January 1920): 349–365; the quoted words are found on p. 353.

16. Leopold quotes J. Muir, *A Thousand-Mile Walk to the Gulf* (Boston: Houghton Mifflin, 1916), p. 98.

17. The Poem by William Cullen Bryant may be found in P. Godwin, ed., *The Poetical Works of William Cullen Bryant*, Volume First (New York: Russell and Russell, 1883), pp. 17–20. The lines Leopold quotes may be found on pp. 18–19.

18. Leopold refers to Arthur Twining Hadley (April 23, 1856–March 6, 1930), a political economist and president of Yale University from 1899 to 1921.

19. Leopold quotes again from Bryant, "Thanatopsis" p. 19, with some slight emendation in punctuation.

20. Leopold probably alludes to J. Burroughs, "Each for Its Own Sake," in J. Burroughs, *Accepting the Universe: Essays in Naturalism* (Houghton Mifflin, 1920): 30–53. On p. 35 these words are found: "The potato bug, if left alone would exterminate the potato and so exterminate itself; …" The entire essay is a blistering attack on anthropocentrism.

21. The words Leopold quotes may be found in R. L. Stevenson, *Virginibus Puerisque* (Teddington: Echo Library, 2006), p. 80.

Index

There is no room in the Index for terms such as "ecology" and "ethics" which occur with great frequency in the text and for which multiple subcategories would be necessary to provide the reader with a useful means of locating a specific item of interest. The analytic Table of Contents complements this index and can provide a supplemental guide to the location of prominent concepts in this book. With few exceptions, names that appear only once in the text do not appear in the Index.

*A Sand County Almanac and Sketches Here
   and There* 7, 8, 10, 13, 17, 19–46, 90, 149,
   162, 170, 177, 205, 212, 221, 260, 268
Asma, Stephen T. 291
astronomy 93, 186, 203, 208, 246, 278
asymmetry 182–183, 191, 193–194, 236
ateleology 27, 81, 203, 218, 232
atman 213–214
atmosphere 4, 6, 83, 150–151, 161, 165, 184,
   187–188, 191, 195–199, 201, 207, 209,
   211–212, 236, 243–244, 266, 271–273,
   280–282, 293, 309
atom(s)(ic(istic))(ized) 29–30, 44, 59, 83,
   85, 90, 93, 100, 103, 111, 116, 183, 187,
   190–192, 197, 264, 269
   social (view of society) (moral ontology)
      60, 100, 111, 241–242, 264, 269, 274,
      278, 289, 292
   sub- 90
Australia(n) 1, 57, 99, 286, 290
Ayer, A.J. 108–110, 143, 147

Bacon, Francis 102, 162, 269
balance of nature 42, 89, 210, 306, 307
beauty 8
   as ecological concept 17, 35, 97
   environmental / natural 79, 255
   in summary moral maxim of the land
      ethic 3, 64–66, 96–97, 150–151, 210,
      212, 221, 234, 300
   of soul 146
Bedichek, Roy 39
belief(s) 35, 172–173, 176, 179–180,
   192, 216, 248
beneficence(ent) 55, 60–61, 69, 78–79, 121,
   296, 300
Bentham, Jeremy 48, 56, 60, 67, 71, 105–106,
   108, 127, 251–252, 275–278, 288
Bergson, Henri 185–186, 189
Berry, Thomas 45
Beston, Henry 19
Bible/biblical 9, 20- 24, 27, 32–33, 39- 41, 99,
   105, 134, 156–157, 165, 170- 172, 179-
   180, 184, 200, 252
Biocentrism(ic)(ists) 6, 8, 11, 166, 206, 207,
   208, 218, 221–233
biocomplexity 270
biodiversity. *See diversity*

biogeochemistry 4, 6, 44, 151, 161, 186,
   192–193, 197–198
biology(ical) 122, 133, 161, 164, 193
   as academic discipline 75, 77, 88, 120, 124,
      196, 199, 294
   evolutionary 3, 7, 26, 39, 41, 44, 81–82, 88,
      112, 115, 120, 138, 149, 202–203, 210, 232
   sciences(tists) 3, 39, 51, 58, 70, 81, 93, 111,
      112, 114–115, 117, 119, 122, 124, 135,
      137, 142–143, 197, 200–202, 293
biosphere 6, 11–13, 68, 151, 183–201, 207, 221–
   222, 225, 231–238, 285, 294, 297–298
biotic community(ies): *See: community(ies)*
"Biotic Land-Use" 87
birds 28, 64, 72, 84, 109, 114, 119, 170, 310
Black, Max 72
Boehm, Christopher 136, 138–139, 147–148
Bormann, Herb 200
Bosanquet, Bernard 107, 180
boundary(ies)
   artificial 208
   between "immediate posterity" and
      "Unknown Future" generations 289
   between inert and living matter 183,
      187–188, 192
   Cretaceous-Tertiary 236
   of biotic communities / (super-)
      ecosystems 5, 93, 208, 294
   of ethics / (moral) communities /
      societies 52, 54–55, 58, 91, 125
   of organisms 183, 208
   of psychological categories 223
   of the atmosphere / biosphere
      187–188, 209
   of the solar system 208–209
   political 91, 270
Bowles, Samuel 136, 138–139, 147
Britain 99, 240
Bryant, William Cullen 167, 169–170, 310
Buddhism(ist) 1, 3, 4, 35, 167, 192–193, 214
Burroughs, John 175–176, 238, 259, 311

Cafaro, Philip 257
capitalism 120, 202, 269
carbon(ate)(s) (dioxide) (CO_2) 29, 83, 151,
   183, 185–186, 188, 195, 197, 201, 212,
   236–237, 244, 267, 272, 281, 348 (n. 6)
   -based energy / molecules 116, 272, 285

ecocentrism 225
ecofascism *See: fascism*
ecofeminism(ists) *See: feminism(ists)*
ecologist(s) 2, 3, 23, 29, 41, 43, 54, 196, 200,
    208–210, 215, 270
  (Anglo-)American 85, 88, 193, 197
  British 24
  community 41, 210
  ecosystem 2, 41, 43, 89, 91, 93–95, 196,
    208–210
  evolutionary 92
  mental eye / ear of 35
  wildlife 58
economy(ic)(s)(ists) 64, 75, 105–106, 124,
    142, 202, 248, 306, 308
  feasibility 34
  individual activity / liberties / (self-)
    interest 34, 66, 67, 87, 130
  health 22
  human / cultural / political 65, 91,
    142,158, 172, 192, 263, 285, 298
  microtine system 23
  neoclassical theory of 10
  of nature 41–43, 54, 65, 85
  relation to land / to members of biotic
    community 47, 64, 87
  resources 155, 303
  value(ation) 34, 37, 68, 97
education 22, 24, 120, 125, 128–129, 134,
    145, 292
egoism 58, 111, 146, 218, 250, 275, 278
Einstein, Albert 101, 181–182, 193–194
electromagnetic 160, 183, 205, 207
Elton, Charles 24, 38, 41–42, 54–55, 65, 70,
    82–87, 92, 95, 98
emergence 2, 22, 53–54, 98, 197, 269
emotion(s)(al)(y) 9, 55, 74, 78–79, 100, 108,
    119, 121, 124, 139, 144, 146, 230, 269,
    295–296
  intelligence 140, 146, 292
  See also feelings, sentiments
empathy 146
enantiomorphy(ic) 182–183, 191–193
energy
  alternative- 270, 281
  cellular 293
  chemical 185–191, 197, 199 208

concept of 30
-consuming 198, 271
cycle 30, 83–84, 184–187, 222
-dissipating 198
(-)flow(s)(ing) / fluxes of 30, 83–85,
    94–97
forms of 83, 184–187
fountain of 42, 83
measurable / mensuration of 42, 88–89
-metabolizing 42, 65
(non-)carbon-based 88–89, 202, 208, 272,
    289
radiant / solar / incoming 184–187, 191
    202
transfer(s) 83, 86, 184–188, 222
transformation(s) 83–89,
    184–188, 199
Engels, Friedrich 123, 133–134
enlightenment 48, 191
entropy 185, 222, 232, 294
epistemology(ical)(ly)
  Aristotle's 162
  Bacon's 162
  concept 172
  ecological 93, 314 (n. 20)
  Judeo-Christian 252
  Kant's 109, 230
  Locke's 100–101
  Modernist 248
  objective 172, 230
  Ouspensky's 162
  Plato's 261
  Pragmatic(ist) 179
  religious 192, 248
  scientific 247–248
equality
  before the law 132
  human 48–49, 193
  of participation 132
  principle of 127, 132, 277, 290, 301
equilibrium(a) 1, 43, 79, 118, 187, 195, 201,
    202, 222, 225, 239, 294, 305–307
erosion 5, 12, 18, 40, 155–156, 210, 242,
    304–308
ethnocentrism 171, 174
Euclid(ian) 99, 101, 182–183, 194
eudaimonia 253–257, 260–261, 265

Mill, John Stuart 55–56, 106, 274, 288
mind(s)(ed) (state of) (collective / group)
    (-body / -matter) (-boggling)
    (-challenging) (economic-) (-less)
    (-numbing) (open-) (planetary)
    (simple-) 6, 23–25, 32, 35, 37, 39, 61,
    76, 81, 94, 100, 105, 107, 109, 113, 114,
    142, 160, 162–163, 181, 189–191, 201,
    203, 217, 241–242, 269, 274, 282–283,
    306, 309
modern synthesis 114, 116, 120, 123
modernism 246–247
modernity 20, 129
module(s) of moral sentiments 135,
    249–250
monoculture(s) 86
Moore, G. E. 70–74, 107, 251
mouse(ice) 23, 27, 34, 125, 129, 213
Muir, John 13, 167, 169–170, 174, 243–245,
    247, 310
mysticism 115
myth 184, 280, 292, 293

Naess, Arne 224, 269
new synthesis 116, 117, 120, 124
neo-Clementsian 196, 198
neo-Darwinian 81, 114–117, 133, 151,
    200- 203
neo-Gleasonian 4, 6, 196, 204
networks 43, 91, 148, 193, 196, 203, 280
Newton, Isaac 99–103, 118, 190, 217, 264
Newtonian(-) 104–105, 183, 264
non-anthropocentric(ism)(ist) 9
    anthropocentrism 175
    Earth ethic 7–12, 165, 177, 206–208, 222,
        231, 301
    (environmental) ethic(s)(al)(ist) 53,
        126–127, 218, 224, 227, 257–258
    evolutionary-ecological worldview 33
    land ethic 12, 67–69, 235, 151–152
    Leopold as 68–69, 159, 166, 168–170, 206,
        237–238, 289, 338 (n. 92), 359 (n.20)
    metaphysical 9, 33, 175
    (holistic) (individualistic) moral
        (attitude) 9–11, 33, 36–37, 167–169,
        175–177, 289
    respect 159, 165, 173
    tautological(ly) 10

non-human 9, 10–11, 25, 36, 119, 127, 144,
    165, 167, 231, 234, 249, 257
noösphere 189–194, 203–207
Norton, Bryan G. 8, 12, 17, 31, 33–35, 37, 94,
    97, 156, 171–176, 179–180
nuclear 134, 148, 204, 234, 239, 298, 299

oceans 5, 84, 150–151, 165, 184, 187–188,
    199, 210, 212, 239, 244, 263, 266, 310
Odum, Eugene P. 1, 3, 42, 88–89, 215, 294
Odysseus 46–50, 156, 298
odyssey (of) evolution (as) 25, 29, 68, 81, 85,
    86, 90, 234, 237, 268, 271, 272, 301
Odyssey 47–48, 156, 298, 321
"Odyssey" 30, 86, 90
oil 216, 248, 266, 282, 303
O'Neill, John 257
ontology(ical) 4, 93
    Gaian / of Earth 208–210
    ghost-in-the-machine 274
    gradient / spectrum 93–94
    moral: holistic / relational 44, 111, 260,
        265, 276, 289, 292, 294
    moral: of Rational Individualism /
        essence-accident / externally related /
        individualistic / (social) atoms(ism)
        (istic) 60, 130, 264, 269–270,
        274–277, 283, 287, 289, 292, 301
    of biotic communities 43, 91–93, 96
    of ecosystems 43, 93, 208, 314 (n. 20)
    of genes 43–44,116
    of land organisms 90
    of social organisms (wholes) 44, 260
    of value 230
    physio-mathematical / material 190
    pluralism 12
    political 242
    questions 41, 43
organicism 43, 87, 89–90, 179
Ouspensky, P. D. 8, 160–165, 173–174,
    180–189, 199, 213, 223, 309
overgrazing 150, 155, 157, 304, 307, 308
oxygen 4, 83, 183–187, 195–198, 201, 207,
    211, 236
ozone 4, 5, 6, 12, 242

pagan 32
Page, Edward A. 286

Parfit, Derek 279, 280, 282–286, 288, 296–297
Pasteur, Louis 182, 184
pastoralism 80, 142, 147
patriotic(ism) 60–61, 69, 112, 134, 296, 300
phenomenology(ical)(ists) 68–69
phenotype(s)(ic) 44, 117, 136, 137, 202
photosynthesis 4, 43
physics 4, 41, 82, 88, 90, 98, 103–104, 164, 173, 181, 190, 203–205, 217, 261, 269, 309
physis 264–265
Piaget, Jean 109–110
Pinker, Steven 140–142, 146
Plato(nic) 37, 41, 44, 48–49, 58, 71, 110, 146–147, 163, 190, 193, 235, 240–241, 250- 256, 261–265, 274, 288
pluralism 12, 34, 173, 257
pollution 5, 94, 157, 187, 210, 247, 250, 255–256, 259, 268, 309
positivism(ist)(s) (post-) 24, 106–110, 115, 142–144, 149, 179, 180–181
poverty 142, 297
Pragmatism(ist) 8, 171–181, 203
predator(s) (-) prey (relationships) 3, 30–32, 43, 83–84, 86 90–91, 95, 129, 211, 230, 241
preservation 20, 32, 65, 100, 227, 243, 257
pre-Socratic(s) 213, 261, 264
Prior, Arthur N. 75
Protagoras(ean) 48, 132, 146, 188, 240
Pryor, Ashley 17, 163–164
Pythagoras(ean) 30, 35 224, 254, 274

race(s)(ism)(ist) 36, 123, 130–131, 134 174–175, 193, 219, 277–278, 291, 297, 310–311
  human 175–176, 238, 259–260
  of plants and animals 191
Rachels, James 37, 124, 126–133, 144, 145
radiation
  cosmic 205
  solar 185,187–188, 202, 209, 236
  ultraviolet 209, 236
rational(ity)(ism)(istic)(ists) 9, 60, 111, 124, 1126–27, 144, 164, 177, 192, 219, 221, 287, 296, 255, 259, 263, 275–277, 279, 289, 296

animal(s) (being(s)) (egoists) (essence) (fools) (humans) (individuals) (monads) (moral agents) (non-/pre-/post-/sub-) 6, 9, 10, 36, 60–61, 76, 104–105, 111, 127, 130, 148, 189, 219, 221, 227, 229–231, 238, 254–255, 259–260, 262, 265, 275–278, 296
  basis for ethics / methods / principle of 125–127, 177, 254, 301
  choice / consciousness / coercion / discourses / interrogation / resolution of ethical disputes 80, 105, 125–126, 190, 245, 296
  individualism 8, 128, 265–289, 295, 301
Rawls, John 111, 132, 146
Regan, Tom 71, 219, 224–227
Riemann, G. F. Bernard 181–183, 194
Riemannian geometry 161, 191, 193–194
relativism 56, 143, 147–149
religion(s)(ous) 167, 175, 189, 278, 310
  Abrahamic / Western 167–169, 250
  affiliation / sectarian 277, 297, 193
  beliefs / "knowledge" / cognition / dogma / epistemology 192, 248
  concept of pollution / piety 240, 250, 252–253, 351 (n. 90)
  Olympian / traditional Greek 10, 262
res cogitans / *extensa* 189, 246
reservoirs 155, 304, 306- 308
respect(ed)(able)(ability) 3, 22, 35, 37, 39, 55, 69, 134, 159, 174, 209, 217–218, 227, 249
  for authority / the (principle of) law / office of the President of the United States 64, 135, 252
  for (biotic) community as such / fellow members of 55, 63–65, 79, 289
  for future generations 159
  for human (animal) rights 65, 227, 300
  for land / nature / of environment 68, 225, 227, 257, 273
  (-)for(-)life (ethic) / living thing (being) (s) (organisms) / teleological centers of 6, 165–166, 177, 175–176, 206–207, 215, 217, 220, 222–225, 227, 232–233, 238, 273, 309, 311
  for pre-natal human life 166
  for private property 57

super-ecosystem(s) 44, 93, 139, 294
super-organism(s) 1–4, 42- 44, 54, 86,
    88–91, 94, 161, 164, 196–198, 242, 293
supra-individual entities 281, 283, 286,
    297–299
symbiosis 81, 138, 196, 294
symmetry 182–183, 227, 236, 239
sympathy(ies)(etic)(ally) 25, 37, 51–53,
    55, 59–61, 64, 69, 72, 78–79, 112, 117,
    120–121, 127–128, 134, 139, 141, 146,
    168, 201, 251, 275
synecdoche 21–22, 39, 87

Tallmadge, John 40, 156
Tansley, Arthur 29, 41–42, 82–83, 93
Taylor, Paul B. 6, 71, 166, 224, 225, 226, 227,
    228, 231–232
technology(ies)(ical) 5, 191–192, 205, 294,
    298
    optimism 191–194
    communication and transportation 148
"The Arboretum and the University" 41
"The Forestry of the Prophets"
    156
"The Land-Health Concept and
    Conservation" 87
Teilhard de Chardin, Pierre 189–190
telos(oi) 3, 26–27, 121, 170, 210, 253, 260
temperature 2, 54, 145, 160, 202–205, 209,
    211–212, 222, 239, 294
terra incognita 43, 156, 219
"The Land Ethic" 7, 13, 17, 35–39, 46–47, 50,
    52, 58, 63–64, 79, 82, 84, 87, 89–90, 94,
    150, 171, 177, 221, 300
theology(ical) 166, 170, 190, 200
thermodynamic(s) 72, 83, 185–186,
    196–198, 203, 232
Thoreau, Henry David 13, 19, 22, 32, 243,
    245, 247, 257–258
tree(s) 13, 18, 20, 31, 81, 95, 136, 156, 164,
    173, 188, 213, 220, 223, 229, 231, 266,
    267, 272, 304–306, 341, 358
tribalism 120
trophic pyramid 84

universal laws 96, 104–105, 148, 227, 275, 276
universalism 56, 249
US Atomic Energy Commission 88
US Senate Committee on Energy 268

utilitarianism 10, 12, 55–56, 60, 65, 67, 71,
    96, 105–106, 127, 251–252, 263, 272–
    278, 282, 284–288, 301
utility 18, 55–56, 63, 105–106, 252–253, 280,
    284–285

value(s)(ing)(able) (good) (worth) 7, 10,
    22–23, 26, 33–37, 246–247, 267, 273–
    274, 303–304, 107, 134, 143, 147–149,
    151, 174
    facts and 36, 70, 134
    instrumental (anthropocentric)
        (economic) (sale) (commercial) 34,
        36–37, 64, 68, 70–71, 87, 97, 295, 166,
        216, 229–231, 295
    intrinsic (cosmic) (inherent) 10, 34,
        36–37, 68, 70–71, 167–168, 230–231,
        238, 257, 259, 295, 311, 175–176, 226–
        227, 229–231, 295
    system (theory) 39, 269–270
van Wensveen, Louke 256–257
Varner, Gary 6, 216
Vernadsky, Vladimir 161, 182–199, 206
village(s)(ers) 132, 260, 261, 282, 290; agrarian
    91; global; 53, 54, 66, 67, 91, 112, 126,
    148, 149, 282, 283, 296, 297, 300
violent(ce) 31, 214, 250, 321 (n.8), 334 (n.56
    & 79)
    changes 74, 95
    conditions of nature 264
    conflicts 192
    in Middle Eastern countries 142
    objective (unreflective) 243
    weather 235
    world of the Titans 110
virtue(s) cardinal 252, 254, 263
    (and) utilitarian(ism) 273–278
    dirty 257
    ethic(s)(ist)(s) (theory) 6, 8, 96, 151,
        157–159, 174, 177, 206, 234, 235–237,
        239, 241–265, 272–274, 286, 288–289,
        301–302
    human 258–259
    intellectual 223, 255–256
    moral 254–256
    new 273
    personal (individual) 255, 258, 273
    professional (of craftsmanship) 158–159
    social(etal) / of city-state 62, 206, 289, 303

vitalism 186
Vogt, William 39

waste(s)(r) 157, 201, 250, 256, 256, 259, 309
   oxygen as 4, 83, 185, 187, 236
   land 130
   of wealth and resources 306
water 10, 23, 30, 35, 43, 54–55, 82–83, 86, 94,
      96, 122, 129, 155–158, 164–165, 185,
      187, 192, 201, 210–211, 220, 234, 236,
      254, 268, 303–305, 308
   column 187
   course 307, 308
   despoliation of (pollution) 158
   fresh 210
   ground- 266
   power(s) 303–304
   quality 211
   rain- 155
   resources 42, 155
   producing 303
   tanks 234
   transport 303
   well- 307
waterfowl 18, 24
watershed 3, 42, 266, 306–307
White, Gilbert 19
White Jr., Lynne 22, 45

Wilson, David Sloan 135–137, 139
Wilson, Edward O. 116–124, 133–135, 139,
     144, 146–148
"When the Geese Return Spring Is Here"
   260, 352
Whitakker, Robert H. 2, 41
wilderness 18, 20, 23, 26, 79, 86, 94, 118, 129,
     135, 183, 225, 310
"Wilderness" 87
"Wilderness as a Land Laboratory" 86
wildlife 18, 33, 58
wildness 28, 32, 243, 257
Williams, George C. 3, 85, 114–116, 119,
     137, 139, 211
Wittgenstein, Ludwig 107–108, 110
wolf(ves) 20, 30- 33, 93, 118, 149, 164, 211,
   267
women 110–111, 132, 136, 142–143, 166, 284
Worster, Donald 88–90
worth (inherent) (intrinsic) 37, 71, 225–229,
   257
   relative 37, 229
Wynne-Edwards, Vero C. 112, 113, 114, 115,
   117

xenophobia 36, 120, 134

Yellowstone 41, 93, 211, 242

CPSIA information can be obtained at www.ICGtesting.com
Printed in the USA
BVOW08s1213270815

415297BV00003B/14/P